W9-DHL-552

Chicago Public Library
C
P
L
REFERENCE
Form 178 rev. 1-94

PROFESSIONAL SPORTS TEAM HISTORIES

FOOTBALL

PROFESSIONAL SPORTS TEAM HISTORIES

MICHAEL L. LaBLANC, Editor

MARY K. RUBY, Associate Editor

Gale Research Inc. DETROIT • WASHINGTON, D.C. • LONDON

This book is printed on acid-free paper that meets the minimum requirements of American National Standard for Information Sciences—Permanence Paper for Printed Library Materials, ANSI Z39.48-1984.

Printed in the United States of America
Published simultaneously in the United Kingdom
by Gale Research International Limited
(An Affiliated company of Gale Research Inc.)

ISBN 0-8103-8861-8

10 9 8 7 6 5 4 3 2 1

Staff

Michael L. LaBlanc, *Editor*
Mary K. Ruby, *Associate Editor*
George W. Schmidt, *Indexer*
Marilyn Allen, *Editorial Associate*
Michael J. Tyrkus, *Assistant Editor*

Linda Andres, Barbara Carlisle Bigelow, Suzanne M. Bourgoin, Catherine A. Coulson, Dean David Dauphinais, Kathleen Dauphinais, Kathy Edgar, Nicolet V. Elert, Marie Ellavich, Peter M. Gareffa, Kevin Hillstrom, Laurie Collier Hillstrom, Anne Janette Johnson, Janice Jorgensen, Denise Kasinec, Paula Kepos, Jane Kosek, Mark Kram, Mary P. LaBlanc, L. Mpho Mabunda, Roger Matuz, Tom McMahon, Louise Mooney, Edward V. Moran, Terrie Rooney, Mary Ruby, Julia Rubiner, Kelly Sprague, Aarti Stephens, Debbie Stanley, Les Stone, Gerald Tomlinson, Roger Valade, Kathleen Wilson, *Contributing Editors*

Marilyn Allen, Kevin Hillstrom, Keith Reed, Mary K. Ruby, *Photo Editors*
Willie Mathis, *Camera Operator*

B. Hal May, *Director, Biography Division*
Peter M. Gareffa, *Senior Editor, Contemporary Biographies*
David E. Salamie, *Senior Editor, New Product Development*

Jeanne Gough, *Permissions Manager*
Margaret A. Chamberlain, *Permissions Supervisor (Pictures)*
Pamela A. Hayes, Keith Reed, *Permissions Associates*
Susan Brohman, Arlene Johnson, Barbara A. Wallace, *Permissions Assistants*

MaryBeth Trimper, *Production Director*
Mary Winterhalter Kelley, *Production Assistant*
Cynthia Baldwin, *Art Director*
Mark C. Howell, *Cover Designer*
Kathleen Hourdakis, *Page Designer*

Cover photos by arrangement with AP/Wide World Photos and NFL Properties

Contents

Introduction ix
Acknowledgements xi
The History of Pro Football 1

American Football Conference

Central Division
Cincinnati Bengals 21
Cleveland Browns 33
Houston Oilers 49
Pittsburgh Steelers 59

Eastern Division
Buffalo Bills 83
Indianapolis Colts 97
Miami Dolphins 119
New England Patriots 133
New York Jets 147

Western Division
Denver Broncos 163
Kansas City Chiefs 175
Los Angeles Raiders 187
San Diego Chargers 209
Seattle Seahawks 221

National Football Conference

Central Division
Chicago Bears 235
Detroit Lions 269
Green Bay Packers 285
Minnesota Vikings 303
Tampa Bay Buccaneers 315

Eastern Division
Dallas Cowboys 327
New York Giants 349
Philadelphia Eagles 375
Phoenix Cardinals 393
Washington Redskins 409

Western Division
Atlanta Falcons 433
Los Angeles Rams 449
New Orleans Saints 471
San Francisco 49ers 489

Index 509

Introduction

Professional Sports Team Histories is a multivolume reference series that chronicles the evolution of four major U.S. spectator sports: basketball, baseball, football, and hockey.

Football, to most of the world, is a term applied to the sport that Americans refer to as soccer. The game Americans call football, unique to North America, evolved from the English game of rugby. The first true American football game was played in 1869 between two eastern universities, Rutgers and Princeton. It quickly spread to other East Coast colleges and eventually to schools throughout the country.

Clubs were formed to promote the new sport, and in 1892 a player was officially paid to play in a game for the first time. Gradually other clubs began hiring professionals—usually ex-college athletes of note. In 1902, a number of clubs joined to form the National Football League (NFL), the first of the professional associations. From these inauspicious beginnings professional football has grown into an American institution, with millions of fans attending games each year and millions more watching on television. With games now broadcast throughout the world and tens of millions of viewers tuning in to the annual Super Bowl, and with NFL exhibition games being played in such distant locales as England, Germany, and Japan, the game has the potential to spread far from its American homeland.

With an extensive prose entry on each NFL team, ***Professional Sports Team Histories: Football*** focuses on the formation and growth of each franchise and highlights the accomplishments of significant players and members of management. The volume also charts the creation of the NFL, the history of the league's precursors, the pioneering teams that engaged in post-World War I play, and the refinement of the game into the sport of the 1990s.

A Source of Convenient Reference *and* Interesting Reading

- **Informative historical essays,** many written by specialists in the field, offer an overview of each team's development from its inception through the 1992-93 season, with coverage of franchise moves, name changes, key personnel, and team performance.

- **A special entry on the history of the sport** follows the development of the game over the years and presents a thorough analysis of the factors that have led to changes in the way it is played.

- **Designed with a broad audience in mind,** the information in ***Professional Sports Team Histories*** is accessible enough to captivate the interest of the sports novice, yet comprehensive enough to enlighten even the most avid fan.

- **Numerous photos**—including shots of Hall-of-Famers—further enhance the reader's appreciation of each team's history.

· **Easy to locate "Team Information at a Glance"** sections list founding dates for each team; names, addresses, and phone numbers of home stadiums; team color/logo information; and franchise records.

· **Additional eye-catching sidebars** present other noteworthy statistics, interesting team-related trivia, close-up profiles of important players and management figures, and capsulized accounts of events that have become a permanent part of sports folklore.

Helpful Indexes Make It Easy to Find the Information You Need

Each volume of ***Professional Sports Team Histories*** includes a detailed, user-friendly index, making it easy to find information on key players and executives.

Available in Electronic Formats

Diskette/Magnetic Tape. ***Professional Sports Team Histories*** is available for licensing on magnetic tape or diskette in a fielded format. Either the complete, four-sport database or a custom selection of entries may be ordered. The database is available for internal data processing and nonpublishing purposes only. For more information, call (800) 877-GALE.

We Welcome Your Comments

The editors welcome your comments and suggestions for enhancing and improving any future editions of the ***Professional Sports Team Histories*** series. Mail correspondence to:

The Editor
Professional Sports Team Histories
Gale Research, Inc.
835 Penobscot Bldg.
Detroit, MI 48226-4094
Phone: (800) 347-GALE
FAX: (313) 961-6599

ACKNOWLEDGEMENTS

Professional Sports Team Histories represents the culmination of nearly three years' effort by a large and diverse group of people. The editors wish to acknowledge the significant contribution of the following individuals and organizations:

• The fine pool of sportswriters and historians who wrote the individual entries, especially Denis J. Harrington, author of *The Pro Football Hall of Fame*; Bernie Kish of the University of Kansas Athletic Department; Joe Lapointe of the *New York Times;* Mark Kram of the *Philadelphia Inquirer;* Steve Marantz of the *Boston Globe;* Jack Pearson of Milwaukee's *Exclusively Yours* magazine; and sports historian Gerald Tomlinson, for sharing their considerable knowledge of the subject matter. When the writers have drawn on reference materials in addition to their own archival resources, we have included a Sources section at the end of the entry. These sources contain a wealth of additional information, and we urge readers to consult these sources for a more detailed understanding of the subject.

• The Pro Football Hall of Fame and NFL Alumni Association, for assistance in securing photos of and information on its members. The Pro Football Hall of Fame is an independent, nonprofit organization designed to honor the significant players, events, and games in the history of professional football. The Museum is open to the public and features four exhibition areas covering the history of football since 1892, a movie theatre showing football action movies, an extensive library, and a Museum gift shop. For more information about the Hall, its Library, Museum, and its publications, contact:

The Pro Football Hall of Fame
2121 George Halas Dr., NW
Canton, OH 44708
Phone: (216) 456-8207

• The media relations departments of the various teams, for their valuable cooperation and assistance in providing photographs, historical materials, information on current players, and for directing us to local sports historians and sportswriters.

• Lauren Fedorko and Diane Schadoff of Book Builders Incorporated, and to Jim Evans of Deadline Inc., for their help in securing knowledgeable and entertaining contributors of team essays.

• The talented and dedicated in-house Gale staff—especially Mary K. Ruby and the Contemporary Biographies and the Biographical References Group staffs; Keith Reed of Picture Permissions; Marilyn Allen, Mike Tyrkus, and Laura Standley Berger of the *Contemporary Authors Autobiographical Series;* Mark Howell and Cindy Baldwin of the Art Department; Patrick Hughes of PC Systems; MaryBeth Trimper, Dorothy Maki, Mary Kelley, and Eveline Abou-El-Seoud of Production; Don Wellman and Maggie Patton of Creative Services; and the entire Marketing and Sales departments—for their invaluable contributions to this series.

The History of Pro Football

Essay by Denis J. Harrington

"It's a game the eleven toughest guys are supposed to win." This was said by no less an authority on the philosophy of professional football than Joe Schmidt, a bandy-legged, barrel-chested linebacker who earned a niche in the Hall of Fame for his particularly aggressive play as a member of the Detroit Lions from 1953 to 1965. Schmidt's response to the probing of a somewhat ingenuous reporter succinctly and pointedly places in perspective the essence of the gridiron sport's mercenary side.

The legendary George Halas, a founding father of the National Football League (NFL) as well as a standout player and the winningest pro coach ever, eyed all potential recruits for his beloved Chicago Bears with one basic requirement in mind: "Speed, size, and all that other stuff must be considered," he said. "But most important, the guy's got to want to hit somebody. If he doesn't like to hit, then pro football's not the place for him."

During the early days of professional football Halas played end for the Decatur Staleys (later to become the Chicago Bears) and distinguished himself as both a devastating blocker and a vicious tackler. He hammered away at the opposition with his fists, forearms, elbows, knees, and head in keeping with the credo, "Do unto others before they do unto you."

From the time of much storied ball carriers Jim Thorpe, Ernie Nevers, Clarke Hinkle, and Bronko Nagurski to celebrated running backs of more modern vintage such as Steve Van Buren, Marion Motley, Jim Taylor, John Henry Johnson, Jimmy Brown, Larry Csonka, John Riggins and Walter Payton, the mindset has been the same: to hit others harder than they can hit you, and hit them first.

Taylor, the Green Bay Packers grinding fullback of the Vince Lombardi era, said: "I always tried to make anybody that tackled me pay the price. The idea was to sting him, intimidate him if possible—let him know I wasn't going down easy."

In the formative years of the Cleveland Browns following World War II it was Motley who pulverized the opposition from the team's famed 34-Trap formation. "On occasion I'd purposely run over a guy," he said. "You do that often enough and he ain't gonna be too eager to get in there. And that's when you can break the big one."

Nicknamed "Diesel" for his locomotive prowess, Riggins powered the Washington Redskins to victory in Super Bowl XVII and then set an NFL single-season record for rushing touchdowns with 24 in 1983. He is regarded as one of the finest short-yardage backs ever to ply his skills in the pro game. "When you see all those legs and arms hanging over into the hole," he said, "you just have to lower your shoulder and plow ahead. If you can't do that you're in the wrong line of work."

Quarterbacks absorb almost as much punishment as those who labor in the football trenches. Johnny Unitas, the great Baltimore Colts field general of the 1950s and 1960s, said, "The game is to hit, and be hit. I knew that from the outset. And it's what I wanted."

But the concept of hitting harbors a singular significance for those men in the NFL who earn a living on the defensive side of the ball. To them, making contact in a particularly violent manner constitutes an art form which serves to satisfy the needs of their somewhat aggressive psyches.

For 13 seasons, from 1960 to 1972, Larry Wilson was widely regarded as the toughest player in the National Football League. Fractures, lacerations, broken teeth, stitches, and contusions of varying magnitudes could not deter him from lining up at his free safety position in the St. Louis Cardinals' secondary. During the balance of one season he never missed a start despite a pair of broken hands.

"My rookie year in the NFL I went to see the trainer with an injury," he recalled. "He just gave me a Band-Aid and said, 'Shake it off, kid. You're a pro now.' I got the idea. Besides, I wanted to be out on the field. I really enjoyed hitting people."

Wilson perfected a daring maneuver which came to be known as the safety blitz. On passing downs he would "cheat up" to within a few yards of the scrimmage line. Then, at the snap of the ball, he deftly slipped through an opening in the protective line of blockers and made for the unsuspecting quarterback with a vengeance.

"I remember the first time I did it," he said, chuckling. "You should have seen the guy's face. His eyes were practically bulging out of their sockets."

Pound for pound no one hit harder than Wilson. He used his body as a virtual battering ram. A classic example of this technique in action involved a rookie wideout who had lauded his own abilities to the media before an outing against the Cardinals. In the course of the game he cut over the middle and leaped to make a catch. He was met in mid-air by a redshirted projectile and crumpled to the scarred turf like a felled bird. While he lay in a heap, devoid of both the ball and his senses, Wilson bent over him and cooed, "Welcome to the NFL, baby."

Someone once said that "linebackers are just fullbacks with their brains knocked out." What did he mean? Simply that the men who form the second line of defense in pro football qualify as instinctual hitters, individuals with a peculiar passion for contact. When mention is made of Dick Butkus, Chuck Bednarik, Sam Huff, Ray Nitschke, Jack Lambert, and Lawrence Taylor, visions of quarterbacks and ball carriers being swarmed under by doggedly ferocious pursuers take shape in the mind's eye.

Perhaps no hit in the history of the NFL was more publized than the one Bednarik, a premier linebacker with the Philadelphia Eagles from 1949 to 1962, administered to New York Giants running back Frank Gifford. As a result of this collision Gifford was forced out of football for more than a year. Bednarik described the situation; "We played our first game in 1960 against the Giants in Yankee Stadium. It was late in the fourth quarter and we were ahead 17-10 but the Giants had a drive going. Gifford ran a little down-and-in pattern as I was coming over from my left-side position. We met head-on. I think of it being like a one-way street with a Mack truck hitting a Volkswagen."

Gifford lay still and had to be taken from the field on a stretcher. A hush settled over the crowd. "They carried Frank off with a towel over his face," recalled Huff, who then played for the Giants. "Everybody thought he was dead." Several days elapsed before Bednarik learned that Gifford had suffered a fractured skull and intracranial bleeding. When he visited the hospital Gifford greeted him with a wan smile and said, "That was a heck of a tackle, Chuck." The public thought so too.

"Even today, people stop me to talk about the hit I put on Gifford," Bednarik said. "If it had been somebody else and another game against a team other than the Giants in Yankee Stadium the play would have gone unnoticed. But it was the Giants, in the Stadium, and Gifford, who went on to become a national celebrity. So I'm still getting a lot of attention because of that incident." Huff later said, "The hit Bednarik put on Gifford is the kind you dream about if you're a linebacker. I have to admit I'm a little envious."

Butkus was the most feared linebacker of his era (1965-1973), and with good reason. He stood three inches above six feet and tipped the beam at 245 pounds. Quick, agile, and ferocious, he seemed to be everywhere at once on the field. When a female fan wrote the Chicago Bears front office requesting a photo of the teams' defensive unit she received a picture of Butkus. He was that dominating. "Dick didn't simply tackle you," said Gale Sayers, the Bears' star running back. "He stomped right over you; up your legs, knees, back."

Paul Hornung, the Green Bay Packers' multi-purpose half-back, said, "With Butkus it was like you were somebody he really hated from his old neighborhood. He'd flat try to take your head off."

Did he actually intend to injure members of the opposition? "Naw, I didn't try to hurt anybody, except maybe on special occasions." When pressed to define such special occasions, Butkus thought a moment before replying, "Oh, league games, usually."

Of late, Giants' linebacker Lawrence Taylor has personified what hitting is all about in the NFL. "There's a sack, and then there's a real sack," he said. "A real sack is when you come in behind the quarterback, and he doesn't know you're there, and you hit him right between the shoulder blades. He goes flying one way, and the ball goes flying the other way, and the coach comes out and asks if you're OK. That's a real sack. I love it. You've got to play like a crazed dog to stay alive and well in this league."

Butkus couldn't agree more. "I loved practice, the games, the hitting," he said. "I loved all there was about pro football. When you put on that uniform, you ought to know what it means, what you're getting into out there. I did, and I loved it."

These few voices echo the sentiments of the many who have graced the NFL with their presence since its inception. Whether they wore leather helmets or no head gear at all, spit out their fragmented teeth with an expression of disdain and sported a broken nose as a badge of honor, or benefited from the more protective technology of recent years, they played with fervor this special trial by combat we know as pro football.

It has been and remains "a game the eleven toughest guys are supposed to win".

In the Beginning

American football evolved from the English game of rugby. In 1869, Rutgers and Princeton staged the first collegiate match and other eastern schools soon added the rough sport to their athletic programs. A set of rules for American football was compiled in 1876.

This new game as engaged in by the various athletic clubs throughout the northeast and upper midwest quickly captured the interest and imagination of the public. As the intensity of these competitions increased, natural rivalries developed between teams in the same region. Winning became important, very important. Before long, the recruiting of larger, faster, and more talented players got underway with such matters as ethics and fairness being largely ignored.

The inevitable ultimately took place in 1892. Yale All-America guard William "Pudge" Heffelfinger accepted $500 from Allegheny Athletic Association (AAA) officials to join their team for a crucial game with the Pittsburgh Athletic Club (PAC). Heffelfinger proved well worth his hire, returning a PAC fumble 35 yards for a touchdown to give the AAA a 4-0 win. Heffelfinger earned the distinction of being the first pro football player.

Not to be outdone, the Pittsburgh Athletic Club acquired the services of triple-threat back Grant Dibert for the entire 1893 schedule. This was the first professional contract to be signed. In 1895, John Brallier broke further new ground when he formally announced his intention to turn pro. He received $10 and expenses to lead the Latrobe YMCA squad against the Jeannette Athletic Club.

The Allegheny Athletic Club registered another first when all professionals were hired to play a brief two-game slate in 1896. A year later, the Latrobe Athletic Association team used paid personnel for the entire season. With the onset of the 1898 campaign the value of a touchdown was increased from four to five points.

Just prior to the turn of the century the Morgan Athletic Club came into existence on the south side of Chicago. With the passing years the team's name changed to the Normals, the Racine (Street) Cardinals, the Chicago Cardinals, the St. Louis Cardinals and, most recently, the Phoenix Cardinals. It now prevails as the oldest organization in pro football as well as the longest continuing franchise in the NFL.

In 1902, two Philadelphia baseball clubs, the Athletics and the Phillies, established pro football teams and joined the Pittsburgh Stars to form the National Football League, the first such confederation in the brief history of the play-for-pay game. Following the inaugural NFL season a World Series of pro football was conducted. The entrants included a team comprised of players from the Athletics, Phillies, and Stars along with the New York Knickerbockers, the Syracuse Athletic Club, the Warlow Athletic Club, and the Orange (N.J.) Athletic Club. Syracuse, led by guard Glenn "Pop" Warner, won the tournament.

The second and last World Series of pro football took place in December of 1903 with the Franklin (PA) Athletic Club, the Watertown Red and Blacks, and a pair of New Jersey teams, the Oreos and Orange Athletic Clubs, competing. Franklin took the title. Shortly thereafter the Massillon (Ohio) Tigers, an amateur team, signed four Pittsburgh pros for an important season-ending contest with an Akron team. Gradually, the center of pro football moved from Pennsylvania to Ohio.

During the 1904 season, seven of the game's top professional teams were located in the Buckeye state with Massillon being the best of the lot. By the end of that year the scoring of a field goal dropped from five to four points and halfback Charles Follis became the first black player to turn professional, joining the Shelby Athletic Club.

With the onset of the 1905 campaign, the Canton Athletic Club, later to be known as the Bulldogs, fielded an exceptionally strong team. But Massillon still managed to win its second successive Ohio League title and were considered to be the best pro aggregation in the land. In 1906, the forward pass gained acceptance as a legitimate offensive play.

Pro football lost much of its public allure due to a 1908 betting scandal and player recruitment improprieties involving the Canton and Massillon clubs. The following season a field goal was further devalued to three points. In 1912, the worth of a touchdown rose to six points. Both standards remain unchanged to this day.

Former Carlisle (PA) College star and Olympic gold medalist Jim Thorpe decided to try his hand as a pro in 1915, signing with Canton for the then munificent sum of $250 a game. He led the Bulldogs to three consecutive Ohio League crowns. In 1919, Earl "Curly" Lambeau organized the Green Bay Packers. The next year an attempt was made to standardize the rules and conduct of pro football. On September 17, 1920, representatives of teams from a four state area convened in Canton. From this meeting came a new and more comprehensive league named the American Professional Football Association (APFA). A prime mover in this alliance was George Halas, manager and head coach of the Decatur (IL) Staleys. By 1921 the APFA was comprised of no less than 22 clubs. That year the Staleys, now situated in Chicago, won the league championship.

The (Real) National Football League

In 1922 the APFA officially became the National Football League. Concurrent with this historical change Halas renamed his Chicago entry the Bears. At that time, he was part owner of the team, the general manager, the coach, the ticket manager, the public relations director and a starting two-way end. He scrapped on the field and off it to achieve the stability of not only the Bears but the NFL as well.

Despite the efforts of NFL leadership the professional game still ran a poor second in popularity to the college version. On Saturdays the major university stadiums were packed with cheering throngs, while the pros played before a relative handful on Sunday afternoons. Halas realized the necessity of legitimizing the NFL in the public view or the league wasn't going to survive.

With this realization foremost in mind he kept a sharp eye out for a collegiate star who might immediately translate into a lucrative attraction as a professional. He didn't have to look farther than a few miles south of Chicago to his alma mater, the University of Illinois. There a swivel-hipped halfback by the name of Harold "Red" Grange was dazzling the scholastic gridiron scene with his electrifying touchdown dashes. Famed sportswriter Grantland Rice wrote glowingly of the elusive Illini, referring to him as the "Galloping Ghost." By any measure Grange was a legend in his own time.

At the earliest possible moment Halas got Grange's signature on a pro contract. Millions of diehard football purists decried this transition but Grange, a poor boy in origin, responded, "If I didn't sign by next year most of these people would have forgotten me. Will they loan me a dollar then?" Given the assistance of an agent, C. C. "Cash and Carry" Pyle, Grange reached an agreement with Halas that afforded him a cut of the gate receipts. This leveraging technique served as a precursor of what has become common practice in the modern era of sports negotiations.

Grange made his professional debut on Thanksgiving Day of 1925, just 10 days after completing a storybook college career. When he emerged from the dressing room dugout at Wrigley Field in a Bears uniform some 36,000 worshippers, the largest crowd in pro football history at that point, greeted him with a roar. The game proved to be anticlimatic as Chicago Cardinals kicker Paddy Driscoll deftly directed his punts away from Grange, limiting him to a longest runback of 20 yards. It was much the same story from scrimmage, as Grange rushed for only 36 yards on the mushy, snowy turf. At day's end, however, he was $12,500 richer.

In early December the Bears embarked on an eight-game tour to showcase their marquee acquisition and enhance the NFL coffers. Fans flocked to see Grange work his ball-carrying magic in Philadelphia, St. Louis, Boston, Washington, DC, Detroit, and Pittsburgh. But the attendance high-water mark was set at New York's Polo Grounds, where 73,000 spectators watched the Galloping Ghost lead the Bears to a 14-7 win over the Giants.

Later that winter the Bears set out on a nine city swing through the South and West. In excess of 75,0000 people pushed their way into the Los Angeles Memorial Coliseum for a look at the headline maker from Illinois. They weren't disappointed in what they saw. When Grange finally slipped off his moleskins it was January of 1926. During the three-month stint he earned nearly $100,000, a phenomenal amount of money for that era. But it was small recompense for what he had attained. With him as the major attraction, the NFL became very much a going concern.

Thus it was ironic that later in the year Grange left the Bears as the result of a salary dispute and went to play for the American Football League (AFL), a hastily concocted invention of his front man, Pyle. The AFL folded after the 1926 season but Grange's team, the New York Yankees, was absorbed into the NFL for the 1927 campaign. He severely damaged a knee against the Bears, which hampered him for the rest of his career.

"I was just an ordinary ball carrier after that," he said. "I didn't play at all in 1928. And when I came back, I couldn't begin to do the things that before came so easily."

Grange performed largely as defensive back for the Bears prior to his retirement in 1934. Meanwhile, Ernie Nevers, a crunching runner from Stanford University, was writing himself into the record book with the crosstown Cardinals. The "Blond Bull," as sports writers liked to characterize him, was a scoring machine. In 1929, he tallied all of the Cardinals points as they whipped the Bears, 40-6. On the following Sunday he personally embarrassed the Dayton Triangles, 19-0. The end result was a total of 59 points in just two games, an achievement no one is ever likely to equal, let alone surpass.

After nearly a decade in business the NFL could boast of 12 participating clubs and having survived the challenge of its first rival league.

The 1930s: Coming of Age

Under the tutelage of Curly Lambeau the Green Bay Packers established themselves as the team to beat. With the slashing jaunts of halfback Johnny "Blood" McNally and the cannon arm of quarterback Arnie Herber the Packers won three NFL titles in a row. Then the bulldozing Clarke Hinkle joined their ball-carrying unit and so the Packers justifiably laid claim to the most explosive offense in the league. But even as Green Bay was pushing to the fore, other franchises were experiencing substantive financial problems.

In 1932, the number of clubs dropped to eight, the lowest membership ever. On a positive note, Bronko Nagurski, the Bears' steamrolling fullback, was receiving extensive coverage in sports pages across the country. He possessed good speed and his 225 pounds were packed on a 6'2" frame with the consistency of cement. Needless to say, he posed big problems for enemy defenders.

Nevers said, "Tackling Nagurski is like meeting a freight train going downhill. First time I had a chance, I hit him high. He just bowled me over and kept going. I darn near got killed. After that I simply tried to trip him up." Added Grange: "When you tackle the Bronk, it's like an electric shock going through your body. If you hit him above the ankles, you can get killed."

Nagurski did come off second best once when he crashed through a phalanx of would-be tacklers and careened off the field into a wall. He rose on unsteady legs and gasped, "Geeze, that last guy really hit me."

The Bears and the Portsmouth Spartans finished the regular schedule tied for the lead, which necessitated the NFL's first playoff game. Because of bitter cold and heavy snow, league officials moved the championship site to Chicago Stadium, an indoor arena. Due to space limitations the field measured only 80 yards and the goal posts were set in from the back of the end zones. The breadth of the playing surface was also constricted by establishing a series of hashmarks 10 yards from the walls that formed the sidelines. After each down the ball was put in play at these designated spots. The Bears defeated the Spartans 9-0 on a disputed pass completion to claim their first NFL crown.

In other developments, the league began to keep statistics for all of its members and a franchise was awarded to Boston. George Preston Marshall, of Washington, D.C., headed a syndicate that established the team designated as the Braves. Later in the year, Marshall bought out his partners to become the sole proprietor of the club.

From the very outset 1933 was a year of change. During their winter meeting, NFL officials decided to write their own rules rather than continue to abide by those that governed college football. Initially, they voted to keep two of the innovations used in the 1932 playoff game—the series of hashmarks set 10 yards in from the sidelines and the goal posts situated on the goal line. They also ruled that a forward pass could be thrown from anywhere, not just five yards or deeper, behind the line of scrimmage.

Later, Halas and Marshall lobbied through a proposal that divided the teams into two geographically defined groups, with the winners to meet in an annual championship game. The league increased to 10 teams with the addition of the Pittsburgh Pirates, the Philadelphia Eagles, and the Cincinnati Reds. Meanwhile, the Staten Island Stapletons suspended operations. Halas took complete control of the Bears and Marshall changed the name of his team to the Boston Redskins.

With each of the clubs consigned to a distinct division, rivalries naturally developed and heightened fan interest. The Bears captured Western honors while the Giants finished atop the Eastern standings. The two clubs vied for the NFL title at Wrigley Field and the Bears prevailed, but barely, 23-21.

On August 31, 1934, the NFL champion Bears went against the best college football talent in the land before 79,432 vocal fans at Chicago's Soldier Field. The contest ended in a scoreless tie, but the pro game gained new and much needed prestige.

Regular league play opened with the former Portsmouth Spartans renamed the Lions and representing the city ofDetroit. With three weeks left in the campaign, the Reds were suspended for insolvency and an independent team, the St. Louis Gunners, was conscripted to complete the Cincinnati schedule. CBS radio broadcast the Thanksgiving Day game between the Bears and Lions for a national audience with famed announcer Graham McNamee doing the play-by-play. Rookie Beattie Feathers of the Bears became the first back in NFL history to rush for 1,000 yards in a season.

Chicago and New York went at it again for league laurels, this time at the Polo Grounds where the field was hard and patched with ice. The Giants were led by halfback Ken Strong, who topped the NFL in scoring the previous year and had just completed another banner campaign. But except for a lone field goal, he was unable to score against the Bears in the first half because of his inablity to change direction on the slippery turf. So Chicago enjoyed a 13-3 advantage at the intermission.

Early in the third quarter, the Giants switched to basketball sneakers for better traction and from that point on Strong hit his stride. In addition to a field goal he tallied two touchdowns and kicked four PAT conversions for a total of 17 points, more than the Bears could amass as a team. It was a performance that defied parallel for 30 years. New York won handily, 30-13.

At the 1935 winter meeting, Eagles' owner Bert Bell suggested that the league conduct a yearly selection of college players with the teams having the poorest records getting the chance to pick first. The measure quickly passed and the first draft was set for early the next year. In other action, officials approved moving the hashmarks another five yards in from the sidelines. In what would be the last recruiting drive by NFL clubs, the Packers signed Alabama All-America end Don Huston.

Triple-threat quarterback Earl "Dutch" Clarke kicked, passed and ran the Lions to a 26-7 victory over the Giants in the 1935 NFL championship tilt.

On February 8, 1936, University of Chicago halfback and Heisman Trophy recipient Jay Berwanger was the first collegian ever to be chosen in an NFL draft. But he declined to join the Eagles, having no interest in pro football. Second pick Riley Smith of Alabama did agree to terms with the Boston Redskins. A second American Football League (AFL) went into business and the Boston Shamrocks became its champion.

Despite the fact that the Redskins won the Eastern Division crown with All-Pro halfback Cliff Battles leading the way, the club did poorly at the gate. This lack of fan support in the Hub City so incensed Marshall that he arranged to play Green Bay, the Western Division winner, for league superiority at the Polo Grounds. The Boston populace gave no indication that it even noticed the snub. The pitch-and-catch combination of Herber and Hutson proved too much for the Redskins and the Packers prevailed, 21-6.

On February 12, 1937, Marshall moved his club to the nation's capital and called them the Washington Redskins. The following day he signed his franchise player, Texas Christian University All-America tailback Sammy Baugh. Almost immediately the Lone Star slinger took charge, passing and punting the club to the top of the Eastern Division. In a deciding contest with the Giants at the Polo Grounds he completed 11 of 15 aerial attempts and the Redskins routed New York, 49-14. A week later against the Bears at frigid Wrigley Field with NFL laurels in the balance, he threw for 335 yards and three touchdowns as Washington squeaked through, 28-21. Meanwhile, the AFL folded in the wake of its second season.

In 1938, rookie Byron "Whizzer" White of the Pittsburgh Pirates was the league's leading rusher. The Giants overcame the powerful Packers, 23-17, at the Polo Grounds to again reign as NFL champions. Marshall, in conjunction with Los Angeles Times sports editor Bill Henry and promoter Tom Gallery, established the Pro Bowl, which would feature the NFL titlists playing an aggregation of all-stars from the other teams.

On January 15, 1939, the Giants edged the Pro All-Stars, 13-10, in the inaugural Pro Bowl. NBC telecast a regular season contest between the Brooklyn Dodgers and the Eagles from Ebbets Field to some 1,000 viewers in the New York City area. For the first time in league annals, more than a million spectators paid their way to watch pro football during the course of the year. Green Bay savored sweet revenge, blanking the Giants 27-0 in Milwaukee to reclaim the NFL title.

The 1940s: War and Peace

With offensive genius Clark Shaughnessy of Standford serving as a consultant, the Bears undertook to master the T-Formation as their new mode of attack. Second-year quarterback Sid Luckman had been tabbed as the man to make the system work. At the outset he experienced difficulty in making the transition from tailback to working behind center. He frequently fumbled the direct snap and found the footwork required to execute handoffs completely foreign to him. For a while he was moved to halfback. Given a second chance, however, he mastered the task.

When the Bears played the Redskins in Washington near the end of the regular schedule, Luckman did little to distinguish himself. And Chicago lost a 7-3 decision. Some observers felt the Bears had been mistaken to change their mode of operation. But Shaughnessy's faith in the T-Formation wasn't shaken. He knew the Redskins won because they had effectively overshifted their linebackers to neutralize the Bears' man-in-motion ploy. So he took Luckman under his wing and together they worked on a means of dealing with the Washington maneuver.

The adjustment was simple. If the Redskins' linebackers shifted to cover the man-in-motion, then Luckman simply pivoted inside and flipped the ball to a second back crossing in the opposite direction toward a split end. The end would block back to the center of the field while the interior of the offensive line slanted over to run interference against a weakened secondary.

On December 8, the teams met again in Washington for the NFL championship. On the first play from scrimmage, the Redskins linebackers shifted with the Bears man-in-motion. As planned, Luckman pitched to the other back running the counter option and he sprinted 68 yards for a touchdown. It was the first of many scores as Chicago went on to win by a 73-0 margin. More than half a century later this stunning defeat remains on the books as the worst beating ever administered in the history of the NFL.

Luckman put up only six passes, four of them connecting for 102 yards and a touchdown. He didn't throw more often because it simply wasn't necessary. But he directed the Bears awesome ground attack to perfection with deft fakes, handoffs and bootlegs that had the Washington defenders guessing all afternoon. Given this mind boggling display of T-Formation power, pro football moved into a new and exciting era without so much as a backward glance.

In 1941, the NFL instituted playoff games to break ties for division honors. This included a sudden death format should the contests be deadlocked at the finish of regulation time. As it so happened, the Bears and Packers closed the year with identical records atop the Western Division. Chicago prevailed 33-14 in the elimination contest and then whipped the Giants 37-9 for the league crown.

Before the 1941 season, Pittsburgh Pirates owner Art Rooney sold the team and then promptly purchased a piece of the Eagles. In 1942 Rooney and Bell traded the Eagles for the Pittsburgh team and renamed it the Steelers. In something of a footnote, the second AFL ceased operations after two seasons.

The deeper involvement of the United States in World War II produced a severe shortage of pro football manpower during the 1942 campaign. But it was still business as usual with the Redskins shading the Bears 14-6 in the NFL title game. In 1943, the league permitted the Cleveland Rams to suspend operations for the season as both the club owners were in the military. Meanwhile, the Steelers and the Eagles merged to play out the schedule and were referred to as Phil-Pitt. Both cities hosted an equal number of home games.

The league granted a new franchise to Boston, approved free substitution, and ruled that helmets were mandatory equipment for all players. Baugh paced the league in passing, punting and defensive interceptions. And Washington defeated New York, 28-0, in a playoff game to claim Eastern Division superiority. But the Redskins fell victim to the Bears, 41-21, in the NFL Championship game.

Prior to the onset of the 1944 season the Cardinals and the Steelers were allowed to merge for the sake of mutual survival. The Boston franchise became known as the Yanks, and Brooklyn dropped its "Dodgers" tag in favor of being called the Tigers. Also, coaching from the bench was approved. The Packers slipped past the Giants, 14-7, to reign over the league for the sixth time.

As the war wound down in 1945 the Brooklyn Tigers quit the NFL for the new All-America Football Conference (AAFC). Late in the season Halas returned from the Navy to take charge of the Bears again. Once more the hashmarks were moved, this time to a point 20 yards in from the sidelines. And a pair of rookies, halfback Steve Van Buren of the Eagles and quarterback Bob Waterfield of the Cleveland Rams, served notice to their more veteran counterparts that change was on the way in the pro football establishment.

Van Buren led the league in rushing and kick return yardage as well as total scoring. Waterfield directed the Rams to a 15-14 win over the Redskins and the NFL Championship. In that game, a Baugh-thrown pass from the Washington end zone struck the cross bar of the goal posts and was ruled a safety, giving Cleveland a precious two points.

Bert Bell, co-owner of the Steelers, took over as NFL commissioner in Jaunary of 1946. That same month league officials determined that a forward pass striking the goal posts should be considered an incomplete attempt. In other action, the Rams were allowed to move their franchise to Los Angeles.

On the eve of the NFL title game Giants halfbacks Frank Filchock and Merle Hapes came under fire for not reporting a bribe offer. Following a hurried investigation of the matter Hapes got benched but Filchock was allowed to play. The Bears took advantage of the unsettling situation to register a 24-14 win and return the league crown to Chicago. Meanwhile, the Cleveland Browns proved they were the best of the eight-teams in the AAFC with a 14-6 championship victory over the New York Yankees.

A back judge was added to the officials who worked NFL games, bringing the crews to five members. Given the presence of a rival conference, the commissioner augmented the drafting process with a first round bonus pick which was assigned by means of a lottery drawing. The Chicago Cardinals became league titlists via a 26-

21 victory over the Eagles, who had made the big game by shutting out the Steelers, 21-0, in a playoff meeting for Eastern Division honors. Once again, the Browns proved they were the cream of the AAFC crop.

In 1948, the NFL approved the use of an artificial tee to enhance the kickoff ritual. Rams halfback Fred Gehrke painted horns on his helmet to initiate the use of equipment designs. And whistles rather than the traditional horns were distributed to all game officials with the exception of referees.

The Cardinals and the Eagles went at it again for league laurels, this time in a blizzard. Philadelphia won, 7-0, on a disputed scoring plunge by Van Buren. Cleveland claimed its third consecutive AAFC crown, battering the Buffalo Bills, 49-7, in the championship contest for a perfect 15-0 record.

Before the weekend wars got underway in 1949 the Boston Yanks became the New York Bulldogs and shared the Polo Grounds with the Giants. Free substitution, adopted once and rejected, was given another trial. By season's end the NFL had experienced a marked change in its configuration.

On December 9, Bell announced that the league was taking in three teams from the defunct AAFC—the perennial champion Browns, the San Franciso 49ers, and the Baltimore club—commencing with the 1950 campaign. The Eagles slogged past the Rams, 14-0, in a driving rain to take the NFL title. Van Buren again rushed for 1,000 yards as did Green Bay halfback Tony Canadeo.

The 1950s: Pro Football Goes National

Unlimited free substitution was restored in January of 1950. This opened the way for platoon football (offensive and defensive units) and specialization in many of the skill positions. American and National Conferences were formed to replace the Eastern and Western Division concept. And Curly Lambeau, founder and head coach of the Packers since 1921, left the Green Bay organization under fire.

In other developments, the New York Bulldogs adopted the name Yanks and divided the players from the former AAFC Yankees with the Giants. A special draft was conducted which allowed the 13 clubs to select from the remaining AAFC personnel. Each team received 10 choices except for Baltimore, which was allotted 15 picks because of its depleted roster.

The Rams and the Redskins arranged to have all of their home games televised, while some of the other clubs had only selected games on TV. But the big subject of discussion around the league concerned how the Browns, an AAFC powerhouse, might be expected to fare against the NFL champion Eagles in the season opener for both clubs on the evening of September 16 at Philadelphia's Municipal Stadium. While Cleveland was dominating "that other league" not a few NFL owners and officials were publicly labeling the club "cheese champs" and "second raters." None of this was lost on the Browns or their coach Paul Brown.

"I remember the attitude of some people in the NFL toward us quite clearly," Brown said. "They figured we had done pretty well with the teams in the AAFC, but they also figured their worst team could beat us."

During the weeks preceding the much anticipated showdown Brown and his players kept to themselves, being careful not to make any inflammatory statements to the media. All the while they were focusing on this game like none other in their careers.

Shortly before the contest, Brown told reporters, "The Eagles may chase us off the gridiron, but we're going out there with no alibis. Quite truthfully, I really don't know what to expect tonight."

In looking back on that time, he recalled, "I was just trying to keep our people from crystallizing emotionally before we got onto the field. We had a couple of years to think about playing in the NFL, about getting an opportunity to play against the clubs that had ridiculed us, and that made us a very aroused group. So we, the coaches, tried kiddingly to get the players not to take the game too seriously. But there just wasn't any way they weren't taking the game seriously."

After a slow first quarter in which the Eagles kicked a field goal for an early lead, the game belonged to the Browns. They forged ahead 7-3 then just kept building on their advantage and won going away, 35-10.

It would have been worse had not a pair of Cleveland scores been nullified by infractions. "The two disallowed touchdowns were due to clipping penalties," Brown said. "But the game films showed they were both missed calls." Philadelphia tackle Bucko Kilroy added, "Cleveland just dominated the game. It was no contest. The score could have been 61-10."

At season's end playoff games were required to determine the winners of both conferences. The Browns defeated the Giants and the Rams beat the Bears. In the NFL Championship matchup Cleveland slipped past Los Angeles, 30-28, to quiet what few naysayers remained. Not a bad debut for "second raters."

The Pro Bowl experienced a rebirth on January 14, 1951 with a new format that featured all-stars from the National and American Conferences playing each other at Los Angeles' Memorial Coliseum. Later that month the league bought control of the struggling Baltimore franchise and made the team's players available in the general draft. Courtesy of the DuMont Television Network, viewers nationwide watched the NFL title game in which the Rams turned the tables on the Browns, 24-17. This was a monumental first for pro football.

Early in 1952 the New York Yanks were reclaimed by the league. Some weeks thereafter a Dallas group took over operation of the team, renaming it the Texans. But they too succumbed to financial problems and the club again became a ward of the NFL. For the remainder of the campaign the team played out of Hershey, Pennsylvania, and was then eliminated from the fold.

The Steelers abandoned the Single-Wing for the T-Formation, the last team in the league to do so. And the Detroit Lions, given the direction of fiery quarterback Bobby Layne, beat the Browns, 17-7, for the NFL crown.

A Baltimore syndicate acquired the holdings of the defunct Texans on January 23, 1953. The new team, dubbed the Colts, promptly put together the largest trade in league history, sending five players to Cleveland and receiving 10 others. In what might be termed a reversal of form, the National and American Conferences were designated as the Eastern and Western Conferences. Jim Thorpe died on March 28. Once again Layne proved to be the difference as the Lions edged the Browns, 17-16, for league honors.

With the onset of 1954, the Canadian Football League began raiding NFL teams for talent. San Francisco fullback Joe "The Jet" Perry exceeded the 1,000-yard rushing mark for the second successive year, a league first. Cleveland rolled over Detroit, 56-10, to claim another NFL title.

During their winter meeting of 1955 league owners ruled that the ball is to be spotted where a tackled runner touches the ground with any part of his body except for the hands and feet. The National Football League Players Association (NFLPA) was formed. For the price of an 80-cent phone call the Colts were able to sign free agent quarterback Johnny Unitas.

Otto Graham passed and ran the Browns past the Rams, 38-14, as they successfully defended their league crown. In the wake of these heroics, Graham retired for the second time. During his career in the All-American Football Conference and the National Football League, Graham had the distinction of quarterbacking Cleveland to 10 championship game appearances in as many years. NBC replaced DuMont as the network that televised the title contest.

Prior to the 1956 season the Giants left the Polo Grounds to play their home schedule in Yankee Stadium. Halas stepped down as coach of the Bears. And CBS began carrying a few league games to select TV markets across the country. New York clubbed Chicago, 47-7, to reign supreme in the NFL.

More than 100,000 fans watched the 49ers and the Rams at the Los Angeles Memorial Coliseum on November 10, 1957. Pete Rozelle became general manager of the Los Angeles franchise. Detroit came from 20 points behind to eclipse San Francisco, 31-27, for Western Conference honors. The Lions then blew out the Browns, 59-14, to become league titlists once more.

Halas reinstated himself as coach of the Bears for the 1958 slate. Cleveland's Jim Brown rushed for an NFL season record of 1,527 yards. But in the Eastern Conference playoff the Giants limited him to only eight yards and prevailed 10-0.

It was Baltimore, Western Conference winner, against New York in Yankee Stadium with CBS telecasting the NFL Championship matchup to more viewers than ever before in pro football history. The millions of people who looked on were treated to what has been called the most dramatic and perhaps the greatest game ever played. After jumping out to an early lead, the Colts had to come roaring back to deadlock the score just seconds before the final gun and then went on to win 23-17 in sudden-death overtime, the first such session with a league title at stake.

Recounting the experience, Unitas said, "I firmly believe the 1958 championship game between New York and Baltimore put professional football on the map. It reached more households than any other sporting event up to that time. Everything involved with the game, I think, served to catch the fancy of the viewing public. The desperate drive at the end of regulation play, the overtime, the strategies employed by both teams, the timing and coordination of the event itself and the trading back and forth in the scoring all worked perfectly to make it a great sales promotion for the NFL."

On January 28, 1959, professional football entered a new era when Vince Lombardi was named head coach of the Green Bay franchise. Later in the year Giants' owner Tim Mara and commissioner Bert Bell died, further diminishing the ranks of the league's old guard. Baltimore and New York met again for NFL honors, but this time the Colts won easily, 31-16.

Meanwhile, yet another American Football League (AFL) was quickly and quietly taking shape. Lamar Hunt of Dallas and a collection of other monied sportsmen moved ahead in businesslike fashion to consolidate plans for the commencement of play during the fall of 1960. Before the year was out no less than two full-scale drafts had been conducted by the eight clubs that comprised the AFL.

The 1960s: A Legend and the AFL Wars

On the same day, January 26, 1960, Rozelle was named the new commissioner of the NFL and Hunt became president of the AFL. The battle was officially underway. However, a verbal no-tampering agreement was reached between the two leagues concerning players' contracts.

NFL franchises were awarded to Dallas and Minnesota. Dallas was to commence play in the fall, while Minnesota had a 1961 starting date. In related action, the Cardinals ownership received permission to move the club from Chicago to St. Louis.

The Eagles held on to defeat the Packers, 17-14, for the NFL Championship. It would be the first and last time a Lombardi-coached team failed to win a title challenge. The occasion also marked the end of the two-way performer, as Philadelphia's Chuck Bednarik played his final game at both center and linebacker. Fittingly enough, it was his tackle in the waning moments of the contest that preserved the Eagles' slim lead.

Legs churning like well-oiled pistons, Green Bay fullback Jim Taylor emerged from a pile of bodies and turned upfield toward the Phildelphia end zone. Just as he did his forward progess was abruptly halted with a muted thud. Powerful arms wrestled him to the snowy turf and held him there until the game-ending gun sounded.

"I was 35 years old at the time," Bednarik recalled. "When Taylor broke through I made the stop on him at the nine-yard line with about 16 seconds left to play. From where I was sitting on him I could see the clock running down. Taylor asked me to get off him in rather strong language, but I didn't comply until time had expired. That day I was in there the entire game at center and left-side linebacker. I did everything but go down on kickoffs. I even snapped the ball for punts, extra points, and field goals. Yeah, I'm the last guy to go 60 minutes. But all things considered, being a part of winning the 1960 championship was the high point of my 14-year career." The Houston Oilers won the inaugural AFL title game, besting the Los Angeles Chargers, 24-16, on January 1, 1961.

End Willard Dewveall of the Bears played out his option and then jumped to the AFL, the first player to jump leagues. Canton, Ohio was designated as the site for the proposed Pro Football Hall of Fame. And NBC received a two-year pact granting the network exclusive radio and TV rights to the NFL Championship game.

In a rematch for the AFL crown the Oilers again took the measure of the Chargers (now in San Diego), 10-3. A week later the Lombardi era got underway with the Packers clubbing the Giants, 37-0, for the NFL championship.

In 1962 CBS contracted to televise all the NFL's regular season games, and a federal district judge in Baltimore ruled against the AFL in its antitrust litigation with the NFL. Green Bay made it two in a row over the Giants, 16-7, for the NFL title, and the Dallas Texans stopped the Oilers, 20-17, in overtime to win the AFL Championship.

Early in 1963 the Texans became the Kansas City Chiefs and the defunct New York Titans found new life as the Jets. Meanwhile, Packers halfback Paul Hornung and Lions defensive tackle Alex Karras were suspended indefinitely for gambling on NFL games. Paul Brown was fired as Cleveland's coach and Don Shula became field boss of the Colts. Jim Brown set a new single-season rushing mark of 1,863 yards.

The Pro Football Hall of Fame was dedicated in Canton, Ohio, and the U.S. Fourth Circuit Court of Appeals reaffirmed that the AFL was not entitled to damages in its antitrust suit against the NFL. Chicago held off the Giants, 14-10, to give Halas a record sixth NFL Championship, and the Chargers turned back the Boston Patriots for AFL honors. CBS signed with the NFL to telecast all regular season games as well as the league championship for a two-year period. Hornung and Karras were reinstated and Pete Gogolak became the first soccer-style kicker in pro football, signing with the Buffalo Bills, who whipped San Deigo, 20-7, for the AFL title. Cleveland blanked Baltimore, 27-0, to top the NFL.

Another official—the line judge—brought to six the members of an NFL game crew. CBS renewed its broadcast agreement with the league for two more years and franchises were awarded to Atlanta (NFL) and Miami (AFL) effective in 1966. The Bills again overcame the Chargers, 23-0, for the AFL crown. Green Bay edged Baltimore, 13-10, in sudden death to finish atop the Western Conference. Then the Packers dumped the Browns, 23-12, to reign in the NFL.

During the spring of 1966 a series of secret meetings between the NFL and AFL led to a merger of the two leagues. Separate schedules were to be maintained through 1969 with a World Championship game (the Super Bowl) featuring the NFL and AFL champions set to begin in 1967 along with a common draft. The leagues would come together officially in 1970. Congress approved the merger, exempting it from antitrust legislation.

New Orleans was awarded an NFL franchise for 1967, and the St. Louis Cardinals became residents of Busch Memorial Stadium. The NFL divided the Eastern Conference into Capitol and Century Divisions and the Western Conference into Central and Coastal Divisions for the 1967-1969 period. CBS and NBC jointly purchased the broadcast rights to the Super Bowl for four years.

On January 1, 1967, the Packers defeated Dallas, 34-27, to win the NFL title and the right to represent the league in Super Bowl I. Their opponent was the Chiefs, who drubbed Buffalo 31-7 for the AFL crown. In the big game Green Bay ran over Kansas City, 35-10, before a national TV audience and 61,946 spectators at Los Angeles Memorial Coliseum.

The "sling shot" goal post replaced the wide H, and a six-foot-wide border around the field became standard in the NFL. Paul Brown, the former Cleveland coach, and several partners were awarded a franchise in Cincinnati by the AFL for the 1968 season.

In one of the most famous playoff games, Green Bay repeated as NFL champion, 21-17, on a last minute quarterback sneak touchdown by Bart Starr against the Dallas Cowboys on a frigid, minus 13 degree afternoon. The Oakland Raiders clubbed Houston, 40-7, to win the AFL title.

On January 14, 1968, the Packers made it two Super Bowl victories in a row with a 33-14 beating of the Raiders in Miami. Lombardi resigned as Green Bay's coach but remained with the club as general manager. Halas retired as coach of the Bears for the fourth and last time. The Oilers moved to the Houston Astrodome, the first NFL club to play in a domed stadium.

Weeb Ewbank, former coach of the NFL champion Colts, directed the New York Jets to AFL honors with a 27-23 win over Oakland. Baltimore swept past the Browns, 34-0, for NFL supremacy.

In one of the greatest upsets in NFL history, the Jets—led by flamboyant quarterback "Broadway" Joe Namath—beat the highly favored Colts, 16-7, in Miami on January 12, 1969 to give the AFL it's first Super Bowl triumph. Lombardi became executive vice-president and head coach of the Redskins. Former Washington owner George Preston Marshall died at 72. Baltimore, Cleveland and Pittsburgh agreed to join the AFL teams to form the American Football Conference (AFC) of the NFL. ABC contracted to televise 13 NFL regular-schedule games on Monday nights during the 1970, 1971 and 1972 seasons.

The 1970s: Miami, Pittsburgh and Change

On January 11, 1970, the Chiefs downed the Minnesota Vikings, 23-7, in Super Bowl IV at New Orleans to even up the count between the NFL and the AFL at two wins each. CBS and NBC signed a four-year TV package with the new NFL. All National Football Conference (NFC) games became the broadcast property of CBS while NBC would cover all the AFC contests. The Super Bowl and the NFC-AFC Pro Bowl telecasts were to be split between the networks.

As commissioner of the enlarged 26-team league Rozelle ruled that the attempt after a touchdown would be worth only a point (there had been a two-point option in the AFL) and designated the scoreboard clock as the official timepiece for all games. In addition, names were to be displayed on the backs of players' jerseys.

Pittsburgh moved into Three Rivers Stadium, while the Cincinnati Bengals leased Riverfront Stadium for their home games. New Orleans Saints kicker Tom Dempsey booted a league record 63-yard field goal against the Lions. And Lombardi died of cancer at 57.

Baltimore edged Dallas, 16-13, with a 32-yard field goal by Jim O'Brien in the waning seconds of Super Bowl V at Miami on January 17, 1971. A week later the NFC whipped the AFC, 27-6, in the Pro Bowl at Los Angeles.

New ballparks were all the rage as the Eagles' home field became Veterans Stadium, San Francisco switched to Candlestick Park, the Cowboys left the Cotton Bowl for Texas Stadium and the Patriots quit Boston for Schaefer Stadium in suburban Foxboro. They became the New England Patriots.

On Christmas Day Miami and Kansas City engaged in the longest pro football game ever, one hour, 22 minutes and 40 seconds actual playing time, with the Dolphins prevailing, 27-24, via a sudden-death field goal by Garo Yepremian. The Dolphins didn't fare as well in Super Bowl VI at New Orleans on January 16, 1972, losing to Dallas by a 24-3 margin.

Once again the hashmarks were moved closer to the center of the field, this time 23 yards, one foot and nine inches from the sidelines. Pittsburgh running back Franco Harris made his much disputed "Immaculate Reception" of a deflected pass to give the Steelers their first postseason victory ever, 13-7, at the expense of the Raiders.

Miami returned to the Super Bowl on January 14, 1973 in Los Angeles to defeat Washington, 14-7, and complete a perfect 17-0 record, the first unblemished regular season and playoff mark in NFL history. The AFC bested the NFC, 33-28, in the Pro Bowl at Dallas.

The Buffalo Bills made arrangements to play in Rich Stadium, while the Giants quit Yankee Stadium to play the remainder of their home games at the Yale Bowl in New Haven, Connecticut.

Running back O. J. Simpson of the Bills became the first back to rush for more than 2,000 yards in a season. The World Football League (WFL) was formed with plans to commence operation in 1974. On January 13, 1974, the Dolphins made their third consecutive trip to the Super Bowl, defeating Minnesota, 24-7, at Houston in the seventh renewal of the big game.

Tampa Bay and Seattle received NFL franchises with both clubs to start play in 1976. Rule changes were made which (1) added overtime periods to regular-season games, (2) moved the goal posts to the back of the end zone, (3) placed kickoffs at the 35-yard line, (4) returned the ball to the point of scrimmage after missed field goals beyond the 20-yard line, (5) eliminated roll blocking and cutting of wide receivers, (6) reduced the penalties for offensive holding, illegal use of the hands and tripping from 15 to 10 yards, (7) prohibited blocking below the waist within three yards of the scrimmage line, and (8) restricted contact with an eligible receiver downfield.

The Toronto Northmen of the WFL pirated running backs Larry Csonka and Jim Kiick and wideout Paul Warfield from the NFL champion Dolphins. Pittsburgh turned back Minnesota, 16-6, in Super Bowl IX at New Orleans on January 12, 1975. It was the Steelers first championship in 42 years of existence.

Referees were equipped with wireless microphones and the WFL folded. The Lions moved to the Pontiac Silverdome, the Saints to the Louisiana Superdome and the Giants to Shea Stadium. On January 18, 1976, the Steelers became only the third team in the NFL to win back-to-back Super Bowls, edging Dallas, 21-17, at Miami. The Packers and Dolphins had turned the trick previously.

The Giants finally took possession of their new stadium in East Rutherford, New Jersey. Pittsburgh beat the College All-Stars in the last contest of the series. St. Louis defeated San Diego, 20-10, in Tokyo, the first NFL game to be played outside of North America.

Minnesota lost again in the Super Bowl, this time to Oakland by a 32-14 count on January 9, 1977 at Pasadena. A record crowd of 103,438 filled the Rose Bowl to watch the proceedings. The NFLPA and the league reached a five-year agreement settling prior legal disputes, monetary allotments, and setting active roster limits at 43 players. Seattle was assigned to the AFC Western Division and Tampa Bay went to the NFC Central Division.

New rules changes allowed defenders to contact receivers only once downfield, and prohibited (1) the headslap, (2) hand blocking to the head, face and throat, and (3) clipping anywhere on the field. Chicago running back Walter Payton rushed for 275 yards to set a single-game NFL record. Dallas blanked the Denver Broncos, 27-0, in Super Bowl XII on January 15, 1978, at the Superdome. The game enjoyed the highest viewership of any program in television history.

A side judge was added to officiating crews. The regular-season slate went to 16 games. Receivers could be impeded only within five yards of the scrimmage line and linemen were permitted to pass block with open hands and extended arms.

The Steelers shaded the Cowboys, 35-31, to annex their third Super Bowl, a league first, on January 21, 1979 at Miami. More rules changes: (1) no blocking below the waist during punts, kickoffs and field goal attempts, (2) no playing with torn, altered or exposed equipment, (3) the no-crackback blocking area was enlarged, and (4) the quarterback couldn't advance the ball when in the grasp of a tackler. Don Shula of Miami, Tom Landry of Dallas, and Chuck Noll of Pittsburgh became the leading coaches of the modern era.

The 1980s: Enter the Frisco Connection

The Steelers made it an unprecedented four Super Bowl victories, downing Los Angeles, 31-19, on January 20, 1980 at Pasadena. Aloha Stadium in Honolulu became the site of the Pro Bowl, with the NFC outscoring the AFC, 37-27.

In other developments, the Rams selected Anaheim Stadium as their new home and the Raiders sued the NFL for the right to move from Oakland to the L. A. Coliseum.

On January 25, 1981, Philadelphia lost a 27-10 Super Bowl decision to Oakland, the first wild-card team to win the big game, at the Superdome. Attendance figures and TV viewership hit an all-time league high.

San Francisco outlasted the Cincinnati Bengals, 26-21, in Super Bowl XVI on January 24, 1982, at the Pontiac Silverdome.

A trial jury ruled against the NFL in its litigation with Oakland, allowing the Raiders to play in the L.A. Coliseum. The regular-season schedule was cut to nine games due to a 57-day NFLPA strike. As a result, the league constructed a 16-team playoff tournament to determine the Super Bowl contestants.

The Redskins bested the Dolphins, 27-17, in Super Bowl XVII on January 30, 1983 at Pasadena. Halas, the last surviving founder of the NFL, died at 88. The United States Football League (USFL) was formed as a spring/summer alternative to the NFL.

Washington returned to the Super Bowl in Tampa on January 22, 1984, only to absord a 38-9 drubbing at the hands of the Raiders.

The Colts relocated to the Hoosier Dome in Indianapolis and the Jets took up residence at Giants Stadium. A number of all-time, single-season marks were set: (1) Miami's Dan Marino threw for 5,084 yards and 48 TDs, (2) Eric Dickerson of the Rams rushed for 2,105 yards on the year, and (3) Redskins' wideout Art Monk caught a single-season record 106 passes. Meanwhile, Walter Payton of the Bears became the all-time leader in rushing yardage.

San Francisco collected its second Super Bowl trophy, outplaying Miami, 38-16, on January 20, 1985 at Stanford, California. More people watched the game than any other live telecast in history. A series of overseas preseason contests were planned for 1986.

In the wake of three campaigns, the USFL folded and brought anti-trust action against the NFL. A judge ruled in favor of the USFL and ordered the NFL to pay retribution of one dollar.

Chicago, with heroic running back Walter Payton and linebacker Mike Singletary, crushed New England, 46-10, in Super Bowl XX on January 26, 1986 at the Superdome.

Preceding the 1986 season use of instant replay to decide close plays was adopted on a limited basis, and the Bears defeated Dallas, 17-6, in the first American Cup game at London's Wembley Stadium. On January 25, 1987, the Giants beat Denver, 39-20, in Super Bowl XXI at Pasadena.

The NFL enjoyed an all-time attendance record of 17,304,463 paying customers during the 1987 season. Instant reply was approved for another year. A 24-day NFLPA strike cut the schedule to 15 games with replacement teams made up of non-NFL players performing from weeks four through six. Cable network ESPN added Sunday night telecasts to the coverage of NFL games.

In a return to the Super Bowl, the Broncos took a 42-10 thrashing from Washington on January 31, 1988, at San Diego. The game was seen live or on tape in 60 foreign countries.

A 2nd Circuit Appeals Court verdict in New York found for the NFL in its suit with the defunct USFL. Instant replay won another stay of execution with the reviewing official to be a member of the regular seven-man game crew. To help speed up games, which were routinely lasting well over three hours, the NFL changed from a 30-second to a 45-second clock that runs between offensive plays and greatly reduces opportunities for stopping the game clock. For example, in the past the clock was automatically stopped for incomplete passes and injuries, and now the clock is started again after the injured are tended to or the ball is placed back on the field following an incomplete pass or an out-of-bounds play. Meanwhile, the Cardinals moved to Phoenix, and Steelers' patriarch Art Rooney died at 87. Tokyo became the site of another American Bowl preseason game.

San Francisco acquired a third Super Bowl trophy, coming from behind to win 20-16 over Cincinnati on January 22, 1989 at Miami, as quarterback Joe Montana deftly led his club downfield for the winning touchdown late in the contest.

Rozelle announced his retirement as NFL commissioner. Former Dallas administrator Tex Schramm was named president of the World League of American Football (WLAF), an adjunct of the NFL. Art Shell became coach of the Raiders, the first African American to hold that position in modern times. D. C. lawyer Paul Tagliabue took over as the new commissioner on November 5.

The 1990s: Upward and Onward

The 49ers bombed Denver, 55-10, on January 28, 1990, in the Superdome to claim their fourth Super Bowl victory, tying Pittsburgh for the most wins in the postseason classic.

For the 1990 season, instant replay lived on and the American Bowl series was expanded to Berlin and Montreal.

Buffalo dropped a cliffhanger to the Giants, 20-19, in Super Bowl XXV on January 27, 1991 at Tampa, as a game-winning field goal attempt by Buffalo's Scott Norwood sailed just wide of winning enduring fame. WLAF began play and instant replay persisted. Paul Brown, founder of the Browns and Bengals, died at age 82.

The Bills lost to Washington, 37-24, in the Super Bowl on January 26, 1992 at Minneapolis' Metrodome. Instant replay died and the Falcons moved to the Georgia Dome in Atlanta. Dallas hammered Buffalo, 52-17, in Super Bowl XXVII on January 31, 1993 at Pasadena. The players won their free agency court battle, initiating a new era for the NFL.

Sources

Books

Aaseng, Nathan. *Football's Cunning Coaches.* Minneapolis: Lerner Publications Company, 1981.

Cohen, Richard & Neft, David S. *The Sports Encyclopedia—Pro Football.* New York: St. Martin's Press, 1990.

Fifty Years of NFL Excitement. New York: NFL Properties, Inc., 1986.

Fitzgerald, Ed. *My Own Story-Johnny Unitas.* New York: Grosset & Dunlop, Inc., 1968.

Harrington, Denis J. *The Pro Football Hall of Fame.* North Carolina/London: McFarland & Company, Inc., 1991.

Leckie, Robert. *The Story of Football.* New York: Random House, Inc., 1974.

Nelson, Kevin. *Football's Greatest Insults.* New York: Perigee Books, 1991.

NFL Special Report. Super Bowl XXVII. New York: NFL Properties, 1993.

NFL Report. New York: NFL Properties, Inc. Fall, Spring, 1992; Fall, 1991.

Sahadi, Lou. *They're Playing My Game-Hank Stram.* New York: St. Martin's Press, 1986.

Smith, Ron. *The Sporting News Chronicle of 20th Century Sport.* New York:Mallard Press, 1992.

The Official 1992 National Football League Record & Fact Book. New York: NFL Properties, Inc., 1992.

The Sporting News Pro Football Guide. St. Louis: The Sporting News Publishing Company, 1991, 1990.

Verdi, Bob. *McMahon.* New York: Warner Books, Inc., 1987.

Washington Redskins Press Guide. Washington Redskins Football Club, Inc., 1992.

Periodicals

Football Digest, July/August/January, 1993; February/March, 1989; September/October/November, 1988; April/May/June, 1987; September/October, 1986.

Pro Football Illustrated Annual, 1988, 1987.

Redskins News, September 6-12, 1988.

Sportscan, November/December, 1987.

American Football Conference

Central Division

Cincinnati Bengals

Paul Brown was living comfortably in LaJolla, California, in 1965, reflecting on a successful 17-year career as head coach of the Cleveland Browns, but something was missing from his retirement. Brown had left the Browns in 1962 with a 158-48-8 record that included seven conference titles and three National Football League (NFL) championships, but after three years of savoring his success, Brown wanted more. He had the urge to return to football, but wasn't sure where or in what capacity.

Brown's son Mike did a study on pro football expansion and recommended Cincinnati as a prospective site for a second Ohio team. The elder Brown then met with Ohio Governor James Rhodes, and the two agreed that the state could accommodate another pro team. Brown had several chances to return to coaching after leaving the Browns, but the conditions he wanted—absolute control of the organization—were lacking. Besides, Brown didn't need the job; he was collecting $80,000 a year from the Browns, was enshrined in the Hall of Fame, and at 59, was at an age when many people are ready to enjoy retirement. It was more than boredom that brought Brown back into coaching. He had a drive that would not allow him to quit to please someone else. And, he wanted to prove that he had not lost touch with the game.

Brown was awarded the franchise on September 27, 1967, and it was scheduled to begin play the following season. "I feel as if I'm breathing again," Brown said after the announcement. Brown hired Al LoCasale as director of player personnel and named the team the Bengals, which had been the name of previous Cincinnati franchises in 1927, 1930, and 1931.

On December 26, 1967, the Bengals acquired their first player, sending two draft picks to Miami for quarterback John Stofa. Cincinnati was awarded 40 players in the expansion draft, but the rest of the NFL owners were less than generous to Brown, who had made a habit of beating them when he was at the helm of the Browns. As UPI (United Press International news agency) reported, "The owners made sure that Brown doesn't start another dynasty too soon."

Cincinnati fared better in the college draft. The Bengals selected center Bob Johnson of Tennessee in the first round, and he would be a fixture in the offensive line through the 1979 season. Other quality draftees that first year were running backs Jess Phillips and Essex Johnson, tight end Bob Trumpy, linebacker Al Beauchamp and tackle Howard Fest.

While Brown was concentrating on putting the Bengals together, a friend wrote to him and asked how he could justify putting his reputation in jeopardy by becoming involved in a new franchise. "I wrote back," said Brown, "and told him 'I couldn't care less about any records. If people aren't understanding enough to know that when you begin a new franchise you've got to go through a wringer, that's too bad.'"

Building the Bengals

Brown enjoyed building the Bengals. He knew the limitations of the team and what to expect during the growing process. He knew there was no pressure to succeed immediately and fill a huge stadium. Cincinnati was playing in 30,000-seat Nippert Stadium until the new Riverfront Stadium, which was approved by city council on the contingency that there would be a pro football team in the city, was completed for the 1970 season.

The Bengals lost their first pre-season game 38-14 to Kansas City before 21,682 fans at Nippert Stadium. They went the entire first half without a first down.

Things improved during the regular season and Cincinnati made a respectable showing. They upset Denver 24-10 and Buffalo 34-23 in their first two home games. The Bengals finished 3-11 that first season. Paul Robinson, a third-round draft pick out of Arizona, where he had been a track star and played only one season of football, won the AFL rushing title with 1,023 yards and was named AFL Rookie of the Year.

Cincinnati continued its rebuilding process through shrewd drafting in 1969. Greg Cook, a quarterback from the University of Cincinnati, was the Bengals' first pick in a draft that also yielded middle linebacker Bill Bergey, defensive end Royce Berry, cornerback Ken Riley, and wide receiver Speedy Thomas.

Other AFL teams stopped referring to the squad as the "Baby Bengals" when they beat Miami 27-21 in the 1969 opener. It was Brown's 300th coaching victory and an impressive debut for German-born kicker Horst Muhlmann, who provided two field goals. The following week, Cook passed for three touchdowns and ran for another as Cincinnati surprised San Diego 34-20.

The Bengals ran their record to 3-0 with a 24-19 victory over Kansas City, but it was a costly win as Cook suffered a serious arm injury when he was hit by Chiefs' linebacker Willie Lanier. He sat out the next four weeks and the Bengals lost all four games. Cook returned to spark Cincinnati to a 31-17 win against Oakland and a 31-31 tie with Houston.

The Bengals finished their second year 4-9-1, but Brown was named AFL Coach of the Year, Bergey was the league's Defensive Rookie of the Year and Cook won the AFL passing title.

Disaster struck before the 1970 season began. Cook's arm went dead at the club's Wilmington College training camp and the young quarterback was placed on the injured list. Virgil Carter, who had been cast off by the Chicago Bears and Buffalo Bills, was signed to quarterback the Bengals.

Cincinnati beat Oakland 31-21 in the opener, but lost its next six games to fall into last place in the AFC Central division. Carter ended the skid when he threw three touchdown passes in a 43-14 romp over Buffalo on November 8th. The following week the largest crowd to watch a sporting event in Cincinnati (60,007) jammed the new Riverfront Stadium to watch Brown upset his old Cleveland team 14-10. Rookie defensive tackles Mike Reid and Ron Carpenter played key roles in the victory.

Team Information at a Glance

Founding date: 1968 (AFL); 1970 (NFL)

Home stadium: Riverfront Stadium
200 Riverfront Stadium
Cincinnati, OH 45202
Phone: (513) 621-3550

Seating capacity: 60,389

Team colors: Orange and black
Team nickname: Bengals
Logo: Tiger stripes

Franchise record	Won	Lost	Tie
(1968-92)	184	187	1

The Bengals' late-season surge continued as they won their last seven games to win the Central Division with an 8-6 record. It was the quickest an expansion team had ever won a division title. Cincinnati clinched the crown with a 45-7 drubbing of the Boston Patriots before a Riverfront crowd of 60,157.

The Bengals met Baltimore in their first AFC playoff game in 1970, but the young squad was no match for the veteran Colts, who came away with a 17-0 victory. Baltimore held Cincinnati to only 139 yards in total offense. Colts' Hall of Fame quarterback John Unitas completed only six of 17 passes for 136 yards, but he had scoring strikes of 45 yards to Roy Jefferson in the first quarter and 53 yards to Eddie Hinton in the final period. Fullback Norm Bulaich helped Baltimore control the ball with 116 yards in 25 carries.

The Bengals, who added Reid, Carpenter and cornerback Lemar Parrish in the 1970 draft, continued to build through that process as they selected quarterback Ken Anderson and tackle Vern Holland in the 1971 lottery. Cincinnati looked invincible as it rolled through a 5-0-1 preseason and crushed Philadelphia 37-14 in the regular-season opener as Carter passed for 273 yards and three touchdowns. Reid sacked Eagles' quarterback Pete Liske five times.

The 1971 season quickly disintegrated, however, as the Bengals lost their next seven games. The most damaging setback was a 20-17 loss to Green Bay in which Carter and safety Ken Dyer were injured. Dyer snapped a vertebrae in his neck and it would be a year before he regained full use of his arms and legs.

A 10-6 loss to Houston may have been the most humiliating defeat in the Bengals' brief history. The Oilers scored on a 48-yard interception return on which no Cincinnati player gave chase. After the game an angry Brown fumed, "I am embarrassed. I just hope we never go through another season like this." The Bengals finished 4-

10 and dropped to last place in the AFC Central, but there was some hope because six of the defeats were by four points or less.

Anderson Named Starting QB

Brown went for defensive help in the college draft in 1972 and selected end Sherman White, safety Tommy Casanova, linebacker Jim LeClair, and cornerback Bernard Jackson; each player had an impact on the team for several seasons. Anderson replaced Carter as the starting quarterback and began a long tenure as the Bengals' number-one signal caller.

Cincinnati's 1972 season unfolded in three stages. The team won four of its first five games, then hit a mid-season slump that saw the Bengals drop four out of five. They recovered to win three of their last four contests to finish 8-6, but couldn't catch Cleveland in the battle for the AFC wild card berth. One of the highlights of the season was a club-record 57 pass receptions by wide receiver Chip Myers.

Brown went shopping for offensive players in the 1973 draft and came away with another impressive haul of college talent. Wide receiver Isaac Curtis was picked in the first round, while running backs Lenvil Elliott and Boobie Clark were taken in the 10th and 13th rounds, respectively. Those additions, combined with the development of Anderson at quarterback, gave Cincinnati game-breaking potential.

It took some time for the new talent to blend as the Bengals split their first eight games in 1973, but they swept their last six to finish 10-4 and win their second AFC Central championship. Once again, though, the Bengals' playoff experience was short-lived as they dropped a 34-16 decision to Miami. The Dolphins rushed for 241 yards—including 106 by Mercury Morris and 71 by fullback Larry Csonka—and built a 21-3 lead.

Miami quarterback Bob Griese completed 11 of 18 passes for 159 yards, including touchdown throws to Paul Warfield and Jim Mandich. Cincinnati's only touchdown was a 45-yard interception return by Neal Craig. Craig's score and a pair of field goals by Muhlmann cut the Dolphins' lead to 21-16 at halftime, but the Bengals wilted in the third quarter as Griese hit Mandich for a seven-yard touchdown and Garo Yepremian kicked a 50-yard field goal for the eventual Super Bowl champions.

Clark, who had wound up the 1973 season with 988 yards rushing and 45 pass receptions, was named AFC Rookie of the Year. Veteran Essex Johnson led the Bengals with a career-high 997 rushing yards and Curtis caught 45 passes.

When Bergey signed with the fledgling World Football League in 1974, Brown "punished" his star linebacker by shipping him to Philadelphia for two first-round picks and a third-rounder in 1977. LeClair, a three-year veteran from North Carolina, replaced Bergey in the middle and the Bengals' defense didn't skip a beat. Cincinnati won four of its first five games to take the early lead in the AFC Central, but the Bengals couldn't keep pace with the Pittsburgh Steelers, who were beginning the dynasty that would bring them four Super Bowl triumphs.

A small consolation in 1974's 7-7 season was the Browns' first sweep. Curtis caught five passes for 117 yards and a touchdown to contribute to the Bengals' 33-7 win in the opener. Four weeks later, Anderson threw three more scoring strikes as Cincinnati beat the Browns 34-24 and tossed four touchdown passes in a 33-6 romp of Kansas City on November 24. The four-year veteran from Augustana College completed a club-record 64.9 percent of his passes. Parrish led the NFL in punt returns with an 18.8 average and had a 90-yard touchdown return against Washington on October 6.

The Bengals got off to a good start in 1975, winning their first six games. LeClair played a major role in a 21-19 victory over Houston by making all four tackles in a goal-line stand. Anderson, meanwhile, took care of the offensive end by throwing three touchdown passes. Cincinnati beat Oakland 14-10 on a 52-yard interception return by rookie Marvin Cobb. The touchdown was his first pro theft. Anderson completed 30 of

46 passes for 447 yards and two touchdowns as Cincinnati improved to 8-1 with a 33-24 victory over Buffalo. It was the 10th highest one-game passing yardage in NFL history. Anderson missed a game with an injury, but backup John Reaves led the Bengals to a 23-19 victory over the Oilers on November 30. A 27-point first quarter carried Cincinnati to a 47-14 rout of San Diego, giving the Bengals an 11-3 record—their best ever.

Earned Wild Card Slot

The Bengals qualified for the playoffs as a wild card team but remained winless in post-season play with a 31-28 loss to Oakland. The Bengals fell behind 31-14, but stormed back behind Anderson's two fourth-quarter touchdown passes. Anderson won his second NFL passing championship, but the Bengals' defense was dealt a serious blow when Reid, who had earned All-Pro status on the defensive line, retired at 26 to pursue a career in music. He later became a popular country composer and singer.

Brown retired as coach on January 1, 1976, ending a 41-year career in coaching. He named his longtime line coach, Bill Johnson, to succeed him. Brown still kept his hand in the operation of the club as he continued to serve as general manager, vice-president, and owner.

In 1976 the Bengals obtained veteran defensive end Coy Bacon from San Diego for wide receiver Charlie Joiner and drafted several outstanding rookies, including two-time Heisman Trophy winner Archie Griffin of Ohio State. Other top draft picks were wide receiver Billy Brooks of Oklahoma and Penn State kicker Chris Bahr.

The Bengals got off to their customary fast start in the AFC Central, winning nine of their first 11 1976 season games. Anderson threw four touchdown passes in a 45-21 triumph over Cleveland. Griffin, who moved right into the starting lineup, rushed for 139 yards and contributed to a 77-yard run as Cincinnati rallied to beat Kansas City 27-24. The team's season hinged on two late-season games with Pittsburgh and Oakland, and Cincinnati lost both. The Bengals bowed 7-3 to the Steelers on November 28 and dropped a 35-20 decision to the Raiders a week later. They finished 10-4, but the two late defeats cost them the AFC Central title and a wild card berth in the playoffs. Cornerback Ken Riley led the AFC with nine interceptions and Bacon had a league-high 26 sacks.

The Bengals had three first-round picks in the 1977 draft and used them on defensive tackles Eddie Edwards and Wilson Whitley and tight end Mike Cobb. In a switch from the normal pattern, Cincinnati started the season slowly, winning only two of its first six games. The Bengals lost the opener 13-3 to the Browns, beat Seattle by 20 points a week later, then dropped a 24-3 decision to the Chargers. Cincinnati then turned its season around, winning six of seven to climb back into playoff contention. The final victory in that surge was a 17-10 win over the Steelers in two-degree

AP/Wide World Photos

Paul Brown

weather at Riverfront. After winning that game, the Bengals needed only a victory over Houston in the final to clinch the division title. They didn't get it, bowing 21-16 as the Oilers' Billy (White Shoes) Johnson ran for 263 all-purpose yards. The Bengals finished 8-6, one game behind division-champion Pittsburgh.

Cincinnati had two more first-round draft picks in 1978 and selected Lombardi Trophy winner Ross Browner of Notre Dame, a defensive tackle, and Washington center Blair Bush. Anderson was injured in the preseason and missed more than a month of the regular season. The Bengals dropped their first eight games and at one point scored only three points in a three-game span. With the team 0-5, Bill Johnson resigned under fire as head coach and was replaced by Homer Rice. Some critics said that Johnson suffered from excessive front-office meddling, but a bigger reason for his lack of success was Anderson's broken finger.

The Bengals' losing streak continued under Rice, but eventually the team began showing improvement and broke into the victory column on October 29, 1978, with a 28-13 upset of Houston that featured touchdown passes of 45 and 57 yards by Anderson. The biggest change Rice made was scrapping Johnson's 3-4 defense and replacing it with a 4-3.

The Bengals' new front four of Gary Burley, Whitley, Edwards, and Browner applied heavy pressure on opposing quarterbacks for the rest of the season and Cincinnati finished with a 4-12 record after ending the year with wins over Atlanta (37-7), Los Angeles (20-19), and Cleveland (48-16).

Some old faces disappeared from the Bengals' roster after the 1978 season. Casanova retired to become a doctor and Trumpy quit for the broadcast booth. Cincinnati's strong finish in that season provided hope for 1979, but it turned into a repeat of the previous year's 4-12 record.

The Bengals started the season 0-6 and got their first victory with a 34-10 upset of the defending Super Bowl champion Steelers. One of Cincinnati's other victories was against playoff-bound Philadelphia. A porous pass defense allowed more points than any other team in the league. The Bengals gave up 51 points to Buffalo, 42 to Houston, and 38 to Dallas and Baltimore. A 16-12 victory over Cleveland in the season finale could not save Rice's job. He was fired and replaced by former Green Bay great Forrest Gregg.

Munoz Signed

The Bengals made a move to bolster their offensive line in the 1980 draft when they picked University of Southern California tackle Anthony Munoz, who went on to become one of the best linemen in the history of the game. The 1980 season got off to a poor start when Anderson was injured in preseason play. The veteran quarterback was bothered by nagging aches and pains all year. He started 12 games but was around at the finish in only two of them; he threw a total of six touchdown passes. The Bengals struggled to a 6-10 record and managed only 244 points, the lowest in the AFC.

The 1981 season was one of change for the Bengals. At the beginning of the year, fans were talking about the new uniforms with striped helmets, pants and jerseys. By the end they were talking about the club's rise to the top of the AFC Central standings. Cincinnati had at least a share of the division lead the entire season and clinched the title on December 6, when Anderson threw two touchdown passes in a 17-10 victory over Pittsburgh. The Bengals finished the season 7-1 with the only loss to San Francisco.

Cornerback Louis Breeden tied an NFL record when he returned an interception 102 yards for a touchdown in a 40-17 victory over San Diego. Anderson, who was benched in the opener and booed for most of September, led the NFL in passing with a 98.5 rating.

One of Anderson's favorite targets was rookie Cris Collinsworth, the Bengals' second-round pick in 1981. Pete Johnson, a massive fullback out of Ohio State, provided the offense with a powerful ground attack.

The Bengals beat Buffalo 28-21 for their first post-season victory. Cincinnati built a 14-0 first-quarter lead on short touchdown runs by Charles Alexander and Johnson but watched the Bills tie the score on a pair of TDs by Joe Cribbs. Alexander scored his second TD on a 20-yard run in the third quarter, but Buffalo hauled in a 21-yard scoring strike from Joe Ferguson to tie the game again. The Bengals got the deciding touchdown on a 16-yard pass from Anderson to Collinsworth.

A week later, Cincinnati defeated San Diego 27-7 in the AFC championship game. The game-time temperature was 11 degrees below zero and the windchill factor was minus 59 degrees. NFL commissioner Pete Rozelle considered postponing the game, but after several medical opinions assured him the players were not in danger, he ordered the contest played. A crowd of 46,302 braved the conditions to watch the game.

The Bengals scored early on a 31-yard field goal by Jim Breech. On the ensuing kickoff, James Brooks fumbled and Cincinnati recovered on the Chargers' 12 yard line. A short pass from Anderson to M. L. Harris quickly made it 10-0. San Diego's Dan Fouts had trouble throwing in the high winds, but managed a 33-yard scoring strike to tight end Kellen Winslow in the second quarter to cut the lead to 10-7.

Fouts led the Chargers deep into Cincinnati territory two other times, but interceptions ended each drive. Shortly before the half, Johnson plunged in from the one yard line to give the Bengals a 17-7 halftime lead. San Diego continued to struggle offensively in the second half, while the Bengals padded their lead with a 38-yard field goal by Breech and a three-yard pass from Anderson to Don Bass.

First Cinci Super Bowl Appearance

Super Bowl XVI, which was played at the Silverdome in Michigan, brought together a pair of teams that had finished 6-10 a year earlier. Cincinnati failed to take advantage of an early scoring chance when the 49ers' Amos Lawrence fumbled the opening kickoff. The Bengals drove to the five before Anderson was sacked for a six-yard loss and then had a pass intercepted.

San Francisco quarterback Joe Montana then engineered an 11-play drive that he capped by diving in from the one. Collinsworth fumbled at the 49ers' eight and Montana began a 92-yard drive that ended with an 11-yard pass to Earl Cooper. Ray Wersching kicked a 22-yard field goal with 15 seconds left in the first half to increase

The Chili Bowl

January 10, 1982 was the coldest January 10 in Cincinnati history, and it might have been the coldest game played in the NFL since the weather folks invented the windchill factor. It was nine degrees below zero at the start of the AFC championship game between the Cincinnati Bengals and the San Diego Chargers, and the winds were gusting up to 35 mph. By the third quarter, the windchill had dipped to an estimated 59 below zero. "I can't ever remember a colder day than this one," said Bengals' coach Forrest Gregg, who had played for Green Bay in the memorable "Ice Bowl" in 1967 against the Dallas Cowboys.

Ron Fimrite, writing in *Sports Illustrated,* noted, "On Sunday in Cincinnati the Amundsen polar expedition wouldn't have made it past the 50-yard line." Strangely enough, it only seemed cold on one side of the line of scrimmage. The Bengals' linemen played in short-sleeved jerseys and Cincinnati quarterback Ken Anderson had plenty of zip on his passes. Chargers' quarterback Dan Fouts, however, seemed to be sailing kites whenever he threw a pass. "You can't throw a ball you can't handle," said Chargers' tight end Kellen Winslow. Anderson scoffed at that by saying, "The ball wasn't hard to handle." Fouts had two costly interceptions, and the Chargers fumbled four times, losing two of them as the Bengals rolled to a 27-7 victory.

the 49ers' lead to 17-0. On the kickoff, Griffin fumbled and Wersching hit another chip shot for a 20-0 lead at the intermission. It was the biggest deficit a Super Bowl team had faced at halftime.

The Bengals began their comeback in the Super Bowl game with an 83-yard drive, with Anderson going the final five on a quarterback keeper. Anderson hit Ross with a four-yard TD pass early in the fourth quarter, but San Francisco got the momentum back when the 49ers made a goal line stand from the one, finally stopping Johnson on the fourth down. Wersching added two more field goals before Anderson and Ross connected on another scoring strike to make the final score 26-21.

The Bengals followed their first Super Bowl appearance with another strong showing in 1982. Anderson passed with such accuracy that he set a single-season record with a 70.6 completion percentage and Cincinnati won the division with a 7-2 mark. The only team with a better record in the strike-shortened season was the 8-1 Raiders, who had moved to Los Angeles.

The New York Jets caught the Bengals sleeping in the playoffs, beating them 44-17 in a first-round game. Freeman McNeil rushed for 211 yards and one touchdown and Wesley Walker caught eight passes for 145 yards and a touchdown to lead the Jets. Anderson completed 26 of 35 passes for 354 yards and two touchdowns, but Cincinnati failed to balance those numbers with a running attack that netted only 62 yards.

Turmoil ruined a promising 1983 season for the Bengals. The NFL suspended Pete Johnson and Ross Browner for the first four games because of drug use. Then the new United States Football League (USFL) snatched offensive coordinator Lindy Infante, and star receivers Collinsworth and Ross came to camp with future USFL commitments.

Cincinnati lost its first three games and six of the first seven to drop out of playoff contention. Anderson missed three games at mid-season because of injury, and Turk Schonert came in to quarterback the team to its first consecutive wins. Anderson regained his job when he was healthy

AP/Wide World Photos

Boomer Esiason

and led the Bengals to a 55-14 victory over Houston. Cincinnati won six of its last nine games to finish 7-9. The Bengals' defense was the best overall in the NFL.

Wyche Takes the Helm

Gregg resigned as head coach after the season and Sam Wyche was named to replace him. It seemed to take the Bengals a while to get used to Wyche's methods in 1984, and they dropped their first five games. Johnson was traded to San Diego for James Brooks, who wound up third in rushing and fourth in receiving on the club.

Anderson missed much of the season with back and shoulder miseries, but Schonert and rookie Boomer Esiason filled in well, leading the Bengals to win eight of their last 11 games. Cincinnati stayed in contention until the final weekend of the season, but fell a game short of

AFC Central champ Pittsburgh with an 8-8 record.

Another slow start—three straight losses to open the season—probably cost the Bengals a shot at the division title in 1985, but just as important were two consecutive setbacks at the end of the season when the title was within reach. Cincinnati finished 7-9, but only a game behind AFC Central winner Cleveland.

Second-year quarterback Esiason replaced Anderson and was protected by a line that was built around Munoz, who was named to his fifth straight Pro Bowl. Rookie receiver Eddie Brown and Collinsworth were Esiason's favorite targets as the Bengals put a team record 441 points on the scoreboard. Unfortunately, they also set a team record in the other direction, allowing 437 points. Curtis retired after a 12-year career that saw him become the club's all-time reception leader with 420, including 53 for touchdowns.

Inconsistency was the word that best summed up Cincinnati's 1986 campaign. Seven times the Bengals scored 30 or more points, including 52 in the season finale against the Jets, but on three occasions they were unable to score ten points and wound up 10-6 and in second place in the division. In week 15, the Bengals needed a victory over Cleveland to win the division, but Browns' quarterback Bernie Kosar completed a 66-yard pass on the first play of the game and Cincinnati never recovered, losing 34-3.

Esiason became one of pro football's top guns, while Brown and Collinsworth earned a combined 120 receptions. Brooks rushed for 1,087 yards and caught 54 passes. The offensive line, led by Munoz and guard Max Montoya out-muscled most of the Bengals' rivals.

The Bengals expected to challenge for a playoff berth in 1987, but instead they found new ways to lose en route to a 4-11 season. One of the worst defeats came against San Francisco when Cincinnati led 26-20 with six seconds left. The Bengals decided not to punt, but failed to run out the clock on a fourth-down sweep at their 30 yard line. The 49ers then hit a pass for the winning TD.

Almost as bad was the game with the Jets when Cincinnati was locked in a 20-20 tie. Breech missed a late field goal attempt, but got a second chance because the whistle had blown for the two-minute warning. That time the kick was blocked and New York returned it for the deciding TD.

The Bengals defense improved in 1987, but that was offset by injuries to Brooks and Collinsworth and a sub-par season by Esiason. Breech led the AFC in scoring with 97 points and Munoz was voted to the Pro Bowl team for the seventh year in a row, although he was unable to play because of a shoulder injury.

Super Bowl Rematch with the 49ers

The Bengals achieved the biggest turnaround in NFL history in 1988, when the team went from 4-11 to 12-4, the AFC Central championship, the AFC title, and a berth in the Super Bowl against the San Francisco 49ers. The Bengals fell 20-16 in the Super Bowl when the 49ers scored on a 10-yard pass from Joe Montana to John Taylor with 34 seconds remaining.

The offense deserved most of the credit for the Bengals' success in 1988. Esiason was the NFL's Most Valuable Player as he passed effectively to Eddie Brown, Rodney Holman, and Tim McGee. Brooks ran for 931 yards.

The new star on the scene was rookie Ickey Woods, who rushed for 1,066 yards and 15 touchdowns. A colorful player, Woods did the "Ickey Shuffle" every time he scored. Munoz, Montoya, and tackle Joe Walter were the bulwarks of the offensive line. Defensive standouts were nose guard Tim Krumrie, safety David Fulcher and cornerback Eric Thomas.

Cincinnati opened the 1988 playoffs with a 21-13 victory over Seattle. Woods rushed for 126 yards and a touchdown, while Stanley Wilson scored twice on short runs. The Seahawks made it close with a pair of fourth-quarter touchdowns. The Bengals' defense, which took a back seat to the offense all season, was the key in the AFC title game as they held Buffalo to 181 yards in total offense and no third-down conversions in a 21-10 Cincinnati victory.

The Bengals played it close to the vest with Woods gaining 102 yards on 29 carries. The rookie from Nevada-Las Vegas scored Cincinnati's first TD on a one-yard plunge in the first quarter. Buffalo tied the game early in the second quarter on a nine-yard pass from Jim Kelly to Andre Reed.

The Bengals regained the lead on Esiason's 10-yard scoring strike to Brooks. Scott Norwood kicked a 39-yard field goal to cut Cincinnati's lead to 14-10 at halftime. The Bengals were unable to put the game away until the fourth quarter when Woods scored from the one, two plays after Bills' cornerback Derrick Burroughs was caught slugging Tim McGee in the end zone, giving Cincinnati a first down at the four.

Super Bowl XXIII was one of the few Super Bowls to live up to its advance billing. Defenses dominated a first half that saw each team sustain a serious injury. San Francisco lost starting offensive tackle Steve Wallace with a broken ankle on the first series of downs and Cincinnati's Krumrie was hurt on a freak play when he planted his foot and his left leg snapped in two places.

The score was tied 3-3 at halftime on field goals by the 49ers' Mike Cofer and the Bengals' Breech. The teams traded field goals again in the third quarter, but after Cofer's second tied the score at 6-6, Cincinnati's Stanford Jennings brought the kickoff back 93 yards for a touchdown.

Joe Montana engineered a San Francisco drive from his 15 to the Bengals' 14. Montana's pass to the end zone went into the hands of Cincinnati cornerback Lewis Billups, but Billups dropped the ball. On the next play, Montana found Jerry Rice in the end zone for a touchdown. Breech kicked his third field goal of the game, a 40-yarder with 3:20 remaining, which give the Bengals a 16-13 lead, but there was still time for Montana to work more of his magic. He started from his own eight and hit short passes to John Frank and Rice, then found Rice for 17 yards to move into Cincinnati territory. Montana finally hit Taylor in the end zone from the 10 to cap the 11-play, 92-yard drive to the winning touchdown. The Bengals couldn't score in the final 34 seconds and San Francisco had its third Super Bowl triumph of the 1980s and its second over Cincinnati.

The Bengals had high hopes for 1989, but they were dashed in the second game of the season when Woods's season, and ultimately his career, ended with a knee injury. Cincinnati won four of its first five games, then blew leads in its next two and staggered home with an 8-8 record. Veteran James Brooks posted a league-high 5.6-yard rushing average, but without Woods the Bengals could not run between the tackles. McGee and Eddie Brown were solid deep threats for Esiason, but Cincinnati still had five games in which it scored fewer than 15 points. Strong safety David Fulcher had an outstanding season, but he was about all the defense had to offer.

The Bengals started the 1990 season with three straight victories, then won only four of their next 11, before closing the year with wins in the last two. Cincinnati, Houston, and Pittsburgh each finished 9-7, but Cincinnati was the division champion. Though Esiason threw 23 TD passes, he was also intercepted 22 times. Woods bounced back from his injury, but Brooks was the Bengals' leading rusher with another 1,000-yard season. The offensive line struggled when Montoya was lost in Plan B and injuries struck Munoz and guard Bruce Reimers.

The Bengals beat Houston 41-14 in the first round of the playoffs. Esiason ran for one touchdown and passed for two others as Cincinnati had 349 yards in total offense. Ten points in the fourth quarter carried the Los Angeles Raiders to a 20-10 victory over Cincinnati the following week. Raiders quarterback Jay Schroeder threw a pair of TD passes, and running back Marcus Allen rushed for 140 yards. Cincinnati had only 182 yards in total offense to Los Angeles's 389.

Disaster struck in 1991 as Cincinnati lost its first eight games, and Wyche lost his composure on the sideline. After the Bengals finished the season 3-13, Wyche was replaced by 32-year-old David Shula, who became the youngest coach in NFL history. The offense failed to score a touchdown in two games and had only one in six other contests. The defense was last in total defense, pass defense, and scoring defense. One bright spot was the development of second-year running back Harold Green, who ran for 731 yards.

Shula started the 1992 season with two straight victories, but the Bengals still wound up 5-11 on the basis of two five-game losing streaks. Esiason finished the season on the bench as David Klingler, the club's first-round draft pick, inherited the quarterback job.

After the season, Esiason was traded to the Jets. Another era ended when Munoz retired after 13 seasons. Green rushed for 1,170 yards, and Krumrie led in tackles with 97. Rookies Carl Pickens, Darryl Williams and Ricardo McDonald had promising seasons. After the season, Ken Anderson returned to the Bengals as quarterback coach in hopes of passing on some of his knowledge to Klingler.

Sources

Books

Clary, Jack, *The Gamemakers,* Follett Publishing, 1976.

Cohen, Richard M., Jordan A. Deutsch, Roland T. Johnson, and David S. Neft, *The Scrapbook History of Pro Football,* Bobbs-Merrill, 1976.

Green, Jerry, *Super Bowl Chronicles,* Masters Press, 1991.

Neft, David S., Richard M. Cohen, and Rick Korch, *The Sports Encyclopedia—Pro Football,* St. Martin's Press, 1993.

The Official NFL Encyclopedia of Pro Football, New American Library, 1982.

Periodicals

Football Digest, April 1982; April 1989; October 1991.

Pro!, November 12, 1978.

Sports Illustrated, January 18, 1982.

Other

Cincinnati Bengals Media Guides, 1963-92, Cincinnati Bengals Football Club.

—*Chuck Klonke*

Cleveland Browns

Cleveland was represented by one of the five original teams in the National Football League, but the Indians, as they were called (and for one year the Panthers) had no connection with the later Cleveland Browns. Nor did the longer-lived Cleveland Rams, a team that began play in 1937 and moved to Los Angeles after winning their only NFL championship in 1945. When the Rams, owned by Dan Reeves, departed for the West Coast, the city of Cleveland—indeed, all of northern Ohio—inherited a brand-new pro football team in 1946, the Browns, in a brand-new league, the All-America Football Conference.

The owner of this Cleveland team was Arthur (Mickey) McBride, a wealthy, tough-minded businessman who also owned, among other things, real estate and taxicab companies in Cleveland, Akron, and Canton. McBride hired a young coaching genius, Paul Brown, to build his team. With McBride supplying the money, the driven and assertive Brown promptly signed Otto Graham as the Browns' quarterback. Other future Hall of Famers came on board, too, including fullback Marion Motley, end Dante Lavelli, lineman Bill Willis, center Frank Gatski, and tackle/place kicker Lou (The Toe) Groza. The powerful, brilliantly coached Browns dominated the AAFC between 1946 and 1949, with an overall 52-4-3 record, including postseason games. Over one stretch they played 29 consecutive games without a defeat.

When the NFL and AAFC merged, the Cleveland Browns, along with the San Francisco 49ers and Baltimore Colts, joined the NFL. By then Paul Brown's namesake football team was solidly established and confident. The Browns soon made believers out of critics who wondered whether an AAFC squad could win games in the National Football League. Cleveland swept to American Conference titles in every season from 1950 through 1955. Their first adversary in an NFL championship playoff was none other than the Los Angeles

Rams (late of Cleveland), a team from which Paul Brown had earlier lured a number of star players. On December 24, 1950, the Browns defeated the Rams, 30-28, to win the NFL championship in their first season. Cleveland repeated as NFL champs in 1954 and 1955. Paul Brown's reputation as a football mastermind was confirmed.

In 1957 Cleveland again won the Eastern Conference title. But the big news for the Browns that year was the signing of their number one draft pick, Jim Brown, a sensational running back from Syracuse University. Brown became an immediate starter and from the very beginning (he won Rookie-of-the-Year honors) until his retirement in 1965 he helped make the Cleveland Browns a title contender every season. The Browns finished first in the NFL Eastern Conference three times, second four times, and third twice. The team's overall regular-season record with Jim Brown in the backfield was 79-34-5.

In January 1963 Paul Brown, head coach and general manager of the Cleveland Browns since their founding, was fired by owner Arthur Modell. The man who replaced him, soft-spoken Blanton Collier, inherited a solid team that included superstar Brown and place-kicking pioneer Lou Groza. Collier directed the Browns with considerable success for the next eight seasons, leading them to one NFL championship, three Conference championships and four Century Division titles.

In the 1970s and 1980s the Browns did not maintain the success of the Paul Brown-Blanton Collier era. They contended at times—1980, 1986, and 1987 were notably good seasons—but the team never won regularly as they had in the past. A succession of head coaches after Collier posted generally mediocre records. Indeed, through 1993, and Super Bowl XXVII, the Cleveland Browns, once the undisputed lords of the NFL, had yet to make their first appearance in the January classic.

The Master Builds a Team

Business magnate Arthur (Mickey) McBride became a football fan after watching the University of Notre Dame, his son's school, pummel an outclassed opponent in 1940. He began attending Cleveland Rams' games and pondering the possibility of adding a pro football team to his other possessions. When a new league, the All-America Football Conference, was proposed in 1944, McBride made it clear that he wanted in. He also made it clear that he wanted a winning team and was willing to spend money to get it.

"Who is the best football coach in the country?" McBride asked sportswriter John Dietrich of the *Cleveland Plain Dealer*. "Paul Brown" Dietrich replied. At age 36, Paul Brown was already a legend in Ohio, having coached the Massillon high school football team to an 81-7-2 record before moving to Ohio State, where in three years his Buckeyes were 18-8-1. At the time McBride asked his question, the dead-serious, prematurely balding Brown was in the Navy, coaching football, successfully as always, at Great Lakes Naval Training Station. McBride, who had been thinking about Notre Dame's Frank Leahy, hired Brown instead.

Brown promptly hired five assistant coaches, much to McBride's surprise, but the new coach and GM assured him that all five were needed. Next he searched for a quarterback, finding one, he was certain, in Northwestern's Otto Graham, a player whose college experience was with the single-wing offense, not with Brown's intended T-formation. But Brown, "The Master," as he came to be called, felt sure that Graham, who had led the Northwestern Wildcats to two wins over Brown's Buckeyes, could handle the change.

Among the other players Paul Brown signed for Cleveland were offensive tackle Lou Groza from Martins Ferry, Ohio; Dante Lavelli, an aggressive, glue-fingered end from Hudson, Ohio; and Mac Speedie, a graceful and deceptive end from Salt Lake City, Utah. Brown chose athletes for their promise and commitment, not for their prior reputations, and consequently his 1946 team looked better on the field than it did on paper.

A contest to choose a nickname for the new team appeared to end with the choice of "Panthers." But when Paul Brown learned that this

TEAM INFORMATION AT A GLANCE

Founding date: 1946 (AAFC); 1950 (NFL)

Home stadium: Cleveland Stadium
West 3rd St.
Cleveland, OH 44114
Phone: (216) 696-5555
FAX: (216) 696-3163
Seating capacity: 78,512

Team colors: Seal brown, orange, and white
Team nickname: Browns, 1950-present (same, 1946-49 in AAFC)
Team logo on helmet: None (solid orange with single white stripe bordered by thinner brown stripes down center)

Franchise record*	Won	Lost	Tie	Pct.
AAFC (1946-49)	52	4	3	.922
NFL (1950-1992)	351	241	10	.593

* Including playoffs

National Football League championships (4): 1950, 1954, 1955, 1964
Eastern/American Conference championships (11): 1950, 1951, 1952, 1953, 1954, 1955, 1957, 1964, 1965, 1968, 1969
Central/Century Division championships (8): 1967, 1971, 1972, 1980, 1985, 1986, 1987, 1989
League/Conference/Division last-place finishes (5): 1974, 1975, 1977, 1981, 1990

was a name already used and, worse, associated with failure, he demanded another. Since a majority of contestants had suggested the name "Browns" anyway—in honor of the team's GM and head coach—he acquiesced, and the Browns were born in name as well as in fact. Not everyone was impressed with the Browns or their league, though. Prior to the AAFC season opener, Earl Layden, commissioner of the NFL, was asked what he thought of the new league. "What new league?" he snapped. "Let them go get a football first, and then play a game."

When the Browns put the football in play on September 6, 1946, before 60,135 fans at Cleveland Municipal Stadium against the Miami Seahawks, few doubted that Paul Brown had molded a competitive team. The Browns buried the Seahawks 44-0, then went on to upend the Chicago Rockets, 20-6, the Buffalo Bills, 28-0, and the New York Yankees, 24-7, after which Yankee head coach Ray Flaherty berated his team for losing "to a team from Podunk with a high school coach."

Like Earl Layden, Ray Flaherty (whose last name Brown thereafter always mispronounced as "Flattery") would come to regret his remark. Paul Brown's team was no fluke. The Cleveland Browns kept on winning. Their toughest rival that year (and for the next three years) proved to be the San Franciso 49ers; after Cleveland had built up a 7-0 season record, the 49ers finally handed the Browns their first defeat, 34-20, before a large and disappointed crowd at Municipal Stadium. The strong Los Angeles Dons then dealt the Browns their second loss, 17-16, on a last-minute field goal.

After these defeats Cleveland returned to its winning ways, ending the season at 12-2-0, crushing the Brooklyn Dodgers, 66-14, in the final regular-season game.

The New York Yankees, winners of the Eastern Division title in the AAFC, met the Browns in postseason play at Yankee Stadium for the league championship. Otto Graham, Marion Motley, and Dante Lavelli starred as Cleveland held on to win again, 14-9, over Flaherty's 10-3-1 Yankees. The "high school coach" was on his way.

"We Start All Over Again"

Paul Brown worried about complacency. As a coach he never let up, and he expected his players to show the same attitude. In 1947 the Browns continued to outplay the opposition, losing only one game, a midseason 13-10 contest to the Los Angeles Dons. Otto Graham completed 61% of his passes to Mac Speedie, "Gluefingers" Lavelli, and other receivers. Marion Motley rushed for 889 yards.

The Browns repeated in 1948, coasting through a 14-0 season. A couple of impressive halfbacks joined the already potent Browns' backfield that year—Dub Jones from the Miami Seahawks and Ara Parseghian from Paul Brown's own alma mater, Miami of Ohio. In 1948, as before, the San Franciso 49ers provided the stiffest competition, falling to the Browns by scores of 14-7 and 31-28. A Cleveland crowd of over 70,000 turned out to watch the hard-fought 14-7 game in Municipal Stadium. Later, in the 31-28 duel, Otto Graham, who had suffered an injured left knee and was not expected to play, hobbled off the bench at Kezar Stadium, San Francisco, and led the Browns to victory. The Buffalo Bills, having won the Eastern Division title of the AAFC, met the Browns in the championship game and were duly routed, 49-7. Coach Brown, a man not given to overstatement, called the 1948 Browns "a team with no weakness."

A Stunning Debut

Today it seems odd that National Football League partisans were so sure the Philadelphia Eagles, champions of the NFL in 1948 and 1949, would roll to an easy win over the four-time AAFC champion Cleveland Browns in the opening game of the 1950 season. The expanded NFL, many thought, was admitting an inferior team (actually three inferior teams, because the Browns were joined by fellow AAFC castoffs the San Francisco 49ers and the Baltimore Colts). The press and fans should have known better, at least by September 16, 1950, and the opening game of the regular season. The Browns had already knocked off a succession of NFL teams in exhibition games, beating the Green Bay Packers, Detroit Lions, Chicago Bears, and Pittsburgh Steelers. Nonetheless, a remarkable number of writers and fans still expected the powerful Eagles under head coach Greasy Neale to make short work of the AAFC upstart Browns. The oddsmakers were a bit more circumspect, giving the Eagles only a three-point edge.

Paul Brown found the predictions amusing: "The press and public were saying how we were going to get whipped 50-0. We knew this would take a little doing because we had players like Otto Graham, Marion Motley, Dante Lavelli, Mac Speedie...." Brown was right, of course. When the dust had settled at Shibe Park, Philadelphia, the Browns had scored in every quarter against the overmatched Eagles, as Cleveland's trap, pass, and screen offense and superb defense gave them a convincing 34-10 win over the defending NFL champs. While Browns' quarterback Otto Graham was named the outstanding player in the game, the entire Cleveland team had functioned as a precisely tuned unit, leading NFL commissioner Bert Bell to say, "Cleveland is the best football team I have ever seen."

Otto Graham

Given the Browns' blistering pace in 1948, many predicted that they would waltz through the 1949 season unbeaten. Overconfident perhaps, they started the season with an inauspicious 28-28 tie against the Buffalo Bills. (The Bills would tie them again, 7-7, later in the season). Four straight wins followed the first loss to the Bills, including a 42-7 rout of the L.A. Dons. But then the Browns were pulverized by the San Francisco 49ers, who rolled over them 56-28.

Paul Brown growled his displeasure with his team's performance, and the following week the Browns humiliated the L.A. Dons, 61-14. A week later Cleveland met San Francisco again and squeaked by the 49ers, 30-28. In the playoffs—divisions having been eliminated because a merger of the Brooklyn Dodgers and New York Yankees reduced the number of clubs to seven—the Browns topped the Buffalo Bills, 31-21, and went on to defeat the 49ers once again, 21-7. The playoff wins gave the Cleveland Browns their fourth and final AAFC championship.

After four seasons in which the Cleveland Browns held sway in the All-America Football Conference, the AAFC went out of business, merging with the National Football League. The very success of the Browns contributed to the league's demise, for many fans concluded that Paul Brown's juggernaut would keep rolling indefinitely, making the AAFC championship a foregone conclusion.

At the end of the 1949 season three of the seven AAFC teams were invited to join the NFL—the Cleveland Browns, San Francisco 49ers, and Baltimore Colts. Many experts at the time thought the Browns would be overmatched by their new competition. As Paul Brown told his troops: "We've been taunted and kidded about playing in an inferior league. It has been said that the worst team in the National League the last four years could beat the best in the All-America Conference."

Winning in the NFL

In 1950 the National Football League, with its three additions, consisted of 13 clubs. Six, including the Browns, were in the American Conference; seven, including the 49ers and Colts, were in the National Conference. A year earlier the NFL's Philadelphia Eagles, under head coach Earle (Greasy) Neale, had racked up an 11-1-0 regular-season record, and then shut out the L.A. Rams, 14-0, in a muddy championship game at Los Angeles. It was this strong and well-coached Eagles' team, powered by halfback Steve Van Buren, a future Hall of Famer, that the Cleveland Browns were to face in their first NFL season opener.

A crowd of 85,000 showed up at Philadelphia's Municipal Stadium to see their Eagles play the presumably outclassed Browns. Most of the fans expected an easy victory, although Philadelphia sportswriter Mort Berry, covering the Browns'

Dante Lavelli

Marion Motley

training camp, had warned his readers that Cleveland's warriors would be no pushovers. After all, the Browns had Otto Graham, Marion Motley, and Dub Jones in the backfield; Mac Speedie and Dante Lavelli at end; Frank Gatski at center; and Lou Groza ready to kick. All of these players were in their prime. And the Browns had something to prove—that they could compete with the best the NFL had to offer. They proved it quickly and decisively, upsetting the Eagles, 35-10. Said the shaken Greasy Neale after the game, "Jeez, they had a lot of guns."

Those guns kept right on firing. Cleveland next breezed past the Baltimore Colts, their old AAFC foes, 31-0. In fact, only one team in the NFL seemed to baffle them. The New York Giants, quarterbacked by Charley Conerly, won 6-0 in their first encounter (the first time in 62 games the Browns had been blanked) and came back to win again, 17-13, the second time they met. The Giants used what head coach Steve Owen called an "umbrella defense" to shut down the Browns' passing attack. These were the only two losses for the Browns in their first year in the NFL, and with the Giants also dropping two (to the Pittsburgh Steelers and Chicago Cardinals), these two American Conference teams were tied at 10-2 at the end of the season.

They met in a playoff game, and at last the Browns found the right combination. In bitter cold weather on an icy field in Cleveland they scratched out an 8-3 victory over the Giants on two field goals and a safety. The Browns then met the Los Angeles Rams, winners of the National Conference title, in the NFL championship game. This was an unusual matchup in that the Rams were still basically the Cleveland team that had won the NFL crown in 1945. Future Hall of Famer Bob

HISTORY

Integrating Pro Football

Professional football was integrated with little fuss in 1946, the same year Jackie Robinson played Triple-A baseball at Montreal. Although the new All-America Football Conference had no written rule concerning black players, Paul Brown was the first to invite a couple of black players to his training camp. They were fullback Marion Motley and guard Bill Willis, whose outstanding play soon made it clear that the Cleveland Browns would be integrated from the outset.

Motley, whom Paul Brown had coached at Great Lakes, said later, "I was 27 years old, married with four children and working in a steel mill when I left for Bowling Green. I knew this was the one big chance of my life...." Willis, whom Brown had coached at Ohio State, made one of the great plays of his career in the playoff game in 1950 against the New York Giants.

With the Browns leading 8-3 in the fourth quarter, Giants' running back Gene (Choo Choo) Roberts broke through the Browns' secondary and seemed on his way to a certain touchdown. Willis, a lightning-fast runner, chased Roberts for 44 yards, bringing him down just short of the goal line to preserve the victory for Cleveland. Both Marion Motley and Bill Willis played for the Browns for eight seasons, on their way to enshrinement in the Pro Football Hall of Fame.

Waterfield was still at quarterback.

The game was played, appropriately, in Cleveland on December 24, 1950, and a seesaw battle ended in the Browns favor when, with the score 28-27 in favor of the Rams and with seconds remaining, Lou Groza kicked a field goal to give the Browns a 30-28 win. "My biggest thrill," said Groza afterwards. The snide remarks about the Browns ceased. It is true, however, that the two other ex-AAFC teams in the NFL fared poorly, the 49s and Colts winning just four games between them and finishing last in the National Conference.

If the Browns had been almost monotonously successful in the AAFC, so were they for many years in the American (later Eastern) Conference of the NFL. That first season set the pattern. Cleveland took six consecutive Conference titles from 1950 through 1955, although the NFL championship eluded them for three straight years after their first-year triumph. The L.A. Rams took the honors in 1951, winning over the Browns, 21-14. Next the Detroit Lions outdid Cleveland twice, 17-7 in 1952 and 17-16 in 1953.

Owner and founder Mickey McBride sold his team to Dave R. Jones in 1953, but the sale had no discernible effect on the Browns' fortunes on the field. Paul Brown, continuing to run the show, obtained tackle Mike McCormack, a future Hall of Famers, prior to the 1954 season.

The Browns returned to their championship form in 1954, going 9-3 that season, then gaining sweet revenge on the Lions in the championship game by romping them 56-10. Otto Graham passed for three touchdowns on that late December day in Cleveland and ran for three more. Another star of the game was rough-and-ready defensive end Len Ford, who picked off two passes by Lions' quarterback Bobby Layne. Ford, a future Hall of Famer, was in his fifth year with the Browns, having been acquired from the defunct L.A. Dons when the AAFC shut down.

In 1955, Otto Graham's last year, the Browns posted a 9-2-1 record and met the L.A. Rams for the NFL title. In Graham's final game, played before 87,695 fans at the L.A. Coliseum, he passed for two touchdowns and ran for two. One of Graham's passes went to veteran receiver Dante Lavelli, playing in his next-to-last season, the other to Ray Renfro, a 1952 recruit from North Texas State. When the game ended, 38-14 in favor of the Browns, coach Paul Brown said, "Graham

PROFILE

Jim Brown

In 1982, when pro coach George Allen named his 100 best pro football players ever, he picked Jim Brown as the greatest running back of all time. No wonder. Through his nine seasons with the Browns, from 1957 through 1965, Jim Brown led the NFL in rushing eight times, seven of them with more than 1,000 yards--and that was when the regular season consisted of 12 games, not 16. In 1963 he reeled off 1,863 yards rushing. His career total was 12,312 yards, a record since surpassed, with an average of 5.22 yards per carry, an all-time high.

Many of Brown's records were later broken by Walter Payton, O. J. Simpson, Earl Campbell, and others (just as some of his Syracuse University marks were erased by Ernie Davis), but consider this: Jim Brown retired from the NFL at the age of 30. Barring injuries--and he had never missed a pro game in nine years--he still had many seasons of record-setting play left. Had he stayed with the Browns rather than defecting to *The Dirty Dozen* (and other, less successful movies), he may have put several of his all-time records virtually out of reach. He still holds the NFL record for touchdowns, 126 to Walter Payton's 125. And he is remembered as one of the best and hardest-to-stop running backs in pro football history.

is the greatest ever to play the quarterback position in pro football."

The 1956 season lent some credence to what some thought was Brown's overstatement. With Graham in retirement, and George Ratterman and Vito (Babe) Parilli at quarterback, the Browns fell to 5-7. A knee injury ended 29-year-old Ratterman's pro career after four games—he had been Graham's understudy for four years—and Babe Parilli took over until he, too, suffered a season-ending (but not career-ending) injury. That left it up to reserve QB Tom O'Connell, acquired from the Chicago Bears, where he had played a single season. O'Connell did quite well for the rest of the losing season, leading the Browns to three of their five wins. He would be back in 1957, but he would soon be overshadowed by one of the greatest running backs of all time.

Jim Brown and His Era

Paul Brown felt that some rebuilding was necessary for the 1957 season and beyond. He hoped to get a quarterback in the December draft, specifically Len Dawson of Purdue. But Pittsburgh, whose 5-7 record in 1956 was the same as Cleveland's, won the coin toss for first choice (after Notre Dame's Paul Hornung had already gone to Green Bay and Stanford's Steve Brodie to the 49ers), and the Steelers picked Dawson. The Browns then decided on a running back from Syracuse University named Jim Brown. In the second round of the draft Cleveland chose a quarterback, Penn State's Milt Plum. Paul Brown traded six veterans to the Green Bay Packers, while other veterans such as Ratterman, Lavelli, and Gaski retired. Only Lou Groza remained from the team that had burst so spectacularly onto the NFL scene in 1950.

At 6' 2" and 228 pounds, Jim Brown combined power, speed, and elusiveness with such devastating effect that Paul Brown designed the Browns' offense around him. A starter in the Cleveland backfield from the first day of training camp, Jim Brown scored no touchdowns (nor did anyone else) in the season opener against the NFL champion New York Giants, but he did gain 89 yards in 21 carries. Lou Groza kicked two field goals to lead the revived Browns to a 6-3 win over New York.

After eight games in 1957 the Browns were 7-1 and on their way to the Eastern Conference championship. Jim Brown had gained 109 yards in a 21-17 victory over the Washington Redskins, but he had not yet had a truly sensational game. Then, in game nine, against the Los Angeles Rams at Cleveland, the rookie running back from Syracuse carried the ball 31 times, gaining 237 yards (an NFL record at the time) and scoring four touchdowns. Brown's great career was underway. He led the NFL in rushing with 942 yards and was named Rookie of the Year.

Although quarterback Tom O'Connell played a major part in the success of the 1957 Browns, too, he was often sidelined with injuries. After the season he took a coaching job at the University of Illinois, and Milt Plum became the Browns' starting quarterback. For the NFL championship game in 1957 against the Detroit Lions, both O'Connell and Plum were ailing. It showed. The Lions, whose own star quarterback, Bobby Layne, was out with a broken ankle but was ably replaced by Tobin Rote, pulverized the Browns, 59-14.

The 1957 championship game aside, Paul Brown had rebuilt well, and yet the glory days were over. The Browns did well in the late fifties and early sixties—but not well enough. In 1958 the Browns and New York Giants finished with identical 9-3 records. A playoff game in New York went to the Giants, 10-0, and the Browns embarked on the unfamiliar path of also-rans. In 1959 they finished in a tie for second with the Eagles, behind the Giants. They came in second to the Eagles in 1960 (the first year of the rival American Football League) and third behind both the Giants and Eagles in 1961.

Jim Brown continued to excel, leading all rushers year after year. His sophomore total of 1,527 yards rushing was not only a record at the time but topped the previous record by nearly 400 yards. Quarterback Milt Plum led all NFL passers in 1960 and 1961. Bobby Mitchell, a newcomer to the Browns' backfield, performed well in tandem with Jim Brown, both men on their way to the Pro Football Hall of Fame. Still, the Browns, although posting winning seasons and generally in contention, could not quite make it all the way.

In the fall of 1961 Paul Brown had his eye on a running back at Syracuse who looked very much like another Jim Brown. His name was Ernie Davis, a young man from Elmira, New York, who in his four years with the Orangemen eclipsed a number of records held by Brown. Paul Brown offered Cleveland's great halfback Bobby Mitchell to the last-place Washington Redskins in return for the draft rights to Ernie Davis. The deal went through amid considerable criticism, some of it from the new Browns' owner Art Modell, who had not been informed of the deal ahead of time. No one will ever know whether Paul Brown made the right move or not, because Ernie Davis, diagnosed as having monclytic leukemia, died at the age of 23 before having played a single Browns game.

Meanwhile, quarterback Milt Plum was publicly criticizing Paul Brown's handling of the team. "The team is in a rut," he told a newspaper interviewer. "It's time to straighten things out. Our offense has become stereotyped."

Following the 1962 season, in which Cleve-

Winning It All in '64

The Browns started off in the NFL in 1950 as if they would dominate it. For a while they did, and yet in all they have won only four league championships through 1992, the most recent one in 1964, before the advent of the Super Bowl. The 1964 Browns, coached by Blanton Collier, quarterbacked by Frank Ryan, and spearheaded by running back Jim Brown, had undoubted strengths, although some cynics called the team the "laugh champs" because so many of their wins came in close games. The Browns would have to be more than a casual joke to win against Don Shula's Baltimore Colts, featuring star quarterback Johnny Unitas and tight end John Mackey.

Although the Browns had shut out no one in the 1964 regular season, they proceeded to shut out the heavily favored Baltimore Colts, 27-0, and capture the NFL championship. Lou Groza kicked a 43-yard field goal in the third quarter to break a scoreless tie. Gary Collins caught three Frank Ryan passes for a trio of touchdowns, and Jim Brown picked up 114 yards on the ground. Lou Groza kicked a second field goal in the last period. When it was all over, Gary Collins' laughed-at pregame prediction, "We are going to win big," had come true.

land at 7-6-1 came in behind the Giants and Steelers, Browns' owner Art Modell did what once would have been unthinkable. He fired Paul Brown. A Cleveland newspaper headlined a column, "It Was Like Toppling the Terminal Tower." To replace Brown, Modell tapped Blanton Collier, a Browns' assistant coach for many years. The soft-spoken Collier inherited a strong offense, sparked by Jim Brown and quarterback Frank Ryan (acquired a year earlier from the L.A. Rams), and a so-so defense. The 1963 Browns started strong, winning their first six games, but then ran aground against the Giants, Steelers, Cardinals, and Lions. Even so, the Browns finished second at 10-4 and were poised for a championship run in 1964.

In addition to Jim Brown and Frank Ryan, the 1964 Browns had two first-rate receivers, Gary Collins, from the University of Maryland, and Paul Warfield, a rookie from Ohio State. They also had a fine running back in Ernie Green and a solid defensive tackle in Dick Modzelewski. The Browns won their five preseason games, then rolled past the Washington Redskins, 27-13, in their season opener. After four games without a defeat, they ran into a fired-up squad of Pittsburgh Steelers and lost, 23-7.

They bounced back with five more consecutive wins before dropping a game to the Packers and, later, the fast-closing Cardinals. It all came down in the Eastern Conference to the Browns' final game against the Giants. It was no contest, as Cleveland crushed the New Yorkers, 52-20, with Frank Ryan passing for 202 yards and five touchdowns. Now, could the Browns upset coach Don Shula's mighty Baltimore Colts?—for it would be an upset: the Colts, led by quarterback Johnny Unitas, were heavy favorites. The Browns could, and did—defeating the Colts, 27-0, to take the NFL championship.

The Browns compiled a slightly better record in 1965—11-3—than the year before, but the championship game was not so satisfying, as the Green Bay Packers chalked up a 23-12 victory.

At the end of the 1965 season, for the second time (the first being 1958), Jim Brown was named the NFL's Most Valuable Player. Nearly everyone expected the 30-year old superstar to play a few more seasons, but Brown, enticed by the prospect of movie stardom, announced his retirement. No one knew his future in acting, but the Browns knew his past in pro football, and they had good reason to worry that victories might be a little tougher to come by without No. 32 in the backfield.

1966 was the last year in which the NFL had a simple two-part East-West split. Starting in 1967 the league consisted of an Eastern Conference with a four-team Capitol Division and a four-team Century Division and a Western Conference with a four-team Coastal Division and a four-team Central Division. This made it much easier for a team to win a preliminary title—but no easier, really, to get to the Super Bowl (the first of these blockbuster games having been played on January 15, 1967).

In any event, the Cleveland Browns finished first in the Century Division in 1967, 1968, and 1969—and then fell by the wayside in postseason play. In 1967 the Browns won the Century Division title, went up against the Cowboys of the Capitol Division, were beaten 52-14, and went home to watch Super Bowl II on TV. Lou Groza, at age 43, was fading a bit, but a number of veterans put in good years, including linemen Dick Schafrath and Bob Hickerson, linebacker Jim Houston, and running backs Leroy Kelly, Paul Warfield, and Gary Collins.

In 1968 and 1969 the Browns survived all but the final contest on the long road to the Super Bowl. They posted a 10-4 record in 1968 and a 10-3-1 mark in 1969. They fought their way past the Cowboys both years, 31-20 (1968) and 38-14 (1969), to take the Eastern Conference crown. But the NFL championship game undid them. The 1968 Baltimore Colts, who had gone 13-1 in the regular season, shut out the Browns 34-0. In 1969 the Eastern Conference champion Browns met the Western Conference champion Minnesota Vikings. The Vikings prevailed, 27-7.

The Disappointing 1970s

On February 1, 1970, the merger of the National Football League and American Football League was announced, resulting in a 26-team NFL divided into an American Conference and a National Conference, each Conference having three Divisions—Eastern, Central, and Western. The Cleveland Browns were assigned to the Central Division of the American Conference, along with the Cincinnati Bengals, Pittsburgh Steelers, and Houston Oilers.

With only three teams to outperform in their division, a few first-place finishes for the Browns would seem assured. But in the mid-1970s a football dynasty made its appearance in that very AFC Central Division—and it was not the Cleveland Browns. The Pittsburgh Steelers, playing in their new Three Rivers Stadium, walked off with six divisional titles from 1974 through 1979 and won four Super Bowls. With the Cincinnati Bengals also showing some power throughout the decade, the Browns not only failed to dominate the NFL in the 1970s, they failed to dominate the one-sixth of it that was designated the AFC Central Division.

In 1970 the Browns compiled a 7-7 record as two new acquisitions, quarterback Mike Phipps and receiver Homer Jones, failed to meet expectations. The loss of Paul Warfield (for draft rights to Phipps) hurt. So did the departure of running back Ron Johnson (in the trade for Jones). After the 1970 season, Blanton Collier was replaced as head coach by Nick Skorich. While Collier's won-lost record had not equaled that of The Master, Paul Brown, it was impressive: 79-38-2. No Cleveland head coach from that day to the present would come close to matching it.

Despite some deficiencies, Nick Skorich's Browns of 1971 rallied for the division championship on a 9-5 season. It was a rollercoaster ride, with Bill Nelsen quarterbacking, since Mike Phipps was not yet ready to take over. Veteran Leroy Kelly continued to shine in the backfield, as did young Bo Scott in his third year with the Browns. Cleveland blanked the Houston Oilers 31-0 in the season opener and edged the potent Baltimore Colts 14-13 the next week.

They built up a 4-1 record, then suffered a string of four losses and seemed to be out of the race. But a 27-7 win over the New England Patriots turned them around, and the Browns, on a roll, finished the season with five straight wins, including a final-game triumph over the tough Washington Redskins. Although the Central Division title put Cleveland on the road to the Super Bowl, the Baltimore Orioles made short work of the Browns in the divisional playoffs, winning 20-3. For Browns' fans it was another wait-till-next-year season.

Whatever the Browns might do in 1972 was sure to be dwarfed by the remarkable achievement of Don Shula's Miami Dolphins, who proved to be the class (to say the least) of the AFC Eastern Division. The youthful Dolphins went 14-0 in the regular season and 3-0 in the playoffs, including a 14-7 Super Bowl win over the Redskins. No team in the NFL had ever before put together an unbeaten, untied skein, including playoffs. Meanwhile, in the Central Division, the Browns were doing all right, although the Steelers were beginning to show Dolphin-like tendencies themselves.

Pittsburgh won the division with an 11-3 record, but Cleveland was close at 10-4, good for a wild-card shot in the playoffs. As it happened, the Browns were paired off against the mighty Dolphins. The Cleveland effort was valiant but futile, the Dolphins winning 20-14. Unhappily, this was to be Cleveland's last gasp of the decade, for beginning in 1973 and continuing through 1979 (the dynastic era of the Steelers) the Browns never finished higher than third in their four-team division and twice occupied the basement.

The descent was rapid, beginning in 1973 and touching bottom in 1974 and 1975. The Browns' problem, in part, was time—the offensive unit, especially the line, was too old, and the development of quarterback Mike Phipps was too slow. With adequate defense, Cleveland still eked out a winning season, 7-5-2, including a 21-16 victory over the strong and improving Pittsburgh Steelers in their second meeting of the season.

But by 1974 even the limited magic was gone. The Browns stumbled through a 4-10 campaign, their worst till then, and head coach Nick Skorich was ushered out the door. His successor, Forrest Gregg, for many years an offensive tackle for the mighty Green Bay Packers, inherited a losing club, and lost.

The 1975 Browns opened the season with nine straight losses, all but assuring themselves of posting the worst record ever. Surprisingly, they then defeated the division-champion Cincinnati Bengals, 35-23, and the next week, less surprisingly, got past the hapless New Orleans Saints, 17-16. The winning streak ended there. The Steelers handed the Browns their tenth loss, and, after a victory over the Kansas City Chiefs, the Browns fell to the Houston Oilers in the final game. That loss gave Cleveland a record of 3-11, ebb tide of the franchise. One bright spot amid the gloom was Gary Pruitt in the backfield, who racked up 1,067 yards in 217 carries for an average gain of 4.9 yards. Another was veteran defensive tackle Jerry Sherk.

Coach Forrest Gregg got a second chance with the Browns in 1976, and he made the most of it. After a feeble start, losing three of their first four games, Cleveland rebounded spiritedly, winning eight of their next nine but losing the finale to Kansas City. Their quarterback dilemma seemed to be solved. Brian Sipe, a San Diego State product and a Brown since 1974, performed well. Running back Greg Pruitt gained an even 1,000 yards, averaging 4.8 yards a carry. All-Pro defensive tackle Jerry Sherk recorded 12 sacks. Defensive back Thom Darden, back from knee surgery, led the club in interceptions with seven.

The 1977 season started on a high note, as the Browns won their first two games. Indeed, they had fashioned a 5-2 mark by midseason and were leading the Central Division. Then things fell apart. The Bengals and the Steelers defeated the Browns by identical 10-7 scores, and in the game against Pittsburgh Brian Sipe suffered a separated shoulder. Milt Mays stepped in as quarterback and directed the team to a 21-7 victory over the New York Jets. After that the Browns dropped four straight. Following the third loss, Forrest Gregg got his walking papers, and Dick Modzelewski coached the final game.

Sam and the Kardiac Kids

Sam Rutigliano took over as head coach for 1978. His tenure would be a mixture of good, bad, and in-between. He inherited some proven talent—quarterback Brian Sipe, wide receiver Reggie Rucker, running back Greg Pruitt, and defensive back Thom Darden. The Browns also had an impressive new tight end, Ozzie Newsome, drafted from the Crimson Tide of Alabama.

For the first three games in 1978 everything clicked. The Browns swept past the 49ers, 24-7; nosed out the Bengels in overtime, 13-10; and subdued the Atlanta Falcons, 24-16. In the fourth game, against Pittsburgh, they fought to a 9-9 tie after four quarters, but the Steelers scored in sudden death, and won the game 15-9. The high-water mark for the Browns that season had passed. They finished the season at 8-8, third in the AFC Central Division.

Rutigliano's crew upped that mark to 9-7 in 1979, winning a couple of their early games on Don Cockroft's clutch field-goal kicking. Then in 1980 the Browns won 11 games, lost five, and replaced Pittsburgh as division champions. Many of the games that season were close and were decided in the final seconds, thus accounting for the team's new nickname, the Kardiac Kids.

Quarterback Brian Sipe had an outstanding season, leading all NFL passers with 4,132 yards. The dynastic Steelers dropped to third place, as the Houston Oilers compiled the same won-lost record as Cleveland, 11-5. The Browns were awarded the division title on the basis of their conference record (8-4 against Houston's 7-5). In the divisional playoffs, the Browns faced the Oakland Raiders, a wild-card qualifier, and lost, 14-12. It was a memorable game highlighted by a risky Sipe pass deep in Raiders territory that was intercepted, giving Oakland a chance late in the game to come from behind, which they did. The Raiders went on to win the Super Bowl. The Browns began to think about next year.

Next year, 1981, was hardly worth remembering. The Kardiac Kids had cardiac arrest, going 5-11 and finishing last in the Central Division. Brian Sipe had another fine year, passing for 3,876 yards, but touchdowns were fewer, and the Browns never really got started. The 1982 season, shortened by a 57-day players' strike, ended with Cleveland at 4-5. A flurry of playoffs ensued, in which the Browns went nowhere, losing 27-10 the Los Angeles Raiders (the team having moved over from Oakland) in the first round.

The Browns improved marginally in 1983, but their late-season drive fell short of giving them a wild-card playoff spot. They ended the season with an impressive 30-17 win over the Steelers, with Brian Sipe tossing four touchdown passes. Sipe would not be back in 1984; he had signed a contract to play for the New Jersey Generals of the new United States Football League.

Head coach Sam Rutigliano, on the other hand, was back—but only for eight games. At that point the Browns' record was 1-7, and owner Art Modell decided that maybe assistant coach Marty Schottenheimer could turn things around. To some extent, he did. The Browns, with solid defense (except in their 41-7 defeat at the hands of the formidable 49ers), won four of their last eight games.

Schottenheimer, Newsome, Kosar & Co.

The new head coach of the Browns kept his team mostly on the ground in 1985 while rookie quarterback Bernie Kosar from Miami of Florida learned the ropes. Even so, veteran Ozzie Newsome gathered in 62 passes to vault him into the number one spot for tight ends on the all-time list. Linebacker Chip Banks and nose tackle Bob Golic sparkled on defense, while running backs Kevin Mack and Earnest Byner each rushed for more than 1,000 yards. The fine individual performances translated into only an 8-8, which nevertheless was good enough for first place in the weak Central Division. Once again, though, the Browns were stopped in postseason play, losing to Miami, 24-21, in the divisional playoffs.

Bernie Kosar was ready to pass in 1986, and with Kevin Mack and Earnest Byner injured at times, he threw a lot, 531 times, and connected with receivers for a total of 3,854 yards. The Browns lost two of their first three games, to the Chicago Bears and Cincinnati Bengals, but after midseason they were all but unstoppable, winning eight of their last nine games, two of them in overtime.

AP/Wide World Photos

Bernie Kosar

AP/Wide World Photos

Ozzie Newsome

Browns fans were exceptionally loud and boisterous. Cornerback Frank Minnifield's remark that the low-profile Browns were a bunch of "dawgs" made up of players no one else wanted was taken up by legions of fans who came to the stadium they had renamed "The Dawg Pound." Armed with dog biscuits and dog masks they proceeded to bark and howl their team to victory.

Most of the games were close until the last two, when the Browns blew away the Bengals, 34-3, and the San Diego Chargers, 47-17. With a 12-4 record this looked like a team with postseason potential; indeed, the Browns behind Kosar, who passed for almost 500 yards, downed the New York Jets 23-20 in overtime during the first round of playoffs.

Next they met the Denver Broncos in the AFC championship game, which proved to be a thriller and is best remembered as the game that culminated with "The Drive." The Browns went ahead 20-13 on Kosar's 48-yard touchdown pass to Brian Brennan with a little over 5 minutes remaining in the game. A mix up on the ensuing kickoff left Denver at their own 2-yard line. Facing first down, 98 yards to go to tie the game, and less than five minutes to play, John Elway led the Broncos on a dramatic and agonizing drive for the game-tying touchdown. The game went into overtime. After the Browns failed to gain a first down following the kickoff, they were forced to punt. Elway then drove the Broncos 50 yards to set up the game-winning field goal by Rich Karlis, putting a sudden end to the Browns' season and completing one of the most memorable comebacks in playoff history, final score 23-20.

In many ways the 1987 season was a replay of 1986. The yawping in the dawg pound was deafening as the Browns, minus star linebacker Chip Banks who'd been traded to the Chargers, racked up a 10-5 record, good for the division title. Once more they won their first-round playoff games, defeating the Indianapolis Colts, 38-21.

That brought them up against the Denver Broncos again, this time for the AFC championship and a trip to the Super Bowl. The game was every bit as exciting as it had been the year before.

A sequence of come-from-behind efforts led by Bernie Kosar and Earnest Byner almost took the Browns to the Super Bowl. But not quite; while Cleveland was driving for the go-ahead touchdown late in the game, Byner fumbled and the Broncos recovered. The game ended with the Broncos on top, 38-33. Just as the Browns' previous Super Bowl run was ended by Denver in a game remembered for "The Drive," this season's run was ended by Denver in a game remembered for "The Fumble."

In 1988 Cleveland fans lamented the early loss of Bernie Kosar, who injured his arm in the first game. As if that weren't enough, second-string quarterback Gary Danielson broke his leg in the second game, and Mike Pagel, the third-string quarterback, suffered an injury in game six. Don Strock, 38, a career back-up on hand for such emergencies, filled in admirably, leading the Browns to victories over the Philadelphia Eagles in game seven and, when called upon later, directing the team to a 28-23 win against the Houston Oilers in the season finale. This final win earned the Browns a wild-card berth and, with it, a rematch with the Oilers, also a wild-card qualifier. Houston eked out a 24-23 victory to advance to the divisional playoffs.

AP/Wide World Photos

David Grayson (56) and Clay Matthews (right) pressure Bills' quarterback Jim Kelly

Following a disagreement about the coaching staff and the direction of the team, owner Art Modelc fired Schottenheimer who departed for the Kansas City Chiefs. The Browns kept right on rolling, winning the division championship with a 9-6-1 record and outlasting the Buffalo Bills in the first-round playoff game, 34-30. As usual, the Denver Broncos were Cleveland's last hurdle in the contest for the AFC championship and a trip to the Super Bowl. As usual, the Broncos prevailed, this time 37-21. Still, the Browns' new head coach, Bud Carson, could take some satisfaction in the season and look forward with hope to 1990.

The 1990 season was horrendous, the worst in Browns' history, as holdouts, surprise retirements, and generally ineffective play resulted in a 3-13 record. Bernie Kosar found himself rushed and harried behind a weak offensive line, but he set an all-time NFL record spanning parts of the 1991 and 1992 seasons by throwing 308 consecutive passes without an interception.

The otherwise inept Browns scored only 228 points to their opponents 462. Small wonder that after nine games (and a 2-7 mark) Bud Carson got the heave-ho. His interim replacement, Jim Shofner, suffered through a 1-6 streak and in February turned over the reins to Bill Belichick, who had begun his coaching career in 1975 at the age of 23 as an assistant with the Baltimore Colts.

Belichick's first two seasons, 1991 and 1992, produced 6-10 and 7-9 records, good for third place in the AFC Central Division each year. In 1992 Bernie Kosar had one of his best seasons ever, completing 66.5 per cent of his passes, but he broke a bone in his right foot twice. In the offseason two pins were inserted in the foot. The worried front office signed quarterback Vinny

Testaverde from the Tampa Bay Buccaneers to back up Kosar in 1993, just as he had years earlier when the two of them played for the University of Miami, Florida.

Sources

Books

Allen, George, with Ben Olan, *Pro Football's 100 Greatest Players,* Bobbs-Merrill, 1982.

Brown, Jim, with Steve Delsohn, *Out of Bounds,* Zebra Books, 1989.

Brown, Paul, with Jack Clary, *PB: The Paul Brown Story,* Atheneum, 1979.

Clary, Jack, *Cleveland Browns,* Macmillan Publishing Co., 1982.

Cope, Myron. *The Game That Was,* The World Publishing Company, 1970.

Harrington, Denis J., *The Pro Football Hall of Fame: Players, Coaches, Team Owners and League Officials, 1963-1991,* McFarland & Company, 1991.

Hollander, Zander, editor, *The Complete Handbook of Pro Football, 1993,* Signet, 1993.

Levy, Bill, *Return to Glory: The Story of the Cleveland Browns,* The World Publishing Company, 1965.

Neft, David S., and Richard M. Cohen, *The Football Encyclopedia: The Complete History of Professional NFL Football from 1892 to the Present,* St. Martin's Press, 1991.

The Official National Football League 1992 Record & Fact Book, Workman Publishing Co., 1992.

Porter, David L., editor, *Biographical Dictionary of American Sports: Football,* Greenwood Press, 1987.

Rutigliano, Sam, *Pressure,* Oliver-Nelson, 1988.

Treat, Roger, *The Official Encyclopedia of Football,* 9th revised edition, A. S. Barnes and Co., 1971.

Periodicals

Sport, July 1989.

Sports Illustrated, January 15, 1990; August 12, 1991; July 26, 1993.

—*Gerald Tomlinson* for Book Builders Inc.

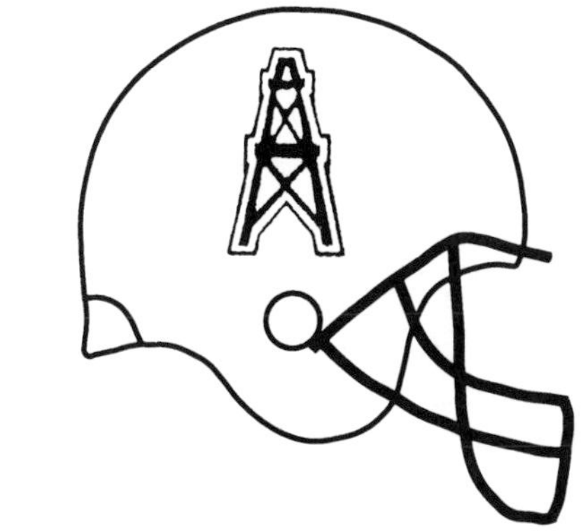

HOUSTON OILERS

The Houston Oilers have seen it all since K.S. "Bud" Adams became one of a group of six owners who founded the American Football League in August 1959. They've known success and they're known failure. They've been embroiled in controversy.

But through it all, the powder blue, red, and white Oilers' uniforms with the oil derrick on the helmets have become one of the most recognizable in professional football.

Adams, a Texas oilman, announced in 1959 that his Houston franchise would join Dallas, Denver, Los Angeles, Minneapolis-St. Paul and New York as the charter members of the new league that would end the NFL's monopoly. He selected the name Oilers for "sentimental and social reasons." John Breen was hired as the club's personnel director. Adams had hoped to play in the 70,000-seat Rice Stadium, but university officials refused permission.

The Oilers' first major controversy occurred when they made Billy Cannon, an All-American halfback from Louisiana State, their No. 1 draft pick. Houston signed Cannon, but a week later they had to file suit to establish the validity of the contract because he had already signed with the Los Angeles Rams. Cannon had decided that he wanted to play in Texas and the judge ruled that he was free to join the Oilers because he was just "a naive country boy."

Cannon's original contract with the Rams was for \$50,000 for three years, but when he signed with Houston he received \$110,000 for three years plus a new Cadillac for his father, a one-armed janitor in Louisiana. "As a kid with some ability and a short life span (in sports) I thought I was entitled to all the traffic would bear," Cannon told *Los Angeles Times* reporter Bob Oates. "I signed every contract that came along and even went to court to chase it. As the judge said, I was naive. I didn't know what the Rams were doing to me."

Both Rams' general manager and Adams had signed Cannon before his last college game, making him a professional. There were several other double signings and the court's awarding of Cannon to Houston set a precedent for players like Cannon's LSU teammate Johnny Robinson and Mississippi's Charlie Flowers.

Lou Rymkus was named the Oilers' first head coach and hired Wally Lemm to coach the defensive backfield. Breen, searching for an experienced quarterback, lured former Chicago Bear George Blanda out of a one-year retirement. "While he's not the greatest quarterback in the world in some departments, he really knows how to take a defense apart," Breen said. Adams leased Jeppesen Stadium, a high school facility, and spent $200,000 on renovations, increasing the seating capacity from 22,000 to 36,000. The Oilers opened their first training camp at the University of Houston.

The Oilers lost their first pre-season game to Dallas 27-10 but came back to beat Denver 42-3 in the home opener before a crowd of 18,500. Houston went 10-4 during the regular season and won the AFL East title with a 31-23 victory over Buffalo.

The Oiler players came from far and wide. Joining Cannon and Blanda were Charlie Hennigan, a wide receiver who had been teaching high school biology. Hennigan taped his final paycheck from the school inside his helmet for inspiration. End Bill Groman was an unheralded rookie from Heidelberg and offensive lineman Al Jamison came from the Canadian Football League. Rymkus blended the group together into a high-scoring machine that took command of the division from the start.

Longest Play

The longest play in Oilers' history occurred during their first year. The long-forgotten Ken Hall, who was a lengendary high school player in Texas, but never lived up to those expectations in college or the pros, returned a kickoff 104 yards for a touchdown against the New York Titans at the Polo Grounds.

At first the Oilers relied on Blanda's passes to Hennigan and Groman but eventually Cannon came on to give Houston a balanced attack. The Oilers beat the Los Angeles Chargers 24-16 on January 1, 1961 in the first AFL championship game before 32,000 fans at Jeppesen. Cannon was the game's Most Valuable Player for his all-around play and Blanda completed 16 of 32 passes for 301 yards and three touchdowns. Each player's winning share from the game was $1,016.42.

The One That Got Away

The 1961 season saw much happening on and off the field. Tight end Willard Dewveall, who had starred at Southern Methodist, became the first player to jump leagues, playing out his option with the Chicago Bears and signing with Houston.

Harris County voters passed a $22 million bond issue to build a domed stadium that would be the Oilers' new home. Adams announced that the team would train in Honolulu. Don Suman was named the club's new vice-president and general manager while Lemm resigned as an assistant coach to enter private business. Six months later, after the Oilers got off to a 1-3-1 start, Lemm was rehired to replace Rymkus as head coach.

The Oilers proceeded to run off ten victories in a row and became the first pro team to score more than 500 points in a season. They won the AFL title for the second year in a row with a 10-3 victory over the Chargers. The biggest change Lemm made was to give the quarterback job back to Blanda, who had been benched by Rymkus in favor of Jacky Lee. Blanda responded with a pro record 36 touch down passes, a pair of 400-yard passing games and effective field goal kicking, including boots of 55 and 53 yards.

Hennigan and Groman continued to be Blanda's favorite targets and Charlie Tolar, dubbed the " Human Bowling Ball", teamed with Cannon to provide a solid ground attack. Lemm down-

TEAM INFORMATION AT A GLANCE

Founding date: 1960 (AFL); 1970 (NFL)

Home stadium: Houston Astrodome
Address: 6910 Fannin St., 3rd Fl.
Houston, TX 77030
Phone: (713) 797-9111
Seating capacity: 60,502

Team colors: Columbia blue, scarlet, and white
Team nickname: Oilers, 1960—
Logo: Oil well

Franchise record:	Won	Lost	Tie
(1960-93)	239	272	6

AFL Championships (2): 1960, 1961

played his part in turning the team around. "I feel like someone who inherited a million dollars in tarnished silverware. All I did was polish it," he said.

The following year Lemm resigned to become head coach of the St. Louis Cardinals of the NFL. Replacing him was former Cardinals coach Pop Ivy. The musical-chairs training camp switched to Ellington Air Force Base in Texas. Blanda and Tolar each had big seasons in 1962 as the Oilers went 11-3 and won their third straight East Division title. Blanda completed six touchdown passes in a 56-17 victory over the New York Titans and Tolar finished with 1.012 yards.

The Oilers won their last seven games and took over first place with a victory over Boston on November 18. Houston lost for the first time in the AFL championship game, but it took a 25-yard field goal by Tommy Brooker in the second overtime period to give Dallas a 20-17 victory. It was the longest pro game up to that time.

The Oilers slumped to a 6-8 record in 1963. The season started with a 24-13 loss to Oakland in the opener and things just got worse. Injuries to Cannon and Jamison damaged the pass blocking and the defense struggled when its top pass rusher, Don Floyd, missed most of the year with a broken jaw.

Houston tried to rebuild on 1964 by drafting Texas All-American tackle Scott Appleton and signing Baylor quarterback Don Trull, who had been a top future pick in a previous draft. Sammy Baugh, who was hired as backfield coach in May, replaced Ivy as head coach less than a month later. Cannon was traded to Oakland for little-known Bob Jackson, Sonny Bishop and Dobie Craig.

Coaching Roulette

Houston's 4-10 season ended with the final game in Jeppesen Stadium, a 34-15 victory over

The Oilers' Greatest Moment

It was the AFL championship game in that Cinderella season of 1961. Lou Rymkus had been fired as head coach after a 1-3-1 start and Wally Lemm replaced him and didn't lose again that year. Many thought the Oilers' string would come to an end when they played the Los Angeles Chargers on Christmas Eve. Surely a defensive wizard like Chargers' coach Sid Gillman would find a way to slow down Houston's high-power offense. It worked, to a certain extent.

The Chargers picked off six of George Blanda's passes and recovered a fumble, but the Oilers countered by intercepting four of Los Angeles quarterback Jack Kemp's throws and recovering two Charger fumbles. Amid the ineptitude on offense, Blanda kicked a 46-yard field goal that gave the Oilers a 3-0 lead. The advantage held until midway through the third quarter when Blanda was forced from the pocket at the Chargers' 35. He sprinted toward the sideline and caught a glimpse of Billy Cannon open over the middle. Cannon made a leaping catch, faked the Los Angeles safety and fell into the end zone for the TD that sealed Houston's 10-3 victory.

Denver. Hennigan was one of the Oilers' few bright spots as he caught a professional record 101 passes. Adams continued to change coaches as Baugh was relieved at the end of the season and replaced by Bones Taylor. Baugh stayed on as an assistant and was joined on the staff by Rymkus, who signed as offensive line coach.

In 1965, the club announced that it wouldn't play in the Astrodome, Houston's new domed stadium, because of "an unrealistic lease agreement." A five-year lease was completed with Rice University for its stadium.

The Oilers also had trouble with their draft picks. The Houston contract of tackle Ralph Neely was declared invalid by an Oklahoma City Federal Court after the University of Oklahoma All-American had signed with both the Oilers and Dallas Cowboys. The club made Tommy Nobis, an All-American linebacker from Texas, its No. 1 draft pick, but he signed with the new Atlanta Falcons of the NFL. The Oilers posted their second straight 4-10 season.

The coaching merry-go-round continued in 1966 when Taylor's contract was not renewed and Lemm was back as head coach. Adams appointed Don Klosterman the new vice-president and GM. The Oilers finished 3-11, their worst record ever.

In 1967, the Oilers became the first team to go from the cellar to the championship as they bounced back with a 9-4-1 record. There were 15 rookies on the rebuilt squad. Blanda was released and Hennigan was traded to San Diego ending an era for the Oilers. The Oakland Raiders spoiled Houston's return to glory by routing the Oilers 40-7 in the AFL championship game. Early in 1968, Adams announced that the Oilers would move into the Astrodome and play there for the season. The contract with Rice was settled and Houston beat Washington 9-3 in a pre-season game at the Astrodome.

Although eleven Oilers were named to various all-star teams in 1968, the club finished with a 7-7 record. Linebacker George Webster was one of four AFL players named to the first combined All-Pro team in 1969. Jim Norton, the last of the original Oilers, retired and his uniform No. 43 was also retired. Despite an up-and-down 6-6-2 season, Houston squeezed into the playoffs under the new wild-card system, but lost to Oakland 56-7 as Raiders' quarterback Daryle Lamonica threw six TD passes.

Klosterman resigned as GM in 1970 to take a similar position with the Baltimore Colts. In one of the most emotional games in club history, the Oilers defeated the Dallas Cowboys for the first time, 37-21, in a pre-season game. Lemm announced late in the season that he would retire at the end of the year. Houston finished 3-10-1, losing 52-10 to Dallas in the final game.

Ed Hughes, who had been backfield coach for the San Francisco 49ers, was named the Oilers' sixth coach to start the 1971 season, signing a five-year contract. Houston selected quarterbacks Dan Pastorini and Lynn Dickey in the first and third rounds, respectively, of the draft. Bob Brodhead was named the team's new GM, but resigned after one month on the job and Breen was given back his old job. Before the season ended, two assistant coaches were fired and shortly thereafter, Adams reported that Hughes' contract had been terminated by mutual settlement. On the field, the Oilers finished 4-9-1.

Rice coach Bill Peterson was hired to replace Hughes, but the Oilers got even worse, posting a 1-13 record in 1972. In the biggest of several trades, Webster was traded to Pittsburgh for wide receiver Dave Smith. When Peterson's two-year record reached 1-18 in 1973, he was fired and Sid Gillman, who had been hired as executive vice-president and general manager, assumed the dual role of coach and GM. The Oilers finished their second straight 1-13 season with a 27-14 loss to Cincinnati.

Gillman announced his decision to stay on one more season as coach-GM, but hired Bum Phillips as his defensive coordinator. John Matuszak, who had been Houston's No. 1 draft pick in 1973, was traded to Kansas City for nose tackle Curley Culp. Culp became an immediate force in the Oilers' new 3-4 defensive alignment and Houston won four in a row and six of their last eight games to finish 7-7, their best record since 1969.

Gillman named Phillips head coach on January 25, 1975, and said he would remain as general manager, but a few weeks later he had to give up that job, too. The decision was announced as "mutual consent" by Adams and Gillman and Phillips was given the added duties as general manager.

The Oilers started fast with five wins in their first six games, including their first victory ever over an NFC team—13-10 over Washington. Pittsburgh stopped the streak with a 24-17 victory on November 10, but the Oilers came back the next week with a 20-19 win over Miami as Billy "White Shoes" Johnson tied an NFL record for touchdowns on kick returns. He had three on punts, including an 83-yarder against the Dolphins, and one on a kickoff. The club finished 10-4, setting a home attendance record, but just missed the playoffs. Johnson's heroics continued after the regular season as he was named MVP of the Pro Bowl after setting a record for kick returns, including a 90-yard kickoff return for a TD.

The Oilers slipped back into their old ways after winning four of their first five games in 1976. They suffered a series of key injuries and lost six in a row and staggered home with a 5-9 mark.

Houston got off to a strong start in 1977 and led the AFC Central after beating Pittsburgh 27-10 on October 9. Pastorini was injured in that game and the Oilers pressed veteran John Hadl into service. By the time Pastorini had recovered, Houston had dropped three straight. With Pastorini's return, the Oilers crushed Chicago 47-0 and won four of their last five to finish 8-6.

Houston obtained the player they felt would lead them over the hump in 1978 when the Oilers traded tight end Jimmie Giles and four draft picks to Tampa Bay for the right to make the first pick in the draft, which they used to take Heisman Trophy winner Earl Campbell of the University of Texas. The Oilers also acquired Pro Bowl offensive tackle Leon Gray from New England, quarterback Gifford Nielsen and wide receiver Mike Renfro.

On October 23, Houston beat the Steelers 24-17 for their first Monday Night Football victory ever. Four weeks later, the Oilers won another Monday night game as Campbell ran for 199 yards and four touchdowns in a 35-30 victory over Miami. Houston clinched a wild-card playoff berth on December 10 with a 17-12 victory over New Orleans. Campbell finished his rookie season with a league-leading 1,450 yards and 13 TDs.

Houston's wild card game was a rematch with Miami and the Oilers beat the Dolphins 17-9 as Pastorini completed 20 of 29 passes. The following week Pastorini led the Oilers to a 31-14 victory over New England. Houston's Cinderella season ended the next week when Pittsburgh scored 17 points during a two-minute span and won the AFC championship game 34-5.

Houston fell into an early hole in 1979 in its quest for a division title when the Oilers dropped a 38-7 decision to Pittsburgh. They recovered to win nine of their next eleven games, beat the Steelers 20-17 on a Monday night, but still finished second in the division with an 11-5 record. Campbell tied NFL records by rushing for 100 or more yards eleven times, including seven in succession, and scored 19 rushing touchdowns. He ran for 1,697 yards.

Playing their first home playoff game since 1961, the Oilers overcame injuries to Campbell and Pastorini to beat Denver 13-7. The following week, again without their offensive standouts, Houston shut down the league's best passing attack with four interceptions by Vernon Perry and beat San Diego 17-14.

The Oilers just couldn't get past Pittsburgh in the AFC title game and lost 27-13 to the Steelers on a pair of touchdown passes by Terry Bradshaw. Pastorini became the scapegoat for the Oilers' playoff demise and was traded to Oakland for quarterback Ken Stabler during the off-season.

Houston started the 1980 season 3-3, including a 31-17 loss to Pittsburgh, but turned the year around on October 14 when the Oilers obtained tight end Dave Casper from the Raiders for three draft choices. Using a two-tight end formation, Houston went 8-2 the rest of the way and one of those victories was 6-0 over the Steelers, which knocked the defending Super Bowl champions out of the playoffs. Campbell rushed for 1,934 yards, the second-highest total in NFL history.

Despite having the same record as the AFC Central champion Cleveland Browns, the Oilers went into the playoffs as the wild card team again, but this time lost to Oakland 27-7 as the Raiders shut down Stabler and Campbell. "The Raiders put in a new blitzing scheme for this game," Stabler said in his autobiography *Snake*. "It had cornerback Lester Hayes and strong safety Mike Davis coming from the left side and they each got me twice. [Ted] Hendricks and each of the ends each got me once apiece. One problem was that our right tackle got hurt and the backup, who because of injuries himself hadn't practiced much, could not make the blocking calls that would have allowed us to pick up the blitzes."

The other problem was there just weren't a lot of adjustments that could be made in the Oilers' conservative old-fashioned offense. The machine just didn't have many adjustables on it. "I felt like a guy who had wandered into Oakland

Bum Phillips

O.A. "Bum" Phillips posted a 55-35 record as head coach from 1975-80, but his trademark cowboy boots and hat and homespun Texas personality overshadowed the way he turned around a struggling franchise. The Oilers won only one game each in 1972 and 1973, but when Phillips became defensive coordinator in 1974 the club rebounded to a 7-7 mark. He took over as head coach the following season and pointed Houston toward the playoffs. The Oilers made the playoffs from 1978-80 but lost each time to the Super Bowl champion. Phillips was fired after the 1980 season, but quickly hooked on with the New Orleans Saints and began that franchise's turnaround.

Phillips, who was popular with his players, didn't miss a trick. Once he was exasperated when Oakland's Ray Guy averaged 45.5 yards a punt and booted a kickoff out of the end zone on the fly. He said, "Let's get a couple of those balls and take them home with us," so the equipment man grabbed a couple balls from the Raiders' sideline and Phillips took them to Rice University to be checked for helium. "That's the craziest thing I've ever heard of," said Guy. "I think they just needed a couple more footballs so they took two of ours home with them." The tests on the balls proved negative, but Phillips couldn't believe it was humanly possible for Guy to be as good as he was.

wearing a flattop haircut, wing-tip shoes and carrying a slingshot, only to be set upon by a band of cutthroats bearing cutlasses. Fortunately, my former teammates took mercy on me. Six of the seven blitzes that got me came from my blind side and could have been hospitalization hits, but the guys just jumped on my back and rode me down."

"Poor Bum. It was even worse for him," Stabler continued. "'They did things and we didn't have the adjustments,' Bum said after the game. 'We were outcoached.' As much as I loved him I had to say he was right." Three days later, Phillips was fired and defensive coordinator Ed Biles was named head coach. Ladd Herzeg became vice-president and general manager. Biles discarded Phillips' two tight end formation and put Rob Carpenter in the backfield to start the 1981 season.

After a slow start, Biles returned blocking back Tim Wilson as Campbell's backfield mate and Campbell responded with 182 yards against Cincinnati and 186 against Seattle. Carpenter was traded to the New York Giants, but Campbell didn't run for 100 yards in any other game that season and the Oilers finished 7-9. Even with his late slump, Campbell gained 1,376 yards and led the AFC in rushing for the fourth straight season.

Late in the year, Biles replaced Stabler with Nielsen. "The Oilers, after Bum left, didn't have much going for them," Stabler wrote. "Ed Biles didn't have Bum's charisma and I don't think guys put out for Biles like they had for Bum."

Best Oilers Linebacker

For a few seasons, former Michigan State standout George Webster was as good as they come, but injuries shortened his career and Robert Brazile's longevity makes him the best linebacker in Oilers' history. Brazile was drafted in the first round out of Jackson State in 1975 and was a perennial all-star through the 1984 campaign. He combined size(6-foot-4, 238 pounds) and quickness and was called Dr. Doom for his ferocious hitting.

Brazile was Walter Payton's teammate in college and some said that Payton developed as a runner by trying to avoid Brazile in practice. He entered college as a tight end, but his toughness made him better suited for defense. Phillips once said Brazile "is the same kid now after becoming a genuine star as he was when he was a rookie. And he has more fun on the field than the rest of the guys."

The Struggle To Survive

Houston's collapse continued in 1982. Biles cut Stabler before the season and gave his job to Nielsen. One week into the regular schedule, Biles decided Nielsen wasn't the man and made a deal with the New Orleans Saints, which Phillips was coaching, for Archie Manning. The Oilers split their two pre-strike games, then dropped seven straight after returning and finished 1-8. Running behind a porous offensive line, Campbell rushed for only 538 yards.

The 1983 season didn't start any better than 1982 had ended. Houston lost its first ten games and Biles was replaced by assistant Chuck Studley. Three weeks into the season, Manning and Casper were traded to Minnesota for draft picks and Nielsen regained his starting job at quarterback.

After seven straight defeats, he was replaced by Oliver Luck. Luck guided the team to wins over Detroit and Cleveland, but the Oilers finished 2-14. Campbell regained his old form and rushed for 1,301 yards and 12 touchdowns.

Houston added one Campbell and subtracted another in 1984. Long-time Canadian Football League coach Hugh Campbell replaced Studley, and Earl Campbell was traded to New Orleans for a first-round draft pick in October. Hugh Campbell brought in former CFL star Warren Moon to quarterback the Oilers and he quickly became the hub of the offense. The improvement wasn't immediate as Houston lost its first ten games, but the Oilers recovered to win three of their last six.

The 1985 season continued to be a struggle as the Oilers wound up 5-11 and Campbell was replaced by defensive assistant Jerry Glanville with two games remaining. One of the big disappointments was first-round draft pick Mike Rozier, the Heisman Trophy winner from Nebraska, who rushed for only 462 yards in his rookie season.

Houston started 1986 with a 1-8 mark before Glanville discarded his conservative ways and opened the offense with Moon and receivers Ernest Givins and Drew Hill. The Oilers were 5-11 for the second straight season. The 1987 campaign brought the Oilers their first playoff appearance since 1980 and began a string of six straight postseason trips. Houston was 9-6, a game behind AFC Central champ Cleveland, as Moon passed for 2,806 yards and 21 touchdowns, Rozier rushed for 957 yards and Hill and Givins combined for 102 receptions and nearly 2,000 yards.

AP/Wide World Photos

Warren Moon

Controversy still visited the Oilers as Adams hinted that he might move the team to Jacksonville, Florida because of low attendance and Glanville was criticized in the local media for errors, and by Pittsburgh coach Chuck Noll for alleged dirty play.

Tony Zendejas kicked a 42-yard field goal in overtime to give Houston a 23-20 victory over Seattle in the first round of the playoffs. The Oilers then fell to Denver 34-10 in the second round. Glanville gained a lot of notoriety during 1988 by leaving tickets at the gate for Elvis Presley and several other deceased celebrities. Less amusing to opponents were the rough play by Houston's defense and special teams. The Astrodome was nicknamed "The House of Pain."

Moon passed for more than 2,300 yards and 17 touchdowns and Rozier rushed for 1,002 yards as the Oilers finished 10-6. They were one of the league's best teams at home, but their inability to win on the road left them tied with Cleveland for second in the AFC Central. Houston nipped the Browns 24-23 in an AFC wild card playoff as running back Allen Pinkett scored two touchdowns, but the Oilers were ousted 17-10 by Buffalo the following week.

Houston was the favorite to win the division title in 1989 and needed only a victory in one of its last two games to take its first undisputed AFC Central title, but the Oilers lost 61-7 to Cincinnati and lost the season finale to Cleveland with 39 seconds remaining on Kevin Mack's touchdown.

Houston took a 9-7 record into the playoffs, but lost the wild card game 26-23 to Pittsburgh on Gary Anderson's 50-yard field goal in overtime. The defeat spoiled a brilliant game by Givins, who had eleven receptions for 136 yards and two TDs.

Those three defeats cost Glanville his job, although the official word was that he resigned. His downfall was his failure to decide on a running back—Alonzo Highsmith, Rozier, Pinkett and Lorenzo White were the candidates—and a club record 148 penalties. The Oilers also lacked an effective pass rush.

Jack Pardee left the University of Houston to replace Glanville and he brought along his run-and-shoot offense. The 1990 season started with a pair of defeats, but eventually Moon and receivers Hill, Haywood Jeffires, Givins and Curtis

Duncan began terrorizing the league.

Moon was on his way to several league-passing records when he dislocated his thumb in Week 15. Cody Carlson replaced him and led the Oilers to a season-ending 34-14 victory over Pittsburgh that put Houston in the playoffs with a 9-7 mark. The post-season was short-lived as Cincinnati beat the Oilers 41-14 in an AFC wild card game.

All Choked Up

Houston won its first AFC Central title in 1991 with an 11-5 record, but for the fifth straight time the Oilers failed to make it past the second round in post-season play. The defense showed great improvement, allowing the second-fewest points in the conference, and Moon was the league's most prolific passer, setting records for attempts (655) and completions (404). On the down side, was a career-high 21 interceptions. Jeffires became the fifth NFL player to catch 100 passes in a season.

Houston, which ended the season with a 4-4 record, beat the New York Jets 17-10 in the first round of the playoffs as safety Bubba McDowell intercepted two passes inside the five to preserve the victory. The Oilers' Super Bowl hopes ended the following week with a heartbreaking 26-24 loss to Denver on David Treadwell's 28-yard field goal with 16 seconds left. Moon was outstanding in the defeat, completed 27 of 36 passes for 325 yards and three touchdowns.

AP/Wide World Photos

A defender's-eye view of Oilers running back Lorenzo White

The Oilers had an up-and-down season in 1992, but still earned their NFL-best sixth straight playoff appearance with a 10-6 record. Carlson replaced the injured Moon and led Houston down the stretch. White emerged as the running back the Oilers had been looking for as he rushed for 1,226 yards. Jeffires led the AFC in receptions for the third straight year, hauling in 90 passes, and Givins topped the conference with ten TD receptions.

The Oilers' Greatest Quarterbacks

George Blanda held that distinction until Warren Moon came along to break all the club's passing records. Blanda came to the AFL after several seasons as a so-so signal-caller in the NFL and quickly led Houston to back-to-back championships. As an Oiler he once threw for 700 yards in a game and threw for 300 or more yards 16 times. In seven seasons with Houston he had 165 TD passes. Blanda was impervious to pressure. He might throw an interception, but would come right back and fire a touchdown pass. He might miss an early field goal, but if the game was on the line he'd hit it.

Moon has passed for 51,428 yards in 14 pro seasons, including six in the Canadian Football League where he led the Edmonton Eskimos to five CFL titles. He also took the University of Washington to the Rose Bowl in 1977. He joined the Oilers in 1984, but is still looking for his first championship with Houston.

The defense ranked first in the AFC and third in the NFL and Houston's offense was second in the conference. No other team could boast such balance, but the Oilers' season ended when they blew a 32-point lead and lost 41-38 to Buffalo in overtime. Houston had beaten the Bills 27-3 in the last game of the regular season. Moon returned for the playoffs and completed 36 of 50 passes for 371 yards and four first-half touchdowns against Buffalo.

Sports Illustrated's Peter King said the Buffalo comeback was "right up there with Bobby Thomson's home run in 1951, the Bill Buckner game of the '86 World Series, Doug Flutie's Hail Mary against Miami and N.C. State's '83 Final Four triumph. However, in terms of a comeback, they'll all have to line up behind this one."

What made the game even more remarkable was that the Bills played the second half without quarterback Jim Kelly, running back Thurman Thomas and linebacker Cornelius Bennett and pass-rushing specialist Bruce Smith was making little impact because of three cracked ribs. Then McDowell returned a pass interception 58 yards for a touchdown at the start of the second half to put the Oilers ahead 35-3. "We choked as a team, choked as player, choked as management," said defensive back Cris Dishman. "How else can you describe it? We completely broke down. We choked."

Givins worried about the future. "I think this game will break this team," he said. The following day, defensive coordinator Jim Eddy and defensive backfield coach Pat Thomas were fired. A few weeks later, controversial Buddy Ryan was named defensive coordinator.

The Oilers were on the spot as the 1993 season began. With several high-priced players and Moon getting along in years, the team had to make a strong showing in the playoffs or it would be time for rebuilding.

Sources

Books

Blair, Sam, and Earl Campbell, *The Driving Force,* Word Books, 1980.

Clary, Jack, *The Game-Makers,* Follett, 1976.

Horrigan, Jack and Mike Rathet, *The Other League,* Follett, 1970.

Neft, David S., Cohen, Richard M. and Rick Korch, *The Sports Encyclopedia: Pro Football,* St. Martin's Press, 1993.

Stabler, Ken and Barry Stainback, *Snake,* Doubleday, 1986.

Twombly, Wells, *Blanda—Alive and Kicking,* Nash, 1972.

The Official NFL Encyclopedia of Pro Football, NAL Books, 1981.

Periodicals

Complete Handbook of Pro Football, 1975-93.

Houston Oilers media guides, 1969-93.

Football Digest, January 1980; February 1983; October 1983; February 1985; February 1988.

Sports Illustrated, January 11, 1993.

—Chuck Klonke

Pittsburgh Steelers

The Pittsburgh Steelers celebrated their 60th season in the National Football League (NFL) in 1992. The fifth oldest franchise in the league, the Steelers were founded on July 8th, 1933 by the now legendary Arthur Joseph Rooney. Originally named the Pittsburgh Pirates, after the city's major league baseball team, they were part of the Eastern Division of the ten-team NFL. Only four other teams in existence at that time have franchises in the NFL today: the Chicago Bears, the Chicago (Phoenix) Cardinals, the Green Bay Packers, and the New York Giants.

When the name "Steelers" is mentioned, football fans of today automatically think of the glory teams of the 1970s, the four-time Super Bowl champions, truly the team of that decade. Some say that Terry Bradshaw, Franco Harris, Mean Joe Greene, Jack Ham, Jack Lambert, Lynn Swann, Mel Blount, and their supporting cast were perhaps the greatest NFL team of all time. What many of today's fans do not realize is that the Steelers experienced years of frustration and mediocrity before winning their first division championship in 1972. In fact, the Steelers posted only eight winning seasons in their first 40 years in the league. This, then, is the story of a proud, old NFL franchise. A franchise born in the depths of depression in a blue-collar town, the coal and steel capital of America, Pittsburgh, Pennsylvania. It is also in many ways the story of one man, Art Rooney, and his love for the game of football and for the city of Pittsburgh.

Art Rooney and the Beginning

Actually, the Steelers began their tenure in Pittsburgh illegally. Lou Sahadi in his *Super Steelers: The Making of a Dynasty* describes the beginning quite well. Art Rooney, affectionately known as "The Chief," loved horses, particularly race horses, and much of his leisure time in the late

1920s and early 1930s was spent at Eastern race tracks. Rooney made a killing on the horses one weekend in New York, winning between $200,000 and $400,000. Being familiar with the National Football League, he telephoned the league president Joe Carr and asked about the possibility of starting a franchise in Pittsburgh. Rooney recalled his decision to purchase an NFL franchise in an interview with Myron Cope: "In 1933, I paid $2,500 for a National Football League franchise which I named the Pirates, because the Pittsburgh baseball team was called the Pirates. I bought it because I figured it would be good to have a league schedule and that eventually professional football would be good."

The only problem was that Pittsburgh had a blue law that prohibited the playing of professional sports on Sundays, the day the NFL played its games. But the fabled Rooney good luck continued. An amendment to repeal the law was expected to be passed before Pittsburgh's first game on September 20, 1933, against the New York Giants. The city council, however, became bogged down with other legislation and the blue law was still in effect the Friday before the game.

Rooney acted quickly. He made sure that one of the city officials who could stop the game would be out of town on Sunday. He invited the other, the superintendent of police, to sit in his box at the game. The contest went off as scheduled with 4,000 fans showing up for the debut of professional football in Pittsburgh. The Giants defeated the Pirates, 23-2, but the blue law was struck down the next week and Rooney was able to play his home schedule.

The Early Years: 1933-1940

The Pittsburgh team kept the name Pirates from 1933 through the 1940 season. Although its baseball namesake was one of the better teams in major league baseball during the 1930s, Rooney's franchise was one of the poorest performing squads in the fledgling NFL. In the eight years they played under the Pirate banner, the "Rooneymen" won only 24 games, with their best season coming in 1936. In that year, the Bucs went six and six and finished second in the league's Eastern Division.

Rooney changed coaches regularly. During their eight years, the Pirates had six head coaches. Jap Douds, a burly tackle and a player-coach, was Rooney's first mentor. Jap was followed by Luby DiMelio (1934), Joe Bach (1935 and 1936), Johnny "Blood" McNally (1937 and 1938) and Walt Kiesling (1939 and 1940). Bach and Kiesling would later resurface as Steeler coaches in the 1950s, thus pointing out a Rooney trait of hiring friends and men he personally liked to head his team.

Throughout Steeler history, Rooney always seemed to have colorful characters on his teams. The first of these was the Pirates' John "Blood" McNally, a star halfback with Curly Lambeau's Green Bay Packers. Seeing the flamboyant McNally as a big box office draw, Rooney signed him in 1937 as a player-coach to replace Bach.

"Blood" was a free spirit, whose off-the-field activities were legendary in pro-football. He gave himself his nickname when he spotted a theater marquee advertising the movie *Blood and Sand.* The name appealed to him and so did the fairer sex. He was a Valentino of the gridiron. Commenting on McNally's coaching ability, Rooney told Cope: "I still believe that John Blood could have been a tremendous coach, if he would just have paid attention. We once played a game in Los Angeles and John missed the train home. John was known to have a good time, of course, so we didn't see him for the whole week. On Sunday he stopped off in Chicago to see his old team, the Packers, play the Bears. The newspaper guys asked him 'How come you're not with your team?' And John said 'Oh, we're not playing this week.' Well, no sooner did he get those words out of his mouth than the guy on the loudspeaker announced a score. 'Philadelphia 14—Pittsburgh 7.' You couldn't depend on John a whole lot."

During 1938, "Blood's" second season as head coach, Rooney shook up the NFL and the sports world by signing Byron "Whizzer" White, the Colorado All-American, for the unheard sum

TEAM INFORMATION AT A GLANCE

Founding Date: July 8, 1933 (franchise purchased for $2,500 by Arthur Joseph Rooney; originally a member of the Eastern Division of the National Football League)

Home Stadium: Three Rivers Stadium
300 Stadium Circle
Pittsburgh, PA 15212
Seating Capacity: 59,600
Surface: Artificial Turf

Team Uniforms: Home—Black jerseys trimmed in gold and white with white numerals; gold pants with black stripe; black helmet with gold stripe
Road—White jerseys trimmed with gold, black, and white with black numerals; gold pants with black stripe; black helmet with gold stripe
Team Nickname: Pirates, 1933-40; Steagles, 1943; Card-Pitt, 1944; Steelers, 1941-42; 1945—
Logo: A round white circle with three modified red, blue, and yellow stars and emblazoned with the word Steelers. (It is the logo of the US Steel Corporation with the word Steelers added)

Franschise record:	Won	Lost	Tie
(1933-92)	363	403	20

NFL Championships (4): 1974, 1975, 1978, and 1979
American Conference Championships (4): 1974, 1975, 1978, and 1979
Central Division, American Conference Titles (10): 1972, 1974, 1975, 1976, 1977, 1978, 1979, 1983, 1984, 1992

of $15,800, making him the highest paid football player in the league. Although White had a great year, leading the league in rushing with 567 yards, passing for 393 yards, and accounting for six touchdowns, the Pirates, as a team, were less than successful.

They finished last in the Eastern Division with a 2-9 record. Not surprisingly, the Pirates had not drawn well at the box office. While the Pitt Panthers, one of the best college football teams in America, routinely drew 35,000 fans for their games at Pitt Stadium, Rooney's Pirates were fortunate to have 3,500 fans show up.

The Pittsburgh franchise retained the name Pirates for two more years without a noticeable improvement in its performance. Whizzer White did not return in 1939, opting instead to go to Oxford, begin his Rhodes Scholar studies, and ultimately be named a Supreme Court Justice. The last two Pirate teams of 1939 and 1940 won a total of three games, finishing in the cellar of the Eastern Division both years.

Rooney finally despaired after the 1940 season ended and sold the team to Alexis Thompson. But when the 1941 NFL season opened, there was still a franchise in Pittsburgh and Art Rooney was one of its owners. The franchise, however, was no longer called the Pirates.

PROFILE **Art Rooney . . .**

Sport never had a better friend than Arthur Joseph Rooney. From his earliest youth athletics held a particular fascination. While still a teenager he fought his way onto the 1920 U.S. Olympic boxing team and later won AAU championships as both a welterweight and a middleweight. He later spent five years as a professional baseball player in the minor leagues, showing considerable promise until an arm injury ended his dreams of making baseball's big time. When forced into more mundane pursuits for the sake of a livelihood he spent his off-hours subjecting life and limb to the rigors of semipro football.

Finally body and brain dictated that his days as a participant were over. He then turned promoter, bankrolling a series of Pittsburgh-area teams given such names as the J. P. Rooneys, the North Side Majestics, and the Hope Harveys. A seed was being planted that would ultimately flower into greater things.

On July 8, 1933, Rooney bought an NFL franchise for $2,500, funds appropriated from a run of good fortune at the race track, or so the story goes. Thus began a long and adventurous association with professional football. He christened his new acquisition the Pittsburgh Pirates, a designation which endured for seven seasons while the team perennially lanquished in the lower echelons of the NFL's Eastern Division. The Pirates didn't draw well for their home games at Forbes Field due to their losing record but also because of the popularity of the resident baseball club and the University of Pittsburgh's gridiron squad.

A New Name and the War Years: 1941-1945

When Art Rooney sold the Pirates to Alexis Thompson after the 1940 season, he soon realized he had made a mistake. He wanted his team back. In a complicated franchise swap prior to the kickoff of the 1941 season, Thompson acquired the Philadelphia Eagles from Bert Bell, the Eagles' coach and owner. Rooney and Bell became the co-owners of the newly renamed Steelers. Rooney had chosen the name to reflect the coal and steel heritage of the city of Pittsburgh.

With Bell handling the Steelers' coaching reins, Rooney watched a pre-season workout for a few minutes, turned to a bystander and commented, "Well, we've got a new team, a new coach, a new nickname, and new uniforms, but they look like the same old Pirates to me." The bystander turned out to be a reporter and "The Chief's" remarks made big news in the papers. Bell turned the team over to Buff Donelli after two games but by midseason Walt Kiesling was back at the helm. The 1941 Steelers may be the only team in NFL history with three different head coaches in one season.

An innately resourceful entrepreneur, he barnstormed the Pirates around central and western Pennsylvania to enhance his financial base and familiarize the public with the pro game. In 1940, he renamed the franchise the Pittsburgh Steelers, and two years later the team experienced its first winning campaign. More losses and red ink ensued until the Steelers finished atop the Eastern Division in 1947. Then it was back to the short end of the score more often than not.

Even though the anguish and disappointment of this period weighed heavily upon him, Rooney would not give up the struggle. "I'll tell you something from the bottom of my heart," he said. "I'd pay to lose money just to keep in this game. I love it that much."

The Steelers remained something of a doormat until Chuck Noll, their 14th head coach, arrived on the scene in 1969. Under his tutelage they won four Super Bowl crowns from 1974 through 1979. Despite this rags to riches transition Rooney remained the same unassuming vendor of solace and comfort, ever concerned with the welfare of others.

John Madden, former head coach of the Oakland Raiders, said, "We had some giant battles with the Steelers, but Art Rooney was always above that. Win or lose, he would treat you the same. There's a saying, 'Shut up until you win, then run your mouth.' He was never like that." Terry Bradshaw, who quarterbacked Pittsburgh's Super Bowl champion teams, said, "Mr. Rooney would give anybody anything he had. He was that kind of a man."

In truth, Rooney always had a hand in his pocket either to acquire needed football talent, to tide over a fellow team owner, or simply to provide assistance wherever it was needed. On more than one occasion he dug deep to help keep the NFL a going concern during World War II. He also played angel to the Pittsburgh Pirates baseball team and other sporting interests in his hometown.

But the most memorable contributions he made were in the area of personal relationships. He spent his life uniting friends closer together and guiding adversaries past their differences into a bond of mutual respect. Even in death the healing effect of his spirit could still be discerned. On August 25, 1988, he passed away at the age of 87. After his funeral service, NFL commissioner Pete Rozelle and Los Angeles Raiders owner Al Davis, bitter foes for many years, shook hands in honor of their departed friend.

During the war years, the club was particularly woeful. From 1941 through 1945 they had three losing seasons, played under three different names, and won an average of three games a year. The lone exception to this dismal era was 1942, when the Steelers made a dramatic turnaround, posting a 7-4 record and finishing second in the Eastern Division to the eventual world champion Washington Redskins. The main reason for their resurgence was a rookie tailback from the University of Virginia, Bullet Bill Dudley.

Although Dudley stood only 5'10", he was what many writers called "a born winner." According to the *Pro Football Encyclopedia:* "He ran slowly but knew how to use his blockers, which hole to hit and when to cut back across the open field. He looked funny passing, but he completed passes, and his running, passing, kick-returning, defensive work, punting, and place-kicking all testified to a competitor's heart burning in a small body."

Dudley introduced himself to the NFL by running 55 yards for a touchdown in the first minute of play on opening day against the Philadelphia Eagles. He went on to lead the league in rushing, carrying the ball 162 times for 696 yards, an average of 4.3 yards a run, and was selected the NFL's Rookie of the Year.

But the next year Dudley joined the Armed Forces, along with many other NFL players, as World War II escalated. With his rosters depleted by the loss of players to the services, Rooney merged the Steelers with the Philadelphia Eagles in 1943 (the Phil-Pitt Steagles) and with the Chicago Cardinals (Card-Pitt) in 1944.

The 1943 Steagles were a decent club by wartime standards finishing with a 5-4-1 record. Philadelphia and Pittsburgh split the home schedule with coaches Earl "Greasy" Neale and Walt Kiesling sharing the reins and pooling their players. The 1944 season may well have been the low point in the history of a franchise with many mediocre seasons. Known affectionately around the league as the "Car-pets," Card-Pitt did not win or tie a game, going 0-10-0. The closest they came to victory was an opening day 30-28 loss to the Cleveland Rams.

Despite the adversity he had experienced with the Steelers during the war years, Art Rooney was optimistic about the future. He hired the University of Pittsburgh's great coach, Jock Sutherland, to head the Steelers for the 1946 season and knew that Bill Dudley would be back with club.

The Postwar Years and the Early Fifties: 1946-1956

During the period from 1946 through 1956 the Steelers field teams were known for their physical toughness but lacked the blend of front office acumen, coaching, and across the board talent to win even a division title. Running the single wing long after it had gone out of vogue, the Pittsburghers played bruising, smash-mouth football.

Tom Landry, then a defensive back with the New York Giants, probably described the feelings of most players in the NFL when he said, "We would much rather play Cleveland twice than Pittsburgh once. The Browns would beat you on the scoreboard, but the Steelers would make you ache all week."

In the first true postwar season, 1946, Rooney pulled a coup. He convinced Doctor John Baines "Jock" Sutherland to accept the job as his head coach. Sutherland, a tall, stern, all-business Scotsman, had produced spectacularly successful teams in the 1930s at the University of Pittsburgh and competitive squads with the NFL Brooklyn Dodgers in 1940 and 1941.

Not only were Steeler fans excited about Sutherland, they were equally aroused by the return of Bullet Bill Dudley from the army. The Sutherland-Dudley combination appeared to bode good fortune for Rooney's team. But in keeping with the black cloud that hung over the franchise, a serious problem arose. Sutherland and Dudley could not get along. In fact, they grew to dislike each other intensely.

However, Dudley's rift with Sutherland did not affect his on-field performance. He led the NFL in rushing (604 yards) and interceptions (ten), spurred the team to a third place tie with a 5-5-1 record, and was named the league's Most Valuable Player. At the end of the 1946 season, Bullet Bill finally answered his hostile coach by quitting professional football and accepting a job as backfield coach at his alma mater, the University of Virginia.

But the Detroit Lions had acquired the rights to him in a trade, and Coach Gus Dorais convinced Dudley to play in the Motor City. He played three years for the Lions and three more for the Redskins before retiring for good.

Had Dudley been a Steeler in 1947, the club probably would have won its first division title. Despite the absence of an established star, Sutherland pushed the team to an 8-4 record and a first-place deadlock with Greasy Neale's Philadelphia Eagles. The teams met at Forbes Field in a playoff game on a cold, snowy day in late December. But playing without their injured rookie tailback, Johnny "Zero" Clement, the Rooneymen lost to the Eagles 21-0. It was the closest they would come to a division championship until 1972.

A personal tragedy struck the Steelers in early 1948. Sutherland, on a spring scouting trip in the South, fell ill with recurrent headaches. Within a week, he was dead from a brain tumor. His place was taken by his top assistant, former University of Pittsburgh star John Michelosen.

"Mike," who kept the Steelers' reins for the next four years, retained Jock's single wing offense running the formation at a time when every other NFL team was filling the air with footballs. But the Steelers of Michelosen had their moments, and their rock-ribbed defense was outstanding. In 1951, the defense, led by tackle Ernie Stautner and cornerback Jack Butler, held their opponents to two touchdowns or less six different times. Michelosen ended his four-year Steeler coaching career with a 20-26-2 record (a .438 percentage), becoming the ninth of Rooney's first ten coaches with a losing career record.

In 1952 the Steelers came out of the dark ages by abandoning the single-wing and installing the T-Formation. Surprisingly, this make over was accomplished by a coach from the 1930s, Art Rooney's good friend, Joe Bach. Bach made Jim Finks, a three-year bench-warmer and former Tulsa passing whiz, his quarterback. The Steelers still lost more than they won, going five and seven in 1952 and six and six in 1953. But the new offense generated excitement, and Finks led the league with 20 TD passes in 1952. Finks, who later became a highly respected NFL general manager, quarterbacked the Steelers for only four years. However, he is fourth on their all-time passing list with 8,854 yards, a remarkable figure for such a short time frame.

Joe Bach was replaced at the beginning of the 1954 season with another of Rooney's "good friends," former Steeler coach Walt Kiesling. Big Kies got the club off to a rousing 4-1 start, the highlight of which was a 55-27 thrashing of the vaunted Cleveland Browns. A week after humiliating the Browns, they won a dramatic 17-7 game against the Eagles before a standing- room-only crowd at Forbes Field. The city of Pittsburgh was ecstatic. Following the victory over the Eagles, the resurgent and highly confident Steelers journeyed to Chicago to meet the winless Cardinals. Ollie Matson ran back the opening kickoff for a touchdown and the Black and Gold never recovered, losing the game 17-14. They won only one contest the rest of the year, and finished the campaign with a five and seven record.

In 1955 and 1956, the Steelers' fortunes continued to sag. They finished four and eight in 1955 and five and seven in 1956. But their biggest mistake, perhaps the biggest one made by any team in NFL history, was their failure to recognize the talents of a young man who grew up in their own city. Looking for a backup quarterback for Jim Finks, Kiesling brought three youngsters, Ted Marchibroda, Vic Eaton, and Johnny Unitas, to the 1955 training camp.

Despite the pleas of Rooney's three young sons to keep Unitas because of his passing skills, Big Walt was unimpressed. Unitas, a native of Pittsburgh and a number nine draft choice from Louisville, never played a minute in the five preseason games. Kiesling let him go, advising Unitas to "try us another time." The man who later was to become one of the game's greatest quarterbacks played the 1955 season with the Bloomfield Rams in the Greater Pittsburgh League for $6.00 a game. A year later, Weeb Ewbank, the coach of the Baltimore Colts signed Unitas for $7,000. The rest, as they say, is history.

Despite winning the final two games of the 1956 season, Walt Kiesling had coached his last game for Art Rooney. Once again, it was time for a change in the Steel City and "Kies" was given the pink slip. Buddy Parker, one of the league's most successful coaches, had abruptly quit as headman of the Lions two days before the first preseason game. Knowing the Texan was available, Rooney signed him to a multi-year contract.

The Buddy Parker Era: 1957-1964

Although the Steelers had been known as a hard-nosed team from the beginnings of the franchise, it was not until Buddy Parker took over as head coach in 1957 that Pittsburgh gained genuine respectability. Parker had won three division titles (1952, 1953, and 1954) and two league championships (1952 and 1953) as the coach of the Detroit Lions.

The Buddy Parker era was marked by two characteristics: he won and he traded away draft choices. Buddy coached the Steelers for eight years and posted winning marks in four of them. His career record at Pittsburgh was 51-48-6, a .514 percentage. Buddy Parker, Jock Sutherland, and Chuck Noll were the only Steeler coaches to post winning career records. But Buddy traded away draft choices at an unheard of clip. In his eight years, the Steelers gave up 50 draft choices, including their first round picks in 1958, 1959, 1961, 1963, and 1965. From 1958 through 1963, of the 42 picks they had available in the first seven rounds of the draft, Parker traded away 36 of the selections.

Parker broke even in his first year at the helm of the Steelers, finishing with a 6-6 record. Immediately upon taking the reins from Walt Kiesling, Buddy engineered a major trade, sending linebacker Marv Matusak plus two number one draft choices to San Francisco in exchange for quarterback Earl Morrall and rookie lineman Mike Sandusky. Even with Morrall, the Steelers were erratic. However, their six wins included victories over the 1956 champions, the New York Giants, 21-10, and the 1958 champions, the Baltimore Colts, 19-13. The defense was excellent once again, holding its opponents to 13 points or less, seven times.

In 1958, Parker was reunited with his fiery leader of the glory days in Detroit, Bobby Layne. Two weeks into the season, Parker traded Morrall and two draft choices to the Lions for Layne. Bobby immediately took charge of the Steelers and guided them to seven wins in their final ten games. In fact, during the last seven weeks of the season the Steelers did not lose, with a 14-14 tie with the Redskins being the only blemish on their record. Many observers felt that at the conclusion of the 1958 campaign, the Pittsburghers were the best team in the entire league.

The Steelers continued their winning ways in 1959 with an opening 17-7 victory over the Cleveland Browns in Pittsburgh. It was their eighth straight regular season game without a loss. But the next week, the Redskins defeated them 23-17. The Steelers won only five more games, finishing fourth in the Eastern Conference with a 6-5-1 record. Rookie Buddy Dial from Rice, who had been cut in pre-season by the Giants, established himself as a deep threat and future NFL star, catching 16 passes for 428 yards and averaging a league-leading 27 yards per catch. Running back Tom "The Bomb" Tracy and receiver Jimmy Orr also had excellent seasons.

1960 and 1961 brought back-to-back losing seasons for the Steelers, their first under Parker-coached teams. During the 1960 season, injuries decimated the club. The heart of the offense, Layne, John Henry Johnson, and Orr were on the shelf at various times throughout the year. The defense remained an intimidating outfit but felt the loss of future Hall of Famer, Jack Butler, who retired after nine brilliant seasons. Parker's team finished strong, though, winning three of the last four games, including a bruising 14-10 victory

How Buddy Parker Came to Pittsburgh

The story of how Buddy Parker ended up in Pittsburgh has a strange and little-known twist to it. In his fine book *The Golden Age of Pro Football: NFL Football in the 1950's*, Mickey Herskowitz relates the following from an interview with Parker:

"I know George Halas would have denied this but I would never have gone to Pittsburgh any other way. I knew what the Steelers had and how they had no money. I went to Chicago and had lunch with Halas and Art Rooney. The deal was I would coach the Steelers for two years and Halas would bring me over to the Bears. That's why I traded so many draft choices away at Pittsburgh. I wasn't building for the future—I had to win right then."

over the always tough Browns, and a thrilling 27-21 win over the eventual World Champion Eagles.

1961 was in many ways a repeat of the previous year. It looked as though Father Time was catching up with the club as key defensive linemen Ernie Stautner, Big Daddy Lipscomb, and Joe Krupa were in the twilight of their careers. The age factor combined with an injury to Bobby Layne, resulted in the worst season of the Parker era, six wins and eight losses.

Sometimes it rains before the sun shines. The disappointing 1961 season was followed by Pittsburgh's best effort since 1947. Parker's 1962 club finished the campaign with a 9-5 record, good enough for second place behind the Giants.

The Steelers second-place finish qualified them to play in the NFL's first ever Playoff Bowl. On January 6th, 1963, one week after the NFL championship game, they met the Detroit Lions in the Orange Bowl in Miami. The Lions, who had lost only three games all year in the tough Western Conference, repeated their opening season victory over Pittsburgh by defeating the Steelers 17-10.

The 1963 season was one of the most unusual in NFL annals. Going into the final game of the season with the Giants, the Steelers, with three fewer victories than New York, could have still claimed the title. This situation arose since ties did not count in the standings and the Steelers had deadlocked Philadelphia twice and the Chicago Bears once. A win in the finale would give them the best won-lost percentage in the Eastern Conference. But it was not to be. The Giants pummeled Pittsburgh 33-17, with Buddy Parker commenting that his quarterback, Ed Brown, "couldn't hit the ground with his hat." The loss gave the Steelers a 7-4-3 record, placing them fourth in the conference.

The season marked Ernie Stautner's final year as an NFL player. After 14 years in the league, all of them in Pittsburgh, and nine Pro-Bowl selections, Big Ernie retired. He later served as an NFL coach, primarily with the Dallas Cowboys, and is a member of the Pro Football Hall of Fame.

1964, Buddy Parker's last year in Pittsburgh, was not a happy one, as the Steelers registered a five and nine mark. But Parker had given Steeler fans much to be proud of. His 1958 and 1962 clubs were particularly strong. Several players like Layne, Butler, Stautner, John Henry Johnson, Lipscomb, and Dial were among the finest in the annals of the NFL. But in the end, the Steelers still had not captured a division title. When the 1964 campaign closed, Art Rooney's franchise may have been as devoid of talent as it ever was.

1965-1968: The Sorry Steelers

The Pittsburgh Steelers performance during the mid-1960s was depressing to their fans and embarrassing to the Rooneys. Under Mike Nixon in 1965 and Bill Austin the next three years, they finished last three times and sixth once. Nixon became the Steelers' head coach by default. Two weeks before the 1965 opener against Green Bay, Buddy Parker quit, stating, "I can't win with this bunch of stiffs." The Steelers played like stiffs, winning only two games, both at midseason, against Philadelphia and Dallas. The 2-12-1 record was the worst in the NFL.

Following the 1965 season, Rooney named Vince Lombardi's top assistant at Green Bay, Bill Austin, as his head coach. Austin lasted three disappointing years in Pittsburgh with his tenure marked by key injuries, a generally nonproductive offense, and an inconsistent defense.

Austin's first year, 1966, was the only one in which the Steelers escaped the cellar. Led by a gimped-up Bill Nelsen, they closed the year with scoring-binge wins over New York, 47-28, and Atlanta, 57-33, to finish with a 5-8-1 record. In 1967, the NFL realigned its conferences once more in an attempt to correct the unwieldy eight-team setup. The Steelers were placed in the Century Division of the Eastern Conference. But the realignment didn't help the club. They won only six games over the next two years, finishing dead last both times.

The only salvaging factor of being the league's worst team is that you draft first. Pittsburgh made the first selection in the 1969 draft. Their pick would mark the beginning of a reversal in the Steelers' 36 years of frustration and ridicule.

1969-1979: Super Steelers; Building the Foundation

Following the disastrous 1968 campaign, Art Rooney made what was certainly the best decision in his long career, hiring a new head coach, Charles Henry Noll. Noll, a native of Cleveland, Ohio, spent seven years as a messenger guard and linebacker for the Cleveland Browns during the mid-1950s. But he was to make his mark as a coach not a player. Renowned as a defensive expert, Noll served on the staffs of two of the game's great football minds, Sid Gillman at San Diego and Don Shula at Baltimore. The 1968 Colts, the last team he was with prior to joining the Steelers, surrendered only 144 points.

Noll quickly decided that he was going to rebuild the Steelers through the draft. The quick-fix trade routine of Buddy Parker would not be used. He was more concerned with a long-range plan than instant success, and Rooney had promised him time. Noll's draft selections from 1969 through 1974 were remarkable. His picks were responsible for building the core of the strongest team in professional football of the 1970s and perhaps of all time. In all, Noll drafted six current Hall of Famers, three in his first 20 picks and four in his first 38.

Look at this list. In 1969, he made defensive tackle Joe Greene of North Texas State his number one choice. The following year it was quarterback Terry Bradshaw of Louisiana Tech and cornerback Mel Blount of Southern. Two Penn Staters were taken in the 1971 and 1972 drafts, linebacker Jack

AP/Wide World Photos

Chuck Noll

Ham and running back Franco Harris. All of these men are now enshrined at Canton.

Other notables drafted during Noll's first six years as head coach were: defensive end L. C. Greenwood of Arkansas AM&N in 1969; defensive end Dwight White and defensive tackle Ernie Holmes of Southern in 1971; wide receivers Lynn Swann and John Stallworth, linebacker Jack Lambert, center Mike Webster, and free agent Donnie Shell in 1974.

When judged solely by the final league standings, Noll's first three years with Pittsburgh were not impressive. In 1969, the Steelers went one and thirteen, with their lone victory coming in the first game against Detroit. Of his first year and the 13 straight defeats, Noll later recalled, "It got harder to take as the year went along. But I felt we were showing some signs of progress. We weren't getting blown off the field."

The Steelers showed steady progress during the 1970 and 1971 seasons as Noll continued to mold the team into a cohesive unit. Although he later stated that he did not consciously set out to build the defense before the offense, that's the way it turned out. By the conclusion of the 1971 season, the famous "Steel Curtain" of Greene, L. C. Greenwood, Ernie Holmes, and Dwight White was in place, and linebacker Andy Russell and Jack Ham plus three future Steeler defensive backfield gems, Blount, Glen Edwards, and Mike Wagner, were also starters.

In 1970, two significant changes took place for the organization. With the NFL-AFL merger, the Steelers moved from the Century Division of the National Football League to the Central Division of the American Football Conference; and the club played its first game in its current home, Three Rivers Stadium.

It took the Steelers four contests before they were winners in 1970, as they extended their regular season losing streak to 16 games. But Noll's charges won five of their last 11 games with a strong midseason run. Although the defense had become one of the best units in the entire league, the offense lacked a complete set of running backs and receivers to complement rookie quarterback Terry Bradshaw. The highly touted Bradshaw found the going tough his first year. Splitting time with Terry Hanratty, he completed only 38 percent of his passes for six touchdowns.

In 1971, Pittsburgh won only one more game than in the previous year, finishing with a 6-8 record and earning the Central Division runner-up spot behind Cleveland. Noll felt they should have done better. "We could have been 9-5 with very little change in our play," he said. "That's why when we went 11-3 the next year and everyone else was surprised, I wasn't surprised at all. I thought we should have been winners earlier."

1972: A Title at Last

The 1972 year was one like no other in the history of the Pittsburgh franchise—a year that lifetime Steeler fans will treasure until their dying day. The Men of Noll won their first ever division crown with a 11-3 record and advanced to the AFC championship game. It was the year of "Franco's Italian Army"—"Gerela's Gorillas"—"Dobra Shunka"—"The Steel Curtain"—and oh yes—"The Immaculate Reception."

Franco Harris of Penn State was the Steelers' first draft choice in 1972. Although the Steelers got off to a good start, going 4-2 after six games, it looked as though Pittsburgh had erred in selecting Harris. He had rushed for only 221 yards and scored one touchdown. But Franco made his "Italian Army" proud for the rest of the season. He ran for 100 yards in six of the final eight games, catching 21 passes for 180 yards, scoring a total of 11 touchdowns, and finishing with 1,055 yards on the ground. Harris became only the fifth rookie in NFL history to gain over 1,000 yards.

In addition to Harris's dramatic first year, several other Steelers had strong performances. Frenchy Fuqua complemented Franco by picking up 665 yards, Ron Shanklin, Frank Lewis from Grambling, and John McMakin of Wake Forest headed a solid core of receivers, and Bradshaw, showing more maturity and savvy passed for 1,887 yards and 12 touchdowns. Roy Gerela,

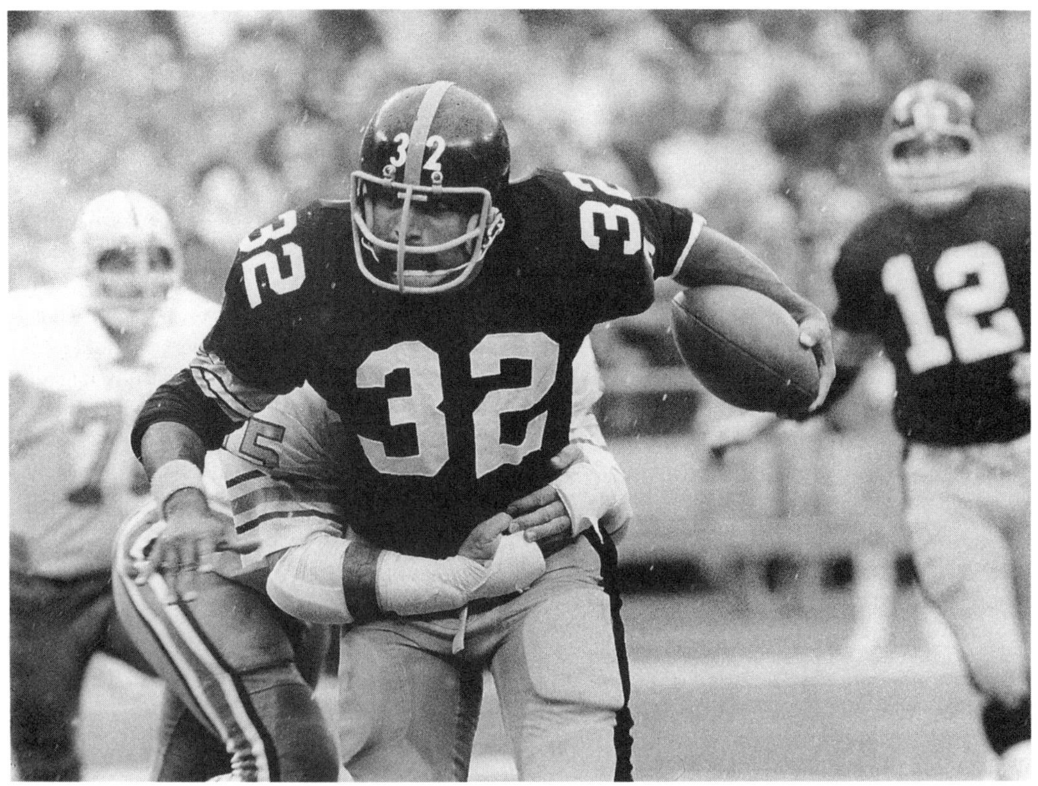

AP/Wide World Photos

Franco Harris (32)

acquired from Houston the previous year, was one of the most dependable placekickers in the league, scoring 119 points. The defense led by Greene, Ham, and Russell was perhaps the best in the entire league, holding Steeler opponents to 175 points and ten or fewer points in seven games.

The Immaculate Reception

Carrying signs like "Run Paisano Run," 50,000 fans trooped into Three Rivers Stadium on December 23, 1972, for the Steelers playoff game against the powerful Oakland Raiders. Despite the fact that the Steelers had won the season opener against Oakland and enjoyed the home field advantage, they were still the underdogs.

The game was a defensive struggle from the opening kickoff. Neither Ken Stabler nor Terry Bradshaw could move their clubs with any consistency. The only scores came on two Gerela field goals, giving the Steelers a 6-0 lead after three quarters. With only 1:13 to play and the ball on the Steelers 30 yard line, it looked like the Steelers would capture the bitterly contested game.

But the tables were abruptly reversed. Facing a long yardage situation with the Steelers in a prevent defense, Stabler dropped back to pass, found no one open, and scooted for the score. George Blanda added the extra point, giving the Raiders a 7-6 lead with less than a minute remaining.

The Steelers took the kickoff and moved the ball to their 40 yard line. Bradshaw needed to complete at least one 15- to 20-yard pass to get Gerela in field goal range. His first three passes against Oakland's prevent defense failed. Now he faced fourth down with 22 seconds on the clock.

Dropping back to try one more pass, Bradshaw frantically looked for an open receiver. He avoided one tackler after another. Now desperate, he spotted Frenchy Fuqua open for an instant at the Raider 37 yard line. Instinctively, he threw the ball. All-Pro defender Jack Tatum rushed over, knocking the ball in the air before it reached Fuqua.

But the ball was still alive and Franco Harris somehow caught it off his shoetops, delicately maintained his balance, and sprinted toward the Oakland goal line. It looked as though the speedy Jimmy Warren would catch him at the 10 yard line. However, Franco turned on the afterburners and went into the end zone unmolested. The Steelers had won 13-7. It was the most dramatic game-winning touchdown in Steeler history and one of the most unbelievable finishes in the annals of the NFL. Thereafter it was simply known as "The Immaculate Reception.".

The following week the Steelers hosted the undefeated Miami Dolphins for the AFC championship. Although they were in the game throughout, the Dolphins prevailed 21-17 on their way to a perfect 17-0 season. 1972 had been an incredible year for Chuck Noll and his "Men of Steel." It had taken the Steelers 40 years to win a division title, but over the next seven years the team achieved a level of success unmatched in professional football annals.

1973: A Wild Card

In 1973, the Steelers continued their excellence, winning ten games and finishing with a record identical to the Cincinnati Bengals. The Bengals were awarded the Central Division Crown, however, using the NFL tie-breaker system with the Steelers qualifying for the playoffs as a wild card. Injuries to key people hampered the Steelers throughout the year. 1972's rookie sensation, Franco Harris, missed several early season games with a bad knee. When Franco was healthy enough to return to the lineup, his running mate Frenchy Fuqua broke a collarbone. Terry Bradshaw was having a banner year until he suffered a shoulder separation at midseason; Terry Hanratty stepped in and was superb, playing his best games in Steeler uniform until he was sidelined with cracked ribs.

The defense continued to shine. Joe Greene, who had established himself as the best defensive lineman in the league, L. C. Greenwood, Dwight White, Andy Russell, Jack Ham, and Mike Wagner all had excellent years. Roy Gerela led the league in scoring with 123 points and was selected for the Pro Bowl along with Greene, Harris (who because of his injuries gained only 698 yards), White, and linebackers Henry Davis and Andy Russell.

The Steeler season ended on December 22 in Oakland with a playoff loss to the Raiders. Coming into the 1973 playoff game, the Steelers had defeated Oakland three straight times, with regular season wins in 1972 and 1973 plus the Immaculate Reception miracle. However, this day belonged to Oakland. Fullback Marv Hubbard scored on a one-yard plunge in the first quarter and the Raiders never trailed, routing the Steelers 33-14. Although the season ended on a sour note, the Steelers were certainly one of the league's premier teams. In 1974, their overall excellence would be clearly demonstrated.

Back-to-Back Championships

The 1974 season brought Pittsburgh its first NFL championship. An indicator of the Steelers' power was shown in the preseason as they zipped through six opponents without a defeat. The regular season was more of the same with the Steelers finishing 10-3- and 1 and easily outdistancing Cincinnati and Houston for the Central Division Crown.

The first championship season was not without its surprises, the biggest being Joe Gilliam winning the starting quarterback job away from

Jack Lambert

Terry Bradshaw. "Jefferson Street Joe," a tremendously gifted passer, started the first four games for the Steelers and was outstanding. But by midseason, he began to falter, and Bradshaw was back in charge of the Steeler offense.

That offense, with either Bradshaw or Gilliam at the controls, was magnificent. Franco Harris again rushed for over 1,000 yards and Rocky Blier, the former Notre Dame captain, overcame a serious Vietnam war injury and established himself as Harris's running mate. Nine different players, including rookie sensations Lynn Swann and John Stallworth, caught ten or more passes. Roy Gerela again led the AFC in scoring, this time with 93 points. The rock-ribbed defense, which held opponents to only 189 points and to seven or fewer points in five games, would be unbelievably dominant during the playoffs and Super Bowl.

The Steelers opened the 1974 playoffs at home against Buffalo. The Bills, with a high-powered offense led by quarterback Joe Ferguson and O. J. Simpson, were considered a formidable foe. But a 26-point second quarter with two TD's each by Harris and Blier put the game out of reach, and the Steelers coasted to a 32-14 victory. The defense held Simpson to 49 yards rushing and the Bills to 267 net yards.

The following week, the Steelers journeyed to Oakland to meet the Raiders. Oakland had upset Don Shula's Dolphins 28-26 the week before, in what most experts considered the real Super Bowl. Although the Raiders were a prohibitive favorite in the game, the Steelers would not be denied.

The Pittsburgh running attack and stout defense were the differences in the game. The score was tied 3-3 at the half on field goals by George Blanda and Gerela. But the Steelers took charge in the fourth quarter, scoring 21 points on two TD runs of eight and 21 yards by Harris and a six-yard scoring pass from Bradshaw to Swann. The Steeler defense completely shut down the Raiders in the final stanza, buoyed by two key pass interceptions by Jack Ham and Jack Lambert. When the gun sounded, Pittsburgh had triumphed 24-13.

Super Bowl IX was played in New Orleans, with the Minnesota Vikings opposing the Steelers. It was the Vikes' third trip to the "Big Game" after losses to the Kansas City Chiefs and Miami Dolphins. This one would be no different.

The only score in the first half came on a safety when Fran Tarkenton fell on an errant pitchout in the end zone to give the Steelers a 2-0 lead. Pittsburgh took control in the second half. The offensive line, which had been spectacular in the first half, continued opening big holes for Harris. (Franco would finish with 158 yards and be named the game's MVP.)

Joe Green and his defensive mates completely shut down Tarkenton and Minnesota's excellent runner, Chuck Foreman. Steeler second half scores came on Harris's 12-yard run and a three-yard pass from Bradshaw to Larry Brown. The lone Vikings score resulted from a blocked

All-Time Pittsburgh Steelers Team

In 1982, in celebration of the Pittsburgh Steelers' 50th anniversary, Steeler fans selected their All-Time Team in balloting conducted by the franchise. Here are the results.

Coach:
Chuck Noll—Dayton (1969-91)

Offense:
Wide Receivers: Lynn Swann—Southern Cal (1974-82); John Stallworth—Alabama A&M (1974-87)
Tight End: Elbie Nickel—Cincinnati (1947-57)
Tackles: Jon Kolb—Oklahoma State (1969-81); Larry Brown—Kansas (1971-84)
Guards: Sam Davis—Allen (1967-79); Gerry "Moon" Mullins—Southern Cal (1971-79)
Center: Mike Webster—Wisconsin (1974-88)
Quarterback: Terry Bradshaw—Louisiana Tech (1970-83)
Running Backs: Franco Harris—Penn State (1972-83); Rocky Blier—Notre Dame (1968, 1970-80)
Kicker: Roy Gerela—New Mexico State (1971-78)

Defense:
Ends: L.C. Greenwood—Arkansas A&M (1969-81); Dwight White—East Texas State (1971-80)
Tackles: Joe Greene—North Texas State (1969-81); Ernie Stautner—Boston College (1950-63)
Linebackers: Andy Russell—Missouri (1963, 1966-76); Jack Ham—Penn State (1971-82); Jack Lambert—Kent State (1974-84)
Cornerbacks: Jack Butler—St. Bonaventure (1951-59); Mel Blount—Southern (1970-83)
Safeties: Mike Wagner—Western Illinois—(1971-80); Glen Edwards—Florida A&M (1971-77)
Punter: Pat Brady—Nevada (1952-54)

punt which Terry Brown fell on in the end zone. The Men of Steel were the victors, 16-7.

After 42 years of frustration, Art Rooney had realized his dream—a National Football League championship. When Pete Rozelle presented Rooney with the Vince Lombardi Trophy, all the world knew the Steelers were now champions.

In 1975, Pittsburgh won its second consecutive NFL title. They dominated the regular season, winning 12 games while losing only two. The defense was superb again, yielding less than 200 points (162) for the second straight year and ten or fewer points in eight contests. The offense also clicked. Franco Harris rushed for a team record of 1,246 yards, Terry Bradshaw passed for 2,055 yards and 18 touchdowns (and only nine interceptions), and Lynn Swann emerged as a premier receiver with 49 catches for 781 yards and eleven TD's.

The Steelers opened the 1975 playoffs with a convincing 28-10 win over Bert Jones and the Baltimore Colts. The defense throttled Jones all afternoon, and Bradshaw directed the Steelers to four touchdowns. The following week, the Raiders came to Pittsburgh, fresh from a 31-28 victory over Cincinnati and anxious to avenge the Steeler's conference championship victory the previous year. In a bruising defensive battle, the Steelers held on for a 16-10 victory as time ran out on Oakland. The Steeler scores came on a 25-yard run by Harris, a Bradshaw to Stallworth 20-yard pass play, and a Roy Gerela field goal.

Super Bowl X turned out to be the most exciting of the first ten Super Bowls. The Steelers were pitted against the NFC's wild card team, Tom Landry's Dallas Cowboys. Dallas opened the scoring in the first quarter on a 29-yard TD pass from Roger Staubach to Drew Pearson. The Steelers knotted the score when Bradshaw hit tight end Randy Grossman with a seven-yard scoring strike. But Tony Fritsch gave the Cowboys a 10-7 halftime lead with a 36-yard field goal.

The Steelers grabbed the momentum in the second half, scoring in the fourth quarter on a safety and two Gerela field goals. The key play in the game, however, was a 64-yard scoring strike from Bradshaw to Swann, giving the Steelers a 21-10 lead. Bradshaw was knocked woozy on the play with a hit by Cliff Harris and had to be helped from the field.

Staubach brought the Cowboys back. He unleashed a 34-yard TD strike to rookie wide receiver Percy Howard to cut the gap to 21-17 with less than two minutes to play. Playing without Bradshaw and with Terry Hanratty as quarterback, the Steelers were unable to move the ball. Staubach had one more chance to engineer one of his patented comeback wins.

But Steelers safety Glen Edwards intercepted a Jolly Roger pass that had been intended for Drew Pearson in the end zone. Time had run out for the Cowboys and the Steelers were champions again. Swann was named the game's "Most Valuable Player," edging linebacker Jack Lambert, whose 14 tackles and intimidating style of play was a key to victory.

AP/Wide World Photos

Terry Bradshaw

1976 and 1977: Close, But No Cigar

In 1976 and 1977, the Steelers again won Central Division titles but fell short of making it to the Super Bowl. Pittsburgh struggled at the beginning of the 1976 season, dropping four of the first five games. After a loss to Cleveland on October 10th and led by an awesome defense, the Steelers finished the season with nine straight victories.

The defense shut out five of their opponents during this remarkable stretch and yielded an unbelievably low total of 28 points. The offense was equally impressive, perhaps even more so, given that they played the entire nine-game winning streak without the injured Terry Bradshaw. Rookie Mike Kruczek of Boston College was thrown into the breach and responded admirably by throwing few passes and relying on the running of Franco Harris and Rocky Blier. Harris had another 1,000-yard year, this time picking up 1,128 yards and scoring a Steeler record of 14 touchdowns on the ground.

Coming off the nine-game winning streak, the Steelers were poised for the playoffs. Bradshaw was healthy and ready to start against the Baltimore Colts. Pittsburgh decimated Baltimore 40-14, looking very much like a team ready to win their third consecutive NFL title. However, Franco Harris and Rocky Blier were hurt late in the game and could not start against Oakland in the conference championship contest. Chuck Noll tried a one back offense against the Raiders with a gimped-up Rocky Blier. But, the Steeler attack sputtered and the Raiders dominated the game, winning by a 24-7 margin.

1977 was the poorest season since 1971 for Pittsburgh. Although they won the Central Division with a 9-5 record, the usually strong defense faltered, giving up 243 points. Both Harris and Bradshaw had good years, with Franco rushing for 1,162 yards and 11 touchdowns and Terry passing for 2,523 yards and 17 touchdowns. Lynn Swann had another outstanding year, catching 50 passes for 789 yards and seven scores.

The Steelers faced the red-hot Denver Broncos at Mile High Stadium in the first round of the playoffs. Pittsburgh was never in the game. The Broncos, led by Craig Morton and the Orange Crush defense, dominated the proud but lifeless Pittsburghers, 34-21.

1978: Champions Again

During the 1977 season Chuck Noll came to realize that he would have to revamp his offense. Despite Franco Harris's proclivity for 1,000 yard seasons, defenses were beginning to stack up the Steeler ground attack. This fact, coupled with the maturing of Terry Bradshaw into an all-around field general and the presence of a pair of the game's most dangerous receivers, Swann and Stallworth, caused the Steeler mentor to change his offense from run-based to pass-oriented.

In 1978, the Steelers filled the air with passes en route to a remarkable 14-2 record. Bradshaw passed for 2,915 yards and 28 touchdowns. Swann led the team in receiving with 61 catches for 880 yards and 11 TDs. It wasn't that Harris and the ground attack had been neglected completely. Franco again had his usual 1,000-yard campaign, rushing for 1,082 yards. The defense, which had been plagued by injuries in 1977, returned to its old stingy self. The 1978 Steelers surrendered only 195 points, holding the opposition to ten points or less in eight of the 16 games.

The Steelers' two regular season losses came to Bum Phillips's Houston Oilers, 24-17 in Pittsburgh, and 10-7 to the Rams in Los Angeles. Otherwise they were sensational, opening play with seven straight wins and capping the regular season with a five-game winning streak.

Pittsburgh's first round playoff opponent was Denver. Despite their sterling record and the home field advantage, the Steelers were concerned. The Broncos had defeated them in the 1977 playoffs and gave them a scare in the regular season finale before bowing, 21-17. Denver opened the scoring with a Jim Turner field goal to take a 3-0 lead. But then the Steelers took charge. On a cold December day with a light rain falling at

Three Rivers, Bradshaw expertly mixed his passing and running games. Franco Harris scored on runs of one and 18 yards and Terry hit Stallworth and Swann with long fourth quarter touchdown passes for a 33-10 victory.

The following week, Pittsburgh played host to Houston. During their championship seasons of 1978 and 1979, the Oilers became a formidable threat to the Steelers in the Central Division; however, this game was decided by halftime. The Steeler defense shut down the powerful running of Earl Campbell, and Dan Pastorini, bothered by cold and rainy weather and the fierce Pittsburgh pass rush, couldn't get the Oiler air game going. Bradshaw moved the Steelers up and down the field at will, directing his team to four touchdowns and a field goal for a 31-3 lead after two quarters. Harris and Rocky Blier scored on runs, and the Steeler quarterback hit Swann and Stallworth with scoring strikes. The final score was 34-5. The Steelers had earned another championship date with Dallas in the Orange Bowl.

In many ways, Super Bowl XIII was a replay of the Steeler-Cowboy confrontation in Super Bowl X. It was an exciting game with plenty of scoring between two high-powered offenses led by two of the greatest quarterbacks in NFL history, Terry Bradshaw and Roger Staubach.

The first half was a see-saw affair with the Steelers scoring first on a 28-yard pass from Bradshaw to Stallworth. Dallas went ahead on a 39-yard pass from Staubach to Calvin Hill and Mike Hegman's 37-yard TD run with a Bradshaw fumble. Before the half the Steelers came right back with two scores of their own on Bradshaw passes. The first was a 75-yard bomb to Stallworth and the second a seven-yard strike to a leaping Rocky Blier. At the halfway mark, Pittsburgh nursed a slim 21-14 lead.

The third quarter was a battle of defenses with the only score coming on a Raphael Septien 27-yard field goal. Midway through the fourth quarter the Steelers struck for two quick touchdowns and seemingly put the game out of reach. The first score came on a 22-yard TD dash by Harris. On the ensuing kickoff, Dallas All Pro defensive tackle Randy White, playing with a heavily wrapped fractured left hand, couldn't handle Gerela's short kick. It was recovered by Dennis "Dirt" Winston at the Cowboys 18 yard line. Bradshaw seized the moment. On the next play he sent Swann deep into the end zone and the acrobatic receiver made a dramatic circus catch for the score. With 6:51 to play, the Steelers had a 35-17 lead.

However, Staubach and the Cowboys refused to die. Roger marched them 89 yards in eight plays hitting Billy Joe Dupree with a seven-yard TD pass. With 22 seconds remaining Staubach threw a four-yard TD strike to Butch Johnson and Dallas was behind by only 35-31. That's the way it ended. Blier fell on Septien's onside kick and the Steelers were champions, becoming the first NFL team to win three Super Bowls.

Bradshaw was named MVP of the game. For the first time in his nine-year career, he passed for over 300 yards, establishing three Super Bowl records: most yards passing (318); most touchdown passes (four); and longest scoring pass (75 yards to John Stallworth). To the press after the game, Terry said, "This son of a gun was fun. Both teams played their game. I want all you guys to say 'By God, this was an exciting game.'"

1979: Four-time Champions

The road to the Steelers fourth Super Bowl title was not as smooth as expected. The major factor in slowing down the Black and Gold Juggernaut was injuries. It wasn't until the sixth game of the regular season that the offensive line played together as a unit. It was even longer before the Steeler Front Four was healthy. Both the offense and defense were hurt by the absence of key players for prolonged periods. Mike Wagner, Dwight White, L. C. Greenwood, Lynn Swann, and Jack Ham were among the 12 starters who missed several games.

Still, the Steelers started strongly, winning the first four games and finishing with a 12-4 record. Terry Bradshaw and the offense were superb, setting a host of records. Defensively, the club was the AFC's best. The Steelers won their sixth straight AFC division crown and matched the Dallas Cowboy record of making the playoffs for eight consecutive years.

Pittsburgh's opening opponent in playoffs was Miami. The Steelers had not met the Dolphins in postseason play since Don Shula's team beat them 21-17 in 1972. This game would be nowhere that close. The pumped-up Pittsburghers scored the first three times they had the football, stuffing the Miami offense after each score and led 20-0 at the end of the first quarter. The outcome was never in question and the Steelers won 34-14 with Sidney Thornton, Stallworth, Swann, Blier, and Harris scoring touchdowns.

The next Steeler hurdle, the Houston Oilers, would be much more difficult to clear. The Oilers drew first blood at 2:30 into the game when Dwight Perry picked off a Bradshaw pass and sprinted 75 yards to pay dirt. The teams then traded Matt Bahr and Tony Fritsch field goals before Bradshaw erupted in the second quarter. First, he hit mammoth tight end Bennie Cunningham with a 16-yard scoring strike, then hooked up with Stallworth on a 20-yard touchdown.

Neither team scored in the third quarter and the Oilers were able to manage only a fourth quarter field goal. Bahr added a three-pointer for the Steelers and Blier finished the Steeler scoring with a four-yard run at the 14:06 mark. The Steelers won 27-13 and were on their way to Super Bowl XIV.

Playing before 103,985 at the Rose Bowl in Pasadena and a record TV audience of 35,330,000 homes, the Steelers won their fourth Lombardi Trophy. But it was far from an easy victory. Matt Bahr opened the game's scoring with a 41-yard field goal. The Rams came right back, scoring late in the first quarter on a one-yard plunge by burly Cullen Bryant. Harris gave the Steelers a short-lived lead with his own one-yard run but the Rams were in front 13-10 at the half on two Pat Corral field goals.

The teams traded third quarter touchdowns. Swann made one of his patented circus catches on a 47-yard pass from Bradshaw, and wide receiver Ron Smith's TD on a 24-yard halfback option pass from Lawrence McCutcheon gave the Rams the lead with only fifteen minutes to play.

The game's turning point came at the 2:56 mark of the fourth period. Faced with a third and long at their 25 yard line, Bradshaw called John Stallworth's number, "60 slot hook and go." Stallworth broke short, hooked out, and headed deep over the middle. In one of the most electric pass plays in Super Bowl history, Stallworth, running at top speed, looked up over his right shoulder and caught Bradshaw's bomb without breaking stride. The 73-yard touchdown and Bahr's extra point gave the Steelers a 24-19 lead. Harris iced the game with his second one-yard TD run for the 31-19 victory.

Once again, Bradshaw was the MVP, having completed 14 of 21 passes for 309 yards and two

Of Quarterbacks Lost

From the early days of their franchise, the Steelers had a knack for failing to recognize the potential greatness in quarterbacks. It all started in 1939 when they traded away the draft rights for their number one selection to the Chicago Bears. The Bears gave the Steelers a journeyman veteran, Ed Manske, and promptly selected Sid Luckman.

In 1955, the Steelers brought Johnny Unitas to training camp and cut him prior to the start of the regular season. Len Dawson, Jack Kemp, Bill Nelsen, and Earl Morrall all played briefly for Pittsburgh before being traded and starring elsewhere.

In 1983, with Terry Bradshaw in the twilight of his career, the Steelers had an opportunity to draft a hometown hero to take his place. But they passed on Pitt's Dan Marino and selected noseguard Gabe Rivera. Rivera's brief six-game career ended with a tragic automobile accident that paralyzed him for life. Marino, of course, went on to stardom with the Miami Dolphins.

scores. Not only was the Steelers' fourth Lombardi Trophy a record, but they also became the first team to win two back-to-back Super Bowls. They were clearly the team of the decade and one of the best of all time. In his postgame comments about Pittsburgh's greatness, Chuck Noll said: "The facts speak for themselves. The Steelers have proven themselves, but this win feels better than the other three. We had to overcome a lot of injuries and we came through."

1980-1989: The Ordinary Eighties

When the Steelers won their fourth Super Bowl in Pasadena, there was a general feeling throughout the NFL that this dynasty would continue well into the 1980s. "One for the Thumb" was the cry greeting the Steelers as they reported to training camp in July of 1980. But the Splendid Seventies became the Ordinary Eighties and Pittsburgh was just another team for the entire decade. They did manage to make the playoffs four times in this ten-year stretch; however, the club was truly a shadow of Chuck Noll's great teams of the previous decade.

Probably the most telling indicator of the Steelers' fall from excellence is a statistic from the 1982 season, three short years after their fourth NFL title. The fabled Steeler defense—the feared "Steel Curtain," known as the NFL's most dominant defense from 1972 through 1979—ranked 22d in the league in yards allowed and 26th in passing yards.

Injuries to veterans were also a major factor in Pittsburgh's decline. Jack Ham, the superb linebacker, never recovered from a broken ankle suffered during the 1979 regular season and retired after the 1982 season. Terry Bradshaw was troubled by an elbow injury, suffered a broken hand, and hung up his cleats after the 1983 campaign. 1983 was also Franco Harris's last year in the Steel City; he finished his career in Seattle, after nursing nagging injuries. By the end of the 1983 season, Rocky Blier, Mel Blount, L. C. Greenwood, Joe Greene, Mike Wagner, John Kolb, Sam Davis, and Lynn Swann had played their last games in the black and gold uniform.

In the strike-interrupted 1982 season, the Steelers finished with a 6-3 record and qualified for the playoff tournament. Their foe was the San Diego Chargers led by quarterback Dan Fouts. In the twilight of his career, Terry Bradshaw had Pittsburgh in the lead late in the game. But Fouts rallied the Chargers with time running out, and the Californians won 31-28.

A year later, Pittsburgh won its first of two division titles of the decade. Cliff Stoudt, taking up the slack for the injured Bradshaw, led the Steelers to ten victories. Franco Harris had one more 1,000-yard season in him, picking up 1,007 yards and scoring five touchdowns, and Jack Lambert and Donnie Shell paced the defense. However, the Steelers were routed by the soon-to-be world champion L.A. Raiders, 38-10, in the first round of the playoffs.

In 1984, Noll's team won the honors in the AFC Central Division again, posting a 9-7 record. Pittsburgh's biggest threat was John Stallworth, who caught 80 passes for 1,395 yards and 11 touchdowns. Quarterback Mark Malone had a highly productive year, throwing for 2,137 yards and 16 touchdowns. Donnie Shell was sensational in the defensive secondary along with linebacker Mike Merriweather, who registered 15 quarterback sacks. The Steelers advanced to the AFC championship game with a thrilling 24-17 win over the Broncos in Denver. But Dan Marino and the hot Miami Dolphins offense buzz-sawed Pittsburgh 45-28 in the conference title matchup.

The Steelers' last playoff appearance of the 1980s came in 1989 when they posted another 9-7 record. Pittsburgh was sparked by the passing of Bubby Brister (2,634 yards and 11 scores), the receiving of Louis Lipps (50 catches for 944 yards and 5 touchdowns), and the running of Tim Worley (770 yards and five touchdowns). Ron Woodson excelled as a kick returner and defensive back. The Steelers played splendidly in the postseason, but came up short. Led by Brister's sharp passing, they upended Houston in overtime in the first round game, 27-23. A week later they

AP/Wide World Photos

Barry Foster (29) eludes Browns linebacker David Brandon for a 12-yard gain.

had the Broncos beat in Denver before John Elway's last-minute magic did them in, 24-23.

The decade of the 1980s also saw the passing of the Steelers' esteemed owner, Art Rooney, who died on August 25, 1988, at the age of 87. He had long since passed the day-to-day operations of the club to his oldest son, Dan. Rooney's legacy, however, will live forever in the hearts of Steeler fans everywhere.

1990-1992: So Long Chuck—Welcome Bill

Chuck Noll's brilliant 23-year head coaching career with the Pittsburgh Steelers came to an end following the 1991 season. He announced his retirement one day after Christmas and four days after a season-ending 17-10 win over the Cleveland Browns. His 209th, and final, victory as the Steelers' head coach had a touch of irony since Noll had begun his NFL playing career with those same Browns in 1953.

The 1990 and 1991 seasons were not particularly memorable. The Steelers played adequately in 1990, posting a 9-7 record, good enough for a three-way AFC Central Division tie. But they were eliminated from the playoffs by their 2-4 division record. Merrill Hoge emerged as a competent runner and pass receiver and picked up 772 yards on the ground. Bubby Brister had his best year as a Steeler by passing for 2,725 yards and 20 touchdowns. But the most consistent Steeler of them all was placekicker Gary Anderson. For the ninth consecutive year, he led Pittsburgh in scoring and, still active, is the all-time leading Steeler scorer with 1,123 points through the 1992 season.

In 1991, Noll's last season, Pittsburgh finished with a 7-9 record. The highlights of the year were season-ending wins at home over two of Pittsburgh's division rivals, Cincinnati and Cleveland. The Steelers alternated Brister and Neil O'Donnell at quarterback and neither one was consistently effective. When the defense gave up 344 points—104 more than it had during the previous campaign—Chuck Noll decided it was time to step down.

The announcement of Noll's successor was in many ways reminiscent of Chuck's hiring in 1969. Pittsburgh again named a young man who was known for his knowledge of defensive football. Bill Cowher, a native of Pittsburgh and the defensive coordinator of the Kansas City Chiefs, became the 15th head coach of the Steelers franchise on January 21, 1992. Only 35 years of age (Noll was 37 when he was named), Cowher was the second youngest head coach in the league (only Cincinnati's David Shula being junior to him).

Cowher's coaching debut was an auspicious one. The Steelers won the AFC Central Division title with an 11-5 record, the best Steeler effort since their 1979 Super Bowl year. Barry Foster, the third year running back from Arkansas, was sensational. He rushed for 1,690 yards, tops in the AFC and second in the entire NFL.

O'Donnell also had a fine year as the Steeler quarterback until he broke a leg late in the season. He passed for 2,283 yards and thirteen touchdowns. The Steelers never recovered from O'Donnell's injury, though, dropping two of their last four games and losing to Buffalo 24-3 in the second round of the playoffs.

The Pittsburgh Steelers' long and glorious history is one of the epic stories of the National Football League. Often the focus of ridicule for their first 40 years of existence, they became the league's top team during the 1970s. Chuck Noll's Steelers of that decade are considered by many to be the best squad ever assembled in the annals of the NFL.

Sources

Books

Blier, Rocky with Terry O'Niel, *Fighting Back,* Warner Books, 1976.

Blount, Roy Jr., *About Three Bricks Shy of a Load,* Ballantine Books, 1974.

Brock, Ted and Larry Eldridge, Jr., *25 Years: The NFL since 1960,* Simon and Schuster, 1985.

Chass, Murray, *Pittsburgh's Steelers: The Long Climb,* Prentice Hall, 1973.

Cope, Myron, *The Game That Was, An Illustrated Account of the Tumultuous Early Days of Pro Football,* Thomas Y. Crowell Publishing, 1974.

Herskowitz, Mickey, *The Golden Age of Pro Football: NFL Football in the 1950's,* Taylor Publishing, 1990.

Neft, David S., Roland T. Johnson, Richard M. Cohen, and Jordan A. Deutsch, *The 1982 Pro Football Weekly Almanac,* Pro Football Weekly, 1982.

Sahadi, Lou, *Super Steelers: The Making of a Dynasty,* Times Books, 1980.

The Sporting News 1975 National Football Guide, The Sporting News, 1975.

The Sporting News 1976 National Football Guide, The Sporting News, 1976.

The Sporting News 1993 Pro Football Yearbook, The Sporting News, 1993.

The Sports Encyclopedia: Pro Football, Grosset and Dunlap, 1974.

Periodicals

Time, December 8, 1975.

Football '86, The Greensburg Tribune-Review, August 24, 1986.

Pittsburgh Steelers Weekly, August 1980; August 1982; July 1983.

—Bernie Kish

American Football Conference

Eastern Division

Buffalo Bills

Professional football returned to Buffalo with the debut of the Buffalo Bills in the American Football League in 1960. Previous attempts to establish a pro football team in the upstate city had failed, but the Bills caught on and eventually prospered. After a couple of losing seasons they began to improve, and in 1964 and 1965, with Lou Saban as head coach and Jack Kemp at quarterback, the Bills emerged as AFL champions. They took the AFL East title again in 1966 but fell to the Kansas City Chiefs in the championship game.

The late 1960s and the entire decade of the 1970s found the Bills in the doldrums, despite the individual brilliance of a few players, most notably running back O. J. Simpson, who played for Buffalo from 1969 through 1977. "The Juice," on his way to the Pro Football Hall of Fame, was the premier running back in the NFL from 1972 through 1976 (the AFL and NFL having merged in 1970). Even with O. J., however, the Bills earned only a single wild-card playoff spot from 1969 through 1977. That was in 1974.

Chuck Knox took over as head coach in 1978, and by 1980 the Bills had worked their way to the top of the AFC Eastern Division. At quarterback was Joe Ferguson (as he had been since 1973 and would be through 1984), ably assisted by running back Joe Cribbs, whose rookie year, 1980, coincided with the Bills' first AFC divisional title. Buffalo won a wild-card shot on a third-place finish in 1981, then faded from contention in the early 1980s.

When the Bills next rose in the standings, their ascent was dramatic—and dynastic. Under head coach Marv Levy, who replaced Hank Bullough late in the 1986 season, Buffalo compiled a 75-40 record through 1992, winning the AFC Eastern Division title five times in a row, 1988 through 1992, and taking the AFC championship three times, 1990, 1991, and 1992.

Among the many stars of the formidable Bills in the early 1990s were quarterback Jim Kelly, running back Thurman Thomas, and wide receiver Andre Reed. The big disappointment for Buffalo fans (and a big one indeed) was that the Bills lost all three Super Bowl games.

Revving Up

By the year 1960 Buffalo had become something of a graveyard for football franchises. In the early 1920s the Buffalo All-Americans were among the top contenders in the new National Football League. Renamed the Bisons in 1924, the team struggled through the late 1920s, finally going belly-up after the 1929 season.

The outlaw American Football League of 1940-41 featured a Buffalo team. And when the All America Football Conference (AAFC) set up shop in 1946, Buffalo was there with an entry, the Bisons (renamed the Bills in 1947, after "Buffalo Bill" Cody). The 1950 AAFC merger with the NFL allowed only three AAFC teams into the expanded league—and Buffalo was not one of them.

In the late 1950s, Detroiter Ralph C. Wilson, Jr., stood ready with his checkbook when the American Football League was being formed. The new Buffalo Bills played their first regular season game on September 11, 1960, against the New York Titans at the nearly deserted old Polo Grounds in upper Manhattan. Buffalo lost, 27-3, then lost the next week to the Denver Broncos, 27-21, before a somewhat larger hometown crowd at War Memorial Stadium.

Finally, against the Boston Patriots on September 23, the Bills won their first game, 13-0. The 1960 Bills, stronger on defense than offense, posted a 5-8-1 record for the season, finishing third in the AFL Eastern Division. Head coach Buster Ramsey, still searching for a capable quarterback, got a second chance in 1961.

Unfortunately for Ramsey and the Bills, the situation at quarterback remained unsettled. Johnny Green and M.C. Reynolds shared the duties, with occasional help from Warren Rabb and Richie Lycas. None performed with distinction. As in 1960, the Bills were best on defense. Among the defensive standouts were end Lavern Torczon, tackle Chuck McMurtry, and linebacker Archie Matsos. Fullback Archie Baker gained the most yards on the ground for the Bills, and the top pass receiver was Glenn Bass. Although this team finished last in the Eastern Division at 6-8-0, it had some promise. But it would not be realized by coach Buster Ramsey, who lost his job at the end of the season.

Lou Saban, formerly head coach of the Boston Patriots and, in his playing days, a linebacker for the Cleveland Browns, inherited the task of making the Bills a winner in 1962. He also inherited some talent, including young offensive linemen Stew Barber, Al Bemiller, and Billy Shaw. Saban brought in fullback Carlton (Cookie) Gilchrist, and after three losses to start the 1962 season, picked up quarterback Jack Kemp on waivers from the San Diego Chargers for $100.

The Bills began to win, going six games without a loss at one stretch. Because of their horrendous start (they had lost five in a row at the outset), Buffalo's record of 7-6-1 was unspectacular, but Lou Saban hoped to see improvement in 1963. So did many football experts, who picked Saban's men to win it all in the upcoming season.

The Bills stumbled at the starting gate, losing three of their first four games before beginning to click. Their record at the end of the regular season was 7-6-1, the same as the year before, but this time it was good enough for a first-place tie with the Boston Patriots. The two teams met in a playoff game at Fenway Park in the snow three days after Christmas. The Bills succumbed, 26-8.

At the Top

The 1964 campaign got off to a blazing start, as the Bills powered their way past nine opponents before losing the tenth game to the pesky Patriots. Cookie Gilchrist led the league in rushing, picking up 981 yards in 230 carries. Pete Gogolak, Buffalo's new place-kicker, made good on 68 percent of his field-goal attempts, also a league-

TEAM INFORMATION AT A GLANCE

Founding date: 1960 (AFL)

Home stadium: Rich Stadium
One Bills Dr.
Orchard Park, NY 14127
Phone: (716) 648-1800
FAX: (716) 649-6446
Seating capacity: 80,290

Team colors: Royal blue, scarlet red, and white
Team nickname: Bills
Logo: Charging buffalo

Franchise record	Won	Lost	Tie
(1960-90)	198	250	8

Super Bowl Appearances (2): 1991, 1992
First-place finishes (AFL East): 1963 (tie), 1964, 1965, 1966, 1980, 1988, 1989, 1990.

leading figure. Jack Kemp, the starting quarterback, usually kept the ball on the ground.

When the rushing attack stalled, backup quarterback Daryle Lamonica sometimes stepped in to throw the long pass. The Bills scored 400 points to their opponents' 242 in compiling a 12-2-0 record, losing a close game to the Oakland Raiders late in the season. The Bills would play the Western Division champion San Diego Chargers for the AFL crown.

The San Diego Chargers, coached by Sid Gilman, were a team to be reckoned with. In the previous AFL championship game they had massacred the Boston Patriots, 51-10. This year they were missing ace receiver Lance Alworth, out with an injury, but they still had Keith Lincoln, the star of last year's triumph. At least they had him for a time.

After jumping out to a 7-0 lead, the Chargers lost Lincoln for the rest of the day when Bills' linebacker Mike Stratton hit him with a clean, crushing tackle that broke one of Lincoln's ribs. With Alworth and Lincoln out, the Chargers' attack wilted, and Kemp's generalship, Gilchrist's running, and Gogolak's kicking carried the Bills to a 20-7 victory and the 1964 AFL championship.

Could Buffalo repeat in 1965? Yes. The Bills managed to win even without Cookie Gilchrist, who had been traded to the Denver Broncos, and wide receivers Elbert Dubenion and Glenn Bass, sidelined with injuries. The defense continued rock solid, Pete Gogolak kicked 28 field goals, and quarterback Jack Kemp directed the team with finesse. The 1965 Bills won ten games, losing only to San Diego, Houston, and, in the final regular-season game, the New York Jets. Their 10-3-1 record gave them another shot at Sid Gilman's Western Division champion San Diego Chargers.

In the game for the AFL title, the Bills lost a star player, offensive guard Billy Shaw, who was knocked unconscious on an early play and missed the first half. But the Chargers, who had trounced the Bills, 34-3 during the season, never got going. The Buffalo defense held, and Jack Kemp, the game's MVP, led the Bills to a 27-0 victory. Said coach Lou Saban, "We whipped them in the trenches."

A week later Saban dropped a bombshell. He was quitting the Bills to coach at the University of Maryland. The team, which had begun to show its age, would be coached in 1966 by Joe Collier, one of Saban's assistants. And the Bills would win—but not quite as convincingly as in the previous two years.

After losing their first two games, Buffalo bounced back to smother Miami, 58-24, and went on to compile a 9-4-1, good for first place in the AFL Eastern Division. This time, though, they could not get past the Western Division champs, losing to the Kansas City Chiefs, 31-7. The loss cost them their chance to play in the first ever Super Bowl against the NFL's Green Bay Packers.

Skidsville

Joe Collier's debut went well, as the Bills edged in the New York Jets, 20-17, in the 1967 season opener. After that, things deteriorated. Jack Kemp had a bad season, and just when the coach needed a talented second-string quarterback, the man he needed was no longer there. The man was Daryle Lamonica.

In a deal with Oakland, quarterback Lamonica, along with Glenn Bass, went to the Raiders in return for quarterback Tom Flores and wide receiver Art Powell. Big mistake. Flores, coming off a fine season at Oakland, never produced for the Bills, while Lamonica, taking over as first-string quarterback for the Raiders, led them straight to the Super Bowl. In the meantime the Bills stumbled through a 4-10-0 season, scoring more than 20 points a game only three times (one of them a 28-21 loss to the Raiders).

The year 1968 was the year of Joe Namath's New York Jets and the first AFL Super Bowl win. It was decidedly not the year of the Buffalo Bills. Jack Kemp was out for the season, injured in a preseason scrimmage. Joe Collier's men lost their first two games, the second one by an embarrassing 48-6 score to the Oakland Raiders. Collier was out the door the next day. Replacing him was Harvey Johnson, the team's head talent scout.

The Bills rallied for one win, a surprising 37-35 triumph over the Jets in game four before collapsing. With Flores and Kemp out of action with injuries, the quarterbacking job fell to rookie Dan Darragh, recently of William and Mary College. He, too, got hurt, and running back Ed Rutowski was pressed into service.

Rutowski had not quarterbacked since high school but by the time he took over it no longer mattered. The Bills, having upended the classy Jets, could beat no one else on their way to a 1-12-1 season. This was a grim outcome, of course, but it did give Buffalo the first pick in the upcoming draft. Bills' Owner Ralph C. Wilson, Jr., had his eye on a running back from the University of Southern California named Orenthal James Simpson—"O. J." or "The Juice," as he was better known—winner of the 1968 Heisman Trophy.

"Juice"

O. J. joined the Bills in 1969 after a somewhat acrimonious holdout. Wilson said the Bills' entire budget for player salaries was $1 million. Why not just give it all to Simpson, he mused, and let O. J. pay the rest of the team? It almost came to that, but not annually. Simpson got a four-year deal worth $950,000. Reporting late, he had to wait for a helmet that would fit and a No. 32 jersey (his college number), since Gary McDermott, a running back, already had the number and was not about to give it up. When McDermott was cut a week before the season opener, O. J. donned No. 32 for the Bills.

The team on which O. J. Simpson was ex-

PROFILE

O. J.

When Orenthal James Simpson, a native of San Francisco, first arrived in Buffalo in 1969, he was met at the airport by the mayor, a beauty queen, and 2,500 Bills' fans. Still, many Buffalonians remained skeptical of their new $950,000 running back.

"O. J.," or "The Juice," had been a sensational athlete at the University of Southern California, where he won the Heisman Trophy, and had played in the Rose Bowl. But he had also publicly disparaged Buffalo, or so the locals thought, by saying, "Sure, I'd rather play in California than in Buffalo," and, "My image of the town is cars stalled in a blizzard with snow piled to the roofs."

When Bills' owner Ralph Wilson, after drafting O. J. with considerable fanfare, made what Simpson and his agent considered an inadequate offer, the negotiations (and tempers) became a bit heated. At one point Wilson snapped, "I'm not sure even Howard Hughes can handle this kind of package." But eventually a deal was struck, and O. J. Simpson joined the Buffalo Bills.

He was not an instant sensation. In fact, for his first three seasons Simpson seemed no more than ordinary. This was partly, perhaps mainly, due to the fact that head coach John Rauch had no intention of letting O. J. carry the ball 30 or 40 times a game as he had in college. "I can't build my offense around one back no matter how good he is," said Rauch. As a consequence Simpson languished, posting routine stats and becoming more and more eager to say goodbye to Buffalo.

What changed his mind was the arrival of new head coach, Lou Saban, who had every intention of building his offense around The Juice. Actually, Saban was not entirely new. He was returning for a second stint with the Bills, having led them to AFL titles in 1964 and 1965. Saban made good on his promise to have Simpson carry the ball. In 1971, the year before Saban arrived, O. J. rushed for 742 yards on 183 carries. In 1972, under Saban, he increased those numbers to 1,251 yards on 291 carries, both league-leading totals. The Juice was on his way.

By the time he left, after playing nine years for Buffalo, he held virtually every one of the Bills' individual rushing records, although recently he has been pursued in some categories (though not very closely yet) by Thurman Thomas. For example, O. J.'s career mark of 10,183 yards gained rushing overshadows Thomas's (through 1992) by about 4,000 yards. In an era when championships for the Bills were nonexistent, O. J. Simpson was a bona fide superstar.

pected to star was hardly a star-quality team. It needed rebuilding. New head coach John Rauch had been a success at Oakland, just as O. J. had been at USC, but the 1969 Buffalo Bills were going nowhere. They won four games and lost ten.

Aging quarterback Jack Kemp, with one eye on the football and the other on politics, was in his final year. John Rauch and O. J. Simpson did not get along. Nonetheless, the rookie from USC gained 697 yards rushing, which was good considering that Rauch favored the passing game, O. J. had been booked for too many far-flung personal appearances, and the Bills' offensive line was only so-so.

The 1969 Bills posted a 4-10-0 record, an improvement but not a stunning turnaround. In 1970, the first year of the NFL-AFL merger (with the new AFC becoming part of the expanded AFL), the Bills were still in trouble. O. J. was injured in game eight and missed the rest of the season. Even so he was the Bills' leading rusher, though gaining only 488 yards.

One of the bright spots in the 3-10-1 season was the performance of rookie quarterback Dennis Shaw from San Diego State. Shaw was an outstanding passer, which meant that Rauch could go with his passing game, leaving O. J.'s running skills under-utilized. In 1970 wide receiver Marlin Briscoe paced the AFC with 57 pass receptions, good for 1,036 yards.

An argument between the Bills' owner and their head coach led to John Rauch's departure. Once again the genial head talent scout, Harvey Johnson, took over, and once again disaster ensued. In 1968 Buffalo under Johnson had gone 1-10-1. In 1971 that dropped to 1-13-0. The Bills lost their first 10 games before salvaging one against the New England Patriots, 27-20. The Bills were shut out four times, twice by the Baltimore Colts. In the first loss to Baltimore, O. J. Simpson was held to minus ten yards rushing.

Saban II and O. J.

Lou Saban had not been entirely happy at the University of Maryland. Among other things, he found that college recruiting was just as stressful as pro recruiting. So when the Denver Broncos made him an offer in 1967 he moved west. Life in Denver proved to be no picnic, however, and near the end of the 1971 season he was ready to pack it in. That coincided perfectly with Buffalo's needs. Ralph Wilson brought Lou Saban back as head coach, giving him a ten-year contract. Saban decided that Simpson should carry the ball a lot more than he had in the past. That suited O. J. fine, and in 1972 he ran for 1,251 yards, tops in the NFL.

After three years of frustration, The Juice became a star. Unhappily for the Bills, Saban's return and Simpson's stardom translated into only a 4-9-1 season, slightly better than New England's record but light years away from Miami's 14-0-0 in that year of the Dolphins. A few bright rays amid the Buffalo gloom were defensive tackle Don Croft, defensive end Robert James, and defensive back Walt Patulski.

Throughout the 1970s two teams dominated the AFC East, the Miami Dolphins and the Baltimore Colts. That left the other three contenders little to hope for but a wild-card opportunity. The Bills, playing their home games at new Rich Stadium in Orchard Park, New York, almost got their chance in 1973 when they compiled a 9-5-0 record, finishing the season with four straight wins.

O. J. Simpson became the first player in pro football history to gain more than 2,000 rushing in a season, picking up 2,003. Rookie quarterback Joe Ferguson had a fine year directing the Bills' offense that was, as Saban had promised, centered on Simpson. When Ferguson passed, the most consistent receivers were Bob Chandler and J. D. Hill.

In 1974 the Bills chalked up another 9-5-0 record after leading their division for part of the season. This time it won them a playoff shot. Opposing them in the first round were the Pittsburgh Steelers under head coach Chuck Noll, champions of the AFC Central Division. The Steelers defeated the Bills, 32-14, and went on to win Super Bowl IX against the Vikings.

The Bills of 1974 were a solid, well-balanced team, the best Buffalo entry of the 1970s. Simpson, favoring a sore knee, gained 1,125 yards rushing, which, while impressive, was well below his previous year's total. Joe Ferguson went to the air more often, hitting wide receivers J. D. Hill and Ahmad Rashad, an ex-Cardinal, with regularity.

The Dolphins were not the overpowering team they had been, and Lou Saban could look forward with some optimism to 1975. But suddenly along came Baltimore, doormats of the Eastern Division in 1974 but now sweeping Miami in two regular-season games, posting a 10-4-0 record, and taking the divisional title.

The 1975 Bills won five of their first six games, while the Colts were losing four of their first five. After that it was all Baltimore. Despite Simpson's 1,817 yards on the ground (with 23 touchdowns, an NFL record) and Joe Ferguson's 2,426 yards in the air, Saban's men could not sustain their drive. The Bills jumped out to a 21-0 lead against the Colts on November 10, only to lose the game, 42-35.

Defense was the Bills' Achilles heel, particularly the defensive backfield, which was riddled with injuries. Simpson was named the AFC's Most Valuable Player (he had been the NFL's MVP the year before), but O. J., who had never liked Buffalo, wanted to be traded. The possibility of that happening cast doubt on the Bills' strength for 1976, particularly when other stars decamped in the off-season, including Ahmad Rashad to the Vikings and J. D. Hill to the Lions.

The Bills finally signed Simpson to a new three-year contract, and he came through in his usual style, gaining 1,503 yards on the ground, but Buffalo went nowhere (except to the bottom) in the standings. Running back Jim Braxton, a strong ground gainer along with Simpson the previous year, hurt his knee in the opener and was out for the season. Quarterback Jim Ferguson went out with a back injury in the seventh game.

1976 was a season to forget. After crushing the Kansas City Chiefs, 50-17, in the fourth game, the Bills lost to the New York Jets, 17-14 in game five. Discouraged, head coach Lou Saban resigned, assistant coach Jim Ringo took his place, and the team proceeded to lose every game thereafter—nine losses in a row for their new head coach. Although the Bills' 1976 record was an abysmal 2-12-0, Jim Ringo got another chance.

It became clear right away that Ringo and his Bills were in trouble. Buffalo lost its first four games before squeaking by the Atlanta Falcons, 3-0, in an upset. After losing two more, one a 56-17 thrashing at the hands of the mediocre Seattle Seahawks, the Bills defeated the New England Patriots, 24-14, and, in the next-to-last game of the season, topped the New York Jets, 14-10, in a battle to avoid the AFC East cellar. In January the Bills said goodbye to Jim Ringo, replacing him with Chuck Knox, fresh from his success as head coach of the L.A. Rams, to try to restore Buffalo's fortunes.

Peaks and (Mostly) Valleys

The 1978 Bills were a distinctly different team from the one that had stumbled through the previous year. Joe Ferguson remained at quarterback, but O. J. Simpson was gone, off to play for the San Francisco 49ers. Rookie halfback Terry Miller stepped into the breach and, after a slow start, finished the season with 1,060 yards rushing. Another newcomer on offense, Frank Lewis, obtained from the Steelers, led all Bills' receivers with 735 yards.

The youthful defense featured a number of rookies, including defensive tackle Dee Hardison and linebacker Lucius Sanford. The Bills improved their won-lost mark to 5-11-0, but gained no ground in their division, as they and the Baltimore Colts shared identical records, tying for fourth place.

Under Chuck Knox in 1979 the Bills won three of their first five games, rolling up 51 points against the Bengals, 48 against the Jets, and 31 against the Colts. Joe Ferguson repeatedly took to the air, hitting Frank Lewis and rookie Jerry Butler early and often. On the ground fullback Curtis Brown and Terry Miller gained the most

PROFILES | **The Passer . . .**

The future of the Buffalo Bills looked bleak in late 1986. The last two head coaches had a combined won-lost record of 14-43, and no improvement seemed imminent. Yet some kind of change was clearly needed.

Back in 1983 the Bills had picked a quarterback, Jim Kelly, in the first round of the draft, but Kelly opted to play for the Houston Gamblers of the USFL, where he went onto set numerous passing records. In 1984 he was the league's MVP.

Just prior to the start of the 1986 season, on August 19, Kelly signed with the Bills and became an immediate standout, completing 285 passes that year to break Joe Ferguson's old mark and amassing 3,593 yards, the second highest total in Buffalo history. In time his name would become synonymous with the "no-huddle" offense.

But even with Kelly's great passing the Bills were losing games in 1986. Finally, on November 3, with seven games remaining in the season, Marv Levy took over as head coach, replacing Hank Bullock. The Bills lost five of the last seven games, but none of them by more than 10 points.

Photo: *AP/Wide World Photos*

yardage, but the Bills' aerial attack was their strength. When it stalled, so did they.

Buffalo lost three in a row after game five and dropped another three straight to end the season. Their 7-9-0 mark gave them undisputed possession of fourth place in the AFC East. Chuck Knox and the Rich Stadium fans had hoped for better.

The Knox-led Bills reached their apogee in 1980. They opened the season with five victories, but then lost a couple to the Colts and the Dolphins. This was clearly an improved team, its running attack aided by the arrival of rookie Joe Cribbs from Auburn University, who rushed for 1,185 yards. The Patriots made a strong bid for the AFC Eastern Division title, but a Bills' win, 18-13, on the final Sunday against the San Francisco 49ers gave the prize to Buffalo.

In the divisional playoff against the San Diego Chargers—a team Buffalo had beaten in a regular-season game—the Bills scored two touchdowns in the second period to take a 14-3 lead. The Knoxmen appeared to be on their way to victory. But San Diego came back with seven points in the third period and ten in the fourth to win the game, 20-14, and with it the division crown.

The Bills came close again in 1981, even though they finished third behind the Dolphins and the Jets. When their 10-6-0 record made them a wild-card qualifier, they proceeded to knock off the Jets, 31-27, to advance to the divisional playoffs. Again they fell by the wayside, losing to the AFC Central Division leaders, the Cincinnati Bengals, 28-21. Attendance at home and on the road, including the playoff game, topped one

Under Levy the team showed improvement in defense against the run and in special teams play. Their confidence improved. Along with his 30 years of coaching experience, Levy also brought a winning attitude to the Bills. After one break-even season in 1987, Buffalo vaulted to the top of the AFC Eastern Division with a 12-4-0 record.

They stayed there for the next few seasons, as the Bills under Levy compiled a 75-40-0 record to make him the winningest coach in Buffalo history. He helped to make Rich Stadium a tough place for visiting teams to win, with his Bills posting a 41-5-0 home record, including playoffs.

Among Bills' quarterbacks, Jim Kelly and Joe Ferguson hold most of the career records, with a few going to Jack Kemp. Head coach, Marv Levy leads all other coaches, his only challenge coming from Lou Saban, who in his two stints posted a combined 70-47-4 mark.

Coached by Levy and quarterbacked by Kelly, the Bills have been a dominant force in the AFC since 1988.

Photo: *AP/Wide World Photos*

million for the second straight year. For the third year Fred Smerlas, a nose tackle out of Boston College, turned in a stellar performance. Joe Ferguson continued to connect with receivers Frank Lewis, Jerry Butler, and Joe Cribbs for major yardage, and on the ground Cribbs again picked up more than 1,000 yards.

Exit Knox

What might have been a good 1982 season dissolved in the 57-day players' strike, and the 4-5-0 Bills received no bid to play in the postseason tournament. Chuck Knox resigned, moving west to coach the Seattle Seahawks. The Bills named Kay Stephenson to take his place. Stephenson decided to concentrate on the running game and built his offense around Joe Cribbs. As in his early days with O. J. Simpson in the backfield, quarterback Joe Ferguson did a lot of handing off, and Cribbs rushed for 1,131.

When Ferguson passed, it was often to Cribbs, whose 525 yards receiving paced all Bills' in snaring the football, although Frank Lewis, Jerry Butler, Byron Franklin, and tight end Tony Hunter were frequent targets, too. Offensive left guard Jim Ritcher put in a fine year. Veteran safety Steve Freeman shone on defense, as did nose tackle Fred Smerlas. The Bills finished with an 8-8-0 record in Stephenson's first season at the helm. Unhappily, the sky was about to fall.

The next three seasons were outright disasters—the downpour before the rainbow. In 1984 the Bills lost their first 11 games en route to a 2-

14-0 record. Before the season began, Joe Cribbs departed for the U.S. Football League and Frank Lewis retired. During the season, Joe Ferguson and Jerry Butler suffered debilitating injuries.

The next season was no better. In fact, it was the same: 2-14-0. Stephenson got the ax after four games and four losses. His replacement, Hank Bulloch, inherited a team with a myriad of problems in every direction. The Bills could neither score nor keep their opponents from scoring. Their 200 points for the season contrasted starkly with the 381 scored against them. The Bills needed a transfusion.

They got one on August 19, 1986, when quarterback Jim Kelly (drafted by the Bills back in 1983 but by now a two-year veteran of the USFL's Houston Gamblers) signed on with Buffalo. They got another on November 3, 1986, when Marv Levy, an experienced hand at both the college and pro level, assumed the head coaching duties upon the departure of 4-17-0 Hank Bulloch. Of nine games the Bills had won only two. They would win only two more in the 1986 season, but the turnaround had begun in earnest.

Kelly, Thomas—and Defense

In the evenly matched AFC Eastern Division in 1987 the Bills were in contention for the title until the closing weeks of the season. But they lost their last two games and fell to 7-8-0, finishing fourth. Jim Kelly ran up a string of 141 passes without an interception before New England's Fred Marion snared one off him in late December.

The defense, which had been so dismal recently, looked good. Defensive end Bruce Smith, in his third season with the Bills, registered 12 sacks and was tapped for the Pro Bowl. Rookie linebacker Shane Conlan from Penn State also won plaudits, as did ex-Colt linebacker Cornelius Bennett.

In 1988 the Bills won 11 of their first 12 games and had the AFC championship in their pocket by mid-November. It was well they did, because they lost three of their last four games. Rookie running back Thurman Thomas, who had been a sensation at Oklahoma State, rushed for 881 yards. Jim Kelly completed 269 passes for 3,380 yards. Wide receiver Andre Reed caught 71 passes to set a new team mark and was named to the Pro Bowl for the first of many times.

Still, the real story of the 1988 season was defense. Shane Conlan, Cornelius Bennett, and Bruce Smith all had banner years. The Bills, 12-4-0, scored 329 points to their opponents' 237, an impressive reversal in a couple of seasons. In the first divisional playoff game played at Rich Stadium, Buffalo defeated the Houston Oilers, 17-10. But the following week at Cincinnati the Bills succumbed to the Bengals, 21-10, in the AFC championship game.

It was something of a miracle that the Bills repeated as division champions. Helping them

AP/Wide World Photos

Thurman Thomas (34)

considerably was the fact that they were the only AFC East team over .500—and that without much to spare at 9-7-0. Their problems were legion. Jim Kelly, Shane Conlan, and Cornelius Bennett lost time to injuries. Defensive back Derrick Burroughs lost his football future to a spinal condition.

Dissension among the players and the resulting annoyance of fans cast a pall over the season. But there were bright spots. One was the performance of backup quarterback Frank Reich, who stepped in when Kelly was injured. Reich helped the Bills rack up three straight wins, including an exciting double-come-from-behind victory, 23-20, against the L. A. Rams. Other bright spots were the brilliance of "the world's best all-purpose running back" Thurman Thomas and the sterling pass receiving of Andre Reed. As had happened the year before, the Bills fell short of the AFC championship, losing in the divisional playoff to the Cleveland Browns, 34-30.

AP/Wide World Photos

Bruce Smith (78)

Three AFC Titles

Under head coach Marv Levy the Bills compiled a 30-24-0 regular-season record between 1986 and 1989—good but not eye-popping. Between 1990 and 1992 the Bills in the regular season went 37-11-0, capturing the AFC crown three times. Levy thus became only the second head coach (the other being Don Shula) to take his team to three consecutive Super Bowls.

Even though the Bills won 13 games in 1990, their divisional competition, Don Shula's Miami Dolphins, stayed in the thick of the fray, winning 12 games, one of them a 30-7 trouncing of the Bills early in the season. But when the chips were down, in the next-to-last game of the season, an injured Jim Kelly gave way to Frank Reich, and Reich completed 15 of 21 passes to lead the Bills past the Dolphins, 24-14.

The 1990 Bills were an outstanding team, solid in all aspects of the game. Quarterback Jim Kelly won numerous awards for his performance, as did defensive end Bruce Smith, linebacker Darryl Talley, running back Thurman Thomas, and wide receiver Andre Reed.

The Dolphins got a wild-card opportunity to avenge themselves on the Bills, but in the divisional playoff Buffalo won again, this time 44-34. In their third straight try for the AFC title, the Bills succeeded. In fact, they succeeded wildly, crushing the Los Angeles Raiders, 51-3, the largest margin of victory in club history. The Bills, as AFC champions, headed for the Super Bowl—and a heartbreaking, last-minute, 20-19 loss to the New York Giants.

In 1991 the championship of the AFC East was never in doubt. The Bills took five straight games before dropping one to the Kansas City Chiefs. They proceeded to win five more in a row and upped their record to 10-1-0. When the Bills ended the season with a 17-14 loss in overtime to the Detroit Lions, their record stood at 13-3-0, the same as the year before. And, as before, they added the divisional title to their laurels, overpowering Kansas City, 37-14.

Super Bowl Jinx

On January 12 the Bills met the Denver Broncos to determine the AFC championship. Once again the men from Buffalo prevailed, though by a slim 10-7 margin. Next it was on to the Super Bowl, where the powerful Washington Redskins (14-2-0) lay in wait. The Redskins had been awesome that season (485 points to their opponents' 224)—and they were plenty tough in Super Bowl XXVI, handing the Bills their second straight Super Bowl loss, 37-24.

The 1992 Bills kept rolling, although this time the Miami Dolphins, coached by Don Shula and quarterbacked by Dan Marino, kept pace. Each team compiled an 11-5-0 record. The AFC East championship went to Miami with a wild-card opportunity for Buffalo. The Bills made the most of it, squeaking by the Houston Oilers, 41-38, in overtime, then knocking off the Pittsburgh Steelers, 24-3, to advance to the AFC championship game. There they faced—who else?—the Miami Dolphins.

Bills' place-kicker Steve Christie, signed from the Tampa Bay Buccaneers to replace Buffalo's all-time scoring leader Scott Norwood, booted five field goals against the Dolphins as the Bills coasted to a 29-10 win—and their third consecutive AFC championship.

In the 1990 Super Bowl, Buffalo had lost to the New York Giants. In 1991 it was the Washington Redskins. This time around they would go up against the rejuvenated Dallas Cowboys in Super Bowl XVII at the Rose Bowl in Pasadena, California. There was no joy in Buffalo on February 1, 1993, the day after the big game, for the Cowboys, under head coach Jimmy Johnson, dismantled the Bills, 52-17.

The MVP of the game was the Cowboys' talented young quarterback, Troy Aikman, who completed 22 of 30 passes for 273 yards and four touchdowns. Aikman even gained more yards on the ground (26) than did the Bills' All-Pro running back Thurman Thomas. So complete was the Bills' annihilation that fans and sportswriters alike began to wonder if the dynastic era for Buffalo might be over, if the Dolphins—or perhaps another AFC East team—might make the future dimmer for Marv Levy's three-time Super Bowl competitors. The test would come in 1993.

Sources

Books

Allen, George, with Ben Olan, *Pro Football's 100 Greatest Players,* Bobbs-Merrill, 1982.

Buffalo Bills 1993 Media Guide, Buffalo Bills Football Team, 1993.

The Complete Handbook of Pro Football, 1993, edited by Zander Hollander, Signet, 1993.

Fox, Larry, *Born to Run: The O. J. Simpson Story,* Dodd, Mead, 1974.

Harrington, Denis J. *The Pro Football Hall of Fame: Players, Coaches, Team Owners and League Officials, 1963-1991,* McFarland & Company, 1991.

Neft, David S., and Richard M. Cohen, *The Football Encylcopedia: The Complete History of Professional NFL Football from 1892 to the Present,* St. Martin's Press, 1991.

The Official National Football League 1992 Record & Fact Book, Workman Publishing Co., 1992.

Porter, David L., editor, *Biographical Dictionary of American Sports: Football,* Greenwood Press, 1987.

Sporting News Pro Football Guide, 1992 Edition, The Sporting News Publishing Co., 1992.

Periodicals

New York Times, January 28, 1991.

Sports Illustrated, October 5, 1964; November 26, 1990; January 21, 1991; December 16, 1991.

—*Gerald Tomlinson* for Book Builders Inc.

Super Bowl XXV

Because of the Persian Gulf War and fears of terrorism in the United States, security was tight at Tampa Stadium on January 27, 1991. Although the 73,813 spectators at this silver anniversary Super Bowl festival were unscathed by game's end, the Buffalo Bills were not as lucky. Favored by seven points, the Bills lost to the New York Giants, 20-19.

With their regular quarterback Phil Simms injured, the Giants started backup quarterback Jeff Hostetler. A 16-yard Hostetler pass to Mark Ingram keyed an early Giants' drive that took them to the Bills' 11-yard line. Matt Bahr kicked a 28-yard field goal, and New York led, 3-0.

Buffalo retaliated quickly, with Jim Kelly completing a 61-yard pass to James Lofton. Stymied at the eight-yard line, the Bills went for the field goal, and Scott Norwood's 23-yard kick tied the game at 3-3. Late in the first quarter, on a Bills' drive that included passes to Andre Reed and Thurman Thomas, Buffalo marched to the Giants' one-yard line. Don Smith ran it in for the touchdown and the extra point gave the Bills a 10-3 lead.

Buffalo made it 12-3 a little later when Jeff Hostetler tripped over Ottis Anderson's foot in the Giants' end zone and the Bill's Bruce Smith nailed him there for a safety. It looked as if Buffalo had taken command, but with less than four minutes to go in the first half, Hostetler engineered an 87-yard drive that ended with a scoring pass to Stephen Baker and a 12-10 score at halftime.

In the third quarter the Bills were blanked, while the Giants drove for another touchdown to take a 17-12 lead. On the first play of the fourth quarter, Bill's running back Thurman Thomas ran 31 yard for a touchdown, and Buffalo bounced back into the lead, 19-17. The Giants still had plenty of time to come back, and they did when a 16-yard Hostetler pass to Mark Bavaro on third down kept a long drive alive, allowing Bahr a 21-yard field-goal attempt. His kick was good, and the Giants edged ahead, 20-19.

Buffalo, with two minutes left, moved the ball from their own 10-yard line to the Giants' 29. With :04 left on the clock it was up to kicker Scott Norwood. The kick, a 47-yarder, was no cinch. Norwood's all-time best was 49 yards, and his best this season was 48. Center Adam Lingner snapped the ball, Frank Reich spotted it, and Norwood kicked. The kick drifted to the right, wide of the goal posts. The game was over, the Bills one field goal shy of a Super Bowl win.

Indianapolis Colts

Few professional football teams have histories filled with as many intriguing, one-of-a-kind stories as do the Indianapolis Colts. For example, critical importance has long been attached to draft choices in the game today, yet the Colts completely defied tradition by picking up their greatest star, one of the greatest in the history of pro football, not via the draft route at all. The club instead found him almost accidentally while he was playing semipro ball. He was, of course, the incomparable Johnny Unitas.

In addition, two of the most successful coaches in Colt history, Weeb Ewbank and Don Shula, received their greatest acclaim after leaving the Colts, Ewbank with the New York Jets, Shula with the Miami Dolphins.

Finally, the Colts were involved in one of the more bizarre trade transactions in any professional sport when the owners of the then Baltimore Colts and the Los Angeles Rams traded franchises.

The Colts have also established a pattern of outstanding turnarounds in team fortunes over the years. The Colts have actually lost more games than they have won over the last 41 years, yet the team has won or tied for ten conference and divisional titles, and has captured three world championships in that time.

At first glance it would seem that the story of the Colts in professional football is a tale of two cities; Indianapolis and Baltimore. It's a bit more complicated than that. The original Baltimore Colt professional football team competed in the old All-American Football Conference from 1947 through the 1949 season.

When that league folded after the 1949 season, the Colts were one of three teams in the league, along with the Cleveland Browns and the San Francisco 49ers, to be absorbed into the National Football League. The team's success, however, did not match that of the Browns and the 49ers, and after one dismal season and a 1-11 record, the club folded.

There was no pro football in Baltimore during the 1951 and 1952 seasons. In 1953, however, businessman Carroll Rosenbloom brought professional football back to the city. He purchased the Dallas Texans, a team that originally started in 1944 as the Boston Yanks before relocating to New York in 1949 (where it was known as both the Bulldogs and the Yanks) and then moving on to Texas. When Rosenbloom brought the club to Baltimore he renamed it the Colts. The franchise remained in Baltimore for 31 seasons through 1983, when it was relocated to Indianapolis by present owner Robert Irsay.

During those three years in the AAFC and the 41 in the NFL, the Colts have won 278 regular season and ten postseason games and have won or tied for ten divisional or conference titles. The Colts have also captured three world championships during that time. The first of those world championships was in 1958-59 under Coach Weeb Ewbank in pre-Super Bowl years; the last was under Coach Don McCafferty in 1970 in Super Bowl V.

Paradoxically, Don Shula, the most successful coach in Colt history in terms of won and loss record (71-23-4 regular season, 4-3 postseason), did not win a Super Bowl until he became head coach of the Miami Dolphins.

Nine Colts have been enshrined in the NFL Hall of Fame: defensive tackle Art Donovan in 1968, defensive end Gino Marchetti in 1972, end Ray Berry and tackle Jim Parker in 1973, running back Lenny Moore in 1975, Coach Weeb Ewbank in 1978, quarterback Johnny Unitas in 1979, linebacker Ted Hendricks in 1990, and tight end John Mackey in 1992. Jersey numbers for Berry (82), Donovan (70), Marchetti (89), Moore (24), Parker (77), Unitas (19), and Buddy Young (24) have all been retired.

In Pro Bowl appearances, both Johnny Unitas and Gino Marchetti were voted in ten times, Jim Parker appeared in eight, Ray Berry and Lenny Moore made it six times each, and Art Donovan, John Mackey, and Chris Hinton were voted in five times each. Marchetti was voted All-Pro nine times, and Parker eight, to lead the Colts in that honor.

Early History of the Colts

After the Miami Seahawks of the newly formed All American Football Conference went bankrupt at the end of the 1946 season, the club was purchased by a group of Baltimore businessmen headed by Bob Rodenberg. One of the group's first moves was to start a fan contest to name the new team. The winning entry, of course, was Colts.

The fledgling owners began the rebuilding process by hiring former Green Bay Packer quarterback Cecil Isbell as the team's new head coach. Isbell, as might be expected, emphasized the passing game. He found a quality performer in Bud Schwenk, who had been backing up the great Otto Graham in Cleveland.

On opening day, September 7, 1947, before a crowd of 27,418, the young Colts and professional football were off with flying colors in Baltimore, topping the Brooklyn Dodgers 16-7. Unfortunately, the team couldn't follow up on that initial success, dropping ten and tying one over their next 11 games. A 14-7 win over the Chicago Rockets late in November gave the Baltimore squad their second win on the way to a 2-11-1 finish. Their performance earned them fourth place in the four-team Eastern Division. Attendance in Baltimore during that first season was 199,861, a big improvement over the 50,151 the franchise had managed in Miami.

During the season, quarterback Schwenk attempted more passes, 327, and completed more, 168, than anyone in the league, and accounted for a total of 2,286 yards. End Lamar Davis and halfback Billy Hillenbrand were his favorite targets. The front office signed former Detroit Lion star halfback Frankie Sinkwich in mid-season, but the old All-American was past his prime and contributed little. The club also picked up a pair of seasoned linemen in tackle John Mellus and guard Augie Lio.

TEAM INFORMATION AT A GLANCE

Founding date: December 28, 1946

Home stadium: Hoosier Dome
Address: P.O. Box 535000
Indianapolis, IN 46253
Phone: (317) 297-2658
Seating capacity: 60,127

Team colors: Royal blue and white
Team nickname: Colts, 1946—
Logo: Horseshoe

Franchise record	Won	Lost	Tie
(1947-92)	288	322	8

Super Bowl wins (1): 1970

The 1948 season proved to be an emotional roller coaster for the young team. In February, knowing that he had to replace the departed Bud Schwenk at quarterback, Coach Cecil Isbell, in a clandestine meeting with All-American Bobby Layne, offered the Texan a then-unheard-of bonus of $10,000 to sign a contract. News of the offer reached Colt fans in Baltimore, who were overjoyed at the prospect of Layne leading the team. But after a period of indecision, Layne crossed up Isbell and the Colts by accepting terms instead with the Chicago Bears of the NFL. Few could understand Layne's choice, as the Bears had the great Sid Luckman as their number-one signal caller, and had already signed Notre Dame All-American Johnny Lujack.

The Colts efforts to secure a quarterback were rewarded from an unsuspected source, however—the Cleveland Browns. With Otto Graham at the top of his game, the Browns awarded their first round draft pick, Y. A. Tittle, to the Colts as part of the league's plan to help the weaker clubs. The infusion of talent dramatically improved the Colts.

With Tittle filling the air with footballs, boasting a new running attack, and help on the line, the Colts opened the season with a huge upset win over the Division Champion New York Yankees, 45-28, before a wild crowd in Baltimore Stadium. Tittle, in his first professional game, threw for four touchdowns. Two weeks later, to prove it was no fluke, they trounced the New Yorkers again in New York, 27-14.

During the year Tittle completed 161 of 289 passes for 2,522 yards, with most of them directed to halfback Billy Hillenbrand and ends Lamar Davis and Win Williams. Isbell built a respectable running attack led by fullback Buzz Mertes and Hillenbrand. Mertes pounded out 680 yards on 155 carries for a 4.4 average. Rookie kicker Rex Grossman had 73 points on 43 straight conversions and 10 of 18 field goal attempts. His field goal total led the league.

The Colts went into the season finale against Buffalo a game out of the lead with a 6-7 mark. At the top of their game, the Baltimore club thrilled a home crowd with a 35-15 win to move into a tie for the division lead. In just his second year at the helm Isbell had taken the club to the brink of a title. After scoring only 167 points in their first season, the resurgent Colts totalled 333 in 1948.

The playoff was scheduled for December 12, again to be played in Baltimore, where the Colt fans were confident of a repeat win. The Colts took a 17-7 lead into the fourth quarter. But then came the play and series of events that Colt fans will never forget. Buffalo quarterback George Ratterman completed a short pass to Bills halfback Chet Mutryn, who caught the ball and appeared to run a number of steps before being belted by two Colt defenders and fumbling. The ball was picked up by John Mellus of the Baltimore team who set off for the Buffalo goal line.

The play was whistled dead, however, as head linesman Tom Whelan ruled that Mutryn never had control of the ball, thus making the play nothing more than an incomplete pass. A few plays later Ratterman threw for a score, and the tide had turned. Another score by Buffalo followed by another interception, and the game was Buffalo's. At least 10,000 enraged Colt fans flooded out on the field after the game, and Whelan was lucky to escape with his life. The Colts protested the game to the league office, but Commissioner Jonas Ingram refused to change the call, and the score stood, Bills 28, Colts 17. The only solace the Colts got was the 49-7 thrashing the Cleveland Browns dealt the Bills in the championship game.

In front office activity, the club was reorganized with 200 stockholders. Jake Embry was named president and Walt Driskill general manager. Guard Dick Barwegen became the first Colt to be named All-League, and attendance for the year totalled 244,502.

Early in 1949 Walt Driskill succeeded Embry as president, the first of two major moves he was to make during the year. After the Colts opened the season with great expectations, four straight lopsided losses—to San Francisco, Los Angeles, Cleveland, and Chicago—cost Coach Cecil Isbell his job. Driskill took over the reins as head coach for the remainder of the year.

The financially troubled AAFC had during this time consolidated from eight to seven teams as Brooklyn and New York merged and the league moved into only one division. It was the last hurrah, however, as the league disbanded after four years of competition. Baltimore was one of three teams, along with Cleveland and San Francisco, that were absorbed into the NFL, while players from the other four clubs were pooled and drafted by the NFL teams.

As one of three selected AAFC teams that were now competing in the National Football League for the first time, the year 1950 should have been exciting for the Colts and their fans. It didn't turn out quite that way, however. In December, the team was purchased by Abraham Watner, who then became the club's president. Three months later, Clem Crowe was named as the new head coach. Neither man enjoyed much success with the Colts.

Officially designated as the 13th team in the NFL, the Colts played a swing schedule, facing each team in the league once instead of playing division teams twice as all the other clubs did. The Colts started out their NFL career by dropping all seven of their pre-season games and their first six regular season contests. The team finally posted a 41-21 win over the Green Bay Packers on November 5 in Baltimore. During the game Colt running back Jim Spavital had a 96-yard run from scrimmage for a touchdown, the longest run of the year for any team.

The only position of any real strength was at quarterback, where Y.A. Tittle and Adrian Burk were deserving of better fate. Tittle hit on 161 of 315 passes for 1,884 yards, while Burk completed 43 of 119 for 798 yards. End Paul Salata was picked up from San Francisco to lead the receivers with 60 catches for 618 yards. Chet Mutryn, an old nemesis from the Buffalo Bills now on the Colt roster, led the club's runners with 355 yards. The team was a sieve on defense, giving up 462 points, an average of 38.5 a game.

Following the season the franchise was dissolved by the league because of financial woes. Watner was paid $50,000 for the team. A year earlier he had paid three times that amount to

George Preston Marshall of the Washington Redskins for infringing on his "territorial" rights. The Cleveland Browns, on the other end of the spectrum, won the NFL Championship.

Some things are supposed to be better the second time around, or so the song goes. The Colts second chance in the NFL most certainly was. After the demise of the Colt franchise in the league following the 1950 season, Baltimore was without professional football for two years. Then, on December 3, 1952, NFL Commissioner Bert Bell issued an unusual challenge to Colt fans to come up with 10,000 season ticket purchases to get their team back. The fans responded admirably, coming up with the goal in just over four weeks. That paved the way to another event.

In January 1953 a group of Baltimore businessman led by Carroll Rosenbloom took over the defunct Dallas Texan franchise and brought it home. Don Kellett was announced as the club's new president, and Keith Molesworth was appointed the new head coach. The team would take the name "Colts" but would keep the old Texan colors of white and blue.

On March 25th the Colts and the Cleveland Browns became principals in one of the biggest, in number if not in importance, trades in the history of the league. Baltimore sent five players to the Browns in return for ten players from the Cleveland franchise. Among those ten was a young running back, Don Shula, and a rookie kicker and defensive back, Bert Rechichar.

Rebirth of the Franchise

A crowd of 23,215 on opening day at Baltimore Stadium was thrilled as the Colts upset the old NFL warhorse Chicago Bears 13-9. In the contest rookie kicker Rechichar not only kicked a 56-yard field goal on his first attempt ever in the pros, but also intercepted a George Blanda pass and returned it for a touchdown. At the time the 56-yarder was a new NFL record. Two weeks later the Colts topped the Bears again in Chicago, 16-14. After a 27-17 win over the Washington Redskins in the fifth game of the season, the young Colts were among the leaders of the league with a 3-2 record. But from that point on it was all downhill, as Baltimore lost its last seven in a row to finish at 3-9.

Postseason honors for club members were highlighted by recognition for Tom Keane, who pulled in 11 interceptions over the course of the season, a total which has not been surpassed to this date by any Colt. Keane was named to the AFL All-Pro Team and to the Pro Bowl. Running back George Taliaferro, guard Dick Barwegen, and tackle Art Donovan were also selected to play in the Pro Bowl classic. Attendance for the year totalled 168,014, an average of more than 28,000 a game. The Colts were back, and they were going to stay.

Colt owner Carroll Rosenbloom turned to the Cleveland Browns again for help, offering the head coaching job to one of Paul Brown's assistants, Blanton Collier. Collier turned down the offer, accepting the head coaching position at the University of Kentucky instead, whereupon Rosenbloom, undaunted, offered the job to another Brown assistant, Weeb Ewbank, who accepted.

The Colts outfought a strong New York Giant club 20-14 in the second game of the 1954 season, then had to wait until the season was nearly over for their second and third wins, over Los Angeles and San Francisco. Don Shula and Tom Keane had five interceptions each to pace the defensive effort, while Buddy Young led the team in kickoff returns, punt returns, and rushing yardage.

End Dan Edwards led the team for the second year in a row in pass receptions, snagging 40 passes over the course of the season, while Gary Kerkorian replaced Fred Enke as the Colts' quarterback, completing 117 of 217 for 1,515 yards. Rookie signal caller Cotton Davidson, the team's number one draft pick, saw little action. Baltimore's sole All-Pro was tackle Art Donovan, who also made the Pro Bowl squad along with defensive end Gino Marchetti and Young.

Gino Marchetti

In Weeb Ewbank's second year as the Colts' top man, the club's improvement became evident even before the season started, with excellent draft choices offering promise for better days. The team was given a bonus pick for the year, which in effect gave them two first round choices. Ewbank used them to select Alan "The Horse" Ameche, the University of Wisconsin All-American fullback and Heisman Trophy winner, and University of Oregon quarterback George Shaw. Both selections had an immediate impact on the club.

Against the Chicago Bears on Opening Day, on the first play from scrimmage, Ameche burst through a hole in the middle of the line and rambled 79 yards for a touchdown. It may well have been the most electrifying debut of any back in league history. The run was a new Colt record for length, as was the 194 total yards Ameche amassed for the game, a 23-17 Colt win.

With Ameche as the club's first legitimate running threat and Shaw at quarterback, and with the addition of other key rookies such as halfback L. G. Dupre from Baylor, end Raymond Berry from SMU, and lineman Dick Szymanski of Notre Dame, the Colts galloped to three straight wins to open the season. But the Bears walloped the Colts in a rematch 38-10 and the club went on to a 5-6-1 mark, good for only a fourth-place finish in the Western Conference.

Improvement over the 1954 season, however, was measurable. In 1954 the club scored only 131 points and gave up 279. In 1955 the club tallied 214 and gave up only 239, a swing of 123 points.

Ameche's 961 total yards rushing for the year was not only a Colt record, it was high for the entire NFL in 1955. Ameche, Donovan, and halfback Bert Rechichar, who led the Colts in interceptions and punt returns, were named as All-Pros. They were joined by teammates Gino Marchetti and Dick Syzmanski on the Pro Bowl squad.

Unitas Arrives

In previous efforts to secure a first-line quarterback, the Colts had devoted first-round draft picks in both 1954 and 1955 to selecting quarterbacks Cotton Davidson of Baylor and George Shaw of Oregon. But in the fall of 1956 a young man with a crewcut and ever-present grin, who had been touted by none of the pro scouts, asked for a tryout. The unheralded youngster, who had been playing semi-pro ball in Pennsylvania, was signed on. A most fortunate move by the Colts, for the player was Johnny Unitas, destined to become one of the greatest professional quarterbacks of all time.

Unitas didn't get his opportunity to star immediately. Behind incumbent quarterback Shaw, the Colts opened the season with an upset 28-21 win over the Chicago Bears, then dropped two, to the Detroit Lions and Green Bay Packers, before facing the Bears again in Chicago on

October 21. In that wild battle, won by the Bears 58-27, Chicago defender Fred Williams broke Shaw's knee with a vicious tackle, and Unitas took over—for the next 17 years. His statistics were only modest for that first year, 110 completions in 198 attempts for 1,498 yards, but Ewbank knew he had found the key to his quest for a championship.

For the year the team finished at 5-7-0, a half game behind their record the year before. First round draft pick Lenny Moore of Penn State became an immediate help, leading the team in scoring with nine touchdowns for 54 points, and forming a highly effective tandem with fullback Alan Ameche as ground gainers. While the Horse bulled for 858 yards in 178 carries for a 4.8 average, the swift Moore added 649 yards and a remarkable 7.5 average.

Johnny Unitas

Moore's 79-yard run for a score against the Green Bay Packers on October 28—a 28-21 Colt win—tied Ameche's record set the year before. The 185 yards rushing Moore totalled for that game was the high point of the year for the team. Bert Rechichar led the Colts in interceptions as well as punting. End Jim Mutscheller again led the club in receptions.

The Colts placed two defensive men on the All-Pro Team, tackle Art Donovan and end Gino Marchetti. Both were also named to the Pro Bowl squad, along with Ameche, Moore, and Rechichar. Although he didn't make any of the honor teams in 1956, a most valuable addition to the club was the big defensive tackle Big Daddy Lipscomb.

The 1957 campaign was a year of streaks for the Colts. First they led off the season with three straight wins, over the Detroit Lions, the Chicago Bears and the Green Bay Packers. Then three losses in a row preceded four more consecutive victories, over the Washington Redskins, the Bears again, the San Francisco 49ers, and the Los Angeles Rams.

At this point in the race the Colts were in first place with a 7-3 mark, a game ahead of both the 49ers and the Lions. But a heartbreaking 17-13 loss to San Francisco, despite an 82-yard touchdown pass from Johnny Unitas to Lenny Moore that gave the Colts a 13-10 lead with two minutes to go in the game, followed by a 37-21 loss to the Rams, broke the Colts' back.

Unitas, who threw for at least one touchdown in every game of the season, completed 172 of 301 for 2,550 yards and 24 touchdowns, leading the league in passing yardage and touchdown passes. Fullback Alan Ameche and halfback Lenny Moore led the ground attack again, while end Ray Berry led the club with 41 catches for 800 yards. Defensive back Milt Davis' ten interceptions led the Colts and tied for the league lead.

Unitas, Davis, defensive tackle Art Donovan, and defensive end Gino Marchetti won All-Pro honors—Donovan for the third year in a row. In the Pro Bowl, the Colts were represented by Unitas, Donovan, Marchetti, Ameche, end Jim Mutscheller, and defensive back Bert Rechichar.

Prior to the 1958 season the team selected massive Jim Parker, an All-American offensive tackle from Ohio State, as their first-round draft pick.

Baltimore Colts ... Champions

When he accepted the head coaching job of the Baltimore Colts in 1953, Weeb Ewbank told Baltimore fans that he'd bring them a championship within five years. Many undoubtedly thought his commentary represented the usual promises new coaches spouted. But Ewbank meant what he said, and he delivered, on the money. In 1958, exactly five years after making that vow, the Colts defeated the New York Giants in a thrilling 23-17 overtime battle to take the NFL Championship. That Colt-Giant battle has been called the greatest pro football game in history. For Colt faithful, it most assuredly was. Disgraced because of poor support of the team in 1950, then without a franchise at all in 1951 and 1952 and without any real hopes of ever getting one again, in only a few short years Baltimore was on top of the pro football world in 1958.

The heroes were many: Ewbank, of course; the incomparable Johnny Unitas, now the top quarterback in all of pro football; fullback Alan Ameche, who scored the deciding touchdown in that epic championship struggle with the Giants; the mercurial Lenny Moore; the glue-fingered Raymond Berry; Big Daddy Lipscomb; and other vital members of the team such as Gino Marchetti, Jim Parker, and Art Donovan. Of the seven Colts who have had their jersey numbers retired, six played on that 1958 squad; of the nine Colts now in the NFL Hall of Fame, seven were with that glorious team.

Early in the year, the team hardly started out as world beaters, winning only two of their six preseason games. But when the regular season began, everything started to come together. The Colts marched through their first six games unbeaten; in the last three games of that streak the club annihilated Detroit, 40-14, Washington, 35-10 and Green Bay, 56-0. The win over the Packers

Raymond Berry

was costly, however, as a hard tackle by Green Bay's Johnny Symank put Unitas in the hospital with three broken ribs and a punctured lung.

With Unitas out indefinitely, George Shaw took over the quarterbacking for the team as the Colts headed into New York for a battle with the eastern powerhouse. Shaw did his share, throwing for three touchdowns, but the Giants came out ahead 24-21 in a bitter fight.

The Colts then beat the Bears and the Rams, and in a wild game in Baltimore against the 49ers, with Unitas back on the field, rallied from a 27-7 halftime deficit to win 35-27. A capacity crowd was delirious, for the win clinched the Western Conference championship for Baltimore. This was fortunate, for the Colts, as they had done the year before, were shut out in their last two games on the west coast, losing to the Rams and 49ers to finish at 9-3.

The championship contest, played before 64,185 fans and many millions more on television, was the first sudden death overtime game played in NFL postseason competition. Tied at 17-17 after four quarters of play, the first team to score in the extra period would reign as champion. The Colts lost the coin flip and had to kick off to the Giants. New York couldn't move the ball and had to punt, and the Colts marched the length of the field. With the ball on New York's one yard line, Unitas handed off to Ameche, and the burly fullback blasted into the end zone.

During the season, while he was able to play, Unitas had connected for 136 of 263 passes for 2,007 yards and 19 touchdowns. As he had done in the 1957 season, he threw for at least one touchdown in every game in which he played. His favorite targets were end Raymond Berry, who caught a league-leading 56 passes for 794 yards, and halfback Lenny Moore, who pulled down 50 for 938 yards.

Ameche again was the team's leading ground gainer, with 791 yards in 171 carries for a 4.6 average, while Moore added 598 on only 82 carries for a 7.3 average, and L. G. Dupre chipped in with 390 yards on 95 trips.

The Colt defensive backfield of Andy Nelson, Ray Brown, Carl Taseff, and Milt Davis grabbed 27 interceptions, and specialist Lenny Lyles, the team's first-round draft pick, became one of the league's top return men with a 103-yard kickoff runback for a touchdown against the Bears and another for 101 yards against Washington.

Ewbank had some great players in the line as well, such as Ray Krouse, Buzz Nutter, Jim Parker, Art Spinney, and Fuzzy Thurston on offense, and Art Donovan, Don Joyce, Big Daddy Lipscomb, Gino Marchetti, Bill Pellington, and Don Shinnick on defense. Six Colts made All-Pro—Berry, Lipscomb, Marchetti, Moore, Parker and Unitas. The same six, along with Nelson and Spinney, were named to the Pro Bowl.

In 1959 the Colts repeated as NFL kingpins, but it took a stirring stretch drive after falling behind the San Francisco 49ers by two games with only five to play. In the season finale, Baltimore scored 24 points in the fourth quarter to come from behind and beat the Rams in Los Angeles, 45-26, to capture the division crown. In the game defensive back Carl Taseff returned a missed Ram field goal 99 yards for a touchdown, tying a league record.

Quarterback Johnny Unitas had a superlative year, completing 193 of 367 for 2,899 yards and an astounding 32 touchdowns, the latter a NFL record, breaking the old mark of 28 set by the Bears' Sid Luckman. And again he threw for at least a touchdown in every game.

End Raymond Berry led the Colt receivers for the third year in a row with 66 for 959 yards, and also paced the team in scoring with 14 touchdowns for 84 points. The three top Colt receivers, Berry, Lenny Moore, and Jim Mutscheller, finished first, second, and fourth in the league. Alan Ameche again led the team in rushing, with 679 yards, while Milt Davis and Don Shinnick, with seven interceptions each, tied for the league lead in that category. Moreover, the Colts finally found a punter who could top 40 yards a kick, Dave Sherer, who averaged 41.8 for the season.

Center Jackie Barkett of Auburn was the team's first round draft pick. All-Pro selections were Berry, Big Daddy Lipscomb, Gino Marchetti, Moore, Andy Nelson, Jim Parker, Art Spinney, and Unitas. Pro Bowlers were Berry, Lipscomb, Mutscheller, Moore, Parker, Spinney and Unitas.

After compiling another 9-3 mark in the regular season, the Colts once again faced the New York Giants for the championship. This time the Colts turned a close contest—9-7 in favor of the New Yorkers after three quarters—into a rout with 24 points in the final stanza. Unitas hit on 18 of 27 passes for 264 yards, threw for two touchdowns, and scored one himself to walk away with MVP honors.

Shifting Fortunes

Although the Colts started out well enough in 1960, shutting out Washington 20-0 in the league opener and then rocking the Chicago Bears 42-7, they lost two of their next three. Three wins in a row put the team back into first place with a 6-2 record, but then they went into a nosedive, losing their last four while the Green Bay Packers swept to the title, their first under new Coach Vince Lombardi.

Quarterback Johnny Unitas, playing for most of the year with a fractured vertebra in his back, nevertheless turned in a gritty performance, completing 190 passes for 3,099 yards and 25 touchdowns. Unitas' consecutive game streak of touchdown passes came to an end during the year when the LA Rams stopped his string at 47. The streak, though, reached a length more than double the old mark of 23 in a row held by Cecil Isbell in the early 1940s.

Alan Ameche suffered a career-ending Achilles heel injury in mid-season. The Colt running attack fell apart as a result, with the leading ground gainer, Lenny Moore, only able to pick up

Jim Parker

374 yards for the whole season. On a high note, Berry caught 74 passes for 1,298 yards, both marks high for the NFL in 1960; the yardage mark is still a Colt record. Johnny Sample led the team in kickoff and punt returns.

Despite that 6-6 record, the Colts still had five All-Pro performers, Berry, Big Daddy Lipscomb, Gino Marchetti, Moore, and Jim Parker. Pro Bowlers included Marchetti, Moore, Parker, Art Spinney, and Unitas.

The Colts recovered from the disappointing 1960 season, compiling an 8-6 mark in 1961. Armed with Unitas, Berry, and Moore, the Colts were still one of the top teams in the NFL. The club played in the league's Western Conference, however, where Vince Lombardi's Green Bay Packers had become one of the greatest teams in pro football history. The Colts were unable to keep pace.

Unitas set new Colt marks for passing attempts (420) and completions (229), good for 2,990 yards and 16 touchdowns. Berry led the team again, for the fifth year in a row, with 75 catches for 837 yards. The old war horse Joe Perry, picked up from the San Francisco 49ers, still had enough left to lead the team in rushing with 675 yards. Steve Myhra hit on 33 of 34 extra point attempts and 21 of 39 field goals for 96 points; the field goals and total points were new Colt highs.

The team's defense, however, had grown increasingly porous. Big Daddy Lipscomb and Johnny Sample had been traded, and Art Donovan had finally begun to feel his years. But although the club's greatest need was defense, the first-round draft choice was Ohio State halfback Tom Matte.

Ewbank Departs

1962 marked Weeb Ewbank's final season at the helm of the Baltimore club. After the magic he had wrought in bringing two world championships to Baltimore, Ewbank deserved a better goodbye party. Quarterback Johnny Unitas was still the consummate pro, but his supporting cast, especially the offensive line, was growing old. On the defensive side, one of the club's all-time fan favorites, tackle Art Donovan, announced his retirement. On September 16, prior to the league opener against the Rams, a special ceremony was conducted to retire Donovan's number 70.

Oddly, the Colts fought the World Champion Green Bay Packers almost even in 17-13 and 17-6 losses, but were blown out of the park by the Chicago Bears, 35-15 and 57-0.

Ewbank's record at Baltimore was 57-52-1 for regular season play, 2-0 in championship games for the NFL title. He left the club to take over the coaching reins of the newly named New York Jets, and within five years duplicated his achievement in Baltimore, leading the underdog Jets to a 16-7 upset win in the Super Bowl against, ironically, the Baltimore Colts.

Shula Takes Over

In January Don Shula was announced as the new Baltimore Colt head coach. Shula's regime stumbled out of the gate, as the club lost five of its first eight games. A spirited stretch run, however, pulled the club up to 8-6 and gave evidence that the Colts were still a strong title contender. Players such as Johnny Unitas, Ray Berry, Gino Marchetti and Jim Parker were perennial All-Pros. Two rookies, future Hall-of-Famer John Mackey at tight end and Bob Vogel at tackle moved into starting roles. Third year man Tom Matte came on impressively during the season, leading the club in rushing, with 541 yards and a 4.1 average; in pass receptions, with 48 for 466 more yards; and in kickoff returns, with 16 for 331 yards.

Unitas set eight club records during the year, including 237 completions for 3,481 yards and 20 touchdowns. The completion total was a new NFL mark. Jim Martin, another newcomer, set a new Colt scoring record with 104 points, garnered on 32 of 35 conversion attempts and 24 of 39 field goal tries. The duo of Gino Marchetti and Jim Parker again were the Colts selected for All-Pro honors. They were joined by Unitas, Berry, and Mackey at the Pro Bowl.

Prior to the 1964 season, Carroll Rosenbloom purchased all of the remaining stock in the club to become sole owner. Rosenbloom was undoubtedly pleased with his investment as he watched the 1964 season unfold. In only his second year as head coach, Don Shula led the Colts to a remarkable 12-2 record, the top regular season mark in the NFL.

Unfortunately, the scoring machine that ran up 428 points during the year floundered in the NFL title game as the Cleveland Browns' stifling defense shut out the Colts 27-0. Johnny Unitas, after another excellent season in which he threw for 2,824 yards, was held to only 95 by the Browns and was intercepted twice. It was possibly his worst showing as a pro.

In addition to a solid season again by Unitas, his old battery mate Raymond Berry reclaimed the Colt pass receiving leadership with 43 for 683 yards. During the year Berry pulled down his 506th pass, a new NFL mark. Lenny Moore also proved to be a pleasant surprise during the season. After sitting out most of the previous two seasons with injuries, many thought Moore was ready to retire. Shula, in fact, tried unsuccessfully to peddle him over the winter. But Moore confounded the critics and his own coach by coming back not only to lead the team in rushing, but scoring 20 touchdowns as well, a new NFL record.

Another Colt mark was set in the 47-27 win over St. Louis, when halfback Tom Matte dashed 80 yards for a score, topping the old Colt record of 79 yards held by both Moore and Alan Ameche.

All-Pro Colts included Gino Marchetti, for the ninth year in a row; Jim Parker, for the seventh consecutive year; defensive halfback Bob Boyd, who led the team in interceptions with nine; Moore; Unitas; and tackle Bob Vogel. Seven Colts made the Pro Bowl squad—Berry, Boyd, Marchetti, Moore, Parker, Vogel, and Dick Szymanski.

In 1965 the Colts took a 9-2-1 record and half game lead over the Packers into a late-season clash against Green Bay. Baltimore hosted the Packers on December 12, a gloomy, foggy day. The elements didn't stop Green Bay, as Packer halfback

Paul Hornung scored a NFL record five touchdowns in a 42-27 Green Bay win. The Colts moved back into a tie for the lead on the last day of the season, however, as they outfought a stubborn Los Angeles Ram team on the coast, 20-17, as the Packers were being held to a tie by San Francisco. A playoff for the conference championship was set for December 26 in Green Bay.

For that tussle, both starting quarterbacks, Johnny Unitas for the Colts and Bart Starr for the Packers, were out with injuries. To make matters even worse for Baltimore, Unitas' backup, Gary Cuozzo, was also hurt and unable to play. Coach Don Shula was forced to use halfback Tom Matte at quarterback, and the latter came up with a courageous effort, armed with a simplified version of the Colts' playbook taped to his wrist.

Despite such desperate measures, the Colts nearly pulled off a victory. Baltimore led 10-7 until the Packers' Don Chandler kicked a tying field goal late in the game. Chandler then won the game on another field goal in the sudden death period. The 13-10 Packer win was their third over the Colts during the year; had Baltimore won any of the three they would have been conference champs.

For the eighth straight year Jim Parker was named All-Pro; he was joined on that honor list by Unitas, Boyd, flanker Jimmy Orr, and tackle Bob Vogel. Pro Bowlers from the Colt squad were Parker, Vogel, Jerry Logan, and John Mackey.

The Colts lost the opening game of the 1966 season to their old nemesis, the Green Bay Packers, 24-3, then spent the rest of the year trying to catch up. A second loss to the Pack on December 10 in Green Bay sealed the issue, and the Colts' 9-5 mark was good only for another second-place finish. Baltimore's key offensive players had passed their prime.

The defense, although aged too, was still among the best in pro ball, however. The linebacking corps was strengthened by the conversion of Mike Curtis from fullback to linebacker; Gino Marchetti came out of retirement and again put in some solid play at defensive end; and the secondary—Bobby Boyd, Alvin Haymond, Lenny Lyles, and Jerry Logan—was a solid unit.

The offense, as it had so often in the past, rode almost entirely on the arm of Johnny Unitas, who threw for 2,748 yards and 22 touchdowns, but also 24 interceptions. Ray Berry, with 56 receptions for 786 yards, and John Mackey with 50 for 829, accounted for one of the best one-two punches in the league.

With the addition of New Orleans to the NFL, bringing total membership to 16 teams, the Eastern and Western Conferences were split into two divisions. The Colts were aligned in the Coastal Division along with the Atlanta Falcons, the Los Angeles Rams, and the San Francisco 49ers. The champion of that division would meet the winner of the Central Division for the Western Conference title; the winner of that tussle would meet the winner of the Eastern Conference for the NFL Championship.

In their new surroundings the Colts swept to a 11-1-2 record, their best performance under Coach Don Shula and the only time the team completed an entire season with only one loss. That 11-1-2 mark, however, was matched by the Los Angeles Rams, and under the league's tie-breaking formula at that time, the Rams were awarded the title on the basis of outscoring Baltimore in their two meetings, which included a 34-10 thrashing the final week of the season. Up until that time the Colts were undefeated and in first place.

Early in the year Don Kellett retired as general manager, and was replaced by Joseph Campanella. Three weeks later Campanella died, and publicity director Harry Hulmes was assigned to take his place.

Quarterback Johnny Unitas enjoyed one of his top years, attempting more passes, 436, and completing more, 255, that at any time in his career. He also had the highest completion percentage, 58.5, that he had ever turned in. His yardage total of 3,428 was his second highest. By the end of the season he had completed more passes, 2,261, for more yardage, 33,340, and for more touchdowns, 252, than any player in NFL history.

Pulling down a major share of Unitas' passes were Willie Richardson, 63 for 880 yards, and John Mackey, 55 for 686. Ground gainers were led by Tom Matte, with 636 yards. In the 24-3 win over Chicago on October 8, Rick Volk returned an interception 94 yards for a touchdown, the longest of the year.

A number of Colt standouts retired during or after the season, including Ray Berry, Jim Parker, and Lenny Moore. Mackey, Richardson, Unitas, and Bob Vogel were voted All-Pro; Mackey, Unitas, Vogel, Richardson, Ordell Braase, Fred Miller, and Rick Volk were named to the Pro Bowl.

Unitas Moves Over

Prior to the 1968 season opener quarterback Johnny Unitas began having pain in the elbow of his throwing arm, so Coach Don Shula worked out a trade deal with New York, giving the Giants a future draft pick for reserve quarterback Earl Morrall. When Unitas's arm didn't respond to treatment, Shula had to go with Morrall, and the journeyman signal caller started for the entire season.

Morrall's performance surprised everyone, including Shula, as his pinpoint passing led the Colts to the best record in the NFL for the year, 13-1, and won him All-Pro honors. He hit on 182 of 317 passes for 2,909 years and led the league with 26 touchdown passes. Shula's insurance paid off.

In the conference championship, the Colts outfought the tough Minnesota Viking club 24-14 on a cold, rainy day in Baltimore. Then in the NFL title game, they crushed the Cleveland Browns 34-0, avenging their only loss during the regular season. But then the honeymoon ended.

Baltimore was a heavy favorite to defeat the upstart New York Jets, coached by their old mentor, Weeb Ewbank, in Super Bowl III. They ran into a buzzsaw, however, in the form of Broadway Joe Namath, who picked them apart all day en route to a 16-7 Jet win. Unitas came off the bench in the second half to lead the Colts to their only score, but it was too little, too late.

Earlier in the year former Baltimore defensive tackle Art Donovan became the first Colt to be elected into the NFL Hall of Fame.

The NFL Realigns

Following a meeting with all team owners on May 17, NFL Commissioner Pete Rozelle announced that the AFL would become part of the NFL the next year, with the Baltimore Colts, the Cleveland Browns, and the Pittsburgh Steelers joining the ten AFL clubs in the NFL's new American Conference, while the 13 remaining NFL clubs would form the new National Conference. The year 1969 marked the last year the two leagues would be separate entities.

Thus in their final year in the Coastal Division of the NFL, the Colts finished at 8-5-1, two and a half games behind division leading Los Angeles. The showing was a disappointing one, coming on the heels of two consecutive years wherein the team lost a total of only two games.

The stigma of their Super Bowl loss seemed to plague the Colts all year. Bob Boyd, Ordell Braase, and Don Shinnick retired after the loss. Quarterback Johnny Unitas was back from the injured list, but was not especially effective. He completed 178 of 327 for 2,342 yards, but only 12 touchdowns. Tom Matte had his best year as a pro, picking up 909 yards and scoring 11 touchdowns.

For the first time since the 1954 season the Colts had only one All-Pro, their punter, David Lee, who led the league with a 45.3 average. Matte, Fred Miller, and Rick Volk were voted to the Pro Bowl team.

Shula Heads South

Following the season Don Shula resigned to take the head coaching job with the Miami Dolphins. He was replaced by Don McCafferty, who became the Colts' seventh head coach. In a front office move, Don Klosterman was named the

Continued on page 112

Nine Colts have been inducted into the National League Hall of Fame—quarterback Johnny Unitas, running back Lenny Moore, receiver Ray Berry, tight end John Mackey, and tackle Jim Parker, all on offense; tackle Art Donovan, end Gino Marchetti, and linebacker Ted Hendricks from the defensive side of the line; and Coach Weeb Ewbank. All of them were with the Colts during the years that the franchise was located in Baltimore.

Art Donovan • Art Donovan, a 6-foot-3, 265-pound defensive tackle, was a member of the original Colt team in Baltimore in 1950. The popular Donovan also played for the old New York Yanks in 1951 and the Dallas Texans in 1952 before the club was moved to Baltimore the next year. The Boston College grad was the first Colt to be inducted into the Hall, so honored in 1968. He was an All-Pro for each of the years 1954 through 1957, and was a member of the Pro Bowl squad five times.

Gino Marchetti • Gino Marchetti, a 6-4, 245-pound defensive end and an alumnus of San Francisco University, was acclaimed as the greatest defensive end in pro football history when the league held its 50th Anniversary celebration in 1969. He was inducted into the Hall in July of 1972.

Marchetti was an All-Pro for nine consecutive years from 1956 through 1964, and played in every Pro Bowl during those years with the exception of 1958, when a broken ankle suffered in the "Sudden Death" playoff game against the New York Giants kept him out. He played his final game for the Colts on December 18, 1966, against the San Francisco 49ers.

Raymond Berry • Raymond Berry, a slim, 6-2, 187-pound end who played his college ball at Southern Methodist University, was a 29th round "future" pick of the Colts in 1954. Thirteen years later, at the end of his career, he was the leading NFL receiver of all time with 631 receptions for 9,275 yards and 68 touchdowns. He earned All-Pro honors three times and played in four Pro Bowl games. He led the NFL in receiving in 1958, 1959, and 1960.

In those years the NFL played a 12-game schedule, and for the three seasons Berry totalled 196 catches, 3,051 yards, and 33 touchdowns. He also holds single-game NFL Championship records for yardage gained receiving (178) and catches (12), both marks set during the "Sudden Death" game. After retiring as a player, Berry headed to the coaching ranks, where he led the New England Patriots to the Super Bowl in 1985. He was inducted into the Hall in July of 1973.

Jim Parker • An extremely strong, 6-3, 277-pound tackle, Parker was the Colts first round draft pick in 1957. He had twice been named as All-American at Ohio State University and had also been awarded the coveted Outland Trophy as the nation's outstanding collegiate lineman.

Parker was named an All-Pro for eight consecutive years—1958 through 1965—and was a member of the Pro Bowl squad for the same years. He played in his final game in 1967, finally forced to the sidelines because of a leg injury. He played in 139 consecutive games, second on the Colt all-time list to Jerry Logan's 155.

Lenny Moore • Lenny Moore, a 1955 Penn State All-American halfback, was the Colts number one pick in the 1956 draft. At 6-1 and 190 pounds, the elusive Moore was one of the most feared running backs of his day. In his rookie year, when he won Rookie of the Year honors, he averaged a startling 7.5 yards a rush. He completed his career with 5,174 yards rushing on 1,069 carries for a 4.8 average. These figures stand today as Colt records.

Moore totalled 12,451 all-purpose yards, adding 6,039 receiving on 363 receptions and another 1,180 on kickoff and 56 on punt returns. His overall receiving average was 16.6 yards a catch, and in 1964 he averaged an astounding 27.5 yards per reception. His 20 touchdowns and 120 points in 1964 are both still Colt highs. His career point total was 678 on 113 touchdowns, which also stand as career records for the franchise.

Weeb Ewbank • Coach Weeb Ewbank led the Colts to consecutive world championships in 1958 and 1959 and compiled a 59-52-1 regular season record with the club over the course of a nine-year career. He left Baltimore in 1962 to take over the head coaching job with the New York Jets, a club he led to the Super Bowl Championship in 1968. The 16-7 win over the Baltimore Colts in that contest has been called one of the greatest upset wins of all time. His overall record in the NFL was 130-129-7 for regular season play, and 4-1 in post season action. He was the only coach to win titles in both the NFL and AFL. Ewbank was inducted into the Hall in 1978.

Johnny Unitas • Johnny Unitas, regarded by many as the greatest quarterback in the history of professional football, retired in 1973 with a barrel full of records. He was the first NFL quarterback to pass for more than 40,000 yards in a career, and still holds the record for consecutive games throwing a touchdown with 47. For four consecutive years he led the league in that statistic. He ended his career with NFL records in passes attempted (5,186), passes completed (2,830), total yards passing (40,239), most seasons with 3,000 or more yards passing (three), most games with 300 or more yards passing (26), and most career touchdown passes (290). He also set several postseason marks. While several of these records have since been broken, Unitas remains one of the NFL's all-time leaders in numerous passing categories. In his record 17 years as a Colt he set 22 major team records, was named as the NFL's most valuable player three times, played in ten Pro Bowls and was named All-Pro five times. He was inducted into the Hall of Fame in 1979.

Ted Hendricks • Ted "The Mad Stork" Hendricks, a towering, 6-7, 215-pound linebacker, played in 215 consecutive games, 70 with the Colts, 14 with the Green Bay Packers, and the final 131 with the Oakland Raiders. He was drafted in the second round by the Colts in 1969 after an All-American performance at the University of Miami. A five-time All-Pro, Hendricks also played in eight Pro Bowls. In his 15 years in the league he used his height to block 25 field goal or extra point attempts and was continuously among the league leaders in quarterback sacks and blocked passes. He recovered 16 opponent's fumbles and intercepted 20 passes over the course of his career, returning the latter for 332 yards. He scored an NFL record four safeties and recorded three touchdowns. In addition to playing on the Super Bowl V Championship Colt team, he was also a member of three Oakland Raider Super Bowl clubs.

John Mackey • John Mackey, the 6-2, 224-pound Syracuse University grad, was recognized as the prototype modern era tight end. An excellent blocker, he also had great hands and exceptional speed for a big man. He retired in 1977 after ten seasons in the NFL in which he pulled in 331 receptions, good for 5,236 yards and 28 touchdowns. Only the second tight end to be inducted into the Hall of Fame, Mackey was voted All-Pro three times and played on five Pro Bowl squads. Voted into the Hall in 1992, he was the ninth Colt to be so honored.

Continued from page 109

team's new general manager.

With Unitas finally showing signs of age, Coach Don Shula gone, and the disappointing 1969 season still fresh in everyone's memory, the odds against the Colts winning the Super Bowl in 1970 were formidable. But under new head Coach Don McCafferty the club swept to a 11-2-1 regular season record and a division title, topped Cincinnati 17-0 in the AFC Divisional Playoff, beat the Oakland Raiders 27-17 for the AFC Championship, then outfought the Dallas Cowboys in Super Bowl V, 16-13. In the Dallas game Colt rookie kicker Jim O'Brien kicked a field goal with only five seconds remaining before a crowd of 79,204 in the Orange Bowl in Miami.

Unitas connected on 166 passes during the season for 2,213 yards and 14 touchdowns. First round-draft pick Norm Bulaich led the team in rushing with 426 yards, while O'Brien hit on 36 of 38 conversions and 19 of 34 field goal attempts for 93 points. Dave Lee, Jerry Logan, Bubba Smith, and Rick Volk were voted All-Pro at the conclusion of the season, while Logan, Smith, and Mike Curtis were named to the Pro Bowl squad.

The club's record in 1971, 10-4-0, was a slight drop from their championship level of performance of the year before, but still earned the team second place in the AFC's Eastern Division, only a half game behind Miami. In the newly-expanded playoff format, however, it qualified them as a wild card entry in the playoffs. The Colts advanced to the AFC Championship game, where they were clobbered by Don Shula's Miami Dolphins, 21-0.

Johnny Unitas was once again injured during the season, and Coach Don McCafferty was forced to use Earl Morrall. The latter held the job until mid-season, when Unitas was well enough to return. Morrall's statistics—84 of 167 for 1,210 yards and seven scores—were actually a bit better than Unitas' 90 of 176 for 942 and only three TDs.

During the year, Norm Bulaich, who led the team in rushing with 741 yards, set a one-game yardage mark against the New York Jets, amassing 198 yards on 22 carries in a 22-0 Colt win. The total still stands as a team single-game rushing record. Ted Hendricks, Bubba Smith, and Rick Volk were named All-Pro, while Smith, Volk, Bulaich, Hendricks, Bill Curry, Mike Curtis, and Bob Vogel were named to the Pro Bowl.

Irsay and Rosenbloom Trade Teams

In July, in one of the most unusual transactions in the history of the NFL, Los Angeles Rams owner Robert Irsay traded his franchise to Carroll Rosenbloom for the Baltimore Colts, and then installed Joe Thomas as Baltimore's vice president and general manager. In the same month Gino Marchetti became the second Baltimore Colt to be elected to the NFL Hall of Fame.

The Colts' first season under the new regime was an inauspicious one. After the team had lost four of its first five games, Thomas began tearing the team apart, first firing Coach Don McCafferty and replacing him with John Sandusky. He then ordered Sandusky to bench Unitas and replace him with rookie quarterback Marty Domres. The Colts went on to win only five of 14 games, their first losing season in 16 years.

Before the season was over, Thomas had traded Unitas to San Diego and peddled off many of the team's top veterans, including Tom Matte, Bubba Smith, Jerry Logan, Fred Miller, Norm Bulaich, Bill Curry, Tom Nowatzke, and Don Sullivan. Watching all of his old teammates depart, Bob Vogel retired. While all this was going on, former Colt Head Coach Don Shula was leading the Miami Dolphins to an unbeaten season and to a Super Bowl Championship.

Domres completed 115 of 222 for 1,392 yards and 11 touchdowns for the season, while Unitas, in his 17th and final season as a Colt, hit on 88 of 157 for 1,111 yards and four touchdowns. For the first time in the club's history no Colt player was named All-Pro. Three made it to the Pro Bowl, however—Bill Curry, Ted Hendricks, and Bruce Laird.

In February 1973 Howard Schnellenberger was named the team's new head coach. With just about all of the team's key veterans gone, however, Schnellenberger and the Colts suffered through a dismal 4-10 season. Second year running back Lydell Mitchell was a lone bright spot, scampering for 963 yards. First-round draft pick Bert Jones started the season at quarterback, but gave way to incumbent Marty Domres after half of the season. No Colts made All-Pro, and only Ted Hendricks was named to the Pro Bowl squad. In July Raymond Berry and Jim Parker were inducted into the NFL Hall of Fame.

Baltimore continued its slide towards the NFL cellar in 1974. The Colts' record of only two wins and 12 losses was their worst performance since their return to the league in 1953. Lydell Mitchell again paced the running attack with 757 yards, and led the receivers as well with 72 catches for 544 yards. The 72 receptions was high for the entire league and was a new league record for running backs.

Bert Jones took over as the team's number-one signal caller and threw for 1,610 yards. No Colts were named All-Pro, and only Mike Curtis was voted to the Pro Bowl. On September 29 Colt VP and General Manager Joe Thomas fired Howard Schnellenberger as the team's head coach and took over those duties himself.

In January of 1975 Thomas divested himself of the team's head coaching responsibilities, naming former Washington Redskin offensive coordinator Ted Marchibroda as head coach. Marchibroda then launched once of the greatest turnarounds in professional football history, directing the club to a 10-4 record that brought the Colts from last in the division to first in one year.

After a decisive 35-7 Opening Day win over the Chicago Bears in the windy City, the Colts dropped four straight and appeared headed for another losing season. But then, beginning with a 45-28 slugfest win over the Jets in New York, the Colts won nine in a row to win the Eastern Division title. Lydell Mitchell became the franchise's first running back to reach 1,000 yards in one season, scampering to 1,193 on 289 carries. He also led the team in scoring with 15 touchdowns for 90 points.

During the year quarterback Bert Jones and second-year wide receiver Roger Carr combined on the longest scoring pass play in the team's history, a 90-yarder, as part of a 52-19 win over the Jets on November 16. Jones came into his own in 1975, completing 203 of 344 passes for 2,483 yards and 18 touchdowns. The defense also improved, led by linebacker Stan White's eight interceptions, a league record for interceptions at that position.

After that tremendous comeback effort, the season ended for the Colts on a losing note. In the AFC Divisional Playoff, Baltimore was eliminated by the defending Super Bowl Champion Pittsburgh Steelers, 28-10.

In August Lenny Moore became the fifth Colt to be inducted into the NFL Hall of Fame. After an absence of four years, Baltimore again had a representative on the All-Pro Team, tackle George Kunz. He, along with Lydell Mitchell and defensive end John Dutton made the Pro Bowl squad.

In 1976 head coach Ted Marchibroda led the Colts to an 11-3 mark and their second straight Eastern Division crown. But, as in 1975, Baltimore was beaten in the first AFC Divisional Playoff game by the Pittsburgh Steelers, 40-14.

During the season the team had amassed 417 points, the second highest total in club history. Lydell Mitchell ran for 1,200 yards, breaking his own record from the year before. He also led in receptions again, hauling in 60 for 555 yards. Kicker Toni Linhart hit on 49 of 51 extra points and 20 of 27 field goal tries for 109 points, the most points ever booted in one season by a Colt kicker. Quarterback Bert Jones threw for 3,104 yards and 24 touchdowns, both highs for him, on 207 completions. He was intercepted only nine times and his completion percentage, 60.4, was higher than any Colt passer had ever achieved. Second-year running back Howard Stevens led the team in both kickoff and punt returns.

Two Colts, defensive end John Dutton and quarterback Jones, were named All-Pro; the same two were joined by Roger Carr, George Kunz, Toni Linhart, and Lydell Mitchell on the Pro Bowl team.

The Colts won their first five games of the 1977 season and nine of the first 10 en route to their third Eastern Division title under Marchibroda, but were eliminated once again in the first round of the playoffs, this time by the Oakland Raiders in two overtimes, 37-31.

For the fifth year in a row running back Lydell Mitchell led the team in rushing, totaling 1,159 yards, and also led the team in receiving for the fourth consecutive year, hauling in 71 for 620 yards. Quarterback Bert Jones hit on 224 passes for 2,686 yards. Despite their division winning season, no Colts were named All-Pro, although Mike Burns, John Dutton, George Kunz, Toni Linhart and Lydell Mitchell represented Baltimore at the Pro Bowl.

Szymanski Named G.M.

In January former Colt player Dick Szymanski (1955-68) was named as the team's new general manager. The team collapsed in dramatic fashion in 1978, blundering to a 5-11 record. It almost seemed as if the three straight AFC Divisional Playoff losses had taken something out of the team. The defensive side of the ball proved particularly troublesome for the squad. The defense was a sieve, allowing 421 points, the most since the franchise re-entered the league in 1953.

Shortly before the beginning of the 1979 season, former head coach Weeb Ewbank was inducted into the NFL Hall of Fame in recognition of his stewardship of championship clubs, both in Baltimore and New York. He was followed into the Hall a year later by John Unitas, another figure from the Colts' hallowed past.

As in 1978, the Colts got off to a miserable start, losing their first five games. A mid-season recovery was followed by another five straight losses and a second 5-11 season, and the handwriting was on the wall for Marchibroda. Despite their won-loss mark, the team had one of the most potent passing attacks in the league. Greg Landry had taken over as quarterback, and he attempted a team record 457 passes, completing 270, also a record, all for a total of 2,932 yards. Joe Washington caught 82 of the lobs, also a new Colt high.

An improved showing under new head coach Mike McCormack brought the team back into contention again in 1980. On November 30 the club's record was 7-6, and it appeared as if a winning season was a good possibility, but a heartbreaking 43-33 loss to the Bengals in Cincinnati and two more losses at home gave the Colts a 7-9 mark and a fourth place finish. The smallest home crowd in 26 years, 29,936, saw the finale against the Kansas City Chiefs, a 38-28 loss.

Bert Jones reclaimed the team's quarterbacking duties and completed 248 of 440 passes for 3,134 yards and 23 touchdowns. Number one draft pick Curtis Dickey paced all Baltimore runners with 800 yards and 11 scores. As in 1978, no Colts were named All-Pro or to the Pro Bowl game.

A Decade to Forget

Coach Mike McCormack's second year as the Colt's skipper resulted in more losses, 14, than any Colt team in history had ever suffered. Opponents ran wild, scoring a total of 533 points, the most ever given up by a Colt team. Had it not been for two victories over the New England Patriots, the Colts would have been completely blanked. Home attendance, which only a few seasons earlier had been averaging close to 60,000, was down to 336,652, an average of only about 21,000.

In December, former Arizona State University coach Frank Kush was named the team's new head coach. Kush proved unable to arrest the team's slide ever downward, however, as the club did not win a game. In a season shortened because of the NFL players' strike, the Colts lost eight of the nine contests they played. A 20-20 tie with the Green Bay Packers late in the year had to serve as the high point of the season.

By virtue of the club's horrible performance the season before, the Colts were awarded the number one selection in the April 1983 NFL draft and picked Stanford All-American John Elway.

Six days later, after Elway said he would not play in Baltimore, the team traded him to Denver for the Broncos' 1983 first round pick, tackle Chris Hinton, reserve quarterback Mark Herrmann, and Denver's first round pick in 1984.

During the course of the 1983 season, Frank Hush's squad forged a major turnaround, winning seven games after winning none in the previous year. At one point the Colts had a 6-4 record, but five losses in the last six games game them a 7-9 mark and a fourth-place finish in the division.

Quarterback Mike Pagel, who first started the year before, had an improved year with 163 completions and 2,353 total yards. Kicker Rohn Stark's 45.3 punting average led the entire NFL and earned him All-Pro honors. Curtis Dickey became only the second running back in Colt history to top a thousand yards, getting 1,122 on 254 carries. Stark was named All-Pro, a rarity for any Colt during this period of the team's existence, while Chris Hinton was named to the Pro Bowl.

A New Home

On March 28, 1984, Colt owner Robert Irsay made millions of pro football fans in Indiana happy when he moved the club franchise from Baltimore to Indianapolis. He enraged an equal number back in Maryland. On April 18 the team opened season ticket sales in its new home; within two weeks more than 143,000 had applied. A week later Irsay's son, Jim Irsay, was named general manager of the club.

After all of this, the season itself was almost an anti-climax. An overflow crowd of 60,388 packed the stadium in Indianapolis on September 2 for the Colts' battle with the New York Jets. To the disappointment of the hometowners, the New Yorkers prevailed 23-l4. The new Colt faithful had to wait until the third home game of the year for a win, 31-17 over the Buffalo Bills.

The team never jelled, however, and finished with a 4-12 record. Despite the lack of success on the field, a new team attendance mark was set, 481,304, an average of more than 60,000 a game. Frank Kush was terminated after the 35-17 loss to the Miami Dolphins in the next to the last game of the season. Hal Hunter served as an interim coach for the final, a 16-10 loss to New England. Following the season Rod Dow-hower was named the team's new head coach.

The team's fortunes did not improve in 1985. In Dowhower's first year, Indianapolis finished at 5-11 and another fourth place finish in the division. With the exception of the strike-shortened 1982 season, when the division setup was scrapped, it was the fifth year in a row that the team had finished fourth.

Kicker Rohn Stark's 45.9 punting average was not only the tops in the league for the year, it was the highest in Colt history. Quarterback Mike Pagel had his best year passing, connecting on 199 of 399 for 2,414 yards and 15 touchdowns. Randy McMillan again led the ground attack with 858 yards and a 4.5 per-carry-average. Colt runners totalled 2,439 yards for the season, tops in their conference. Stark and Chris Hinton represented the team on the Pro Bowl squad.

For the second time since the move to Indianapolis three years earlier, a Colt coach was replaced in mid-season. This time it was Rod Dowhower, who was given the ax in 1986 after the team lost its first 12 games. The naming of Ron Meyer as his replacement had immediate effect, as the Colts won their last three games to finish at 3-13. Despite the late rally, however, Indianapolis finished in fifth place in the division. It marked the team's ninth consecutive losing season.

Rohn Stark again led the NFL in punting average, this time with a 45.2 average. Rookie Jack Trudeau took over at quarterback, passing for 2,225 yards on 204 of 417 passes. No Colts were named All-Pro, but Ray Donaldson, Chris Hinton, and Stark were voted onto the Pro Bowl squad.

Under head coach Ron Meyer's direction, the Colts put together their first winning season since moving to Indianapolis, their first in fact in ten years. The season hardly started off as if a winning year was on hand, as the Colts dropped their first two regular season games, both of which were played at home. But with the addition of running back Eric Dickerson and a vastly improved defense, the team won nine of its next 13 to finish at 9-6.

The record was good enough for first place in the Eastern Division. (Only 15 games were played in the league during the year as one contest for each team was canceled due to a NFL player strike.) Dickerson had been acquired from the Los Angeles Rams in a three-way trade in which the Colts sent first round draft pick Cornelius Bennett to the Buffalo Bills and the Rams received six draft choices and two players.

Dickerson became the third Colt running back to top a thousand yards in a single season, just topping the mark with 1,011 in 223 carries. On December 27, in the regular season finale, Dickerson galloped for 196 yards in a win over Tampa Bay, the second-highest running total in Colt history. In the playoffs the Colts dropped their fifth consecutive post season contest, losing to the Cleveland Browns 38-21.

Dickerson was named All-Pro for his efforts, and along with Dean Biasucci, Duane Bickett, Ray Donaldson, Chris Hinton, and Ron Solt, represented Indianapolis at the annual Pro Bowl game.

Despite a second straight winning season in 1988, the Colts did not qualify for the playoffs. During the campaign Eric Dickerson set a number of club records, including total yards rushing (1,659) and total carries (388). He shattered Lydell Mitchell's old team rushing mark by 459 yards. He also tallied four touchdowns against Denver on October 31, a game witnessed by 60,544 fans, a new attendance record for the team in Indianapolis. It was also the first Monday night game played by the team in Indianapolis.

In 1989 the Colts lost their opening game, the sixth consecutive year the club had done so. The Colts were competitive, however, in part because of the arrival of fleet wide receiver Andre Rison, their first round draft pick. The club harbored hopes for a winning season until the season finale, a 41-6 drubbing at the hands of the New Orleans Saints.

During the year defensive back Keith Taylor ran back seven interceptions a total of 225 yards for a club and league record 32.1 average. Another club mark was set by punt returner Clarence Verdin, who ran back 23 of them for 296 yards and a 12.9 average. That average was higher than any Colt punt returner had ever managed in more than four decades.

On the offensive side of the ball, quarterback Jack Trudeau completed 180 of 362 passes for 2,317 yards, with his favorite target Bill Brandy, who caught 63 for 919 yards, the highest yardage total in receiving by a Colt player in a decade. Eric

AP/Wide World Photos

Eric Dickerson

Dickerson had his third 1,000 yard season for the Colts, totaling 1,311 on 314 carries, the second highest rushing total in club history. There were no Colt All-Pros, although Dickerson, Ray Donaldson, and Chris Hinton made it to the Pro Bowl.

In 1990 Ted Hendricks became the eighth Colt to be inducted into the NFL Hall of Fame. The induction of the "Stork," as he had long been known, served as a reminder to the club of its glory days, when the Colts were routinely regarded as a championship contender.

Prior to the 1990 season the Colts gave up their first round pick from the previous year, Andre Rison, along with six-time Pro Bowler Chris Hinton and their first round pick in 1991 to the Atlanta Falcons for the rights to Illinois quarterback Jeff George. In his first year as a pro George hit on 181 of 334 passes for 2,152 yards and 16 scores.

Eric Dickerson, meanwhile, had his worst year in the NFL with only 677 yards. The team as a whole, however, continued its pattern of mediocrity. The Colts stumbled out of the box, again losing their first two games on their way to a 7-9 season, the first losing one under Ron Meyer.

The 1991 season was a complete disaster for the Indianapolis Colts; the 15 losses the team suffered was an all-time high and only a 28-27 squeaker over the New York Jets in the tenth game prevented the season from being a washout. Meyer was fired after five games and replaced by Rick Venturi. After the season, former coach Ted Marchibroda, who had been the Buffalo Bills' offensive coordinator for the previous five years, was lured back to his old post.

The Colts also gave up on running back Eric Dickerson, who had not only made his displeasure in Indianapolis most evident, but had experienced his worst season in the pro ranks, managing only 536 yards on 167 carries for a career low 3.2 average. Punter Rohn Stark continued his amazing string of season, however, averaging 42.6 yards a kick for the year, the tenth straight season he had averaged 40 yards or more for the club.

Jeff George attempted and completed more passes than anyone in Colt history, putting the ball in the air 485 times and completing 292 for 2,910 yards. The offensive line assigned to protect him, however, was a poor one. George took a heavy beating from opposing teams throughout the season.

In Ted Marchibroda's first term as the Colts' head coach in 1975, his 10-4 record, after the previous year's mark of 2-12, was hailed as the biggest turnaround in NFL history. In 1992, in his return to the job, he did it again. Indianapolis' 9-7 finish, following the 1-15 debacle of 1991, was by any account a significant achievement.

Buttressed by the addition of young stars such as defensive tackle Steve Emtman, the Colts dramatically improved their defensive totals. The offense, however, continued to struggle, and George was injured for part of the season, but replacement Jack Trudeau filled in admirably. The season also gave long-suffering Colts fans some hope that their long playoff drought might end sometime in the near future.

—Jack Pearson

MIAMI DOLPHINS

Entering the American Football League as an expansion team in 1966, the Miami Dolphins launched their story in impressive fashion. In their first regular season game, against the Oakland Raiders on September 2, 1966, Miami receiver Joe Auer took the opening kickoff and galloped 95 yards for a touchdown. The history of the Dolphins would echo that achievement—but not immediately. Miami lost the opener to the Raiders, 23-14, and finished in a tie for last place in the Eastern Division of the AFL in 1966 under head coach George Wilson. Three more losing seasons preceded the remarkable breakthrough that made the Dolphins an NFL powerhouse (the AFL having been merged into the NFL in 1970) and saw their head coach, Don Shula, who took over in 1970, go on to become the winningest coach in pro football history.

In the early years of the franchise the stars included quarterback Bob Griese (whose No. 12 jersey became the first Dolphin number to be retired), fullback Larry Csonka, wide receiver Paul Warfield, center Jim Langer, and guard Larry Little. After 1981 the name Dan Marino, like that of Don Shula, became almost synonymous with the Miami Dolphins. In a recent Dolphins' media guide the exploits of quarterback Dan Marino take up more than 28 pages. Marino has set a number of all-time NFL passing records over the years, including the only 5,000-yard passing season (5,084 yards, 1984) in the history of the pro game. He ranks as one of the great quarterbacks of all time.

Since the 1970 merger of the National and American football leagues, the Dolphins have won more games than any other team in professional football. They have the best regular-season record and the highest winning percentage of any NFL team during that span. Indeed, from 1970 through 1992 the Dolphins, with a 229-113-2 regular-season mark, have the best winning percentage (.669) of any of the combined 105 teams in the four major professional sports in the United States—the National Football League, Major League Baseball, the National Basketball Association, and the National Hockey League. The Dolphins have suffered only two losing seasons over this 23-year period.

New Kids in the AFL

In March 1965 Joseph Robbie, a Minneapolis lawyer, met with American Football League Commissioner Joe Foss in Washington. Foss suggested that Robbie apply for an AFL expansion franchise in Miami. Upon learning from Mayor Robert King High of Miami that the Orange Bowl stadium would be available for a pro team, Robbie forged ahead. When the AFL executive committee voted its first expansion, Miami got the nod. The franchise went to Joe Robbie and television star Danny Thomas for $7.5 million.

In the first round of the AFL's college draft Miami chose quarterback Rick Norton from the University of Kentucky and running back Jim Grabowski from Illinois. In the twelfth round they chose Tulsa wide receiver Howard Twilley, a player who would be a Dolphin stalwart for more than a decade. Miami got another long-termer in the 31-player expansion draft, tackle Norm Evans from the Houston Oilers. Evans would put in ten good seasons for the Dolphins. Most of the original players would be gone, however, by the time the team started to post winning records in the 1970s.

The head coach who inherited these draft picks was George Wilson, hired in late January 1966 after eight years as head coach of the Detroit Lions and a year as an assistant coach with the Washington Redskins. Wilson, known as a fine handler of players, was generally pleased with the players the Dolphins had chosen from among the rookies and rejects. Nevertheless, problems were apparent at all positions in Miami's inaugural season, particularly at quarterback, where injuries eventually led George Wilson, Jr., the coach's son, to play the position for a while.

The Dolphins' first win, a 24-7 triumph over the Broncos, came on October 16, 1966, with George Wilson, Jr., at quarterback. Miami defeated the Houston Oilers, 20-13, the Sunday after that, then lost six straight before edging Houston again in the final game, 29-28, to finish at 3-11-0 in their first season.

For the final game the quarterbacking was done by John Stofa. Wilson expressed satisfaction with the outcome: "Those fans were sure making noise behind us and urging us on." The problem was, there were too few of those fans. Despite co-owner Danny Thomas's smiling salesmanship of the team, there were only 20,045 spectators at the cavernous Orange Bowl as the Dolphins closed out their first year.

When the 1967 season began, the Dolphins had a new quarterback, rookie Bob Griese of Purdue, chosen in the first round of the March draft. When Stofa broke his ankle in the season opener against the Broncos, Griese took over and directed the team to a 35-21 win. But after that the Dolphins lost eight games in a row and were faced with the prospect of a worse season than 1966.

Then in game ten, with 61 seconds remaining on the clock, Griese hit wide receiver Howard Twilley with a 31-yard touchdown pass for a come-from-behind 17-14 victory over the Buffalo Bills. After losing a hard-fought contest to the Oilers, the Dolphins, with a 2-9-0 record, went on a rampage, clobbering the San Diego Chargers, 41-24, with Griese completing eight passes to rookie receiver Jack Clancy. Next week, against the Boston Patriots, Miami again scored freely, racking up a 41-32 win. A loss to Houston in the season finale gave the Dolphins a 4-10-0 record for the season.

Optimism ran high in 1968. In the first round of the draft Miami chose Syracuse University fullback Larry Csonka. The Dolphins also signed halfback Jim Kiick of Wyoming, tackle Doug Crusan of Indiana, and safety Dick Anderson of Colorado. On August 31 an AFL-record crowd of 68,125 packed the Orange Bowl to see an interleague game between Miami and the NFL's Baltimore Colts. The Colts, coached by Don Shula

Team Information at a Glance

Founding date: 1966

Home stadium: Joe Robbie Stadium
2269 Northwest 199th Street
Phone: (305) 620-5000
Seating capacity: 73,000

Team colors: Aqua, coral, and white
Team nickname: Dolphins
Logo: Leaping dolphin wearing a football helmet featured against a stylized coral hoop

Franchise record*	Won	Lost	Tie
(1966-92)	260	164	4

*including playoffs

at the time, prevailed, 22-13. Miami wide receiver Jack Clancy suffered a left knee injury in a game that took him out for the season. When the regular season started, running back Jack Harper and tight end Doug Moreau were also sidelined with injuries. The tank at the Orange Bowl that held the dolphin "Flipper," mascot of the team, was also a casualty, ruined by the salt that had to be added to the water in it.

The 1968 Dolphins started poorly, losing to Houston, then to Oakland, then succumbing to the Kansas City Chiefs, 48-3. "Bring back Flipper," cried the fans.

Flipper stayed away, but the gridiron Dolphins barged back, trouncing the Oilers in their second meeting of the season, 24-7, tying Buffalo, 14-14, and beating the Cincinnati Bengals, 24-22. But the rest of the season was uneven, and the Dolphins came in at 5-8-1, good for third place in the AFL Eastern Division. On the ground, rookies Larry Csonka and Jim Kiick worked well in tandem, while in the air Bob Griese connected for 2,473 yards, a club record at the time.

Coach Wilson appeared pleased with the progress of the Dolphins, but owner Robbie was not. "We could have done much better," Robbie said. "We were spotty all year." Nor did he rush to give Wilson a new contract. When he did offer one, it was for a single season. The message was clear: produce or leave.

Wilson and the Dolphins did not produce in 1969. Several of the losses were close, but not until the seventh game, against the Buffalo Bills, did Miami manage to win. By then George Wilson's fate was probably sealed. Certainly it was sealed at the end of the season, with the Dolphins back in the cellar at 3-10-1.

And yet Miami had the nucleus of a first-rate team. Bob Griese, Larry Csonka, Jim Kiick, and Howard Twilley were joined in 1969 by linebacker Nick Buoniconti, obtained from the Patriots in a trade. Another trade brought guard Larry Little, a future Hall of Famer, from the San Diego Chargers. And the Dolphins signed several outstanding rookies that year, among them defensive end Bill Stanfill, defensive tackle Bob Heinz, cornerback

Lloyd Mumpford, and halfback Mercury Morris. Neither George Wilson nor Joe Thomas, the Dolphins' head talent scout (who resigned after the 1971 draft), would be around to share in the triumphant days ahead.

Don Shula Leads the Way

The Dolphins new head coach was Don Shula, hired away from Baltimore, where his Colts had posted a glittering 73-26-4 record between 1963 and 1969. George Wilson left Miami gracefully, saying, "I wish Don all the luck in the world. I think he'll succeed in a big way. This team is just about ready."

Wilson was right. The team was ready. In 1970 the Dolphins vaulted into second place in the Eastern Division of the new American Conference of the National Football League (the AFL and NFL having merged). Their 10-4-0 performance made them a wild-card qualifier for the playoffs. Wilson had helped to build the team, but it was under Shula that Miami jumped all the way from the basement to a shot at Super Bowl V.

The Dolphins lost their first game under Shula, falling to the Boston Patriots, 27-14. But brighter Sundays lay ahead. Miami defeated the Houston Oilers, Oakland Raiders, New York Jets (for the first time ever), and Buffalo Bills before running into the Cleveland Browns. The Browns, minus star wide receiver Paul Warfield, whom they had traded to the Dolphins earlier in the year, shut out Miami, 28-0, before 75,313 fans in the Orange Bowl, the largest crowd in their history up to that point. The club then took a shellacking at Baltimore the following week, losing to the Colts, 35-0.

After a third consecutive loss, this one to the Philadelphia Eagles, 24-17, the Dolphins turned up the heat and won the last six games of the regular season. One of these wins was a 34-17 drubbing of the Colts, and another—the final game—was a 45-7 romp over the Buffalo Bills.

The Dolphins' first playoff game pitted them against the Raiders in Oakland on December 27, 1970. Miami took a 7-0 lead on a Griese-to-Warfield touchdown pass. But the Raiders fought back, building up a 21-7 margin in the fourth quarter. Griese tossed a short pass to wide receiver Willie Richardson in the end zone to make the score 21-14, but the Dolphins could pull no closer. Although the Dolphins would sit out the Super Bowl, the franchise had done far better in 1970 than anyone had really expected. The team was young, and the future looked bright.

The Dolphins were so good in 1971 that Miami sportswriters rushed out to sign book contracts to chronicle the ascendancy. They should have waited a year, as it happened, for 1972, not 1971, stands out as the season of seasons. Still, 1971 was a fine one for the Dolphins. The Miami

Larry Czonka

offense had talent aplenty, with cool, imaginative quarterback Bob Griese, stellar deep receiver Paul Warfield, steady short receiver Howard Twilley, power rushers Larry Csonka and Jim Kiick, and lightning-fast running back Mercury Morris.

When fourth down arrived and the Dolphins were within kicking range, Garo Yepremian could be counted on. Indeed, the Miami placekicker paced the NFL with 117 points. The 1971 Dolphins finished with a 10-3-1 record, barely nosing out the Baltimore Colts for the AFC Eastern Division title by beating the Green Bay Packers in the final week of the regular season while the Colts were being upset by the New England (formerly Boston) Patriots.

In the divisional playoff game, on Christmas Day, 1971, Miami and Kansas City tangled in the longest game in pro football history (82 minutes, 40 seconds). In the second overtime, with the score tied 24-24, the Dolphins advanced far enough into Chiefs' territory to permit Yepremian to try for a 37-yard field goal. He put the ball through the uprights and Miami won, 27-24, advancing to play the Colts for the AFC crown.

In the regular season the Dolphins had won one and lost one against the Baltimore club led by Johnny Unitas. This time around it was no contest, as the Dolphins blanked the Colts, 21-0. It was the first time in 97 games and seven seasons that Baltimore had been shut out. The Dolphins advanced to the Super Bowl, where they faced the Dallas Cowboys. For Dolphin fans, Super Bowl VI, played at Tulane Stadium in New Orleans, proved to be a gloomy anticlimax to a great season. The Cowboys dominated from start to finish in an easy 24-3 win. Sharp passing by Roger Staubach and a 252-yard Dallas rushing attack humbled Shula's squad and thwarted Miami's first bid for the world championship.

Then came 1972. There has never been another season like it in NFL history. Even before it got underway, the Miami front office was happy, having sold a then-record 69,303 season tickets. Yet all did not go smoothly. On October 15, after four straight Miami wins, quarterback Bob Griese went out with a broken right leg and dislocated

Paul Warfield

ankle. Thirty-eight-year-old Earl Morrall, obtained on waivers from Baltimore, replaced him. Miami kept on winning.

On December 16, in their last regular season game, the Dolphins shut out the Colts 16-0. It was their fourteenth consecutive victory, making them the only team ever to have gone 14-0-0 in the regular season. The Miami defense, known as the "No-Name Defense" because of its lack of well-known players, allowed the fewest points in the NFL.

Fullback Larry Csonka and running back Mercury Morris each rushed for 1,000 yards or more—the first time in NFL history that one team could boast of two 1000-yard rushers in the same season.

After defeating the Cincinnati Bengals, 34-16, in the American Conference playoff game, the Dolphins triumphed again, 21-17, over the Pitts-

UNSUNG HEROES | **Miami's No-Name Defense**

The Dolphins owed much of their success in 1972—a perfect 17-0-0 season—to their so-called No-Name Defense. Of course, many of the No-Names became well known as time passed and the victories accumulated. But when the season started, the only familiar name among the Miami defenders, at least to most fans, was that of middle linebacker Nick Buoniconti. He had been a star at Notre Dame and later for the Patriots in the American Football League. Buoniconti, an attorney in the off-season (and after his retirement from pro football), was the graybeard on defense at age 31. When the AFL merged with the NFL in 1970, Buoniconti was chosen as the all-time AFL middle linebacker. "He's really not tall enough (5'11") to play middle linebacker," head coach Don Shula once observed, "but he's always in the right place. And he's quick as a cat."

In an article in *Sports Illustrated,* writer Tex Maule noted, tongue in cheek, that Buoniconti "is flanked by outside linebackers Nos. 57 and 59," thus emphasizing his teammates' lack of name recognition. No. 57 was Mike Kolen from Auburn University, a Dolphin from 1970 through 1977, and No. 59 was Doug Swift from Amherst, a member of the Miami club from 1970 to 1975. Among the best known of the other No-Names (as the season progressed) were ends Manny Fernandez and Bill Stanfill, tackle Bob Heinz, and safeties Dick Anderson and Jake Scott.

There were several occasions during the Dolphins' famous perfect season in which the club was in danger of falling. Each time, the defense did its part to snare victory. In their second encounter against the New York Jets in 1972, with the Dolphins going for their tenth consecutive win, the Jets took a 14-7 lead prior to halftime and threatened to score again, intercepting an Earl Morrall pass and gaining a first down on the Dolphins' nine-yard line. The Miami defense held, however, and the Jets were forced to settle for a field goal.

The Dolphins still had to fight back from a 17-7 deficit, which they did successfully. Running back Mercury Morris led the way, picking up 107 yards in 23 carries. The Miami defense continued to hold, the Dolphins began to score, and (on the heels of their 52-0 trouncing of the New England Patriots the week before), they were happy to settle for 28-24 victory over New York.

After the game, Shula said, "We have had a big-play defense all year, and it made the big plays today just when we needed them." The No-Name Defense continued to make the plays. The Dolphins won four more regular season games, both of their AFC playoff games, and emerged victorious from Super Bowl VII at Los Angeles to cap their flawless season.

burgh Steelers to take the AFC title. That made it 16 straight victories in the 1972 campaign, leaving January's Super Bowl VIII as the last remaining hurdle on the road to a perfect record.

On January 14, 1973, in Los Angeles, the Dolphins beat the Washington Redskins, 14-7, to secure the world championship and complete the season with a 17-0-0 record, the only team to be unbeaten and untied throughout an entire NFL season.

A Winning Decade

Not only were Don Shula's Dolphins apparently invincible, they were also young. A second perfect season seemed a real possibility to many, but in the second game of the 1973 season Miami lost a heartbreaker to Oakland, 12-7, after which they resumed their winning streak. In the next to last game of the season, however, the Baltimore Colts upset them, 16-3. An easy final-game win over the Detroit Lions, 34-7, gave the Dolphins, divisional winners in a walk, a 12-2-0 regular-season record.

The No-Name Defense held opposing teams to 150 points over the course of the season, while the classy Miami offense of Griese, Csonka, Warfield, Little, and the rest piled up 343 points. Once again the postseason play of the Dolphins was close to flawless; they brushed aside Cincinnati, 34-16, in the divisional playoff, defeated Oakland, 27-10, to capture an unprecedented third consecutive AFC crown, then defeated the Minnesota Vikings, 24-7, in Super Bowl VII at Rice Stadium in Houston.

In the game against the Vikings, fullback Larry Csonka carried the ball 33 times and gained 145 yards on the ground, a Super Bowl record. So dominant were Shula's Dolphins that they invited comparison with Vince Lombardi's great Green Bay Packer teams of earlier days.

Nor were they finished yet. In 1974 the Dolphins' 11-3-0 mark earned them another first place in the AFC East. There were signs of trouble, though. That March the short-lived World Football League signed Larry Csonka, Jim Kiick, and Paul Warfield to play for a new Toronto team in 1975.

AP/Wide World Photos

Don Shula

Then a seven-week players' strike, from early July through mid-August, saw a number of veteran players, including Jim Langer and Mercury Morris, cross the picket line, which created further internal bitterness.

During the 1974 season, injuries to key players—among them Csonka, Warfield, and Morris—slowed down the Dolphin attack. All in all, Miami's march toward the divisional title through this miasma of trouble was a remarkable one.

In the final regular-season game at the Orange Bowl on December 15, the Dolphins fell 24 points behind the New England Patriots. After 30 consecutive wins (not including preseason games) at the Orange Bowl in Miami, it looked as if the team would finally succumb. But with quarterback Earl Morrall passing for 288 yards, the Dolphins roared back to win, 34-27. The momentum did not carry over into postseason play, however, as Oakland took the semifinal game, 28-26, thwarting the Dolphins' bid to win a fourth straight AFC championship.

For four seasons, beginning in 1975, the Dolphins encountered frustration in a variety of ways. In 1975 offensive stalwarts Csonka, Kiick, and Warfield were off playing in the WFL, while injuries decimated the Miami defensive unit, sidelining, among others, Nick Buoniconti, Bill Stanfill, Manny Fernandez, Dick Anderson, and Bob Heinz.

The Dolphins had some good days, as when they buried the New York Jets, 43-0, on October 19, intercepting Joe Namath six times. They also had some bad days, as on November 23, when Bob Griese suffered torn tendons in his right foot in a contest against New England, giving way to the 41-year-old Earl Morrall. Morrall subsequently hurt his knee. That left the quarterbacking duties to third-stringer Don Strock, who performed creditably in a 31-21 victory over the Buffalo Bills.

But Miami's 10-4-0 overall record, the same

as Baltimore's, included two losses to the Colts. On that basis, the NFL awarded first place in the AFC Eastern Division to Baltimore, leaving the Dolphins out of postseason play for the first time in Don Shula's six years at the helm.

After an injury-plagued 1976 season in which Miami fell to 6-8-0, the team rebounded to tie the Baltimore Colts for the divisional lead in 1977 despite the retirements of Nick Buoniconti and Earl Morrall. Bob Griese donned eyeglasses in 1977 after having difficulties with his contact lenses. The spectacles did not affect his performance. On Thanksgiving Day he became the first quarterback since 1972 to throw six touchdown passes in a game, contributing to a 55-14 rout of the St. Louis Cardinals. It was a record high score for the Dolphins and included record high yardage for them of 503 yards.

Once again, though, the league's tiebreaker system worked against the Dolphins. This time the Colts won the title on the basis of a better conference record (9-3-0) than Miami's (8-4-0). Both teams posted 10-4-0 records overall. For the third straight year the Dolphins sat out the playoffs.

In 1978 Miami again tied for the divisional lead with an 11-5-0 mark, the same record posted by New England. But the Patriots, having done better against Eastern Division opponents, were awarded the title. This time, though, the Dolphins got a wild-card chance in the playoffs, only to lose to the Houston Oilers in the first round. Aided by five Dolphin turnovers and subpar passing by sore-ribbed Bob Griese at the Orange Bowl, the Oilers, quarterbacked by broken-ribbed Dan Pastorini, plodded to a 17-9 victory.

Apparently, the only sure way for Miami to capture the AFC Eastern Division title was to win more games than anyone else. The club did so in 1979. Larry Csonka, now 32, was back after one season in the WFL and three seasons with the New York Giants. The 1979 Dolphins won their first four games, stumbled, then took three of their last four, and ended the season with a 10-6-0 record, good for undisputed first place. Miami never got past the divisional playoffs, however. The Pittsburgh Steelers (eventually the Super Bowl champions) took their measure, 34-14, in a game at Pittsburgh.

The Dolphins, a strong team throughout the 1970s, never quite recaptured the magic of 1972, their perfect season. Still, from 1970 through 1979 their cumulative regular-season record under Don Shula was 104-39-1. They appeared in three Super Bowls, winning two. Five players from this great decade for the Dolphins have since been elected to the Pro Football Hall of Fame: Larry Csonka, Bob Griese, Jim Langer, Larry Little, and Paul Warfield.

End of an Era

The 1980 season saw two superstars fade into the sunset. One was hard-driving fullback Larry Csonka, who tried to renegotiate his contract after a good season in 1979. Instead, the Dolphins released him. The other was Bob Griese, the Dolphins' "thinking man's quarterback" since 1967, whose ailing right shoulder kept him on the bench for much of 1980. He did come off it to engineer a couple of fourth-quarter rallies, but after the October 15 loss to the Baltimore Colts, Griese did not play again.

His replacement, rookie David Woodley from Louisiana State, performed well but was not the quarterback of the future. Despite solid defense, the 1980 team lacked a certain spark and could do no better than a third-place finish behind the Patriots and Jets.

After 1980 the Dolphins took the AFC Eastern Division title for five straight seasons. Shula, who recorded his 200th NFL coaching victory in 1981, confirmed his reputation as a master strategist by continuing to win even as his coterie of Hall-of-Famers from the 1970s departed.

Six-time All-Pro guard Larry Little retired before the 1981 season. Young linebacker Rusty Chambers was killed in an automobile accident in Hammond, Louisiana. Shula built with what he had. David Woodley did the quarterbacking, spelled now and then by veteran Don Strock.

GREAT MATCHUPS | **December 17, 1984**

On December 17, 1984, the Miami Dolphins defeated the Dallas Cowboys, 28-21, for their 14th win of the regular season. The Dolphins had lost only to the San Diego Chargers in overtime (34-28) and the L.A. Raiders (45-34). The club subsequently charged through the playoffs to secure the AFC Championship. The Super Bowl would be a major disappointment for Miami fans, though, as the San Franciso 49ers won handily.

But the game against the Cowboys was one for the record books—literally. When Dolphin quarterback Dan Marino connected with wide receiver Nat Moore on a 22-yard pass in the first quarter, he surpassed Dan Fouts's all-time single-season passing record of 4,802 yards. Five plays later, on a scoring pass from Marino to Mark Clayton, the Dolphins set an NFL record for the most touchdowns in a season, 67. The Dolphins added three more TDs in the game to give the team the current record of 70 regular season TDs.

Finally, yet another milestone was set by Marino in the contest against the Cowboys. Marino completed 23 of 40 passes for 340 yards in the game; in doing so, the talented young quarterback became not only the holder of the single-season passing record, but, with 5,084 aerial yards, the only quarterback in league history to top 5,000 yards.

Other records fell that day as well. Wide receiver Mark Clayton gathered in three touchdown passes to give him 18 for the season, a record at the time (since surpassed by the 49ers Jerry Rice). Two players broke a Dolphin team record in the game—wide receivers Mark Clayton and Mark Duper—both of whom erased the prior Miami marks for number of pass receptions and reception yardage in one season. Clayton caught 73 passes for 1,389 yards; Duper snared 71 for 1,306 yards.

Apart from the record-shattering performances, the game against the Cowboys was exciting right down to the wire. Dallas tied the game, 21-21, with one minute and 40 seconds left to play. That proved to be enough time for Dan Marino. With 51 seconds left, he threw a touchdown pass to Mark Clayton that covered 63 yards. It was Marino's fourth scoring pass of the game, and it gave the Dolphins their 28-21 victory.

Third-year running back Tony Nathan led the Dolphins in rushing, while wide receivers Duriel Harris and Jimmy Cefalo (comprising something of a No-Name Offense) registered the most yards on pass receptions.

The Dolphins cruised to an 11-4-0 first-place finish, but lost their AFC playoff game to the San Diego Chargers in overtime in a thrill-packed, high-scoring game at the Orange Bowl on January 2, 1982. Reserve quarterback Don Strock came off the bench with the Dolphins down by 24 points. The team rallied behind him, and by the end of the third quarter the score was 31-31. Early in the fourth quarter a 12-yard sweep by Tony Nathan gave Miami the lead, but the Chargers scored again, with 58 seconds remaining, to tie the game.

For 13 minutes and 52 seconds of overtime, neither team scored. Then San Diego's Rolf Benirschke kicked a 29-yard field goal to give the Chargers a 41-38 victory. The Pro Football Hall of Fame named this contest "NFL's Game of the '80s." It was the first time in NFL history in which both quarterbacks—Miami's Don Strock and San Diego's Dan Fouts—passed for more than 400 yards.

In the strike-shortened 1982 season a 7-2-0 Dolphins team qualified for the 16-team postseason Super Bowl Tournament. They wasted no time in beating everyone in sight—downing the Patriots, 28-13, the Chargers, 34-13, and the Jets, 14-0. Meanwhile, the NFC Washington Redskins were advancing in similar style. On January 30, 1983,

PROFILES | **A Tale of Two Quarterbacks**

AP/Wide World Photos

Miami Dolphin franchise owner Joe Robbie called quarterback Bob Griese the "cornerstone of the franchise." Griese, inducted into the Pro Football Hall of Fame in 1990, posted a .698 winning percentage (91-39-1) under coach Don Shula from 1970 through 1980. He was a consensus All-Pro quarterback in 1971 and 1977 and made six appearances in the Pro Bowl. Indeed, Griese held all the important Dolphin passing records—until Dan Marino arrived on the scene in 1983.

Marino **(left)** was an instant sensation. By the end of the 1992 season his statistical accomplishments were eye-popping, as shown by a few of his passing records in comparison with those of Hall of Famer Bob Griese (and Griese fully deserves his place in Canton's showplace of pro football). Griese threw 192 touchdown passes in his AFL/NFL career. Through the 1992 season Marino had thrown 290 scoring lobs.

Griese's lifetime aerial yardage totaled 25,092—putting him in fairly exclusive company. Marino, however, had racked up 39,502 yards in the air by the end of the 1992 season. Griese completed 1,926 passes in 3,429 attempts for a healthy 56.2 percent completion percentage. Marino, though the 1992 season, had completed 3,128 passes in 5,284 attempts for a completion percentage of 59.2 percent.

From 1984 through 1992 Dan Marino led the Dolphins to a remarkable 24 fourth-quarter comeback victories. In the 1992 season alone he directed six comeback wins in the final quarter of the game—against the Browns, Seahawks, Falcons, Oilers, Jets, and Patriots. In these fourth-quarter comebacks (two of them in playoff games), he completed 158 of 256 passes (61.7 completion percentage) for 2,175 yards with 17 touchdowns. The 6'4", 225-pound quarterback, a 1983 graduate of the University of Pittsburgh, rewrote the record book at Pitt; he is doing the same to NFL record books.

the Dolphins and Redskins met in Super Bowl XVII at the Rose Bowl in Pasadena, California. Gathered to watch were 103,667 spectators in the stands and an estimated television audience of 115 million. The Dolphins led with ten minutes to play, but a fourth-quarter Redskin attack gave Washington a 27-17 victory.

On April 26, 1983, the Dolphins selected quarterback Dan Marino from Pitt in the first round of the draft, the 27th player chosen overall. This gave Miami an abundance of riches at quarterback—Marino, Woodley, and Strock. On October 9 Dan Marino made his first start, as did wide receiver Mark Duper (drafted in 1982), and together they put on quite a show against the Buffalo Bills. Marino passed for 322 yards, while Duper gathered in seven aerials for 202 yards. Although the Bills won in overtime, 38-35, there was little doubt that Marino and Duper would play major roles in the future of the Dolphins.

Indeed, for the rest of the season the team won nine of ten games to post a 12-4-0 record and move into postseason play. This time they were stopped early as the wild-card Seattle Seahawks upset them, 27-20, in the divisional playoff.

In 1984 the Dolphins started as if to reprise their 1972 perfect season, winning 11 games in a row at the outset. The dream died at the hands of the Oakland Raiders on December 2, 45-34, the day on which Dan Marino broke the all-time NFL record for touchdown passes in a single season by tossing his 37th. Other records fell, too, a couple of weeks later in this 1984 campaign. On December 17 against Dallas, the last game of the regular season, Dan Marino became the first quarterback in NFL history to pass for more than 5,000 yards in a season.

Three days after Miami defeated the Cowboys, 28-21, concluding a 14-2-0 season, the Associated Press named Dan Marino as the NFL's Most Valuable Player. The quarterback looked sharp a week later as he led the Dolphins to a 31-10 playoff win against the Seattle Seahawks. On January 6, 1985, he passed for 421 yards and four touchdowns in the AFC championship game against the Pittsburgh Steelers.

Mark Duper chalked up 148 yards receiving as the Dolphins triumphed, 45-28, and advanced to the Super Bowl. There they met the NFC's San Francisco 49ers—and once more suffered a Super Bowl defeat. Two of the great quarterbacks of the modern era, Dan Marino and Joe Montana, called the signals in this match at Stanford Stadium in California, which the 49ers dominated, winning 38-16. The Dolphins failed to score in the second half, while San Francisco continued to add to its halftime lead. Miami's so-called Killer Bee defense lacked much sting against the Montana-led 49ers.

1985 proved to be the last of Miami's division titles for a while. At the beginning of the season, it looked as if doomsday had arrived already. After nine games the Dolphins' record stood at 5-4-0, hardly the shape of a championship season. But somehow Shula got his players' act together, and the Dolphins won their last seven games. A noteworthy victory came on December 2 against the Chicago Bears. Miami's 38-24 win was the only defeat suffered all year by the potent Bears.

Despite the momentum of seven straight Dolphin victories, the unheralded Cleveland Browns nearly upset them in the first-round playoff game. Only two touchdowns in the final 17 minutes by fullback Ron Davenport enabled the Dolphins to nip the Browns, 24-21. No such heroics marked the AFC championship game. The New England Patriots, previously consistent losers at the Orange Bowl, came to life on January 12, 1986, and waltzed past the Dolphins, 31-14.

Goodbye to Orange Bowl Glory

Since early 1984 Miami fans had known that a new multi-purpose stadium would be built in northern Dade County. In late 1985 Joe Robbie officially broke ground for the new 73,000-seat facility, then called Dolphin Stadium. The team posted an 8-8-0 record in 1986, their last year playing in the Orange Bowl. The high point of the season was a 45-3 rout of the New York Jets on November 24. At that point the Jets were 10-1-0, but Miami running back Lorenzo Hampton's spectacular effort—148 yards rushing on 19 carries (a 7.8 average), including two touchdowns—sparked a dazzling Miami offense. Dan Marino completed 29 of 36 passes for 288 yards and four touchdowns.

Except for that game, the season was mostly forgettable, including the final loss on December, 1986, in the Orange Bowl to the New England Patriots, 34-27. In their 21 years at the Orange Bowl the Dolphins had compiled a brilliant home record of 110-38-3.

The Dolphins moved to their new home in 1987—Joe Robbie Stadium, as it was now called. They still had some clout on offense with quarterback Dan Marino and wide receivers Mark (Super) Duper and Mark Clayton. Also adding punch to the attack was rookie running back Troy

Stradford from Boston College.

What the Dolphins lacked was defense, and it cost them. Only the last-place Jets allowed more points in the AFC Eastern Division. The most lopsided victory for the Dolphins all season was a 42-0 shellacking of the Kansas City Chiefs on October 11 in the first regular-season home game played at Joe Robbie Stadium.

Somewhat unhappily, though, the Dolphins and Chiefs who played on this historic occasion were "replacement" teams, the NFL Players Association having gone out on strike. Only after three weeks of replacement-team games (and one missed date) did the "real" Dolphins take the field again. Their 8-7-0 record tied them with the New England Patriots for second place in the AFC East.

Miami fans hoping for improvement in 1988 were disappointed early and often. The Dolphins showed little defensive ability and, surprisingly, mounted a rather puny offense as well, except for the reliable Dan Marino and the consistent Mark Clayton. Mark Duper, though, had a drug-shortened season that clouded his otherwise outstanding career. Head coach Don Shula, overseeing perhaps his weakest team ever, was fortunate to escape with a 6-10-0 record. That mark gave the Dolphins sole possession of last place, an unfamiliar address for them. It was not a Shula-like season.

Neither was 1989, although it was marginally better. Dan Marino, struggling with a succession of injuries, still managed to pass for 3,997 yards. A shakeup in assistant coaches, the arrival of rookie running back Sammie Smith, and the placekicking of Pete Stoyanovich—he booted a Miami-record 59-yard field goal against the Jets in November—were among the highlights of a break-even season (8-8-0). After 11 games in 1989 the Dolphins boasted a 7-4-0 record and seemed headed for the playoffs. But they lost all but one of their last five games, and for the fourth season in a row missed the playoffs.

On January 7, 1990, Joseph Robbie, founder and owner of the Dolphins, died of respiratory failure at the age of 73.

It was clear that some new faces would be needed on the Dolphin roster for the 1990s. But the new faces would not be those of the head coach or the starting quarterback. Don Shula, already a legend, stood on the verge of breaking George Halas's career total of 325 wins in the National Football League. Dan Marino, one of the great quarterbacks of all time, neared the 40,000-yard mark in career passing, a plateau reached by only three others (Fran Tarkenton, Dan Fouts, Johnny Unitas)—and Marino was nearly five years ahead of any of them in getting there.

But the Dolphins needed a tougher defense and a more balanced offense. Marino could surely pass, but the receivers were growing long in the tooth, and the running attack was an anemic one. Better defense in 1990, keyed by cornerback Tim McKyer and linebackers John Offerdahl and Hugh Green, helped boost the Dolphins back into contention. Their 12-4-0 record, ordinarily good enough for first place, earned them only second place as the Buffalo Bills marched to their third straight Eastern Division title.

It did give Miami a wild-card playoff shot, however, and the Dolphins eked out a 17-16 win over Kansas City at Joe Robbie Stadium. Miami's Pete Stoyanovich kicked a 58-yard field goal in the game, an NFL playoff record. In the AFC Championship Game, played in the snow and ice at Rich Stadium, Buffalo, the Dolphins lost to the Bills by a 44-34 margin. Miami's offensive standouts were Dan Marino (32 completions and 323 yards in 49 pass attempts), Mark Duper (three receptions for 113 yards), and Sammie Smith (99 yards on 21 carries).

Miami fell back to the break-even mark in 1991, finishing third at 8-8-0. But then in 1992, the 20th anniversary of the Dolphins' perfect season, the team jumped off to a 6-0-0 mark by mid-October. A couple of losses, to the Colts and the Jets, brought them down to earth, but they recovered and ended the regular season atop the AFC Eastern Division at 11-5-0. The Dolphins clinched their trip to the playoffs with a 19-17 come-from-behind victory over the New York Jets on December 20 at Joe Robbie Stadium. In this game Dan Marino threw his 290th career touchdown pass in the NFL to tie Johnny Unitas for second place on the all-time list in that category.

The Dolphins rolled over San Diego, 31-0, in the divisional playoff. But in the AFC Championship Game the wild-card Buffalo Bills took advantage of five Miami turnovers—three fumbles and two interceptions—to fashion a 29-10 win. Once again the Bills represented the AFC in the Super Bowl. Miami fans, disappointed as they were by that outcome, can take comfort in the continued presence of Don Shula and Dan Marino, insurance that the Dolphins will remain competitive for some time to come.

Sources

Books

Braucher, Bill, *Promises to Keep: The Miami Dolphin Story*, Dodd, Mead, 1972.

Greene, Harvey, and Scott Stone, *Miami Dolphins 1993 Media Guide*.

Harrington, Denis J., *The Pro Football Hall of Fame: Players, Coaches, Team Owners, and Officials, 1963-1991*, McFarland & Company, 1991.

Hollander, Zander, ed., *The Complete Handbook of Pro Football, 1993,* Signet, 1993.

Neft, David S., and Richard M. Cohen, *The Football Encyclopedia: The Complete History of Professional NFL Football from 1892 to the Present*, St. Martin's Press, 1991.

Porter, David. L., ed., *Biographical Dictionary of American Sports: Football,* Greenwood Press, 1987.

Sahadi, Lou, *Miracle in Miami: The Miami Dolphins Story,* Henry Regnery Company, 1972.

Sporting News Pro Football Guide, 1993 Edition, The Sporting News Publishing Co., 1993.

Periodicals

New York Times, December 18, 1984.

Sports Illustrated, November 27, 1972; January 8, 1973.

—*Gerald Tomlinson* for Book Builders Inc.

New England Patriots

When the upstart American Football League was created in 1959, the last franchise awarded went to a Boston group that—after a fan contest—named the team the Patriots. In a sense, the Patriots have never caught up with the competition. The New England Patriots 33-year existence has been one of off-the-field turmoil and on-field heartbreak, characterized by moments of high drama and low comedy.

While the Patriots have never won a Super Bowl, they have demonstrated a consistent soap opera quality that always has entertained their fans, if not satisfied them. Lacking financial stability under the founding family, the Sullivans, the Patriots for years careened from crisis to crisis, be it the lack of a home stadium, a multimillion-dollar lawsuit by former stockholders, or the defection of the general manager/head coach to a college job two weeks before a post-season playoff game.

Never able to displace Boston's other professional teams—the Red Sox, Celtics, and Bruins—in the hearts of New England fans, the Patriots nonetheless have had a few moments when they dominated the region's sports pages. In 1985, they defied the odds by becoming the only team ever to win three playoff games on the road, earning a berth in Super Bowl XX in the process.

Yet, it was typical of the franchise that its highest moment would lead to humiliation, in the form of a 46-10 drubbing by the Chicago Bears. In weeks after the Super Bowl, a time that should have been gratifying and joyous, the Patriots were hit by revelations of drug usage by several of its most prominent players.

Throughout their rocky existence, the Patriots have been graced by several standout performers whose individual brilliance could not be dimmed. Steve "Doc" Grogan, a player who made several comebacks in a 15-year career from 1975-90, covered nearly 30,000 yards by air, a franchise record.

John Hannah, a nine-time Pro-Bowler at offensive guard, showed that big men can also have speed as he was always able to stay ahead of swift running backs on sweeps. Wide receiver Stanley Morgan (1977-89), whose magic hands grabbed over 10,000 yards worth of passes, averaged a remarkable 19.4 yards per catch.

Running backs Jim Nance, Sam Cunningham, Tony Collins, Craig James and John Stephens led the team in rushing over consecutive seasons. Nance led the team for six straight seasons (1965-70) while Cunningham led for five straight (1975-79). In the early years, quarterback Babe Parilli (1961-67), connected for over 16,000 yards to lead the way, while Gino Cappelletti (1960-70) is the Patriots all-time top scorer with 42 touchdowns, 176 field goals, and 342 extra points, for 1,130 points.

Other scoring leaders include kicker John Smith (1974-77 and again from 1979-82) and kicker Tony Franklin. These were just some of the Patriots' franchise players who sometimes helped the team to achieve the impressive heights.

But, even after years of growing pains, the Patriots were almost in the same state of chaos following the 1992 season that they were in 1960. Owner James B. Orthwein, a St. Louis-based financier, was threatening to put the team up for sale unless local city and state officials came up with the funds to build a Boston-based $700 million sports and convention center megaplex project to replace Sullivan Stadium in the small town of Foxboro. Orthwein had purchased the franchise from the financially-strapped previous owner, Victor Kiam, in May, 1992.

No Place Like Home

Meanwhile, Connecticut Governor Lowell Weicker and other Connecticut officials were pushing a proposal to build a stadium to lure the Pats away from Massachusetts. The uncertainty of the situation was ironic, because it was reminiscent of the early days when founder Bill Sullivan and several local businessman were awarded a franchise but had no place for the team to play.

From 1960 to 1965, the Patriots called four different venues home. When Sullivan announced in 1959 that he was bringing professional football to New England, not many took notice. After all, other semi-pro and pro football teams had come and gone in the area and all of them were losing propositions both on the field and in the investors' pocketbooks.

In 1926, the Boston Bulldogs were the town's team. Then the Boston Shamrocks arrived in 1936, disbanding just a year later. The Redskins played in Boston for four years in the mid-1930s before moving out of town, eventually to become the Washington Redskins. And then, in 1940, the Boston Bears came and went. Later came the Yanks, who lasted as long as an average college student, starting in 1944 before the team went bankrupt in 1948. So, when Sullivan made his announcement, many looked at it as just another flash-in-the-pan franchise.

According to Joe Fitzgerald's *Minutemen of the Gridiron,* when Sullivan made his announcement at the Hotel Somerset on a cold and rainy November night, he wasn't prepared to name the team, identify any of its players, its coach, or even where the games were going to be played. Sullivan wouldn't even disclose the names of the nine other partners who, like him, put up $25,000 each to start the team. But Sullivan, who was a president of a large petroleum company, was a smart businessmen, and those who knew him knew that if anyone could make a professional football team a success in Boston, it would be him.

Sullivan and his partners were awarded the franchise on November 16, 1959. He immediately involved the general public by holding a contest to see who could name the new home-town team. It was, of course, the Patriots. But, at the beginning, they were the Boston Patriots. And, like the colonial-era Minutemen after whom they were named, they were trying to secure a home.

The team first started playing at the field of the old Boston Braves baseball team at Boston University, now named Nickerson Field. The squad played an exhibition game and defeated the Buffalo Bills—a team against whom they were

Team Information at a Glance

Founding date: Novermber 16, 1959 (AFL); 1970 (NFL)

Home stadium: Foxboro Stadium
Rt. 1
Foxboro, MA 02035
Phone: (508) 543-8200
Seating capacity: 60,794

Team colors: Red, white, and blue
Team logo: A stylized Minuteman
Team nickname: Patriots; Pats

Franchise record	Won	Lost	Tie
(1960-92)	216	247	9

Division first-place finishes: (4) 1963 (AFL East), 1976 (tie), 1978, 1986
Super Bowl appearances: (1) 1986

picked as three-touchdown underdogs—28-7. The team's first real game, however, didn't go quite as well. In front of a crowd of 21, 597, the Pats fell to the Denver Broncos, 13-10.

The team's first win didn't come until they hit the road and defeated the New York Titans at the Polo Grounds in New York, 28-14. In that game, defensive back Chuck Shonta recovered a fumble on the final play of the game and returned it for a touchdown.

Lou Saban Built First Team

The Pats first coach was Lou Saban, a former captain of the Cleveland Browns which won four championships in the 1940s. Saban was just a college coach, however, when he signed a three-year contract with the Patriots. His Western Illinois team was undefeated in 1959. Running back Ron Burton was the first, first-round draft pick for the Pats while running back Gerhardt Schwedes, out of Syracuse University, was the team's first territorial pick. Running back and kicker Gino Cappelletti retired in 1971, after leading the team in scoring from 1960-69.

In that fabled first season, where the Pats finished up 5-9-0 to finish fourth in the AFL East, Jim Colclough led in pass-reception yards with 1,949 while Alan Miller was the leading rusher with 416 yards on 101 carries. They were quarterbacked by 34-year-old Butch Songin. In their second season Songin was replaced by Vito "Babe" Parilli who held the job until 1967.

Just three years into their existence, the Patriots won the first and only AFL divisional playoff game, 26-8, over the Bills at War Memorial Stadium in Buffalo. Parilli and Cappelletti led the way with Parilli throwing touchdown strikes of 59 and 17 yards to Larry Garron while Cappelletti cleared four field goals of 28, 12, 33 and 36 yards. The Pats, however, lost the 1964 AFL title game to the Chargers, 51-10, at San Diego's Balboa Stadium.

In that contest Garron suffered a concussion which minimized the Patriots' offensive attack. Charger Keith Lincoln was a one-man wrecking crew against the Pats, rushing for 200 yards while adding over 100 yards in receptions. After their disappointing opening season, the Pats went on to finish with back-to-back 9-4-1 records for consecutive second place finishes in the AFL East.

In 1963, when the Pats moved to Fenway Park, their 7-6-1 record was good enough to finish first in their division. Garron was the team's leading rusher from 1963-64 while Jim Nance was the leader from 1965-70. Saban, known for being hard on his players, was replaced five games into the 1961 season by Mike Holovak, who logged a 7-1-1 record the rest of the way. Holovak, taciturn and dignified, would remain as the coach for 7 ½ years, compiling a 53-47-9 record.

That 1964 Season

The Pats regrouped in 1964 after the big loss to San Diego in the previous year's AFL championship. After losing all of its exhibition games—a tradition as strong as New England's unpredictable weather—the team won its season opener at Oakland, 17-10. In its second game of the season against the Chargers, the Pats avenged their title loss with a 33-28 victory, led by Cappelletti's field goals of 41, 32, 37 and 38 yards.

With a 5-2-1 record a little over halfway through the season, trailing the 8-0 Bills led by former Patriot coach Saban, the Pats had to play perfect ball to catch them. Led by Parilli and Cappelletti the team went on to defeat Oakland, Buffalo, Denver, Houston and Kansas City.

That set up a showdown for first place between the 10-2-1 Pats and the 11-2 Bills at a snowy Fenway Park. The Bills won the game and the East crown, 26-14, continuing a trend of disappointments in crucial games that has characterized the franchise. Cappelletti, with 155 points on the season, won the scoring crown while Holovak was named the coach of the year.

However, the 1965 season was a disappointment, with the Pats finishing 4-8-2 after a miserable 0-6-1 start. In 1966 the team rebounded to an 8-4-2 record, good for second place in the AFL East. It would be the last winning season the Pats would enjoy at Fenway, as the aging squad went on to finish 3-10-1 in 1967 and 4-10-0 in 1968. Perhaps homesickness—or more accurately, not having a permanent home—led to a tough stretch for the Pats.

The year of 1963 marked the first year the Patriots played at Fenway Park. One game, against New York, was played at Boston College because of a conflict with a Red Sox game, but outside of that, the Patriots and Red Sox co-existed harmoniously.

But subsequent events underscored the problems in sharing Fenway Park. In 1967, the Patriots had to play a "home game" at San Diego. A year later, the Pats played a home game against New York in—of all places—Alabama, because no local venue was available. The team moved to Boston College for one season in 1969 and then moved to Harvard a year later.

Home at Last

Their problems were solved in 1971 with the opening of Schaefer Stadium in Foxboro, a small town midway between Boston and Providence. Schaefer Stadium, later named Sullivan Stadium, finally was a place the Patriots could call home. The 60,000-seat open-air facility was built for $20 million and had few of the luxuries characteristic of other NFL stadiums.

From 1967 through 1973, the Pats were 28-70-1. It wasn't until the 1974 season—when the squad finished at .500 with a 7-7-0 record—that the losing streak came to a halt. Why did the team's performance decline in the late 1960s and early 1970s? In Fitzgerald's account, Sullivan blamed himself for allowing the team's best players to grow old without bringing in quality young talent.

Sullivan, a former public relations man for the Boston Braves baseball team, likened the Patriots troubles to those he had seen with the Braves. "I can remember when I was working for the Braves in 1948, the pennant year," Sullivan said. "Everybody knew the same team would have trouble winning again in 1949 because the players were getting too old. There was a reluctance to tamper with success, though, and in the long run it hurt the Braves. And I'd have to say it's hurt the Patriots very badly, too."

Holovak was replaced by Clive Rush in 1969. Rush, however, only lasted a season and a half. Despite a three-year contract, Rush was released just seven games into the 1970 season. Rush, popular with the players, was sensitive and emotional. At times he would ask his players how he was doing, and by the end of his tenure he was often seen by reporters talking to himself.

The Pats sorely needed a replacement for quarterback Parilli, and they got a suitable one in 1970 with Joe Kapp who the year before had led the Minnesota Vikings to a Super Bowl. But even Kapp wasn't enough, as the Pats finished 2-12-0 for a fifth-place finish.

It took four seasons at the Pats' new home of Schaeffer Stadium before the they played winning football. After the .500 season in 1974, however, the Patriots faltered the next year to finish 3-10-0. When the Patriots moved into Schaeffer Stadium in 1971, they made Stanford quarterback Jim Plunkett their No. 1 draft pick. Winner of the Heisman and Maxwell trophies, Plunkett was the cornerstone of a rebuilding period. Although Plunkett enjoyed only one winning season as a Patriot, he was an on-field leader with a shotgun arm, racking up almost 10,000 aerial yards in four years to receivers such as Reggie Pucker, Randy Vataha, and Mack Herron.

After the 1970 season, in anticipation of their move to their suburban Foxboro home, the Boston Patriots for a short time renamed themselves the Bay State Patriots. But that name was unpopular with fans, and on March 22, 1971 they became the New England Patriots. More than anything, the new name was a marketing ploy, designed to bring in fans from the other New England states while giving the old fans a fresh perspective.

And while the first half of the 1970s was not kind to the Patriots, the second half certainly was. From 1976 to 1980, the Patriots compiled a 50-26-0 record. John Mazur, Rush's assistant, took over as the new head coach in 1970 and remained until 1972 when he was replaced by interim coach Phil Bengston.

Coaching Stability

The revolving door to the coach's office was finally slowed down in 1973 with the hiring of Chuck Fairbanks, who stayed through 1978 and compiled a 46-40 record. Fairbanks, who led the University of Oklahoma team to five bowl appearances in six seasons, was chosen by Sullivan after a nationwide search. In order to lure Fairbanks to New England, Sullivan agreed to give him the dual role of general manager/coach.

Fairbanks quickly put together the pieces of a contender. He traded running back Carl Garrett in order to secure a first-round draft pick. He picked up John Hannah, a 270-pound guard out of Alabama, Rose Bowl standout Sam Cunningham from Southern Cal, and Darryl Stingley, one of Purdue's top-three receivers ever. While the team wasn't winning yet, the spirit of the early winning years slowly returned. Plunkett, who was selected for the AFC's 1971 All-Rookie team at quarterback, completed over 50 percent of his passes in 1973.

While the season ended at 5-9-0, there were some highlights that suggested better days ahead. Against the Dolphins at the Orange Bowl, where the Pats had a long history of failure, they came back from a 20-0 deficit to narrowly lose, 23-16. The squad went on to defeat the Colts, 24-16, and the Bears, 13-10. The 1974 squad's record improved to 7-7-0. But when the next year's team dropped to 3-11 Fairbanks decided that a dramatic change was necessary. He made perhaps the biggest trade in franchise history, sending Plunkett to the San Francisco 49ers for four draft picks.

It was a risky move, because Plunkett had long been the team's leader, both on and off the field. But Fairbanks extracted heavy payment, getting two first-round draft picks that year and a first- and second-round draft pick the following season. Those picks became defensive back Mike Haynes, center Pete Brock, defensive back Raymond Clayborn, and wide receiver Stanley Morgan, all key components to the strong teams of the late 1970s.

Grogan Takes Over at QB

In 1976 Steve Grogan, acquired out of Kansas State a year earlier, took over as quarterback, a job that would be exclusively his for the next seven years. Grogan was a gutsy bruising runner who used the bootleg effectively in his early years. Later, after suffering several injuries, Grogan developed a more cautious style and learned to pass with a softer touch.

The 1976 team finished 11-3-0 and qualified for the franchise's first NFL playoff game, and its first playoff since 1963. In the AFC wild card playoff game, the Patriots fell to Oakland (the eventual Super Bowl champion), 24-21, in the final 10 seconds on a controversial roughing the passer call.

At the Patriots 27-yard-line, the defense looked as if it had stopped the Raiders' potent offense, on a third and 18 situation, when a Ken Stabler pass fell incomplete. But nose tackle Raymond Hamilton was hit with a dubious roughing the passer penalty by referee Ben Dreith. The Raiders suddenly found themselves with a 1st and 10 on the New England 13.

Five plays later, Stabler rolled around left end for the game-winning touchdown. The loss was stunning, coming after Grogan had put together scoring drives on the Patriots' first two possessions.

In 1977, the Patriots continued to play winning ball, this time ending up 9-5-0 to finish third in their division. In 1978 they continued to improve, finishing 11-5-0 to finish on top in the AFC East, while overcoming the tragic loss of one of their best players. Wide receiver Darryl Stingley suffered a career-ending injury during an exhibition game with the Oakland Raiders in August.

Stingley, a fifth-year veteran out of Purdue, was trying to catch a pass on a pattern over the middle when he was hit by Raiders strong safety Jack Tatum, known for his "clothesline" tackles, since outlawed, that utilize an extended arm to catch an oncoming or airborne oppponent by the neck.

Stingley was taken to Eden Hospital in Castro Valley, just outside of Oakland, where it was found that he had a flexion injury to his spinal cord. A bone surrounding the spinal cord in his neck was fractured, cracking his vertebra and leaving him permanently paralyzed from the neck down. The Patriots' wide receiver was just 26 years old at the time.

Tatum, who later recounted the incident in his autobiography *They Call Me Assassin,* said after the game, "I knew it was serious. We just sort of hit head to head. When he went down he never moved. He was in the air when I hit him. We almost hit head on. I knew it was a good shot ... you hate to see anybody get hurt, but I was just doing my job."

Coaching Confusion

During the tragedy-shrouded season, the squad went on a seven-game tear and never lost two games consecutively. The squad's come-from-behind victory, 26-24, over the Buffalo Bills on December 10, secured the franchise's first outright divisional championship. But the season ended as it began—in turmoil. Before the last game, Fairbanks made a surprising announcement that he would be leaving New England to coach college ball at the University of Colorado. Prior to the last game against Miami in the Orange Bowl, Billy Sullivan suspended him.

Fairbanks' assistant coaches Ron Erhardt and Hank Bullough took over as co-coaches, and the Patriots lost to Miami, 23-3. Fairbanks was reinstated for the playoff game against Houston, but the team was demoralized and confused and lost, 31-14. In that game, the Oilers led 21-0 at half-time, as quarterback Dan Pastorini riddled the Patriots' struggling secondary, completing 10 of 13 passes for 184 yards. The Patriots briefly threatened in the second half on a 24-yard option-pass from running back Andy Johnson to wide receiver Russ Francis, and a touchdown pass from Tom Owen (in for Grogan) to Francis.

Erhardt became the head coach for the next three seasons and experienced success for his first two. The 1979 squad ended up 9-7-0 while the 1980 edition finished 10-6-0. After the squad's 2-14 record in 1981, Erhardt was gone. On December 16, 1979, the Patriots finished the season with a 27-23 conquering of the Minnesota Vikings. In that game, Harold Jackson (1,013) and Stanley Morgan (1,002) become the first Patriots to reach the 1,000-yard receiving plateau.

In 1982, Ron Meyer, the head coach at SMU from 1976-81, became the eighth head coach in Patriots history. Meyer's first season, shortened by a strike, ended at 5-4. In 1983, under Meyer, the Pats went 8-8. By that time Meyer had become unpopular with his veteran players for instituting rules that restricted their off-field freedom. Midway through the 1984 season, with the team's record at 5-3, Meyer was replaced by Raymond Berry.

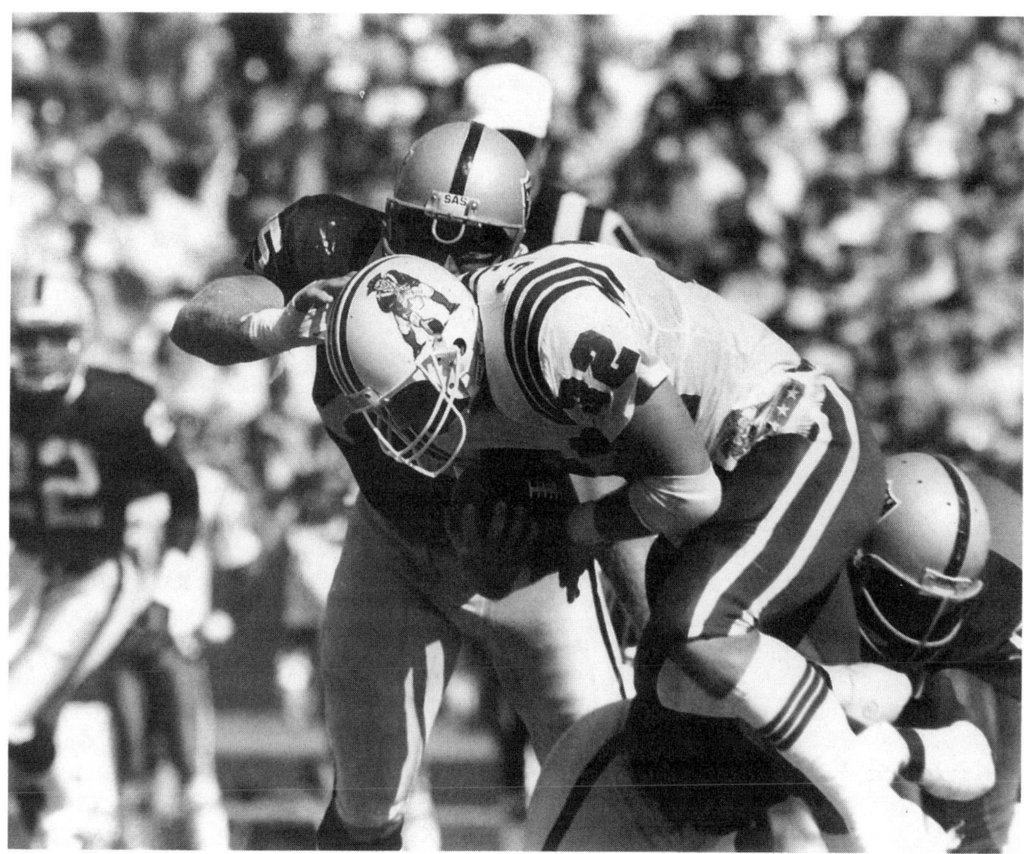

AP/Wide World Photo

Craig James (32)

Patriots Head Coaches

1960-61: Lou Saban 7-12-0
1961-68: Mike Holovak 52-46-9
1969-70: Clive Rush 5-16-0
1970-72: John Mazur 9-21-0
1972-73: Phil Bengston 1-4-0
1973-78: Chuck Fairbanks 46-39-0
1979-81: Ron Erhardt 21-27-0
1982-84: Ron Meyer 18-15-0
1984-89: Raymond Berry 48-39-0
1990-90: Rod Rust 1-15-0
1990-92: Dick MacPherson 8-24
1993—: Bill Parcells

Berry Leads Pats to Super Bowl

Berry, a Hall of Fame receiver with the Baltimore Colts, led the Patriots to their greatest moment. Although he finished out the 1984 season with a mediocre 4-4 record, Berry earned the respect of his players with a straightforward no-nonsense style of communication. The 1985 season culminated with the team's first and, so far, only Super Bowl appearance, and gave New England fans a bittersweet moment.

The Patriots were led by second-year quarterback Tony Eason, who threw for over 2,000 yards; running back Craig James, who rushed for over one thousand yards; tailback Tony Collins, who average 10.6 yards per reception, and linebacker Andre Tippett, a fierce pass rusher.

Just as amazing as their Super Bowl berth was the manner in which they got there. The Patriots, historically a weak road team, had to win three playoff games on the road to make Super Bowl XX. The team was dubbed "The Road Warriors" after completing the three-game sweep. It started at Giants Stadium in East Rutherford, New Jersey, on December 28, against the New York Jets in the AFC East wild card game. The Patriots won, 26-14, in a game with many heroes. Eason hit 12 of 16 passes for 179 yards while kicker Tony Franklin tied an NFL playoff record by completing four field goals. The Jets were also generous hosts, giving up five turnovers, four of which led to Patriots' points.

The team then headed to the L.A. Coliseum to meet the Raiders, and came away with a 27-20 win, thanks again to some timely Raiders turnovers (three fumbles and three interceptions). Trailing 17-7, the Pats went on an 80-yard, 10-play drive that ended with a Craig James 2-yard TD run behind the blocking of John Hannah, cutting Oakland's lead to 17-14.

The second of two interceptions by Ronnie Lippett led to a 45-yard Franklin field goal to tie the game at 17-17. While many praised the Patriots for their accomplishment, most thought the season would be over when they headed to the dreaded Orange Bowl to tango with the Miami Dolphins for the AFC championship on January 12.

The Patriots had won only once previously at the Orange Bowl, in 1966, and had lost 19 straight there. The Dolphins were also 6-0 in AFC finals. But New England fans were hopeful. Homes, restaurants and other such businesses carried signs reading, "Squish the Fish." The team had done the impossible all season, so why not again? The Patriots rewarded their optimism with a 31-14 victory. Eason led the way with three touchdown passes of 4, 1, and 2 yards to Tony Collins, Derrick Ramsey, and Robert Weathers.

Suddenly, Super Bowl fever seized New England. Fans were accustomed to watching the Bruins and Celtics win championships, but the Patriots had long been a source of frustration and ridicule. With the Dolphins already wrapped in newspaper, next up were the NFC champion Chicago Bears. The slogans became "Berry the Bears" (in tribute to head coach Raymond Berry) and "Skin the Bears." But true to form, off-field events distracted the team's preparation. A few days before the game, it was announced that star wide receiver Irving Fryar had sliced a tendon on his little finger while putting away a knife in the kitchen. Fryar's availability was in question. One newspaper later reported Fryar was actually stabbed by his pregnant wife during a domestic dispute. Fryar denied the report. By game time, he was in uniform and ready to play.

During the days prior to the game, owner Bill Sullivan asked an investment banking house in New York to find a buyer for the team. Sullivan said he did this to assess the true value of the team. Sullivan was under financial pressure from former stockholders who had sued him over the terms of a stock buyout in 1976. The suit threatened to cost Sullivan millions.He said that if the courts ruled against him, he would likely have to put the team up for sale. Said Sullivan, "It would be difficult to continue."

Crushed by the Bears

But the off-field stories, as big as they were, took a back seat to what was to come. The game,

AP/Wide World Photos

Andre Tippett (56) sacks Jets' quarterback Ken O'Brien during the 1985 AFC playoffs

played at the SuperDome in New Orleans on January 26, was at the time the most widely-watched TV show in history with 127 million viewers, topping the previous high of 121.6 million for the final episode of *M*A*S*H* in 1983. The massive audience witnessed the most lopsided defeat in Super Bowl history, to that point. Chicago's 46-10 victory was overwhelmingly decisive. For the Pats, the loss was comparable to the 51-10 beating suffered against San Diego in the 1963 playoffs.

Bears noseguard William "Refrigerator" Perry dominated. Perry stopped the Pats running game and harassed both their quarterbacks. Chicago quarterback Jim McMahon made good on his own boasts and ran for two touchdowns while completing 12 of 20 passes for 256 yards. Chicago's time of possession, 39:15, was almost twice that of New England's. The Pats scored first when Tony Franklin nailed a 36-yard field goal just 1:19 into play.

But the Bears scored 13, 10, and 21 points over the next three quarters to put the game away. Tony Eason was ineffective against the Bears, failing to complete a pass or get a first down pass or first down. Grogan, who had led the Patriots to six straight wins when Eason was injured during the season, replaced Eason in the second quarter.

Although Grogan was intercepted twice and was sacked four times (once for a safety) he managed to throw an 8-yard touchdown pass to Irving Fryar in the fourth quarter. It was the only touchdown the Bears' defense had allowed in three playoff games. Not many doubted coach Berry when he said after the game, "We gave it everything we had."

But the end of the Super Bowl was only the beginning of a long winter. The next day, defensive end Julius Adams, the team's No. 2 draft choice in 1971 out of Texas Southern, announced his retirement. Prior to the 1986 season, Hannah announced his retirement. Perhaps the greatest player in Patriots history, Hannah finally gave in to injuries—torn rotator cuffs.

Team Tackled Drug Problem

Following the Super Bowl, the Patriots surprised other NFL teams and caused internal strife by voting to adopt a volunteer drug-testing program, a first in professional sports history. The vote had come about after Berry had reportedly threatened to quit because he was upset about alleged drug abuse by players. Six players reportedly admitted to Berry that they used illegal drugs, and their names were released to the press by General Manager Patrick Sullivan.

New England Patriots player rep Brian Halloway, one of only seven Patriots to vote against the testing, said that Sullivan broke one of the conditions of the one-year program—confidentiality—when he released the names of the alleged drug users. Holloway said, "I can guarantee you with the release of those players' names, that you have seen the end of the voluntary program with the Patriots." In February, the NFL Players Association protested the Patriots drug-testing vote. The program, the group said, violated the collective bargaining agreement.

Meanwhile, the Sullivans, facing the same financial problems, announced that Sullivan Stadium and Foxboro Raceway could be sold in the near future. The Sullivans still had the 10-year-old stockholder suit hanging over their head. Finally, the stockholders' case was settled. Sullivan ended up paying about $3 million to former stockholders, well below the $18 million they were demanding. Now Sullivan could hold onto his team.

The 1986 season went well for the Pats, proving that there was indeed life after losing the Super Bowl. They won the AFC East with an 11-5 record. But once again the season ended in frustration, with a playoff loss at Denver, 22-17. The squad won its season opener against the Indianapolis Colts in dominating fashion, 33-3, and then went on to defeat the Jets, in a rematch of the previous year's AFC wild card game, 20-6.

After losses to Seattle and Denver, the Patriots matched and then surpassed the Super Bowl season's winning streak by winning seven straight.

PROFILE

The Sullivan Family

For their first 30 years of existence, the New England Patriots were synonymous with the Sullivans. William Sullivan, Jr. forged the family's link to professional football in 1959 when he led a team of 10 investors who put up $250,000 to bring a charter franchise of the American Football League to Boston. From the beginning, Sullivan was undercapitalized and was never able to recover financially until he finally sold the team three decades later.

Sullivan, a 1937 graduate of Boston College, was raised in Lowell where his father worked as a town clerk, newspaper correspondent, and fight promoter. He held public relations posts at Boston College, Notre Dame and the Naval Academy before taking his skill to professional baseball and the Boston Braves in 1946. After a hiatus from sports as an executive in a petroleum company, he invested $8,000 to return to professional sports at the helm of the Boston Patriots. Sullivan took the lead in strengthening the AFL.

In 1962, he was elected AFL president for the first of two consecutive terms, and during his tenure the AFL signed a $36 million contract with NBC. Sullivan also served as a representative during the AFL-NFL merger talks in 1965. Sullivan eventually took control of the team as president and majority stockholder. In 1975, he faced his greatest threat as head of the team when a group led by his son, Charles Sullivan—the team's executive vice-president and chief legal and financial adviser—sought control of the Sullivan clan.

Like his father, Chuck Sullivan also took an active role in the league as a member of the NFL Management Council. Billy Sullivan kept his entire family involved in the Patriot organization during his reign. Along with Chuck, he brought son Pat into the fold after he graduated from Boston College in 1976. Pat Sullivan quickly moved up the ladder from his first post on the stadium operations staff to publicity assistant in February 1977, to stadium manager.

The family's reputation for bargaining, however, created a deep chasm between management and the players throughout their era. Disputes between Pat Sullivan and agent Tony Pennacchia as well as those between Chuck Sullivan and agent Howard Slusher led to drawn-out negotiations and countless holdouts. The result was a chronic alienation of the team's veteran leaders like All-Pro cornerback Mike Haynes and All-Pro offensive linemen John Hannah and Leon Gray. In 1979, following a contract dispute, Gray was dealt for a first-round draft pick.

The 1980s were marked by Pat Sullivan's rise through the ranks. He became general manager in 1983 and a member of the team's board of directors in 1985. By this time, however, the Sullivans were mired in financial problems and looking to sell the team. Despite Pat Sullivan's signing successes, by 1988 the hunt for an owner was intensifying as were the Sullivan's troubles. One reported suitor was Donald Trump, but nothing came of it. Another business group represented by Boston attorney Robert Popeo sued the Sullivans in an effort to gain control of the team.

The Sullivans were soon negotiating with several prospective buyers as they met with Fran Murray, Robert Tisch, and Paul Fireman before finally reaching an agreement with Victor Kiam to ease their financial difficulties. With Kiam in control, Patrick Sullivan remained as the team's general manager. In late 1989, Kiam gave Sullivan a directive to improve the team for the 1990 season. But Sullivan's handling of the Lisa Olson sexual harassment case displeased Kiam, and his role was reduced. When Kiam brought in Sam Jankovich to run the team's day-to-day operation, on December 20, 1990, the Sullivans lost their last shred of power within the organization.

The family's last official tie to the New England Patriots was severed a little over a month later when Patrick Sullivan resigned as general manager on January 29. Always combative, Billy Sullivan has sued the NFL for over $300 million, claiming that he was forced to sell the team at less than its market value. The Sullivans, for all their well-documented problems, were passionate owners who took a hands-on approach to management. While the media, and fans alike, criticized Bill Sullivan for his obvious nepotism, he always stood his ground and defended his family's involvement.

Week after week, the Patriots marched through the Pittsburgh Steelers, Buffalo Bills, Atlanta Falcons, Indianapolis Colts, Los Angeles Rams, the Bills again, and then the New Orleans Saints. After two losses to the Cincinnati Bengals and the San Francisco 49ers, the Patriots won again at the Orange Bowl, defeating the Miami Dolphins, 34-27. But Denver's defense was too strong in the playoffs, and Eason was unable to find the magic that had pulled the Patriots through the previous year.

Labor Disputes

Prior to the 1987 season, the relationship between Patriots management and union leaders deteriorated after NFL owners refused to grant protection for union representatives on the 28 clubs. The five-year collective bargaining agreement that had settled a 57-day strike in 1982 was expiring. Player reps felt they were being penalized by management, and those rumors seemed to be confirmed when Patriot offensive tackle Brian Holloway, the NFL Players Association vice president, was traded to the Los Angeles Raiders.

The NFL Players Association contended that the league was trying to "break the union" by having teams cut and trade away player reps. The association's vice president, Gene Upshaw, said of the Holloway trade, "This is just the most unbelievable act I've ever seen. They're not just harassing (union representatives), they're getting rid of them, they're firing them." Berry said that the trade was not based on Holloway's union activity.

The possibility of a strike worried Patriots management more than most, as the franchise was now $30 million in debt. General Manager Pat Sullivan said, "Naturally, we can't afford a strike. We are hoping it works out because we need the money. We don't need it tomorrow but we can't sustain three more years of unhappy fans." Sullivan said that attendances after the 1982 strike averaged 13,000 fewer fans per game than before the strike. It wasn't until the big 1985 season that alienated fans started to return to Sullivan Stadium.

As the season began, it was announced that Grogan, who had been a back-up to Tony Eason in 1985 and 1986, would be the Pats' starting quarterback. In the season opener, Grogan led the squad to a 28-21 win over Miami by connecting 14 of 20 passes for 150 yards. Tony Collins had 95 yards of rushing along with three pass receptions.

But the Pats could not regain their playoff form, and finished 8-7-0, tied for second in the AFC East. Notably, in 1987, cornerback Raymond Clayborn broke Gino Cappelletti's consecutive game streak of 152, reaching 161. Clayborn's streak ended on November 29 when he couldn't suit up against Philadelphia at Sullivan Stadium because of a knee injury suffered a week earlier against the Colts.

Under New Management

In July, 1988, the Patriots retired the number 57 worn by 14-year linebacker Steve Nelson. Nelson, who played in three Pro Bowls, led the team in tackles for eight seasons. The same month, the Sullivans finally sold the team—after years of threatening to do so—to Victor K. Kiam II, chief stockholder and CEO of Remington Products, Inc., out of Bridgeport, Connecticut.

Kiam became one of the most active National Football League owners by serving on the NFL Properties Executive Committee. Bill Sullivan remained the team's president while Francis Murray, the minority owner, was named the vice chairman of the franchise. The Kiam, Murray, Sullivan connection became known as KMS Limited.

While things were new upstairs, the old guard was still succeeding on the field. Later, during the 1988 season, veteran wide receiver Stanley Morgan caught his 500th career pass on a 19-yard reception against Seattle. Coach Berry's 1988 team finished a respectable 9-7-0, a remarkable feat considering the team's struggling offense. The brunt of the offense was carried on the

Patriots' Year-by-Year Team Records

1960: 5-9-0, fourth in AFL East
1961: 9-4-1, second in AFL East
1962: 9-4-1, second in AFL East
1963: 7-6-1, first in AFL East
1964: 10-3-1, second in AFL East
1965: 4-8-2, third in AFL East
1966: 8-4-2, second in AFL East
1967: 3-10-1, fifth in AFL East
1968: 4-10-0, fourth in AFL East
1969: 4-10-0, tied for third in AFL East
1970: 2-12-0, fifth in AFC East
1971: 6-8-0, third in AFC East
1972: 3-11-0, fifth in AFC East
1973: 5-9-0, third in AFC East
1974: 7-7-0, tied for third in AFC East
1975: 3-11-0, fifth in AFC East
1976: 11-3-0, tied for first in AFC East
1977: 9-5-0, third in AFC East
1978: 11-5-0, first in AFC East
1979: 9-7-0, second in AFC East
1980: 10-6-0, second in AFC East
1981: 2-14-0, fifth in AFC East
1982: 5-4-0, third in AFC East
1983: 8-8-0, second in AFC East
1984: 9-7-0, second in AFC East
1985: 11-5-0, tied for second in AFC East
1986: 11-5-0, first in AFC East
1987: 8-7-0, tied for second in AFC East
1988: 9-7-0, tied for second in AFC East
1989: 5-11-0, fourth in AFC East
1990: 1-15-0, fifth in AFC East
1991: 6-10-0, fourth in AFC East
1992: 2-14-0, last in AFC East

back of running back John Stephens while Berry played musical quarterbacks with Grogan, Eason, and newcomer Doug Flutie. The offense failed to score more than 30 points in any single game, and in six games, it scored 10 points or less.

The struggle continued into the 1989 season with the team finishing 5-11, with the aging Grogan once again the starting quarterback and Stephens again the leading rusher. Berry, who had a 49-39 record, was fired and replaced by defensive coordinator Rod Rust. Still, from 1987 to 1989, the Patriots were an attraction, mainly because of local hero Flutie who broke the picket line to play ball with the Patriots in 1987.

Flutie, best known for his Hail Mary pass against University of Miami when he was suiting up for Boston College, was an immediate favorite with the Patriots' fans. Perhaps the most popular college athlete in Boston history, Flutie came to the Patriots with the public's expectation that he would duplicate the magic of his Heisman-winning BC career. And while Flutie managed to deliver a few exciting victories, he proved inconsistent and incompatible with Berry.

The 1990 season, under coach Rod Rust, was a disaster. Eason and Flute were gone, and new quarterback Marc Wilson was backed up by the veteran Grogan. The squad finished up 1-15, and suffered the ignominy of a lawsuit filed by a female sportswriter for the *Boston Herald,* Lisa Olson, who claimed she was verbally and sexually harassed in the Patriots' locker room after a game. Pat Sullivan apologized to Olson on behalf of the team, but Olson wanted an apology from the players themselves. The event escalated when Kiam was allegedly overheard saying, "She's a classic bitch. No wonder the players don't like her." The NFL, following an investigation, fined three players.

Lowlights of the 1990 season included a 42-7 whipping by the New York Jets, at the time one of the worst teams in football. As AP sportswriter Howard Ulman said, "Every time it seems the Patriots hit rock bottom, they chisel out to a lower level." Hope returned in the dead of winter, December, 1990, when Kiam named Sam Jankovich, University of Miami's athletic director, as Patriots CEO and general manager.

Jankovich's first move was to fire Rust and replace him with Dick MacPherson, Syracuse's head coach for 10 seasons. MacPherson brought a spark back to the team with his upbeat personality and animated manner.If a player made a great pass reception, or a key tackle, MacPherson was there to pat him on the back. Unfortunately for MacPherson, however, he didn't experience much success. Despite having veterans like Fryar, who was fifth in club receptions with 240, and cornerback Ronnie Lippett, seventh in interceptions with 22, the Patriots struggled.

The 1991 team improved to 6-10, but sank again in 1992, finishing 2-14. Frustration was running so high that when the 2-13 Patriots met the Miami Dolphins in the final game of the season, many debated whether the Pats should play to lose in order to gain the No. 1 pick in next year's NFL draft. MacPherson was fired after the season, and a few days later, Jankovich resigned.

New Owner—New Location?

On May 11, 1992, Kiam sold the team to James Orthwein, a St. Louis-based financier who was portrayed as a temporary owner who would stabilize the franchise before selling the team back to local ownership. His real goal, however, was to bring an NFL expansion franchise to St. Louis, where he lived and was a major shareholder in the Anheuser-Busch brewery.

Other NFL owners, as well as Patriots fans, were concerned that Orthwein's secret plan was to move the Patriots to St. Louis. Prior to the 1993 season, Orthwein indicated that the team might be moved unless a new stadium is built in Boston.

A new era began in the spring of 1993 with the hiring of Bill Parcells—head coach for the New York Giants from 1983-90 (88-52-1 with two Super Bowl titles) as head coach. Parcell's hiring immediately stimulated season ticket sales. Parcells has been compared to 1970s skipper Chuck Fairbanks. He likes to do things his way, without interference from club ownership.

His first major move was the drafting of quarterback Drew Bledsoe, a Washington State University standout. As the 1993 season got underway, it appeared that the Patriots would be led by a rookie quarterback for the first time since 1971, when Jim Plunkett took the reigns. It also appeared that along with a new coach, new quarterback, and new logo, a new tradition of winning was taking hold.

Sources

Books

Fitzgerald, Joe, *New England Patriots, Minutemen of the Gridiron,* Prentice-Hall.
New England Patriots 1991 Media Guide.
New England Patriots 1986 Fact Book.
Fox, Larry, *The New England Patriots,* Rombeck, Rochard, 1990.
Ives, Alan, *New England Patriots Trivia.*

Periodicals

Inside Sports, February 1982.
Sporting News, August 27, 1990; January 7, 1991.
Sports Illustrated, December 3, 1990.

—*Steve Marantz*

New York Jets

On January 12, 1969, the New York Jets under Head Coach Weeb Ewbank made football history. They became the first team in the nine-year-old American Football League to win the Super Bowl, defeating the mighty (and heavily favored) Baltimore Colts 16-7 in Super Bowl III. The Jets' quarterback, Joe Namath, had told the media three days before the game: "I think we'll win. In fact, I'll guarantee it." Broadway Joe, having helped translate his boast into reality, pointed out later, "We beat Baltimore in every phase of the game. If ever there was a world champion, this is it."

It was good for the Jets to savor the moment, for it was the only one of its kind they would have in more than 30 years of trying. The original New York Titans, formed in 1960, played .500 ball a couple of times, always performing before puny crowds, but that was the best they could do. The renamed New York Jets, under new ownership and new Coach Ewbank, had more class from the very outset, but they produced no better a record until 1967, when a 7-2-1 start faded into an 8-5-1 finish. Still, it was the Jets' first winning campaign. Then came 1968, an 11-3-0 regular season record, an Eastern Division title, an AFL championship, and a stunning Super Bowl victory. The Jets had another fine year in 1969, but were upset by the Kansas City Chiefs in the playoffs.

Never again did the Jets scale the heights. Except for 1981 and 1982, with the "New York Sack Exchange" of Joe Klecko, Mark Gastineau, and others, plus a couple of AFC second-place finishes in 1985 and 1986, the team became one of pro football's also-rans. Under head coaches Walt Michaels and Joe Walton the Jets compiled fair won-lost records but earned no Super Bowl rings. Walton gave way to Bruce Coslet in 1990. Quarterback Ken O'Brien, running back Freeman McNeil, wide receiver Al Toon, and others turned in some fine performances in the 1980s, but the Jets entered the 1990s still looking for the kind of powerful and balanced team that would permit an optimistic prediction of the sort Joe Namath had made back in January 1969.

Harry Wismer's Titans

When 26-year-old Lamar Hunt, son of Texas oil billionaire H. L. Hunt, tried to buy himself a National Football League team, he got little encouragement from commissioner Bert Bell. Deciding to form a league of his own, young Hunt approached another oil-rich young man, K. S. (Bud) Adams of Houston. Lamar Hunt figured that with a guaranteed team in Dallas, his hometown, and another in Houston, he could attract investors in other cities. And he did, lining up Denver, Houston, and Minneapolis (which later dropped out), before turning his sights toward the Big Apple.

In New York Hunt approached Bill Shea, who was too busy with baseball and the nascent Mets to get involved, but Shea suggested Harry Wismer, who had made a name for himself as a sports broadcaster and had then branched out as a businessman. Although Wismer was well-to-do, he was no Lamar Hunt, and the football team he founded—the New York Titans—suffered from a chronic lack of cash.

Nevertheless, he signed Sammy Baugh, one of the all-time greats of pro football as his head coach. Baugh was a Hall of Fame quarterback who played for the Washington Redskins back in the 1940s. And the Titans lined up some pretty fair players, among them quarterback Al Dorow, receivers Don Maynard and Art Powell, and linebacker Larry Grantham.

The Titans opened their debut season, 1960, against the Buffalo Bills in the run-down old Polo Grounds in upper Manhattan, a stadium which the baseball Giants had abandoned after the 1957 season. It was an auspicious start on the field, as the Titans won 27-3, although attendance then, and later, was far from promising. The Titans won three of their first four games, then suffered a tragedy that cast a pall over the rest of the season.

In an October 2 game against Dallas, 25-year-old second-string guard Howard Glenn was knocked out and took a long time to recover. Still, he seemed to be alright. But playing the next week against the Houston Oilers, he complained of tiredness, became hysterical in the clubhouse, lapsed into a coma, and died. The autopsy revealed a broken neck. It was assumed he had been seriously hurt the previous week in Dallas, but the injury had gone undetected.

The Jets finished the season at 7-7-0, well behind the Houston Oilers.

They opened the 1961 season just as they had the year before, winning three of their first four games while playing before virtually nonexistent crowds. Passing was their strength, defense their weakness. Owner Harry Wismer made plenty of noise about his dissatisfaction with Titan Coach Sammy Baugh and AFL commissioner Joe Foss. Wismer, losing more money than he could afford, may have seen a ray of hope in the fine performance of All-Star halfback Bill Mathis, who gained more yards than anyone else in the AFL except Houston's Billy Cannon. But the Jets merely reprised their 7-7-0 record of the previous year.

By 1962 Harry Wismer was out of money, and the New York Titans, never popular, were out of fans. Wismer replaced Sammy Baugh with another Hall of Famer, affable Clyde (Bulldog) Turner. The season was a disaster. In November the Titan players' paychecks bounced, and commissioner Joe Foss, determined not to see the New York franchise fail, ran the team with league funds. Clearly, Wismer was out. New ownership was needed.

Amid the financial chaos and in front of mostly empty seats (36,161 fans in all for seven home games), the Titans won a few times on the field, five to be exact, while losing nine. The team relied heavily on passing, with Art Powell, Don Maynard, and Dick Christie doing most of the receiving. Once again, the Titans could rely on their defense hardly at all.

Team Information at a Glance

Date of first game: September 11, 1960

Home stadium: Giants Stadium
Meadowlands Sports Complex
East Rutherford, NJ 07073
Phone: (201) 935-8500
Seating capacity: 76,891

Team colors: Kelly green and white
Team nickname: Titans, 1960-1962; Jets, 1963-present
Team logo on helmet: Base color Kelly green, with word "Jets" in modern, forward slanting white capital letters; stylized profile of a jet plane, also in white, above the word, extending forward from the "J" in "Jets"

Franchise record*	Won	Lost	Tie	Pct.
(1960-1992)	218	269	8	.448

* Including playoffs

Super Bowl wins (1): 1969
American/National Football League championships (1): 1968
Eastern Division championships (2): 1968, 1969
League/Conference/Division last-place finishes (7): 1962, 1963, 1973, 1975, 1980, 1987, 1989

Enter the Jets

If pro football was becoming show business, as it seemed to be, what better owner for a New York team than the head of television for the vast entertainment complex, Music Corporation of America (MCA)? David A. (Sonny) Werblin proved to be just what the ailing franchise needed. His partners were Leon Hess of the Hess Oil Company, Townsend B. Martin of the old-money Martins, and Philip H. Iselin, a garment-industry magnate, later joined by stockbroker Donald C. Lillis. The press got word of the purchase of the bankrupt franchise on March 15, 1963. Two days later, on St. Patrick's day, Sonny Werblin would be 53 years old. Werblin had always loved the color green, perhaps because it reminded him of both his birthday and his bankroll. In any event, the New York Jets—for that was to be the Titans' new name—would play in uniforms of Kelly green and white.

The Jets bought out the second year of Bulldog Turner's contract and hired a new head coach, Weeb Ewbank, recently let go by the Baltimore Colts. Ewbank began building a team for 1963 that would remind fans as little as possible of the past. He picked up some Baltimore castoffs, including fullback Mark Smolinski and offensive ends Dee Mackey and Bake Turner. At quarterback he installed veteran Dick Wood, cut from the Denver Broncos. Wood could pass well but could run only with difficulty, given his taped and braced knees. Ewbank designed his offense to protect the fragile Wood. It worked, but only up to a point. The Jets finished the season with a 5-8-1 record. As Ewbank admitted later, "Wood isn't the kind of quarterback you win championships with."

In 1964, two years after the Titans had played to empty stands at the Polo Grounds, the Jets began setting AFL attendance records at their new home, Shea Stadium—45,665 for the opener against the Denver Broncos, 60,300 for a midseason game against the Buffalo Bills. Fans saw an improved team that included fullback Matt Snell, placekicker Jim Turner, and middle linebacker Ed (Wahoo) McDaniel. ("Tackle by guess who?" blared the Shea public address announcer. "Wahoo," the fans screamed back.)

Dick Wood, still at quarterback, passed for 2,298 yards, and his backup, newcomer Mike Taliaferro from the University of Illinois, added 341. Taliaferro, whom the NFL Giants had tried to sign, expected to replace Wood soon as the Jets' starting quarterback. Another newcomer, a star of the future, was guard Dave Herman of Michigan State, also snatched from the rival Giants. Despite these acquisitions, the 1964 Jets did no better in the won-lost column than they had the year before. They finished at 5-8-1, just as in 1963.

The $400,000 Man

In 1965 Sonny Werblin, buoyed by skyrocketing attendance and the AFL's lucrative NBC television contract, went after two of the most highly touted college quarterbacks in recent memory. One was John Huarte of Notre Dame, winner of the Heisman Trophy in 1964, whom the Jets signed to a $200,000 contract. No announcement of this signing was made immediately, because Werblin was pursuing an even hotter prospect—the University of Alabama's supremely gifted quarterback, Joe Willie Namath.

It cost Werblin at least $400,000 to sign Joe Willie, who at 6'2"; 200 pounds, and in need of knee surgery, might or might not be a bargain at that startling price. He was worth every penny, as it turned out, although he began the 1965 season on the bench, with Huarte assigned to the taxi squad. Weeb Ewbank's starting quarterback was Mike Taliaferro—for a number of losing games.

Then Joe Willie went in. Namath proved (though not instantly) that the Jets' search for a quality quarterback was over. He was their new QB—"Broadway Joe"—ladies' man and nightlife swinger though he might be. The Jets won five of their last eight games in 1965, to finish with that old familiar 5-8-1 record. But this was a new football team, not just because of Joe Willie Namath but also because of several other rookies, among them tight end George Sauer, defensive end Verlon Biggs, and defensive tackle Jim Harris.

The Jets seemed to have a good chance to compile a winning record in 1966 (it would be their first), especially when they got off to a 4-0-1 start, including a 52-13 massacre of the Houston Oilers. In the Houston game Joe Namath completed five touchdown passes, and rookie halfback Emerson Boozer got his first chance to carry the ball for the Jets. Boozer carried five times, one a 39-yard touchdown run.

But as the season progressed, the Jets seemed to get worse rather than better. The next time they faced Houston they were blanked 24-0. Namath was intercepted four times, and his sarcastic explanation of the loss—"We were all out getting drunk the night before"—did nothing to cheer up disenchanted Jet fans. When the team blew a game against the Oakland Raiders, a Shea Stadium fan tossed coffee on Namath in the runway.

The Jets finished the 1966 season with a disappointing 6-6-2 mark. Another AFL team, namely the Kansas City Chiefs, represented the junior circuit (and lost to the NFL's Green Bay Packers) in Super Bowl I, January 15, 1967.

Sooner or later the Jets were bound to put together a winning season. When in 1967 the team jumped off to a 7-2-1 record, that happy milestone was assured. It even looked as if the Jets might capture their first Eastern Division title, since they led Houston by one game at the time. But the Jets then dropped three straight before salvaging the season finale, beating the San Diego Chargers 32-21.

Their 8-5-1 record gave them second place behind the Oilers' 9-4-1. Injuries to fullback Matt Snell and halfback Emerson Boozer hurt their chances, as did failures on pass defense. Yet Joe Namath completed 258 of 491 passes, good for 4,007 yards, the first 4,000+ season ever—and the only one ever recorded in a 14-game schedule. Don Maynard caught 71 passes for 1,434 yards, while George Sauer gathered in 75 for 1,189 yards. This was an offense with clout.

Weeb Ewbank

"We Can Win It All"

Usually it is the coach and not the owner who loses his job. But in the spring of 1968 Sonny Werblin, at the request of his four partners, sold out to them. The partners had been unhappy for some time. They resented being kept in the dark about major trades and other important decisions. "I want to find out what's happening with my money," Leon Hess said.

They were increasingly unhappy, too, about the Jets' late-season cave-ins and the inability of Head Coach Weeb Ewbank to prevent them. When Donald Lillis, the president who succeeded Werblin, died after a few months at the helm, Phil Iselin took over. Iselin made it clear that Ewbank and the Jets must win and keep on winning in the upcoming season. Joe Namath was sure they would. He told reporter Larry Fox, "I think we can win it all, and if I have a halfway good season I know we'll do it."

The Jets squeaked by the Kansas City Chiefs 20-19 in the 1968 season opener at Kansas City. Joe Namath, with the assistance of Don Maynard, Emerson Boozer, and Matt Snell, kept his team in possession of the ball for nearly the last five minutes of the game. Next week they won again on the road, beating the Boston Patriots 47-31. In their third road game of the new season, against the Buffalo Bills, they were expected to win easily. They didn't. Five Namath passes were intercepted (a sixth was nullified by a penalty), and three were run back for touchdowns. The Bills triumphed 37-35, their only win all season. Namath was philosophical. "Even good pitchers get knocked out of the box," he said.

At home at last the Jets edged the San Diego Chargers, 23-20, coming from behind in the final minutes. But then the Denver Broncos arrived in town and handed the Jets a 21-13 defeat, their second loss in three games, both of them upsets. With a 3-2 won-lost record and Joe Namath's penchant for tossing long passes into the hands of enemy receivers, the Jets, while leading the AFL Eastern Division, were hurting.

They stopped hurting the next week in Houston, topping the Oilers 20-14 for the first of four straight victories. On November 3, 1968, in their rematch against Buffalo, place-kicker Jim Turner

OOPS!

Heidi-Night Football

The Jets were playing a crucial game against the Oakland Raiders at the Oakland Coliseum on Sunday, November 17, 1968. If the Jets won, they would clinch a tie for the AFC Eastern Division title. The game was a nip-and-tuck affair, with the lead changing several times. When the Jets' Jim Turner kicked his third field goal of the day, New York led 29-22, with about nine minutes left in the game. But the Raider quarterback, Daryle Lamonica, marshaled an 88-yard drive that ended with a 22-yard touchdown pass to Fred Biletnikoff. Unfazed, Jet quarterback Joe Namath hit Don Maynard with a pass for a nine-yard gain, then another for a 42-yard gain. A penalty against the Raiders put the ball on their 18-yard line, from which Jim Turner booted yet another field goal. With 65 seconds left in the game, it looked as if the Jets had won, 32-29.

Back at NBC-TV in New York City they seemed to think the same thing. The game was running long—19 penalties plus time-outs having pushed it well beyond the anticipated two and a half hours. As it happened, NBC was planning to run a special children's show that night, the old favorite *Heidi,* starting at 7:00 p.m. New York time. With the game almost over, NBC made the decision to switch to *Heidi,* which they did. Angry fans picked up their telephones to complain. There were so many calls the switchboard broke down. Some fans called police emergency numbers, tying up New York City's emergency response system for several hours. Others called New York Telephone and the *New York Times.*

It was bad enough that Jet fans missed the last 65 seconds of the game. But what happened in those last seconds was infinitely worse. Daryle Lamanica directed a march down the field, then tossed a pass to Charlie Smith, who raced into the end zone. The Raiders led, 36-32, with 45 seconds remaining. There still might have been enough time for Joe Namath to lead the Jets to victory, but the question became moot when the Jets' kickoff receiver, Earl Christy, fumbled at the 12-yard line. Preston Ridlehuber, a Raider reserve back, grabbed the ball and took it into the end zone. The game ended: Raiders 43, Jets 32.

At 8:20 p.m. WNBC-TV ran a streamer across the bottom of a pleasant Alpine scene in *Heidi.* It informed viewers that the Raiders had scored two touchdowns to win the game and advised them to watch for "Details on the 11th Hour News." Few fans were mollified. Even NBC president Julian Goldman admitted, "I missed the end of the game as much as anyone else."

accounted for 19 points in the Jets' 25-21 win. He kicked six field goals—from the 32, 9, 32, 27, 35, and 27 (plus one point after touchdown)—to tie an AFL record.

After defeating Houston for the second time, 26-7, Namath and the Jets faced the formidable Oakland Raiders. NBC television switched from the Jets-Raiders game to a special showing of the movie *Heidi,* with 65 seconds remaining in the game. The Jets were leading 32-29. When the game ended (as protest phone calls flooded the wires at NBC), the Raiders had won it 43-32.

Earlier in the season Weeb Ewbank had posted a newspaper headline on the Jets' bulletin board: "Will the Jets Blow It Again?" That is, would the team go into its familiar December nosedive? After the loss to the Raiders, who knew?

The players had been growing beards and mustaches as good-luck tokens, but the Jets would need more than facial hair to beat the Chargers, Dolphins, and Bengals. Not to worry. The Jets pulverized San Diego 37-15 and breezed past the Dolphins 35-17.

By then (because of the Oilers' loss to Kansas City) Weeb Ewbank's crew had already clinched the divisional title. Nonetheless, they went on to defeat Cincinnati 27-14, and Miami again 31-7, finishing with an 11-3-0 record, their best ever by far. But they would still have to beat their nemesis, the Western Division champion Oakland Raiders, in order to advance to the Super Bowl.

In fact, their opponents could have been the Kansas City Chiefs, because Kansas City and Oakland finished in a dead heat in the Western Division, 12-2-0. But the Raiders trounced the Chiefs 41-6 in a playoff, and the stage was set for an Oakland-New York confrontation.

The Oakland Raiders, *Heidi*-night victors over the Jets, were a tough aggregation, coached by Johnny Rauch and led by quarterback Daryle Lamonica along with one-time quarterback, now place-kicking phenom, George Blanda.

A crowd of 62,627 turned out at Shea Stadium to watch the game. The Jets jumped off to a 10-0 first-quarter lead on a 14-yard Namath to Maynard pass and a 33-yard Jim Turner field goal. Early in the second period Lamonica hit Fred Biletnikoff with a 29-yard touchdown pass, closing the gap to 10-7. Field goals by Turner and Blanda made the score 13-10 in favor of the Jets at halftime. In the third period a Raider drive stalled at the one-yard line and Blanda kicked the short field goal to tie the score 13-13.

With less than a minute left in the third period Namath connected with a pass to tight end Pete Lammons. Jim Turner booted the extra point, and the Jets were back in the lead, 20-13. A fourth-quarter Blanda field goal narrowed it to 20-16. Raider defensive back Butch Atkinson, a rookie, intercepted a Namath pass at the Jets' 37-yard line and carried it to the five. When Pete Banaszak took it over on the next play, the Raiders led for the first time 23-20.

But with 8:18 remaining, the game was far from over. Namath passed to Sauer and Maynard and a Turner PAT quickly made it 27-23 in favor of the Jets. More than seven minutes remained on the clock, but neither side scored again. The Jets were AFL champs and Super Bowl-bound. At the victory dinner Weeb Ewbank thanked the wives of all the Jet players for their help and sacrifice. Joe Namath, free-spirited bachelor, added, "I just want to thank all the broads in New York."

Over in the NFL the Baltimore Colts under Head Coach Don Shula had compiled a 13-1-0 regular-season record and gone on to defeat the Minnesota Vikings and Cleveland Browns to advance to Super Bowl III. On January 12, 1969, at the Orange Bowl in Miami, the New York Jets, 18-point underdogs, took on the Colts. Joe Namath had issued his "guarantee" of a New York victory (almost as legendary today as Babe Ruth's supposed called home run), but few put much faith in it.

Even though the great but sore-armed Johnny Unitas would not be quarterbacking for the Colts, his place being taken by Earl Morrall, most observers thought the Baltimore team was too overpowering for Joe Namath and his brash New Yorkers. Morrall had subbed brilliantly for Unitas that season, and the Colts had beaten everybody in the supposedly stronger NFL.

Both teams moved the ball in the first half, but only the Jets moved it over the goal line. At halftime New York led 7-0—the first time an AFL team had been ahead in a Super Bowl game. Nothing changed dramatically in the second half. When Jim Turner kicked a field goal for the Jets, widening their lead to 10-0, the Colts' future Hall-of-Fame quarterback, Johnny Unitas (who said he felt okay), began warming up behind the bench.

Babe Parilli replaced Namath, whose thumb was giving him problems, and Parilli hit Sauer with a short pass, after which Turner kicked his second field goal, and the Jets went up 13-0. In came Johnny Unitas. Coach Ewbank admitted later that this move scared him. Sportswriter Larry Fox wrote in *Broadway Joe and His Super Jets,* "Sore arm? This guy could beat you from an iron lung."

Unitas got nowhere on his first series, Namath came back into the game, and early in the final quarter Jim Turner kicked his third field goal of the day to give the Jets a 16-0 lead. Although Unitas could be brilliant in the closing minutes of a game, he was not at his best on this occasion. He did avoid a shutout, handing off to Jerry Hill for a touchdown with less than three minutes to play. The final score: 16-7. Namath's guarantee held. The AFL had proved its mettle.

Jet fans hoped for an encore, and there was one—at least at the Eastern Division level. The

1969 Jets rolled through a 10-4-0 season, with all four losses coming at the hands of Western Division teams. In the divisional playoffs the Jets lost to the Kansas City Chiefs (the eventual Super Bowl winner) 16-10. The Jet offense clicked again that year (the year of baseball's "Miracle Mets"), with Joe Namath leading the way. Matt Snell, Emerson Boozer, Don Maynard, George Sauer, Pete Lammons, and Bill Mathis all gained good yardage in this, the last season of the AFL as a separate league. Starting in 1970 the National Football League was scheduled to absorb the American Football League, leaving its teams intact but making some divisional realignments and creating the National and American Football Conferences of the NFL.

Injuries and Losses

The Jets—now, in 1970, in the Eastern Division of the AFC, along with the Baltimore Colts, Miami Dolphins, Buffalo Bills, and Boston Patriots—lost a number of key players to injuries and lost several games as a consequence. Joe Namath suffered a broken wrist, and Al Woodall, a second-year quarterback out of Duke University, took over for him. Matt Snell, Emerson Boozer, and Don Maynard all lost playing time because of injuries. Their replacements, including running back George Nock and tight end Rich Caster, kept the offense on the move.

The Jets lost a few close games, finishing with a 4-10-0 mark and taking third place (out of five) in the new AFC Eastern Division. Weeb Ewbank had no reason to celebrate, but he thought he could count on better luck, if nothing else, in 1971.

The Buffalo Bills put in a truly horrendous season in 1971, which was a good thing for the battle-weary Jets because it gave them two of their six wins and kept them out of last place in the AFC's Eastern Division. Joe Namath lost time to injuries again, as did Matt Snell. George Sauer quit football. The Jets were shut out by Baltimore and New England (formerly Boston), and devastated by the Dallas Cowboys, 52-10. They did win their last two games, though, avenging themselves on New England 13-6, and then slapping Cincinnati 35-10.

Joe Namath was healthy in 1972, but the Miami Dolphins, clearly the class of the division, romped to a 14-0-0 season, while the Jets, weak on defense, had to settle for a 7-7-0 second-place finish. Stats give some idea of the problem. In the regular season the Dolphins scored 385 points to their opponents' 171. The Jets tallied almost as many points, 367, but gave up a whopping 324 to the other teams.

Fullback John Riggins, who had joined the Jets from the University of Kansas Jayhawks the year before, rushed for 944 yards, and Emerson Boozer picked up 549. (This was the year, though, that Larry Csonka and Mercury Morris of the Dolphins each rushed for 1000 or more yards.) Late-season injuries sidelined both Riggins and Boozer, blunting the Jets' attack.

Weeb Ewbank's last season as head coach of the Jets was disappointing. Don Maynard, he of the original 1960 Titans, was released before the 1973 season began. When it did begin, the defense proved remarkably strong, but now the offense had become ragged. On September 23, playing against Baltimore, Joe Namath injured his right shoulder. Two weeks later, against Miami, Al Woodall went out with an injured left knee. That left 22-year-old free-agent rookie Bill Demory to do the quarterbacking. In his first pro start he kept the ball on the ground for 58 running plays. Bobby Howfield kicked three field goals, and the Jets beat the New England Patriots 9-7. But the season was a 4-10-0 flop.

The Jets' new head coach for 1974 was Charley Winner, Weeb Ewbank's son-in-law. Winner did not live up to his name, and the Jets began playing poorly, winning only one of their first eight games. But then the troops rallied to win their last six games, posting a 7-7-0 record and earning Winner a second season as coach. He flunked out. After a 2-1 start, the Jets dropped eight straight games. After the sixth of these losses, Charley Winner was fired, and Ken Shipp took over for the rest of the season. Under Shipp

PROFILE Joe Willie Namath

The New York Jets have had one indisputable superstar in their history—quarterback Joe Willie Namath from Beaver Falls, Pennsylvania, and the University of Alabama, where Bear Bryant called him "the best athlete I've ever coached." Namath played for the Jets from 1965 through 1976, and although he quarterbacked for a team that often lost, suffered from bad knees, threw many interceptions, and was accused of being a New York media darling, he was inducted into the Pro Football Hall of Fame in 1985. Few doubted that he deserved it.

The high point of Namath's career was the 1968 season, when he "guaranteed" that the underdog New York Jets would win the Super Bowl, and then went on to spark that victory. Joe Willie took every honor in sight for his 1968 regular-season and Super Bowl performances: AFL Player of the Year, Hickok Pro Athlete of the Year, the George Halas Award as Most Courageous Player, Most Valuable Player in the Super Bowl, and quarterback on every All-AFL and combined All-Pro team. Moralists might shake their heads over his Fu Manchu mustache and his swinging life style, but it was hard to argue with his success in that glorious Jets' season.

Joe always acknowledged that he was "a pretty confident guy," noting that a quarterback needs "the ability to throw, to read defenses, to call plays, to lead the team"—and adding that "nobody has ever played the position of quarterback any better than I do." Although Namath could do what he said, he did have a penchant for overstatement. When George Allen picked his 100 greatest pro players, he included Joe Willie—but put him fourteenth on his list of quarterbacks, behind Sammy Baugh, Sid Luckman, Johnny Unitas, Terry Bradshaw, and nine others.

Yet Namath was good, very good. He had class, charisma, and courage. His damaged knees were a constant problem, making it hard for him to get out of the pocket and evade a rushing defense. Even so, he often passed for more than 300 yards in a game. And he is the only player in pro football history to pass for more than 4,000 yards in a single 14-game season, racking up 4,007 yards in 1967, the year before his greatest season and his Super Bowl prediction.

the Jets won one game and lost four, giving them an overall 3-11-0 mark.

Things continued to deteriorate. For 1976 the Jets hired Lou Holtz off the campus of North Carolina State. Holtz faced a major rebuilding task. The much-injured Joe Namath was 33 years old. His heir apparent at quarterback, Richard Todd, started six games in this second-straight 3-11-0 season. When Holtz unexpectedly resigned before the final game, the rebuilding job went to his replacement, Walt Michaels, a gruff, tough old-timer who had played for the Cleveland Browns in the nineteen-fifties. Michaels named Richard Todd as his starting quarterback in 1977 but continued to acquire rookies for the future. Todd and the kids, including wide receiver Wesley Walker and offensive tackle Marvin Powell, suffered through a third consecutive 3-11-0 season.

Nevertheless, by 1978 the nucleus of a first-rate Jet team was in place. On offense, in addition to Walker and Powell, the Jets had Clark Gaines, Ken Long, Scott Dierking, and Bruce Harper, the latter a superb kickoff receiver. When Richard Todd, the starting quarterback, was injured in an early game against the Washington Redskins, Mike Robinson stepped in and racked up 2,002 yards passing.

The 8-8-0 record of the youthful 1978 Jets earned Walt Michaels recognition as NFL coach of the year. After turning in another .500 year in 1979, with Richard Todd at quarterback after Robinson injured his thumb in preseason horse-play, the Jets thought they were ready to contend in 1980. They soon proved otherwise, losing their first five games and finishing the season at 4-12-0. In mid-December they even lost to the New Orleans Saints 21-20, allowing the Saints to record their only win against 15 losses.

The New York Sack Exchange

The high hopes of 1980 had faded so quickly and completely that few fans expected much in 1981. At first the Jets seemed ready to fizzle again, losing their first three games. But then something remarkable happened. The Jets drubbed the Houston Oilers 35-17, sacking quarterback Kenny Stabler seven times, and went on to tie the strong and unbeaten Miami Dolphins the next week 28-28.

Their record was still only 1-3-1, but the Jets seemed inspired. In their next game, against New England, the Jets' defense sacked the Patriots' quarterback Steve Grogan eight times. In the Shea Stadium stands appeared a cloth banner reading "N.Y. SACK EXCHANGE." An assistant trainer for the Jets noticed the sign and was inspired to start a humorous in-house newsletter based on the name. The media picked it up, and soon the four players most responsible for the sacks had acquired their nickname. The four: Joe Klecko, Mark Gastineau, Marty Lyons, and Abdul Salaam.

The Jets won ten of their last 13 games in 1981, and the members of the New York Sack Exchange with their near-record 66 sacks were a big factor in the turnaround. Highly effective, too,

Saga of the New York Sack Exchange

A banner in the stands sometimes gets a fleeting moment of television time, but few banner slogans ever go on to become part of the game's history. One that did was a fan's cloth sign reading "N.Y. SACK EXCHANGE." It was noticed and immortalized by an assistant trainer for the Jets, who spotted it at Shea Stadium in 1981 during a game in which the Jets' defense caught New England Patriots' quarterback Steve Grogan eight times behind the line of scrimmage. In midseason Frank Ramos, publicity director of the Jets, picked up on this nickname when Pepper Burrus, the man who was first struck by it, kept putting it into a humorous weekly "stock report" on the achievements of the Jet defense. The Burrus report went only to the New York team and office personnel, but when Ramos began publicizing it, the name "Sack Exchange" caught the nation's fancy. Fans who perhaps had never thought much about Joe Klecko, Mark Gastineau, Marty Lyons, and Abdul Salaam became aware of them. Football defense, seldom an object of adulation even among faithful fans, caught the spotlight.

A memorable moment occurred on Tuesday, November 24, 1981. It did not occur on the field. On that day, in the middle of the afternoon, trading on the floor of the New York Stock Exchange stopped when four invited Jets—Klecko, Gastineau, Lyons, and Salaam, members of the "New York Sack Exchange"—arrived by limo, walked across the floor of the exchange, and were greeted by enthusiastic cries of "Jets! Jets! Jets!" After lunch with the brokers, the four players were ushered to a balcony overlooking the floor of the exchange, and this time the cheering traders added another word to their chant: "Defense! Defense! Defense!"

Not all was sweetness and light on the Sack Exchange, however. Since the previous season, Mark Gastineau had been performing what he called a "sack dance" each time he nailed the quarterback. His teammates were not amused and gave him unflattering nicknames such as "Scarecrow," after the character in *The Wizard of Oz* who lamented, "If I only had a brain." At one point the New York *Daily News* headlined a story, "Klecko, Lyons Despise Gastineau." Naturally, this did nothing to clear the air. Still, if the sacks (and the Jets' success) had continued at a blistering pace in 1982 and beyond, the Sack Exchange would have had a longer life. As it was, the Jets began losing, and the nickname began fading from public consciousness.

were center Joe Fields, offensive tackle Marvin Powell, and defensive back Darroll Ray. Quarterback Richard Todd passed for 3,231 yards, Freeman McNeil rushed for 623 yards, and Wesley Walker caught passes good for 770 yards and nine touchdowns.

The Jets almost threw away a postseason bid when the Seattle Seahawks upset them, 27-23, but Michaels' men bounced back to win their last two and nail down a wild-card shot at the Super Bowl. Their 10-5-1 regular-season record was second to the Dolphins' in the Eastern Division of the AFC. But in the first-round playoff the Jets fell to the Buffalo Bills 31-27, and Coach Walt Michaels, no sentimentalist, walked into the team meeting the next day and snapped, "I hope you enjoy your f—-ing New Year's!" That was it. End of speech.

The strike-shortened 1982 season came to a close with the Jets at 6-3-0. A "Super Bowl Tournament" followed, designed to winnow the ultimate NFL winner from 16 teams, eight from each conference. The Jets got off to a blazing start, routing the Cincinnati Bengals 44-17, in the first round.

Next they met the Los Angeles Raiders and, playing before a crowd of more than 90,000 fans in the L.A. Coliseum, the Jets capped a fourth-period drive with a 45-yard pass from Richard Todd to Wesley Walker at the Raiders' one-yard line. Scott Dierking took it in, Pat Leahy kicked the extra point, Lance Mehl intercepted two Raider passes in the final three minutes, and the Jets won 17-14. Next stop: the AFC championship game against the Miami Dolphins in the Orange Bowl.

Walt Michaels was furious when he saw the playing field at the Orange Bowl. It had been raining for most of the week in Miami, and there was no tarpaulin covering the field. Michaels thought the omission was intentional, that it was intended to slow down the speedy Jets and tip the scales toward the slower, ball-control offense of the Dolphins. Whether intentional or not, it had that effect.

The Jets never got moving in the mud, and New York, with a 7-0-1 record against Miami over the last four seasons, lost the game 14-0. Richard Todd had no success at all. He was intercepted five times, three times by Dolphin linebacker A. J. Duhe. "It was futility," said Jet center Joe Fields. Walt Michaels thought so, too, and skipped the season-ending team meeting. Following the Pro Bowl in Honolulu, the Jets announced Michaels' dismissal. They handed the reins to offensive coordinator Joe Walton.

Jet Lag

No head coach of the New York Jets has compiled a winning record while with the team. Even Hall of Famer Weeb Ewbank posted only a 73-78-6 mark with the Jets. Sammy Baugh, coaching the fledgling Titans, broke even at 14-14-0, while Walt Michaels, whose Jets won frequently over his last two seasons, finished with a career mark of 45-49-1. When Joe Walton stepped into the head coaching job for the 1983 season, he seemed to be in a good position to break that .500-or-under tradition. But when he was fired after the 1989 season, his record had slipped to 54-59-1.

Joe Walton's first season, 1983, was a disappointment. The Jets dropped to 7-9-0, tying the Baltimore Colts for last place in the AFC East. Quarterback Richard Todd had a so-so season, and Freeman McNeil went out with an injury. The next season—the Jets' first at the Meadowlands in New Jersey—was no better. In fact, it was the same, as New York (or was it now New Jersey?) finished at 7-9-0 after a surprising 6-2-0 start.

Richard Todd was gone, and Pat Ryan started at quarterback. After taking some hard jolts, Ryan was replaced later in the season by Ken O'Brien, a first-round 1983 draft choice from the University of California-Davis. The Jets won their last two games in 1984, but just prior to that they had lost six straight.

Don Shula's Miami Dolphins had been capturing AFC Eastern Division title since 1981, and 1985 was no exception. However, in 1985 the Jets rose up to challenge them, as did the New England Patriots. It looked as if the Jets had found the quality quarterback they needed in Ken O'Brien.

A fine passer, O'Brien got plenty of support from sensational rookie Al Toon, not to mention old pros Freeman McNeil, Wesley Walker, and Mickey Shuler. O'Brien was sacked 62 times, a record, but the Jets' own Sack Exchange veterans Joe Klecko and Mark Gastineau were standouts on defense. The Jets won 11 games, lost five, and gained an AFC wild-card position. The Patriots gained one, too, and the two teams met at the Meadowlands to determine which would advance to the next round. The answer was New England as the Jets fell, 26-14, and the Pats marched onward toward the Super Bowl.

1986 started out as the best season in Jets' history. They roared off to a 10-1-0 record and appeared to be unstoppable. Al Toon and Wesley Walker were hauling in Ken O'Brien passes as the Jets swept past everyone in sight (except New England). But suddenly it ended. Injuries piled up. Ken O'Brien slumped. The Jets lost to Miami 45-3 in game 12, then lost by narrower margins to the Rams and 49ers, and ended the season in utter humiliation, losing to the Steelers 45-24, and the Bengals 52-21.

Even so, the Jets' 10-6-0 record earned them a wild-card opportunity. To the surprise of many, the Jets turned up the heat and beat the Kansas City Chiefs 35-10. Next they faced the Cleveland Browns—and nearly carried the day again, losing in overtime 23-20.

Both Pat Ryan and Ken O'Brien were capable quarterbacks, but the team as a whole went into a tailspin in 1987. Age and injuries and Joe Walton's increasingly bizarre behavior took their toll. The Jets fell to 6-9-0 in 1987, struggled back to 8-7-1 in 1988, and then plummeted to 4-12-0 in 1989.

Klecko was gone in 1987, Gastineau in 1988, and Walton himself—as had long been rumored—got the ax at the end of the 1989 season. A new general manager, Dick Steinberg from the New England Patriots, came in to try to straighten things out. He obtained Bruce Coslet, formerly with the Cincinnati Bengals, as head coach.

The situation improved, but Coslet had inherited a demoralized team. The Jets' 6-10-0 record in 1990 did not earn them a playoff bid, but since many of their losses were close, a guarded optimism prevailed for 1991.

Much was expected from halfback Blair Thomas, a second-round draft pick in 1990, notwithstanding his somewhat disappointing rookie season. He disappointed again, but the Jets upped their record to 8-8-0, giving them their first wild-card opportunity in five years. Although they lost in the first round to the Houston Oilers 17-10, Bruce Coslet seemed to be on track in his rebuilding effort.

The Jets swooned in 1992, ending up with a 4-12-0 record and forcing owner Leon Hess and General Manager Dick Steinberg to look outside for some new personnel. The biggest name they added to the roster was that of quarterback Boomer Esiason, a bona fide superstar from the Cincinnati Bengals.

Two other expensive additions, tight end James Thornton from the Chicago Bears and running back Johnny Johnson from the Phoenix Cardinals, bolstered the offense. Another acquisition, free safety Ronnie Lott from the L.A. Raiders, was expected to sharpen the defense. Whether these new faces, plus established veterans such as fullback Brad Baxter and safety Brian Washington, would propel the Jets into the upper reaches of the AFC Eastern Division remained to be seen.

Sources

Books

Allen, George, with Ben Olan, *Pro Football's 100 Greatest Players,* Bobbs-Merrill, 1982.

The Complete Handbook of Pro Football, 1993, edited by Zander Hollander, Signet, 1993.

Fox, Larry, *Broadway Joe and His Super Jets,* Coward-McCann, 1969.

Gilman, Kay Iselin, *Inside the Pressure Cooker: A Season in the Life of the New York Jets,* Berkley Publishing, 1974.

Harrington, Denis J., *The Pro Football Hall of Fame: Players, Coaches, Team Owners and*

League Officials, 1963-1991, McFarland & Company, 1991.

Klecko, Joe, Joe Fields, and Greg Logan, *Nose to Nose: Survival in the Trenches of the NFL,* William Morrow, 1989.

Neft, David S., and Richard M. Cohen, *The Football Encyclopedia: The Complete History of Professional NFL Football from 1892 to the Present,* St. Martin's Press, 1991.

Porter, David L., editor, *Biographical Dictionary of American Sports: Football,* Greenwood Press, 1987.

The Official National Football League 1992 Record & Fact Book, Workman Publishing Co., 1992.

Periodicals

New York Times, November 11, 1968; November 18, 1968; January 13, 1969.

Sports Illustrated, December 2, 1985; September 15, 1986.

—*Gerald Tomlinson* for Book Builders Inc.

American Football Conference

Western Division

Denver Broncos

The Denver Broncos came into being in 1960 as a charter member of the American Football League (AFL). For most of their first decade, the Broncos held down last place in the AFL's Western Division, although they did rise as high as third place on a break-even record in 1962. When Cincinnati joined the league as an expansion team in 1968, the Bengals briefly took over the cellar, but the Broncos moved up only a single step in the standings. Even so, the Denver teams of the 1960s were not without stars. Quarterback Frank Tripucka threw 24 touchdown passes in the 1960 inaugural season, still a Bronco record. Wide receiver Lionel Taylor was a standout performer for much of the decade, as was fullback and kicker Gene Mingo. In 1967 rookie halfback Floyd Little came aboard to add punch to the formerly weak Denver running game.

In 1970, with the merger of the AFL and NFL, Denver sank to the basement again. But the arrival of head coach John Ralston in 1972 signaled the beginning of the Broncos' ascent. With Charley Johnson at quarterback and such defensive stalwarts as Lyle Alzado and Paul Smith, the team began to challenge for leadership in the AFC Western Division. Finally in 1977, under head coach Red Miller—sparked by quarterback Craig Morton and the famed Orange Crush defense—the Broncos went to the Super Bowl, where they suffered the first of their four losses in the January classic.

Denver finished on top of the AFC Western Division again in 1978 but lost in the divisional playoffs. When the Broncos faded over the next two seasons, Red Miller got the ax, and Dan Reeves became the new head coach. Under Reeves the Broncos were mediocre at first, despite fine defense by Randy Gladishar, Louis Wright, Rulon Jones, and others. Then came the arrival of quarterback John Elway in 1983. Elway, ably assisted by running back Sammy Winder and (prior to the debut of the "Three Amigos") wide receiver Steve

Watson, led the team to a first-place finish in 1984 and all the way to the Super Bowl in 1986, 1987, and 1989. The Three Amigos—wide receivers Vance Johnson, Mark Jackson, and Ricky Nattiel—played a major role in Denver's success in the late 1980s.

After losing Super Bowl XXIV to the San Francisco 49ers, the Broncos stumbled in 1990, regained their footing in 1991 (losing the AFC Championship Game to the Buffalo Bills), but then dropped to 8-8-0 and third place in 1992. Dan Reeves, who had compiled a solid 110-79-1 record at Denver, was fired. His replacement, Wade Phillips, whom Reeves had brought in as defensive coordinator four years earlier, faced a rebuilding job, particularly on offense, although John Elway remained reliable and often brilliant. One of the Broncos' key acquisitions was star running back Rod Bernstine from the San Diego Chargers.

Began in the AFL

Bob Howsam, who owned the minor league baseball franchise in Denver, was looking for a way to fill the new South Stands he had built at Bears Stadium. A professional football team seemed like the answer, and when Lamar Hunt of Texas put the wheels in motion to create a new league, the American Football League, Howsam expressed interest.

His interest led to an AFL charter franchise in Denver. A contest among fans led to the name "Broncos." Howsam hired Frank Filchock, an ex-NFL quarterback with pro coaching experience in Canada, as the Broncos' head coach. Filchock was vouchsafed two assistant coaches and some used uniforms from the out-of-business Copper Bowl. The team trained at the Colorado School of Mines. Fans purchased a mere 2,600 season tickets.

Nonetheless, the Denver Broncos became the first AFL team to win a regular-season game, defeating the Boston Patriots, 13-10, in a Friday night game in Boston. The Bronco quarterback leading the attack was the aging and much-traveled Frank Tripucka, who doubled as an assistant coach. Tripucka, a Notre Dame star from the 1940s, proved effective despite his advancing years, as did Gene Mingo, a fullback and kicker, who had served in the U.S. Navy in lieu of college. Mingo scored 21 points in a game against Los Angeles, a record that holds as the most for a Denver player in one game. The Broncos bolted off to a surprising 4-2-0 start in 1960 then dropped their five last games to finish at 4-9-0, last in the four-team Western Division of the AFL. The first all-AFL team included one Denver player—safety Goose Gonsoulin.

The Broncos moved up one notch in the Western Division in 1961 but only because the Oakland Raiders were so abysmal. Denver's 3-11-0 record edged Oakland's 2-12-0. Relying entirely on the passing skills of Tripucka and backup quarterback George Herring, the Bronco offense soon stalled. Wide receiver/split end Lionel Taylor, blessed with good hands but little speed, scored only four times on 100 receptions.

At the end of the season Coach Frank Filchock got his walking papers and was replaced by Jack Faulkner, a former San Diego assistant coach. It was Faulker who ordered the orange uniforms that became so widely known a few years later. Actually, he ordered burnt orange, but the manufacturer delivered bright orange, a fortunate mistake, as it turned out.

The 1962 season started impressively for Jack Faulker and the Broncos, who won their opener at the University of Denver stadium before a sellout crowd of 28,000. They went on to build a 7-2-0 record before losing to the Boston Patriots—and every other team thereafter. For the season they went 7-7-0, good for second place in their division.

Glowing promises were made for 1963. Frank Tripucka, however, was nearing the end of his playing days—he retired after two games in 1963—and the Bronco ownership lacked the money to compete with NFL clubs for top players. Denver drafted several outstanding prospects—Merlin Olsen among them—but then could not afford to sign them. The team's record, 2-11-1 in 1963,

TEAM INFORMATION AT A GLANCE

Founding date: 1960 (AFL); 1970 (NFL)

Home stadium: Mile High Stadium
1900 Eliot Street
Denver, CO 80204
Phone: (303) 433-7466
Seating capacity: 76,273

Team colors: Orange, royal blue, and white
Team nickname: Broncos, 1960-present
Team logo on helmet: Base color royal blue, with large capital "D" in orange outlined in white, inside of which is a profile of a white bucking bronco with royal blue highlights

Franchise record	Won	Lost	Tie
(1960-1992)	235	242	10

American/National Football League championships (4): 1977, 1986, 1987, 1989.
American Conference championships (4): 1977, 1986, 1987, 1989.
Western Division championships (7): 1977, 1978, 1984, 1986, 1987, 1989, 1991.
League/Conference/Division last-place finishes (9): 1960, 1963, 1964, 1965, 1966, 1967, 1970, 1971, 1990.

showed it. The Broncos were clearly in need of a shakeup. For starters, they needed a capable first-string quarterback to replace Tripucka. What they got instead was a game of musical chairs.

"The Next Best Thing to an Open Date"

Coach Jack Faulkner, making an unusual temporary trade, put Houston's Jacky Lee at quarterback. Lee had no success at all behind the porous offensive line, and when the team lost their first four games by wide margins, the coach was bid good-bye. Enter Mac Speedie, formerly a star receiver for the Cleveland Browns. The 1964 Broncos never got going, despite the presence of some good individual players such as split end Lionel Taylor, fullback Billy Joe, and safety Goose Gonsoulin.

The Broncos hoped for better days in 1965 with the acquisition of two proven backfield stars—fullback Cookie Gilchrist from the Buffalo Bills and halfback Abner Haynes from the Kansas City Chiefs. For the first time ever the Bronco offense was built around the running game. A new assistant coach, Red Miller, summed up the Broncos of those days. "We had fun," he said. "We weren't any good, but we had fun." Opposing players, on the other hand, were joking that a game against the Broncos was "the next best thing to an open date." Denver finished last again in 1965, although they won twice as many games (four) as they had in 1964.

When the Broncos opened their 1966 season, they were without Cookie Gilchrist, whom they had dealt to the Miami Dolphins following some harsh words between the fullback and the front office. The opener did not augur well, as the Houston Oilers buried the Broncos, 45-7. Denver failed to make a first down all afternoon. The Broncos could neither score (earning only 196 points for the season) nor keep their opponents from scoring (allowing 381 points). Trying to find a capable performer on the Bronco team was like trying to find a pearl in a sausage. Only the kick returners, including Abner Haynes, Goldie Sellers, and Nemiah Wilson, did their jobs well. The usual starting quarterback, John McCormick, was just another face on the carousel. Head Coach Mac Speedie, lasting only two games into the 1966 season, was succeeded by Ray Malavasi, one of his assistants. The Broncos finished last once more, 4-10-0.

The only direction to go was up. Two events in 1966 and 1967 seemed to make that possible. One was the signing of Lou Saban to coach the Broncos. Saban, an ex-linebacker for the Cleveland Browns, had a well-deserved reputation as a head coach. He had directed the Boston Patriots and Buffalo Bills as well as the University of Maryland Terrapins, and Denver fans thought Saban would turn things around in 1967. The other key event was the announced merger of the AFL and NFL. It would not take place until 1970, but meanwhile the AFL–NFL bidding war over draft choices would end. Denver, a chronic loser in that war, might now be able to sign a few top draft picks.

The Broncos indeed did benefit from the new draft, choosing and signing star halfback Floyd Little from Syracuse University in 1967. Lou Saban made major changes in his effort to build a future winner, trading two first-round draft choices to San Diego in return for quarterback Steve Tensi. The Broncos needed a quarterback for sure, but Tensi, out of Florida State, never lived up to his promise.

By the late 1960s, Denver had, after a tepid start, become a city of enthusiastic football fans, and Tensi took the flak for what continued to be a losing record. Tensi jokes made the rounds. Coach Saban, it was said, had asked his quarterback how many footballs he, the coach, was carrying in a bag over his shoulder. "If you guess right," Saban said, "I'll give you both of them." Tensi thought for a moment and replied, "Three."

Although the 1967 Broncos finished last in the AFC Western Division in 1967, help was on the way. It came via expansion. In 1968 a new team, the Cincinnati Bengals, became the fifth entry in the AFC West. If all went well for Denver, the Bengals would finish last, displacing the Broncos from the cellar. And so it came to pass. The 1968 Broncos, playing their home games in newly enlarged and renamed Mile High Stadium, won five games and lost nine—not a great record, but good enough to relegate Cincinnati to last place. For the first time in six years Denver escaped the basement.

Of course, Denver fans had expected more than that from their new head coach, and when the 1969 Broncos did not seem to improve (5-8-1), the crowds grew restless and the boos continued. Injuries hurt the team in 1969, partially obscuring the fact that the Broncos now had some real talent, not only Floyd Little (who missed five games because of injuries) but also defensive linemen Rich Jackson and Dave Costa and rookie cornerback Bill Thompson. Still, if Lou Saban was truly creating a contender, he was doing it slowly. The merger of the AFL and NFL in 1970 sent the Cincinnati Bengals to the Central Division of the new American Conference and left the Denver Broncos in the four-team Western Division with the generally more successful Oakland Raiders, San Diego Chargers, and Kansas City Chiefs.

Quarterback troubles continued to plague the Broncos. In 1970 Steve Tensi, a question mark anyway, was out with injuries for most of the season. His backup, Pete Liske, had subpar passing skills, and rookie Al Pastrana did not look like a future star. What the Broncos did have was a pair of first-rate running backs in Floyd Little and rookie Bobby Anderson. Little led the AFC in rushing with 901 yards. Anderson chipped in with 368. When Denver started the season with four wins and one loss, it looked as if a winning season (or at least a break-even season) might be in the offing. But the Broncos started losing, and by the time they played San Diego, they were 5-7-0. Two wins would give them .500.

Against San Diego the score was tied 17-17 with 11 seconds to go. Quarterback Al Pastrana kept the ball and carried it to the Chargers' 35-yard line. The obvious call was for a field-goal attempt. But when Pastrana, the only Denver player who could call a timeout, was tackled on the keeper play, he was knocked cold. The clock ran out and the game ended in a tie. The season ended in a 5-8-1 disappointment for Lou Saban and the Broncos. When, if ever, would the head coach's moves pay off?

They certainly would not in 1971. In the opening game of the season against the Miami Dolphins, the score was tied, 10-10. Saban, deciding not to gamble, had the Broncos run out the clock in their own territory. After the game he said, "Half a loaf is better than none at all." The strategy may have been right, but the psychology was wrong. Furious Denver fans began calling him Half-a-Loaf Saban. After nine games and a 2-6-1 mark in 1971, Lou Saban called it quits. Jerry Smith, the offensive line coach, filled in for the rest of the season.

The Road Upward

No head coach had yet compiled a winning record with the Broncos. That would change with John Ralston, the new man in charge. Ralston, a college coach whose Stanford Cardinals had appeared in a couple of Rose Bowls, could see right away that he needed a starting quarterback and didn't have one. Steve Tensi had retired at the age of 28. ("Football is not fun anymore," he reportedly said.) Steve Ramsey, a good backup quarterback, was not the answer. Ralston wasted no time, trading for the Houston Oilers' Charley Johnson, a veteran quarterback, who, if not the future of the franchise, was nonetheless an experienced and capable team leader. Defensive linemen Rich Jackson and Dave Costa were traded away, but Lyle Alzado and Paul Smith remained in place, and halfback Lloyd Little was at the top of his form.

While it was hardly a team for the ages, the 1972 Broncos were a team that gained third place in the AFC Western Division, the Broncos' best finish (5-9-0) in ten years. And 1973 proved to be even better. When the Broncos defeated the Chargers, 42-28, in the next-to-last game of the season, they were assured of their first winning season ever. Oakland beat them in the final game, 21-7—a Denver win over Oakland in that game would have given the Broncos the divisional title. As it was, the Broncos had to settle for a 7-5-2 final mark. John Ralston, named coach of the year, began to dream of a Super Bowl trip in 1974. The dream was premature; although Denver did have a chance in the last game of the season to improve on its previous year's record, a 17-0 loss to the Chargers ended even that more modest aspiration. The 7-6-1 finish earned Ralston a new contract.

But in 1975 the team dipped below .500 again. Running back Otis Armstrong, who had led the AFC in rushing in 1974, suffered an injury and was sidelined. Tight end Riley Odoms, an All-Pro choice in 1974, tailed off a bit in 1975. Quarterback Charley Johnson and halfback Lloyd Little had reached the end of their careers and retired when the season ended.

John Ralston returned as head coach in 1976, and the Broncos enjoyed their best season so far, mounting a serious challenge for the divisional crown. After losing their opening game to the Bengals, 17-7, the Broncos won three straight blowouts at home, crushing the Jets, 46-3, the Browns, 44-13, and the Chargers, 26-0. Otis Armstrong was on his way to a second consecutive 1,000-yard rushing season. Unfortunately for Denver, the Oakland Raiders were on their way to a 13-1-0 record, and unfortunately for coach Ralston, the Patriots embarrassed the Broncos,

38-14, late in the season. Although Denver's 9-5-0 record, their best ever, might have argued for Ralston's staying on, he resigned under fire in January. His successor was Robert (Red) Miller, the offensive coordinator of the Patriots. Also, in what was considered a minor trade, the Broncos acquired veteran quarterback Craig Morton from the New York Giants.

Broncomania

By 1977 the Broncos—and Bronco orange—had become synonymous with Denver. The club sold 74,000 season tickets and had a waiting list of 15,000. Clearly, the fans were expecting great things of their football team in the near future. They were not disappointed. The Broncos' 3-4 defensive unit, nicknamed Orange Crush (prompting sales of the soft drink to soar), featured All-Pros Lyle Alzado, Rubin Carter, Randy Gradishar, Tom Jackson, Bill Thompson, and Louis Wright, along with Joe Rizzo.

How well quarterback Craig Morton would perform was an open question. But the team could expect impressive punt returning from young Rick Upchurch and topnotch kicking from 36-year-old Jim Turner.

The Broncos bolted off a 5-0-0 start in 1977. Opposing teams found it tough indeed to score against the Orange Crush. In those first five games only the Seattle Seahawks' offense (with 13 points) reached double figures against the formidable Denver defenders. Craig Morton—the 26th quar-

Orange Crush and Broncomania

The color orange has been associated with the Denver Broncos ever since the early 1960s, when a manufacturer delivered bright orange uniforms instead of the subdued burnt orange that had been ordered. Nothing much was made of the color at first. But then, a decade later, when John Ralston was head coach, the Broncos' Boosters Club began to pass out pieces of orange cotton cloth for the fans to wave.

Several years after that, Channel 9 sportscaster Bob Kurtz, noting the Broncos' stalwart defense (second in the AFC in points allowed and in rushing defense), coined the phrase Orange Crush to describe the new 3-4 formation—three linemen and four linebackers, with the then new position of nose tackle. The Broncos nose tackle was Rubin Carter, (6 feet; 252 pounds), an All-American defensive tackle two years earlier at the University of Miami. A fifth-round draft pick, Carter could bench-press 525 pounds and, even with all his bulk and strength, could move as quickly as a cat.

Orange Crush mania was short-lived, lasting from 1977-78, although the players who powered it were mostly long-term Broncos. Nose tackle Rubin Carter played through 1986. Linebacker Randy Gradishar was a Bronco from 1974 through 1983. Lyle Alzado, a hulking 6'3", 250-pound defensive end, whose steroid use would end his life prematurely, was already playing his seventh season at Denver when Broncomania struck.

The soft drink called Orange Crush had been a fairly weak seller in Colorado before Bob Kurtz applied the name to the Bronco defense. Joe Iacino, the man who distributed Orange Crush in the area, was ecstatic. "It's like the Fourth of July," he said. "I can't keep the shelves full." He added that he was pleased "not just because it's helping our company, but because the fans deserve it." The fans also evidently deserved—and received—Orange Crush T-shirts—65,000 of them were sold in the first 48 hours after reaching the department stores.

With the Broncos at 6-0-0 in 1977, the mayor of Denver proclaimed "Orange Sunday" in honor of the second game of the season against the Oakland Raiders. Oakland spoiled the day, however, beating the Broncos, 24-14, at Mile High Stadium. Broncomania and Orange Crush madness lived on for another year or so, and then, like all fads, receded into memory.

terback in the Broncos' brief history—quickly proved to Red Miller that he could do the job. Denver's record stood at 12-1-0, their only loss being to the Oakland Raiders in midseason, when the Broncos met the Dallas Cowboys in the regular-season finale.

The Denver-Dallas matchup was a preview of the Super Bowl, perhaps, because Dallas, at 11-2-0, seemed to be a likely Super Bowl entrant, as did Denver. Neither team showed much in the 14-6 Dallas victory. The Cowboys' offense moved no better than anyone else against the Orange Crush. Craig Morton, with a hip injury, played only briefly.

Both Dallas and Denver, whose 12-2-0 records were the best in the league, were looking forward to the playoffs. For Denver that meant first facing the Pittsburgh Steelers with Franco Harris and Mean Joe Greene. The game, played on Christmas Eve, went to the Broncos, 34-21, before 75,011 fans at Mile High Stadium, the largest crowd ever to watch a sporting event in the state of Colorado. Broncomania reigned. The color orange was everywhere. On television, Dickens's *A Christmas Carol* was preempted for filmed highlights of the Broncos' win over the Steelers. A Denver man sold his 23-year-old Buick (no transmission) for $600. The appeal: four tickets to the upcoming playoff game on New Year's Day against the Oakland Raiders for the AFC title and a shot at the Super Bowl.

The Road to Super Bowl XII

John Madden's Raiders, a wild card qualifier at 11-3-0, had already beaten the Broncos once in the regular season. Not this time. Before 74,982 spectators at Mile High Stadium the Broncos held a 7-3 lead at halftime on a touchdown pass from Craig Morton to Haven Moses. Midway through the fourth quarter the Broncos had built the lead to 20-10, but the Raiders came back to cut the lead to 20-17 with 3:16 remaining. Denver received and let the clock run out. Haven Moses turned a cartwheel as fans surged onto the field.

At the Louisiana Superdome in New Orleans the Dallas Cowboys, coached by Tom Landry, took a 13-0 lead over Denver at halftime, and it could have been worse. The Denver offense was shut down. In the third quarter Jim Turner kicked a 47-yard field goal to make it 13-3. But nothing really worked for the Broncos that day, and the final score was Dallas 27, Denver 10. "It hurts too much inside to cry," said defensive end Lyle Alzado. But coach Red Miller promised, "We'll make it here again." And they would—but not with Miller at the helm.

In 1978 and 1979 identical 10-6-0 records carried Denver to the playoffs, first in a repeat match against the Pittsburgh Steelers (the Steelers winning, 33-10, in 1978), then against the Houston Oilers (the Oilers winning, 13-7, in 1979). The Broncos won the AFC Western divisional title in 1978 but not in 1979, when they were a wild-card qualifier. Fan interest remained high despite postseason disappointments. Season ticket renewals approached 100 percent. In 1979 Rick Upchurch set the all-time pro football record for punt-return yardage, surpassing Emlen Tunnell's prior mark of 2,209 yards.

In 1980 the Broncos slipped to 8-8-0. Red Miller started young quarterback Matt Robinson, acquired from the Jets, but soon went back to Craig Morton as the offense sputtered. Kicker Fred Steinfort, a product of Boston College, booted 26 field goals to tie for the league lead. One of them was a booming 57-footer. Injuries hurt the defense, although linebacker Randy Gradishar continued to shine. Against the Cleveland Browns he intercepted a pass at the Bronco seven-yard line and toted it 93 yards for a touchdown.

In February 1981 Edgar F. Kaiser, Jr., purchased the Denver Broncos from principal owners Gerald H. Phipps and Allan R. Phipps. New ownership brought a new general manager, Grady Alderman, and a new head coach, Dan Reeves. While Red Miller's 42-25-0 record with the Broncos could hardly be faulted, it was nonetheless a coup for Denver to sign Reeves, who had been Tom Landry's heir apparent on the coaching staff of the Dallas Cowboys.

The Dan Reeves Decade

Under new head coach Dan Reeves the Broncos stayed in the AFC Western race for most of the 1981 season. Old-timers Randy Gradishar, Bill Thompson, and Bob Swenson put in All-Pro seasons, although the stingy Bronco defense became more generous with points late in the campaign. Reeves gave veteran wide receiver Steve Watson a starting role, and Watson responded with an All-Pro season of his own. Rookie fullback Rick Parros from Utah State also looked good. Late-season losses dropped Denver to 10-6-0, the same as the San Diego Chargers. A better divisional record gave the Chargers the title.

Strike-shortened 1982 saw the Broncos fall to 2-7-0 and fail to make the 16-team playoff tournament. It was a lost season anyway. But Denver hit the road to recovery in 1983, signing quarterback John Elway via a trade with Baltimore. Elway, a sensation at Stanford University in baseball as well as football, was the most publicized college prospect since Joe Namath in 1965. He started the first five games at quarterback for the Broncos then gave way to Steve DeBerg, reclaiming the assignment when DeBerg was injured. Elway's rookie stats were less than sensational, but Reeves knew he had found his quarterback. The 9-7-0 Broncos of 1983 earned a wild-card playoff bid, but fell to the Seattle Seahawks, 31-7, at the Kingdome.

It was rock-solid defense that provided much of the impetus for a 13-3-0 season in 1984. Despite Randy Gradishar's retirement and Bob Swenson's injuries, the defense held Bronco opponents to a mere 241 yards, while the offense—led by John Elway, running back Sammy Winder, and wide receiver Steve Watson—produced enough points to keep winning. Indeed, after being blanked, 27-0, by the Chicago Bears in the second game of the season, the Broncos reeled off ten straight victories, the most in their history, before losing close games to the Seattle Seahawks and Kansas City Chiefs near the end of the season. In postseason play the Broncos went up against a familiar rival, the Pittsburgh Steelers, and succumbed, 24-17. In the final quarter, with the score tied 17-17, Pittsburgh's Eric Williams intercepted an Elway pass and returned it to the Denver two-yard line with 2:45 to play. Two plays later the Steelers went up by a touchdown. It ended that way after two more Denver possessions. An AFC championship, not to mention a trip to the Rose Bowl, would have to wait at least another year.

The 1985 season saw John Elway advance toward the superstardom he seemed sure to achieve. The Bronco team, on the other hand, had a sometimes impressive but ultimately frustrating time of it, losing two close games to the Raiders late in the season to thwart their chance at the division title. The Broncos' 11-5-0 record would ordinarily have qualified them for a wild-card spot, but both the Jets and Patriots were also 11-5, and the intricate NFL rules gave those two teams the nod. Elway passed for 3,891 yards, a Bronco record, while his 4,144 total yards on offense also set a new Denver standard. Steve Watson and Sammy Winder continued to star, while, on defense, Karl Mecklenburg recorded 13 quarterback sacks, another team high.

Although the 1986 Broncos did no better on paper in the regular season than they had in 1985—11-5-0—they marched straight to the AFC Western Division title, the AFC championship, and a meeting with the New York Giants in Super Bowl XXI at the Rose Bowl in Pasadena. They started off by winning six straight games before the Jets finally stopped them at the Meadowlands. In the last half of the season they alternated wins and losses as their efforts seemed to weaken somewhat. On offense John Elway was a one-man sensation, while the defense, strong at the outset, was anchored by end Rulon Jones, cornerback Louis Wright, and linebackers Karl Mecklenburg and Rickey Hunley.

In the 1986 playoffs the Broncos engineered two come-from-behind victories on their road to the AFC title. First, they recovered from a 17-13 deficit to edge the New England Patriots, 22-17. The two big plays of the comeback drive were John Elway's 48-yard pass to Vance Johnson and Rulon Jones's sack of Patriot quarterback Tony

PROFILE

Enter (and Exit) Dan Reeves

When Edgar F. Kaiser, Jr., a businessman from Vancouver, British Columbia, purchased the Denver Broncos in 1981 for something over $30 million, he decided to replace head coach Red Miller. No one could fault Miller's record at Denver, which was 42-25-0 after succeeding John Ralston in February of 1977—just in time to lead the Broncos to Super Bowl. But now, after a disappointing though not disastrous 8-8-0 season in 1980, the new Bronco owner wanted a different head coach.

The man Kaiser chose was 37-year-old Dan Reeves, the offensive coordinator of the Dallas Cowboys. Reeves had played for the Cowboys for eight seasons, a running back who finished his career as the Cowboys' fifth all-time leading rusher (at the time). He then served as Tom Landry's backfield coach before moving up to the defensive coordinator's job. A tough-minded, no-nonsense leader, Reeves was a Landry favorite and was widely regarded as Landry's successor as head coach of the Cowboys. Instead, he took over the Broncos.

Reeves's disciplined approach seemed to be what Denver needed. Starting in 1983, when the Broncos were wild-card qualifiers, into the late 1980s, when they went to the Super Bowl three times, Dan Reeves' teams were always competitive. He compiled a 110-79-1 coaching record through 1992, and when premier NFL coaches were discussed, his name was sure to be among them. As late as 1991 his Broncos won the AFC Western Division title, putting together a 12-4-0 record, just missing the AFC championship on a close 10-7 loss to the rampaging Buffalo Bills.

The 1992 Broncos fell to 8-8-0—the same mark that had proved to be Red Miller's Waterloo. Yet many observers were surprised when Pat Bowlen, the team's owner since 1984, did not renew Dan Reeves's contract. The head coaching job went to affable, easygoing Wade Phillips, Reeves' defensive coordinator. Over the years the pure-business, succeed-or-else approach of Dan Reeves had begun to wear on his players. All-Pro linebacker Karl Mecklenburg, a Bronco since 1983, said flatly he would not have played in 1993 if Reeves had returned. Whether the laid-back style of Wade Phillips or the hard-driving manner of Dan Reeves—who soon took over the head coaching duties for the New York Giants—was best for the Broncos would perhaps become clearer with the passage of time.

Eason in the end zone for a safety with 1:37 left on the clock. Next, the Broncos fought back from 20-13 margin in favor of the Cleveland Browns to record a 23-20 overtime win and capture the AFC championship. Elway led a long touchdown drive in the final minutes of play to give Denver a 20-20 tie. In overtime the Broncos worked the ball to the Browns' 15-yard line. Rich Karlis, who had played an important part in the victory over the Patriots, kicked the three-pointer to sink the Browns. It was then on to Pasadena and Super Bowl XXI, where the New York Giants lay in wait.

Super Bowl XXI, played before a crowd of 101,063, started well for the Broncos. Karlis put Denver on the board first by kicking a 48-yard field goal, and by halftime the Broncos held a slim 10-9 lead. But the third quarter was all New York's, as the Giants scored 17 unanswered points to take a lead that would hold up until the end. The passing of John Elway and kicking of Rich Karlis sparked Denver's offense, but when the clock ran out the Giants were on top, 39-20.

Twice More to the Super Bowl

Dan Reeves's star quarterback, John Elway, was nonpareil in 1987, aided by the "Three Amigos," as they were called—wide receivers Vance Johnson, Mark Jackson, and Ricky Nattiel. In midseason the Broncos went to the shotgun

PROFILE John Elway: Fourth-Quarter Comeback King

From 1983 through 1992 Bronco quarterback John Elway directed a total of 31 fourth-quarter, game-saving drives. In those games the team posted a 30-0-1 record. One of Elway's finest hours (or, more accurately, 15 minutes) came on January 4, 1992, in the AFC Championship Game against the Houston Oilers. At one point in the first half the Oilers led 21-6 and seemed to be in control. But then, with six minutes left in the half, the Broncos' Steve Atwater intercepted a Warren Moon pass.

Photo: *AP/Wide World Photos*

John Elway connected on six passes in six attempts, and Steve Sewell threw one for one, as the Broncos drove 88 yards downfield. Running back Greg Lewis carried it over from the one-yard line. David Treadwell's conversion made the score 21-13 at halftime. In the third quarter the Broncos called on Treadwell to attempt a 49-yard field goal. He put the ball through the uprights, the longest field goal in Denver's postseason history, closing the gap to 21-16. But the Oilers, on their next drive, advanced to the Broncos' 25, and a Houston field goal made the score 24-16 in their favor.

Thus trailing in the fourth quarter, Denver started from its own 20-yard line. Nine plays later, facing a fourth-and-four situation at the Houston 41, Elway tossed a short pass to wide receiver Michael Young, who broke away for a 26-yard gain. Three plays later Greg Lewis again barrelled in from the one, making the score 24-23 in favor of the Oilers. When Houston's next drive stalled, Elway took over at the Denver two yard line with 2:07 minutes and no time outs remaining. After gaining short yardage, the Broncos faced a fourth-and-sixth decision at their own 28. Elway dropped back to pass then ran upfield and out of bounds for a seven-yard gain and a first down.

Three plays and three incomplete passes later, Elway had to deal with another fourth-down situation. He dropped back again, started to run, then passed to Vance Johnson, who raced to the Houston 21 for a 44-yard gain. After Steve Sewell picked up short yardage rushing, two more plays took the clock to 20 seconds. David Treadwell came in to kick. He booted the football 28 yards for three points and a 26-24 Bronco victory.

"I'm numb," said Bronco coach Dan Reeves in the immediate aftermath, but added, "When you've got No. 7, anything is possible." John Elway, of course, was wearing jersey No. 7.

offense, an attack that proved potent whether the Broncos were passing or running. The defense, usually reliable, experienced injuries, retirements, and reorganization. A players' strike at the beginning of the season resulted in three games in 1987 being played by "replacement teams." Denver lost the first of these to the Houston Oilers, 40-10, but won the next two. The Broncos' regular-season record was 10-4-1, good for first place in the AFC Western Division.

In postseason play the "real" Denver Broncos sent the Oilers packing, 34-10, then moved on to the AFC Championship Game against the Cleveland Browns. It was a rematch between 1986's AFC rivals. This time the Broncos seemed determined to avoid catch-up football. They took a 21-3 lead into halftime. That margin evaporated quickly in the second half, however, as the Browns, led by quarterback Bernie Kosar, evened the score at 31-31. With Elway passing to Rickey Nattiel and Sammy Winder, the Broncos went up 38-31 with just over four minutes to play. A Browns' rally fell short, but a safety closed the gap 38-33, the final score. For the second year in a row the Broncos advanced to the Super Bowl.

The story of Super Bowl XXII is encapsulated in the second quarter, during which the Washington Redskins piled up 35 points to erase a 10-0 Bronco lead and put the game on ice. The game started very differently. On the first play from scrimmage John Elway connected with a 56-yard touchdown bomb to Ricky Nattiel. On the Broncos' next possession, the offense powered its way to the seven-yard line, Rich Karlis kicked a field goal, and Denver held a 10-0 edge. They never scored again.

The Broncos' Super Bowl record dropped to 0-3. Although they were one of the dominant NFL teams of the 1980s—along with the Miami Dolphins, Washington Redskins, San Francisco 49ers, and Buffalo Bills—they were never able to capture the ultimate prize.

John Elway came up with a sore arm in 1988. The Broncos acquired Hall of Fame-bound running back Tony Dorsett from the Dallas Cowboys, but he was long past his prime. Denver skidded to 8-8-0. The main problem was defense. Elway recovered sufficiently to pass for 3,309 yards, while aging Tony Dorsett picked up enough yards on the ground to place him second behind Walter Payton among the NFL's all-time rushing leaders. At the end of the season Dan Reeves fired most of the defensive coaches, including coordinator Joe Collier, who had been with the team for 20 years. Wade Phillips, the son of former NFL coach Bum Phillips, replaced Collier. Top draft pick Steve Atwater, a safety man, signed on, as did free-agent cornerback Wymon Henderson. Tony Dorsett faded into the sunset.

The Broncos charged back in 1989 to capture the AFC crown and trek once more to the Super Bowl. Improved defense helped considerably, with veteran linebackers Karl Mecklenburg and Simon Fletcher getting needed support from the newcomers and from a new defensive strategy. In 1988 opposing teams had scored 352 points against the Broncos; in 1989 they scored a mere 226. Elway was a bit off in 1989, but rookie running back Bobby Humphrey rushed for 1,151 yards. In the divisional playoff game against the Pittsburgh Steelers, Denver gained a come-from-behind 24-23 victory before 75,868 fans at Mile High Stadium. A week later in Denver they captured the AFC championship by defeating the Cleveland Browns, 37-21. John Elway threw for 385 yards and three touchdowns.

The Broncos' momentum did not carry over to Super Bowl XXIV, where, at the New Orleans Superdome, the San Francisco 49ers, paced by quarterback Joe Montana, scored two touchdowns in each quarter and buried Denver, 55-10. It was the biggest margin of victory in Super Bowl history. The 49ers gained 461 yards to the Broncos' 167. Defensive coordinator Wade Phillips was not happy. The game was simply no contest.

As if in repentance, the Broncos plummeted to the AFC Western Division cellar in 1990 on a 5-11-0 mark. Quarterback John Elway had a so-so year, sophomore running back Bobby Humphrey sprained his ankle early on, and the defensive unit was riddled with injuries. Nevertheless, by season's end, Elway had passed for

3,526 yards, Humphrey had rushed for 1,202 yards, and five-year veteran Mike Horan had compiled the best punting stats in the NFL—none of which staved off frequent defeat for the Broncos. Head Coach Dan Reeves, who had undergone preseason surgery to clear blocked arteries, suffered his worst season since strike-skewed 1982. Yet few doubted that Reeves and the Broncos would rebound.

The first game of the 1991 season pitted Denver against the 1990 Central Division champs, the Cincinnati Bengals. The Broncos pounded the Bengals, 45-14, to record the biggest opening day win in their history. After falling to the L.A. Raiders, 16-13, they put together three straight wins then lost a game every three weeks or so thereafter, finishing at 12-4-0.

Undisputed AFC West champs for the fifth time in eight years, the Broncos met the Oilers in postseason play. In a hard-fought game at Mile High Stadium, Denver eked out a 26-24 win over Houston, coming back from a 21-6 deficit. Their Super Bowl hopes ended a week later in Buffalo, however, as the Bills, quarterbacked by Jim Kelly, hung on to win, 10-7.

The 1992 season marked the end of Dan Reeves' long and successful tenure as head coach of the Denver Broncos. Few expected him to depart, but an 8-8-0 record coupled with the need for an overhaul, particularly on offense, spurred Broncos' owner Pat Bowlen to announce that Reeves's contract would not be renewed for 1993. Reeves's replacement, Wade Phillips, had been installed as defensive coordinator five years earlier by the departing head coach.

Bowlen, determined to position the Broncos for another run at the Super Bowl, shopped aggressively for the talent to achieve that goal. Denver signed running backs Rod Bernstine and Robert Delpino, along with offensive linemen Don Maggs and Brian Habib. He also inked a new four-year contract with "the franchise," quarterback John Elway, superstar for a decade and a likely shoo-in for the Pro Football Hall of Fame.

Sources

Books

Alzado, Lyle, with Paul Zimmerman, *Mile High: The Story of Lyle Alzado and the Amazing Denver Broncos,* Atheneum, 1978.

The Complete Handbook of Pro Football, 1993, edited by Zander Hollander, Signet, 1993.

Denver Broncos Media Guide, 1993.

Neft, David S., and Richard M. Cohen, *The Football Encyclopedia: The Complete History of Professional NFL Football From 1892 to the Present,* St. Martin's Press, 1991.

Paige, Woodrow, Jr., *Orange Madness: The Incredible Odyssey of the Denver Broncos,* Thomas Y. Crowell, 1978.

Porter, David L., editor, *Biographical Dictionary of American Sports: Football,* Greenwood Press, 1987.

Sporting News Pro Football Guide, 1993 Edition, The Sporting News Publishing Co., 1993.

Periodicals

New York Times, March 10, 1981; January 5, 1992.

Sports Illustrated, October 17, 1977; October 19, 1981.

—*Gerald Tomlinson* for Book Builders Inc.

Kansas City Chiefs

Few people remember the second trans-Atlantic flight or the second expedition to the North Pole. A casual football fan will very likely remember that Joe Namath's New York Jets were the first American Football League team to win a Super Bowl, but not many recall that another former AFL squad, the Kansas City Chiefs, did it a year later.

The Chiefs entered professional football as the Dallas Texans and were one of the most successful teams of the 1960s and early 1970s. Their rivalry with the Oakland Raiders provided some epic battles. Kansas City experienced some lean years during the 1980s, but under coach Marty Schottenheimer's direction the Chiefs are back among the NFL's elite.

The history of the Chiefs began in 1958 when Lamar Hunt, a wealthy, 26-year-old Texan, failed in his attempt to buy the Chicago Cardinals and move them to his native Dallas. Hunt then spoke to NFL commissioner Bert Bell about an expansion franchise for Dallas and was turned down. He went back to Mrs. Walter Wolfner, the widow of Cardinals' founder Charles Bidwell, and was turned down again.

Frustrated, Hunt returned to Dallas and hit upon a brilliant idea. "It was like a light bulb coming on," he said. He figured that because men in Minneapolis, Houston and Denver had also tried to buy the Cardinals and had also been rebuffed, they might be interested in a new league.

Hunt contacted K.S. "Bud" Adams in Houston and Bob Howsam in Denver and found them enthusiastic about the idea. In the summer of 1959, he officially launched the American Football League with charter members in Dallas, Denver, Houston, Minneapolis, Los Angeles and New York. Later that year, Boston and Buffalo also joined the new league. Hunt had hoped to coexist peacefully with the NFL, but when the older league announced plans to expand to Dallas and Houston the seeds of war were planted.

"Hunt fought the battle with talent, money, brains and foresight," wrote Dick Connor in *Great Teams' Great Years: Kansas City Chiefs.* "And he waged his battle with three men who remained with him for years—until long after the AFL was finally absorbed into the NFL. One of these men was Hank Stram, who joined Hunt almost at the start. Stocky, vain, inventive and a brilliant football tactician, Stram had spent a long apprenticeship as an assistant coach in college. The second man was Jack Steadman, an SMU man like Hunt, who had shown a preference for business affairs and a talent for management. The third man was Len Dawson, a quarterback the NFL had discarded as a failure.

"Together this unlikely quartet—a millionaire, a tailor's son, a businessman and a backup quarterback who had been waived by every team in the NFL—created one of pro football's most imposing records," Connor wrote. "They survived the lean years and the humiliation of having to leave Dallas in 1963 for a new start in Kansas City. They survived more hardships in Kansas City before moving into national prominence in 1966 as the first AFL team to challenge the reign of the NFL's Green Bay Packers. That they lost the game (35-10) mattered little in perspective."

Hunt was the cornerstone of the new league and the other owners recognized his contribution. "Before there was a player, coach or general manager in the league there was Lamar Hunt," said former Patriots' owner Billy Sullivan. "Hunt was the cornerstone, the integrity of the league. Without him there would have been no AFL."

A Strong Show Of Faith

The Texans had strong home-state ties during their first season in the Cotton Bowl. The quarterback was Cotton Davidson, an All-American from Baylor. Fullback Jack Spikes had been an outstanding player at Texas Christian and Abner Haynes had starred at North Texas State. After winning five straight pre-season games, the Texans drew 51,000 fans for their final exhibition against Houston, a 42-3 victory.

Haynes led the new league in rushing with 875 yards and in touchdowns with nine. The Texans had a flashy, high-scoring club and only three close losses kept them from challenging for the division championship. A variety of promotional ploys helped Dallas average 24,500 for their home games, the highest attendance in the league.

E.J. Holub, the Texas Tech All-American center described as "the best football player in America" by many scouts was drafted first by both Dallas teams. Hunt considered it a major victory for the new league when Holub agreed to play for the Texans. Hunt also signed three more quality rookies for the 1961 season—Southern Methodist's Jerry Mays, Fred Arbanas of Michigan State and Ohio State's Jim Tyrer.

The revitalized Texans won four of their five pre-season games and three of their first four during the season. Spikes was then injured and his absence from the running attack put even more pressure on Davidson's already erratic passing. Dallas fell into a six-game losing streak, then rallied to win three of its last four and finished second in the Western Division at 6-8.

Don Klosterman was named the club's player personnel director in 1962 and Stram made his most important acquisition when he invited Dawson, whom he had once coached at Purdue, to try out for the Texans. Another key addition was Curtis McClinton, a 6-foot-3, 227-pound running back who had enough speed to run the high hurdles at Kansas. With Dawson directing Haynes and McClinton, the Texans clinched the division title in November and finished with an 11-3 record.

Arbanas, fully recovered from a back injury that kept him out for the 1961 campaign, was instrumental in Dallas' turnaround with his receiving and blocking. His contribution to the ground game helped Haynes to his greatest year, which included 1,049 yards and a record 13 rushing touchdowns. Dawson, who threw 29 TD passes, was voted Player of the Year. McClinton was the league's top rookie and Stram earned Coach of the Year honors. Dallas won the AFL

Team Information at a Glance

Founded in 1960 as the Dallas Texans (AFL);
moved to Kansas City and changed name, 1963;
joined the NFL, 1970

Home stadium: Arrowhead Stadium
1 Arrowhead Dr.
Kansas City, MO 64129
Phone: (816) 924-9300
Seating capacity: 78,097

Team colors: Red, gold, and white.
Team logo: An arrowhead bearing the letters "KC"
Team nickname: Texans, 1960-63; Chiefs, 1963—

Franchise record:	Won	Lost	Tie
1960-92	229	219	12

Played in first Super Bowl (defeated by the Green Bay Packers, 35-10), 1966
Winners of Super Bowl IV (defeated the Minnesota Vikings, 23-7), 1969

championship when Tommy Brooker kicked a 25-yard field goal in overtime to beat the Houston Oilers 20-17.

"I remember in the huddle," McClinton said. "Some of the guys started to say something to Tommy about the kick and somebody else hushed them up, afraid they would make Tommy nervous. But Tommy just looked at us and laughed. 'Don't worry about it,' he said. 'It's all over now.'" Holub snapped the ball, Dawson placed it on the 25-yard line and Brooker delivered his 14th field goal of the year, clearing the crossbar by 10 feet to end what was then pro football's longest game. After 77 minutes and 54 seconds, the Texans had become the AFL's third champion.

The length of the game, however, was only one topic of post-game discussion. After regulation time expired, Dallas won the coin toss. Stram, confident of his defense but fearful of his team's punting, chose to defend the goal that would force Houston to go against a strong wind. He instructed Haynes to tell the officials. But Haynes, the team captain, fumbled the assignment. He stated that Dallas chose to kick. Houston then elected to defend the goal Stram wanted.

"The players were excited and tugging at Abner," explained Stram. "He just didn't understand the options." Johnny Robinson took Haynes off the hook when he intercepted a pass at the Texans' 40 to end Houston's first possession of the overtime.

Plagued By Disaster

The AFL's stay in Dallas ended in 1963 when H. Roe Bartle, the mayor of Kansas City, invited Hunt to move his team to the Missouri city. Bartle promised to enlarge Kansas City's Municipal Stadium and guaranteed Hunt three times as many season ticket sales as the Texans had in Dallas.

Impressed with the inducements and the fact that the nearest pro football rival was 250 miles away, Hunt announced on February 8, that he was shifting the franchise to Kansas City and renaming it the Chiefs. "People say Dallas is a poor sports town, but I think the situation of having two teams has been the fault here," Hunt said. "I anticipated a one-team city."

He also said that he hadn't expected how much television would hurt. "While one team is trying to sell tickets to a home game in the Cotton Bowl, the other team is beaming its game into town free. I can't be bitter at the city. And I can't be bitter at the situation that has existed. I don't think they (the NFL) did the right thing. What they did was wrong for pro football."

Hunt suggested that his move to Kansas City might be the first step in inter-league operation. "Obviously, the leagues could never get together until the Dallas situation was resolved," he said.

There was a lot of confusion with the two new teams in Dallas. A national magazine once placed ads in the Dallas dailies, telling them about an upcoming story on Tom Landry, "the brilliant young coach of the Dallas Texans." And when the Kansas City-based Rockne Club of America honored Stram as coach of the year after the 1962 season, they sent the letter in care of the Cowboys.

The first of several tragedies visited the franchise in 1963 when Stone Johnson, a rookie running back, suffered a broken neck returning a kickoff in a pre-season game and died eight days later.

Kansas City opened the regular season with a 59-7 victory over Denver, but the new-look Chiefs with rookies Ed Budde, Buck Buchanan and Bobby Bell in the lineup, managed only one win and two ties in their next nine games and finished 5-7-2.

Ten regulars were hurt at one time or another during the 1964 season. McClinton broke a hand in training camp and it bothered him all year. Holub tore up a knee and missed the last five games. Robinson, the outstanding defensive back, suffered a rib injury in November and was out for the year. Arbanas was mugged on a Kansas City street and blinded in his left eye.

Burdened with such misfortune, the Chiefs played erratically and finished 7-7. Attendance was disappointing. Seven home games at Municipal Stadium drew only 126,881 and when the AFL owners' meetings were held, there was discussion about the Chiefs' future in Kansas City.

Among the bright spots in 1964 was the emergence of rookie running back Mack Lee Hill, who was signed as a free agent. The Chiefs drafted Gale Sayers, the spectacular breakaway runner from Kansas in the first round in 1965, but the Chicago Bears won him in a bidding war.

Some of the sting of losing Sayers was soothed by the emergence of fourth-round pick Otis Taylor, a big-play receiver from Prairie View. Haynes, who had been the AFL Comeback Player of the Year in 1964, was traded to Denver for linebacker Jim Fraser and cash.

Tragedy struck again in 1965 when Hill died on the operating table after routine knee surgery. He was being prepared for return to his hospital

Talented Toes

Since moving from Dallas to Kansas City in 1963, the Chiefs have used fewer place kickers in 30 years than some teams use in a season. Tommy Brooker, the hero of the overtime championship victory against Houston in 1962, kicked for the Chiefs until he was replaced by Mike Mercer in 1966.

Jan Stenerud, who became the first full-time kicker elected to the Pro Football Hall of Fame, took over in 1967 and kicked through the 1979 season. He was replaced by Nick Lowery, who has been on the job since 1980. Lowery entered the 1993 season as the second-most accurate kicker in NFL history with an 80.1 field-goal percentage.

bed when it was discovered that Hill's body temperature had soared to 108 degrees. After a desperate battle that included ice water enemas and alcohol baths, Hill was pronounced dead.

The Chiefs finished the 1965 season with a 7-5-2 mark and three of the defeats were by three points or less.

Intercepted

Running back Mike Garrett, the Heisman Trophy winner from Southern Cal, was drafted in the 20th round in 1966. Garrett was also drafted by his hometown Los Angeles Rams, but the Chiefs signed the swift runner the team needed for $400,000. "In the past we ground out yardage inch by inch," Stram said. "We moved by bus. Now we travel by jet."

A crowd of 43,885, the largest ever to see a sporting event in Kansas City, turned out to see the home opener with Buffalo. The Chiefs lost 29-14, but after the game, in the middle of the field, Stram and Bills' coach Joe Collier negotiated a trade. Kansas City got kicker Mike Mercer for a fifth-round pick. The deal solidified the one weak link in the Chiefs' attack.

Mercer proved his worth in a title-clinching 32-24 win over New York in late November by kicking 32, 15, 47 and 33-yard field goals. Garrett, whose lateral quickness gave Kansas City a genuine outside threat, was second in the AFL in rushing with 801 yards and his 5.45 yards-per-carry was the league's best average. Dawson led the AFL in passing and Taylor caught 58 passes for a 22.4 average. The Chiefs finished 11-2-1, three games ahead of Oakland in the West Division.

Using their flashy I-formation offense and an assortment of defenses, Kansas City confused and outplayed Buffalo in winning the AFL championship 31-7 to gain a berth in the first Super Bowl. The city went wild and more than 6,300 fans bought tickets for the first AFL-NFL matchup at the Los Angeles Coliseum. The Chiefs played Vince Lombardi's Packers close, trailing 14-10 at the half, but Green Bay took charge in the second half and posted a 35-10 victory.

"I sincerely felt that we could win," Stram said. "And I think our people felt that way. I'll never forget it. One of our players walked into the locker room and blurted out, 'We've got them. They're a bunch of old men, getting tired. They're not in real good shape.' "And they really felt that way," Stram continued. "Then all of a sudden it blew up in the second half with the quick interception."

One play, an interception by Willie Wood at the Green Bay 45 in the third minute of the second half, turned the game. Wood returned to the Chiefs' five and on the next play Elijah Pitts raced into the end zone and turned a close game into a 21-10 Packers' lead.

"I would like to think that one play doesn't make that much difference, but in this case it did," Stram said. "Our personality changed. We diverted from our game plan, from the things we had set out to do and had accomplished the first half."

A Slow Recovery

The loss to Green Bay prompted an emphasis on defense in the Chiefs' 1967 draft. They got linebacking strength in Maxwell Trophy winner Jim Lynch of Notre Dame and Little All-American Willie Lanier from Morgan State. Specialists Jan Stenerud and Nolan "Super Gnat" Smith were also selected.

Interest in the team skyrocketed. Season ticket sales which reached 22,000 in 1966 went over 30,000 in 1967. The seating capacity in Municipal Stadium was increased from 40,000 to 47,000. In June, the voters in Jackson County approved a $43 million general obligation bond issue for construction of a sports complex that would feature both a football and baseball stadium. A two-thirds approval was required and the bond carried with 67 percent of the vote.

The Chiefs started well in 1967, but injuries to center Jon Gilliam and linebackers Holub and Lanier weakened the middle of the offense and defense. Kansas City scrambled for three straight wins at the end of the year to finish in second place with a 9-5 record. Stenerud, a Norwegian from Montana State, led the league in field goals with 21, while Smith, the 5-6, 154-pound sprinter from Tennessee State, led the AFL in kickoff return yardage.

Kansas City's offensive power was depleted early in the 1968 season by injuries to running backs Bert Coan and Garrett and receivers Taylor and Gloster Richardson. The offense scored no touchdowns in a 20-19 loss to New York. Stram improvised, bringing quarterback Jacky Lee and running back Robert Holmes off the bench, and both played well in a 34-2 win over Denver in Week 3. Dawson returned the following week to direct a 48-3 rout of Miami.

The Chiefs ran their winning streak to six, en route to a 12-2 finish and a first-place tie with Oakland in the West Division. In the playoff game, the Raiders built a 21-0 lead in the first quarter and coasted to a 41-6 victory. All the Kansas City scoring came in the second quarter when the Chiefs ran 10 plays inside the Raiders' 10-yard line and could manage only two field goals.

A 6-0 pre-season was a sign of things to come for the Chiefs in 1969. They started the regular season with a comfortable win over San Diego and Boston, but in the 31-0 win over the Patriots, Dawson injured his knee and was replaced by Lee for Game 3 against Cincinnati. Kansas City lost the game 24-19 and lost Lee with a cracked bone in his ankle. Mike Livingston became the third QB in three weeks and helped turn things around in a 26-13 victory over Denver that ignited a seven-game winning streak.

Two months into the season, Dawson returned. The Chiefs finished with an 11-3 record, second to Oakland's 12-1-1, but it was the first year of a new playoff system that pitted the first and second-place finishers in opposite divisions against each other in the first round. Kansas City relied on its strong defense to turn back the defending Super Bowl champion New York Jets 13-6, while the Raiders crushed Houston 56-7.

The Chiefs, who had lost to Oakland twice during the regular season, rallied from an early 7-0 deficit to win 17-7 in the AFC championship game. "I dwelt on that championship thing," Stram said of his brief halftime message. "I said I thought we were a little tight, but that we could work it out. And I said it had been going on for six months, and now we were within 30 minutes of a championship." At that point he paused and looked at his team. "We have it in the grasp of our hands. All we have to do is squeeze."

Jim Otto, Oakland's veteran center, summed up the rivalry between the Chiefs and Raiders. "We're like tough old partners of an unhappy marriage, each knowing just where to kick, scratch and scream to cause each other the most anguish.

Media Mayhem

Kansas City's opponents in Super Bowl IV in New Orleans were the Minnesota Vikings and the Chiefs used the game as a crusade for the American Football League. They wore patches on their jerseys saying "AFL-10," which referred to the 10-year existence of the AFL, the league that would become extinct in the new NFL setup.

Oddsmakers had established the Vikings as two-touchdown favorites, but the Chiefs came out with three Stenerud field goals and a second-quarter fumble recovery on the Minnesota 19 that led to Garrett's five-yard touchdown run and a 16-0 halftime lead. A 46-yard pass from Dawson to Otis Taylor in the third quarter sealed Kansas City's first Super Bowl championship 23-7.

Dawson was the subject of a major controversy during the week before the Super Bowl when NBC used his name and those of some other athletes in connection with the story on the arrest of a Detroit gambler. Dawson, within days of what could be the most momentous game of his career, fought to regain his composure as he listened unbelievingly to the words coming from the television set in Stram's hotel suite.

When he met with the press after the story broke, Dawson admitted that he knew the gambler, Donald "Dice" Dawson, but only casually. Len Dawson said he had met Donald Dawson some 10 years earlier when he played for Pittsburgh, but he never had business dealings with him and didn't know why his name would have been in the gambler's possession when he was arrested.

The next morning Dawson reread the statement to his teammates. Stram asked if there were any questions. "Yeah," said Holub, "Have our tickets come in yet?" "When Lenny explained his side, we had no doubts whatever," one Chiefs' veteran said. "We never had anyway. If you knew Lenny, you knew there was nothing to it."

Dawson endured a hard week. "Lenny said he'd never been through anything like it," said his roommate Johnny Robinson. "I know it hit him real hard. It ate him up inside, and it looked to me as if he aged five years from Tuesday to Thursday."

Dawson set a Super Bowl record by throwing only 17 passes, but he also set a record by completing 70.7 percent of them. Garrett, Holmes, Warren McVea and Wendell Hayes had gained 151 yards against the Purple People Eaters. The Vikings finished with only 67 yards.

"The Chiefs' defensive line looked like a redwood forest," said Minnesota QB Joe Kapp. "They took the running game away from us. We went into the game wanting to run the ball, and their defense was able to take it away. They didn't do a lot different defensively than we had anticipated. We were well prepared. It was our intention to stay away from Bobby Bell's side of the field as much as we could. But that line—like a redwood forest in California—just seemed to block things out sometimes."

Dashed Hopes

During the 1970 regular season, relations soured between Stram and Garrett and Garrett was traded to San Diego. Despite key injuries, the Chiefs' record after 12 games was 7-3-2. They traveled to Oakland and lost 20-6, then dropped the final game to San Diego 31-13 as Garrett haunted them with his best day of the year, 95 yards.

Stram opened up the offense again in 1971 with the help of receivers like rookie Elmo Wright and Morris Stroud. Taylor emerged as one of the best pass-catchers in the game, leading the NFL in yards gained on receptions. Ed Podolak became the new running star and the linebacking trio of Lanier, Bell and Lynch was among the league's best.

After an opening loss to San Diego, the Chiefs won five straight. In the next-to-last game with Oakland, a late field goal by Stenerud gave the Chiefs a 16-14 victory and the Western Division title. Stram awarded game balls to all 40 players. The team finished with a 10-3-1 record, 1 ½ games ahead of Oakland.

But on a balmy Christmas afternoon, in the AFC playoff against East Division champion Miami, Kansas City dropped a 27-24 double-overtime decision. The game went into overtime when the usually reliable Stenerud missed a 32-yard field goal with 31 seconds to play.

The Chiefs were leading 24-17 when Miami QB Bob Griese marched the Dolphins down the field. With 1:26 remaining, he completed the 76-yard drive with a five-yard scoring strike to tight end Marv Fleming. It was after this that Stenerud missed the field goal that would have won it.

"I was on the wing and looked downfield toward the goalposts and those uprights looked about that far apart to me," said Lynch, holding his thumb and forefinger an inch apart. "And it got smaller and smaller. I knew it wasn't good. I had a good angle, but I really had to look. Jan allowed for the wind and there was none. People looking from our bench thought it was good."

By the time the second overtime period had rolled around, both teams were weary. Finally, Dolphins' fullback Larry Csonka broke loose on a 29-yard run to the Chiefs' 36. Three running plays took Miami to the 30 and Garo Yepremian came on to kick a 37-yard field goal that ended the 82-minute marathon.

Two years later the memory of the game still

haunted Stenerud. "I suppose that if you look at it from an unselfish point of view it was a fantastic game. But in my mind, it does not stick out as a great football game. It will stick out as a personal disaster," Stenerud said.

All-Star safety Johnny Robinson retired in 1972, but Dawson ended speculation that he would do the same by signing a two-year contract. Kansas City fans were introduced to their new Arrowhead Stadium with a seating capacity of 78,097.

The Chiefs opened the regular season with a loss to Miami, but eventually recovered to 5-3 with a 27-14 victory over the Raiders. Consecutive losses to Pittsburgh, San Diego and Oakland put Kansas City out of contention and the Chiefs finished 8-6—second in the West. The future no longer looked bright.

The Mean Season

The defense continued to play with its customary vigor in 1973, but the offense began showing new holes. Dawson was hurt most of the time and gave way to longtime backup Pete Beathard, who had returned for his second tour of duty with the Chiefs.

Beathard couldn't get the team going, so Stram gave Livingston a chance and he generated some excitement by getting the team into first place in late November. A 14-10 loss to Denver and a 37-7 drubbing by the division-leading Raiders knocked Kansas City out of contention and the Chiefs finished 7-5-2.

The Chiefs were 3-4 midway through the 1974 season, but then lost consecutive games to the New York Giants and San Diego and wound up 5-9 for the first losing record in 11 years. Age began to show. Dawson was 39, and the offensive linemen were older, slower and ready to be replaced. The defensive front four also needed overhauling. Stram, the only coach in the team's history, was fired at the end of the season and Paul Wiggin, an assistant with the San Francisco 49ers was named to succeed him. The highlight of the season was Emmitt Thomas' league-leading 12 interceptions.

Wiggin directed his young, inexperienced club to four victories in five games early in 1975, including a 34-31 upset of the Dallas Cowboys in a Monday night game. But then injuries hit and by the end of the year, Wiggin was scrambling for healthy bodies. A 24-21 victory over Detroit was the only bright spot in the last six games and the Chiefs again finished 5-9 and third in the Western Division. After 19 seasons, the last 14 with the Dallas-Kansas City franchise, Dawson announced his retirement.

Wiggin suffered through four straight losses at the start of the season as he continued his rebuilding program in 1976. Livingston, who seemed on the verge of becoming the regular QB several times in previous years, took over as the starter and improved considerably as the season progressed. The Chiefs won two of their last three games, including an impressive 39-14 victory over Cleveland, to finish 5-9 for the third straight year.

The poorest season in club history cost both Wiggin and his successor, Tom Bettis, their jobs in 1977. Kansas City lost its first five games before taking advantage of San Diego fumbles to score twice in 31 seconds for a 21-16 win.

The next week Cleveland crushed the Chiefs 44-7 and Wiggin was fired. Bettis was promoted to head coach and the players dedicated the next game to Wiggin and beat Green Bay 20-10. But six straight losses closed out a 2-12 campaign and Bettis' contract was not renewed. The heart of the Kansas City defense also departed as 11-year veterans Lynch and Lanier retired after the season.

Running On Empty

Marv Levy, the former head coach of the Montreal Alouettes of the Canadian Football League, was named head coach in 1978. He drafted for defense and took Art Still, a defensive end from Kentucky, in the first round. Levy installed the Wing-T as his offense.

The Chiefs only passed for seven touchdowns, but they had the second-most productive ground game in the league as a record five backs—Mark Bailey, Tony Reed, MacArthur Lane, Arnold Morgado and Ted McKnight—ran for at least 100 yards in a game. The highlight of the 4-12 season was a 23-0 victory over the Chargers in which the Chiefs intercepted five San Diego passes.

Quarterback Steve Fuller of Clemson was the club's first-round draft pick in 1979. Early in the season he replaced the veteran Livingston and improved from a 1-3 start to a 7-9 finish. Despite a gradual shift from the Wing-T, the running game remained effective but the passing attack was disappointing with only seven TDs. Late in the season the defense began making strides, holding Baltimore to seven points and Tampa Bay to three.

Despite injuries to key starters in 1980, the Chiefs recovered from an 0-4 start to finish 8-8. The defense came of age with defensive backs Gary Barbaro and Gary Green and Still playing key roles. Fuller suffered a knee injury late in the season and Bill Kenney took over at quarterback and led Kansas City to two victories in its last three games.

Kenney held the job at the start of the 1981 season and the Chiefs reversed their pattern of slow starts and came out winning. Linebacker Thomas Howard returned a fumble 65 yards for a touchdown with less that two minutes remaining in the opener and Kansas City beat Pittsburgh 37-33.

On October 11, the Chiefs routed Oakland 27-0 as Kenney passed for 287 yards. Two weeks later, Kansas City defeated the Raiders again to take over first place in the AFC West with a 6-2 record. Two losses followed, but wins over Houston and Seattle put the Chiefs back in first.

Three more losses eliminated the Chiefs from the playoffs, but a season-ending 10-6 victory over the Vikings left Kansas City 9-7 for its first winning record since 1973. Rookie Joe Delaney rushed for a club-record 1,121 yards.

Things started going badly in May 1982 when Delaney required surgery to repair a detached retina. The offense suffered from his reduced availability and Levy's constant shuffling of quarterbacks Fuller and Kenney. The Chiefs lost their first four games after the players' strike and finished 3-6.

Fans lost interest and Kansas City beat the Jets 37-13 in the final game before a turnout of only 11,902, the smallest regular-season crowd since the move to Missouri. It was the final game for veteran center Jack Rudnay and also for Levy, who departed after a five-year stint that produced no playoff appearances.

Another tragedy hit the Chiefs in 1983 when Delaney drowned while trying to save a child. New coach John Mackovic was forced to give the offense a new look by turning the passing game loose. With Fuller traded, Kenney became the starter and had a fine season. Receiver Carlos Carson was his favorite target with 80 receptions for 1,351 yards.

Barbaro left for the United States Football League after a contract dispute, but he was replaced by Deron Cherry. The inconsistent play and 6-10 record failed to interest the fans and only 11,377 showed up for the home finale.

The Chiefs won their first two games and their last three in 1984, but struggled in between and wound up 8-8. The glaring weakness on offense was an erratic running game in which rookie Herman Heard was the workhorse with 684 yards in 165 carries, but he scored only four TDs.

Kenney broke his thumb in the pre-season and Todd Blackledge ran the offense until Kenney returned in relief in a 31-13 victory over San Diego on October 14. Green was traded to the Rams, but the defense had outstanding seasons from Still and Cherry while rookies Bill Maas and Kevin Ross made significant contributions. The low point of the season occurred in November when the Chiefs lost 45-0 to Seattle and dropped a 17-16 decision to winless Houston.

A seven-game losing streak in the middle of the 1985 season left Kansas City with a 6-10 record. Kenney was again plagued by injuries and so was Still. Once more the running attack sputtered. On the bright side, Cherry was All-Pro and

AP/Wide World Photos

Steve DeBerg

had four interceptions in one game, and receiver Stephone Paige broke an NFL record with 309 yards on eight receptions in a 38-34 victory over San Diego. It was the 14th straight season in which Kansas City missed the playoffs.

Fumbled Attempts

In 1986 the Chiefs had their first winning season since 1981 and earned a spot in the post-season for the first time since 1971, but Mackovic was fired after the 10-6 campaign, blamed for the team's poor offense and general disharmony. His successor, special teams coach Frank Gansz, produced a unit that blocked 11 kicks, including four by Albert Lewis, and had six touchdown returns.

In the final game against Pittsburgh with the Chiefs needing a victory to make the playoffs, the special teams accounted for all three touchdowns in a 24-19 win. The first playoff appearance in 15 years was a disappointment as Pat Ryan passed for three TDs and Freeman McNeil ran for 135 yards to lead the New York Jets to a 35-15 victory.

Gansz wasn't the genius as head coach that he'd been as assistant and the Chiefs dropped back into the Western Division cellar in 1987 with a 4-11 record. Kansas City won its opener, then plunged into a franchise-record nine game losing streak. Nose tackle Maas was the only bright spot in a defense that finished next-to-last.

The offense showed some spark with Christian Okoye, a native of Nigeria, leading all rookie runners with 660 yards. Carson gained 1,044 yards on 55 catches and Kenney played well after regaining his starting QB job.

Kenney struggled at the start of the 1988 season and Gansz replaced him with veteran journeyman Steve DeBerg. DeBerg passed for 2,935 yards, the second-highest total in club history at the time, but there was no balance in the offense as Okoye struggled with injuries. Cherry had an All-Pro season at safety, but the other Pro Bowlers in the secondary, Lloyd Burruss and Lewis, had injury problems. Still was traded to Buffalo at the beginning of the season and Maas was injured after eight games so the Chiefs lost any ability to stop opposing runners and finished 4-11-1.

Kansas City traded its first-round draft pick and its second selection to Detroit so that the Chiefs could move up one spot and draft defensive end Neil Smith of Nebraska. Although Smith became a find with two Pro Bowl appearances, the Lions took Chris Spielman with the second-round pick and he also became a perennial Pro Bowler.

The Chiefs fired Gansz and made Marty Schottenheimer their seventh head coach on January 24, 1989. Schottenheimer had guided Cleveland to two AFC championship game appearances, but he got off to a slow start in Kansas City. In their first six games, the Chiefs lost eight fumbles and threw 13 interceptions. Not surprisingly, they were 2-4 and far behind division-leading Denver.

Once Kansas City settled down, it became one of the better teams in the league. Okoye led the NFL in rushing with 1,480 yards and 12 touchdowns. DeBerg survived two early benchings to finish strong. He generated four wins in the last five games and the Chiefs wound up 8-7-1 and a half-game from the playoffs. Rookie linebacker Derrick Thomas, who had 10 sacks, keyed a defense that finished first in the conference.

High Hopes

Kansas City got out of the blocks quickly in 1990, winning three of their first four games. The club then struggled, splitting its next six, before tearing up the league in the home stretch, winning six of the last seven to finish 11-5 for the best record since the Super Bowl season of 1969.

The Chiefs' defense accounted for 60 sacks, six blocked punts, 25 fumble recoveries and 20 interceptions. Thomas had a league-high 20 sacks, including an NFL-record seven in a 17-16 loss to the Seahawks.

DeBerg had an outstanding season despite playing the last two games with a broken finger on his passing hand. He passed for 23 touchdowns and threw only four interceptions. Okoye was bothered by injuries most of the year, but Barry Word picked up the slack by rushing for 1,015 yards. The Chiefs trip to the playoffs was a short one as they lost 17-16 to Miami in the first round as Dan Marino threw a pair of fourth-quarter touchdown passes to overcome a 16-3 Kansas City lead.

Kansas City had another fine 10-6 season in 1991, but the QB situation was unsettled as DeBerg was benched in Week 15. His replacement, Mark Vlasic, was injured after only two quarters of the regular-season finale and DeBerg came back to rally the Chiefs to the second round of the playoffs. The offense was unable to make the big plays, but running backs Okoye and Word combined for 1,715 yards rushing and 13 TDs. Rookie Harvey Williams also made a significant contribution. The defense was strong with Smith and Thomas

AP/Wide World Photos

Christian Okoye

playing well in front of a secondary that did a good job of hiding its age.

In the first playoff game ever at Arrowhead, the Chiefs chalked up their first post-season win since Super Bowl IV when they forced six Los Angeles turnovers in a 10-6 victory over the Raiders. The following week, Buffalo's dynamic offense proved too much as the Bills won 37-14 in the second round as QB Jim Kelly passed for 273 yards and three Tds and running backs Thurman Thomas and Kenneth Davis combined for 175 yards.

The Chiefs battled through an injury-filled season in 1992 and needed three defensive touchdowns in their last game to qualify for the playoffs with a 42-20 win over Denver that left them with a 10-6 mark. Plan B signee David Krieg threw a pair of TD passes in the finale. Runners Okoye, Word and Williams had disappointing seasons as they combined for only 1,317 yards.

The offense continued to sputter in the playoffs as Kansas City dropped a 17-0 decision to San Diego in the first round. First-round draft pick Dale Carter of Tennessee was the AFC Defensive Rookie of the Year.

Sources

Books

Cohen, Richard M., Deutsch, Jordan A., Johnson, Roland T., and Neft, David S., *The Scrapbook History of Pro Football,* Bobbs-Merrill, 1976.

Connor, Dick, *Great Teams' Great Years: Kansas City Chiefs,* McMillan, 1974.

Dawson, Len, with Sahadi, Lou, *Len Dawson: Pressure Quarterback,* Cowles, 1970.

Green, Jerry, *Super Bowl Chronicles,* Masters Press, 1991.

Horrigan, Jack and Rathet, Mike, *The Other League,* Follett, 1970.

McGuff, Joe, *Winning it All,* Doubleday, 1970.

Neft, David S., Cohen, Richard M., and Korch, Rick, *The Sports Encyclopedia: Pro Football,* St. Martin's Press, 1993.

The Official NFL Encyclopedia of Pro Football, New American Library, 1981.

Periodicals

The Complete Handbook of Pro Football, 1975-1993.

Football Digest, October 1983; November 1987.

Pro Football Weekly, September 19, 1993.

Other

Kansas City Chiefs media guides, 1969-93.

—Chuck Klonke

Los Angeles Raiders

They are as intimidating on the football field as off. They're known for hitting hard, and their boss is known for playing hardball. The team's detractors dislike their style of play and let-the-chips-fall-where-they-may attitude, but no one could argue that the National Football League's Los Angeles Raiders aren't winners.

The Raiders have been playing their brand of football since 1960 and were the winningest team for thirty years. They have also proved to be the winningest team in professional sports in America—their record from 1963 through 1990 showed 269 victories, 130 losses, and 11 ties for a .674 winning percentage.

Since 1967, when the Raiders won the American Football League championship and went to the Super Bowl, they have been a playoff team 17 times. In addition, the Raiders have played in 12 championship games, won or shared 14 division titles, and won the AFL championship, three American Conference titles and three NFL titles via the Super Bowl. Much of the credit rests with owner/president Al Davis, a 1992 inductee into the Pro Football Hall of Fame in Canton, Ohio.

Talk about the Raiders and there is no way to avoid talking about Al Davis, who's been involved in more aspects of the game than any Hall of Famer. There have been great quarterbacks, coaches, skill players, and linemen as well—all of whom helped bring great success to a franchise sometimes referred to as the "Pride and Poise Boys."

Among the Hall of Fame inductees who spent time with the Raiders are tackle Ron Mix (inducted in 1979), center Jim Otto (1980), quarterback and placekicker George Blanda (1981), defensive back Willie Brown (1984), guard Gene Upshaw (1987), wide receiver Fred Biletnikoff (1988), tackle Art Shell (1989), linebacker Ted Hendricks (1990), and owner Davis (1992).

While these players contributed to the Raiders' success, many also helped foster a bad boys image for the team. Whether they were or not, they were often considered the renegades in silver and black, a characterization that Davis and the whole organization has embraced. It is that image that has made Raiders clothing and souvenir items perennial best-sellers nationwide. The Raiders' logo itself—a shield depicting a pirate wearing a helmet, with a patch over his left eye and crossed cutlasses behind his head—seems to suit the team's image.

"The Raiders may not be choirboys, but everything seems to turn out well on the football field," observed Jim Plunkett in his book, *The Jim Plunkett Story: The Saga of a Man Who Came Back.* Plunkett wasn't one of the classic bad-boy Raiders, but as the quarterback he led them to the Super Bowl championship in 1981 and was the game's most valuable player. Upshaw voiced the same sentiment: "We're not a bunch of choirboys and boy scouts. They say we're the halfway house of pro football. Well, we live up to that image every single chance we get."

Tom Flores, former Raiders quarterback who served as coach from 1979 through 1987, said in a 1984 article in *PRO!* magazine: "There's a little mystique involved in wearing that silver and black uniform.... It's a quiet toughness. It comes across from our veterans to our young guys without really preaching it. To be a Raider you have to be a winner. To be a winner you have to have total dedication, a burning desire to be the best, and a willingness to do whatever it takes ... a willingness to work hard, to play the game the way we like to play the game—tough, aggressive, attack football."

This philosophy of winning was instilled by Davis and has characterized the Raiders from their infancy into the 1990s, when they continued to win big with players considered cast-offs by most other teams. Many of them, including Jim Plunkett, had been lifted from scrap heaps and waiver lists, when their careers seemed to be waning.

Davis was described in a 1981 pro football annual as the man who "loves a fight and will pick one rather than suffer the agonizing serenity of non-combat." In addition, Davis' instinct "has helped his team, purposely populated by a collection of misfits and very nice guys, to win an extraordinary number of NFL games through the years."

Team Built From Ground Up

The Raiders' history begins in 1959 when Lamar Hunt of Dallas, Texas, organized the American Football League (AFL), which sought to rival the NFL by going after top-notch college and pro players. On January 30, 1960, just three days after the AFL adopted its first 14-game schedule, a group of eight Oakland investors was awarded a franchise initially intended for Minneapolis. The college draft selections were inherited from the Minnesota organization, which had opted to hold out for a possible NFL expansion team.

"Dons" and "Senors" were considered as nicknames before the "Raiders" name was selected. Eddie Erdelatz became the coach and was called the "personality boy of the AFL and also one of the most optimistic in the game" by the 1961 *Pro Football Handbook.* The Raiders' first game was at home (initially Kezar Stadium in San Francisco) against the Houston Oilers who won, 37-22. Originally they hoped to play at the University of California's stadium in Berkeley, but university regents wouldn't allow it, so the team shared Kezar Stadium with the NFL's San Francisco 49ers.

Oakland won just nine of 42 games during its first three seasons, and averaged only 9,612 fans a game in 1960, a figure that dropped to 7,655 the next year at Candlestick Park in San Francisco. By 1963, however, average attendance climbed to 10,985 at their first Oakland site, Frank Youell Field, which remained the Raiders' home until 1965.

Jim Otto, a 205-pound linebacker from the University of Miami, was the center during the early years. He recalled those days: "Me and the American Football League were both rookies the

Team Information at a Glance

Founding date: 1960, in Oakland, CA;
moved to Los Angeles in 1982

Home stadium: Los Angeles Memorial Coliseum
Address: 332 Center St.
El Segundo, CA 90245
Phone: (213) 322-3451
Seating capacity: 92,516

Team colors: Silver and black
Team nickname: Raiders
Logo: A black shield with a helmeted player wearing an eye patch, set against a background of two crossed swords

Franchise record	Won	Lost	Tie
(1960-92)	287	179	11

same year. It was kind of a good thing.... Everyone was given the same kind of shot to make the ballclub. If you wanted to play badly enough you stuck around. We lost some real cliff-hangers, like 52-28 and 41-7.... We had a young club and we made a lot of mistakes." They had a fairly respectable 6-8 record in 1960, thanks to players like Otto, guard Wayne Hawkins, and quarterbacks Flores and Babe Parilli. But for the next two years Oakland's overall record was 3-25.

In January of 1961 Ed McGah, Wayne Valley, and Robert Osborne bought out others involved in the ownership syndicate, and McGah became president. The team lost its first two games, which were now being played in Candlestick Park, 55-0 to Houston and 44-0 to San Diego. While Erdelatz claimed he didn't know what to do about the situation, McGah had some ideas. He fired Erdelatz and replaced him with assistant Marty Feldman.

Osborne, discouraged by the dismal 2-12 season, sold his interest in the club in May of 1962, leaving McGah and Valley as controlling partners. Valley issued an ultimatum to Oakland city officials: "Either build us a stadium or we move." He got his wish, but in the meantime a high school stadium, Frank Youell Field, was provided with temporary stands to boost seating capacity to 20,000 for the Raiders. It was so small that even if the club sold every seat for every game it would have lost money. The league's television contract helped keep the Raiders financially solvent during the season.

To help make Oakland and Denver more competitive, that summer the AFL installed a special draft of veteran players specifically for those teams. It didn't seem to help. The Raiders lost their first 13 games in 1962. After the first two losses, Bill "Red" Conkright replaced Feldman as coach. Finally, the Raiders won a game, beating the Boston Patriots 20-0, and season ticket sales the next year rose from 1,500 to 2,000.

"We had some very low moments," recalled Otto; "I never got bitter, though. I never asked to be traded. Oakland gave me a chance to play pro football, so I felt I owed them a certain amount of loyalty. But it was embarrassing, [the] things that just kept happening. One time we were practicing in another town and it was on a Little League ballfield. When the Little Leaguers came, their coaches kicked us off."

Enter Al Davis on January 15, 1963. Formerly an assistant with the San Diego Chargers, Davis became head coach and general manager on a three-year contract. "What I want is enough time and money to build the Raiders into a professional football team," he told McGah and Valley. He began to reorganize immediately by hiring a new business manager, director of player personnel, and ticket manager. He signed split end Art Powell, who had played out his option with the New York Titans. He got Flores back from an extended illness and coaxed several players away from other teams, including former tight end Clemon Daniels, who would set the AFL record for 1,099 yards rushing as a running back.

The AFL tried again to help Oakland, establishing a special draft of players from other franchises to try and get the Raiders and Titans up to competitive snuff. The New York Titans went from a 5-9 record in 1962 to a 5-8-1 record in 1963, an improvement of one tie game. Oakland, however, showed a great deal more promise. When the Raiders outlasted Houston 52-49 in December, it

AP/Wide World Photos

Raiders owner Al Davis

was their eighth consecutive victory after a 2-4 start. They finished just one game out of the playoffs with a 10-4 record, well on their way to the success that would become their trademark. A month later the AFL signed a five-year, $36-million television deal with NBC, and the league, along with Oakland, never looked back.

Al Davis's Changes Pay Off

The 1963 *Fawcett's Pro Football* magazine quoted McGah on the 33-year-old Davis: "This is a young, dynamic man and we have full confidence he can put together an organization that will be second to none in professional football." In the 1964 preseason annual, *Pro Football Stars,* the Raiders were called "the miracle club of the league," citing nine excellent trades by Davis as well as his organizational abilities. Said Otto: "When Al Davis came, you could see the difference. We started doing things first class instead of third class. He cleaned house immediately.... We all started scrambling for our jobs." Otto needn't have worried—he was unanimously selected the AFL All-Star of the Decade for the 1960s.

Construction on the 54,000-seat Oakland Coliseum began in February of 1965, and it opened in September of the following year as the Oakland-Alameda County Coliseum. Meanwhile, the war between the AFL and NFL to sign college players reached its peak in 1966. NFL teams signed 75 percent of the 232 players they drafted, while the AFL inked only 46 percent of its 181 selections. Of the 111 common draft choices, 79 signed with the NFL, 28 with the AFL, and four went unsigned. Altogether the leagues spent $7 million on draft choices that year.

Joe Foss had resigned as AFL commissioner in April, and Davis replaced him for four months, leaving John Rauch to take over as Oakland's head coach. Davis rejoined Oakland as managing general partner in July when Milt Woodard became AFC commissioner. In the meantime, secret negotiations were taking place for a merger between the two leagues. Davis did not deny that he was instrumental in negotiating that union, but a commentary in *Petersen's Pro Football* annual some years later contradicted this view, stating that "in truth he was completely unaware of the negotiations." NFL Commissioner Pete Rozelle announced the merger in June, and suddenly Oakland was in the AFC—the American Football Conference of the NFL.

The Raiders finished second in the AFC West with an 8-5-1 record in 1966, including a 32-10 loss to Kansas City at the debut of the Coliseum, before 50,746 spectators. The Chiefs went on to beat Buffalo for the conference title, then lost 35-10 to the Green Bay Packers in Super Bowl I. Oakland, though, wouldn't be the bridesmaid for long. Davis traded Flores and Powell in 1967 to Buffalo for quarterback Daryle Lamonica and wide receiver Glenn Bass. He obtained receiver Bill Miller from Buffalo in another deal, and cornerback Willie Brown from Denver. Blanda had been cut loose by Houston and Davis grabbed him. Upshaw, a rookie from Texas A&I, immediately established himself as one of the league's best blockers.

The Raiders, who were 1-13 just five years earlier, now led the league with a 13-1 record, and beat Houston 40-7 for the conference title. However, they lost Super Bowl II, 33-14, to the Packers in a game that featured the first $3 million gate in pro football history. Biletnikoff said that he and the Raiders were "a little bit in awe" of the Packers then because "we'd never played Green Bay and we just couldn't cope with it." Running back Pete Banaszak said Lamonica would ask receivers in the huddle what might work, "and he'd get no answers." For his part, Lamonica was named AFC player of the year, having thrown for 3,228 yards and 30 touchdowns. He also earned the nickname "The Mad Bomber," in reference to his penchant for throwing long and successful passes.

Oakland came back in 1968 with a 12-2 record, squaring off against Kansas City in the playoffs. The Raiders won easily, 41-6, to represent the AFC West against AFC East champs, the New York Jets, a contest New York won, 27-23.

Then, led by quarterback Joe Namath, the Jets triumphed in a 16-7 Super Bowl III upset over the Baltimore Colts, establishing once and for all the quality of the former AFL teams.

Television Viewers Miss Raiders' Comeback

Earlier that season, the Raiders had beaten the Jets, 43-32, by scoring two touchdowns in the last 42 seconds. The game became legendary in football history due to the storm of protest from NBC-TV viewers who missed the great comeback because the network cut away from the final 65 seconds of the game to the movie *Heidi*. The "*Heidi* Game" revealed the immense popularity of professional football, and it also resulted in a change of network policy to air football games no matter how long they ran overtime.

The NFL celebrated its 50th anniversary in 1969. That summer Davis got some help with his busy docket in the form of Al LoCasale, AFL player personnel director and administrator, who came aboard as executive assistant to the Raiders. A few months earlier, Davis had decided to bring in a new coach to replace Rauch, though he told Rauch's assistants they still had a job if they wanted one. After the draft he asked John Madden, a 32-year-old assistant, if he wanted to be the new coach. "I said, 'Hell, yes,'" Madden recalled.

Said Davis of his somewhat surprising choice: "The Oakland Raiders' job was one of the most sought-after in the business. A lot of coaches wanted it. Some very big names were in touch. But I saw potential for growth, for excellence, in John. Some people walk into a room and dominate it. I'm like that. Other people become great within the framework of an organization. I knew intuitively John Madden was a candidate for such greatness. He just had to grow. Call it insight. *Gestalt*. What[ever] you want. John Madden was my choice because he best fit the organization and its future."

Oakland tied a record in 1969 by capturing the AFC West championship for a third consecutive year, posting a 12-1 record for Madden behind the leadership of quarterback Daryle Lamonica. He had set a pro record in a 50-21 October victory over Buffalo by throwing six touchdown passes in the first half against Rauch's new team. The Raiders crushed Houston 56-7 in the playoffs, but wound up on the short end of a 17-7 score in the conference title game against Kansas City. The Chiefs went on to beat Minnesota 23-7 in Super Bowl IV. For the 1960s, the Raiders finished with a 77-58-5 regular season record. From the time Davis arrived it was 68-25-5—including an amazing 37-4-1 over the three most recent years.

Otto was an all-league or all-pro selection throughout the 1960s. Other Raiders honored during those years included running backs Clem Daniels and Hewritt Dixon; wide receivers Art Powell, Warren Wells, and Biletnikoff; defensive backs Brown, Fred Williamson, Dave Grayson,

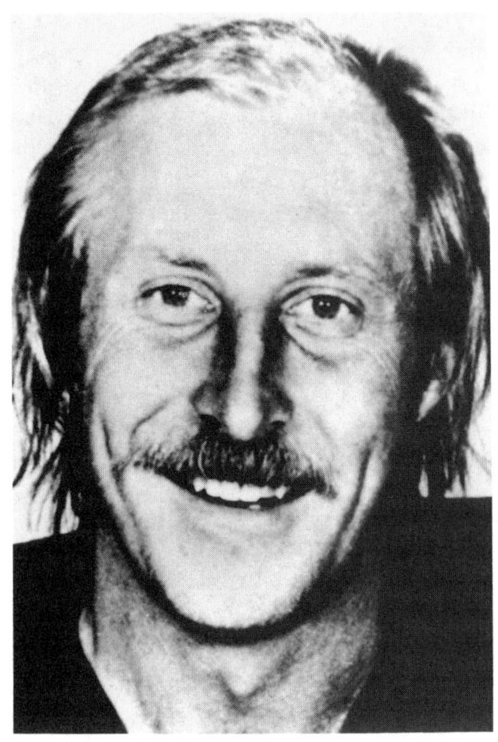

Fred Biletnikoff

and Kent McCloughan; guards Wayne Hawkins and Upshaw; tackle Harry Schuh; tight end Billy Cannon; Lamonica; defensive end Ben Davidson; defensive tackles Tom Keating and Dan Birdwell; and linebacker Dan Connors.

Cannon had a long, distinguished career as a running back and most people thought he was through, but Davis converted him to a tight end and he became an all-pro at the position. Williamson, nicknamed "The Hammer," fit the brash Raider mold perfectly; he took his attitude with him when he left the game to star in movies. Along with the likes of Upshaw, Brown, Davidson, Schuh and others, the arrival of Lamonica and Biletnikoff late in the decade would prove vital in the coming years.

George Blanda, meanwhile, had bounced around a number of places, since his start with the Chicago Bears in 1949. He was with Baltimore in 1950, went back to the Bears for eight years, retired in 1959, revived his career from 1960 through 1966 at Houston, then put in nine more years with Oakland. Despite his age, he helped the Raiders countless times with field goals, point-after kicks, and as an erstwhile backup to Lamonica and others. His leadership and his advice to young players also was significant. Blanda was named the NFL's Player of the Year for the 1970 season, primarily for leading the Raiders to five consecutive wins with passing and kicking heroics late in each contest.

"He is one of the all-time great pros," said Davis, who was two years younger than Blanda. In 1971 Blanda backed up Lamonica and was ahead of up-and-coming Ken Stabler on the depth charts. It was Blanda's 21st season of professional football. "They needle me because I have to go through bed check at age 44," Blanda said of his younger teammates. "What do I care? If you play the game, you abide by the rules."

Under Madden and Flores, the 1970s saw the Raiders garner 100 more victories, with only 38 losses and six ties—a .715 winning percentage. Season ticket sales passed the 50,500 mark—49,000 more than their first year. A 20-6 triumph in December of 1970 over Kansas City gave them an unprecedented fourth consecutive AFC West championship. Then they beat Miami 21-14 in a playoff game at Oakland, earning a spot in the conference title game against the Colts, who won 27-17 in Baltimore. The 1971 season featured a nine-week unbeaten string by Oakland to start the season, but Kansas City would take the division title with a 16-14 victory in December. While an 8-4-1 record would seem great to some, it was a disappointment for Oakland.

As Lamonica affirmed in a *Football Digest* story: "We've been a bridesmaid too many years now. The guys know it was a frustrating season last year. I think they basically feel like I do right now—they will work that little extra and get prepared a little more mentally and just start from the exhibition season and carry right into the league."

Playoff Hopes Dashed by "Immaculate Reception"

Glory returned in 1972 when the Silver and Black won their fifth AFC West crown and welcomed aboard such new players as defensive lineman Otis Sistrunk, linebackers Phil Villapiano and Gerald Irons, and fleet wide receiver Cliff Branch. But the season's bubble burst in the playoffs against Pittsburgh. The Raiders lost, 13-7, on what has become known as the "Immaculate Reception" by rookie Franco Harris of a Terry Bradshaw pass that deflected off Oakland defensive back Jack Tatum and Steelers receiver Frenchy Fuqua.

Oakland was leading the game, 7-6, with Stabler in as quarterback for the flu-ridden Lamonica. Pittsburgh got the ball back with 1:13 remaining and Bradshaw proceeded to throw three incompletions. He saw Fuqua open on fourth down at the 20-yard-line of Oakland. The ball and Tatum, considered the hardest hitter in the game, arrived at the same time. Harris caught the deflection on his fingertips just above the ground and ran the ball into the end zone for the winning touchdown.

Officials scrambled to determine if the play was legal. If the ball deflected Fuqua to Harris the play would be illegal; at that time it was against the rules to have a forward pass deflect from one offensive player to another. However, the officials determined that the ball careened off Tatum.

"I was zeroing in on the receiver, not the ball," Tatum recalled. "I never touched it; it never touched me." Said Stabler, "I guess that's football, but I can't accept it. It doesn't seem fair. What an awful way to lose." In his 1979 book, *They Call Me Assassin,* Tatum asserted: "To this very day, because of my angle of attack and the position of Frenchy's body, I think it was an illegal play.... If the game had been played in Oakland, that play would have gone down as an incomplete pass."

The new season brought a chance to try again. Oakland startled the football world by selecting Ray Guy as their top draft choice, the first time a punter was ever picked in the first round.

On September 23rd, the largest Coliseum crowd to date gathered for the Miami-Oakland game. The Dolphins had finished the previous season with a perfect 17-0 record, culminating with a Super Bowl win. But on this day Blanda would kick four field goals to beat Miami, 12-7, and end their unprecedented winning streak. Oakland went on to defeat Denver, 21-17, for its third straight AFC West title and its sixth in seven years. The team took revenge against the Steelers with a 33-14 victory in the playoffs, but Miami won its third successive AFC title by topping the Raiders, 27-10.

Although Lamonica had been the winningest quarterback and top touchdown passer in pro football for the previous six years, in 1973 he was replaced by Stabler, who was getting frustrated sitting on the bench. The Raiders had drafted him in 1968 out of the University of Alabama, but he hurt a knee and was on the taxi squad as a rookie. He went back to college in 1969, then rejoined the team in 1970, once again occupying a seat on the bench. Fed up, he stormed into Madden's office early in the 1973 season and demanded to play or be traded. Madden threw him out—only to make him the starting quarterback a few days later. The Raiders were becoming a running team—particularly with Marv Hubbard to carry the ball—and Stabler was more mobile than Lamonica, a two-time NFL most valuable player who had thrown 26 more TD passes than anyone else in the span of the past six years. "Daryle hadn't done anything wrong," Madden wrote in his 1984 book, *Hey, Wait a Minute,* "Kenny just seemed to want the job more."

Stabler recalled the incident thusly: "I left the meeting and went out on the practice field feeling relieved. I was loose and decided to have a good time. I completed everything that I threw. I was popping the ball all over the field. After practice, Madden came up to me and said, 'You're starting this week. You're our quarterback. We're going to win with you the rest of the year.'"

Nicknamed "The Snake" for his ability to slither away from would-be tacklers, Stabler ignited the slumping Raiders to an 8-2-1 finish and another spot in the AFC championship game. Lamonica signed with the Southern California Sun of the new World Football League at the end of the season.

In 1974 Oakland began a nine-game winning streak on September 22nd with a 27-7 drubbing of Kansas City and locked up its seventh division crown just ten games into the season. The Raiders finished with a 12-2 record and ended Miami's bid for a fourth consecutive Super Bowl appearance by beating the Dolphins 28-26 in a thrilling home game in the conference playoffs. The game began with Miami's Nat Moore returning the opening kickoff for a touchdown and climaxed with Stabler, falling forward in the grasp of a tackler, lobbing a 8-yard game-winning touchdown pass to Clarence Davis, who barely clutched the ball away from a Miami defender, with 26 seconds remaining.

During his years with Coach Bear Bryant's Crimson Tide at the University of Alabama, Stabler led the team to the Orange, Cotton and Sugar bowls . When he started to win with Oakland, analysts were calling him the "best left-handed quarterback since Frankie Albert." In one

1974 game Stabler completed 25 of 29 passes for a percentage of 86.2, eclipsing the 85.7 percent NFL record held previously by fabled Sammy Baugh. Frustration, though, dogged Stabler in the AFC title game when the Raiders were defeated by their old nemesis Pittsburgh, 24-13, to advance to the Super Bowl. The Steelers won the Super Bowl, 16-6 over Minnesota.

"[Stabler's] total performance cannot be equated with a single bitter loss to the Steelers when all the chips were shoved to the center of the table," wrote John Kuenster in *Football Digest* the following spring. Stabler completed 178 of 310 passes for the season for 2,469 yards and a league-best 26 TDs. "I was told dozens of times that I wouldn't make it big in the NFL simply because I threw with the wrong hand," Stabler remarked. Former defensive back Jim Tatum said the perfect quarterback "would have Ken Stabler's mind inside Terry Bradshaw's body. I'm not taking a slap at Bradshaw's mental capacity; it's just a fact that Stabler is a physical wreck." Stabler would endure several knee and other surgeries over his career.

Marv Hubbard Sets Records, Gains Reputation

During the period from 1971 to 1974, Marv Hubbard was the Raiders' running star. He led the team in rushing yardage, including 1,100 yards in 1972. Madden described Hubbard as having "an angelic face" even though he "was one of the toughest, fightingest guys I've ever known." Madden said Hubbard used to get in bar fights in his hometown in upstate New York near the Pennsylvania border, then grab the victim around the neck, make up, and buy him a drink.

Another Hubbard story concerns his ability to punch his fist through a glass window and pull it back without cutting himself. According to Madden, it was something he'd do often. As Madden tells it, Hubbard would give the bartender at one particular establishment $50 and tell him to give it to the dry cleaning business next store to pay for the window he was about to break. Then he'd break it, showing off his skill to his friends. He did it a number of times, Madden said, and finally the woman who owned the cleaners called the Raiders and insisted that it stop or she'd sue.

Another Hubbard legend involved his roommate, kicker George Jakowenko, who just wasn't Hubbard's kind of guy. "What's wrong with him?" Madden asked. "He wears pajamas," Hubbard replied. Madden said Jakowenko's wife called him one day and complained that she wanted a different roommate for her husband because Hubbard was "a bad influence."

About the time Hubbard's Raiders career was coming to a close in 1975, linebacker Ted Hendricks' term was just beginning. Obviously cut from the same cloth as Hubbard, he once rode a horse onto the practice field. "Ted Hendricks was a free spirit long before it was fashionable to be a free spirit," Madden wrote in his book. "When he joined the Raiders, he looked around and announced, 'Everywhere I've been, I've been the screwball on the team—in college, with the Colts, with the Packers—but here I'm just a

Monday Night Magic

The Los Angeles Raiders and *Monday Night Football* seem to have been made for each other. Since ABC television began broadcasting the games during prime time in 1970, no team has been more dominant than the Oakland/Los Angeles Raiders. Heading into the 1993 season, the Raiders sat atop the list with a .744 winning percentage on Monday night, a 29-10-1 record. Their closest competitor was Seattle at .668, with an 11-5 record.

When asked if the Monday night televised games present additional pressure to win, former coach John Madden replied: "No more so than if we were playing a game in a parking lot in front of 10 customers.... The important thing is to win, no matter when or where the game is being played."

COACH OF THE YEAR

In the Raiders' first 33 years, five of their head coaches were named National Football League Coach of the Year:

— 1963, Al Davis
— 1967, John Rauch
— 1969, John Madden
— 1982, Tom Flores
— 1990, Art Shell

normal guy.'" Hendricks summarizes his influence similarly: "We're responsible for many rules changes. There's the no-clothesline [tackling] rule. The no-spearing rule. The no-hitting-out-of-bounds rule. No fumbling forward in the last two minutes of the game. No throwing helmets. The no-stick'm [on your fingers] rule.... So you see, we're not all bad."

Also among the cast of characters was middle linebacker Dan Conners. Madden said Connors once needed a wrist operation but told the doctor the incision would ruin his modeling career. "How's that?" the doctor wondered. "I model wrist watches," Connor said. The doctor made the incision on the underside of the wrist. Another time he went golfing and shot 144 for 18 holes. Madden told him, "You should've cheated." Connors replied, "I did cheat. I still shot 144."

Then there was Ben Davidson, the 6-foot 8-inch, 280-pound hulk who later was one of Madden's beer commercial co-stars. Davidson also landed several small parts in films, including *M*A*S*H,* as well as several television shows. He had a handlebar mustache and rode a motorcycle, and "more than any other player, Ben created the image of the Raiders as Hell's Angels with shoulder pads," Madden wrote. "Off the field, Ben Davidson is one of the gentlest people I know. And one of the nicest." Davidson fit the Raider philosophy, expressed by a *PRO!* magazine writer in 1984, "The Raiders' basic rule is that bigger is better, their philosophy being that bigger people wear down smaller people by the fourth quarter."

Another "character" was cornerback Skip Thomas. According to Madden, one Saturday Thomas was watching Evel Knievel do one of his daring motorcycle jumps on TV. Thomas went outside behind the team's motel, put a board against the fence to make a ramp, and put some hay on the other side to cushion the landing. Then Thomas proceeded to put on his Raiders helmet and walk to his motorcycle. Fortunately, an equipment man had alerted Madden in time for Madden to talk Thomas out of the jump.

While at training camp in September of 1974 Otto retired, thereby ending a brilliant career. During the 1975 season the team became the winningest franchise since 1960. It also played its first-ever overtime game, a 26-23 decision over Washington. The Raiders clinched their eighth AFC West title in nine years with a 37-34 overtime victory over Atlanta. Blanda's four extra-point kicks against Kansas City in December made him the first player to score 2,000 career points. A 31-28 squeaker over Cincinnati advanced the Raiders to the AFC championship game, but there was more frustration as Pittsburgh slipped past Oakland 16-10 and went on to defend its Super Bowl crown, 21-17, over Dallas.

Super Bowl Victory at Last

The 1976 season brought more victories. The Raiders won the division once again and achieved football's best record, 13-1. They knocked off New England (24-21) and Pittsburgh (24-7), to become AFC champ. The Raiders went on to whip Minnesota, 32-14, in Super Bowl XI before a record crowd of 103,424 at the Rose Bowl stadium in Pasadena, California, and a TV audience of 130 million. More than 20,000 fans greeted the new world champs at the Coliseum in Oakland upon their return. Madden was named Coach of the Year and Davis, Executive of the Year for the second time in a row.

Biletnikoff was the Super Bowl MVP, having

caught key passes near the goal line to set up three touchdowns. But the award "should have been shared by Oakland's superb offensive linemen Gene Upshaw and Art Shell," insisted an analyst for *Football Digest* the following spring. "They whipped the Vikings like no one else. They were crushing. Devastating." The publication quoted *Philadelphia Bulletin* writer Ray Didinger: "Military historians claim the Raiders stole their offense from Hannibal's old playbook. When those elephants came thundering over the Alps, they must have looked a lot like Gene Upshaw and Art Shell leading an Oakland end sweep.... The Raiders' idea of finesse is to reduce a defense to rubble, then put a torch to it."

In the first half of the Super Bowl, 26 of 33 Oakland running plays against the Vikings went to the left side, with blocking responsibilities resting with the 270-pound Shell, Upshaw at 260 pounds, and tight end Dave Casper at 230 pounds. Clarence Davis rushed for 137 yards, an 8.56 average for his 16 carries, and Stabler was 12 of 19 passing for 180 yards.

Clarence Davis was apparently not enamored of the Raiders bad-guy image. "They say we recruit our defensive backfield from Central Park. They say we're a bunch of thieves and cutthroats. I guess we've shut up the critics now," he asserted. "We took all the criticism and we just kept building and maturing," Upshaw said, reflecting on the overall season. "That's the kind of team we have. There's a closeness on this team.... When [Stabler] says a sweep, a pass or whatever, we do it. We don't even question it. If he didn't call it, it wasn't the right play. That's the total confidence he has in us."

Stabler said about his team: "We've won so often, we've come from behind so many times, we feel nothing is impossible. Most of all, I have great faith in my own ability. I firmly believe I'll find a way to win every game." About Biletnikoff, he raved: "What he does no longer amazes me. There are people who will argue with me, but I think he's the greatest pass receiver of all time. He has caught over 500 passes (536 to that point) and I think he caught half of them standing on his head." Biletnikoff, however, was self-deprecating when asked why he got stopped by the goal line three times without scoring. "Getting caught is nothing new for me," he said. "I've been getting caught like that for the past 12 years. I can't run away from anybody, including the officials."

Another of the Raiders' standouts in that era was Otis Sistrunk, obtained from the Rams along with a fifth-round draft choice in exchange for a fourth-rounder. Sistrunk, a Raider from 1972 through 1979, did not go to college. While steam rose from his shaved head as he stood on the sidelines of a Monday night TV game, ABC color analyst Alex Karras—apparently noticing no college listed in the press guide for Sistrunk—said he was from "the University of Mars."

When the Raiders began the 1977 season they were working on a 13-game winning streak. They ran it up to 17 before losing to Denver—only twice in NFL history had any team won more games in a row. Oakland clinched the playoffs for the 10th time in 11 years when it beat Minnesota, 35-13, on December 11th. The next week they nipped Kansas City, 21-20, to become the first NFL team to win 150 league games since 1960. The following week the Raiders defeated the Colts, 37-31, in a double-overtime thriller in the AFC playoffs. A 20-17 loss at Denver in the conference championship game, however, thwarted the defending Super Bowl champs.

John Madden Retires

In 1978 Madden became the 13th coach in league history to reach the 100-victory plateau when Oakland downed the Chiefs 20-10 in November. However, the club lost five of eight games in its division, finishing with a 9-7 record and missing the playoffs for the first time since 1971. Frustrated, Madden retired and Flores was named his successor.

Although the Raiders continued to thrive after Madden's departure, it was the end of an era. Madden, a dedicated and enthusiastic leader was one of the most successful coaches of his era. He went on to win greater recognition through TV beer commercials and as a color commentator on CBS football games and is considered among the best (and certainly most down-to-earth) in the business.

Following Oakland's Super Bowl triumph against the Vikings, a *Football Digest* article described Madden this way: "The Oakland Raiders' head football coach doesn't look like a long-range planner who believes hard work will pay off in future years. He has a way with his players and a touch for the pro game that is almost mystical and too elusive for diagrams, charts and detailed schedules. But like all successful NFL coaches, Madden, the big man with curly red hair and an innocent smile, is dedicated to the smallest detail."

One of his more colorful players, defensive end John Matuszak, said, "the relationship of John Madden to his players is better than that of any coach in the NFL. He's fantastic because there is no bull with him. He tells you what your goals are, what your job is. Then he steps back out of the way. It's up to you to accomplish. He's a good one."

Gregg Jordan, in the 1977 Petersen Publishing's *Pro Football Annual,* said of Madden: "He had the image of a puppet; created in obscurity and molded to jump when Al Davis pulled the strings. But at Pasadena [in the Super Bowl against Minnesota] there were no strings attached and Madden was revealed as his own man."

Madden said he enjoyed his stay with Oakland because Davis was "the only boss I had to answer to, which also made it easier, not harder.... I've always felt sorry for a coach with several names above his on the Club Directory in the media guide.... Almost any time a club has that many bosses, the coach is going to want a new coach."

Madden noted in his book that a mitigating factor in his decision to quit coaching was the terrible tragedy that occurred during his final season. New England receiver Darryl Stingley was paralyzed after a hard mid-air tackle by Tatum, although he said he didn't think the tackle was any harder than Tatum's others. "I was ready to retire," Madden said. "I had 103 wins in 10 years. I had my Super Bowl ring. I had my ulcer."

The Stingley disaster happened in a preseason game August 12, 1978. Tatum's hit broke the former Northwestern University star's neck in two places and caused spinal cord damage that would keep him in a wheelchair the rest of his life. Tatum went to see him at the hospital, but was turned away because no visitors were allowed. Tatum thought Stingley didn't want to see him, and although Stingley was bitter about what happened, he was also angry that Tatum didn't visit. Madden was able to muscle his way in by obtaining a scrub gown from the hospital which enabled him to skirt the visiting rules.

"It was a fairly good hit, but nothing exceptional," Tatum said of the tackle. "When the reality of Stingley's injury hit me with its full impact, I was shattered." In his book, Tatum criticized the NFL for not having more rules against certain rough play, but "I'll play the game the way the rules are written. I am supposed to hit people and destroy the play and the harder I hit them, the better I can do the job."

Ironically, when comedian Bob Hope introduced Ohio State star Tatum years earlier on his TV show featuring Associated Press All-Americans, Hope joked: "Jack Tatum ... what a hitter. Tatum can straighten your spine quicker than Ben Casey. Why, he's so tough even his fingernails have muscles.... Jack's mother told me that he was just a normal kid ... except he liked to ram his head into fire hydrants."

Said Tatum about his reputation: "I'm no psychopath. But I and others like myself learned early in our careers that in football the name of the game is hitting and to play it well you have to play it hard." Teammate Clarence Davis once got Tatum in serious trouble by granting an interview with a newspaper reporter who thought he was Tatum. Davis said of the Pittsburgh receivers in the upcoming game, "Ain't none of them worth a damn." He called the running backs, "chicken, all of them chicken." And of the whole team he said, "Mister, if I told you the Steelers were gutless

Raiders Super Bowl Records

Raiders players through 1993 held 12 Super Bowl records for the following:

— Longest Run: Marcus Allen, 74 yards, Super Bowl XVIII.
— Most Rushing Touchdowns, Game (tie): two, Pete Banaszak (XV) and Marcus Allen (XVIII).
— Longest Pass Completion: 80 yards, Jim Plunkett to Kenny King (XV).
— Longest Pass Reception: 80 yards, King from Plunkett (XV).
— Most Pass Interceptions, Career (tie): three, Rod Martin (XV, XVIII) and Jack Squirek (XVIII).
— Lowest Percentage, Passes Had Intercepted, Career: 0.00, Plunkett (XV, XVIII).
— Most Pass Interceptions, Game: three, Rod Martin (XV).
— Most Yards on Interceptions, Career: 75, Willie Brown (II, XI).
— Most Yards on Interceptions, Game: 75, Brown (XI).
— Longest Interception Return: 75, Brown (XI).
— Most Touchdowns on Interceptions, Game: one, Brown (XI), (shared).
— Highest Average Gain, Career: 9.6 yards, Marcus Allen (XVIII).

wonders that would be a compliment." Needless to say, Tatum had some explaining to do to a few of his friends who were Steelers.

After Madden's departure in 1979, Flores became the pro game's first Hispanic head coach. "I think you'll find Tom has an inner strength as tough as anyone from any walk of life," Al Davis said. Flores had played with the Raiders for three years under Davis, though he missed the 1962 season with a lung ailment. Davis traded him to Buffalo in 1967 and he later was on the Kansas City team that won Super Bowl IV. He joined Madden's staff in 1972.

In 1979, Flores installed an offense with two tight ends, featuring Dave Casper and Raymond Chester, both of whom made the Pro Bowl. Although the passing game flourished, the running attack faltered, finishing 24th in the league. Oakland was in the playoff picture going into the last game, but lost 29-24 to Seattle for their second straight 9-7 record and non-playoff season. However, in the 1970s the Raiders had compiled a regular season record of 100-38-6, with six division titles, one conference, and a Super Bowl championship.

At 34 years-old, Upshaw closed out the decade as the oldest player on the team. The 13-year veteran—the last ten as captain—declared: "Two more years of football and I'll switch to politics. I think someday I could be governor." His wife, Jimmye, told the NFL program magazine *GameDay* that "Gene's a doer—not a sit-around person.... He's involved."

Upshaw was at that time vice-president of the NFL Players Association (he eventually became president). He was also on the board of governors of California Junior College, served with the Alameda County Planning Commission, the Oakland Boys Club, and the Boy Scouts of America. Upshaw chaired various fund-raising drives for charities, including the American Cancer Society, sickle cell anemia, cystic fibrosis, and the Special Olympics. Despite all that, he was still a Raider and thus his reputation as a tough guy sometimes won out.

The 1980s began with an all-time Raiders rushing record and a new quarterback. On September 28th, Mark van Eeghen broke the Raiders' all-time rushing record. The next week quarterback Dan Pastorini, who had come from Houston in exchange for the knee-scarred Stabler, suffered an injury against Kansas City. That gave Jim Plunkett, a former Heisman Trophy winner from Stanford, an opportunity.

Plunkett had previously led the underdog Stanford team to Rose Bowl victories against both Michigan and Ohio State. He was the NFL's top draft pick in 1971, going to New England. Plunkett played every down that season and threw 19 touchdown passes, but by 1975, Patriots fans were booing him. He asked for a trade and got it, heading to San Francisco in return for three number one draft picks, a number two pick, plus quarterback Tom Owen.

Plunkett was released in 1978, however, on the heels of an exhibition game in which he had 11 consecutive incompletions, by the 49ers new general manager, Joe Thomas. "I felt like the world was caving in on me," Plunkett said. Subsequently picked up by the Raiders, Plunkett came off the bench after Pastorini broke his leg during the fifth game only to throw five interceptions. This performance, however, didn't deprive him of the start a week later against San Diego, a game the Raiders won. Plunkett won five more in a row, eventually ending the regular with a nine of 11 record.

Plunkett Leads Team to Another Super Bowl Victory

The next stop was Cleveland. In sub-zero weather, the Silver and Black edged the Browns, 14-12, advancing to the AFC title game in San Diego. They outlasted the Chargers, a mighty offensive team, 34-27, and once again advanced to the Super Bowl. Oakland won Super Bowl XV at the Superdome in New Orleans, beating Philadelphia 27-10 for the Raiders' second world championship in five years. The persistent Plunkett was the game's MVP.

"I've always said that the key to Jim Plunkett is how he is handled by his head coach," Plunkett quoted former 49ers coach John Ralston in his book *The Jim Plunkett Story: The Saga of a Man Who Came Back*. "Jim has days when he isn't going to do well. Just pat him on the back and he'll come back and perform well the next week. Jim needs continual reassurance.... Tom Flores is the kind of guy who doesn't rant and rave. He is the ideal kind of coach for Jim Plunkett and deserves a real pat on the back for the season Jim had."

Davis said Plunkett had a great training camp in 1979: "I thought we'd be better off with him than with Stabler as our starter. But you know coaches. They resist change. Remember that Stabler blasted me [in the press] that year. He sensed I liked Plunkett better. Stabler won one of five championship games the years he was with us. I think with Jim we'd have won two more."

Madden spoke of Davis' penchant for picking up discards and re-energizing them into stars. "Yes, the Raiders took a few players that other teams had given up on—not that Al and I thought we had a magic formula to reform them," Madden said. "Our reasoning was, when a player's back is against the wall, when he realizes that no other team wants him, when he knows that the Raiders will be his last stop, that's when he should realize that if he doesn't shape up, his career will be over. We also never gave up much, if anything, to get that type of player."

Tatum, in his book, agreed with Madden's assessment: "The essence of Al Davis' success stemmed from the fact that he wasn't afraid to bring in washed-up players or so-called troublemakers. He was building a team and judged a man solely by his talents and what he could do for the Raiders. As an Oakland Raider, I am given the flexibility to be myself. It's always been that way with the Raiders, and I like it." However, he said Davis was tough in contract negotiations. "I don't fault the man for doing his job," Tatum said, "but he does make it difficult for an athlete when it comes time to talk about new contracts."

One highly touted player who kicked around the league without really doing much until joining the Raiders in 1976 for a seven-year stay was John Matuszak. He was, like so many other Raiders, considered somewhat of a character. The week of Super Bowl XV Matuszak told reporters, "I've had enough parties for 20 people's lifetimes. I've grown up. I'll keep our young fellows out of trouble. If any players want to stray, they gotta go through ol' Tooz."

The next night, "ol' Tooz" was out dancing four hours past curfew. Philadelphia coach Dick Vermeil huffed that if Matuszak was his player he'd fine him $10,000 and send him home. Said Plunkett, "Vermeil might lose his mind if he woke up one morning and found that he was the coach of Oakland, not Philadelphia. Dick believes in strict discipline and regimentation. Most Raiders players would need a dictionary to look up those words, because they're never used in Oakland." Flores fined Matuszak $1,000 and forgot the matter.

Lyle Alzado, the defensive end once regarded as the best defensive player in the NFL, was an integral part of that Super Bowl team. The 1980 season was his first with Oakland, where he stayed through 1985. "You can play in great games and win great games and be on teams with great players," he said, "but there is a special feeling when you win the Super Bowl.... If your goal is to be the best player you can be and the outcome is being on the best team in the NFL, that's what it's all about."

Alzado, who turned to acting after his retirement, died in 1993 of complications attributed to his use of steroids for body building. Having once commented that he had never met a man he didn't want to fight, Alzado said of a failed comeback try in 1990: "I was a violent player and I missed that. I couldn't drive around the streets and pull people out of cars and beat the hell out of them. The bottom line is that I like to kick butt, and I felt I could still do that."

If Davis wasn't resurrecting the career of an Alzado or a Matuszak, he was discovering someone who otherwise might not have received much attention; Mark van Eeghen of Colgate was a typical example. Davis liked to say, "I can watch a guy for 10 seconds and tell if he's a player." He only saw van Eeghen working out in shorts and gym shoes indoors on the rainy day he visited Colgate, but Davis drafted him on the third round. Taking over for fellow Colgate grad Marv Hubbard, who was traded, van Eeghen led the team in rushing from 1976 through 1980. In 1977 van Eeghen became only the third Raider to reach the 1,000-yard season rushing mark, totaling 1,012 yards.

Plunkett's 1980 Cinderella season didn't carry over into 1981. Oakland fell to fourth place with an uncharacteristic losing record of 7-9, and never won more than two consecutive games. Midway through the season, Plunkett, center Dave Dalby, Chester, and Upshaw were replaced by younger players. Wide receiver Bobby Chandler and van Eeghen spent most of the season on the injured reserve list. In 1982 running back Marcus Allen of Southern California was the club's top draft choice. It would prove to be an excellent pick.

Davis Moves Team to Los Angeles

The early 1980s proved to be a turbulent time, not so much for the team itself as for Davis, who

AP/Wide World Photos

Lyle Alzado

AP/Wide World Photos

Marcus Allen (32)

was being thwarted by the league in his attempts to move the franchise to Los Angeles. The Raiders and the Los Angeles Coliseum Commission filed an antitrust suit against the NFL and the matter went to trial in Federal District Court in Los Angeles on May 11, 1981. The suit contended that the league violated anti-monopoly statutes in blocking the proposed move to the Coliseum, where the Raiders would replace the Rams, who were moving to Anaheim. A mistrial was declared August 13th when the jury was unable to reach a verdict. But early in 1982, a jury ruled against the league, clearing the way for the move.

The Los Angeles Raiders debuted in an August exhibition game in which they defeated the Packers, 24-3, in the Los Angeles Memorial Coliseum. In the regular season opener, they surprised the Super Bowl champion 49ers, 23-17, in San Francisco. Because of a 57-day NFL players strike, the Raiders didn't make their regular season home debut until November 22nd, when they overcame a 24-point deficit to edge the Chargers 28-24.

On December 12th in Kansas City, the Raiders beat the Chiefs in the final seconds, 21-16, to clinch their 17th winning season in 18 years and earn the 200th victory in the franchise's history. Six days later they recorded the first million-dollar gate at a home league game, while downing the Rams 37-31. The Silver and Black won the abbreviated season's AFC West crown with an 8-1 record, proceeded to beat Cleveland 27-10 in the opening playoff round, then suffered a 17-14 setback to the New York Jets in round two.

The Raiders garnered a different kind of victory in April of 1983, when a federal court jury awarded the team nearly $35 million in compensatory damages from the NFL for antitrust and bad faith violations. The Los Angeles Memorial Coliseum was awarded almost $15 million in the same ruling. Later in the year, the California State Superior Court upheld the Raiders' move to Los Angeles by ruling against the city of Oakland. The court said that Oakland did not have the right to acquire the Raiders through condemnation in what came to be called the Eminent Domain case.

Davis' team opened its 1983 season with a 20-10 victory over Cincinnati. Two weeks later, E. W. McGah, the only remaining original partner of the franchise, died at the age of 84. According to the Raiders' media guide, McGah "added stability and credibility to the franchise for three decades." In November the Raiders clinched their 18th winning season in the last 19 years by besting Buffalo in the final seconds 27-24. That put them in the playoffs against Pittsburgh before an AFC-record playoff crowd of 92,434. The crowd witnessed a 38-10 triumph that propelled the team to the conference championship game against the Seattle Seahawks, who fell victim to the Silver and Black 30-14.

Once again the Raiders advanced to the world championship game—Super Bowl XVII at Tampa Stadium in Tampa, Florida. They faced off against the National Conference champs, the Washington Redskins, before more than 72,000 spectators and a worldwide radio and television audience pegged at 125 million. Los Angeles won easily, 38-9, for its third Super Bowl title in eight years. The Raiders received a ceremonial key to their home city at City Hall in May of 1984.

Among the featured stars of that 1983 championship team was tight end Todd Christensen. "I love saying, 'The purpose of life is to maximize your emotional income,'" he said. "For six months after the Super Bowl my emotional income runneth over. You couldn't measure on a Richter Scale the incredible amount of gratification I felt." Christensen led the team with 92 catches for 1,247 yards and 12 touchdowns, amazing statistics for a position that normally involves more blocking than receiving. He was another castoff who made good. Drafted as a running back from Brigham Young by the Dallas Cowboys in 1978, he spent a year on injured reserve and was waived. The New York Giants picked him up, only to release him after one game in 1979. During the next couple of weeks he had tryouts with Green Bay, New England, Chicago and Philadelphia.

"When 'Orphanage West' finally picked me up," Christensen said of the Raiders, "I was just happy to be employed anywhere." Flores asked him at the 1980 minicamp what position he wanted to play and he said tight end—even though All-Pros Casper and Chester were on the team. He played on special teams for a while, but eventually Casper was traded, Chester retired, and in 1982 Christensen became the starter.

Another key player during this time was linebacker Rod Martin, who had been drafted by the Raiders in the 12th round in 1977 after an All-Pacific Eight conference season at Southern Cal. He was later traded to San Francisco, where the 49ers picked his brain for information on the Raiders prior to a preseason game between the two teams. Then, without even allowing him to play in the game, the 49ers promptly released Martin. Eventually, the Raiders asked Martin to replace one of their injured linebackers. Four seasons later he found himself basking in the limelight as a star of Super Bowl XV, having intercepted three passes in that victory over the Eagles.

Another Super Bowl XV star was middle guard Reggie Kinlaw, who also happened to be a 12th-round draft choice. "It took me a long time to get over that stigma of being a 12th round draft choice," Martin told *GameDay* magazine in a 1984 article. "Even though I finally made All-Pro, you'll still hear broadcasters say, 'That's Rod Martin. He was a 12th round draft choice and he wasn't supposed to make it.'" In relating the story of Martin's selection, Madden said the Raiders got down to that spot in the draft and didn't know who to pick. He pointed out to the other Raiders officials at the draft that "they probably have more guys just running around at Southern Cal, just hanging around there, who are better players than anyone we're talking about." Madden decided to call his old friend John Robinson, the coach at University of Southern California. "He asked me if Martin had been drafted yet. When told he wasn't, Robinson said, 'Hell, he's better than anyone who's been drafted all day. He'll make it and he'll play.' So I said that was good enough for me and we drafted him."

Meanwhile, on the persistent legal front, in July the California State Superior Court again upheld the team's move to Los Angeles. Four months later on November 5th, the United States Supreme Court upheld the Raiders' victory in the antitrust case, refusing to alter previous favorable decisions made by other federal courts.

The 1984 campaign marked the Raiders' 25th anniversary. It began with a 24-14 triumph over the Oilers in Houston on September 2nd. Two weeks later in Kansas City they edged the Chiefs, 22-20, to earn Flores his 50th league victory. In November, with a 21-7 home decision over Baltimore, the Raiders clinched their 19th winning season, en route to a playoff berth. A 24-3 Monday night victory over Detroit at the Pontiac Silverdome raised the Raiders' record on the Monday night TV games to 22-3-1. The season ended 12 days later at Seattle in a 13-7 loss to Seattle in a wildcard playoff game.

Legal Issues Finally Resolved

Although their legal entanglements had still not been sorted out, the Raiders opened their first Southern California preseason training camp in Oxnard in 1985. The team sponsored Family Day at the local high school and drew 12,000 people. In September the Chamber of Commerce held the largest sports banquet they had ever had in order to honor the Raiders. Then in November the California State Court of Appeals ruled in favor of the Raiders in the Eminent Domain case, saying the proposed exercise of eminent domain by the city of Oakland would violate the commerce clause of the U.S. Constitution.

AP/Wide World Photos

Raider Howie Long (75) sacks Lion quarterback Chuck Long

The following February the matter still was being debated, but the California State Supreme Court again upheld the decision of the State Court of Appeals. It wasn't until June 30th, though, that the matter finally was put to rest, when the U.S. Supreme Court upheld the franchise's move to Los Angeles, refusing to alter prior favorable decisions by the California courts.

Los Angeles won its division with a 12-4 record behind quarterbacks Marc Wilson and Plunkett. The big 1985 season pushed Flores to the 70-victory level, but there was disappointment after a 27-20 loss to New England in the playoffs before 89,000 fans at the Coliseum.

An unsung Raider got some recognition in June of 1985. George Anderson, the team's head trainer since 1960, was inducted into the National

Athletic Trainers' Association Hall of Fame. He was responsible for pioneering safety devices for the prevention of knee injuries, one of which came to be known as the "Anderson Knee-Stabler" brace. Anderson was also a pioneer in the use of one medication that promoted quick healing in injured athletes—a substance called Dimethylsulfoxide, or DMSO.

He found the liquid being used at the horse race track where it was applied to an affected area of a horse, causing an analgesic reaction. The applied area would heat up as blood rushed to the area. Healing time was reduced markedly. He started trying DMSO on players' injuries with great success, although there were drawbacks. "An injured Raider, having daily applications of DMSO, would reek like a forgotten sack of cleaned fish left out in the hot sun," wrote Bob Svihus in *Raider: How Offensive Can You Be!!*. "The cry of 'rotten clams' was often screamed across the training room to any DMSO test case."

The Raiders' 14-10 victory over Seattle in October of 1986 was their 200th league triumph against an AFC team. In November the Raiders posted their 50th league victory since their relocation in 1982 by beating Cleveland, 27-14. It was an uncharacteristic year, however, with an 8-8 mark that put them fourth in their division and out of the playoffs.

In 1986 Plunkett managed to wrestle the quarterback job away from Marc Wilson, who had been a top Raiders draft selection. Wilson was to get the position back the following year, though. "The 38-year-old Plunkett has been resilient in his 14-year NFL career," commented writer Bob Cox in *The Sporting News 1986 Pro Football Yearbook*. "Twice in his seven years with the Raiders he has risen from the football graveyard to the glorious heights of Super Bowl victories."

The Raiders' downward movement continued in 1987 as they finished with a poor 5-11 record. They improved in 1988, but at 7-9 they were still under .500. However, the Raiders' still-impressive final 1980s regular season record stood at 89-63. Flores called it quits before the 1988 campaign, winding up with 91 victories, including two world championships. Mike Shanahan, offensive coordinator of the Denver Broncos, was his replacement. At 36 he was the league's youngest coach and was expected to revive the Raiders' passing game. However, Shanahan lasted only until the 1989 season was underway. With a commitment to returning the Raiders' to the achievements of the past, Davis hired Art Shell to succeed Shanahan on October 3rd. Shell became the first African-American head coach in the NFL since 1921.

Some critics felt the constant court wrangling had taken a toll on Davis and drew his attention away from monitoring the team and finding under-utilized talent that could blossom with the Raiders. "It appears that owner Al Davis' intent is to return to the aggressive style that once was the Raiders' trademark," writer Ric Bucher said. "Davis seems to be returning too, in a sense, after being distracted for almost seven years by court battles and by his wife suffering a prolonged illness that nearly took her life." As Ron Lynn, defensive coordinator for the San Diego Chargers, assessed, "So much of the Raiders is Al Davis. What they do depends on decisions he makes. He wasn't there to make those decisions, or at least give them his full attention."

Bo Jackson Joins Club

Marcus Allen was a perennial All-Pro during the 1980s and became the team's all-time rushing leader. Others who were All-Pro or all-conference included Hayes, Hendricks, Guy, Martin, Christensen, Long, tackle Henry Lawrence, cornerback Mike Haynes, linebacker Matt Millen, middle guard Bill Pickel, safety Vann McElroy, kick returner Tim Brown, defensive end Greg Townsend, and running back Bo Jackson.

Jackson, the Heisman Trophy winner from Auburn University in Alabama, was an outstanding baseball player as well and played with the Kansas City Royals during baseball season. Later Jackson played with the Chicago White Sox after a football injury in 1990 led to hip replacement

Courtesy of Los Angeles Raiders

Bo Jackson

surgery that ended his football career. "Bo Jackson as a full-time running back would be the best in the league," one unidentified NFL general manager had said. As Shell pointed out, "We have Bo Jackson from the second week in October—if his baseball team is done—until the end of the season. We're happy to have that. We understand the situation and have accepted it.... I'm glad when he plays football it's on our side."

Before Jackson's arrival in 1987, Allen was the go-to guy for the Raiders, leading them in rushing from 1982 through 1988. Included were three consecutive 1,000-plus seasons, culminating with a 1985 total of 1,759 yards and 11 touchdowns. When Jackson became running back, Allen was only called on to play while Jackson rested. He later shared playing time with veterans Roger Craig and Eric Dickerson before joining the Chiefs.

The Raiders had selected Allen on the first round of the 1982 draft, based solely on their own scouts' advice. The only team in the NFL that didn't belong to a scouting combine, the Raiders were apparently the only ones who didn't have doubts about Allen. "In Allen, the best all-around back in the league, all they got was the guy who, barring serious injury, will be the heart and soul of their offense for years to come," penned a writer for the September 1984 issue of *PRO!* magazine.

In their 31st season in 1990, Davis began nudging the Raiders backs to their former attack-oriented defense and power-running, deep-passing offense. In August they played an exhibition game against the New Orleans Saints in London's historic Wembley Stadium, then opened the regular season at home with their 150th home victory, beating Denver 14-9.

The Raiders attained overall league triumph number 275 with a 38-31 December win at Detroit and later that month locked up their 14th division title with a 17-12 triumph over the Chargers. Completing a 12-4 season, the Silver and Black went on to defeat Cincinnati 20-10 at home in the AFC playoffs' second round, but were crushed in the conference championship game by Buffalo, 51-3.

The 1991 season included an exhibition game in Japan against Miami. For the year, the Raiders were third in the AFC West with a 9-7 mark, losing 10-6 to Kansas City in the wild card playoffs. Earlier that year, Davis received the first NFL Players Association Award of Excellence "for his contributions to the men who played the game." Davis was becoming a regular fixture in Canton, Ohio, as a Hall of Fame presenter to former Raiders, including Shell, whom he called "a magnificent blue-collar worker." Davis himself was honored in 1992; John Madden was the presenter.

The Raiders had a modest 7-9 record that year, but they opened their 1993 season with an impressive 24-7 victory over a good Minnesota team—it appeared they might be headed back to

PROFILE

Shell's Game

When Al Davis promoted Raiders offensive line coach and Hall of Famer Art Shell to the head coaching job a month into the 1989 season, it was the first time since 1921 that an African-American became a head coach in the National Football League. In 1921, Fritz Pollard became the NFL's first black head coach when he was a player and co-coach with the Hammond Pros of Indiana."It is an historic event," Shell said. "I understand the significance of it. I'm proud of it. I can't believe the color of my skin entered into this decision. I was chosen because he felt I was the right person this time." Remarked Davis of Shell's appointment: "If this is an historic event it'll really be meaningful and historic if he is a success. I have watched this guy with our young players through the years. I've watched him with the older guys. He can communicate. He can inspire people to be great." Tom Flores, the Raiders head coach 1979-87, became the NFL's first Hispanic head coach when Davis gave him the job. "If you don't let your race get in the way, you have a better chance of accomplishing your goals," Flores said later, while a general manager with the Seattle Seahawks. "The challenge isn't because I am Hispanic. The challenge is to see if I am good enough to succeed."

Photo Courtesy of the Los Angeles Raiders

their more familiar position atop the division. At the offensive controls was another Davis resurrection project, former New York Giants Super Bowl quarterback Jeff Hostetler.

When he signed as a free agent after nine years with the Giants, the Raiders hoped it would be the end of what had been a frustrating search for a quarterback. The search had encompassed former Redskins' Super Bowl quarterback Jay Schroeder and a top draft pick, Todd Marinovich, who left the University of Southern California early amid controversy over his problems with substance abuse.

Davis and his staff still had a knack for finding top-notch players as proven by the number of All-Pro and all-conference selections in the early 1990s. Those chosen included guard Steve Wisniewski (a first-round pick in 1989), Townsend, punter Jeff Gossett, kicker Jeff Jaeger, safety Ronnie Lott (another wily veteran who proved his glory days were not yet finished), center Don Mosebar (a first-round choice in 1983), kick returner Tim Brown (first round, 1988), and cornerback Terry McDaniel (first round, 1988).

Throughout most of the Raiders' history, Al Davis has been an important constant. Some doubted he would ever be elected to the Hall of Fame because of his problems with the league concerning his desire to move his franchise from Oakland. The Raiders' accomplishments were far too significant to ignore, however, and Davis, who has among the best credentials as well as a tradition of excellence, was recognized for his achievements.

Sources

Books

Los Angeles Raiders Media Guide, El Segundo, CA: Los Angeles Raiders, 1993.

Madden, John, with Dave Anderson, *Hey, Wait a Minute,* New York: Villard Books, 1984.

Neft, David S. and Richard M. Cohen, *The Football Encyclopedia,* New York: St. Martin's, 1991.

Official National Football League 1993 Record and Fact Book, New York: NFL Properties Inc., 1993.

Plunkett, Jim and Dave Newhouse, *The Jim Plunkett Story: The Saga of a Man Who Came Back,* New York: Arbor House, 1981.

Pro Football Handbook, edited by Don Schiffer, New York: Pocket Books, 1961.

Svihus, Bob, Wayne Hawkins, and Dave Dalby, *Raider: How Offensive Can You Be!!* Carmel, CA: TriRaid Productions, 1987.

Tatum, Jack with Bill Kushner, *They Call Me Assassin,* New York: Everest House, 1979.

Periodicals

Don Heinrich's Pro Preview, 1984.

Fawcett's Pro Football, 1963.

Football Digest, November 1971; January 1972; July/August 1972; December 1973; January 1975; March 1975; October 1975; April 1977; December 1990.

GameDay, December 15, 1979; September 2, 1984; October 7, 1984; November 22, 1984; December 10, 1984.

Insider! 1988; spring 1989; summer 1989; fall 1989; winter 1990; spring 1990; winter 1991; winter 1992.

NFL Report, fall 1988; winter 1989; spring 1990; summer 1990; fall 1990; fall 1991; fall 1992.

Petersen's Pro Football Annual, 1977; 1981.

PRO!, August 1981; September 1984.

Pro Football Stars, 1962; 1964.

Pro Quarterback, January 1978.

Sporting News Pro Football Yearbook, 1986.

Street and Smith's Football Yearbook, 1960.

—*Larry Paladino*

San Diego Chargers

The San Diego Chargers have never been backward about passing. From the embryonic days under legendary Sid Gillman through the era of "Air Coryell" and beyond, the Chargers and passing have been nearly synonymous—Jack Kemp to Lance Alworth, John Hadl throwing to everybody, Dan Fouts flinging the ball all over the field, and now, Stan Humphries making his bid to join that group of legendary passers. The forward pass has been foremost in the Charger mentality from the day the franchise was constituted as an original member of the American Football League back in 1960.

On August 14, 1959, six representatives met in Chicago with the idea of forming a new professional football league. One of them was hotel magnate Barron Hilton. Eight days later in Dallas, a second meeting was held. The group decided on the name "American Football League." A historic venture began.

On October 14, former Notre Dame football coaching legend Frank Leahy was named general manager of Hilton's franchise, which was located in Los Angeles to give the new league a foothold in the major West Coast city.

Two weeks later, the new team was named "the Chargers." Gerald Courtney of Hollywood won an expenses-paid trip to Mexico City and Acapulco for submitting the winning entry in a name-the-team contest. Hilton liked the name because it symbolized electricity, a horse charging, and, best of all, his hotel chain's new credit card.

Searching for a head coach, the fledgling franchise decided it needed a high-profile guy to combat the rival Los Angeles Rams of the established National Football League. Who better than Sid Gillman? Already a legend for his all-guns-blazing offensive style, Gillman had the added advantage of having just been let go as coach of the Rams. And maybe some disaffected Rams fans would follow Gillman over to the Chargers.

The Los Angeles Chargers

Gillman was given a three-year contract on January 7, 1960, and later that spring Hilton hosted a party at his Santa Monica home to unveil his team's new uniforms. Quarterback Kemp and Hall of Fame tackle Ron Mix were there wearing the Chargers' blue and gold uniforms bearing the distinctive lightning bolt down the both sides of the pants and on the helmet. Kemp was a quarterback long before he audibled to the political field where his name has now become familiar. At that time he was just another NFL quarterback reject, having played with the Steelers, Giants, and 49ers.

Another NFL reject was 41-year-old kicker and former Ram Ben Agajanian. End Dave Kocourek was one of a group of players who migrated down from the Canadian Football League that the haughty NFL had thumbed its nose at. Mix symbolized the hopes of the new league because the Chargers outbid the Baltimore Colts, who had made him their number one draft choice, for his services.

They also won a legal battle for fullback Charlie Flowers, who enjoyed the wooing so much he signed contracts with both leagues. Gillman took on the role of general manager in the summer when Leahy resigned due to failing health, and the franchise got off to a good start in every way save attendance.

High-stepping rookie running back Paul Lowe, later to make the Chargers' Hall of Fame, returned the first exhibition game kickoff 105 yards on August 6 to help his team defeat the New York Titans, 27-7. More than a month later, on September 10, a crowd of 17,724 at the Coliseum saw the new team score twice in the fourth quarter of its first regular season game to score a 21-20 victory over Dallas. The team won eight of its last nine games, surviving tragedy when leading receiver Ralph Anderson died of a diabetes attack in November. Kocourek caught 40 passes, four less than Anderson, but had the most yards (662-614). Kemp was rated the league's best passer. Lowe led the team with 855 yards.

The Chargers' 10-4 was best in the West Division, qualifying them for the first AFL championship. They lost, 24-16, at Jeppeson Stadium to host Houston. Quarterback George Blanda, already an aging performer at 32 but with a decade of football ahead of him, threw a seven-yard scoring pass to Bill Groman to give Houston a 17-9 lead in the third quarter. Lowe capped a long drive with a two-yard touchdown, pulling Los Angeles to within a point, but Billy Cannon came out of the backfield and took a Blanda pass 88 yards to give the Oilers the first AFL title.

A week earlier, though, Hilton had made a decision that would have a great impact on the Charger franchise. His team had drawn an average of 15,665 for its seven home games—considerably less for the final two, although it was obvious the team had gotten a handle on Gillman's complicated offensive schemes. The Chargers were churning out points the way its owner's hotel chain went through soap and shampoo, averaging 26.64 points. Take away two shutout losses in the first five games plus a 3-point defeat midway down the stretch and it was scoring 33.63 points per contest. In its last four, it scored 52, 41 twice, and 50.

It was like Fifth of July fireworks to Hilton. He lost $900,000 that first season and must not have liked bragging to his high-rolling friends about a team that didn't light up the cash register like it lit up the scoreboard. So on December 23, 1960, he said he'd listen to what San Diego had to say about relocating his franchise. What San Diego told him was to "Come on down." The city, tired of sitting under Los Angeles' sun, was seeking its own identity. It formed a committee charged with getting a major league baseball franchise, a pro football team, and a place where both of them could play.

Turnaround in San Diego

On February 10, scarcely five weeks after his team lost the first AFL championship game, Hilton announced that the Chargers would be

TEAM INFORMATION AT A GLANCE

Founding date: 1960 (AFL); 1970 (NFL)

Home stadium: Jack Murphy Stadium
Address: P.O. Box 609609
San Diego, CA 92160-9609
Phone: (619) 280-2111
Seating capacity: 60,750

Team colors: Navy blue, gold, and white
Team nickname: Chargers
Logo: Lightning bolt

Franchise record	Won	Lost	Tie
(1960-92)	233	225	11

moving to San Diego to play in an enlarged Balboa Stadium (to which an upper deck would be added, enlarging it to 34,000 seats). The move paid immediate dividends, both financially and on the field. San Diego won its first 11 games, finished 12-2, won the West, and nearly doubled its average attendance to 27,859.

Barron still lost money, but was making progress. He had tweaked the NFL's nose by outbidding it for defensive end Earl Faison. A 315-pound rookie, Ernie Ladd, anchored the middle of the defensive line, and middle linebacker Chuck Allen, a mere 28th round draft choice, was a sensation until breaking his ankle with the year nearly done.

The Chargers hosted the second AFL title game, losing again to Houston, this time 10-3, before a crowd of 29,556 as Blanda, flushed out of the pocket, threw 35-yards to Cannon in the third quarter for the only touchdown in the game. Kemp tried to rally his team in the defensive struggle, passing his team deep into Oiler territory early in the fourth quarter but having to settle for a George Blair 12-yard field goal. Houston's Julian Spence picked off a Kemp pass on the Oiler 30 with less than two minutes to play, one of four interceptions by his team. The Chargers picked off six passes in the defensive struggle. Kemp dropped to fifth in the QB rankings but fired 15 TD passes and 2,686 yards, nearly half to Kocourek (1,055). Lowe ran for 767 yards and scored nine touchdowns.

Those were giddy times—the teen-age years for the league even though it was just two years old. Kemp threw, Mix blocked, Lowe ran, Paul Maguire punted, and All-AFL cornerback Dick Harris led a high-interception secondary. But a large portion of the roster was made up of revolving door players: in, around, and out—sometimes more than once. Rejects, retreads, and renews.

The year was another financial beating for Hilton but not nearly as bad as the first. If television money was keeping the league alive, TV itself was hurting league attendance. Why pay good money to go out and watch the games when you could stay at home and see them for free? But slowly that began to change.

The 1962 season was a downer, 4-10, as injuries plagued San Diego. The Chargers' troubles began in the off-season when linebacker Bob Laraba was killed in an automobile accident. Lowe broke an arm in an exhibition game, and before the season ended 11 starters missed seven or more games. One of the injured was Kemp, who suffered a broken hand. Gillman got in on the gaffes by putting his quarterback on waivers to get him on the reserve list. Buffalo claimed him for $100.

But things were looking up. Another 1961 draftee was fullback Keith Lincoln, who steadily improved as a runner after blocking most of his first year. Quarterback Hadl came in 1962 and guard Walt Sweeney in 1963. And a real lightning bolt zigged out of the sky to strike the Chargers in 1962: wide receiver Alworth. San Diego had secretly signed Alworth in the fall to a two-year contract worth $40,000 plus a $10,000 bonus, so Oakland drafted him and immediately traded him to the Chargers for three draft choices.

Hadl learned the hard facts of pro quarterback life his rookie season, completing just 41 percent of his passes and throwing 24 interceptions. He ranked seventh of the eight starting quarterbacks in the AFL. Lowe's yards went to Lincoln (574) and Bobby Jackson (411) while Don Norton passed Kocourek at the top of the receiver's list with 771 yards and 48 catches.

Hadl went back to the bench in 1963 as veteran NFL quarterback Tobin Rote, who had guided the Detroit Lions to an NFL championship in 1957, put things together. Rote had spent the three previous seasons playing for Toronto of the Canadian Football League, but quit and was persuaded to replace Kemp.

Lowe became the franchise's first 1,000-yard rusher (averaging 5.7 yards for 177 carries) while Alworth blossomed to lead the team with 61 receptions for 1,205 yards and 11 touchdowns. Alworth, Faison, Lincoln, Mix, and Rote all had All-AFL seasons. Rote was the top-rated passer in the league, completing 59 percent of his passes for 2,510 yards. He threw 20 touchdowns and had 17 intercepted.

For Alworth, who had spent most of his rookie season injured, it was the first of seven straight 1,000-yard receiving seasons. He earned his nickname "Bambi" for his youthful, innocent features plus the stag-like way he would streak downfield, gracefully leap to catch a pass, then twist and dart for extra yardage when he came down. He was perhaps the first highlight film receiver and certainly his excellence helped the AFL gain respect in the football world. He set records with catches in 96 consecutive games and touchdown receptions in nine straight games. Alworth showed his toughness in 1966 when he played with two broken hands through much of the season, finally going out of the lineup due to a pulled hamstring. But he still led the league in all receiving categories.

Alworth Joins Winning Team

The 1963 season saw the Chargers win five of their first six games en route to an 11-3 record and their third first-place West Division finish in four seasons. This despite two losses to the up-and-coming Oakland Raiders as Gillman's high-powered offense scored the most points in the league. The second loss to Oakland, 41-27, came with two games to play and left the Chargers with a one-game lead. But San Diego edged Houston and hammered Denver, 58-20, behind Lowe's 183 yard, two-touchdown game, to clinch.

San Diego hosted Boston in the title game and this time delighted a crowd of 30,127 with a 51-10 thrashing of the Patriots as Lincoln accounted for 349 yards total offense, 206 rushing, and 123 passing.

Lincoln set the tone for the day on the second play of the game when he shot through the middle for a 56-yard run to set up Rote's two-yard scoring sneak. When San Diego got the ball back, he scooted around end for a 67-yard score, and Lincoln scored a third time with a 25-yard pass from mop-up man Hadl in the fourth quarter. Former Cleveland Browns quarterback Otto Graham said after the game, "If the Chargers could play the best in the NFL, I'd have to pick the Chargers."

The only thing the Chargers lost in 1963 came prior to the season, when a strong-willed, driven assistant coach defected to become both head coach and general manager of the Raiders at the age of 33. That man was Al Davis.

San Diego and the league came of age in 1964. The flashy show the Chargers put on in the 1963 championship game contrasted sharply with the deadly dull defensive-minded Chicago Bears, who won George Halas an NFL championship the same year. The Chargers win came on the heels of an overtime AFL title game the year before, a contest that kept viewers nailed to the set.

The two games helped convince NBC it could use the league as a counter to CBS's Sunday telecasts of NFL games. The AFL signed a five-year contract with NBC for $36 million, replacing the pact with ABC which let the league survive its infancy. The Chargers set a record when a crowd of 34,865 showed up to Balboa Stadium on Thanksgiving Day to watch Buffalo defeat San Diego, 27-24.

The franchise did win its fourth AFL West title in five years when it whipped the New York Jets, 38-3, on December 6. The season marked the point at which Hadl assumed the mantle of leadership from the 36-year-old Rote, who had a sore arm. Hadl was second to Len Dawson among league quarterbacks despite a relatively low amount of passes (274). His touchdowns outnumbered his interceptions, 18-15. Rote got enough playing time to rank 11th but had a 9-15 TD-interception ratio. Alworth gained 1,235 yards and scored a league best 13 times while Lincoln (632) and Lowe (496) combined for 1,128 yards.

A six-game winning streak in the middle of the season gave San Diego the title in an AFL West where the other challengers outstumbled the 8-5-1 Chargers. The more experienced Rote got the call in the title game and drove San Diego 80 yards in four plays, the last a 26-yard TD pass to Kocourek. A key play happened on San Diego's next possession. Lincoln caught a short pass in the flat only to be flattened by Buffalo linebacker Mike Stratton, popping the ball loose and breaking one of the running back's ribs. Since Alworth was already out because of a knee injury, the Chargers were unable to move the ball against the Bills the rest of the game. Kemp, the ex-San Diego quarterback, and Buffalo took control for a 20-7 victory.

The success of the Chargers led to the start of construction on a new stadium in 1965, shortly after San Diego copped its fifth AFL West title in six years. Rookie linebackers Rick Redman and Dick Degan, defensive end Steve DeLong plus cornerback/return artist Leslie 'Speedy' Duncan came in to give fresh legs to the sturdy defense while running back Gene Foster reported to help Lincoln at fullback. But the glory days for the team's early core were coming to an end. Faison and Ladd were both playing out their options and the team would not hold off the Raiders much longer.

Hadl had emerged as one of the league's top tossers — still second to Dawson—and Alworth gained an incredible total of 1,602 yards with a league-leading 14 touchdowns. Lowe set a league mark by rushing for 1,121 yards and Duncan was a demon on returns. But this 9-2-3 team could not dent Buffalo's hard-hitting defense in the AFL championship game, watched by 30,361, even with all its weapons. Kemp hit Ernie Warlick with an 18-yard touchdown pass five minutes before halftime and, after the Chargers punted, Butch Byrd returned the kick 74 yards down the sideline to put Buffalo ahead, 14-0, in a game it eventually won by a 23-0 count.

It was the fifth straight AFL title game quarter in which San Diego had not scored and it was to be the last. The Chargers would not return to post-season play until after the league had merged with the rival NFL. They lost an owner, four players in an expansion draft, and bulwarks Faison and Ladd to contract disagreements.

Hilton sold the franchise on August 25, 1966, to a group of 21 businessmen headed by Eugene V. Klein and Sam Schulman for $10 million, at the time a record for a pro football team. At year's start, the expansion Miami Dolphins drafted tight end Kocourek, guard Ernest Park, and defensive backs Dick Westmoreland and Jimmy Warren off the San Diego roster. Contract disputes with

Gillman found Ladd going to Houston and Faison to Miami.

Allen suffered a broken ankle and missed most of the year but the addition of rookie Gary Garrison gave Hadl another receiving option besides Alworth. San Diego won its first four games that year, but then opponents discovered they could run the ball down the Chargers' throats. San Diego finished third, 7-6-1. Alworth still managed to lead the league with 1,383 yards and 13 touchdowns. And Dawson again beat Hadl out for the honor of top AFL quarterback. The defense disintegrated down the stretch in 1967, costing the Chargers their last four games and putting them third again, 8-5-1.

One bright spot was the dedicating of San Diego Stadium August 20 with a crowd of 45,988 watching Detroit defeat San Diego, 38-17, in an exhibition game, its first meeting with an established NFL team. The stadium's first sellout, 52,611, came December 3 in a 41-21 loss to Oakland. Alworth squeezed past the 1,000-yard barrier by 10 yards, but Hadl dropped two notches in the quarterback standings to fourth. Willie Frazier caught more passes than Alworth, and the new rushing leader was Dickie Post.

Gillman's Reign Ends

Three losses in the last four games left San Diego 9-5, third for the third straight year in 1968. An 8-6 1969 brought the fourth in a run of six straight thirds for the Chargers. It also brought an end to the Gillman era as coach. With five games to go, stomach ulcers and a chest hernia induced Gillman to relinquish his duties to offensive backfield coach Charlie Waller. The Chargers won their last four games—Alworth catching pass in his 96th straight on December 14—after dropping Waller's opener. Gillman remained as GM as the AFL officially passed out of existence. A resurgent Alworth had league highs with 68 receptions and 1,312 yards. A weak running game made Hadl throw the ball more than anybody, but his 32 interceptions contributed to him ranking fifth among AFL quarterbacks in 1968.

In 1969, Hadl cut his throwing but again was fifth in the quarterback standings. Alworth squirmed by 1,000 yards by three but led the league with 64 receptions. The pass rush that had been largely nonexistent since Faison and Ladd left contributed to the team intercepting just five passes during the entire 1970 campaign. At the end of the season, Klein persuaded Gillman to return as head coach and Waller to coach the offense. Garrison assumed Alworth's role as the primary receiver in 1970—"Bambi" slipping to just 608 yards on 35 catches at the age of 30—but Hadl led the league with 22 TD passes and was second among QBs again, this time to Daryle Lamonica.

A link with the franchise's beginning years was severed when Alworth was traded to the Dallas Cowboys, to finish out his career with two seasons of part-time duty. Harland Svare was brought in to replace Gillman as general manager, a move which foreshadowed his leaving in the middle of the 6-8 1971 campaign due to traditionally fatal differences of opinion with the owner. Ex-Rams Coach Svare found himself in Gillman's hot seat on the field, although Garrison and rookie Billy Parks capably replaced Alworth.

Mike Garrett led the runners with 591 yards but had no help, and the Chargers were forced to throw again. Hadl threw more than 400 times for 3,075 yards and 21 TDs to rank fourth in the league. Svare, not one to let a telephone sit unused, made 21 trades in 221 days prior to the start of the 1972 season. But the Chargers started a string of four straight fourth-place (last) finishes in the AFC West as GM Svare's cast of oldsters (John Mackey, Deacon Jones, Lionel Aldridge, etc.) and malcontents (Duane Thomas) ran out of gas for Coach Svare. The Chargers won just four games, the fewest since their third season, lost nine, and tied one. Garrett gained 1,031 yards.

It didn't help that offensive coordinator Bob Schnelker's penchant for ball control didn't mesh with Hadl's penchant for throwing the ball. Player-coach clashes can be found under the same listing as coach-owner tussles—see 'Sure Way To Lose.'

Veteran Johnny Unitas—now there's a ball control artist if there ever was one—was brought in on January 22, 1973, and three days later Hadl (his rating down to 10th) was dispatched to the Rams for defensive end Coy Bacon and running back Bob Thomas. But the zing was gone from Unitas' arm after 17 years of throwing for the Colts. He ended the season with a back injury, watching third-round draft choice Fouts calling signals, but not until completing a 30-yard pass to Garrett that made him the first QB to throw for 40,000 yards. Also gone—not even arrived, in fact—was top draft choice Johnny Rodgers. The Heisman Trophy winner had elected not to sign with San Diego and went to Montreal of the CFL instead.

Svare benched Garrett (obtained in a 1971 trade with Kansas City) early in the season, Garrison went out with an injury, and receiver Dave Williams was released in mid-year, calling San Diego "a zoo." After eight games, Svare seemingly agreed because he turned the coaching part of his duties over to assistant Ron Waller. Waller finished out the 2-11-1 season and was replaced at the start of 1974 by Tommy Prothro, longtime UCLA coach who went to the Los Angeles Rams in 1971.

Prothro had been fired following the 1972 season when the club changed ownership and lost five of its last six games. Some of the trades Prothro made with the Rams backfired but didn't stop "The Great Pumpkin" from making more deals like shipping venerable guard Sweeney, 32, and the aging Deacon Jones to gaffer-loving George Allen of Washington.

Meanwhile, owner Klein, Svare, and several Chargers were implicated in a drug scandal, which brought them fines and probation by Rozelle.

The Chargers improved to five wins and one bright spot surfaced when Prothro claimed rookie running back Don Woods off waivers from Green Bay on September 17. Woods set a standard for rookies by running for 1,162 yards that season and was named Rookie of the Year, but in 1975 San Diego lost its first 11 (two in overtime). They beat Kansas City, 28-20, and followed up with win number two, their last, against the Jets. Injuries to Woods and Bo Mathews put quarterbacks Fouts and Jesse Frietas under siege.

Svare resigned as GM on January 20, 1976, and was replaced by long-time Rams executive John Sanders, who had joined the organization 11 months earlier. The team won its first three games and four of its first six before going 2-6 the rest of the way. But Fouts, tutored by a young offensive coordinating wizard named Bill Walsh, began his maturation as a quarterback despite having just one quality receiver, Charlie Joiner (obtained from Cincinnati for Bacon), who gained 1,056 yards. Fouts led the AFC with 359 passes and 208 completions to rise to eighth as a statistical quarterback.

Three defensive linemen drafted in 1975—first rounder tackle Gary Johnson, plus second-round picks tackle Louie Kelcher and end Fred Dean—were instrumental in returning the Chargers to the conference's upper echelon. San Diego got back to .500 and into third place in 1977. Unfortunately, Fouts got into a salary squabble with management and "retired" for most of the season, eventually returning for the last four games. James Harris, obtained from Los Angeles for a draft choice, replaced him.

The pieces were now in place for a return to prominence, but "The Great Pumpkin" didn't even make it to Halloween. Prothro quit after the Chargers got off to a 1-3 start in 1978 and Don Coryell, once the coach at San Diego State and recently resigned as coach at St. Louis, was chosen to succeed him. The year had begun on a good note when Alworth became the first AFL player selected to the Pro Football Hall of Fame. It also ended in an upbeat fashion as San Diego closed with seven wins in eight games, good for fourth at 9-7 and clear evidence that "Air Coryell" was off the ground.

Fouts Leads Streak

Fouts, now the number two quarterback in the AFC behind Terry Bradshaw, had Joiner and number one draft choice John Jefferson (1,001 yards) as deep targets. Back Lydell Mitchell, acquired from the Colts, was available for running and for dump-offs. The two top 1979 draft picks were packaged in a deal to Cleveland so San Diego could draft tight end Kellen Winslow (who broke his leg in October). Coryell also shored up the defense with veteran cornerback Willie Buchanon from Green Bay and got excellent play from veteran Wilbur Young when Kelcher suffered a preseason knee injury.

Fouts had four 300-yard passing games in a row (a record) in an NFL record 4,082-yard season that made him the number one quarterback in the AFC. Joiner (72-1,008) and Jefferson (61-1,090) both topped 1,000 yards receiving. San Diego won six of its last seven games to return to first place in the AFC West with a 12-4 mark. That put the Chargers in the playoffs against old nemesis Houston.

In this contest, Fouts outthrew his Houston counterpart, Gifford Nielsen, 3-1 (333-111) but Nielsen hit the one that counted—a 47-yard touchdown pass to Mike Renfro. It negated an 8-yard fourth-quarter scoring run by San Diego's Mitchell and gave Houston a 17-14 victory.

AP/Wide World Photos

Dan Fouts

Winslow, Jefferson (his 1,340 led the AFC), and Joiner were all 1,000-yard receivers in 1980 with Fouts (ranked second to Cleveland's Brian Sipe) again flinging the ball all over what late in the season was renamed Jack Murphy Stadium in honor of the late sports editor of the San Diego Union. Dean held out for more money and missed the first two games of the season. Fouts threw for a club record 444 yards in one game, but it still took five wins in the last six games to get the Chargers, who started the season with four straight wins, to 11-5 and into the playoffs. The team clinched the AFC West title on the final Monday night of the season, beating Pittsburgh, 26-17, with Winslow catching 10 passes for 171 yards.

Fouts again hit the 300-yard mark in the playoffs (22-37—314), but it took ten fourth-quarter points to net San Diego a 20-14 opening round victory over Buffalo. Rolf Benirschke's 22-yard field goal and Fouts' 50-yard scoring strike to Ron Smith with 2:08 to play got the job done. That put San Diego up against division rival Oakland, which had the same record as the Chargers but lost first place on the tie-breaking procedure in the AFC title game. The two had split their regular season meetings, but the Raiders blitzed the Chargers with 21 first-quarter points and a 28-14 halftime lead. Jim Plunkett, hauled from the bench when Dan Pastorini broke a leg, completed 14-of-18 passes for the day and snuck for a 5-yard score. Oakland held on for a 34-27 win and became the first wild card team to both play in and win the Super Bowl.

Fouts led the league in all the throwing categories including 30 touchdowns and another NFL record of 4,715 yards. His mechanical arm again put Winslow, Joiner, and Jefferson over 1,000 yards and Chuck Muncie, acquired in a 1980 trade with New Orleans to give the running attack more punch, ran for 827 yards.

Another echo of Faison and Ladd struck San Diego in 1981 as both Jefferson (Green Bay) and

Dean (San Francisco) were traded after bitter salary disputes. Yet the Chargers still managed to capture a third straight AFC West crown, again clinching on the final Monday night of the season. This time Oakland was the victim, 23-10.

Wes Chandler was obtained from New Orleans to join Joiner and Winslow as primary Fouts' targets—and again San Diego placed three receivers above 1,000 yards. Fouts maintained his lofty ratings (third this time) while Muncie ran for 1,144 yards. The offense scored 40 points or more four times during the season but the defense, feeling the loss of Dean's pass-rushing talents, gave up 40 three times. It took four wins in the final five games to put the 10-6 team in the playoffs, this time edging Denver in the tie-breaker for first place.

San Diego stunned Miami with 24 first-quarter points as Fouts had a 433-yard passing game. But the Dolphins fought back and finally tied the score, 38-38, on Don Strock's (397 yards passing himself) 50-yard touchdown toss to tight end Bruce Hardy. Fouts got San Diego into position so Benirschke could kick a 29-yard field goal 13:52 into overtime to put the Chargers into the AFC championship game for the second year in a row.

They got frozen out of the title. The game was played in Cincinnati on a January 10 day when the temperature was 11 degrees below zero with a wind chill of 59 below. San Diego could only dream of the warmth back home and the warmth two weeks hence when the Super Bowl would be played indoors, in the Pontiac Silverdome.

The Bengals got a field goal, recovered a Chargers fumble on the kickoff, and converted that into a touchdown for a 10-7 lead. Fouts hit Winslow with a 33-yard touchdown pass, but interceptions ended two other forays and Cincinnati added 17 more points to the margin.

A slip to second with a 6-3 record marked the 1982 strike season, with San Diego making the playoffs for a fourth straight year despite an increasingly porous defense. December victories by 41-37, 50-34, and 44-26 scores characterized the team.

Fouts put on his usual passing show (333 yards) and hit Winslow with TD passes of 8- and 12-yards in the fourth quarter to pull out a 31-28 victory over Pittsburgh in the first round of the playoffs. But Miami intercepted Fouts five times in the second round and the host Dolphins eliminated the Chargers, 34-13. Even with just nine games, Chandler made it over 1,000 yards and Fouts threw for 2,883. Anderson beat him out for number one again, though.

Coryell switched to a 3-4 defense in 1983 in hopes of better utilizing his personnel, but the team was still unable to mount a consistent pass rush. In addition, troubles on the offensive line (veteran Russ Washington was unexpectedly cut and Doug Wilkerson missed the first four games with a broken arm) hurt the ground game. So when Fouts suffered a mid-year shoulder injury the Chargers were doomed to a tie for fourth, 6-10, in the AFC West. Fouts still ranked third among his peers and Winslow was 88-1,351, but Muncie was down to 886 yards and increasingly at odds with his coach.

Construction expanding Jack Murphy Stadium to 60,100 was completed May 1, 1984, and on August 1, Klein sold a majority interest in the Chargers to apartment builder Alex G. Spanos of Stockton. "This is the culmination of a dream, a lifelong dream. I'm a very happy man," Spanos said four weeks later upon his confirmation as owner by his league counterparts. But when construction of the stadium was complete, the team began to fall apart.

Muncie, whom Coryell felt had a bad attitude, was traded to Miami—only to be returned (to sit out the season on suspension) when he failed a drug test. Winslow sat out a game to underscore dissatisfaction with his contract—then suffered a season-ending knee injury October 21.

The Chargers dropped to fifth, 7-9. A 3,740-yard season (completing 63 percent of 507 attempts) kept Fouts among the league leaders but his TD passes dropped to 19 and none of his receivers gained more than 800 yards. Ernest Jackson, an eighth-round draft choice in 1983, ran for 1,179 yards.

But the record brought changes. Old mainstay Kelcher was traded to San Francisco before the 1984 season for draft choices; back James Brooks went to Cincinnati for fullback Pete Johnson, later dealt to Miami as a substitute for Muncie; and Gary Johnson went to San Francisco in late September for more draft choices. Jackson was traded to Philadelphia for draft choices at the start of the 1985 season, and that left the Chargers without a ground game. Back Lionel James was too small to take the pounding as a runner but he was great at catching passes out of the backfield, leading the AFC with 86. The defense still couldn't stop anybody so 8-8, fourth place, was where the club finished.

Two receivers were over 1,000 yards (James and Chandler, with Joiner just missing) as Fouts, now 34, threw 27 TD passes and 3,638 yards. However, soft-tossing Mark Herrmann threw 200 passes as his backup. Coryell had his contract extended at the end of the season—but a 1-7 start in 1985 prompted him to resign. Al Saunders became the youngest head coach in the league at age 39. Saunders promised an end to the point-a-minute defenses and turned Fouts from a long-range bomber into a short-game man, even if he did receive a couple of concussions in the process. The Chargers finished 3-5 for a last-place 4-12 mark.

Nobody gained 900 yards receiving that year for the Chargers, and Fouts slipped to tenth under the change in throwing philosophy. There was no running game to take the pressure off, so Fouts threw 22 interceptions.

There was another strike in 1987, and games by replacement teams counted in the standings. San Diego's were 3-0, contributing to an 8-1 start that spotlighted an improved defense led by linebacker Billy Ray Smith. But Fouts was finally starting to show his age and, even though the Chargers needed just two wins in its last six games to get to the playoffs, they lost all six. The offense managed just seven touchdowns in the last eight games, San Diego wound up third, 8-7, and Fouts retired during the winter. He ranked 22nd his final season.

Jack Murphy Stadium hosted the 1988 Super Bowl, and Washington defeated Denver, 42-10.

The search for a new Fouts (Steve Fuller, Babe Laufenberg, Mark Malone, and Mark Vlasic were the candidates) occupied much of 1988 as the emphasis switched from passing to running. Gary Anderson gained 1,119 yards (5.0 average) and set records of 34 rushes and 217 yards in a December 18 game. A six-game losing streak in the middle of the season doomed Saunders, who lost his job the day after the 6-10 season ended, even though San Diego captured four of its last six. Dan Henning, 46-year-old former Chargers quarterback (1966, backed up Hadl) and Atlanta head coach, succeeded Saunders and the defense showed sharp improvement.

Defensive ends Lee Williams and rookie Burt Grossman plus linebackers Smith, Leslie O'Neal (number one pick in 1986) and Gary Plummer put pressure on the passer and helped the Chargers hold opponents to 20 points or less in their last 14 games. But the offense was like Anderson—a no-show all year—as former Bears quarterback Jim McMahon failed to deliver the goods in another 6-10 campaign. Fullback Marion Butts proved a find as a seventh-round draft choice with a club record 39 carries in one game.

Beathard Reshapes Chargers

Spanos set the tone for the future, though, on January 3, 1990, with the naming of former Redskins' GM Bobby Beathard as his team's GM. The new man had a mild connection with the Chargers, having spent six exhibition games trying to make the franchise's very first roster as a defensive back. Beathard, whose specialty was spotting talent on the discard pile and in out-of-the-way places, had grown bored with Washington's success and was looking for a new challenge.

He found it in a TV booth in 1989 but discovered he missed the never-ending challenge of the talent hunt even more. The measure of Beathard is that 27 members of his 1982 Super Bowl champion Redskins he signed as free agents.

PROFILE

Sid Gillman

If any team symbolized the new age of razzle-dazzle professional football, it was the San Diego Chargers of Sid Gillman. Gillman's staff in those pre-techno days consisted of four of the best and brightest minds in the game. In addition to the head coach, considered the father of the modern passing game, there was his long-time aide Joe Madro; defensive backfield assistant Jack Faulkner, later to coach the Denver Broncos; defensive coach Chuck Noll, empire builder with Pittsburgh; and a young receivers coach named Al Davis. Yes, that Al Davis.

Gillman and his aides all scouted and recruited players, specializing in athletes. But they also had to be signable, so while the other clubs had nice draft lists but "Who He?" rosters, the Chargers had players. Usually with one big name mixed in for credibility. The beauty of the Chargers was their athleticism. And the fact that they were maybe 20 years ahead of their time in the way they played.

San Diego had Jack Kemp, a quarterback who loved the deep game and could really stretch a defense. Paul Lowe was a high-stepping running back who could follow his blockers or flash out by himself. Lance Alworth became a Hall of Fame receiver for the Chargers after not catching a lot of passes as a wingback at Arkansas. He'd work short, middle, long, hooks, outs, posts, ... anything. But his speciality was the leaping, cutting downfield catch that earned him the nickname "Bambi." Ron Mix was a great blocking guard and San Diego had the prototype massive defensive line anchored by Ernie Ladd, the first 300-pounder outside Les Bingaman, and pass-rushing defensive end Earl Faison.

Lowe had been cut by the San Francisco 49ers and was working in the mail room of the Beverly Hilton in Los Angeles. Barron Hilton and his son Conrad owned the Chargers as well as the hotel line. Lowe pestered the elder Hilton for a tryout until he got it. Paul Maguire, best known today as a television commentator, was recruited by Gillman for The Citadel and then recruited once again for the Chargers. Dave Kocourek was a tight end Gillman moved to wideout while Keith Lincoln developed gradually into a punishing slashing fullback.

Gillman started the NFL film exchange when he coached the Rams. He got interested in working with film because his father owned movie theaters in Minnesota. He made up reels of film on particular plays for each position, showing how the best guys in the league ran things, and gave them to his players to study. "With Sid's offense," Alworth used to say, "it was just a matter of time. The only thing we worried about was who was going to get the ball next. Every week Sid would draw up a game plan, and he knew it would work, and we knew it would work, and so did the guys we were playing." If Gillman had time, the other team was in trouble.

The only AFL title Gillman's Chargers won came in 1963 (they were beaten by Kemp and the Buffalo Bills the next two years), when Gillman had an extra week's preparation. San Diego had beaten Boston twice, 17-13 and 7-6, during the regular season but the Patriots had been difficult because of an aggressive, blitzing defense. But while Boston was beating Buffalo, 26-8, in a playoff game, San Diego was sitting home making preparations as an outright conference champ. "That's all Sid needed, that extra week," Kocourek said. "He put in a motion scheme that just ate 'em alive. We gave them slot formations and trips (three receivers) to one side. They never knew where we were coming from."

The result was a 51-10 lambasting, and only the fact the Chargers were outmuscled by the Bills (Alworth missed the first game with an injury and Lincoln suffered a broken rib in the first quarter, leading to 20-7 Bills' win) in the next two title games kept the Chargers from wider recognition as one of the great teams of all time. But from 1960-65 the franchise won five AFL West titles and overall championship.

Hilton sold the Chargers in .1966 to a group headed by Gene Klein. Money got tight, contract squabbles ensued and within a couple of seasons it was all over. It took 14 years to get back to the playoffs.

Only three times in 11 years did the Redskins have a number one choice as he preferred to trade them rather than draft high in the round.

The first season in the Beathard regime was a duplicate of the one before it, 6-10, but up a notch to fourth place. Billy Joe Tolliver was inconsistent at quarterback. His best move was a handoff to Butts, who jumped his production to a club record 1,225 yards. Five straight losses at the start of the 1991 season and eight defeats in the first nine games led to a 4-12 mark and the sacking of Henning when it was over. If a lack of a solid ground game doomed the Chargers during their playoff years of 1979-82, the lack of an air attack was crippling.

John Friesz, a sixth-round choice in 1990, was the latest in the string of quarterback hopefuls. Again, his best play call was a handoff to Butts or Rod Bernstine, or a dumpoff pass to Ronnie Harmon. The call went to Bobby Ross, who had done well at both Maryland and Georgia Tech and had some pro experience from spending four seasons as an assistant with the Kansas City Chiefs (1978-81). Ross got his welcome back to pro football when Friesz, his nominal starter, suffered a season-ending knee injury in the first preseason game.

Beathard turned to his Washington roots in getting a replacement, culling third-stringer Humphries. Humphries relieved veteran Bob Gagliano in the season opener, then started the rest of the way. San Diego lost its first four as Humphries settled in, but won 11 of the last 12 to make the Chargers the first team ever to overcome such a start and still make the playoffs. San Diego's 11-5 record was good for its first first-place finish since 1981.

By season's end, San Diego's offense rose from 13th in 1992 up to sixth. The passing game went from 24th to seventh as Harmon caught 79 passes and Anthony Miller 72 for 1,060 yards and seven scores. Linebacker Junior Seau, Beathard's first number one choice for San Diego, plus O'Neal, defensive end Chris Mims (number one in 1992), safety Stanley Richard (number one in 1991), and cornerback Sean Vanhorse (Plan B, Detroit) keyed a defense that rose to fourth in the AFC from 19th the season before and became tops against the rush.

Humphries balanced his ground and air games in the playoffs against Kansas City. The defense blanked the Chiefs, and Butts' 54-yard scoring run in the third quarter broke a scoreless tie. That advanced San Diego to the second round of the playoffs, where Miami's defense stung Humphries with four interceptions in rolling to a 31-0 victory. The Dolphins scored 21 points in the second quarter to take the Chargers' ground game away from them, then concentrated on the air game.

Sources

Books

Klein, Gene, & Ray Fisher, *First Down and A Billion,* Morrow, 1987.

Neft, David S., Richard M. Cohen, and Rick Korch, *Sports Encyclopedia: Pro Football,* 11th edition, St. Martin's, 1993.

Porter, David L., Ed., *Biographical Dictionary of American Sports: Football,* Greenwood Press, 1987.

Riffenburgh, Beau, *The Official NFL Encyclopedia,* NAL, 1986.

Periodicals

Sports Illustrated, February 1, 1988; September 7, 1992.

—*Richard Shook*

SEATTLE SEAHAWKS

The Seahawks joined the NFL as an expansion team in the mid-1970s. Like most expansion teams, the players were a mixture of aging marginal castoffs and wide-eyed eager rookies, and they made their mark by doing what they did best—that is, throwing the ball—even if they weren't *that* good at it.

The Seahawks started out with a left-handed quarterback, Jim Zorn, who was quick on his feet (which was good, because he had to be given the rush protection his front line afforded him) and loved to throw the ball. So the early Seattle team quickly grew to rely on Zorn to run them out of trouble. Zorn running or throwing to receiver Steve Largent quickly became a team staple.

Dancing and darting is fine for certain things, but not winning championships. At least not by itself. A champion team can have a running quarterback, but he ideally should be running by choice, not necessity. Zorn ran because he had to. But when the franchise corrected, it overcorrected, eventually turning to a coach noted for his love of keeping the ball on the ground.

Seattle became a strong team under Chuck Knox. It could line up and knock you off the ball. It switched from the free-lancing Zorn to Dave Krieg, who could run a ground-oriented attack and still throw with the best of them. Injuries and ill fortune stalled the Seahawks' promising running attack. But its defensive wall was growing stone by stone. By the mid-1980s it was developing a terrific pass rush and the team began to rely on its stone wall defense. The team had achieved stability. The front office had a long-range game plan and it stuck to it. But Knox and the Seahawks grew apart. And following the 1991 season, they agreed to part.

Tom Flores, who played quarterback under Al Davis and then came back to coach for his mentor, was already on the scene as organization boss. Flores knew what it took to win a Super Bowl, (he'd already won one). So he returned to coaching with the experience and confidence to win a title. The Seahawks saw in him the master carpenter with a plan and some finishing touches that the team needed.

Seattle Lands a Franchise

The Seahawks were founded with an idea of how to get the job done and, with some exceptions, have stayed the course until they thought progress was no longer being made. It started in earnest in 1972, when the area began its serious drive to land pro football. It paid off on June 4, 1974, when the National Football League announced Seattle would have a franchise to begin play with the 1976 season.

Seattle Professional Football, Inc., was headed by Lloyd W. Nordstrom, with partners Herman Sarkowsky, D.E. "Ned" Skinner, Howard S. Wright, M. Lamont Bean, and Lynn P. Himmelman. It got the franchise for $16 million. Two years earlier the group had been instrumental in getting construction started on the 65,000-seat domed stadium, the Kingdome.

Nordstrom never lived to see his dream turn into reality, dying of a heart attack January 20, 1976, while vacationing in Mexico. Control of the franchise remained in the family when brother Elmer was named to succeed him as majority representative. John Thompson, executive director of the NFL Management Council, was hired to become general manager and oversee the football operation.

The name "Seahawks," chosen by 151 entrants in a "name the team" promotion, was selected June 17, 1975, from among 1,741 different names submitted on 20,365 entries; the moniker seemed appropriate for the region from which the franchise would draw its fans. Season tickets applications were accepted and 24,168 were delivered the first day. Applications were closed 27 days later with 59,000 purchased.

That December, the team signed a 20-year lease to play its home games in the recently completed Kingdome. Then came the fun part—choosing coaching staff and players. An assistant coach of the Minnesota Vikings, Jack Patera, was selected January 3, 1976, as the man to mold Seattle's first NFL team. Patera had experience on both sides of the ball as a linebacker-guard from 1955 through 1961 with Baltimore, the Chicago Cardinals, and Dallas.

Building the Team

On March 30, 1976, Seattle chose 39 veterans in the allocation draft, among them defensive backs Lyle Blackwood and Dave Brown, linebacker Mike Curtis, tackle Norm Evans, center Fred Hoaglin, and wide receiver Sam McCullum. Faded roses, to be sure, but enough to get the Seahawks through the long night of their first season or two.

The distinction of being the first player Seattle chose in a draft went to Notre Dame defensive tackle Steve Niehaus, who started for the Irish as a freshman. Another key draftee proved to be one of three second-round choices, Sherman Smith, a quarterback converted to running back. Largent, picked up from Houston for the cost of a 1977 eighth-round draft choice, began an illustrious career with 54 catches for 705 yards and four touchdowns.

A discard who panned out was quarterback Jim Zorn, perhaps unwanted in some places because he threw with his left hand. Niehaus was named defensive Rookie of the Year and Zorn his offensive counterpart. Maybe the Seahawks weren't good, but they were exciting. Zorn flitted all over the field as befitted a man who spent a good deal of the time dodging tacklers. In fact, he tied for second on the team in rushing yards that first season with 246.

There was an Expansion Bowl on October 17, and Seattle beat fellow newcomer Tampa Bay, 13-10, with Curtis blocking a Bucs field goal attempt with 42 seconds to play to preserve the victory. The franchise's other victory in that 2-12 season was a 30-13 home win November 7 against Atlanta. Smith became the first Seahawks back to

Team Information at a Glance

Founding date: 1972; began competing in 1976

Home stadium: Kingdome
11220 N.E. 53rd St.
Kirkland, WA 98033
Phone: (206) 827-9777
Seating capacity: 64,981

Team colors: Blue, green, and silver
Team nickname: Seahawks
Logo: Stylized seahawk head

Franchise record:	Won	Lost	Tie
(1976-1992)	114	130	0

gain 100 yards with 124 on 14 carries in the game.

Now the task was to improve. Zorn threw 27 interceptions, but it was the defense that needed the most work. Seattle allowed conference highs in points (429), first downs (323), passing yards (2,770) and rushing yards (2,876).

Holding the second choice in the 1977 draft presented Seattle with a dilemma. The Seahawks could keep the selection and take the second-best collegian, or they could put the pick up for bid. They opted to play *Let's Make a Deal.* And the Cowboys wanted Tony Dorsett so badly they were willing to give the Seahawks their first-round pick (14th overall) plus three in the second round to get the future Hall of Fame running back.

Tackle Steve August was the first of the choices, followed by tackle Tom Lynch and linebackers Terry Beeson and Peter Cronan. Seattle traded one second-round choice to the Rams for center Geoff Reece and a lower second-round pick (Cronan), then returned a second-round choice to Dallas for wide receiver Duke Fergerson. On the whole, hindsight says you'd rather have a Dorsett. But who knows what would have happened to him running behind Seattle's line? For a team that needed help in so many places, Seattle didn't do badly.

August played eight years for the team, starting 90 of 97 games. Lynch started 48 games in four seasons before being traded to Buffalo for a draft choice that turned out to be tight end Pete Metzelaars (13 starts in three seasons before being traded to Buffalo for wide receiver Byron Franklin, who appeared in 33 games in three seasons). Beeson started 67 games in 5 years, Cronan was a backup for four years, Fergerson started eight times in three years, while Reece made token appearances and was gone.

Originally placed in the NFC West, Seattle was switched to the AFC Western Division when the NFL realigned to finalize its meshing with the old AFL in 1977. That meant the Seahawks would be slugging it out with Oakland, San Diego, Denver, and Kansas City.

The troika of Zorn, Smith, and Largent got a stout young offensive line to work behind, including fourth-round pick center John Yarno, and helped Seattle compile the best second-year record any expansion team has ever had, a 5-9 mark that put it fourth. The Seahawks won their final two, the first a 34-31 victory over Kansas City that doomed the Chiefs to last place.

Zorn missed the first four games of the season with an injury, an early indication of the price to be paid for all his running around. His interception total, 19, still exceeded his touchdown passes by one. The top draft choice, Keith Simpson, saw spot duty at corner-back before shifting to free safety in 1979, while No. 2 pick Keith Butler quickly settled in at right linebacker.

A third straight year of progress saw Seattle compile a winning record, a 9-7 that was the best third-year expansion mark and one that left the Seahawks just one game outside 1978's playoff pool. Four wins in their last five games made most people stop thinking of the Seahawks as an expansion team and earned Patera nods as Coach of the Year.

AP/Wide World Photos

Chuck Knox

Zorn outthrew everybody in the conference and made Largent the top receiver with 71, with which he gained 1,168 yards. Zorn led the conference in attempts (443), completions (248), and yardage (3,283). Fullback David Sims led the conference with 15 touchdowns but unfortunately had to retire due to a neck injury the next year.

Worked on Defense

Hidden by the record was the fact that the defense led the conference in penalties and was breaking down at critical times. As a consequence, the top draft choices in 1979 went to that side of the line. Defensive tackle Manu Tuiasosopo was the first, linebacker Joe Norman second, and linebacker Michael Jackson third. Patera reached into his Minnesota past during training camp to get veteran defensive end Carl Eller in a trade for the disappointing Niehaus.

A 1-4 start showed the team wasn't quite ready for prime time pressure. The defense remained easy to score on, gave up the most penalty yardage, and was soft on third down. Some of this was disguised by the Zorn Flying Circus. Patera would fake field goals and keep his offense on the field for fourth downs in an effort to keep the defense just where it belonged—on the sidelines.

Still, the Seahawks regrouped to win seven of their last nine games for another 9-7 record, tying Oakland for third place. Largent topped 1,000 yards receiving again, Zorn moved up to fourth among quarterbacks, and his touchdown passes (20) exceeded his interceptions (by two) for the first time.

The need for a presence on the defensive line motivated Patera to trade Buffalo two draft choices for the 10th player in the 1980 selection process, defensive end Jacob Green. Second pick Andre Hines, a tackle, was a bust, but the club did its homework well and came up with a gem in the 10th round, tackle Ron Essink of little Grand Valley (Michigan) State.

The next step for Seattle was a misstep. The team was 4-3 after beating the New York Jets, 27-17, October 19. It didn't win another, losing nine straight to finish 4-12. Smith had suffered a knee injury in the third game and then the offensive line broke down, putting Zorn on the run again. Jackson and Green played well but the defense still couldn't shut down offenses when it had to.

Safety Kenny Easley was the top choice to help the defense in the 1981 draft, but save minor tinkering, the cast of characters was largely the same. Guard Edwin Bailey, a fifth-round pick, started 15 games, while Theotis Brown was obtained from St. Louis in mid-season to shore up the ground game.

Losses seldom turn a season around in a positive way, but a 32-0 thrashing in the Kingdome at the hands of the New York Giants left the Seahawks embarrassed, 1-6, and boiling mad. Brown arrived and the Seattle ground game was no longer pitifully inept. He gained 583 yards the rest of the way to help the team win five of its nine remaining games.

Zorn suffered a broken ankle while Seattle was blowing a 24-3 lead, losing to Oakland, 32-31. Krieg, who had thrown two passes the previous year, took over for the final three games. He led the team to a 27-23 upset of the hot Jets and two weeks later closed out the season, guiding the Seahawks to a 42-21 victory over Cleveland.

Largent caught his 1,000 yards again and Zorn was fifth in the quarterback standings, his interceptions down to nine and his TD tosses at 13.

AP/Wide World Photos

Jim Zorn

He completed 59 percent of his passes and looked poised to take the next step up.

Shuffle Behind the Scenes

Herman Sarkowsky stepped down as managing general partner and was replaced by John Nordstrom. Mike McCormack, former head coach at both Philadelphia and Baltimore, was brought in to head football operations. The result was not good. Speculation immediately began (denied of course) that McCormack was brought in to supersede, if not replace, GM Thompson and Coach Patera.

Original Seahawk McCullum was cut before the opener, causing widespread resentment among those left on the roster. McCullum was the club's player representative, and 1982 was a year of mammoth labor unrest, eventually resulting in a players' strike that lasted eight games. Seattle's players talked of a one-game strike for the opener, their way of protesting the decision. Bitterly, they finally agreed to play. The players felt McCullum was cut for non-football reasons since his 1981 production (46 catches, 567 yards, 12.32 per catch, 3 TDs) was not a dramatic falloff from his 1980 numbers (62, 874, 14.09, 6). He played two more seasons with Minnesota as a part-timer.

Patera switched from Zorn to Krieg at quarterback with costly results. Seattle lost both games, then the league's players walked out. During the strike, Thompson and Patera were both canned and McCormack took both jobs. McCormack restored Zorn to the starter's job, which helped ease the players over to him. Green and Easley showed marked improvement to enable the team to right itself with a 4-3 finish.

The top eight teams overall in each conference qualified for the playoffs under the strike-caused setup, but Seattle, though its 4-5 record tied for eighth, was left out because of the tie-breaking procedure. Could it take the next step up?

Having been named president and general manager of the team, McCormack lured in Chuck Knox so he could return to the front office. Knox had been a highly successful coach at Los Angeles (1973-77) and Buffalo (1978-82), winning six division titles and making seven playoff appearances. He had quit at both places. Chuck Allen, former star middle linebacker with San Diego, was named director of scouting and assistant GM.

Knox liked his running backs, plus the offensive linemen it took to block for them. By the time his tour with the Seahawks was over, "Ground Chuck" had nothing to do with hamburger in Seattle. Sizing up his personnel, and noting Seattle's first draft choice was too low to get the player he wanted, Knox used the same strategy that had worked so well for Dallas in Seattle's second season.

He traded first-, second- and third-round choices to Houston, which had the third choice overall, to get the prime time player he wanted: running back Curt Warner of Penn State. Knox traded to get guard Reggie McKenzie from Buffalo (12th round choice) and center Blair Bush from Cincinnati (first round 1985), also adding tight end Charles Young. Sherman Smith was traded away in training camp.

Seattle lost its opener, but Warner showed his worth in the second game as he accounted for 24 of a club record 57 rushes, gaining 128 yards in a 17-10 victory over the New York Jets. Warner ended up leading the conference with 1,449 yards rushing. Zorn opened the season at quarterback for Knox but may have had trouble adjusting to the new handoff offense rather than the style of running and throwing the ball—all over the lot—that he was used to.

Seattle defeated the (now Los Angeles) Raiders, 38-36, on October 16, despite Zorn's 4-of-16 passing, because it generated eight turnovers and eight sacks. But trailing Pittsburgh 24-0 at the half the following week, Knox went to Krieg with mixed results in a 27-21 loss.

Playoff Prospects

Krieg started the next week, Seattle repeating its win over Los Angeles, 34-21, and ran the team the rest of a season that included three wins in its final four games to clinch the franchise's first playoff berth. The Seahawks were 9-7, tied for second behind the Raiders. Krieg ended up the second-ranked passer in the AFC, connecting 61 percent of the time, and his touchdowns outnumbered his interceptions, 18-11. Despite the emphasis on running the ball, Largent again surpassed 1,000 receiving yards.

The first playoff opponent for Seattle was the team it had tied in the standings, Denver, which had rookie John Elway learning his trade behind Steve DeBerg. Krieg threw for 200 yards and three touchdowns while Warner gained 99 yards in a 31-7 victory that sent Seattle to Miami for the second round. Warner gained 113 yards against the Dolphins, including a 2-yard touchdown that capped a 66-yard, 5-play drive late in the fourth quarter to give the Seahawks the lead in a 27-20 victory. Now it was back to Los Angeles for the Raiders.

Though Seattle had beaten the Raiders twice during the regular season, Los Angeles was a veteran-laden team. It showed. They shut down Warner completely, holding him to 26 yards, while Marcus Allen shredded the flexible Seahawk defense for 154. The Raiders put heavy pressure on Krieg, intercepting him three times. The more mobile Zorn was picked off twice but did throw two TD passes late in a 30-14 loss that stopped a Knox team one game shy of the Super Bowl for the fourth time in his career.

Knox was acknowledged as Coach of the Year in some quarters while Easley was both All-Pro and a Pro Bowl selection. Warner played in the Pro Bowl. The successful season again masked a defensive deficiency. Seattle was one of the easiest teams in the conference to run on, pass against, and score against.

The top draft choice was Terry Taylor, a cornerback, while the No. 2 was Daryl Turner, a burner to take the heat off possession receiver Largent. Knox traded for another tackle, Bob Cryder, then dealt August away in mid-year.

The defensive alignment was switched from 4-3 to 3-4 to take advantage of personnel and perhaps generate a bit better pass rush. The defense cut 115 points off the scoreboard from the previous season, slashed 70 first downs, got a dozen more sacks and sharply reduced yardage allowed.

Disaster struck in the first game of 1984 when Warner suffered a serious knee injury that put him out for the season. But the defense accepted the challenge, posting three shutouts. Knox had Krieg switch from an emphasis on handing off to a game plan oriented toward throwing the ball. This loosened defenses for the bevy of backs he used in an attempt to replace Warner's production.

Largent gained 1,164 yards with 74 passes while Turner added 715 with 35. Krieg was intercepted 24 times but countered with 32 TD passes and a total of 3,671 yards passing. An eight-game winning streak assured Seattle a spot in the playoffs, but the Seahawks lost their last two games, the last a showdown with Denver for the AFC West championship, 31-14.

Knox won more acclaim as Coach of the Year while Easley was cited the NFL Defensive Player of the Year by two national media outlets. The defense allowed the fewest points (282) and had the most sacks (55) in club history and also forced 63 turnovers, second-most in NFL history.

Seven Seahawks played in the Pro Bowl—cornerback Dave Brown, Easley, kicker Norm Johnson, Krieg, Largent, nose tackle Joe Nash, and special teams star Fredd Young—while Green replaced Krieg among the seven as an All-NFL player.

Its 12-4 record gave wild card entrant Seattle the home field against the defending Super Bowl champion Raiders in the playoffs and the Seahawks responded with a 13-7 victory. In the second quarter, Turner caught a 26-yard touchdown pass from Krieg, who threw just 10 times in the game, and Johnson kicked a pair of second-half field goals.

Seattle went to Miami again, but the Dolphins borrowed from the Raiders' successful tactics of the year before and stuffed the Seahawks' running game in a 31-10 decision. Off the field, the team announced it was signing a long-term lease to shift its base in 1986 to Northwest College in suburban Kirkland, where administrative of-

PROFILE

Steve Largent

How does a 5-foot-11, 190-pound receiver with no speed come to set National Football League records? Perseverance, for one thing. Durability, quickness, and hard work also come to mind—all qualities possessed by Steve Largent, holder of the NFL record for consecutive games catching a pass plus assorted other honors garnered during his career with the Seattle Seahawks.

AP/Wide World Photos

Largent surely will become Seattle's first Pro Football Hall of Fame player when the five-year waiting period ends. He retired in 1989, having caught a pass in his last 177 consecutive games. His reception yardage total of 13,089 is second in NFL history, as are his 100 career receiving touchdowns. Largent holds the NFL record for career receptions, 819, shares the mark for 70-catch seasons with six, and his 10 seasons of 50 or more receptions are tied for second on the all-time NFL list.

But Largent wasn't fast in high school—just a 4.8 40-yard dash. By the time he was through at Tulsa, his time was down to 4.65. "There's a difference between being fast and being quick," Largent noted. "And there is such a thing as football speed. Track guys run like crazy. But put the guy who holds the world record in the 100 on a football field, get a defensive back to jump in front of him, and he'll probably break his ankles trying to stop or change direction. The way you run on a track—with body lean and on the balls of your feet—is different from how you run pass routes. To run routes, you have to have more body control."

PROFILE

The Houston Oilers drafted Largent on the fourth round when he finished playing at Tulsa. He was waived after the fourth exhibition, too naive by his own admission to know that pro rookies learn as much in the classroom as they do on the field. The expansion Seahawks, on the advice of former Tulsa quarterback and coach Jerry Rhome, put in a claim and traded Houston an eighth-round pick for Largent. Rhome had been a Tulsa assistant when Largent played there and became quarterbacks/receivers coach.

"Steve dropped everything," Rhome recalled of Largent's first day of practice with the Seahawks. "He fell all over the place. [Coach] Jack Patera pulled me aside and asked, 'This the guy you've been raving about?' I went over to Steve and found he'd worn himself out traveling to get here. So I said, 'Look, I'll guarantee you make this team. I'll see to it you won't get cut.' And Steve told me, 'I promise I won't do this tomorrow.'"

He didn't, and two weeks later he came off the bench in the season opener to make a typically spectacular diving catch. "If Seattle hadn't been running an offense I was familiar with," Largent noted, "I wouldn't have made the team." Largent credits the Seattle system and the two quarterbacks, Jim Zorn and Dave Krieg, who practiced extra with him, for making his exceptional career possible. "I'm not saying anybody could have come in here and done what I've done," he said. "But I'm not saying I'm a great football player. I've also been very lucky."

fices and practice facilities would be built on 12 acres of land.

Without a first-round pick in the 1985 draft, not sure whether Warner could come back and unsure of how effective he would be if he did, Knox opted for fullback Owen Gill as his team's top pick in the second round. Gill never played for Knox, highlighting a very poor draft that hurt the club's development.

Warner came back with 66 yards on 17 carries in the opener, a 28-24 victory at Cincinnati in which he scored the game-winning touchdown on an 11-yard run with 7:07 to play. But the season proved Seattle unable to get up to the next level. The Seahawks won two and lost two all season long. Their 8-8 log found them watching the playoffs on television—this despite continued fine play by the defense.

Warner did gain 1,094 yards, Largent led the AFC with 1,287 receiving yards and extended his consecutive game catching streak to 123, but Krieg slumped badly. The quarterback threw 20 interceptions as Seattle went from plus-24 in the turnover tables to plus-3. He did throw 27 touchdowns and passed for 3,602 yards.

Fullback John L. Williams was Seattle's No. 1 choice in the 1986 draft, and cornerback Patrick Hunter was the next choice, groomed to take over in 1987. Tackle Ron Mattes, drafted seventh the year before, became a starter after his year of seasoning.

The 1986 season began with Krieg still erratic, and he was benched in favor of second-year man Gale Gilbert despite the team's 5-3 record. Zorn was no longer an option, long since having departed the scene. Seattle quickly found consistency—three straight losses. Krieg was restored, the team closed with five straight wins, and Knox must have wondered why he hadn't made the switch back earlier. His team missed the playoffs for the second straight year.

Warner ran for an AFC-best 1,481 yards, Williams added 538, and Largent had 1,070 yards while setting an NFL record by catching passes in 139 straight games. Green had 12 sacks but Easley did not start in six games due to injury.

Next, Seattle won and lost with the same move. It won the right to chose first in a supplemental lottery—but lost because the player everybody wanted was Brian Bosworth, a linebacker who turned out to be a monumental flop. The Boz's feats couldn't match his mouth, as things turned out. Linebacker Tony Woods, the top regular draft choice, started seven games while Hunter took over opposite Taylor at cornerback, making possible the trade of Dave Brown to Green Bay. Free agent Melvin Jenkins also played well in the defensive backfield.

Overall the defense slipped a little, contributing to a season that was disappointing despite a 9-6 record that put Seattle second in the AFC West and back into the playoffs. Krieg's slump and an excellent offensive line induced Knox to go more with his ball-control ground offense, although Warner fell 15 yards shy of 1,000. Williams added 500 but Largent's receiving total fell to 912 as Krieg passed for less than 200 yards in nine games. Largent did become the all-time pass-catching leader with 752, but all statistics were influenced by the regular player's strike that caused them to miss four games, three filled by replacements.

Warner missed the playoff game with an injury and there's little doubt it influenced the outcome: a 23-20 Houston win achieved on a 42-yard field goal in overtime. Seattle had just 29 yards rushing and 250 yards total offense. It was Krieg's 12-yard fourth-quarter scoring pass to Largent that got the game into overtime.

AP/Wide World Photos

David Wyman (92)

Franchise ownership changed August 30, 1988, with developer/entrepreneur Ken Behring buying the team from the Nordstrom family in conjunction with Ken Hofman. Without a No. 1 due to the supplemental selection of Bosworth, the Seahawks traded their fifth-round pick in the 1988 draft plus first- and fifth-round selections in 1989 to Phoenix for quarterback Kelly Stouffer. They looked to replacements at wide receiver by taking Brian Blades and Tommy Kane in the second and third rounds.

A shoulder separation knocked Krieg out of action for seven games early in the season, but he returned November 13 against Houston to direct a 10-play drive that let Johnson break a 24-24 tie with a game-winning field goal with a second to play.

Two weeks later Krieg equalled his club record with five touchdown passes against the Raiders. His superlative play down the stretch would let him finish second in the AFC quarterback ratings.

Seattle finished up with a 9-7 record, but that was good enough this year to place one game up on Denver and two ahead of Los Angeles. It was the third divisional title for Knox.

Largent became the NFL's all-time leader in reception yards during the season, his season's total down to 645 as both Williams (58-651) and the rookie Blades (40-682) surpassed him. Williams became a bona fide double threat because he rushed for 877 while Warner topped 1,000 by 25 yards.

Seattle got pushed around in the playoffs

again, though, going out to eventual Super Bowl loser Cincinnati, 21-13, in the first round. If Seahawks' fans thought 29 yards rushing was pathetic in 1987's playoffs, what must they have thought of this game's 18? Krieg threw for 297 yards but it was 21-0 at halftime.

After the season, McCormack was fired and replaced with former Super Bowl winner Tom Flores of the Raiders, who had tired of coaching and quit two seasons earlier. The trade of inside linebacker Fredd Young to Indianapolis early in the 1988 season brought Seattle a first-round draft choice to replace the one it had given Phoenix for Stouffer, plus another one for 1990. They took tackle Andy Heck first and in the second round got center Joe Tofflemire, who finally became a starter in 1992.

Venturing into the '90s

A four-game losing streak just before the stretch run kept Seattle out of the playoffs at 7-9. Krieg was benched in favor of Stouffer but tried to bail the club out with hot play at the end, guiding the team to three wins in four games. However, the turnover ratio went back to minus-15, thanks to just nine interceptions and a team record 43 fumbles.

Largent closed out his career with his streak of pass-catching games intact at 177, but he totaled just 28 receptions and 403 yards as he missed six games with a broken elbow. His 13,089 yards and 100 touchdown catches (he also ran for one) are the second highest totals in NFL history, while his 819 catches are a league best.

Warner's production fell off to 631 yards, and Williams, who caught 76 passes for 657 yards, ran for 499. Krieg still was rated seventh among quarterbacks. The need for more beef on the defensive line motivated Seattle to ship both its first-round choices in the 1990 draft so it could move up and take New England's place in the third slot.

The Seahawks wanted defensive tackle Cortez Kennedy and returned to the 4-3 defense. Kennedy confirmed their judgment when he was selected for the Pro Bowl in his second season and named NFL Defensive Player of the Year in his third. As part of the deal, Seattle also got New England's second-round choice and took linebacker Terry Wooden, knowing Bosworth would have to retire because of a shoulder injury. The Seahawks went for safety Robert Blackmon with its other second-round selection.

Seattle opened with three straight losses but closed 9-4. An inability to win some close games kept the Seahawks out of the playoffs. Sacks dropped to 33 and giveaways outnumbered takeaways by six, which Krieg contributed to by throwing 20 interceptions. His touchdown tosses slipped to 15 as he slid to 11th in the rankings.

Retired Uniform to Honor Fans

The Seattle Seahawks have just one retired uniform number—and it isn't even a player's. The Seahawks were the first pro sports team to retire a uniform in honor of the support of its fans. Seattle retired a jersey with the number 12 on it, for '12th man,' and presented it on Dec. 15, 1984, to Mr. and Mrs. Randy Ford of Tukwila, Washington, who originated the idea.

The club does have a "Ring of Honor" around the 200 level of the Kingdome to pay tribute to exceptional individuals associated with the NFL team. First to be honored was wide receiver Steve Largent in 1989, followed by quarterback Jim Zorn in 1991. Former cornerback and current assistant coach Dave Brown was honored August 22, 1992, while broadcaster Pete Gross was inducted November 30 of the same year. Gross broadcast every game but seven from 1976 until his death from cancer two days after the ceremony.

All of these inductees first joined the organization when it was formed in 1976.

Derrick Fenner succeeded Warner as the chief ground threat, gaining 859 yards, while Williams ran for 714 and caught 699 yards worth of passes. Fenner led the AFC by equalling club records with 15 touchdowns and 14 rushing TDs.

The inability of Krieg to take the club to a championship level prompted the search for someone who could. That began with the selection of Dan McGwire, younger brother of Oakland Athletics' first baseman Mark McGwire, and the first quarterback Seattle had selected in the first round. Seattle also drafted a replacement for venerable Norm Johnson, taking John Kasay in the fourth round. Johnson, who found a home in Atlanta, made 5-of-6 from the 40-49 yard lines but made just 8-of-14 from 30-39 yards and 1-of-3 longer than 50.

Knox signed a two-year contract extension right after the draft but fled back to the Los Angeles Rams after 1991 turned out to be a disappointing fourth-place, 7-9, season. Krieg broke his thumb in an opening-game loss and missed six games, which started a season of quarterback roulette. Perennial backup Jeff Kemp got a win and two losses, McGwire then got his baptism, and the Seahawks were 3-4 when Krieg returned.

They lost five of their last seven, and when it was all over Knox and Seattle decided it was time for a fresh face on the sidelines. Williams ran for 741 yards but a 3.9 average while adding 499 through the air. Blades finally put a wide receiver back on the top of the pass-catching list with 70, good for 1,003 yards, but he scored just two TDs. Krieg was fourth in the QB ratings, his TD-interception ratio at 11-12, but the team only scored 276 points.

Flores, now familiar with the personnel after two seasons with the organization, decided to get back into coaching and agreed to replace Knox. Recognizing the need for help on offense, Flores took tackle Ray Roberts first. The long link with Krieg was severed when the quarterback was let go, winding up with Kansas City and was understudying Joe Montana at the start of 1993.

The offense deteriorated in 1992 as it went through three quarterbacks. Journeyman Stan Gelbaugh wound up starting the last eight games when both Stouffer (7 starts) and McGwire suffered season-ending injuries in consecutive games. Chris Warren, primarily a kick returner since he was drafted in 1990's fourth round, stepped up and gained 1,017 yards. Williams ran for only 339 but resurfaced as a pass-catcher with 74 for 556 yards. However the club was only able to score 140 points, fewest ever in a 16-game schedule. The defense led the AFC in fewest first downs allowed, 247, but too often took the ball away for an offense that merely gave it away again.

The price of a 2-14 season is a lot more than 16 weeks, but the payback is on draft day. Flores knew he was going to get his quarterback to build on, either Washington State's Drew Bledsoe or Rick Mirer of Notre Dame. New England drafted first and took Bledsoe, but Flores had no misgivings about Mirer, who showed in the exhibition season he would do no worse as a starter than the trio who shared the job in 1992.

Flores also got the backing to dip into the free agent market. He signed Ferrell Edmunds, a five-year veteran who was a two-time Pro Bowl tight end with Miami. He also signed wide receiver Kelvin Martin off the Super Bowl champion Dallas Cowboys and linebacker Kevin Murphy from San Diego, plus possible bench help in 35-year-old center Ray Donaldson and guard Mitch Frerotte.

Sources

Books

Neft, David S., Richard M. Cohen, and Rick Korch, *Sports Encyclopedia: Pro Football,* 11th edition, St. Martin's, 1993.

Riffenburgh, Beau, *The Official NFL Encyclopedia,* 1986.

Periodicals

Sports Illustrated, October 20, 1986.

—Richard Shook

National Football Conference

Central Division

Chicago Bears

The creation, history and success of the Chicago Bears—the entire National Football League (NFL), for that matter—can be summed up in two words: George Halas. It is perhaps symbolic that Halas and professional football were born in the same year, 1895. An incredibly enthusiastic, dedicated and multi-talented individual, Halas is justifiably credited with doing more for the sport of professional football than any other individual in the history of the game.

The first pro football game in the United States was played on August 31, 1895, in Latrobe, Pennsylvania, between a group fielded by the Latrobe YMCA and a club from nearby Jeannette. Latrobe won, 12-0.

A quarter of a century later, on August 17, 1920, Halas and a number of other football enthusiasts were gathered in the showroom of Ralph Hay's Hupmobile dealership in Canton, Ohio. Sitting around the room on the fenders and running boards of the autos, the group formed what was to become today's NFL. Halas was all of 25 years old at the time.

In today's world of high finance, when a single player can command several million dollars in salary, it is amusing to look back on the modest economies of those hard-pressed days. "We decided that it would cost $100 per team to enter the league," Halas recalled in later years. "We awarded franchises to 11 teams, then sat back and crossed our fingers. I guarantee you that there wasn't a hundred dollars among all of us in the room that day. But we wanted the new league to have credibility, so we established what we regarded as a stiff entry fee." One of the franchises went to Halas's team, the Decatur Staleys, the forerunner of the Chicago Bears.

Halas was always a sports enthusiast, and was an outstanding player in both baseball and football as a youth. He was a star tackle at only

140 pounds at Crane Tech High School in Chicago, and later as an end at the University of Illinois, at not much more in weight. It was at Illinois, playing for Coach Bob Zupke, that the idea of forming a professional league began to form in Halas's mind. "We had just won the Big Ten Championship," Halas recalled, "and Zup looked around the locker room at his graduating seniors and said, 'It's too bad, just when all of you begin to know something about football, I lose you. Football is the only sport where a player's career ends just when it should be beginning.'"

The coach's words stuck with young Halas. After graduation, he joined the Navy and became an ensign at Great Lakes Naval Training Station just north of Chicago, which, happily for him, had a great football team. In the Rose Bowl of 1919, played between service teams, Great Lakes shut out the Mare Island Marines, and Halas was the star of the game with two touchdown receptions.

Halas was also a good enough baseball player to have a brief tryout with the New York Yankees during the summer of 1919, the year before Babe Ruth was to join the team. After his short baseball career, Halas joined a professional football team in Canton, Ohio, where he was thrilled to earn the then magnanimous salary of $100 a game.

A year later, Halas went to work for a sports loving industrialist in Decatur, Illinois by the name of A. J. Staley. The latter's company was called the Staley Starch Works. It already had an established semi-pro baseball team managed by Hall of Famer Joe McGinnity. Halas, the company's athletic director, soon convinced Staley to sponsor a football team as well. And thus it was that the Decatur Staleys, managed and coached by Halas and with Halas playing end, came into being. In their first season they lost only one of 13 games.

The team's roster included a number of names that would become famous in coming years: in addition to Halas, there was Ed Sternaman, Jimmy Conzelman and Charley Dressen, the latter of whom would become a major league baseball manager. Halas found that it was more of a problem for him to find teams to play and agree on a playing site and date than it was coaching and winning the games themselves. "I wrote to my old boss, Ralph Hay of the Canton Bulldogs," he said, "and suggested that it would be easier for all of us if we formed a league and played a set schedule."

George Halas

That letter led to the historic meeting in the Canton auto showroom. Jim Thorpe, the world famous Carlisle Indian football All-American and Olympic star was named as the league's first president. The organization billed itself as the American Football Association—the name change to the NFL would come two years later, at Halas's request.

Franchises were awarded to the Akron Pros, Canton Bulldogs, Cleveland Panthers, Dayton Triangles, Halas and his Decatur Staleys, Hammond Pros, Kenosha-Chicago Cardinals, Massilon Tigers, Muncie Tigers, Rochester Jeffersons and Rock Island Independents. Mas-silon and Muncie disbanded before the season began.

Staley enjoyed watching his team perform and the publicity it brought to his company, but

TEAM INFORMATION AT A GLANCE

Founding date: 1920

Home stadium: Soldier Field
Address: Halas Hall
250 North Washington Rd.
Lake Forest, IL 60045
Phone: (708) 295-6600
Seating capacity: 66,946

Team colors: Navy blue, orange, and white
Team nickname: Bears
Logo: Letter "C"

Franchise record	Won	Lost	Tie
(1920-92)	567	362	42

NFL Championships (8): 1921, 1932, 1933, 1940, 1941, 1943, 1946, 1963
Super Bowl Victories: 1985

the economy was down and he decided that he simply couldn't afford the team any longer. He sent for Halas and suggested that he take over the ownership of the team and to move it to Chicago, where there was more chance for its success. He also gave Halas $5,000 to get the new club started and asked only that the name, "Staleys," be continued for one more year. Halas quickly agreed.

Halas Takes Over

Incredibly, a football team that was to become a multi-million franchise was not only given away, a bonus was attached in the bargain. Halas took Sternaman along as co-owner, a move which was to cost him a good deal of money in later years when the two split up. Halas and Sternaman negotiated a deal with William Veeck, owner of the Chicago Cubs baseball team, to play at Wrigley Field for a rental of 15 percent of the gross take of each game. (In 1922, Halas, a rabid Cubs baseball fan, changed the name of the Staleys to the Bears, primarily because of his love of the Cubs.)

In addition to being co-owners of the new franchise, Halas and his partner "Dutch" Sternaman were also starters on the team itself, Halas at end and Sternaman in the backfield. For the record, the first win by the Chicago Bears, or Decatur Staleys as they were known, in the NFL was a 20-0 shutout over the Moline Indians in 1920. The team's record in that first year of existence was 10-1-2; the only loss came in a one-point decision to their cross-town rivals, the Racine-Chicago Cardinals, 7-6.

Of the 13 teams in the league in 1920, only those two, the Bears and the Cards, have stayed in existence to this day. The Cardinals have moved twice since, to St. Louis and then to Phoenix. The Green Bay Packers, who were playing as an independent in 1920, did not enter the league until 1921. The Bears and the Packers have played each other 145 times through the 1992 season, more than any other teams in professional football. During the 1920 season, Chicago gave up only 21 points in 13 games, shutting out 10 teams and allowing single touchdowns in a 25-7 win over Kewaunee, a 28-7 win over Hammond and the 7-6 loss to the Cards. The team reportedly paid each of its players $1,900 in salary.

A championship in only their second year in the league would undoubtedly have been looked upon by just about anyone as a tremendous achievement; for Halas and Sternaman, however, it was only natural. Both men felt the club should win every game it played, and that confidence rubbed off on their players.

As in their first year, Chicago won ten games and lost only one, and again it was by the narrowest of margins, this time a 7-6 loss to the Buffalo All-Americans. Prior to that loss, Chicago had won its first seven games, beating Waukegan, Rochester, Dayton, Detroit and Rock Island twice. After the conclusion of the season, Jim Thorpe stepped down as NFL president. He was replaced by Joe Carr, who had been manager of the Columbus Tigers.

The league expanded in 1922 to include the addition of teams in Louisville, Marion, Milwaukee, Racine and Toledo. Three teams, Cincinnati, Cleveland and Detroit, dropped out.

There were two significant name changes during the year. Both were George Halas's doing. First, after completing his obligation to continue calling the team the "Staleys" for one year after moving it to Chicago, he renamed it the Chicago Bears. Then, during a league meeting with other owners during the year, he proposed changing the name of the league from the American Professional Football Association to the National Football League. There was little opposition; few people said no to Halas in those years.

The Bears' 9-3-0 mark, which included losses to the Chicago Cards twice and to the Canton Bulldogs, was good enough for second place in the standings, behind an undefeated Canton squad and their 10-0-2 record. Chicago did edge the Rock Island Independents twice, 10-6 and 3-0, to give that team its only two losses of the year. In the first player purchase by any team in the league, the Bears bought tackle Ed Healey's contract from the Rock Island Independents for $100.

The Canton Bulldogs again swept through the season unbeaten in 1923, posting an 11-0-1 mark that included a 6-0 win over the Bears on October 21 in Wrigley Field. The only other loss by the Bears was an opening day setback to the Rock Island Independents, who gained a measure of revenge for the two beatings the previous year. Chicago's record, however, was good enough for second place among the league's 20 teams.

Prior to the season Evansville had dropped out, but new clubs included Duluth and St. Louis as well as Cleveland, which came back in with new owners. During that 1923 season Halas, playing defensive end, scooped up a fumble by an Oorang Indian runner and ran it back 98 yards for a touchdown, a record that stood for half a century.

For the third year in a row the Chicago Bears finished second in the National Football League standings in 1924, this time only a half game back of the Cleveland Bulldogs. Cleveland's record was 7-1-1; the Bears were 6-1-4. The Chicago club's only loss was a tough 14-10 decision to the Bulldogs in the season's second game.

Through its first five years in the league the Bears had actually tied more games, nine, than they had lost, eight. Their overall mark of 44-8-9 was good for a .846 winning percentage (.795 as computed today.) In the early years of the league ties were disregarded in figuring winning percentage; today ties count as a half game won and a half game lost. Standings were determined by a team's winning percentage.

Red Grange

The Arrival of Red Grange

Professional football and the NFL had been in existence for five years, but it was not until the 1925 season and the signing of the fabulous Harold "Red" Grange by the Chicago Bears that the game truly fired up the public imagination. Grange, who had an incredible career at the University of Illinois, was the most publicized player of his era.

Whereas crowds in the first few years of the league had usually been measured in the hundreds, Grange's emergence on the scene brought thousand of fans to the game. A wild throng of more than 36,000 filled Wrigley Field on November 26 for Grange's debut against the Chicago Cardinals.

The game, which ended in a scoreless tie, was actually the 11th of the season for the Bears. Grange was still in college and had just completed the last game of his senior year before signing a pro contract with the Bears. A week later 28,000 turned out to see Grange lead the Bears to a 14-13 win over the Columbus Tigers, the first of six games the Bears were to play in a two-week span.

In Philadelphia the crowd exceeded 35,000, and in New York it topped 73,000. With Grange's own personal press agent, "Cash 'n' Carry" Pyle handling much of the promotion, the six-game tour gained more headlines for professional football than all of the games of the previous five years. The Bears finished the season with a 9-5-3 mark; the .643 winning percentage was the lowest in Halas's six years as the team's coach.

Coming within a whisker of the league championship the following year, the Bears finished at 12-1-3, a game behind the Frankford Yellowjackets and their 14-1-1 mark. During the season the Bears and the Green Bay Packers fought three monumental battles. The two rivals tied twice, 3-3 and 6-6, with the Bears winning the third game, 19-13. The Bears only loss came in another great struggle, 7-6 to Frankford.

Enthusiasm throughout the league stirred up by Grange helped put 31 teams into professional ball in 1922 in the NFL and nine more in a new league formed by Grange, who had left the Bears, and his colorful manager Pyle. Grange played for the New York entry in the new loop, called the American Football League (AFL). But most of the teams were playing on a shoestring, and after only a year of competition, the AFL and 10 of the new teams in the NFL had folded.

Although the 1927 Bears finished third in the league—behind the New York Giants and the Green Bay Packers—the club had solace in afflicting both of the Pack's losses. The champion Giants finished at 11-1-1, the Packers at 7-2-1 and Chicago at 9-3-2. Grange had brought his New York Yankee team into the NFL, where they finished at 7-8-1, but they managed to give the Bears their worst loss of the year, 26-6, In the third game of the year Grange suffered a serious knee injury in a collision with George Trafton of the Bears, an injury from which he never fully recovered.

After starting off the 1928 season with wins over their crosstown rival the Chicago Cards and the New York Giants and a tie with the Green Bay Packers, the Bears floundered to a 7-5-1 mark and a .636 winning percentage, the lowest in their nine-year history. For the first time Halas's crew lost two games in the same season to the Green Bay Packers, 16-6 and 6-0, after an early season 12-12 deadlock. The Bears finished in fifth place, behind champion Providence, which had an 8-1-2 record, Frankford, Detroit, and Green Bay.

The Bears' less than sparkling performance might have been attributed to advancing age in key players such as Halas, Paddy Driscoll and George Trafton, as well as a growing animosity between Halas and Sternaman, who owned the other half of the Bears.

Sternaman no longer played halfback but did insist on calling the shots on much of the Bear offense, As one Bear lamented, "We had two offenses; one devised by Halas, the other by Sternaman. No one knew what to expect on any play, Men ran into each other, The team lacked timing." The Bears were clearly in trouble in the tug of war between the two men, and the worst was still to come.

Meanwhile Grange's knee did not respond to treatment, and the once-great star decided to retire. He spent the year on the vaudeville circuit and making a movie; it seemed that the Grange name was still magic, whether on stage, in front of a camera or on a football field. Grange's retirement didn't even last a year, but the "Iceman" could never recapture the speed and elusiveness that had made him the scourge of the league.

Six games into the 1929 season the Bears' record was 4-1-1, but the club lost eight of their last nine games. It was the first losing season for the Bears, and even worse, the team lost all three of its games to the team that had become their number-one rival, the Green Bay Packers.

The Bears finished ninth in a twelve team field, far back of the Packers and their undefeated mark of 12-0-1. A highlight—or lowlight—of the year occurred in the 40-6 loss to the Chicago Cardinals on November 28, a game in which Card star runner Ernie Nevers tallied four touchdowns and four extra points, a league scoring record.

Owner-coach-player George Halas, disgusted over the Bears' woeful record, decided that the club needed a major overhaul. So, at the age of only 34, he retired as a player and fired himself and Sternaman as the coaches. For a new mentor he dipped into the nearby college ranks, hiring Lake Forest Academy's coach, Ralph Jones.

Bronco Nagurski

Most of the professional teams of the day were utilizing the old Notre Dame box or single wing formation on offense. Jones installed a refined T-formation with split ends and a man in motion, an offensive concept designed to make best use of the talents of the team's star halfback, Red Grange.

Jones also added two more significant weapons, rookies Bronko Nagurski, a powerful fullback, and Carl Brunbaugh, a quarterback. Brunbaugh became the Bear's first great signal caller, while Nagurski, at six-feet two-inches and 230 pounds, soon developed into one of the most feared runners in the league. Halas had offered Nagurski a one-year contract for $5,000, but the former Minnesota Gopher held out for a two-year pact. Halas gave in.

The Bears signed another star runner from the college ranks, Joe Savoldi of Notre Dame. But because Savoldi was still an underclassman, league president Joe Carr fined the Chicago team $1,000. The club could have saved the money; Savoldi was cut after only four games. With Grange and Nagurski in the same

Bronko Nagurski

backfield, there was no place for him to play.

Under Jones the Bears returned to their winning ways. Early on, struggling with Jones' new systems, the team lost three and tied one of their first six games before righting themselves to sweep seven of the last 10, improving to a 9-4-1 mark. On defense the Bears gave up as many as two touchdowns in only two games and only 71 points for the entire season, holding opponents to just over five points a game.

The Bears and their crosstown rivals, the Cardinals, made history in 1930, when they played pro football's first indoor game in Chicago Stadium. The field, including the end zones, was only 80 yards long, however, which meant that the goal lines were only 60 yards apart.

Coach Jones' promise to turn the Bears into a champion took a slight detour during 1931 as a multitude of injuries held the team to an 8-5 record, well behind the title-winning Green Bay Packers' 12-2 mark. The Bears had the consolation of beating their neighbors to the north in two of the three games they played during the year. A 26-0 win over Brooklyn on November 22 was the 100th for the Bears franchise. Also during the year also the league office initiated the selection of an All-Star team. Red Grange was the only Bear to make that first team.

The 1932 season, in which the Bears were to win their second NFL championship, was also one of the strangest in the club's long history. Despite having two of the greatest running backs in the game, Red Grange and Bronko Nagurski, the Bears' scoring punch was almost nonexistent in the first month of the season; in fact the club did not score a point through their first four games. The first three were scoreless ties, the fourth a 2-0 loss to the Green Bay Packers. After the sixth week of the season the Bear's league record was 1-1-4, while the Packers were 5-0-1.

The Packers had only one tie through their first 10 games and looked like an absolute shoo-in for their fourth straight league title. But Green Bay faltered at the end, losing their last two games to Portsmouth and the Bears to finish at 10-3-1, while Portsmouth and the Bears tied for first place, the Spartans at 6-1-4, the Bears at 6-1-6.

With the two teams finishing in a dead heat, the first time it had happened in league history, Halas and Harry Snyder, the owners of the two clubs, got together and decided on a playoff. That also was a first for the young NFL. The original plans were for the game to be played in Chicago at Wrigley Field on December 18, but frigid weather and a snowstorm prior to the game changed everything. The two owners agreed to move the contest indoors, to Chicago Stadium.

Dirt already covered the floor, as a circus had just left town. As with the Bear-Cards game two years earlier in the Stadium, the field was only 60 yards long, and the stands were right up to the sides of the 145-foot wide field. In those days, after an out-of-bounds plays, the rules called for the ball to be placed in play only one yard inside the sidelines. Because of the stands, it was agreed to move it in 10 yards. Other rule changes for the game prohibited field goals, called for kickoffs to be made from the 10 yard line, and limited teams to three downs instead of four.

Early in the fourth quarter, Dick Nesbitt of the Bears intercepted a pass by Spartan back Ace Gutowski and returned it to the seven yard line. On first down Nagurski smashed to the one, but then lost a yard on his next attempt. On third down Nagurski took a handoff and ran toward the line of scrimmage, but at the last instant he leaped into the air and tossed the ball to Grange in the end zone for a touchdown.

Portsmouth screamed that the play was illegal—and it was; rules at the time called for all passes to be thrown from at least five yards behind the line of scrimmage. But the referees refused to change the call, and the score stood. A safety was added later, and the Bears won, 9-0.

From that game came two important rule changes, which greatly changed pro offenses in the future. The first called for the ball to be placed in 10 yards from the sidelines instead of one after all out-of-bounds plays, which created the field's hashmarks; the second eliminated the "five yards behind the line for passing" rule. During the year the league also began keeping individual statistics; the leading pass receiver for the season was the Bears' Luke Johnsos with 24 catches for 321 yards. In addition, three Bears made the All-Star Team: Bronko Nagurski, Roy Carlson and Johnsos.

Coach Ralph Jones promise that the Bears would win a title in three years was fulfilled; paradoxically, it cost him his job. Halas, chomping on the bit on the sidelines and in the owner's box over the last three years as the Bears returned to respectability, could contain himself no longer. All's fair in love and war, Halas thought, no one loved the Bears more than he did, and what went on every Sunday in the trenches surely was a form of warfare. In two bold moves Halas solved his major problems. First borrowing every cent he could, he bought out Sternaman's half-interest in the team for $38,000, then he gave Jones his walking papers and hired himself back as head coach.

The Bears were atop the world of professional football in 1933, with George Halas again at the helm. Halas, ever the innovator, took the team out of Chicago for the first time for training camp, to the Notre Dame campus. The idea was soon taken up by every other team in the league. With Red Grange and Bronko Nagurski carrying the pigskin, Keith Molesworth passing, Bill Hewitt and Luke Johnsos catching, and George Musso, Roy Lyman and Nagurski on defense, the club had the most talented aggregation in the NFL.

Chicago won its second consecutive title with a 10-2-1 record, then captured the first divisional playoff for the championship in league history, a hard fought 23- 21 win over the New York Giants.

Jack Manders, the Bears' rookie placekicker, was the difference in the game, making good on three field goals and one conversion for 10 points. The two Bear touchdowns came on passes from an improbable source—Nagurski. The first was an eight yard toss to Bill Karr; the second was on a 14-yard pass to Hewitt, who lateraled to Karr. At the conclusion of the season, end Bill Hewitt, guard Joe Kopcha and fullback Bronko Nagurski were the Bear representatives on the league's All-Star Team.

During the 1933 season football, which had been gradually slimming down over the years from the fat bladder it had been originally, finally took its modern day shape. It was impossible to drop kick accurately, so that practice faded out, but the rules changes and new emphasis on offensive strategy greatly improved the passing game.

For the first time in their historyin 1934, the Bears finished regular season play unbeaten and untied, winning 13 straight and scoring a team record 286 points while holding the opposition to only 86. Unfortunately, the team lost the division playoff for the NFL championship to the New York Giants, a team they had beaten twice during the regular season, in the famous "sneaker game."

The game was played in December in the Polo Grounds in New York, and the turf was frozen solid. At the halfway point in the contest the Bears had fought to a 10-3 lead. During halftime the Giants' coach, Steve Owen, instructed his players to pull off their cleated shoes and gave them basketball shoes to wear instead. With their light sneakers, the Giants were able to move far better and quicker over the frozen ground and ran away from the befuddled Bears, scoring 27 quick points to win the game and the title, 30-13. Chicago's only scoring was on a one-yard plunge for a touchdown by Bronko Nagurski and two field goals and an extra point by Jack Manders.

Placekicker Manders was again the Bears top scorer for the season with 79 points, a total that also led the league. Bear halfback Beattie Feathers became the NFL's first thousand-yard back, just passing that mark with 1,003 yards on only 101 carries for a phenomenal average of ten yards a carry.

It would be 22 years before another Bear, Rick Casares, would top the 1,000 yard figure for one season. Feathers, incidentally, was injured prior to the Giant championship game and did not play. The Bears placed four players on the annual All-Star squad, end Bill Hewitt, guard Joe Kopcha, halfback Feathers and fullback Bronko Nagurski.

Prior to the season opener the Bears took on the College All-Stars in the first of those games sponsored by the Chicago Tribune Charities. The game was played before 79,432 in Soldier Field and proved to be a major disappointment to Halas and his crew as the college boys held the powerful Bears to a 0-0 tie. The team also played their first Thanksgiving Day game during the 1934 season, topping the Detroit Lions, 19-16.

The 1935 campaign was another odd one for the Bears. Their 6-4-2 record and .600 winning percentage was only a game behind division-leading Detroit's 7-3-2 mark, but it was also the same record that the Chicago Cards had, and the two tied for last place in the four-team division. The Green Bay Packers at 8-4-0 were in second place. Red Grange retired after the season. His play in the past few years, due to injuries, had not been up to his earlier prime, but he was still a crowd favorite.

A major decision during the year involved the adoption of the college draft, which was set to begin before the 1936 campaign. In that draft the Bears' selection was West Virginia tackle Joe Stydahar. Both Bear guards, Joe Kopcha (he for the third year in a row) and George Musso, as well as end Bill Karr, were named to the All-Star Team.

After six consecutive wins—against Green Bay, Philadelphia, Pittsburgh (twice), the Cardinals and Detroit—to open the 1936 season, the Bears had first place in the division all to themselves. A 21-10 loss to the Packers was followed by three more one-sided victories over the Giants, the Redskins and the Eagles, and it appeared that the team was on its way to a title. That path was plowed under, however, as the team lost their final two games, to Detroit, 13-7, and to the Cardinals, 14-7.

The Bears' record of 9-3-0 was a game and a halfback of division champ Green Bay, which went on to top the Boston Redskins for the NFL championship. For the first time since the inception of the All-Star Team selections, no Bear player made the squad.

With only one loss—to the Green Bay Packers—and a tie to mar their regular season, the Bears won their fourth divisional crown in six years in 1937 with a 9-1-1 mark. But just as happened after the undefeated 1932 season, the team faltered in the playoffs. This time they dropped a heartbreaker to the Washington Redskins and their sensational rookie quarterback, Sammy Baugh, 28-21 before only 15,870 frozen fans in Wrigley Field.

Sid Luckman

The game was a see-saw battle throughout. The Redskins scored first, followed by 14 straight points by all-purpose back Jack Manders of the Bears, who scored on a ten-yard run, caught a 37-yard scoring pass from Bernie Masterson, and kicked both extra points. But behind the passing of Baugh—18 of 33 for 335 yards and three touchdowns—the Redskins fought back from a 14-7 halftime deficit to take the game and the championship. The Bears' player share for the game was $128 each.

Manders again was the league's top scorer with 69 points on five touchdowns, 15 extra points and eight field goals. Bears on the All-Star Team were second-year tackle Joe Stydahar and guard George Musso.

In 1938, for the first time in eight years, the club was without the incomparable Bronko Nagurski, who had retired. In their worst showing since 1929 the Bears finished the 1938 season with six wins and five losses. Still, Chicago was only two games behind division leading Green Bay's mark of 8-3-0. Chicago players on the NFL's All-Star Team were Stydahar—for the second year in a row—and guard Dan Fortmann.

In the college draft prior to the 1939 season, the Bears made two most significant choices: Sid Luckman, a quarterback from Columbia, was their first pick; Bill Osmanski, a Holy Cross fullback, was their second. Both would play key roles in the years to come.

Close losses to Green Bay and the New York Giants in games that could easily have gone either way doomed Coach George Halas's squad to a second-place finish, only a game behind the division leading Packers, who went on to take the league championship. Both games against the Packers were great battles, with Green Bay winning 21-16 in Green Bay, and the Bears taking the return engagement, 30-27.

Chicago set a new team scoring mark for the year with 298 points, a total that included 44-7 and 48-7 drubbings of "that other team" in the city, the Cardinals. Jack Manders led the team in scoring for the sixth time in seven years, this time with 50 points. Rookie fullback Bill Osmanski pounded out 699 yards to lead not only the team, but the entire league. Bear tackle Joe Stydahar was named to the league All-Star Team for the third consecutive year, along with guard Dan Fortmann and rookie Bill Osmanski.

During the year league President Joe Carr died and was replaced by Carl Storck.

The Monsters of the Midway

The Bears' walloping of the Green Bay Packers 41-0 in the 1940 season opener for both clubs should have been a portent to the rest of the league of what was to come. Although the team finished the regular season with the same record, 8-3-0, as they had in 1939, they not only won their division, but obliterated the Washington Redskins 73-0 in the league championship in what has been called the most perfectly played game of all time. Halas's legions were now, most assuredly, "The Monsters of the Midway."

That rout, which witnessed the unveiling of the T-formation, signaled the beginning of pro football's modern era. Washington was actually slightly favored prior to the game, and had a better regular season mark (9-2-0) than did the Bears, and had defeated Chicago 7-3 in Washington earlier in the year. For all intents and purposes, the game was over after the first quarter.

The Bears had won the flip and chose to receive. On the second play of the game Bill Osmanski sped around left end and dashed 68 yards for a touchdown. The second time Chicago had the ball the Bears' young quarterback, Sid Luckman, led the team on an 80-yard drive and stole over from the one to score the second touchdown. Then Joe Maniaci followed Osmanski around left end on a 42-yard scamper, and all of a sudden it was 21-0.

The only score in the second quarter was a 30-yard pass from Luckman to Ken Kavanaugh. Hampton Pool intercepted a Sammy Baugh pass to open the second half and sped 19 yards for a score. Later in the game George McAfee also intercepted a pass, this one from Roh Zimmerman, and returned it 34 yards for another score. In all, ten different Bears scored 11 touchdowns; six different players scored seven extra points.

The All-Star Team, which had been selected before the championship game, had only two Bears in its lineup: Joe Stydahar, who made the squad for the fourth year in a row, and Dan Fortmann, on the team for the third consecutive year.

The Bears' 1940 college draft pick was center Clyde "Bulldog" Turner of Hardin-Simmons, who is now in the Bear Hall of Fame. The Detroit Lions made an attempt to win Turner away from the Bears, for which the league office fined them $5,000, a major amount at that time.

World War II

With war clouds on the horizon, the 1941 Bears followed up their spectacular championship game win of the previous year with their fifth NFL title. After finishing the regular season tied with Green Bay, each with ten wins and only one loss, the Bears dismantled the Packers 33-14 in the playoff for the division crown, then crushed the New York Giants 37-9 in their second championship game rout. The contest was played only two weeks after the Japanese attack on Pearl Harbor, which kept attendance down to only 13,341.

Many Bears, as well as players from all NFL teams, were soon destined for service in the war. Young Bussey, the Bears' backup quarterback to Sid Luckman, would be killed in action before World War Two was over.

During the regular season the Bears, led by Luckman's passing, chalked up 396 points, nearly 100 more than they had ever scored before in one year. The team opened with a 25-17 win over Green Bay then ran off four more wins before bowing to the Packers in their second meeting, 14-16. That game was the Bears' only loss of the year.

Luckman was named to the league's All-Star Team for the first time, as was running back George McAfee and center "Bulldog" Turner, while guard Dan Fortmann made it for the fourth year in a row. Former Notre Dame "Four Horseman" Elmer Layden was named as the league's new Commissioner, replacing Carl Storck.

The Bears were guided to their second undefeated and untied season through the first six games of 1942 by Coach George Halas, who then left for service in WWII, and for the remaining five games by Heartley "Hunk" Anderson and Luke Johnsos, who had served as assistant coaches under Halas.

In the divisional playoff for the championship the Bears' opponent again was the Washington Redskins, and this time the 'Skins came out on top, 14-6. In the game, played before

36,006 in Washington, D.C., the two teams battled through a scoreless first quarter. In the second stanza Bears guard Lee Artoe grabbed a loose ball and rambled 50 yards for Chicago's only score. The point after was unsuccessful. Then the Redskins, led by the league's top quarterback Sammy Baugh, took over. Baugh completed a 25-yard scoring strike to Wilbur Moore for the go-ahead touchdown before halftime, then led the team to a second score, a one-yard plunge by Andy Farkas in the third quarter to ice the game.

The year was the last in which the NFL office selected the All-Star Team; thereafter the choices would be by the wire services, including the Associated Press (AP) and United Press International (UPI). For the first time five Bears made the squad: Luckman at quarterback, Dan Fortmann (for the fifth time) at guard, "Bulldog" Turner at center, Lee Artoe at tackle and Gary Famiglietti at fullback, the latter two for the first time. Turner, a "Bulldog" on defense as well as a center on offense, led the league in interceptions with eight.

During regular-season play in 1943 the Bears, with most of their veterans in the service, fought to a 8-1-1 record, with only an opening game 21-21 tie against the Green Bay Packers and a 21-7 loss to the Redskins late in the season to mar their record.

Sid Luckman became the first Bear quarterback to throw for more than two thousand yards in a single year; he had been the first to exceed one thousand two years earlier. With all-purpose back Harry Clark as his prime target, Luckman completed 110 of 202 for 2,194 yards and an astounding 28 touchdowns, the most scoring passes any quarterback has ever thrown for the Bears. Keep in mind that those 28 touchdown passes came in only 10 games—projected out to a 16-game schedule the total would be 45.

Luckman's quarterback rating at the end of the season was 107.8, tops in the league and the highest ever for a Bear. En route to his overall totals Luckman tossed for seven touchdowns in a single game, a 56-7 thumping of the New York Giants on November 14.

Clark, in addition to being Luckman's favorite target and the leading receiver on the team, also led the Bears in rushing with 556 yards in 120 attempts, in scoring with 60 points, in punt returns with 158 yards, in kickoff returns with 13 for 326 yards, and he even led the team with five interceptions on defense. It was to be his last year as a Bear, however, as he was off to join the war effort, and when he did return home, he opted to the new All-America Football Conference.

Still in shape from working out on his farm in northern Minnesota, 34-year-old Bronko Nagurski came out of a five-year retirement to try to help his former team. Nagurski played in the line during nearly all of the year until the final game of the season against the Cardinals. The Bears needed a win to clinch the division title. Trailing 24-14 late in the third quarter, the Bears needed a lift. Co-coach "Hunk" Anderson asked Nagurski to move back into his old fullback spot, and it was as if he had never been gone. Nagurski responded with 84 yards in 16 carries and a touchdown, leading the Bears to a wild 35-24 comeback win. He later said that the game gave him his greatest thrill in football.

For the fourth year in a row the "Monsters of the Midway" were in the NFL championship game, and for the third time it was against the Washington Redskins. The playoff against Washington was billed as a battle between the two top quarterbacks in the game, Sammy Baugh of the Redskins and Sid Luckman of the Bears.

The Chicago ace was the overwhelming winner, at least on this occasion, throwing for five touchdowns, completing 15 of 26 passes for 286 yards and running for 64 more. Nagurski, in his last game as a pro, added 34 yards on 11 carries and scored the Bears' first touchdown. Baugh, on the other side of the line, threw for two touchdowns before being knocked out of the game with a concussion in the second half. Luckman, Clark, center "Bulldog" Turner and guard Dan Fort-mann, the latter for a record sixth time, were named to the league All-Star Team.

Any hopes the team had for a repeat as champions in 1944 were quickly dashed as the Bears lost their first two games, 42-28 to the Green Bay Packers and 19-7 to the Cleveland Rams. After a tie with Detroit on October 27 the club righted itself to take five of the last six. It was too late to catch the Packers, however, who finished with a 8-2-0 mark and went on to win the NFL title with a 14-7 win over the New York Giants. Bears honored on the All-Star Team for the year were Luckman and Turner.

Papa Bear Returns

For only the second time since their creation a quarter century earlier, the Bears suffered a losing season in 1945. The team had to win its last two games against Pittsburgh and the Chicago Cardinals just to achieve a 3-7-0 season. It was to be the last year that the team would be coached by the unique combination of Hunk Anderson and Luke Johnsos. In their three and a half seasons running the team, the pair had guided the Bears to an overall record of 23-12-2 and a league championship. They weren't losing their jobs because anyone was unhappy with their work or level of competence. It was just that "Papa Bear" was back home again.

George "Papa Bear" Halas, in fact, was quite probably the causative factor in those last two wins. On Thanksgiving Day the team was practicing when Sid Luckman noticed a middle aged man in a naval uniform walking along the sidelines. When the man waved, Luckman saw it was Halas, shouted, and the team went wild. The 20-7 win over the Steelers and the 28-20 victory over the Cards in the final two games could easily be attributed to Halas's return.

In the Chicago Bear press guide and in other pro football histories dealing with that time, Anderson and Johnsos are credited with being the co-coaches for the entire 1943 season; in reality Halas was calling the shots from the time Luckman noticed him.

Other Bear veteran began coming back into the fold, including Hugh Gallarneau, Ken Kavanaugh, George McAfee and Joe Stydahar. When McAfee reported in for the, game against Pittsburgh, Halas told him he would only use him sparingly. Halas was good to his promise; McAfee only played 12 minutes, but he scored three touchdowns in that time. The postwar era had begun, Papa Bear was back, and the Bears were ready.

In 1946—for the seventh year in a row—the "Monsters of the Midway" opened up the season against their top rival, the Green Bay Packers. The game was played in Green Bay, and Halas's team made things miserable for the Pack, winning easily, 30-7, on their way to a 8-2-1 season. In the championship playoff Chicago belted the New York Giants 24-14 before a title game record crowd of 58,346 in the Polo Grounds. Sid Luckman tossed for one score and scampered 19 yards for another.

Under Halas's stern control, the Bears had put together an amazing comeback from their 1945 performance, not only returning to their accustomed winning ways, but capturing their division crown and going on to take the NFL championship as well, their seventh league title.

During the year the rival All-American Conference began play with teams in Brooklyn, Buffalo, Cleveland, Los Angeles, Miami, New York, San Francisco, and, to Halas's ire, Chicago. The UPI was given the responsibility of selecting the annual All-Star Team; Bears on their squad included Turner and Kavanaugh. The team's first pick in the annual college draft was Notre Dame All-American Johnny Lujack.

An 8-4 record is nothing to be ashamed of, but for the Chicago Bears of 1947, it was a major disappointment. Halas and his crew were leading their division by a full game going into the next to the last game of the season against the Los Angeles Rams, needing a win to clinch the title. The Rams, however, spoiled the day for a full house at Wrigley Field, edging the Bears 17-14.

Chicago went into the season finale against the Cardinals with the two teams tied for first place with identical records of 8-3. On the first play after the opening kickoff Cardinal quarterback Paul Christman launched an 80-yard touchdown pass to speedy halfback Babe Dimancheff, and the Bears spent the rest of the day trying to catch up. They never did, and the Cardinals won, 30-21. The Cards went on to defeat the Philadelphia Eagles 28-21 for the NFL title.

Quarterback Sid Luckman put the ball in the air 323 times during the season, completing 176 passes for 2,712 yards, all new Bear records. Two Bear receivers also were responsible for new Bear highs. Jim Keane caught 64 passes, best in the league. His total yards receiving, 910, was a new Bear high, as was the 13 touchdowns caught by another Bear receiver, Ken Kavanaugh.

All-Star representatives from the Bears were Kavanaugh for the second year in a row, tackle Fred Davis and Luckman, the latter for the fifth time. Early in the year Bill Hewitt, one of the all-time great ends in Bear history, was killed in an automobile crash.

The Chicago Cardinals were again the spoiler of the Bears' titles hopes in 1948. The Bears got off to four straight wins at the beginning of the season, including a 28-17 win over the Cards, and went into the last game of the season with a 10-1 mark, tied with the Cards for the division lead. But in the big game the Cards again prevailed, edging the Bears 24-21 in a thriller. The season was to be the last as the Bear starter for quarterback Sid Luckman.

Earlier Coach-Owner George Halas opened up his wallet to outbid the All-America Football Conference for three prized rookies, Johnny Lujack, whom they had drafted two years earlier; another quarterback, Bobby Layne, and huge Notre Dame tackle George Connor. Lujack received $18,000, Layne $10, 000 and Connor $22,500 and a no-cut contract, all exceptional deals in those days for rookies. Lujack, drafted by the Bears as the future replacement for Luckman at quarterback, played the year primarily on defense and led the Bears in interceptions with eight. Bears on the All-Star team were guard Ray Bray and, for the fifth time, "Bulldog" Turner.

The Los Angeles Rams were the spoilers for the Bears in 1949, topping the Chicago club twice early in the year 31-16 and 27-24, the last of the two dropping the Bears to a 3-3 record on October 30. The club rebounded to win its last six games, including a 51-21 route of the Cardinals in the season finale, but it wasn't enough as they finished at 9-3, a game behind the 8-2-2 Rams.

During the year Johnny Lujack emerged as one of the top quarterbacks in the league, throwing for 2,658 yards and 23 touchdowns on 162 completions in 312 attempts. In the finale against the Cards Lujack threw for 468 yards—a Bears single- game passing yardage record that still stands—and six touchdowns. Earlier in the year Halas had peddled the team's other young quarterback, Bobby Layne, to the New York Bulldogs. Guard Ray Bray was the only Bear named to the annual All-Star team.

At the conclusion of the season the rival All-America Football Conference disbanded, with three clubs moving into the NFL: Cleveland, San Francisco and Baltimore.

New Competition

A 9-3 record in 1950 was good enough for a tie with Los Angeles for the division title, but in the playoff against the Rams, the Bears were defeated 24-14. In the NFL championship the Rams in turn were defeated by the American Conference leaders, the Cleveland Browns, 30–28. It was Cleveland's first year in the NFL after winning four consecutive titles in the old All-America Football Conference (AAFC).

With the addition of the three teams from the AAFC, the NFL continued to have two divisions, but instead of calling them the Eastern and Western Division, they were now the American and National Conferences. The Bears were in the National Conference along with the New York Giants, the Detroit Lions, the Green Bay Packers, the San Francisco 49ers and the Baltimore Colts.

Bear quarterback Johnny Lujack, a triple-threat scoring back, led the club in scoring for the third year in a row, this time with 109 points on 11 touchdowns, 34 extra points and three field goals. The 109 total points was a new Bear scoring mark.

Leading the team for the fourth straight year were end Jim Keane with 36 receptions and George McAfee in punt returns with 284 yards. Two former Notre Dame All-Americans, George Connor and Lujack, along with guard Dick Barwegan, were named to the All-Star Team.

With the free substitution rule adopted by the league, teams were now able to split their squads into offensive and defensive units, and players would no longer be required to play both ways. Because of this, the 1950 season was the last in which just a single All-Star team was selected; in the future there would be an All-Star Team for defense as well as offense.

The Bears got off to a good start in 1951, winning five of their first six, but then went into a tailspin, losing four of their last six to drop out of contention. For the year the Bears finished at 7-5, only a game behind conference-leading Los Angeles but in fourth place, as Detroit and San Francisco were tied for second at only a half-game out. It was one of the closest races for the title in many years. It was to be Lujack's last year as the Bears' quarterback. The triple-threat back had injured his shoulder early in the 1950 campaign and never fully recovered.

Two Bear players were selected to three positions on the All-Star Team. Dick Barwegan was named at end, while big George Connor, who continued to play two ways, was named at tackle on both defense and offense.

Losing Seasons

For the Bears, a losing season was an abnormality. The 1952 season was only their third season under .500 in their 33 years of play. Four years earlier Coach George Halas had a remarkable stable of quarterbacks in Sid Luckman, Johnny Lujack and Bobby Layne, but now Luckman was retired, Lujack was forced to quit because of an injured shoulder, and Layne was leading the Detroit Lions to the conference championship. Halas was stuck with two unproven youngsters, Steve Romanik and George Blanda. The only Bear to make the All-Star team was George Connor, who made it again both on offense and defense.

If Bear fans thought the 1952 season was like a bad dream, then 1953 must have been a nightmare. The club's 3-8-1 record represented the lowest winning percentage in its history. Even worse, the Bears' perennial All-Star center, "Bulldog" Turner, had retired, and now no one from the "Monsters of the Midway" years of the early 1940s was left on the team.

Quarterback George Blanda was erratic at best; it was said he was more accurate as a place kicker than as a passer, and in fact he would go on to earn Hall of Fame status for his kicking prowess.

One high point of the season came late in the year when the Bears knocked the Los Angeles Rams out of the running for the conference crown, winning a hard fought 24-21 contest. George Connor again made both the defensive and offensive All-Star teams.

With Coach George Halas cracking the whip, the Bears returned to respectability in 1954, coming back from three early season losses to post an 8-4 record and capture second place behind a strong Detroit Lions squad. The Bears won their last four games of the year, including a 27-24 win over the Lions, avenging an opening day 48-23 loss.

Halas put new life into his sputtering offense with the addition of a few key players. One was rookie end Harlon Hill, a lanky speed-

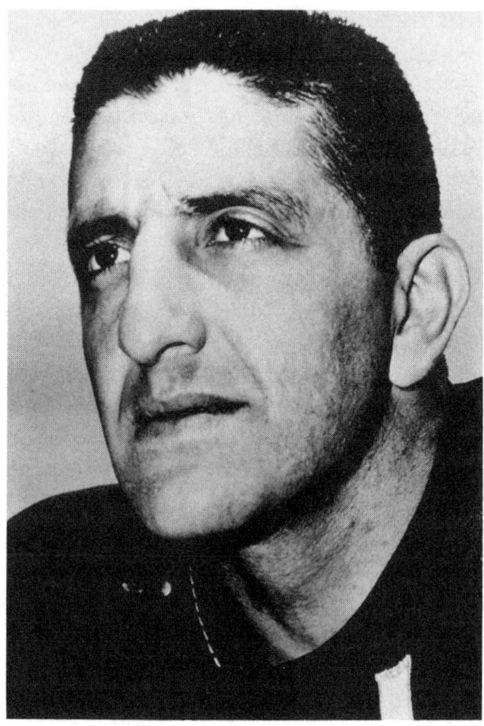

Bill George

ster who would tie a Bear record with 12 touchdown receptions and set another with 1,124 yards in catches. The others were ex-Brown fullback Chick Jagade, and two offensive linemen, Stan Jones and Larry Strickland. Hill was the only Chicago player on the annual All-Star Team.

Halas Retires (Again)

Early in September of 1955, George Halas announced that he would be retiring at the end of the season. It would be the third time that the fiery leader had stepped down as the team's mentor; he had retired at the end of the 1929 season and had left the team in 1942 for duty in WWII.

The Bears opened the season with three straight losses, including heartbreakers to Baltimore and San Francisco, before racking up six wins in a row and eight of their last nine. The team was riding high and in first place when they were bombed by the Cardinals 53-14 in a huge upset. Chicago finished with a 8-4 record, only a half game behind the conference leader, Los Angeles, at 9-3-1.

During the year Ed Brown became the club's main signal caller, and Rick Casares its top power runner. Whereas only one Bear made the All-Star team in 1954, in 1955 five Bears were elected: end Harlon Hill, tackle Bill Wightkin and guard Stan Jones on offense, and Bill George and George Connor (in his last year) on defense.

John "Paddy" Driscoll, a long-time assistant under Halas and a Bears' running star in the 1920s, took the helm in 1956 and drove the club to their first conference title in six years. Shrugging off an opening day loss to the Baltimore Colts, the Chicago team reeled off seven straight wins. Their 9-2-1 record was a half-game better than the Detroit Lions.

After getting trampled by the Lions 42-10, the Bears won the return match in Chicago, 38-21, on the last day of the season to win the Western Conference championship The regular season drive to the top took it all out of the Chicago squad apparently, as the New York Giants ran all over them in the NFL title game, 47-7. The 40-point loss was the worst ever suffered by the Bears in either postseason or regular season play.

During the year Bear fullback Rick Casares pounded out a league-leading 1,126 yards on 234 carries and scored 14 touchdowns, 12 of them by rushing, all new highs for the team. It was only the second time that a Bear running back had topped 1,000 yards in the team's history. Ed Brown turned in a fine effort at quarterback, throwing for 1,307 yards on 96 completions to lead the league. His favorite target, end Harlon Hill, pulled down 47 passes for 1,128 yards, beating his own Bear total yardage record by four yards.

Five Bears were honored by being selected to the All-League Team: on offense, Casares, center Larry Strickland, guard Stan Jones and Hill, and on defense, middle guard Bill George.

After the great performance by the team in Paddy Driscoll's first year as head coach, the Bears stumbled out of the gate in 1957, losing their first three games en route to a lackluster 5-7 fourth-place finish. Center Larry Strickland and linebacker Bill George made the All-Star Team.

Following the season team owner George Halas decided that Driscoll was not the coach of the future for the team and that there wasn't anyone available to do the job as well as he could himself, whereupon he reassumed the head coaching job after an absence of two years.

Halas Returns (Again)

With Papa Bear calling the shots again, the Bears moved back into contention with a rejuvenated offense in 1958. Their drive toward the top, however, was thwarted by the Baltimore Colts, the eventual conference winner, who torpedoed the Bears 51-38 in the first game between the two, then shut them out 17-0 in the return match in Wrigley Field. Bill George was named to the All-League Team for the fourth consecutive year, the only Bear to make the honor squad.

The Bears' 8-4 record in 1958 was duplicated in 1959. Chicago was again plagued by a poor start, losing four of their first five games, including an opening day 9-6 loss to the Green Bay Packers and their new head coach Vince Lombardi, before getting it all together to sweep their last seven games. The Bears did manage to gain some measure of satisfaction by earning a split of their two games with the conference champion Baltimore Colts.

Offensive guard Stan Jones and linebacker Bill George were named to the annual All-Star Team, the latter for the fifth time.1960

In 1959 the Bears' inability to win early on was their downfall. In 1960 the club won three of its first four, but after a tie with the Lions lost five of the last seven. Going into the December 4 game against the Green Bay packers, the Bears had a 5-3-1 record; the Packers were 5-4. Green Bay won that game, 41-13, and also its last three to take the conference title; the Bears dropped their last three, two by shutouts, 42-0 to the Browns and 36-0 to the Lions.

Being selected for the annual Pro Bowl was gradually becoming more important than being named as an All-League selection. Bear players named to the Pro Bowl in 1961 were defensive end Doug Atkins, linebacker Bill George, guard Stan Jones and flanker Johnny Morris.

The NFL expanded its season from 12 to 14 games in 1961, opening play two weeks early to make room for the two additional games. Despite being blown out by the Minnesota Vi-

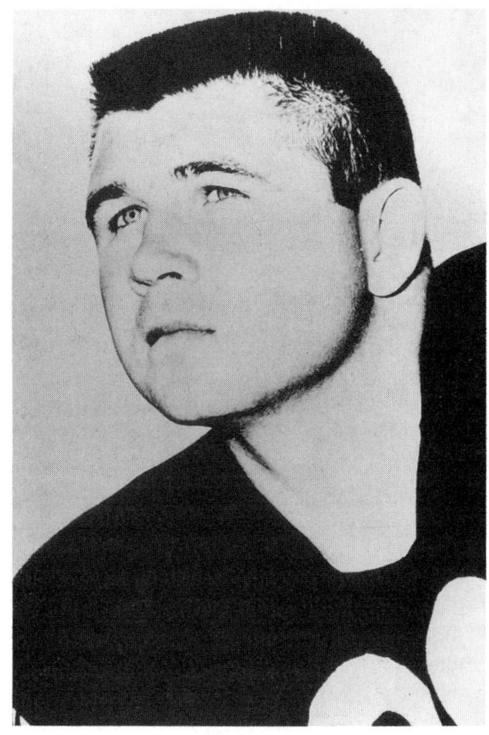

Mike Ditka

Doug Atkins

kings 37-13 in the opener, the Bears took five of seven during one stretch, including two wins over the Baltimore Colts, on their way to an 8-6 season. The only team to top the Bears twice was Lombardi's powerful Green Bay Packers, on their way to the NFL championship.

Leading the Chicago club in scoring with 12 touchdowns was rookie tight end Mike Ditka, who would eventually become the Bears' head coach. The burly Ditka, who also led the team in receptions with 56 and total yards receiving with 1,076, had been the team's number one draft choice. Bears in the Pro Bowl were Doug Atkins, Mike Ditka, Bill George and Stan Jones.1962

Improvement on both offense and defense continued into the 1962 season, but the Bears again could not contain the Green Bay Packers, losing 49-0 and 38-7 in the two most lopsided losses ever suffered to their northern rivals. The team ended the year at 9-5-0.

During the season the Bears went into the air more than at any time in their history. Quarterback Bill Wade threw 412 times and completed 225 for 3,172 yards, all new highs for the team. The total yardage mark is still a record. Wade also threw for 466 yards against Dallas in a thrilling 34-33 win on November 18 to come within two yards of Johnny Lujack's record. A primary reason for the Bears reliance on the passing game were injuries to two key running backs, Rick Casares and Willie Galimore.

Doug Atkins, Joe Fortunato and Richie Petibon anchored the defense, and along with offensive end Mike Ditka, were named to the Pro Bowl. Roosevelt Taylor had more interceptions, nine, than anyone else in the league. Much of the success of that defensive unit could be credited to the system installed by assistant coach George Allen.

The Dominance of Defense

The 1963 season was marked by one of the greatest defensive efforts by the Bears or any team over the last few decades. In an era of high scoring offenses, Coach George Halas's fearsome squad held seven of their 14 opponents to a touchdown or less and allowed only 144 points for the entire season. To put that total into perspective, the Bears had allowed 302 and 287 in the two previous years. The great defensive effort culminated in the Bears first NFL championship in 17 long years.

On their way to the title the Bears topped the reigning champs, the Green Bay Packers, 10-3 and 26-7. In the championship game, the Bears outfought the New York Giants, 14-10, with quarterback Wade scoring two touchdowns on keepers. In the game the Bears had five interceptions, the Giants none.

The team placed a record eight players on the Pro Bowl squad: tight end Mike Ditka, defensive end Doug Atkins, linebacker Joe Fortunato, fullback Joe Marconi, safety Richie Petibon, center Mike Pyle, defensive back Roosevelt Taylor and quarterback Bill Wade. For Atkins it was the seventh trip. In the newly created NFL Hall of Fame, 13 players were elected in the initial balloting. Three were Chicago Bears: founder-player-coach George Halas, halfback Harold "Red" Grange and fullback Bronko Nagurski.

Unfortunately, everything came apart for the Chicago Bears in 1964. The team opened with four straight road games, and lost three of them, to the Packers, the Colts, and the 49ers. Then, after a win over the Rams in Wrigley Field, the club proceeded to lose four in a row on their way to a very discouraging 5-9 record, all of this following an NFL championship. The defense, which had given up only 144 points the year before, allowed 379, the most ever by a Bear squad.

Gale Sayers

Tight end Mike Ditka, for the fourth time, as well as linebacker Joe Fortunato and flanker Johnny Morris were selected to play in the Pro Bowl. Morris grabbed 93 of Wade's passes for 1,206 yards, totals that led the league and were new Bear records as well. Three more members of the Chicago club were selected to the Hall of Fame, tackles Ed Healey and Roy "Link" Lyman and center George Trafton.

1965 was an odd season of streaks for the club: they lost their first three games, then won four in a row, and after a single loss, won five in a row to finish at 9-5. But the big story in 1965 was the emergence of the club's two top draft picks, Gale Sayers and Dick Butkus, both of whom would go on to All-Pro status as rookies and would become the brightest stars in the Bear heavens in the years to come.

Led by the mercurial Sayers, the Bears' offense generated 409 points for the year, more than any other Bear team in history. Part of that scoring total was a 61-20 pasting of San Francisco on December 12, atoning for an earlier 52-24 win by the 49ers. Sayers, probably the most thrilling back to come into the league since the heyday of Red Grange in the 1920s, led the entire league with an astonishing 22 touchdowns for 132 points. That total was not only the high for the league, it was the most points ever for a Bear running back. Butkus, meanwhile, became the most feared middle linebacker in the league. Quarterback Rudy Bukich also led the league with 176 completions in 312 attempts for 2,641 yards and 20 touchdowns.

Five Bears made the All-Pro squad—in addition to Sayers and Butkus, Doug Atkins was named for the eighth time, and tight end Mike Ditka and linebacker Joe Fortunato for the fifth time each. Former Bear star running back and later head coach John "Paddy" Driscoll, quarterback Sid Luckman and guard Dan Fortmann were selected to the NFL Hall of Fame during the year.

The following year marked the end of the war between the NFL and the new American Football League (AFL). The two leagues agreed to a merger, with the NFL absorbing the AFL and splitting into two conferences. The agreement also set up the first Super Bowl, matching the conference winners.

Another excellent performance by Gale Sayers was one of the few things that kept Bear fans happy during 1966. The headlines were filled with negative reports—Owner George Halas and the club were taking Assistant Coach George Allen to court to prevent him from leaving the Bears; flanker Johnny Morris and other key players were lost to injuries; quarterback Rudy Bukich was having a terrible year; some players, including Doug Atkins and Mike Ditka, became openly critical of Halas; and the Green Bay Packers were again the cream of the league, beating the Bears twice during the year.

But Sayers was another story. He led the Bears in rushing and kickoff returns and hauled in 34 passes. His rushing total, 1,231 yards, and his total yardage from rushing, receiving and kick returning were new marks for the Bears, and the total yardage figure was a new high for the league as well. His 197 yards on 17 carries against the Vikings on December 18 was also a new single game mark for the Bears. He was an obvious selection to the Pro Bowl, and was joined there by Dick Butkus and Richie Petibon.

Two former Bears were named to the Hall of Fame, running back George McAfee and center "Bulldog" Turner.

The Bears returned to the winning side of the ledger for the 1967 campaign, albeit barely, with a 7-6-1 mark. The big news, however, was the third and final retirement of the team's remarkable coach, George Halas, the winningest head coach in the history of the league. Halas's career, actually longer than that of the league itself, included 326 wins, 151 losses and 32 ties. On the field, Bear-Packer contests were invariably all-out battles, no matter how either team was doing against the rest of the league. In 1967 the title-bound Packers were to win their 11th NFL championship and second Super Bowl, but they had all they could do to handle the Bears in two bellringers, 13-10 and 17-13.

Only two Bears made it to the Pro Bowl, Sayers and Dick Butkus. It was the fewest number of Bear representatives at the event since it began in 1951. Former Bear tackle Joe Stydahar was named to the Hall of Fame prior to the season.

A New Coach

Chicago finished at an even 7-7 in 1968 under their new coach, Jim Dooley, the first time they ever finished with a .500 season. They lost four of their first five games before running off a four-game winning streak. The Bears' fortunes suffered a double blow in the third game of the season against the Vikings when quarterback Jack Concannon suffered a broken collarbone and understudy Rudy Bukich had a shoulder separation. Later in the year Gale Sayers also was lost with torn ligaments in his knee.

Prior to that injury Sayers had set a new single game rushing total with the Bears, 205 yards against the Green Bay Packers on November 3. A 28-27 loss to the Packers on the final day of the season prevented a winning season for Dooley in his first year.

Placekicker Mac Percival hit on 25 extra points and 25 field goals to lead the club in scoring with an even 100 points. Sayers was joined by teammates Dick Butkus and safety Roosevelt Taylor on the Pro Bowl squad.

The 1969 season was unquestionably the worst in the history of the team. Seven straight losses to open the year, four of them by less than a touchdown, preceded a 38-7 thumping of another weak club, the Pittsburgh Steelers, before

Dick Butkus

ending with six more losses and a 1-13 mark.

Bear fans had little to cheer about during the season, except when Gale Sayers was carrying the ball. He again led the Bears and the league in rushing with 1,032 yards on 236 carries. Both Sayers and linebacker Dick Butkus were named to the Pro Bowl, each for the fifth consecutive year. In an off-field headline, Bears' owner George Halas was elected President of the NFL's National Conference.

Chicago opened the 1970 season with two hard fought wins, the first over a strong New York Giant club, 24-16, the second by a 20-16 margin over the Philadelphia Eagles. The club then went into a tailspin, losing eight of their next ten games before ending the season with solid decisions over the Green Bay Packers, 35-17, and the New Orleans Saints, 24-3, to finish at 6-8, a definite improvement over the previous year.

Gale Sayers was hurt again and was lost for most of the season, as was quarterback Bobby Douglas with a broken wrist. Bears' fans as well as football fans everywhere were saddened by running back Brian Piccolo's death from cancer.

Their was some good new, however. Jack Concannon stepped in to have his best year at quarterback, completing 184 of 385 passes for 2,130 yards. Flanker Dick Gordon led the league with 71 receptions good for 1,026 yards. No Bear receiver has reached that 1,000 mark since then. Kick returner Cecil Turner also provided a few thrills, returning four kickoffs for touchdowns to tie an NFL record. He also led the league in kickoff returns with a 32.7 yards per return average.

The Bears said goodbye to Wrigley Field after many years; beginning in 1971 the club would play all of their home games in the much larger Soldier Field. The Bears also played their first ever Monday Night television game, topping the Detroit Lions 28-14 on October 5.

Another 6-8 finish in 1971, especially the loss of the club's last five games of the season, spelled the end for Coach Jim Dooley. Prior to the season-ending nosedive, the team seemed to be a solid contender with a 5-2 mark at the year's midpoint. Former Bear offensive guard Abe Gibron was named to replace Dooley. Linebacker Dick Butkus was named to the Pro Bowl for the seventh time; receiver Dick Gordon for the second.

Chicago's 1971 offensive statistics were hard to believe; the club led the entire league in rushing, but were dead last in passing. This inconsistency was a main reason for the Bears 4-9-1 record. Head coach Abe Gibron's first year at the helm was also star halfback Gale Sayers' last; his torn up knees made it impossible to continue.

During the season quarterback Bobby Douglas set a new league record with 968 yards rushing. Ron Smith's average of 30.8 yards per kickoff return also led the league, and four Bears were named to the Pro Bowl: Dick Butkus, Dick

Gordon, Bobby Joe Green, and Cecil Turner.

The team's woes continued in 1973 as the Bears managed but three wins, and only one against a division opponent. They lost their last six games, scoring only one touchdown over the last three and finished with a 3-11 record.

Dick Butkus scored the first touchdown of his professional career by picking up a Houston fumble in the end zone on October 28, helping the Bears to a 35-14 win. However, a chronically bad knee forced the All-Pro linebacker to retire at the end of the season. In two seasons Coach Abe Gibron had lost two of the greatest athletes ever to play for the Bears, Gale Sayers and Dick Butkus.

The team again had the league's top kickoff returner. This year it was rookie Carl Garrett, who averaged 30.4 yards per return. The year was Bobby Joe Green's last as the team's punter. After 12 years, he too retired. The only Bear to make the Pro Bowl was defensive tackle Wally Chambers.apse

After splitting their first six games of 1974, the Bears experienced a complete offensive collapse in mid-season. In four straight games they did not score a touchdown and managed only nine points total. They ended the season at 4-10. Head coach Abe Gibron, with a woeful three year record of 11-30-1, the worst performance ever by a Bear coach, was given his release.

Former NFL linebacker Jack Pardee was named as the new coach, the first non-Bear to hold the post. For the first time, no Bear was named to the Pro Bowl. During the year former Bear linebacker Bill George was elected to the Hall of Fame, and in a major front office move, Jim Finks became the team's new vice president and general manager.

Payton Arrives

Since their inception in 1920, the Bears had been blessed with a long list of top running backs—Red Grange, Bronko Nagurski, Rick Casares, and Gale Sayers, to name but a few. Quite possibly the greatest of them all emerged on the scene during the 1975 campaign—Walter Payton. Not as strong perhaps as Nagurski nor as flashy as Sayers, Payton would go on to gain more yards and score more touchdowns than anyone in the history of professional football.

But even with Payton in the lineup the Bears could manage only four wins, the same total that the deposed Abe Gibron had chalked up. It was also their seventh consecutive losing season. The 379 points allowed by the Bears tied the old record set by the 1964 team.

On offense, however, the Bears did manage to score in every game, an achievement that had not occurred in ten years. Payton led the Bears in rushing with 679 yards and the entire NFL in kickoff returns, averaging 31.7 yards per return. He and tackle Wally Chambers were named to the Pro Bowl. Former Bear tackle George Connor was elected to the Hall of Fame, the 15th member of the team to win the honor.

With just nine more points the Bears could have won ten games in 1976. Their 7-7 season was marked by one point losses to the Vikings, 20-19, and the Raiders, 28-27, and a four point loss to the Lions. It was, however, a step up from Coach Jack Pardee's first-year mark. There was also a big turnaround in points scored and allowed over the two years. Whereas in 1975 the Bears managed only 191 points and allowed 379; in 1976 they scored 253 and allowed only 216.

During the year Walter Payton came into his own as one of the premier running backs in the league, rushing for 1,390 yards on 311 carries, more than double his rookie production, and scoring 13 touchdowns. Bob Avelini took over the passing chores for the team, accounting for 1,580 yards. On the defense, end Jim Osborne set a new mark for sacks with 15 for 129 yards in losses. Tackle Wally Chambers was the only Bear selected to play in the Pro Bowl.

After losing five of their first eight games of the 1977 campaign, the Bears came on strong late in the season, winning their last six in a row. For the first time in 14 years the Bears made it into the playoffs, where, unfortunately, they ran into a Dallas Cowboy buzzsaw and lost, 37-7. The defeat was the deciding factor in Coach Jack Pardee's resignation, for the nine wins by the club were certainly nothing to quit over; they were the most for the team in 12 years.

Walter Payton led all NFL runners with 1,852 yards, averaging 5.5 yards a carry. His total yardage and 339 carries were new Bear records, as was the 275 yards in a single game he scampered for in a 10-7 win over Minnesota on November 20. Payton also ran for 205 yards in a 26-0 win over Green Bay on October 30. He again led the Bears in scoring with 14 rushing and two receiving touchdowns for 96 points. Bob Avelini connected on 194 passes in 293 attempts for 2,004 yards and 11 touchdowns. His favorite receiver was Scott Jones, who grabbed 50 passes for 809 yards.

AP/Wide World Photos

Walter Payton

Payton and cornerback Allan Ellis were named to the Pro Bowl, and former star running Back Gale Sayers was inducted into the Hall of Fame. Following Pardee's exit, Minnesota Viking offensive coordinator Neill Armstrong was named as the team's new head coach.

The Neill Armstrong era began well enough in 1978 with wins over St. Louis, San Francisco and Detroit in the club's first three regular season games. The fourth game, however, a 25-19 overtime loss to Oakland, started the club on an eight-game losing streak, their longest ever in a single season. The Bears righted themselves at season's end, though, finishing with a 7-9 record. The year marked the beginning of a 16 game schedule in the NFL. Chicago's sole representative on the Pro Bowl squad was Walter Payton, who again turned in a sparkling effort, running for 1,395 yards and pulling down 50 passes for 480 more.

In 1979 Chicago returned to double-figure wins for the first time since the championship year of 1963 and also returned to the playoffs. For the second year in a row Coach Neill Armstrong's squad finished strong, winning seven of their last eight to end up at 10-6 after a poor start. In the playoffs, however, the team again stumbled, losing to the Philadelphia Eagles, 27-17, in a first round clash.

Walter Payton again was almost the entire offensive show, running for 1,610 yards on 369 carries, the latter a new club high, and scoring 16 touchdowns. He also caught 31 passes for 313 yards on his way to his fourth Pro Bowl appearance. Former Bear middle linebacker Dick Butkus was inducted into the NFL Hall of Fame during the year.

The 1980s

Two overtime losses, to Green Bay in the opener and then to Cincinnati later in the 1980 season, marked another disappointing year for the club. After a promising 1979 season, Bear faithful were expecting a bit more. Six early losses, all by less than a touchdown, were too much to overcome and the club floundered to another 7-9 losing season.

One highlight of the year was the team's 61-7 thrashing of perennial rival Green Bay on December 7, avenging the earlier loss to the Packers and dealing them their worst defeat in history. As usual Walter Payton afforded the crowds their money's worth, pounding out 1,460 yards, his fifth season in a row over the thousand-yard mark. Vince Evans became the team's signal caller and threw for 2,039 yards in his initial effort. Walter Payton, defensive end Dan Hampton and safety Gary Fencik were named to the Pro Bowl, Payton for the fifth time.

More disappointmentwas in store for 1981. A 1-6 start in the first half of the season and the wolves began to howl for Coach Neill Armstrong. Two overtime wins over San Diego and Kansas City, followed by wins in the last three games could not save Armstrong and his staff, and all were given their walking papers after the season.

For the sixth year in a row running back Walter Payton topped the thousand-yard mark, fighting his way to 1,222 hard-earned yards. No Bear running back, in fact, had ever run for more than a thousand yards even two years in a row, and the history of the club was filled with great backs.

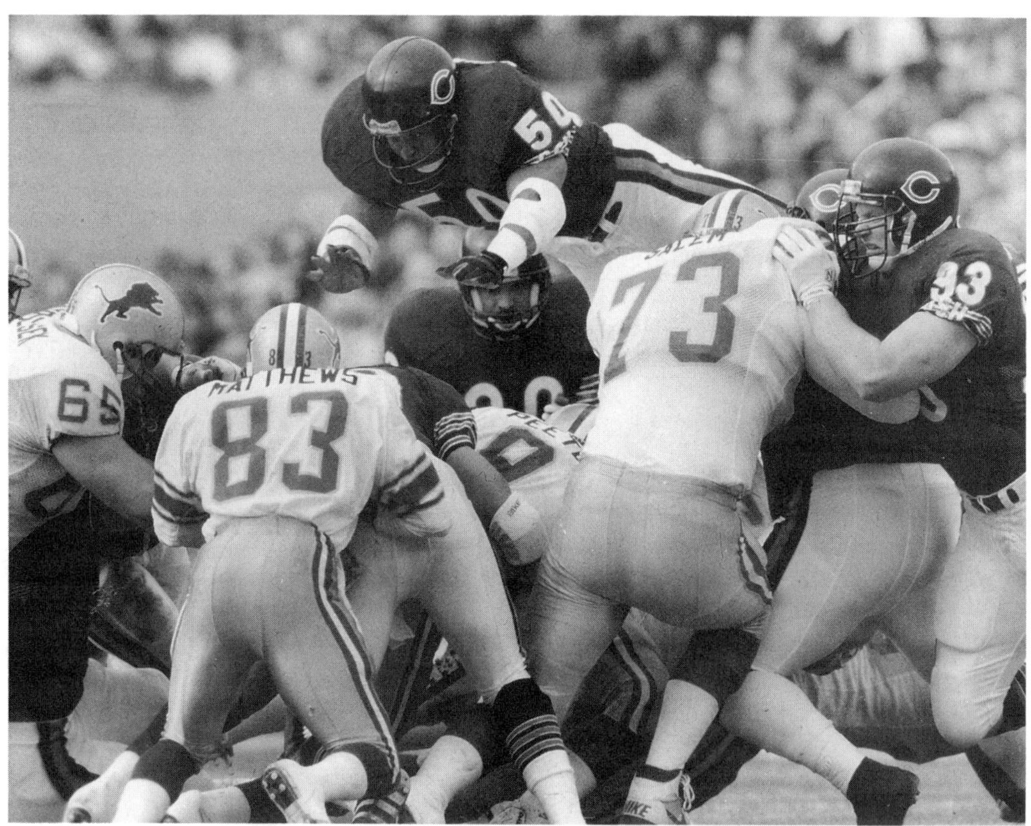

AP/Wide World Photos

Mike Singletary

Quarterback Vince Evans turned in the best performance of his brief career, airing the ball 436 times for 2,354 yards, the highest passing figure for a Bear in 16 years. Payton was Evans' favorite target, grabbing 41 passes for 379 yards. A more dubious honor was achieved by kicker Bob Parsons, who punted 114 times during the long season, the only time in Chicago Bear history that 100 or more punts were necessary in a single season. In postseason honors, former Bear quarterback-kicker George Blanda was inducted into the NFL Hall of Fame, and safety Gary Fencik was named to the Pro Bowl.

"Iron Mike" Takes Over

In January of 1982 Bears owner George Halas announced Coach Neill Armstrong's successor: former Bear tight end Mike Ditka, who had been serving for the past several years as an assistant offensive coordinator with the Dallas Cowboys.

Halas, who had led the Bears to one championship after another in the early years and had coached the club to its last NFL title in 1963, was 86 years old and in failing health when he named Ditka as his personal choice to lead the Bears back to respectability.

The appointment of Ditka astounded many, including players and veteran Chicago sportswriters who remembered the heated shouting arguments between Halas and Ditka during the latter's playing career. It was Ditka who had coined the famous phrase about Halas: "George Halas tosses nickels around like manhole covers." The volatile Ditka had left the Bears in 1967 when Halas traded him to the Philadelphia Eagles for quarterback Jack Concannon. The trade had followed a lengthy contract dispute between Halas and Ditka. But now Halas saw Ditka as a mirror image of himself.

Ditka's debut several months later hardly got a chance to get off the ground before the Bears and players from all other clubs in the league went on strike. Chicago played only nine games in the strike shortened season, losing six of them. The abbreviated season also caused the elimination of both Chicago-Green Bay games, the first time in the two teams' long history that they did not meet.

Walter Payton's record string of thousand-yard performances was also broken, although he again led the Bears in rushing yardage with 596. At quarterback, rookie Jim McMahon took over full-time duties. The team's only representative at the annual Pro Bowl was defensive tackle Dan Hampton. Inductees into the Hall of Fame during the year included Bear defensive end Doug Atkins and tackle-guard George Musso.

Coach Mike Ditka's first full year as the Bear's mentor had a tough beginning as the team lost three of its first four games in 1983, each by only three points and two in overtime. The Chicago team came on strong in the second half of the season, winning five of six, including decisions over division rivals Tampa Bay, Minnesota and Green Bay. Halfback Walter Payton and linebacker Mike Singletary were named to the Pro Bowl squad.

The season was more notable for its off-the-field turmoil than the team's performance. In August general manager Jim Finks resigned after nine years with the club and was replaced by Jerry Vainisi. On October 31, the Bears' founder-owner George Halas died at age 88. Two weeks later, Edward McCaskey, who had served the team for 17 years as its vice president and treasurer, was named to succeed him as chairman of the board. McCaskey, Halas's son-in-law, thus became only the second chairman of the club in its 63-year history.

The club's performance under Coach Mike Ditka improved markedly in the 1984 campaign, as the team won 10 games and qualified for postseason play for the first time in five years. Their Central Division title was their first ever. In the playoffs, their 23-19 win over the Washington Redskins was their first postseason victory in 21 years. Unfortunately for the Bear faithful, however, the San Francisco

AP/Wide World Photos

Jim McMahon (9)

49ers, on their way to the NFL championship, shut out the Bears 23-0 in the second round.

En route to a 1,684 yard rushing mark, Walter Payton broke Jim Brown's NFL career total yardage rushing record. Payton was also the club's receiving leader in 1984, with 45 catches for 368 yards. Second-year defensive lineman Richard Dent set a club mark with 17.5 sacks for 140 yards in losses; both figures are still Bear high marks.

For the first time in 19 years the Bears placed five players on the Pro Bowl team: Todd Bell, Richard Dent, Dan Hampton, Mike Singletary and Walter Payton.

In the front office, business manager Rudy Custer announced his retirement after 38 years with the team.

1985: That Championship Season

Super Bowl Champions! It was one of the most glorious chapters in Chicago Bear football history. Sadly, however, George Halas was not around to see the triumphant 1985 season. When Halas had named his protege, Mike Ditka, as the team's new head coach in 1982, Chicago fans had been promised a championship. In three years that promise was fulfilled.

Ditka and his legions put together one of the most outstanding performances the league had ever witnessed, scoring a team record 456 points and allowing only 198. They shut out their two playoff opponents, the New York Giants, 21-0, and the Los Angeles Rams, 34-0, before going on to crush the New England Patriots 46-10 in the Super Bowl. It was the Bears' first Super Bowl title and ninth NFL championship.

During the game the team set seven championship game records, including most points and largest margin of victory. The contest was also viewed on television by a record number of people. The next day coach Ditka and his squad were welcomed by a half-million fans in a ticker-tape parade through downtown Chicago.

On their way to the crown the team compiled a 15-1 record, won a second straight NFC Central title and placed a league record nine players in the Pro Bowl: tackle Jim Covert, defensive ends Richard Dent and Dan Hampton, safety Dave Duerson, center Jay Hilgenberg, quarterback Jim McMahon, halfback Walter Payton and linebackers Mike Singletary and Otis Wilson.

Rookie kicker Kevin Butler led the league in scoring with 144 points on 51 extra points without a miss and 31 of 38 field goals. The point total shattered the team point record set by Gale Sayers in 1965. Payton fought for 1,551 yards during the season, the ninth time he had topped the thousand yard mark, and again led in receptions with 49, good for 483 yards.

Quarterback McMahon had his finest season as a pro, hitting on 178 of 313 passes for 2,392 yards and 18 touchdowns. Speedster Willie Gault, who led in receiving yardage with 704 on 33 catches, also led the club in kickoff returns with a 26.2 yards per return average. On defense, Richard Dent followed up his 1984 performance with a league leading 17 sacks, good for 133 yards in losses.

The 1986 Bears put together another outstanding record, 14-2, on the heels of their 15-win season in 1985, for 29 regular season wins in two years, the highest two-year total of any team in NFL history. On defense the team allowed an NFL record-low 187 points, an average of only 11.7 a game. The Washington Redskins put a damper on the Bears' hopes for repeating as Super Bowl champs, however, topping Chicago 27-13 in the first round of the playoffs.

Kicker Kevin Butler hit on 36 extra points and 28 field goals for 120 points, a two-year total of 264, the highest in Bear history. Walter Payton had his final thousand-yard rushing season, struggling for 1,333 yards in his 12th year. Willie Gault paced Chicago receivers with 42 catches for 818 yards, but Dennis Gentry replaced him as the team's kickoff return specialist, leading not only the Bears but the entire league with a 28.8 average.

The Bears again led all NFL teams in Pro Bowl representatives, with seven: offensive tackle Jim Covert, safety Dave Duerson, linebackers Wilbur Marshall and Mike Singletary, defensive tackle Steve McMichael, center Jay Hilgenberg and running back Walter Payton. It was the ninth and final Pro Bowl for Payton, the most ever for a Bear up to that time.

Another strike-shortened season in 1987 saw the Bears win their fourth consecutive Central Division title, posting a 11-4 mark. It was also the fourth straight winning season for the club, a feat last accomplished from 1948 to 1951. In the first round of the playoffs the Washington Redskins again upset the Bear applecart, coming back from a 14-0 deficit in the second quarter to defeat the Chicago club, 21-17.

Second-year running back Neal Anderson took over the rushing yardage leadership for the team, after 12 straight years by Payton. Anderson added 467 yards receiving on 47 catches to his rushing total of 586 yards to pace both Bear categories, while Willie Gault hauled down 35 passes for 705 yards. Five Bears, safety Dave Duerson, center Jay Hilgenberg, linebackers Wilbur Marshall and Mike Singletary and defensive tackle Steve McMichael were named to the Pro Bowl team.

Walter Payton announced his retirement following the 1987 season. In his finale at Soldier Field he rushed for 79 yards and two touchdowns. "Walter Payton Day" was celebrated prior to the game, and Payton's jersey number—34—was retired, the 11th Bear number to be so honored.

Another great regular-season performance, and another postseason disappointment were in store for Bears' fans in 1988. During the year the Bears posted 12 wins, tied for the top spot in the entire league, but after disposing of Philadelphia in the first round, 20-12, they were eliminated by eventual Super Bowl Champion San Francisco, 28-3. Over the previous five seasons, 1984 to 1988, the Bears had won 62 regular season games under Coach Mike Ditka, more than any team in the NFL had ever won over the same number of years, but they had only one Super Bowl title to show for it.

Individually, kicker Kevin Butler topped the club in scoring for the fourth straight year with 82 points, and Neal Anderson climbed over the thousand-yard mark for the first time with 1,106 yards in 249 carries. For the fourth straight year the team had five or more players on the Pro Bowl squad: running back Anderson, guard Mark Bortz, safety Dave Duerson, center Jay Hilgenberg and linebacker Mike Singletary. In ceremonies at the NFL Hall of Fame in Canton, Ohio, Ditka became the 21st Chicago Bear to be enshrined.

1989: A Year of Contrasts

Opening with four straight wins, over Cincinnati, Minnesota, Detroit and Philadelphia, Coach Mike Ditka's crew seemed on their way to another fine season. But then, beginning with a tough 42-35 loss to the Tampa Bay Buccaneers on the road, the club proceeded to drop ten of its last 12 games.

Included in that stretch was the bitterly disputed 14-13 "Instant Replay Game" loss to the Green Bay Packers, in which television replays showed that the Packers had committed a penalty on the game's winning play. The incident angered Ditka to the point that he had an asterisk placed after the loss in the Bears' press guide.

Highlights of the year included defensive end Richard Dent's 82nd career sack, a new Bear mark, and the performance by kicker Kevin Butler, 24 straight successful field goal attempts (carried over from the previous season) which was a new league record. Despite Butler's kicking prowess, halfback Neal Anderson, with 15 touchdowns and 90 points, led the team in scoring. Anderson also rushed for 1,275 yards on 274 carries, his second year in a row over the thousand-yard figure, and his third straight leading the team. He also pulled down 50 passes for 474 more yards.

Injuries derailed quarterback Jim McMahon, but understudy Mike Tomczak filled in, connecting on 156 of 306 passes for 2,058 yards and 16 touchdowns. Dennis Gentry led the club in kickoff returns for the fourth straight year, this time averaging 23.8 yards per return. Three Bears were named to the Pro Bowl: running back Neal Anderson, center Jay Hilgenberg and linebacker Mike Singletary.

With Coach Mike Ditka cracking the whip, the Bears returned to the winning side of the ledger in 1990, posting an 11-5 mark and regaining the Central Division championship. The Bears had charged off to a 9-1 record, tops in the entire league. In the first round of the playoffs the Bears parlayed three field goals by Kevin Butler and a second quarter touchdown heave from Mike Tomczak to tight end Jim Thornton for a 16-6 win over New Orleans. Tomczak had taken over the quarterbacking duties after Jim Harbaugh had suffered a shoulder separation in the 14th game of the season.

In that first playoff contest, Neal Anderson rushed for 102 yards and Brad Muster added another 71, while Tomczak threw for 166 yards on 12 completions in 25 attempts. The story changed in the second round as the New York Giants shut down the Bear running game, holding Anderson and Muster combined to only 27 yards in 16 attempts. Tomczak threw for 205 yards on 17 completions but was intercepted twice as the Giants rolled, 31-3.

Neal Anderson managed 1,078 yards for the year, his third over a thousand. Jim Harbaugh took over as the team's quarterback, passing for 2,178 yards in his first full season. During the year Harbaugh also completed a team record 173 passes without an interception. Defensive back Mark Carrier's ten interceptions led the league. Carrier was one of six Bears who earned Pro Bowl recognition, along with back Neal Anderson, guard Mark Bortz, defensive end Richard Dent, center Jay Hilgenberg and linebacker Mike Singletary.

A second consecutive 11-5 season in 1991 saw Coach Mike Ditka win his 100th game as the Bear's coach, a 27-13 win over the Green Bay Packers at Soldier Field. The club's record earned them a wild card berth in the playoffs, where they were upset by the Dallas Cowboys 17-13.

Kicker Kevin Butler led the club in scoring for the sixth time, hitting on 32 conversions and 19 field goals for 89 points. Neal Anderson was also a repeat leader, rushing for 747 yards despite missing nearly half of the season with injuries.

Second-year starter Jim Harbaugh launched 478 passes during the season and completed 275 of them for 3,121 yards, all new highs for the Bears. He threw for 15 touchdowns but also suffered 16 interceptions. Wendell Davis was on the receiving end of 61 of those passes, good for 945 yards, the most for a Chicago receiver in 21 years. Defensive end Richard Dent led the team in sacks with 10.5, the seventh time he had paced the club in that department.

Bears in the Pro Bowl were halfback Neal Anderson for the fourth time, safeties Mark Carrier and Shaun Gayle, center Jay Hilgenberg for the seventh time, and middle linebacker Mike Singletary for the ninth time, which tied Walter Payton's team record for total appearances. Stan Jones, a standout Bear tackle of the late 1950s and early 1960s, became Chicago's 22nd addition to the Hall of Fame, the most of any team in the NFL.

Throughout the 1990 and 1991 seasons, the friction that had begun to fester between Bears' president Michael McCaskey and Coach Mike Ditka was growing closer to the breaking point. It was not Ditka's performance or lack of success as a coach so much as it was his general demeanor. His violent temper tantrums against players, fans and the media and the many thoughtless things he was reported to have said were becoming an embarrassment to the club. But whereas it is most difficult to fire a legend such as Ditka when the club is winning, the sad 5-11 performance in 1992 afforded the volatile coach little protection.

In late December, following the team's final game, a 27-14 loss to the Dallas Cowboys, Ditka was given his walking papers. The overall dim performance for the year was difficult to understand, for at the end of the seventh week of the season the Bears, with a 4-3 record, were seemingly in the middle of the title chase. Eight losses in their last nine games, however, sealed the team's—and Ditka's—fate.

Offensively, the club never seemed to be able to put it all together. Key running back Neal Anderson was limited to 582 total yards rushing, his lowest total since his rookie year. Jim Harbaugh had an apparently solid year as the team's quarterback, throwing for 2,486 yards on 202 completions, but lost his starting job late in the season to backup Peter Tom Willis, after throwing an interception on a play in which he ignored Ditka's orders. Ditka's subsequent rage was witnessed by millions on television.

Kicker Kevin Butler, who became the focus of Ditka's wrath after failing on a field goal attempt, hit on 34 straight extra points and 19 of 26 field goals to pace the team in scoring with 91 points. For only the second time since the Pro Bowl was established, there were no Bears named to the classic event. In addition to the losing season and the dismissal of Ditka, Bear fans were also saddened with the retirement of perennial All-Pro linebacker Mike Singletary.

Into The Future

Although he had just led the Bears through a disastrous 5-11 season, their worst performance since the woeful days of the mid-1970s, Coach Mike Ditka's dismissal by club President Michael McCaskey was not greeted with approval in all quarters. Ditka's tirades and volatile personality had grated on many fans and sportswriters; others, however, saw in him the embodiment of what Chicago Bear football was all about.

McCaskey soon silenced his critics—for the time, in any case—with the announcement of Ditka's successor as the team's new mentor, Dave Wannstedt, defensive coordinator of the NFL Champion Dallas Cowboys. The appointment came as a great surprise to many, for Wannstedt had been considered as the frontrunner for the vacant New York Giants coaching job, and Washington Redskin defensive coordinator and former Bear defensive standout Richie Petibon was the top contender for the Chicago job.

Wannstedt, 40, was credited with building the Dallas defense into the best in the NFL. The Cowboys held their opponents to an average of 15.2 points and only 245.8 yards per game. In many ways Wannstedt also had similarities to his predecessor. Both were from Pennsylvania, both played football at the University of Pittsburgh, and both served as assistants with the Dallas Cowboys before taking on the head coaching job with the Bears.

—Jack Pearson

GOLDEN BEARS

It is testimony to the success of the Chicago Bear franchise and the quality of the athletes who have played for the team over the years that 23 Bear players have been elected to the National Football League (NFL) Hall of Fame in Canton, Ohio, more than any other professional football team. Bears' players inducted as charter members of the Hall of Fame were the team's founder-owner-player-coach George Halas and two of the greatest running backs in the history of the game, Harold "Red" Grange and Bronko Nagurski. Here are brief looks at those Golden Bears.

1963 Inductees (Charter Members)

George Halas • Founder, 1920; player, 1920-29; coach, 1920-68; owner, 1920-1983. The guiding light for the Chicago Bears over 63 years, George Halas was unquestionably the most influential figure in the history of the game. He not only founded the Chicago Bear franchise, he was the key figure in the formation of the National Football League as well. At the time of his death in 1983, his 326 wins as coach of the Chicago Bears were the most wins by any coach in NFL history.

During the first decade of the club, Halas also played end on the team, on offense as well as defense. His 98-yard return of a fumble by Jim Thorpe in 1923 stood for 50 years as an NFL record. Although there were no selections of all-league players during the individual years in the 1920s, Halas later was selected as an NFL All-Pro for that decade.

Halas interrupted his own coaching career four times. He first turned over the reins of the club to Ralph Jones, from 1930 through 1932. In 1942, when he left for naval service in World War II, he appointed two of his assistants, Luke Johnson and Hunk Anderson, as co-coaches until his return. Then, in 1956, he again retired himself as the team's head coach and named former Bear star John "Paddy" Driscoll as the new mentor. Coincidentally, in 1933 and 1946, when Halas resumed his coaching duties, the team won world championships. He resumed coaching again in 1958, and within five years had led the team to another NFL title. *The Sporting News,* Associated Press, and United Press International named him Coach of the year in 1963 and 1965.

During the 1940s his teams truly earned the nickname, "Monsters of the Midway," winning four Western Conference crowns and three world championships and putting together four tremendous years in which their regular season and postseason record was a phenomenal 41-6-1. His 1940 team, which annihilated the Washington Redskins 73-0 for the championship, was voted as the greatest professional team of all time by the National Academy of Sports Editors in 1963. Halas retired for the final time from coaching on May 27, 1968, with a career record of 326 wins, 151 losses and 32 ties. He died on October 31, 1983, at age 88.

Harold "Red" Grange • Running back and defensive back 1925 and 1929-34. Grange, the "Galloping Ghost," was one of the most publicized college football players of all time. He joined the Bears on Thanksgiving Day, 1925, only ten days after playing his final college game with the University of Illinois. At a time when pro football crowds often numbered in the hundreds, he attracted wild throngs of 70,000 in the Polo Grounds in New York and 75,000 in the Los Angeles Coliseum during the 1925 "Tour," 18 games in two months primarily set up to showcase Grange's talents. He left the Bears in 1926 to play for New York of the rival American Football League. After New York joined the NFL the next year, Grange suffered a severe knee injury playing against, of all teams, the Bears. After sitting out a year, he rejoined the Bears in 1929 and played halfback on offense and safety on defense until his retirement in 1934.

Bronko Nagurski • Fullback, tackle 1930-37 and 1943. Called the most powerful running back of his time, big Bronko was as valuable on defense as he was on offense. He joined the Bears in 1930 after an All-American career at the University of Minnesota. He retired in 1937, but returned for a single year of play in 1943 when the Bears were shorthanded due to wartime depletions.

1964 Inductees

Ed Healey • Tackle 1922-27. Picked up by Coach Halas from Rock Island in 1921 in exchange for $100 in gate receipts, Healey was called the most versatile tackle of all time by Halas. After his retirement he served as the first President of the Chicago Bears Alumni Association.

Roy "Link" Lyman • Tackle 1926-34. Credited with pioneering such defensive moves as shifting, slanting and stunting, Lyman played for two championship teams at Canton and another at Cleveland before joining the Bears and picking up a third title with Chicago in 1933.

George Trafton • Center 1920-31. A perennial All-NFL choice at center, Trafton had the reputation of being a tough, mean player, exactly the kind of player that Halas was always looking for. In one game in 1920 against Rock Island, he knocked four players out of the game in the first 12 minutes of play.

1965 Inductees

John "Paddy" Driscoll • Running back 1920 and 1926-29; coach 1956-57. Called the NFL's first "franchise" player, Driscoll was a triple threat to score as a running back, receiver and drop kicker. He was also a punter. His 50-yard field goal as a Chicago Cardinal in 1925 was the NFL record for many years. He served as the club's head coach in 1956 and 1957, compiling a 14-10-1 record.

Danny Fortmann • Guard 1936-49. A ninth-round pick in the NFL's first college draft in 1936, Fortmann became a starter in his rookie year and, at age 20, was the youngest starter in the league. A deadly tackler on defense, he served as the signal caller for the offensive line. He earned All-NFL honors from 1938 through 1943. During his eight years with the Bears the team finished first five times, second twice, and third once.

Sid Luckman • Quarterback 1939-50. A second-round pick in 1939, Luckman quickly developed into one of the finest quarterbacks in the history of pro football. He still holds the Bears' all-time records for attempted passes, 1,744, completions, 9.04, yards gained, 14,686, touchdowns, 137, and average yards per pass attempt, 8.42. He is also the Bears' record holder in passing efficiency for a single season with a rating of 107.8 in 1943.

1966 Inductees

George McAfee • Running back, defensive back 1940-50. The Duke All-American quickly gave the Bears evidence of his value, returning a kickoff 93 yards for a touchdown in his first game; his career punt return average of 12.8 yards per return is still an NFL record. He scored a total of 234 points on 22 rushing, 11 receiving and six return touchdowns. On defense he still ranks fifth in Bear total interceptions with 25.

Clyde "Bulldog" Turner • Center and linebacker 1940-50. The Bears' first-round pick in 1940 from Hardin-Simmons, Turner was a flawless snapper and an excellent blocker who earned All-NFL honors six times. He also could play guard or tackle, if needed, and even running back, scoring on a 40-yard touchdown run in 1944. On defense he led the league with eight interceptions in 1942 and ran back an interception 97 yards for a touchdown in 1947.

1967 Inductee

Joe Stydahar • Tackle 1936-46. Stydahar was the first player ever drafted by the Bears. He became an All-NFL tackle in his second year and won that honor for four straight years. His career was interrupted in 1943 and 1944 by service in World War II.

1971 Inductee

Bill Hewitt • End 1932-36. A four time All-NFL end, Hewitt was the last NFL starter to play without a helmet. He caught 101 passes for 1,606 yards and 25 touchdowns.

1974 Inductee

Bill George • Linebacker 1952-65. Voted into the Pro Bowl and on the All-NFL Team for eight straight years, George played a record-tying 14 years for the Bears. He joined the team in 1952 as a middle guard and is credited with creating the middle linebacker position when he dropped back off the line in the 1954 season. During his career he had 18 interceptions.

1975 Inductee

George Connor • Tackle, linebacker 1948-55. The first of the big but mobile outside linebackers, Connor won All-NFL honors five times. In 1951 and 1952, when few NFL players were still playing on both offense and defense, he won All-NFL plaudits on both. Injuries forced his early retirement.

1977 Inductee

Gale Sayers • Running back 1965-71. Among Sayers' many awards and achievements in an all-too brief career was being named to the NFL Hall of Fame at only 34 years of age, the youngest player ever elected. Sayers burst on the pro football scene like a rocket in 1965, amassing 2,272 net yards rushing, receiving and returning kicks as well as scoring an NFL rookie record 22 touchdowns. Included in that spree were six touchdowns against the San Francisco 49ers in a 61-20 Bear win. A fourth-round pick in the 1965 draft, Sayers was selected NFL Rookie of the Year in a close vote over teammate Dick Butkus. He was named to five Pro Bowls and was the offensive MVP in three of them. He led the league in rushing in 1966 and 1969 and totalled twenty 100-yard rushing games for his career. A second major knee injury in 1970 put an end to his brilliant career. He is third on the all-time Bear rushing list and averaged five yards a carry on his way to setting 23 team records.

1979 Inductee

Dick Butkus • Middle linebacker 1965-73. Described as the greatest—and meanest—linebacker of all time, Butkus was a heralded All-American out of the University of Illinois when drafted by Coach George Halas in 1965. He immediately took charge of the Bear defense, beating out the club's incumbent middle linebacker and Hall of Famer Bill George in his rookie year. Voted into the Pro Bowl in his second year, he repeated in every one of his remaining years in the league. He is first on the Bears' all-time list, and second in the NFL, in fumble recoveries with 25 and is second all-time on the Bears in causing turnovers, with 47.

1981 Inductee

George Blanda • Quarterback, kicker 1949-58. The NFL's all-time leader in seasons played, 26, Blanda totaled 340 games, scored 2,002 points and passed for 26,920 yards. Blanda holds Bears' records in two categories, having scored in 63 consecutive games and having made 156 consecutive extra points, and he is fourth in club history in scoring with 501 points. He retired in 1959 but returned to play seven more years with Houston and nine more with Oakland. He was voted Male Athlete of the Year in 1970. When he retired for good he was one month short of his 49th birthday.

1982 Inductees

Doug Atkins • Defensive End 1955-66. A three-time All-NFL Pick and an eight-time Pro Bowler, Atkins was acquired in a trade with the Cleveland Browns. He was named the outstanding lineman in the 1959 Pro Bowl and anchored the Bear defensive line for more than a decade.

George Musso • Tackle, guard, defensive tackle 1933-44. Musso was the first player to win All-NFL honors at two different positions, as a tackle in 1935 and as a guard in 1937. He was signed by Coach George Halas for only $90 a game and five dollars in expenses in 1933. He was elected team captain in his fourth season and kept the title for the rest of his career.

1988 Inductee

Mike Ditka • Tight end 1961-66, coach 1982-92. Big Mike's outstanding career as a Chicago Bear includes six years as a player, from 1961 through 1966, and 11 more as the team's Head Coach, from 1982 through 1992. Ditka was pro football's first prototype tight end. He played in five Pro Bowls and on two World Championship teams, the Bears in 1963 and Dallas in 1971. He caught 56 passes in his first year en route to winning Rookie of the Year honors. He still holds a number of Bear records, including the most consecutive games with a reception, 49, most receptions by a rookie, 56, and most touchdown receptions by a rookie, 12. During his playing career with the Bears he pulled down 316 passes, third on the all-time Bear list, good for 4,503 yards and 34 touchdowns. Ditka was the first tight end to be enshrined in the Hall of Fame and is only the second man in pro football history to be on a winning team in the Super Bowl as a player, assistant coach (with Dallas) and head coach. He is among an elite group of former NFL players who went on to become successful head coaches.

When he joined the Bears prior to the 1982 season, the club had enjoyed only two winning seasons in the previous 14 years. He guided the team to three Central Division titles and a Super Bowl championship. The 50 regular season wins he led the team to from 1984 through 1987 were the most ever won over a four-year period in the history of pro football. Selected as Coach of the Year in both 1985 and 1988, his 11-year record included 112 wins and 68 losses for a .622 winning percentage. He is the only coach in Bear history to lead his team to five postseason appearances.

1991 Inductee

Stan Jones • Tackle, guard 1954-65. Although he began his career at tackle, he switched to guard at the end of his first season and became an eight-time Pro Bowler. Jones played offense and defense in 1962 before switching solely to defense in 1963, the year the club won the championship. One of the first NFL players to concentrate on weightlifting, he was always in top condition and missed only two games in 11 seasons.

1993 Inductee

Walter Payton • Running back 1975-87. The leading ground gainer in NFL history, Payton fought for a total of 16,726 yards on 3,838 carries, all league highs, and scored 110 touchdowns, also an NFL record. He rushed for more than a thousand yards ten times. He was also an excellent receiver, catching 482 passes for 4,538 yards and in fact was the Bears' leading pass receiver six times. He led the team in rushing for 12 consecutive years, doubling Rick Casares' old mark of six straight.

Payton was voted into a record nine Pro Bowls, holds 27 Bear records and eight NFL marks. Payton excelled in all areas of the offense, and led the league in kickoff returns in 1975 with a 31.7 yards per return average. In the playoffs he rushed for 632 yards and caught 22 passes for 178 more. His total of 750 points was the most for the Bears until topped by Kevin Butler during the 1992 campaign. His total of 16,726 yards rushing is more than the total of any other three backs in Bear history, and his 110 touchdowns more than twice that attained by any other Bear.

DETROIT LIONS

The history of the Detroit Lions begins in 1930 at Portsmouth, Ohio, where a National Football League team called the Spartans finished far down in the standings. A year later, when quarterback Earl (Dutch) Clark arrived, the fortunes of the Spartans improved dramatically, and the team fought it out for the NFL championship (never quite getting it) with the Chicago Bears and Green Bay Packers in 1931, 1932, and 1933. In 1934 Detroit radio executive George A. Richards bought the franchise for $8,000 and moved it to Detroit, renaming the team the Lions.

The Detroit Lions played their first NFL game at the University of Detroit Stadium on September 23, 1934, beating the New York Giants 9-0 before 12,000 fans. Coached by George (Potsy) Clark and quarterbacked by Dutch Clark, the Lions, one of six teams in the NFL's Western Division, finished second in 1934 to the undefeated Chicago Bears. A year later they won the division title and went on to defeat the New York Giants for the NFL championship. The Lions were a winning team throughout the 1930s but fell on hard times in the 1940s, going 0-11-0 in 1942 and 1-10-0 in 1946, despite the presence of individual stars such as center/linebacker Alex Wojciechowicz.

For Lions fans there was no finer decade than the 1950s. Detroit won four division titles and three NFL championships between 1952 and 1957. Coached by Raymond (Buddy) Parker, the Lions posted a 28-7-1 record from 1952 through 1954, winning back-to-back NFL crowns the first two of those years. Their quarterback was future Pro Football Hall of Famer Bobby Layne. Other great Lions of the 1950s—also bound for the Hall of Fame—were halfback Doak Walker, linebacker Joe Schmidt, defensive back Jack Christiansen, and defensive back and punter Yale Lary.

There were no encores after coach George Wilson's successful 1957 season. In 1967 Joe Schmidt took over as head coach, but the Lions sat out all postseason action until 1970, when a second-place finish earned them a wild-card shot. Another drought followed.

The Lions moved into their new, air-supported, 80,000-seat domed stadium, the Silverdome, in Pontiac, Michigan, for the 1975 season. They responded by winning as many games as they lost (7-7-0). But not until 1980 and 1981 were they in contention for a playoff berth. After losing out both times, they qualified in strike-shortened 1982 and then won the NFL Central Division title in 1983. Their Super Bowl hopes were dashed by a 24-23 defeat at the hands of the San Francisco 49ers in the divisional playoff game.

The rest of the 1980s saw the Lions struggle mainly to stay out of the Central Division cellar. But in 1991, under head coach Wayne Fontes, they turned in a solid 12-4-0 season, captured the Central Division title, and won their divisional playoff game, but missed a trip to the Super Bowl by losing, 41-10, to the eventual world champion Washington Redskins. In 1992 they plummeted to 5-11-0 and shared the NFL Central basement with the Chicago Bears.

From Portsmouth to the Motor City

For the 1930 season a strong, independent pro football team in Portsmouth, Ohio, joined the 11-team NFL. The Portsmouth Spartans, coached by Hall (Tubby) Griffen, finished at 5-6-3, far down in the standings, and hired a new head coach. He was George (Potsy) Clark, who quickly brought in an array of new players, the most outstanding of whom was quarterback Earl (Dutch) Clark, a tricky open-field runner, stellar safety, and talented dropkicker from Colorado College.

In addition to the versatile Dutch Clark, coach Potsy Clark obtained rookie back Glenn Presnell from the University of Nebraska and linemen Maury Bodenger, George Christensen, Gover (Ox) Emerson, and Bill McKalip (all future Lions stars). Thus strengthened, the Spartans breezed through an 11-3-0 season, after starting with eight straight wins, finishing second behind the mighty Green Bay Packers.

Portsmouth claimed third place in the NFL in 1932 and second place in the newly created Western Division of the league in 1933. The official all-NFL team honored two Portsmouth players: quarterback Dutch Clark and back Roy (Father) Lumpkin. In 1933 the Spartans lost two key games to the Chicago Bears, the first one on a Bronko Nagurski touchdown late in the fourth quarter, moments after Portsmouth's Ernie Cadell had gone over to give the Spartans a 14-10 lead.

But a more serious problem than losses to the Bears faced the team in the Depression year of 1933. A series of missed paydays signaled the difficulty. The Portsmouth franchise was struggling financially. When help came, it was not from anyone in that small Ohio River city, the hometown of Branch Rickey and Roy Rogers, but from a man in the bustling industrial city of Detroit.

The Lions Roar

George A. Richards, a Detroit radio executive, purchased the Portsmouth Spartans franchise on June 30, 1934. He moved the team to Detroit, at that time the fourth largest city in the nation, renamed it the Lions, and retained Potsy Clark as head coach. Perhaps no team in the history of pro sports has made a more impressive debut. Between September 9, 1934—the Lions' first regular-season game—and October 28, Potsy Clark's Detroit team blanked the New York Giants, 9-0; the Chicago Cardinals, 6-0; the Green Bay Packers, 3-0; the Philadelphia Eagles, 10-0; the Boston Redskins, 24-0; the Brooklyn Dodgers, 28-0; and the Cincinnati Reds, 38-0.

When a team finally scored against them (the Pittsburgh Pirates on November 4), the damage was slight, for the Lions, although allowing a touchdown, crushed the Pirates in that game, 40-7. It might have seemed that Detroit was on its way to the Western Division title. Not so. While the Lions were pulverizing the opposition, so were

TEAM INFORMATION AT A GLANCE

Date of first game: September 23, 1934

Home stadium: Pontiac Silverdome
1200 Featherstone Road
Pontiac, MI 48342
Phone: (313) 335-4131
Seating capacity: 80,500

Team colors: Honolulu blue and silver
Team nickname: Lions, 1934—
Team logo on helmet: Base color silver, with solid blue profile of rampant lion outlined in white

Franchise record*	Won	Lost	Tie
NFL (1934-1992)	370	398	25

* Including playoffs

Super Bowl appearances: (0)
National Football League championships (4): 1935, 1952, 1953, 1957
National/Western Conference championships (5): 1935**, 1952, 1953, 1954, 1957
Central Division championships (3): 1983, 1991, 1993
League/Conference/Division last-place finishes (7): 1942, 1946, 1947, 1948, 1955, 1968, 1979

**Called Western Division

George Halas's Chicago Bears—and just as decisively. The Bears went 13-0-0. The Lions, by contrast, were upset by the Green Bay Packers, 3-0, on November 25, and then dropped two straight games to the Bears, 19-16 and 10-7, finishing the season in second place at 10-3-0.

This first Lions team was loaded with talent. In addition to the stellar backs—Dutch Clark, Ernie Caddel, Glenn Presnell, Father Lumpkin, Ace Gutowsky—the Lions were well served by ends Bill McKalip and Harry Ebding, guards Maury Bodenger and Ox Emerson, and tackle George Christensen. If the Bears and the always-tough Packers could be beaten, Potsy Clark had the team to do it. And in 1935, the Lions' second year in the NFL, they did it. Their powerful ground attack was led by veteran rushers, the best in the league, plus rookie Bill Shepherd from the University of Maryland. Detroit's 7-3-2 record was good for the divisional title and a spot in the championship game against the NFL East's New York Giants. Steve Owen's Giants, a very solid team, were no match for the Lions, who won the game, 26-7, and with it the 1935 NFL crown.

Although the Lions had winning seasons from 1936 through 1939, they were always bested in the divisional standings by the Chicago Bears, the Green Bay Packers, or both. In 1938 the Lions moved into a new home, Briggs Stadium (shared with the city's baseball franchise, the Tigers), and stayed in contention with the Packers until the final game of the season. They finished at 7-4-0. Rookies Lloyd Cardwell, a halfback from the University of Nebraska, and Alex Wojciechowicz, a center from Fordham, attracted notice and seemed to promise hope for the future.

But veteran quarterback Dutch Clark, who held the dual role of star player and head coach in 1937-38, was sidelined with a bad ankle. In 1939 he left to become head coach at Cleveland. That year marked the end of an era, for Ernie Caddel retired, Ace Gutowsky was sold to the Dodgers, and George Christensen went to Brooklyn as an assistant coach.

In 1940 Fred Mandel of Chicago bought the club, now mediocre except for rookie back Byron (Whizzer) White, who put in two fine seasons for the Lions, 1940-41, before leaving for Yale Law School and, eventually, the U.S. Supreme Court. Detroit broke even in 1940, with a 5-5-1 record, fell to 4-6-1 in 1941, and then in wartime 1942 the Lions, with no attack and no defense, plunged to 0-11-0.

Still, Mandel remained cheerful. Head coach Charles (Gus) Dorais took over in 1943, and by 1944 he had engineered a turnaround. The Lions climbed to 6-3-1 in 1944 and 7-3-0 in 1945, both marks good for second place. One of the standout players in 1943-44 was Frank Sinkwich, a versatile back from the University of Georgia and winner of the Heisman Trophy in 1942. Sinkwich entered the military in 1945 and suffered a career-ending injury (although he played briefly for the New York Yankees of the AAFC in 1946).

The end of World War II saw no resurgence of the Lions. Detroit, still under Gus Dorais, beat the Pittsburgh Steelers in 1946—and no one else. At 1-10-0 they could only improve, which they did in 1947, going 3-9-0. The big news of 1947 was the arrival of halfback Bill Dudley from the University of Virginia. Future Hall of Famer Dudley wasted no time in making his presence felt, leading the Lions in scoring (66 points on 11 touchdowns), punt returns (averaging 16.5 yards), and kickoff returns (averaging 23.9 yards.) He also intercepted five passes, good for 104 yards and one touchdown.

In 1948 the Lions got new ownership—a syndicate headed by Detroit businessman Edwin J. Anderson—and a new coach, aging Alvin (Bo) McMillan, whose only experience had been at the college level. But for the third year in a row the Lions, at 2-10-0, brought up the rear in the NFL's Western Division. Rookie quarterback Fred Enke and halfback/end Cloyce Box provided a ray of hope on offense, but the defense was nonexistent, giving up 407 points to the Lions' 200. With a defense that poor, changes were inevitable, and McMillan began acquiring players with defensive skills, including middle guard Les Bingaman and a couple of backs with a flair for interception, Don Doll and J. Robert (Jim) Smith. The 1949 Lions finished one step out of the cellar, 4-8-0.

Layne, Walker, and Victory

1950 is a key year in the history of the Detroit Lions: Their days as a punching bag were over. Although Bill Dudley had departed for the Washington Redskins, the Lions added a glittering group of newcomers to the team. Heading the list were star quarterback Bobby Layne, purchased from the New York Bulldogs, and versatile halfback Doak Walker, a rookie from Southern Methodist University. Also new and notable were end Leon Hart from Notre Dame (like Walker, a Heisman Trophy winner) and tackle Thurman McGraw from Colorado A&M.

The 1950 Lions finished fourth, 6-6-0, in the new seven-team National Conference of the NFL, an arrangement created to absorb three teams from the defunct AAFC. Bo McMillan, whose coaching record for the Lions from 1948 through 1950 read 12-24-0, was instrumental in building a well-balanced, competitive team from the debris he had inherited. His successor in 1951, Raymond (Buddy) Parker, would be the fortunate beneficiary.

Attendance soared at Briggs Stadium in 1951

as the new-look Lions fought it out with the Los Angeles Rams and San Francisco 49ers for the top rung of the National Conference ladder. They lost out by dropping a 21-17 contest to the 49ers on the last Sunday of the regular season.

But the pieces were now all in place; the team featured not only Bobby Layne, Doak Walker, Leon Hart, and Thurman McGraw, but two other stars from the Class of 1950 as well—rushing ace Bob Hoernschemeyer in the backfield and Lou Creekmur on the offensive line.

Bobby Layne

The 1952 Lions still had to contend with the explosive L.A. Rams, who matched the equally impressive Lions in the standings with a 9-3-0 record. They met in Los Angeles in late December for a playoff game to determine the conference championship. The Lions prevailed, 31-21, and advanced to the NFL title game against the Cleveland Browns.

These Browns, with Otto Graham at quarterback, were the dynastic team in the American Conference in the early 1950s. Cleveland was off a bit in 1952, though, and remained off in the title game. The Lions marched to a 17-7 victory on a quarterback sneak by Bobby Layne, a 67-yard run by Doak Walker, and a field goal by Pat Harder.

In 1953 Detroit stood all alone at the top of the Western Conference (renamed after three years of being called the National Conference) with a record of 10-2-0. The veterans performed well. Second-year offensive guard Dick Stanfel was named the team's MVP, and several talented rookies put in impressive seasons, among them linebacker Joe Schmidt (from Pitt), halfback Gene Gedman (Indiana) and offensive linemen Charley Ane (USC), Harley Sewell (Texas), and Ollie Spencer (Kansas).

The Lions faced the Cleveland Browns once again in the playoff game for the NFL championship. In a down-to-the-wire contest, Bobby Layne hit Pat Doran with a long pass in the end zone to tie the score at 16. Doak Walker kicked for the extra point to give the Lions a 17-16 lead. With just two minutes left, Cleveland quarterback Otto Graham (having one of his worst games ever) had his first pass intercepted, and the Detroit Lions were champions for the second year running.

There were no surprises in 1954—at least not during the regular season. The Lions won the Eastern Conference title again, 9-2-1, while the Cleveland Browns, after a shaky start, also won the divisional title.

Bobby Layne, who received as much publicity for his late-night revels as for his on-field play, never let the partying interfere with his passing or play calling. Doak Walker, with five touchdowns, 11 field goals, and 43 extra points, led the team in scoring. On defense Les Bingaman, a 320-pound, seven-year veteran, diagnosed plays brilliantly and brought down opposing ball carriers with crunching effectiveness.

In the last game of the regular season the Lions subdued the Browns, 14-10, and approached the championship game with high hopes of taking their third straight NFL crown. It was not to be. On December 26 the Browns destroyed the Lions, 56-10. Doak Walker's 36-yard field goal in the first quarter and Lew Carpenter's 52-yard run to set up a touchdown in the second quarter were the bright spots in a dismal day for Detroit.

The unhappy championship game of 1954 proved a portent, for in 1955 the Lions plunged from the heights to the depths. There were two main reasons: One was that Bobby Layne had injured his throwing arm in a mishap with a horse in the off-season; another was that defensive stalwart Les Bingaman and ace receiver Cloyce Box had both retired. Layne missed no playing time, but the zip was gone, and the Lions lost their first six games, then split the last six for a 3-9-0 record.

Despite a few favorable signs, such as the arrival of Heisman Trophy-winning halfback Howard (Hopalong) Cassady, a pessimist might have predicted the end of a dynasty. But, in fact, 1955 was just a single, surprising flop in the Detroit Lions' success story from 1952 through 1957. The Lions nearly bounded back to the top in 1956. With one game to play, they led the Chicago Bears by half a game. And that last game was against Chicago, a team the Lions had easily beaten, 42-10, a couple of weeks earlier.

But this time disaster struck—or rather the Bears' defensive end Ed Meadows struck. He slammed into Bobby Layne, blindsiding him, and the Lions' quarterback was out with a concussion for the rest of the game. The Bears won, 38-21, nudging the Lions into second place.

The biggest shock of the 1957 season occurred before the Lions had even played their first pre-season game. Head coach Buddy Parker, speaking at a Detroit Boosters' banquet, complained that the team looked terrible and said he wanted no part of it, "so I'm leaving Detroit. As a matter of fact, I'm leaving tonight." And he did. His assistant, George Wilson, stepped in to try to pump some life into the drowsy Lions. He succeeded. Detroit hung in there throughout the season against San Francisco and Baltimore, finally emerging in an 8-4-0 dead heat with the 49ers. Needing a playoff win to qualify for yet another championship shot at the Cleveland Browns, the Lions prospects seemed iffy.

Bobby Layne was out with a broken leg, which at the end of the season left the quarterbacking to former Green Bay Packer Tobin Rote. The ex-Packer filled in admirably. Among those starring on defense during the season were linebacker Joe Schmidt, tackles Lou Creekmur and Charley Ane, and defensive backs Jack Christiansen, Yale Lary, and Jim David.

In the 1957 season the Lions had won one game and lost one against San Francisco. In the Western Conference playoff, they won another one, squeaking by, 31-27. The Lions—a far better team than Buddy Parker had anticipated when he quit—prepared to meet the Cleveland Browns on December 29 for the NFL title.

No one watching the Lions-Browns game that day would have predicted that the Detroit dynasty was ending. With Bobby Layne still sidelined, Tobin Rote led the team to a stunning 59-14 rout of the Browns. Although the Browns, like the Lions, were in their last year of 1950s dominance, the arrival that year of superstar running back Jim Brown masked the fact that the great days of the Browns were over.

Second Best—At Best

George Wilson would remain as head coach of the Lions through 1964, but neither he nor any succeeding coach could return Detroit to the top spot. The decline looked bad at first—fifth place in the Western Conference in 1958 and 1959. After two games in 1958 the Lions traded the near-legendary Bobby Layne to the Pittsburgh Steelers, leaving Tobin Rote as their starting quarterback.

That might have worked out, but injuries dogged the team, and age was creeping up on the other veteran stars. A promising rookie defensive tackle, Alex Karras, joined the team in 1958, and the next year Nick Pietrosante, a fine running back from Notre Dame, came on board. Both would play their part as the 1960 Lions snapped

HISTORY

Lions 59, Browns 14

A high point in Detroit Lions' history—perhaps *the* high point—occurred on December 29, 1957, at Briggs Stadium, Detroit. The Lions, facing their perennial 1950s rivals, the Cleveland Browns, routed the Browns, 59-14, to win the NFL championship. This was a particularly sweet victory, because the last time the two teams had met to decide the issue, in 1954, Cleveland had overwhelmed the Lions, 56-10. In fact, even being in the championship game in 1957 was a bit surprising. Head coach Buddy Parker had quit in disgust before the season started, saying the Lions were a team going nowhere. George Wilson, his assistant, inherited the top job and guided Detroit to victory.

Bobby Layne, the Lions' regular quarterback, had suffered a broken ankle four weeks earlier, and backup quarterback Tobin Rote was calling the plays. Rote, an ex-Packer, was no novice. He had led the team to three victories at the end of the regular season and was comfortable in the position—comfortable enough to change his head coach's orders on a key play. With the Lions leading 17-7, Rote completed a series of passes that moved the ball to the Browns' 26-yard line.

There the attack stalled, fourth down and 11 yards to go. Coach Wilson sent in kicker Jim Martin. "The play came off the bench," said Rote later in the Lions' dressing room, "and the play was to try for a field goal. Some of the fellows thought we ought to 'go for broke,' so I changed the play in the huddle." In a play the Lions had been working on but had never used, Rote took the snap and pretended to hold the ball for Martin. Then he stood up, rolled out to his right, and fired a perfect pass to rookie end Steve Junker, who was all alone on the five-yard line. Junker crossed the goal line untouched. The extra point made the score 24-7 in favor of the Lions. By halftime the score was 31-7, and the second half went about the same way.

The Lions had come a long way from their pre-season lethargy, when then head coach Buddy Parker complained, "I never have seen a team in training with less 'go' than the 1957 Lions." After the championship win, George Wilson praised the Lions' team spirit and admitted they had gotten some good breaks in the game. Coach Paul Brown made no excuses for his battered Clevelanders. He said, "The Lions were a great team today."

back into contention.

There were new faces aplenty in 1960 (the first year of the new American Football League), including rookie tackle Roger Brown and rookie end Gail Cogdill. From the Chicago Cardinals came two key players, linebacker Carl Brettschneider and defensive back and future Hall of Famer Dick (Night Train) Lane. From the Cleveland Browns came quarterback Jim Ninowski. The Lions won their last four games to nail down second place in the NFL West, behind Green Bay.

They repeated that finish in 1961 and 1962, both times behind Vince Lombardi's perennially powerful Packers. In 1961 the Lions' 8-5-1 record had a curious twist. Every one of the team's five losses occurred at home, in the supposedly friendly confines of Briggs Stadium, while on the road the Lions were unbeatable.

Except for a 49-0 humiliation at the hands of the San Francisco 49ers, the Lions' defense, featuring Roger Brown, Alex Karras, Yale Lary, Night Train Lane, and Joe Schmidt, was among the best in the NFL. In 1963, when Detroit posted a sparkling 11-3-0 record, the Lions scored 315 points to their opponents' 178. But the Packers, at the peak of their power under Lombardi, went 13-1-0, scoring 415 points to their opponents' 148 and capturing the Western Conference title.

In 1963 Commissioner Pete Rozelle suspended Detroit tackle Alex Karras and Green Bay halfback Paul Hornung for betting on NFL games. The loss of Karras hurt the Lions' defense, as did a succession of injuries, and the team slipped to 5-8-1. Earl Morrall did a first-rate job at quarterback, but the offense as a whole lacked punch. The situation improved marginally in 1964, despite an aging defense, a so-so offense, and frequent injuries. Detroit chalked up a winning record, 7-5-1, on the strength of a 31-14 victory over the Colts and a 24-7 win over the 49ers in the last two games of the season.

William Clay Ford, a grandson of auto pioneer Henry Ford, purchased the Lions in November 1963 for $4.5 million. By 1965 he showed his annoyance with the team's performance by firing all of George Wilson's assistant coaches. Wilson pondered the matter briefly, then submitted his own resignation.

Dick "Night Train" Lane

Harry Gilmer, the new head coach, decided to go with Milt Plum as his starting quarterback. Earl Morrall was dealt to the New York Giants, for whom he starred. The Lions slid to 6-7-1 in 1965 and 4-9-1 in 1966. Plum, injured in mid-season 1966, gave way to Karl Sweetan, who had played semipro ball the year before. Sweetan began hitting wide receiver Pat Studstill with some regularity. Studstill, a one-season wonder, gathered in 67 passes in 1966, good for 1,266 yards and the NFL lead in that category. Another player who made good copy was soccer-style place-kicker Garo Yepremian, a native of Cyprus, who kicked four field goals in one quarter (six in the game) against the Minnesota Vikings in November.

But a 4-9-1 record was not what owner Ford had in mind, and head coach Harry Gilmer departed. His replacement was Joe Schmidt, the great linebacker for the Lions in the 1950s and early 1960s. Schmidt, having served as linebacker coach for the team after retiring as a player, now took over as the man in charge.

Still Not King of the Jungle

The 1967 reorganization of the Eastern and Western Conferences into two four-team divisions each, meant that a team could finish no worse than fourth. The 1967 Lions, assigned to the Central Division of the Western Conference, finished third, winning five games, losing seven, and tying two.

The Lions' two most valuable players that season were both rookies. Mel Farr, a running back from UCLA, rushed for 860 yards on 206 carries. Lem Barney, a defensive back from Jackson State, intercepted 10 passes to tie for the NFL lead. Farr and Barney would soon help to spark a Lions' mini-revival under Joe Schmidt, but not before the team fell to the cellar in 1968.

More rookies, more rebuilding, more injuries—and the 1968 Lions faded after a couple of decisive wins early in the season. After losing the opener, a 59-13 drubbing by the Dallas Cowboys, Detroit came back to smother the Bears, 42-0, in the next game and then sneak past the Packers, 23-17, in game three. But that was it. Injuries and ragged play set in.

Nevertheless, the Lions had some fine young players, including a sorely needed new quarterback, Bill Munson, acquired from the Los Angeles Rams, where he had been playing intermittently in the shadow of Roman Gabriel. The Lions also added wide receiver Earl McCulloch and tight end Charlie Sanders to gather in Munson's passes.

Sportswriters saw the nucleus of a good team here, and 1969 proved them right. Although the Lions were no match for the newly dynastic Minnesota Vikings under head coach Bud Grant, they were better than anyone else in their division, romping through a 9-4-1 season to take second place.

The 1970 season was a landmark of sorts for Detroit in that it saw the Lions' only playoff action between 1957 and 1983. Joe Schmidt's team came through with solid performances from established veterans, such as tackle Alex Karras, linebackers Mike Lucci, Paul Naumoff, and Wayne Walker, and cornerbacks Lem Barney and Dick LeBeau. The Lions blanked the Giants, 24-0, the Cardinals, 20-0, and the Rams, 28-0, on their way to a 9-4-1 record. This was not good enough to top the Vikings (12-2-0) but it did earn the Lions a wild-card playoff opportunity. They failed to advance beyond the first game, however, as the Dallas Cowboys beat them by the odd (for football) score of 5-0.

Starting with the 1970 season the Lions settled into second place in the NFC Central Division, finishing behind the Vikings in 1970, 1971, 1972, 1974, and 1975, and behind the Packers in 1973. None of these were especially poor years for the Lions, but they were disappointing ones.

A tragic event occurred on October 24, 1971, in a home game against the Bears, when Detroit wide receiver Chuck Hughes collapsed and died of a heart attack on the field. Another tragedy befell the Lions after Joe Schmidt resigned in

Joe Schmidt

1973. The Lions named Don McCafferty their new head coach, but after one full season (6-7-1), McCafferty died of a heart attack prior to the 1974 season. Rick Forzano then took the helm for a couple of break-even seasons, including 1975, the Lions' first season in their glittering new home, the Pontiac Silverdome.

Team leaders in the early 1970s included defensive back Lem Barney (headed for the Pro Football Hall of Fame), center Ed Flanagan, running backs Dexter Bussey and Steve Owens (the Lions' first 1,000-yard rusher—1,035 yards in 1971), running back Altie Taylor, tight end Charlie Sanders, and the alternating quarterbacks, Greg Landry and Bill Munson.

In 1976 the Lions slipped to third place in the NFC Central Division, behind the Vikings and Bears, and stayed there in 1977 when the

AP/Wide World Photos

Billy Sims (20)

expansion Tampa Bay Buccaneers became the fifth team in the division. Lions' head coach Rick Forzano gave way to Tommy Hudspeth after four games in 1976, and Hudspeth left after a 6-8-0 season in 1977.

Monte Clark assumed the head coaching position in 1978, and his first two seasons were as forgettable as any others for Lions' fans in the 1970s. Indeed, 1979 was even more forgettable, because, after winning seven games in 1978, Detroit posted a grim 2-14-0 mark in Clark's sophomore season. Incredibly, the Lions had been pre-season favorites to win the Central Division title. Quarterback Gary Danielson's pre-season knee injury hurt their chances considerably, and the season soon unraveled.

The Lions' poor showing did have an upside, though; it gave them first pick in the 1980 college draft. And they used it wisely, choosing 1978 Heisman Trophy winner Billy Sims, a brilliant running back from the University of Oklahoma.

Billy Sims, Briefly

With Billy Sims in the backfield and Gary Danielson healthy, the Lions had a clear shot at first place in the Central Division. They blew it. After winning their first four games with ease, they ran into a buzz saw in Atlanta, losing 43-28, then lost two of their next three games. Although Detroit's 9-7-0 mark at the end was the same as the Minnesota's, the Vikings took the title on the basis of a better conference record. Nor did the Lions qualify for a wild-card shot at Super Bowl XV. Billy Sims, in his first year in the NFL, rushed for 1,303 yards and a league-leading 13 touchdowns.

The Lions' prospects in 1981 were every bit as bright as they had been the year before. But Gary Danielson hurt his wrist, and backup quarterback Jeff Komlo failed to engineer victories. Coach Monte Clark turned in desperation to benchwarmer Eric Hipple, who came through handsomely. With Billy Sims rushing for 1,437 yards and Hipple passing for 2,358 yards, the Lions managed to salvage an 8-8-0 season—and barely miss the NFC Central title on a 20-17 loss to Tampa Bay in the Silverdome on the last day of the regular season. The strike-shortened 1982 season ended with the Lions, at 4-5-0, losing to the Washington Redskins, 31-7, in the first round of the elaborate 16-team postseason Super Bowl Tournament.

And then, after several years of mediocrity, the Lions finally put together a respectable season. 1983 was no piece of cake for Detroit, though. After their first four games the Lions found themselves staring at a 1-4-0 record and the possibility of early elimination. From that point on, they were very tough to beat, rolling over Green Bay, 38-14, in the turnaround game. The Lions got outstanding performances from defensive end William Gay, right tackle Doug English, and linebackers Ken Fantetti and Roosevelt Barnes—not to mention Billy Sims.

At season's end the Lions' 9-7-0 record barely nosed out three other teams, the Packers, Bears, and Vikings, all at 8-8-0. Still, it was enough. Detroit would face the San Francisco 49ers in a divisional playoff game, their first since 1970. But high hopes for the playoffs came to dust. In a close battle, the Lions succumbed, 24-23.

1984 was bad news from beginning to end. The Lions lost early and often, but never by more than four points until the Denver Broncos belted them, 28-7, in game six. By then they were 1-5-0, and things improved very little as the season wore on. The 4-11-1 next-to-last-place finish was bad enough, but even worse was a knee injury to Billy Sims in an October 21 win over the Vikings. The injury ended not just the season for Sims but, as it turned out, cut short his career as well.

In a mere five seasons for the Lions, the classy running back piled up 5,106 yards, the highest career total for any Lion until Barry Sanders burst on the scene in the late 1980s. (Dexter Bussey in his 11 years in the Lions' backfield, 1974-84, amassed 5,105 points, one shy of Sims's total.) When the 1984 season ended, so did Monte Clark's seven-year tenure as Detroit's head coach.

The Good, the Bad, and the Future

Darryl Rogers, Clark's successor as head coach, experienced little success, although in 1985 the Lions were well-nigh unbeatable at the Silverdome. They won six games in a row there, but meanwhile they were losing regularly on the road, finishing with a 7-9-0 record. Billy Sims's knee injury kept him from playing, and quarterback Eric Hipple handed off to James Jones instead, who led the team in rushing with 886 yards.

Many observers looked for improvement in 1986, but the Lions failed at home and on the road alike, blowing leads, losing once to feeble Tampa Bay, and generally dismaying their fans as they dropped to 5-11-0. Although fullback James Jones shone again, and second-year offensive tackle Lomas Brown performed notably, the team as a whole lacked spark. For the third year in a row, no Lion was chosen for the Pro Bowl.

In 1987 and 1988 things only got worse, at least in the standings. Detroit's 4-11-0 in 1987

PROFILE

Barry Sanders

It took running back Barry Sanders just four seasons to become the Lions' all-time rushing leader. On November 22, 1992, he surpassed Billy Sims's record of 5,106 yards, ending the season with 5,674—an average 4.8 yards a carry.

The road to the top in pro football was not easy for the "blockish, Scripture-spouting" Sanders, as writer Austin Murphy called him in *Sports Illustrated*. The 5'8", 203-pound Sanders was virtually ignored by Division I-A college scouts when he played for North High School in Wichita, Kansas.

Weighing 180 pounds as a high school senior, he received just two scholarship offers, from Oklahoma State and hometown Wichita State. He chose Oklahoma State, where he starred from the outset, setting 13 NCAA season records in three years and winning the Heisman Trophy as a junior.

When Oklahoma State was placed on NCAA probation after the 1988 season, Sanders asked the NFL for permission to enter the pro draft a year early.

The NFL granted Sanders's request, and the Lions chose him in the first round. They were less concerned about Sanders' size than the colleges had been. "Look at his legs in the huddle," said Lions' offensive coordinator Mouse Davis. "His legs are as big as the guards' legs."

Sanders rewrote the Lions' record book for rushing in his rookie year. He galloped for 1,470 yards, eclipsing Billy Sims' mark, on his way to becoming the NFL Rookie of the Year. He gained more than 1,000 yards rushing in each of his first four seasons, a feat accomplished by just three other running backs in NFL history (Eric Dickerson, Earl Campbell, and Tony Dorsett). He was named a Pro Bowl starter in each of his first four professional seasons.

Fast and elusive, Sanders is very hard to stop. Bears' defensive end Trace Armstrong described him as being "like a little sports car. He can stop on a dime and go zero to 60 in seconds." Walter Payton, the NFL's all-time leading rusher, remarked after seeing Sanders play, "I don't know if I was ever *that* good."

Photo: *AP/Wide World Photos*

and 4-12-0 in 1988 put them in a tie for last place in the NFC Central Division each year. Quarterback Chuck Long, the Lions' first round draft pick in 1986, played well in 1987, then sat out much of the 1988 season because of injuries. Long, who had made the record books in 1986 with a touchdown completion on his first pass as a pro, had been touted as a big part of the Lions' future, but 1988 made observers wonder. On a more positive note, punter Jim Arnold got plenty of work both seasons and was twice named to the Pro Bowl.

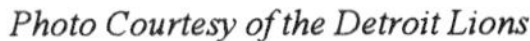

Photo Courtesy of the Detroit Lions

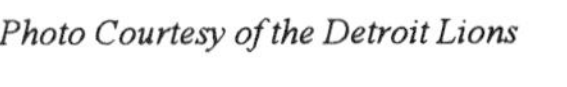

Chris Spielman

Photo Courtesy of the Detroit Lions

Jim Arnold

Darryl Rogers survived 11 games of the 1988 season (2-9-0) before being bid adieu. Wayne Fontes, the team's defensive coordinator, took over as interim coach, coaxed a 2-3-0 finish out of the struggling Lions, and was given the head coaching job for 1989.

Fontes promised to bring excitement back to the Silverdome and to "restore the roar." At first the Lions could only whimper, losing eight of their first nine games under the new head coach. But the team was truly better than that. In the backfield they had rookie running back Barry Sanders, the 1988 Heisman Trophy winner from Oklahoma State, not to mention rookie quarterback Rodney Peete, a first-team All-American at Southern Cal.

Down 1-8-0, the Lions really did begin to roar, winning six of their last seven games to salvage a respectable 7-9-0 third-place finish. Barry Sanders rushed for 1,470 yards, averaging 5.3 yards a carry, and scoring 14 touchdowns—all conference-leading figures. But the dazzling Detroit offense, dubbed the "Silver Stretch" for its run-and-shoot attack, got minimal help from the defense and in 1990 managed only another third-place finish (6-10-0).

Barry Sanders, on his way to breaking Billy Sims career rushing record, piled up 1,304 yards on the ground. Quarterback Rodney Peete improved markedly. Offensive tackle Lomas Brown had another outstanding season. On defense (not the Lions' strong suit) linebackers Michael Cofer and Chris Spielman stood out.

The 1991 season was what fans in the Silverdome had been waiting for ever since the Silverdome was built. Although the Lions were routed, 45-0, by the Washington Redskins in the season opener, they rebounded immediately to win five games in a row. They faltered a bit in mid-season, but got a second wind and reeled off

The Lions' First Season

In 1933 the Portsmouth Spartans had won six games and lost five, finishing a distant second in the NFL Western Division to George Halas's talent-laden Chicago Bears. It was hardly news, then, that when the Spartans became the Detroit Lions in 1934, the team to beat would be the Bears.

For seven games the Lions were invincible—unbeaten, untied, and unscored upon. In the seventh game Detroit crushed the Cincinnati Reds, 38-0, with Earl Clark, the "flying Dutchman from Colorado College," as the *New York Times* called him, scoring two touchdowns, drop-kicking a field goal, and adding two extra points on drop kicks. Other Lion touchdowns were contributed by Glenn Presnell, Father Lumpkin, and Ace Gutowsky. The only disappointment was the size of the crowd. Coach Potsy Clark's Detroit Lions had returned to play a homecoming game in Portsmouth, Ohio, and only about 4,800 fans turned out.

With the Lions at 7-0-0, having scored 118 points to their opponents 0, where were the Bears? The Bears were also at 7-0-0, having scored 155 points to their opponents 41. And, interestingly, the last two games of the 13-game season would pit the Lions against the Bears. The only question was, would both still be undefeated by game 12? Both went to 10-0-0, but then the Lions hit a snag. On November 25 the Green Bay Packers upset them, 3-0, while the Bears were defeating the Chicago Cardinals, 16-7. Still, Detroit could win it all by taking those last two games from the Bears.

The Lions hosted the Bears on Thanksgiving Day, 1934. At halftime, sparked by the running of Ace Gutowsky, Detroit led, 16-7. But the Bears fought back in the second half to win, 19-16, before 26,000 disappointed fans in Detroit. That ended the championship race. Even if the Lions were to prevail in the final game, the Bears would take the divisional title. As it happened the Bears won game 13 as well, again by the margin of a field goal, 10-7, giving them the first perfect record in NFL history. The Lions' 10-3-0, ordinarily good enough for first place, earned them second.

six straight victories at the end of the season.

All this was good for a 12-4-0 record—the most wins in the history of the club—and a first-place finish in the Central Division. Detroit then polished off the Dallas Cowboys, 38-6, in the divisional playoff. This brought them head to head with the powerful Washington Redskins, this time with the NFC championship on the line. These Redskins, who had opened the season by battering the Lions, battered them once again, 41-10, to send Wayne Fontes's men limping home to watch the Super Bowl on television.

But they could look forward with a certain optimism to 1992, or thought they could. Alas, despite some fine individual performances, including Barry Sanders' always electrifying running, 1992 was a major disappointment.

The Lions won only five games, while losing 11, leaving sportswriters and fans to wonder if that 1991 championship season had been only an isolated triumph, like 1983, rather than the beginning of a 1950s-style Detroit Lion resurgence.

Sources

Books

Allen, George, with Ben Olan, *Pro Football's 100 Greatest Players*, Bobbs-Merrill, 1982.

Harrington, Denis J., *The Pro Football Hall of Fame: Players, Coaches, Team Owners and League Officials, 1963-1991*, McFarland & Co., 1991.

Hollander, Zander, editor, *The Complete Handbook of Pro Football*, Signet, 1993.

Murray, Mike and James Petryka, editors, *De-*

troit Lions 1993 Media Guide, Detroit Lions, 1993.

Neft, David S., and Richard M. Cohen, *The Football Encyclopedia: The Complete History of Professional NFL Football from 1892 to the Present*, St. Martin's Press, 1991.

The Official National Football League 1992 Record & Fact Book, Workman Publishing Co., 1992.

Porter, David L., editor, *Biographical Dictionary of American Sports: Football*, Greenwood Press, 1987.

Sporting News Pro Football Guide, 1993 Edition, The Sporting News Publishing Co., 1993.

Periodicals

New York Times, October 29, 1934, December 30, 1957.

Sports Illustrated, July 3, 1989, September 10, 1990, October 14, 1991.

—*Gerald Tomlinson* for Book Builders Inc.

GREEN BAY PACKERS

The Green Bay Packers rank as one of the National Football League's proudest franchises, with a history dominated by a number of the most legendary figures ever to step on the gridiron. Indeed, the images of great Packer figures from the past such as Vince Lombardi, Bart Starr, Jim Taylor, Paul Hornung, and Ray Nitschke are particularly enduring ones.

Moreover, there has always been an "underdog" flavor to the club. Of all of the 35 metropolitan areas in the United States and Canada that support major league football, baseball, or basketball, all have populations in excess of a million people, save one—Green Bay. In fact, with a population of only 200,000 Green Bay ranks *158th* in size in the United States. It can truly be said that the scrappy Packers are America's only small-town major league football team.

The Packers are also the only professional franchise in major league football, baseball or basketball that is community-owned. There are in excess of 1,800 stockholders; none have ever received any dividends; none have even asked for any. Any profit motives seem to be of secondary importance to the prospect of keeping the historic franchise in its Green Bay home. After all, the Green Bay Packer club is the only team that has both remained in its original city and kept its original nickname since the league began play in 1921.

Despite all of the media attention in recent years devoted to the success of NFL franchises in San Francisco, Miami, Dallas, Pittsburgh, Chicago and Washington, D.C., the Green Bay Packers still have garnered more championships—eleven—than any other team. The Packers have won three consecutive national titles on two separate occasions; no other team has achieved that feat on even one occasion.

The Pack simply dominated football in the 1960s, winning numerous championships, including the first two Super Bowls. Today when the

Earl "Curly" Lambeau

names of great football teams are mentioned, anyone with even a cursory knowledge of the National Football League's long history inevitably includes teams fielded in the 1960s by the Green Bay Packers. Those teams were led by celebrated coach Vince Lombardi, perhaps the best football coach ever to lead a professional team.

Birth of the Packers

According to a recent Packers Press Guide, the birth date of the team was a muggy summer evening on August 11, 1919. Two young men from the small but bustling Wisconsin city of Green Bay—Curly Lambeau and George Calhoun—had gathered together a group of their friends and former schoolmates for a meeting to form a professional football team. All in the group were rough-and-tumble athletes. The location of this seemingly innocuous meeting was the editorial offices of the old Green Bay *Press Gazette.*

Lambeau and his cohorts had no way of knowing it then, of course, but their meeting was to be the beginning of one of the most incredible sagas in American sports history.

Professional football in those early years after World War I bore little resemblance to the high-powered, multi-billion dollar industry of today. The teams then were rag-tag outfits made up of local athletes; most of the communities involved were small, midwestern towns: Menominee, Marinette, Stambaugh, Ironwood, and Rock Island. There were no teams in cities such as New York, Los Angeles, Dallas, or Chicago. Television or radio coverage was nonexistent and newspaper reports on the relatively new game were sparse. Most games were played in open fields with no grandstands.

A disorganized league in those early days, good players migrated from team to team and from game to game pretty much as they pleased. Attendance at games ran anywhere from less than a hundred to a thousand or more. Often the majority of the fans were players' families and friends. There were no salaries to speak of, for players or team officials. If income was generated at all, it was accomplished via a passing of the hat during halftimes. Only two major team sports generated any interest in that era—professional baseball and college football.

It was on the high school level, however, where the teenage Lambeau's star first began to shine. Although Lambeau's given name was Earl Louis, he was known as "Curly" to everyone because of his abundance of natural, wavy hair. Good looks and charm aside, Lambeau was a natural athlete and leader. He was a star halfback and a senior in high school when the school's football coach went off for service in World War I. With no one to replace the departed coach, 17-year-old Lambeau took over and guided the team through to the end of the season.

The next fall Lambeau went on to college, to the University of Notre Dame. Because of the war, freshmen were permitted to play, and the Notre Dame coach, the immortal Knute Rockne, quickly assessed Lambeau's abilities—especially

Team Information at a Glance

Founding date: 1921

Home stadium: Lambeau Field
P.O. Box 10628
Green Bay, WI 54307
Phone: (414) 496-5700
Seating capacity: 59,543

Team colors: Dark green, gold, and white.
Team nickname: Packers
Logo: The letter "G"

Franchise record	Won	Lost	Tie
(1929-1990)	472	388	37

League Championships (11): 1929, 1930, 1931, 1936, 1938, 1939, 1944, 1960, 1961, 1962, 1965.
Super Bowl Wins (2): 1966, 1967

his passing talents. (The two were to go on to help revolutionize the game of football by emphasizing passing as an offensive weapon; Rockne accomplished this on the college level, Lambeau in the pros.) Although Lambeau served as the backup to another Fighting Irish great, the All-American George Gipp, in the Notre Dame backfield, he saw considerable playing time and in fact scored the team's first touchdown in a season opener against Case.

Lambeau's college football career was cut short soon after that first season when he came down with a severe attack of tonsillitis. The illness forced him to leave school and return home to Green Bay. He was offered and took a job with a local firm called The Indian Packing Company, for the then-impressive salary of $25 a month. Lambeau quickly decided that he no longer needed a college education, and he cancelled all plans to return to Notre Dame. But the game of football was ever in his mind.

Certain that there were a sufficient number of skilled players such as himself in the Green Bay area, Lambeau made plans to form a team. In an effort to drum up interest, he and his friend Calhoun called that fateful meeting together. In addition to the two of them, others at that momentous occasion included Nate Abrams, Tubby Bero, Jim Coffeen, Riggie and Dutch Dwyer, Fritz Gavin, Sam Powers, Gus Rosenow, Charlie Sauber, and Carl and Martin Zoll. This unassuming group became the basis for the Green Bay Packers.

Not all of the attendees at that 1919 planning session called by Lambeau to form a team actually went on to become players. Calhoun, for example, was a cigar-chomping newspaperman who later served as the team's business manager and self-appointed promoter. He also was the one who "passed the hat" for donations during halftimes in the first year of play. All were from the Green Bay area except Powers, who hailed all the way from Marinette, 56 miles up the coast. Lambeau, as might be expected, was named the team's coach and captain.

Other town football teams had actually existed in Green Bay prior to that 1919 meeting. Football in America, on a level other than high school or college play, had its inception as far back as August 31, 1895, when the YMCA team of Latrobe, Pennsylvania, took on and beat another Pennsylvania club from Jeannette, 12-0.

During that 1895 season, a few other town teams cropped up in that area. Only a year later Green Bay also fielded a town team, the first community in the entire United States outside of western Pennsylvania to do so. That group, incidentally, was started and coached by a Green Bay native, one Tom Silverwood, who had played football for the University of Wisconsin.

The team had only one paid player—Tom Skenadore, an Oneida Indian who had gained his experience at the famous Indian school, Carlisle. In any event, the team soon folded, as did a few other half-hearted attempts over the next two and a half decades.

Those town teams of the era were considered "professional" in that the play was supposed to be for money. In stark reality few if any of the teams made any profit at all. Players and coaches maintained their involvement, as Lambeau recalled later, for one reason only—the love of the game.

Lambeau talked his employers at the Indian Packing Company into donating $500 for uniforms. "All they asked for was that the name 'Indian Packing Company' be printed on the sweaters," Lambeau later recalled. The company also provided the team with use of an athletic field for practice purposes; the facility also served as a spot in which to play games if other fields were not available. Given the name on the playing jerseys and their growing association with the Indian Packing Company, the name "Packers" naturally evolved. No other name was ever really considered.

"All of the players agreed that if we made any money, we'd split it up at the end of the season," Lambeau said. The season split for that first year was all of $16.75 per player, less than $1.50 per game. Out of that they were expected to pay their own medical bills and expenses.

The involvement of the Indian Packing Company with the football team was practically over for the season when the company was purchased by the Acme Packing Company. The company remained a "packing" company, however, and the name Packers stuck.

On the field, that initial Packer team was a whopping success. The club posted an unbeaten 10-0 mark in which the team scored 565 points and allowed but six points the entire season. Beloit, Wisconsin, down on the Illinois border, also had a strong town team, and Lambeau challenged them to a post-season game with the winner to be the "state champion." The Beloit club played under the misleading name "The Fairies."

The game was played at Beloit, and proved to be a rugged, hard-fought battle. The Packers trailed 6-0 with time running out in the fourth quarter, but had reached the Fairies' three-yard line. On the next play Lambeau slashed off tackle for an apparent touchdown, but the referee ruled the Pack offside and penalized them five yards.

On the next play Lambeau dashed around end and scored again, but again the referee called the team offside. Now the Green Bay contingent was back to the 13-yard line, with only seconds remaining. Lambeau called time to set up a play and told each of the other members of the team to stand absolutely still until after the ball was snapped—and even then not to move. They followed his instructions, the center passed the ball back to Lambeau, who again raced around end to score.

But unbelievably, the referee again blew his whistle and called an illegal motion penalty over Lambeau's outraged protests. Lambeau remained convinced throughout the remainder of his life that the game was fixed. In any case, the score stood, and Green Bay suffered its only loss of the year.

Commenting on the early years of pro football, the Packers' Press Guide recalls, "there were no gates where tickets to the games could be sold, because there were no fences around the fields. Spectators just walked over to the sideline, or drove up close to the field with their cars, and watched. There were no stands. Some people sat on their cars and watched, but more preferred to walk up and down the sidelines with the movement of the teams. By moving with the play they always had a good view and were close at hand if any form of a donnybrook were to take place. In fact, when things got really hot and heavy, the crowd often spilled right out onto the field. It's hard to believe today, but the crowd would actually surround the players out on the field as they scrimmaged, and offered suggestions on plays and strategy."

At halftime of these early-era contests, both teams grabbed blankets and whatever was around that was hot to drink and moved to opposite ends of the field. Spectators would form a tight circle around the players and continue to offer advice. This practice was actually encouraged at times, for the ring of people standing around the shivering players offered a degree of protection from the bitter winds that whistled into Green Bay during late fall and early winter games.

The Packers' second season (1920) was similar to their first, except that some 3,000 seats were put up at Hagemeister Park in Green Bay, the team's home field. Marcel Lambeau, Curly's father, built the stands as well as a fence around the field. No longer could passers-by simply stop and watch the action free of charge. An admission charge of 50 cents was instituted.

Green Bay was tied 3-3 by the Chicago Boosters in the 1920 opener. The Packers then won six straight—all shutouts—including a 7-0 revenge win over the hated Beloit Fairies. But the latter club took the rematch 14-3 to dash the Packers' hopes for an unbeaten season. Green Bay completed its last year as an independent town team with three more wins for a 9-1-1 record. Over the course of their first two seasons of play, the Packers scored 792 points while giving up only 36.

At Canton, Ohio, meanwhile, a meeting had been held on September 17, 1920, in the automobile agency of Ralph Hays, owner of the Canton Bulldogs. A league called the American Professional Football Association was formed, with the great Jim Thorpe as its president. There were 11 teams in the league—the Packers were not represented—but the league folded in less than a year.

On April 30, 1921, however, many of the same teams got together and formed a new league, the American Professional Football Association. At Lambeau's urgent request, two officials of the Acme Packing Company, which now owned the Packers, came up with the entry fee of $50. Green Bay joined the league.

The league's first champion was the Decatur Staleys, coached by George Halas; the Packers finished fourth. A total of 13 teams competed that first year. In addition to Decatur and Green Bay, the league included Akron, Buffalo, Canton, the Chicago Cardinals, Cincinnati, Cleveland, Columbus, Dayton, Detroit, Rochester, and Rock Island. Later in the year, at Halas's suggestion, the league changed its name to the National Football League.

Of the original members, only the Packers are still competing where they started and in their original hometown. The Staleys were moved by Halas from Decatur to Chicago in 1922 and renamed the Bears. The Chicago Cardinals, the only other charter member in existence today, moved to St. Louis in 1960 and then on to Phoenix, Arizona. All told more than 50 cities have been in and out of the league since its inception.

The Packers nearly became one of the casualties in 1922 when the league boss, Joe Carr, booted them out of the league because they were using college players on their squad under assumed names. The practice was widespread throughout the league, but Carr was determined to use the Packers as an example to the rest. He returned the $50 franchise fee to the Acme Packing Company.

Lambeau didn't give up all that easily. He scraped up another $50 of his own money to buy back the franchise. The problem was he had no form of transportation or the necessary funds to get to the league meeting in Canton to file his application. In desperation he turned to one of his cohorts, Don Murphy, for help.

Murphy, who was an avid fan but most certainly no football player, agreed to sell his car, a Marmon roadster, to finance the trip—*if* Lambeau would agree to let him play for one minute in the Packers' opening game the following season. Lambeau agreed, and the two went to Canton and bought back the franchise for that $50. Murphy started at tackle on Opening Day against Duluth and retired happily after that one minute of play.

Along with new league members based in Toledo, Ohio, and Racine and Milwaukee, Wisconsin, one of the most intriguing additions to the NFL in 1923 was a club called the Oorang Indians, organized by Jim Thorpe and made up entirely of Native Americans, most of whom played at Carlisle. The team lasted only two years before folding.

The Packers continued to have their problems off the field during the 1920s. Plagued by bad weather and subsequent poor attendance, the team was nearly bankrupt. But the resourceful Lambeau again saved the day by talking local businessmen into a $12,500 loan. A non-profit corporation was set up to run the team. For only five dollars a Green Bay citizen could buy a share of the team and get a series box seat in the bargain. The shares were all snapped up, and another $5,000 was raised. The Pack had weathered the financial storm that swamped many other early NFL teams.

Recordkeeping was spotty at best in the early years of the league. It was not until 1921 that the names of the players on the rosters were recorded by the NFL office. It was not until the 1933 season that even rudimentary statistics were kept. Even the Packers, who possess one of the more complete statistical records of their club history, list none of the players from the 1919 or 1920 teams (though the club holds the names of more than 1,100 players who wore the Packer uniform since 1921).

During the Packers' first year of NFL play in 1921, there were 35 players listed on their roster. Ten were running backs, one was a quarterback, eight were ends and 16 were centers, guards, and tackles. In that bygone "Iron Man" era, there were no safeties, no linebackers, no punting and placekicking specialists. Most players played on both offense and defense.

On the playing field, player-coach/mother hen Lambeau did well enough to keep the Packers near the top in the league standings every year through 1927, when they finished second to the New York Giants. They dropped to fourth in 1928, then won their first championship in 1929 after Lambeau persuaded three star players from other teams to join the Packers. Those three—halfback Johnny "Blood" McNally, guard Mike Michalske, and tackle Cal Hubbard—went on to become All-Pros and key members of the Packer mystique.

The stories of Johnny Blood's exploits, on and off the field, could fill a book. There's the tale of how he chose the name, "Blood," for himself after seeing it on a movie marquee advertising "Blood and Sand," a Rudolph Valentino hit of the day. There are many more tales that seem to contradict his almost genius-level intelligence.

As a player, he had speed, courage and spirit. He was a runner, a passer, a receiver and a kicker, as well as a defensive wizard. Known as a player who ignored injuries that would have felled other players, Blood played best when the games were the toughest. When the Packers were far ahead, he would clown. Off the field, he broke training and curfew, missed trains, buses and bed checks. He drove Lambeau and his teammates to distraction, yet they were fascinated by him and his daring, both on and off the field.

Packer lore contends that on one occasion, when the Packers were in Los Angeles for a game, Blood locked himself out of his hotel room by mistake. It was well after curfew when he returned from a wild night on the town, and Lambeau was sitting in the lobby, waiting for him. Blood remembered that he had left the window of his fifth floor room open. He went up via the back stairs to another player's room, a room that was across an open court from his own. Although there was a blinding rain, Blood leaped from one ledge more than eight feet across to his own room, went in and crawled into bed.

Lambeau Brings A Championship To Green Bay

On November 24, 1929, the Packers brought an unblemished 10-0 record to New York and handed the also-unbeaten Giants a 20-6 beating in front of 25,000 at the Polo Grounds. Ten of the 11 Packer starters played the full 60 minutes. A scoreless tie with Frankfort preceded two more wins, including the season finale against the hated Bears, giving the Green Bay club a 13-0-1 record, the only time the team has enjoyed an undefeated season.

During that year the Packers beat the Bears three times, holding them scoreless in each. There were only three touchdowns scored against the Packers all year. After that season finale against the Bears, the team came home to a rousing welcome by a huge crowd at the railway station. The happy throng escorted them to City Hall, where Lambeau and his legions were given the keys to the city. Although the Packers had been in existence for ten years, it was really on that specific occasion that the long love affair began between the city and its team.

With increased financial backing, Lambeau now was able to attract additional gridiron stars from other parts of the country to bolster his beloved Pack. Although Lambeau's days as a player had come to an end, he was at the height of his career as a coach. The 1929 championship was followed by league crowns in both 1930 and 1931. The Green Bay Packers, as they were to be known under Vince Lombardi decades later, were hailed as the finest professional football team in America.

Green Bay did not make it four titles in a row in 1932, even though they won ten games, three more than the league champion Bears. Green Bay's league record vas 10-3-1, which was computed to a .709 percentage. The rules at that time did not take tie games into account, and thus the percentage was arrived at by dividing the games won, ten, by 13, the total of games won and lost. Chicago had a record of 7-1-6, which translated into an .875 winning percentage utilizing that odd formula, and thus was considered the champion.

The 1933 campaign was almost a disaster for the Packers, on and off the field. The club had its first losing season ever, winning six, losing seven and tying one. During one of the games in Green Bay a fan fell from the stands and sued the franchise for $25,000. A subsequent judgment nearly took the club to bankruptcy. Another stock sale was started, a board of directors was named to run the organization, and once again Lambeau's team endured.

During the early years of the NFL, Green Bay was actually only one of four cities in the state that had franchises in the league. The others were Kenosha, Racine, and Milwaukee. With transportation problems a major factor in that era, it would have seemed that each of those other teams—closer to Chicago and other midwestern cities—would have had a better chance to survive than Green Bay. None of the other three, however, had Curly Lambeau.

Lambeau's status as an immortal figure in the Packer pantheon is due to several factors. He was the founder of the team; without him the Green Bay Packers surely would not have come into being. Of course he was much more than merely the founder; he was a star player, the team's only coach through its first three decades, and its guiding spirit.

Lambeau put together a tremendous record as a coach. From the inception of the team in 1919, the Packers under Lambeau played their first 26 years with only one losing season. His teams captured six NFL Championships and, from 1921 to 1949 racked up 212 wins, 106 losses and 21 ties in NFL play to establish Lambeau as one of the winningest coaches in league history. Small wonder, then, that the modern-era Packers play their home games at a stadium named in Curly's honor, Lambeau Field.

Hutson Takes Center Stage

By the mid-1930s the Lambeau era was far from over. One reason that it extended on through World War II and beyond was the arrival of the incomparable Don Hutson. Hutson, signed by Lambeau after considerable effort, was an All-American end from the University of Alabama who had scored three touchdowns for the Crimson Tide in their 29-13 win over Southern California in the 1935 Rose Bowl.

Because he played for the College All-Stars that fall against the pros, he was late reporting for practice with the Packers, and was held out of the first game. The majority of the Packer veterans, however, weren't sure that any amount of practice was going to make a professional football player out of the slim Southerner.

After hearing of his exploits in the Rose Bowl, they had envisioned a much bigger and tougher-looking player. What they saw instead was a quiet, almost frail-looking youngster, just over six feet tall and weighing in at only 177 pounds. There were more than a few snickers. The Packers' opponents in the second game that season were the fearsome Chicago Bears, and the sports writers had a field day speculating how the Monsters of the Midway would chew up the rookie and spit him out.

George Halas and the Bears were certain that Lambeau was going to have his quarterback, Arnie Herber, throw a long one to Hutson the very first time the Packers had the ball. They were right. On that first play from scrimmage, Packer back Johnny Blood was positioned out to the right as a flanker, only yards from the sidelines. Hutson, at left end, split wide to the other side. Only the two of them went downfield on the snap. The others, including the other end, Milt Gantenbein, and fullback Clarke Hinkle, stayed in to block for Herber. Blood dashed straight downfield at full speed, pulling two defenders with him. Herber faded back, back, almost to his own end zone, appearing to be watching Blood, and even pumped the ball twice in his direction.

Hutson, meanwhile, had zoomed off the line directly toward Gene Ronzani, the Bear defensive back on that side. As he neared Ronzani, he dipped his shoulder, momentarily cut outside, then shot upfield sharply, leaving Ronzani completely out of position to defense the play. Herber then turned toward Hutson and lofted a bomb more than 60 yards in the air.

Hutson took the ball over his shoulder without breaking stride and sped untouched across the goal line for a touchdown. With the ensuing extra point, the Packers led 7-0, and that's the way the game ended. The Hutson era had begun. The snickers were silenced forever, as Hutson went on to become the terror of the league, setting new league records for receptions, total yardage, and total points scored.

With Hutson catching and Herber and then Cecil Isbell throwing, the Packers won three more World Championships, in 1936, 1939 and 1944. Hutson's touchdown on that opening play against the Bears in 1935 was the first of 105 he was to score for the Packers in 11 seasons. He caught a total of 488 passes for 7,991 yards and scored 823 points. Hutson's statistics are even more astounding in light of the fact that NFL teams played only ten or 11 games a season in those days, as opposed to the 16 a season today.

"Hutson was the Babe Ruth of football," said Buckets Goldenberg, the Packer's All-Pro guard. "No one could stop him. He was also a great defensive back, too. They never threw in his area. He was a sure, tough tackler."

As a touchdown threat, Hutson had no peers. For example, he leads all the Packer ends in history with 99 touchdown receptions; second and third places are held by Max McGee and James Lofton, with 50 and 49. Hutson's touchdown receptions rank him third on the all-time NFL list in that category, behind only Jerry Rice and Steve Largent. Indeed, Hutson originated the whole concept of pass patterns, today used by every team in professional football.

After Hutson retired following the 1945 season, Lambeau's position with the Packers began a steady decline. Many people in the Green Bay area felt that Lambeau had "gotten too big for his britches." Lambeau was the author of most of his troubles. He was spending less and less time in Green Bay and with the team; he became arrogant and domineering. He left his wife, Marguerite, which did even more to alienate him from the Packer faithful. He had taken up with the movie set out in Hollywood and was photographed regularly with stars and starlets. Packer management for the first time ever began to question his lifestyle and expenses. They even questioned his football expertise.

After three lackluster years following the Second World War, during which his teams went 7-4, 6-5, and 6-5, things really took a nosedive for Lambeau in 1948 and 1949. The Packers posted miserable 3-9 and 2-10 records, only the second and third losing seasons in the entire history of the team and the first time they had ever suffered two such years in a row. Coming so soon on the heels of the 1944 championship, the losing seasons were even harder to take.

Memories are short, and Lambeau was no longer the most popular man in town. The last straw, perhaps, came when he attempted to put together a takeover of the Packer board of directors. But the bid failed, and for the first time Lambeau didn't have his way. He resigned to take a job as coach of the rival Chicago Cardinals. An era had ended in Green Bay, and some fans wondered if they would ever see another championship-calibre team.

To replace the legendary Lambeau, the Packer board turned to their arch-enemies, the Chicago Bears, and hired Gene Ronzani. Unfortunately, Ronzani's clubs could do no better than two 3-9 seasons and a 6-6 mark before he was let go with two games left in the 1953 campaign.

The Packers overhauled their front office operation and coaching staff in 1954, hiring former Packer great Verne Lewellen as the team's new general manager and naming Marquette University football mentor Lisle Blackbourn as the new head coach. But during the next four years under the likeable Blackbourn, the Packers won only 17 games while losing 31, including six losses to the Bears. Blackbourn also was fired.

In 1958, another well-liked coach, Packer assistant Ray "Scooter" McLean, was given the reins of the team. Scooter was destined to go on to guide the Pack to their worst performance ever, a horrible 1-10-1 record. Even the lone win was a harrowing experience. Green Bay had a 38-7 lead over Philadelphia and barely hung on to win 38-35 as the Eagles mounted a furious comeback. McLean did not wait to get the axe. He quit and took a job with the Detroit Lions as an assistant.

During Blackbourn's tenure a new million-dollar stadium was built by the city through a bond issue, with the Packers committed to pay for it through a rental agreement. The new City Stadium was dedicated on September 29, 1957, with then-Vice President Richard Nixon the principal speaker at halftime. The Pack made the dedication a success on the field, upsetting the Chicago Bears 21-17. The stage was set for the coming of a short, stocky Italian from New York.

There has unquestionably been more copy written about Vincent Lombardi than any other

How's This for Stock Value Increase?

The Green Bay Packers are the only community owned team in major professional sports. The more than 1,800 stockholders own a total of 4,627 shares, for which they paid $5 per share. There are no more shares available. Wouldn't it be interesting if the Packer Board of Directors decided to sell the team? Given the club's current estimated value of $125 million, that would make every one of those $5 shares now worth in excess of $27,000 each.

coach or player in the history of professional football. He certainly entered a dismal situation in the wake of that 1958 season: the Packers, after decades of being one of the top teams in the NFL, were now the laughingstock of the league. League officials were actually considering whether to drop the franchise. It became a major task to come up with any creditable leader to take on the reins of the team.

The Lombardi Era Begins

By the time the NFL meeting in January of 1959 began, the situation was becoming desperate. Out of the blue, the name of Vincent Lombardi, coach for the offense of the New York Giants, was put forth. The two men who had made the suggestion, however, were two of the more respected men in pro football, league commissioner Bert Bell and Cleveland Browns head coach and general manager Paul Brown. Some time before, Green Bay scout Jack Vainisi had tried to get the Packer board to consider Lombardi as a head coach, but at the time they wanted someone with a head coaching background. Time had changed their minds.

They made an effort to talk to Lombardi, but at first he said he wasn't really interested, that he was reluctant to leave New York, his home. He finally agreed, but insisted on a five-year contract as both head coach and general manager and the opportunity to wield almost unlimited authority. On his first day in Green Bay he told the Packer board, "Gentlemen, I want it understood that I am in complete command here." And he was.

"He treated us all alike," joked tackle Henry Jordan. "Like dogs." Jordan was also the quipster who said, "When Coach Lombardi says to sit down, I don't even look for a chair." Packer buffs love to tell the story of the time Lombardi came home late at night from the office and slipped into bed next to his wife, Marie, who said, "God, your feet are cold." Whereupon Lombardi supposedly answered, "Marie, you can call me Vincent when we're alone."

Vince Lombardi

Lombardi and his Packers gave the world of sport a portent of things to come in the very first game of the 1959 season, upsetting George Halas and the Chicago Bears 9-6. The team went on to win seven games and lose five, the first winning season for the Packers in 12 years. Lombardi was unanimously voted Coach of the Year.

The improvement continued in 1960, as Green Bay finished 8-4 and won the Western Division title. The subsequent 17-13 loss to the Philadelphia Eagles for the NFL title was to be the last title championship loss Lombardi would ever suffer while leading the Packers.

Green Bay went on to capture NFL Championships in 1961, 1962, 1965, 1966, and 1967, an achievement never duplicated in the history of professional football. That 1962 team—one that completely crushed the New York Giants 37-0 in the title game—has been called one of the finest football teams in the history of the sport. Lombardi's teams became the standard of football excellence, and the Packer franchise correspondingly became one of the most successful in the NFL.

The startling turnaround in the team's fortunes was accomplished in less than a decade.

During his tenure as head coach of the Packers, Green Bay compiled an 89-29-4 regular season record; even more outstanding was his record in post-season play, where Packer teams won nine times in ten games and collected the first two Super Bowl victories.

It is interesting to examine the list of Green Bay Packer players named to the All-Time "modern era" Packer team—the modern era being basically those years after World War II and after the NFL opted to two-platoon play. Of the 11 players on that offensive team, wide receivers Max McGee and Boyd Dowler, tackles Forrest Gregg and Bob Skoronski, guards Fuzzy Thurston and Jerry Kramer, center Jim Ringo, tight end Ron Kramer, quarterback Bart Starr, halfback Paul Hornung, and fullback Jim Taylor all were part of the Lombardi era.

Of the two specialists on this All-Time team, punter Dick Deschaine and placekicker Don Chandler, the latter, Chandler, was a Lombardi player; and on defense, ends Willie Davis and Lionel Aldridge, tackles Henry Jordan and Dave Hanner, linebackers Ray Nitschke, Fred Carr, and Dave Robinson, and defensive backs Willie Wood, Herb Adderley, Bob Jeter, and Bobby Dillon, all played for Lombardi.

Did these pro football greats, ten of whom have been named to the NFL Hall of Fame, assure Lombardi's greatness as a coach? Or did Lombardi spur them to greatness as players? Many of the above-mentioned stars were on that Packer team in 1958 when they won only one game all season long.

Moreover, other Packer stars such as Thurston, Davis and Jordan were picked up from other teams who didn't think they had much of a future as players. Lombardi took these castoffs and made them into champions. Furthermore, two more of these All-Team players, Willie Wood and Herb Adderley, joined the Packers as rookie offensive players in 1959. Lombardi transformed them into defensive specialists, and they went on to the Hall of Fame.

In his comprehensive anthology on the life and times of Lombardi, *The Vince Lombardi Scrapbook*, author George Flynn describes the man. "He was called tyrannical, vindictive, cruel, short-tempered, a martinet, and a S.O.B. He was also termed tender, understanding, compassionate, friendly, warm, dynamic, considerate and a saint. And he was actually all of these."

With all of the stories about Lombardi, Flynn wrote, most often forgotten is the uniquely American one, that of the man from an immigrant background who struggled for years to become a success in his chosen field. Most observers forget that Lombardi was 46 years old before he got his first head coaching job in pro football. The only other head coaching job he had was at a high school.

Ray Nitschke

Lombardi waited patiently for his career to develop. He got discouraged, but he never quit; and when he got his shot, nothing could keep him from his goal. "Without question, Lombardi was the most famous sports personality of the sixties," Flynn said. "He transcended that limited area of sports as no man before him had done. He also won as no coach before him had done in such a very short time."

Social scientists, psychologists and others use his desire for achievement as an example when criticizing sports and the competitive American system, Flynn noted. Businessmen in all walks of life use Lombardi as their patron saint for success; he signifies the sacrifices they demand of themselves to be successful. All leaders are compared to him, and many wrap the "Lombardi Credo" around themselves whenever talking about their own commitment to discipline, sacrifice, and hard work. But few people in any walk of American life have ever been as committed and hard-working as Lombardi.

"To Lombardi, winning and making the effort to win again were what life was all about. He had no understanding of those who questioned why winning was so important and why winning all the time was such a goal. To him, it was not winning for winning's sake but the constant struggle to improve oneself, to work to the limits of one's ability and then go a little beyond. To him, the basic fundamental was to use the talent God gave you to the fullest. As he so often told his team, 'The spirit, the will to win, and the will to excel, are the important things that transcend the game itself,'" Flynn wrote.

Wellington Mara, the owner of the New York Giants, said "I think he could have been president, and he could have been pope. In other times and other circumstances, he might have been Alexander the Great and conquered the world.

Jim Taylor (31)

Or he might have been St. Francis Xavier and converted it."

Vince Lombardi was a most successful football coach, but he was much, much more. The things people have said and written about him even to this day are not the kind of things written about a mere sports figure.

Bart Starr, the benchwarmer he transformed into one of the greatest quarterbacks in the history of professional football, recited one of Lombardi's most famous quotes: "The quality of any man's life is in direct proportion to his commitment to excellence." It was a credo that he instilled in every one of his players, Starr said. "I'll always feel sorry for those football players that never had the chance to play at least one game for Coach Lombardi."

Betty Lombardi, his sister-in-law, once said, "There was something in him that you just don't find in people today, and I guess that's why the admiration and respect are still there. He was such a deeply moral man, so dedicated and so strong. And also so kind."

Writer Bill Heinz, who helped Lombardi with his book, *Run to Daylight,* said: "Vince Lombardi was probably the most vital human being I have ever met in my life. I have a special pantheon of heroes of my own whom I have collected in more than 30 years in this business. I call them my Armageddon squad because they're not going to win that last battle, but they are going to make a great show before they go. Vincent is not only on that squad—he's the leader!"

Father Guy McPartland, who played for Lombardi at St. Cecilia's High School in New York, was, as was the entire country, greatly saddened by Lombardi's sudden death from cancer in 1970. "When I read in the newspapers when he died where someone said he was one of the greatest if not the greatest coach ever, that he knew how to win, but that this was one game he couldn't win, I thought to myself, that isn't true. That's the one game he won going away, that was a rout, he won life by a rout. He may have lost a few ball games in his coaching career, and time may have run out on some of his games, but in the game of life he won by such a big score that it wasn't even close."

Bart Starr (15)

Following the second Super Bowl Win and his third consecutive title in 1967, Lombardi turned the head coaching duties over to his defensive coach, Phil Bengtson, and then a year later announced he was leaving the Packers and would manage and coach the Washington Redskins. Despite Lombardi's resignation, it was hoped that Bengtson, a part of the Packer coaching staff for years, would carry on the team's winning ways.

After taking the 1968 season opener with a convincing 30-13 win over the Philadelphia Eagles, however, the Pack had to settle for a 6-7-1 finish, their first losing season since pre-Lombardi days. An improvement to 8-6 in 1969 was followed by a lackluster 6-8 performance in 1970, after which Bengtson turned in his resignation.

Continued on page 300

The Green Bay Packers . . .

The Packers have won more championships that any other team in the NFL. The club's history is one which has been marked by a standard of excellence in championship play that is reflected in Green Bay's .833 winning percentage in such contests. With ten victories in 12 contests, the Packers have established themselves as one of the top big game franchises in sports history.

1936—Green Bay 21, Boston Redskins 6. The game was played at the Polo Grounds in New York because the Redskins were in the process of being moved by owner George Marshall from Boston to Washington. A crowd of 29,545 saw Don Hutson gather in a 45-yard touchdown pass from Arnie Herber in the opening minutes, and the Pack controlled the game from the point on.

1938—New York Giants 23, Green Bay 17. Again played in New York's Polo Grounds. Green Bay overcame an early 9-0 Giant lead but could not hold off the New York team in the second half. In the second period Herber lofted a 50-yard scoring strike to end Carl Mulleneaux to cut the Giant lead. After New York forged ahead 16-7 in the second half, Clarke Hinkle crashed over from the six-inch line following another Herber bomb, a 66-yarder to Wayland Becker. The Packers then forged ahead on a field goal by Tiny Engebretsen, but the Giants stormed back with a long scoring drive. A crowd of 48,120, a playoff record, saw the game.

1939—Green Bay 27, New York Giants 0. In the first NFL Championship game ever to be played in Wisconsin (at State Fair Park in Milwaukee), the Packers made playoff history by winning the first shutout ever in NFL title play. Despite 35-mile-per-hour winds, both Herber and Cecil Isbell passed for touchdowns in leading the Pack to the world championship before 32,271 spectators. Green Bay's first score came when Milt Gantenbein gathered in a Herber pass. In the third quarter another long scoring toss, this one by Isbell to Joe Lewis, and a 29-yard field goal by Engebretsen, put the game out of reach. In the final stanza another field goal, by Eddie South, and a scoring plunge by fullback Eddie Jankowski, added to the total.

1944—Green Bay 14, New York Giants 7. Again the Polo Grounds in New York was the scene of a bitter battle between the two long-time NFL antagonists, before a crowd of 46,016. With Hutson used primarily as a decoy, the Packers utilized a devastating ground game led by fullback Ted Fritsch. Fritsch scored both Packer touchdowns, the first on a two-yard plunge, the second on a 26-yard pass play. The hero of the game, however, was veteran Joe Laws, a 34-year-old all-purpose back, who set a playoff record with three interceptions on defense, while leading all ground gainers with 74 yards on 13 carries.

1960—Philadelphia Eagles 17, Green Bay 13. Played before a crowd of 67,325 at Franklin Field in Philadelphia, the game was the first—and last—championship game of any kind lost by Lombardi. The Pack jumped out ahead 6-0 on two short field goals by Paul Hornung. The Eagles moved ahead 10-6 on a scoring strike from Norm Van Brocklin to Tommy McDonald and a subsequent field goal by Bobby Walston. Green Bay stopped the Eagles on the Packer four yard line in the third quarter, then retook the lead on a seven-yard touchdown pass from Bart Starr to Max McGee. A 58-yard kickoff return by Ted Dean, however, placed the Eagles in fine field position, and Philadelphia eventually punched it over on a short run by Dean. The Packers gamely battled back and were threatening to score when Packer fullback Jim Taylor was brought down by a host of Eagle defenders only yards from the goal as time expired. After the game, Lombardi assured his team that they would be back in the championship the next year, and that they would win. He was right on both counts.

1961—Green Bay 37, New York Giants 0. This was the single game that transformed the Packers into the premier football dynasty of the 1960s. Hornung, on leave from Army duty, scored a record 19 points in the first NFL title game ever played in Green Bay. A record Packer home crowd of 39,029 delightedly watched as Green Bay erupted for 24 points in the second quarter. In all, the Green and Gold scored seven times against what had been the NFL's top defensive team. The Packer defense was equally as devastating, intercepting four Giant passes and completely shutting down New York's high powered passing offense. The victory by the Packers was termed one of the most decisive in the history of the NFL championship. In less than three years, Lombardi had taken the most pathetic club in all pro football and transformed it into what many feel was the greatest team of all time.

1962—Green Bay 16, New York Giants 7. In a brutal rematch for the NFL Championship on an unusually cold and windy day in Yankee Stadium, the Packers again won it all. The Pack defense was nothing short of awesome. The only Giant score came on a blocked kick in the third quarter. Green Bay linebacker Ray Nitschke, with two interceptions and his usual brand of devastating defense, took Most Valuable Player honors. Fullback Jim Taylor led the Pack attack with 85 hard-earned yards, and Jerry Kramer kicked three field goals.

1965—Green Bay 23, Cleveland Browns 12. Played before a throng of 50,777 at Lambeau Field on a surface turned into a quagmire by melting snow, the Packers again became world champions. Packer backs Paul Hornung and Jim Taylor combined for more than 200 yards, while the Browns' vaunted All-Pro running back Jim Brown was held in check. Green Bay took an early lead on a 47-yard scoring pass from Bart Starr to end Carroll Dale. After Cleveland took a 9-7 lead, Packer placekicker Don Chandler put two through the posts, and Starr iced the contest by leading the Packers on a 90-yard march culminated by Hornung's 13-yard sweep around end.

1966—Green Bay 34, Dallas Cowboys 27. At the Cotton Bowl in Dallas Bart Starr turned in one of his finest performances, passing for four touchdowns. In the closing moments Packer defensive back Tom Brown thwarted the Dallas bid to tie the game with an end zone interception of a Don Meredith fourth down pass from the two yard line. A crowd of 74,152 included thousands of Packer faithful. The NFL Championship safely tucked away, the Pack went on to win Super Bowl I.

1967—Green Bay 21, Dallas Cowboys 17. The contest is better known as the "Ice Bowl," and was played at Lambeau Field in Green Bay before 50,861. With the thermometer registering 16 below zero at game time, and the wind chill factor an arctic 37 below, the Packers fought to their third championship in a row and fifth in seven years under Lombardi's guidance. Bart Starr scored the winning touchdown on a one yard sneak into the end zone on fourth down, with only seconds remaining. The Packers went on to secure a victory in Super Bowl II.

Super Bowl I, January 15, 1967—Green Bay 35, Kansas City Chiefs 10. What better team to launch the Super Bowl series than the Green Bay Packers? Lombardi's legions didn't let the NFL down as they outclassed the American Football League Champion Kansas City Chiefs 35-10. A crowd of 61,946 witnessed the contest in Los Angeles's Memorial Coliseum. The game was highlighted by the passing of Bart Starr, who earned MVP honors, an unexpected performance by veteran end Max McGee and a key interception by All-Pro safety Willie Wood.

After leading by only 14-10 at halftime, the Pack broke open the game with three second-half scores. The first of those was set up by Wood's interception and 50-yard return. McGee, filling in for injured Boyd Dowler, grabbed seven receptions for 138 yards and two touchdowns after catching only three passes during the regular season. Elijah Pitts ran for the other two scores. Starr completed 18 of 23 passes and hurled two touchdowns. The Packers collected $15,000 per man for winning, the largest single game share in NFL history up to that time.

Super Bowl II, January 14, 1968—Green Bay 33, Oakland Raiders 14. Before 75,564 in the Orange Bowl in Miami, the Packers captured the second Super Bowl with a convincing 33-14 win over the Raiders. The victory would mark the last for Vince Lombardi as a Packer coach, ending a nine-year era in which his teams won six Western Conference crowns, four NFL titles and the first two Super Bowls ever held. After a pair of field goals by Don Chandler, the Packers moved out to a 13-0 lead with a 62-yard scoring strike from Bart Starr to Boyd Dowler. Chandler added two more field goals, Donny Anderson tallied on a two-yard scamper and defensive stalwart Herb Adderley scored on a 60-yard interception and return to pull the Packers out to an insurmountable 26-point lead. Starr was again named the game's Most Valuable Player, completing 13 of 24 passes for 202 yards. In the two Super Bowl wins Starr was 29 for 47 for 452 yards and three touchdowns.

Lean Years For The Pack

The Green Bay board then turned to the college ranks and selected Dan Devine, who had turned in superlative efforts at Arizona State, Missouri, and Notre Dame. After a woeful 4-8-2 mark in 1971, Devine led the Pack to a fine 10-4 record in 1972, bowing to the Washington Redskins 16-3 in the divisional playoff. That one-year return to winning ways was short-lived, however, as the Packers then sank to 5-7-2 and 6-8 marks, and Devine resigned at the end of the 1974 season.

The sorry won-loss record was not the only reason why Devine opted to get out of town. In an effort to build a winner for the 1974 season, Devine put together the infamous trade for quarterback John Hadl that has been called one of the most foolish in league history. To acquire Hadl, a 35-year-old nearing the end of his career, Devine gave the Los Angeles Rams the Packers' first-, second-, and third-round draft picks for 1975, as well as their first- and second-round choices in 1976. No one will ever know how much help the Packers could have obtained with those picks; with Hadl, who only stayed with the Packers for a season and a half, the Pack finished with 6-8 and 4-10 records.

On December 21, 1974, Bart Starr, one of the most successful field generals in pro football history, accepted the challenge to lead his old club out of the NFL doldrums. Starr agreed to a three-year contract as head coach and general manager of the Packers. Fans had to settle for three more years of losing before Starr was able to manage a 8-7-1 mark in 1978. But despite a high-powered passing offense built around quarterback Lynn Dickey, the Packer faithful then had to wait four more years before enjoying another winner, as the Pack posted a 5-3-1 record in the strike-shortened 1982 season. In the playoffs that year, the Packers topped the Cardinals 41-16 but then lost to the Cowboys in the second round. Following another mediocre 8-8 season in 1983, Starr was relieved of his duties.

Starr was replaced on Christmas Eve, 1984, by his former teammate, Forrest Gregg, one of the premier offensive tackles ever to play the game. Unlike Starr, Gregg had served as a head coach elsewhere before taking on the Packer job, and had led the Cincinnati Bengals into the Super Bowl three years earlier. After an injury-ridden 1-7 start in 1984, the Packers rallied to finish at 8-8.

AP/Wide World Photos

Reggie White (left)

The next year was almost a repeat performance, with a multitude of injuries, a 3-6 start and an 8-8 finish. Gregg made wholesale changes in the team personnel over the winter, but to little avail, as the Pack sunk to 4-12 and 5-9-1 marks. Gregg resigned under pressure and on January 15, 1988, was named as the new head coach for his alma mater, Southern Methodist University.

Nineteen days later Lindy Infante, the Cleveland Browns offensive coach, became the tenth head coach in Packer history. Recognized throughout the league as an offensive innovator and very popular with the media as well as fans, Infante was able to put together only one winning season in his four years at the helm.

His final year in 1991 was especially disappointing. The Packers' "Magic Man," Don Majkowski, who had enjoyed a tremendous season in 1989, was able to play only half a year before succumbing to injuries. That, combined with the absence of a running attack, made for a long and losing season. Year-end statistics revealed that the Packer runners totaled only 1,389 yards on the ground all season long, a pitiful 87 yard-per-game average. It was the lowest average the team had ever experienced since records had been kept, and only the second time in their history that the club averaged less than a hundred yards a game on the ground.

For decades Packer fans had been as loyal as any in the country, but the frustrations of the 1991 season resulted in concerted booing and catcalls for the first time in decades. The displeasure was evidenced in attendance as well. At the December 15 game against the Detroit Lions in Green Bay, only 43,881 showed up for the game, leaving close to 15,000 empty seats, and on November 24 in Milwaukee, only 42,132 attended, resulting in some 14,000 empty seats. The poor record, coupled with dwindling fan support, culminated with the dismissal in November 1991 of Executive Vice President Tom Braatz, who had held the reins of the team for five years, and the dismissal of Infante the next month.

Hope springs eternal, the saying goes, and Packer fans were encouraged by the hiring of long-time NFL administrator Ron Wolf as the new Vice President and General Manager, and then six weeks later by the naming of highly-regarded San Francisco 49er assistant coach Mike Holmgren as the new head coach.

Holmgren has a reputation for offensive expertise and served as the 49ers offensive coordinator for two years under Head Coach George Seifert, and three as the team's quarterback coach under Bill Walsh. He had not been a head coach on either the college or professional level; but of course, neither had Lombardi.

Holmgren promised to make the Packers competitive again in the tough National Football Conference. His impact was felt immediately, as the Packers posted a winning 9-7 mark in 1992. Certainly he has some talent to work with as he attempts to right the Packers' ship. Sterling Sharpe is regarded as one of the game's finest wide receivers and Brett Favre is one of the game's most exciting young talents at quarterback.

Moreover, the Packer front office illustrated its commitment to winning when it signed free agent defensive lineman Reggie White, one of the game's most dominating defensive players, to play for the Pack in 1993. How successful he will be remains to be seen, but Packer football fans hope a new dynasty forms and surges into the Super Bowl from the icy confines of Green Bay, Wisconsin.

—Jack Pearson

MINNESOTA VIKINGS

In their 30-plus years as members of the National Football League, the Minnesota Vikings have enjoyed and endured several distinct cycles. Perhaps the best symbol of these shifts is their playing environment, which changed from a venue marked by extremes determined by the whims of nature to one that is artificial and controlled.

First, the Vikings were a struggling but colorful expansion team, created at the beginning of the boom era for their sport. Next, they were a powerhouse that four times came close, but fell short, of the ultimate prize, a team that drew its identity from the sometimes harsh climate it called home and the stone-faced, calculating persona of its coach.

After that, the franchise deteriorated, struggling through mediocre years on the field and an identity crisis off it, churning playing personnel and management executives while the fans adjusted to the new, sterile environment of a domed stadium.

Finally, as they continued well into their fourth decade, the Vikings have regained stability in leadership and have thus returned to a position of competitiveness in the league, led by a head coach whose race alone makes him an historical figure in league annals and whose abilities could help lift the Vikings to a more prominent place in the history books of the sport. The story of the Minnesota Vikings ranges from the coaches like Norm Van Brocklin, Bud Grant, and Dennis Green to quarterbacks as varied in playing style and personality as Fran Tarkenton, Joe Kapp, and Jim McMahon.

Along the way came a colorfully-named defensive line—the Purple People Eaters—and a major, unsuccessful business decision—the Herschel Walker trade—that ultimately helped the Dallas Cowboys build a Super Bowl championship team.

The Vikings Join the NFL

The saga of this successful franchise begins early in an era of competition between the established National Football League and the newly-created American Football League. The professional game, limited in scope and impact through the 1950s and still secondary to college football, seemed poised for explosive growth in the decade of the 1960s. Many investors wanted to buy into the business, as members of either the NFL or the new circuit. The AFL held its organizational meeting in 1959 in Minneapolis, which was to be one of eight charter members of the new league.

A businessman named Max Winter headed a group of investors seeking a team for Metropolitan Stadium, which had been built in suburban Bloomington in the late 1950s, originally to lure major-league baseball. The first baseball team that seemed interested was the New York Giants, which operated a minor-league team in the area. But the Giants moved to San Francisco in 1958 at the same time the Brooklyn Dodgers moved to Los Angeles.

Minnesota instead got the Washington Senators, who took the name "Minnesota Twins" to represent the Twin Cities of Minneapolis-St. Paul, beginning in 1961. (A new version of the Washington Senators was created in the expansion of baseball's American League that season, although that franchise eventually moved to Texas and became the Rangers).

Minnesota's football defection from the AFL became apparent on November 22, 1959, at the Minneapolis meeting. According to author David Harris, in his book *The League: The Rise and Decline of the NFL*, it was learned there that the NFL had decided to "expand."

"That 'expand' translated as raiding the AFL was apparent when Max Winter opened the Minneapolis meeting with the announcement that his Vikings were dropping out and joining the other league," Harris wrote. "While Winter was still explaining himself, Harry Wismer (who operated the New York franchise) came running in from the neighborhood news stand with an armful of local papers announcing the NFL's plans for Minnesota."

Jim Klobuchar, a columnist for the *Minneapolis Star-Tribune*, covered that meeting for the Associated Press and has written about the Vikings, in a variety of roles, for their entire history. In an interview for this essay in late 1993, he recalled Winter's strategy. "The group put pressure on the NFL by courting the AFL," he said. "The first player draft was here (in Minneapolis). Then Bert Bell (the NFL commissioner) and George Halas (the owner of the Chicago Bears) saw this and they decided this territory was too good to let go to the AFL. So they made a counter-offer. The original owners wanted to be in the NFL anyway, so they accepted."

Winter had first approached the NFL about a franchise in 1955. He had come to America from Mahrishostrau, Austria, at the age of 10. Among his many businesses, Winter invested in women's hair care and vending machines and real estate. He was the co-owner and general manager of the Minneapolis Lakers basketball team from 1947 to 1957. Like the Dodgers departing Brooklyn, the Lakers had left for Los Angeles in the late 1950s. At the time, the National Basketball Association was hardly the big business it later became. Minnesota wouldn't again have professional basketball until the late 1980s.

The switch of the Winter group to the established league threatened the birth of the AFL, according to *The Sports Encyclopedia: PRO FOOTBALL, The Modern Era*. "Commissioner Joe Foss, the former South Dakota governor chosen by the team owners to run the league, faced a major problem when the Minneapolis owners quit the circuit," the authors wrote. "This strategic move by the NFL shut the new circuit out of the Midwest and almost killed it in the cradle, but the upstarts did not give up. After several days of discussion, the league owners turned down a bid from an Atlanta group and instead granted the eighth franchise to a syndicate from Oakland, California." That team, the Oakland Raiders, became one of the AFL's most successful franchises.

Team Information at a Glance

Founding date: 1961

Home stadium: Hubert H. Humphrey Metrodome
9529 Viking Dr.
Eden Prairie, MN 55344
Phone: (612) 828-6500
Seating capacity: 63,000

Team colors: Purple, gold, and white
Team nickname: Vikings
Logo: Stylized horn on helmet based on headgear worn by ancient Vikings

Franchise record	Won	Lost	Tie
(1961-1992)	257	216	9

Land grabs such as these in Minnesota and Oakland were typical of the 1960s in the realm of sports business. Until after World War II, most major professional sports leagues were based in the populated cities of the Northeast quarter of the country. But jet airplane transportation had brought distant cities closer together in terms of travel time while television, traveling through the air in a different way, was bringing images of distant places into people's living rooms. The generally healthy economy brought increases in people's leisure time and disposable income, and sports leagues were about to increase their presence in the entertainment industry. The 1960s were to see a gold rush for territory and nearly a doubling of the number of professional teams in the four major sports.

Klobuchar, the journalist, recalled that Minnesota had an edge over some other prospective sites because it had built a stadium even before it had the guarantee of big-league teams. "The only reasons these things happened is that they had built the stadium," he said. "It was a minor-league stadium originally, with 15,000 seats, but the framework was there for expansion."

The name "Vikings" was chosen because many people who live in the region were of Scandinavian descent. According to *The World Book Encyclopedia*, the original Vikings of northern Europe "were fierce pirates and warriors who terrorized Europe from the late 700s to about 1100....Among the Scandinavians, the expression 'to go a-viking' meant to fight as a pirate or warrior," according to *World Book*.

The official mascot of the football Vikings dresses as a Viking warrior and can be seen leading the cheers along the sidelines. The sport caught on with the public, but the games weren't necessarily sellouts at first. College football was still king in the land of 10,000 lakes, and the Golden Gophers drew the sellout crowds.

"The University of Minnesota was very strong at the time, they had won a national championship in 1960," Klobuchar said. "So, in 1961, when the Vikings opened, the attendance for the first game was about 30,000. Pro football didn't have the massive appeal. The big season ticket sale came later, when television created the high impact and then Bud Grant put together winning teams later in the decade."

That first game was played on Sept. 17, 1961, before 32,236 customers at Metropolitan Stadium. The Vikings defeated the Bears by a score of 37-13. The coach of Minnesota was Norm Van Brocklin, a former quarterback. His quarterback, for the last three and one-half quarters of that game, was a rookie from the University of Georgia named Francis Asbury Tarkenton. To this day, Tarkenton's name, of all those who have worn the purple and white of the Vikings, is probably most associated with the club.

Within five minutes after entering the game, Tarkenton threw his first touchdown pass. He threw two more in the third quarter and a fourth later, and scored one touchdown himself. Tarkenton finished the game with 17 completions in 23 attempts for 250 yards.

And he did something else, something that set him aside from other quarterbacks. Instead of taking the ball on pass plays and standing in one area to either succeed or fail and risk a "sack" tackle, Tarkenton often chose to run from side to side in order to avoid defensive rushers and create more time for his receivers to get free of coverage.

It wasn't really a planned play, but it wasn't a panic move, either, because Tarkenton managed to keep his poise while on the run, his eyes searching the field for the open man. This vacating of the pass pocket and its group of blockers was called "scrambling," and no pro quarterback before or since has done it better. When asked why he scrambled so much, Tarkenton said he got the idea from watching games on television and seeing pro quarterbacks accept sacks when their pass pocket collapsed. "I'd sit there and I'd say, 'God, do something,'" he wrote in his book, *Tarkenton*. "Don't just accept defeat."

That first team finished with a record of 3-11 and the home attendance average was 34,586. The roster was made up mostly of castoffs from other teams. The leading rusher was Hugh McElhenny, who carried 120 times for 570 yards. Van Brocklin, who coached the Vikings in their first six seasons, was a colorful and controversial man who didn't mind scolding his players in public. In their second season, the Vikings went 2-11-1. Records in subsequent years were 5-8-1, 8-5-1, 7-7 and 4-9-1.

"The coach was totally unpredictable," Tarkenton wrote. "He could be the most charming guy in the world, and the next day he would be the most obnoxious. He could be sweet as a lamb or raise holy hell. You never knew which way he was coming from, so you were never in a stable situation." Van Brocklin called Tarkenton "Peach" because he was from Georgia or "P.K." for "Preacher's Kid." "If you could throw," he told his young quarterback on one occasion, "you'd be a real menace."

Another of the more colorful original Vikings was Jim Marshall, a defensive end who had played at Ohio State University before spending one year in the Canadian League and another with the Cleveland Browns. He played with Minnesota from 1961 through 1979, setting a league record, for a defensive player, of 270 consecutive games as a Viking, but that wasn't the only reason he was regarded as remarkable.

A few months before joining the Browns, when stationed at an army training camp, Marshall was stricken with encephalitis. He lost 40 pounds but still reported to camp and played. In 1966, he was involved in a play that is still part of many film anthologies. In San Francisco, Marshall picked up a 49ers fumble and ran for the end zone—the wrong end zone. He traveled 66 yards to his own end zone. He had accidentally given the 49ers two points for a safety, although, to Marshall's considerable relief, the Vikings still won by a score of 27-22.

In 1964 Marshall accidentally shot himself in the side while cleaning a gun. He began selling wigs to women. He was given a genius rating on a brokerage test. He modeled men's clothes. He became a skydiver. He was hospitalized when a grape lodged in his windpipe during training camp. While visiting United States soldiers during the Vietnam War, he underwent a tonsilectomy that resulted in severe hemorrhaging. And in 1971 he went on a snowmobile trip in the Grand

Teton Moutains of Wyoming.

According to a Vikings publication called *The First Fifteen Years,* the trip resulted in an accident. "Marshall's snowmobile went over a cliff and nearly crushed him on that trip in the midst of a blizzard," the story said. "Marshall later said, 'It was the toughest thing I've ever encountered in my life. I thought we were going to die." One of the 16 people in his group didn't survive. In his book *RASHAD: Vikes, Mikes and Something on the Backside,* former Vikings pass receiver Ahmad Rashad called Marshall "a Viking among men, and a giant among Vikings."

"Every one of us wants to be the baddest dude in the valley," Marshall told Rashad. "That's what it was all about." Part of the initiation ritual for a new Viking player, Rashad said, was to make a trip to training camp in a car with Marshall driving. A trip that took two hours for most drivers took 45 minutes for Marshall because Marshall drove his car fast. "He was thrilled by danger," Rashad wrote.

After the 1966 season, the personality of the Vikings underwent a drastic change. Marshall remained, but Tarkenton was traded to the New York Giants. He would play there for five years before returning to Minnesota. He was feuding at the time with Van Brocklin, who resigned and went on to coach the Atlanta Falcons. The next coach, Bud Grant, would build the best teams of Minnesota's first 30 years.

Bud Grant Takes the Helm

Grant had been a local hero long before he joined the Vikings. Born in Superior, Wisconsin, Grant won nine varsity letters at the University of Minnesota from 1946 through 1949. He played football, baseball, and basketball. After college, he played two seasons in the National Basketball Association, for the Minneapolis Lakers, and was on two championship teams. After that, he switched to football, joining the Philadelphia Eagles.

He then moved to the Canadian Football League as a player because the Winnipeg Blue Bombers offered him a better salary. Grant also coached the team for 10 years and won the Grey Cup, the CFL's championship trophy, four times. "Canada had comparable players then, and they were paying more money in some cases," Grant said in an interview for this essay. "It was professional football and I coached for 10 years. I enjoyed Winnipeg very much, but coming to Minnesota was coming home for me."

The frosty climate of the Canadian provinces prepared Grant well for Minnesota, one of the NFL's coldest outposts, especially late in the season. Even Grant's appearance seemed to suggest winter. He wore his hair in a silver crew cut and looked at people with what was often called an icy gaze. He rarely showed emotion.

In his book, Tarkenton compared Grant's competitiveness to something "animalistic." "He's the guy in the jungle," Tarkenton wrote. "Patient. Driven but careful. You get the feeling that one way or another he will get what he came for." In an interview for this essay, Tarkenton said Grant "commanded respect as well as anyone I've ever known and he did it without yelling or intimidating or chewing people out.... He never put himself up as an offensive or defensive genius," Tarkenton said. "But everybody knew that he was the leader. He just wasn't overbearing. He's a very wisened man."

Although his first Minnesota team was 3-8-3, Grant's next teams finished at 8-6 in 1968, at 12-2 in 1969, at 12-2 in 1970, and at 11-3 in 1971. Much of the mystique of the Vikings of that era came from their ability to win close games, late in the season, in the cold weather of Metropolitan Stadium.

Like many legends, it doesn't always stand up to close inspection, at least not in all cases. The Vikings lost their share of playofff games at home in December, to San Francisco in 1970 and to Dallas in 1971. But Grant won a few, too, and the impression sent out over television was that he had a team immune to weather.

Rashad recalled the psychological aspect of Minnesota's defense of their home turf. "The

Vikings always ran out for the warmups with this big facade, like we weren't cold," Rashad wrote. "Of course, we were freezing. But the other teams didn't know that, not for sure. They would be looking at us out of the corners of their eyes, thinking 'How come these guys look so warm? They must be some bad dudes.... We knew you could play with numb fingers and frozen feet, which gave us an edge. A lot of times I caught passes without ever feeling the ball, just this heavy thump against my frozen hands."

Grant didn't allow his players to use heaters on the sidelines or hand warmers or long underwear or turtleneck shirts under the jersies. His theory was that if you thought about getting warm you weren't thinking about football. "We probably would have preferred better playing conditions all the time, but the fact of the matter was we weren't going to have them," Grant said in an interview for this essay. "So, we could lament that, like the Rams or the 49ers would, or we could just live in it, which we did. I was used to bad weather, so my background and approach to it helped out."

In the 1980s, when Grant was still coaching the Vikings, the team moved to a domed stadium in downtown Minneapolis. "The things that bothered me about going into the dome is that it took the coaching out of it," Grant said. "There's more things I could do in outdoor weather, even just windy days, or on wet fields, or on poor turf. With frozen fields or snowy days, there were things in my background and experience I could exploit maybe a little bit. Little things that I lost when I went inside. For example, there are stadiums where the wind goes in one end and out the other, so you can actually be kicking with the wind, depending what side of the field you are on, for four quarters. Or, the scoreboard, for example, in December, doesn't allow the field to thaw for the first 20 yards because the sun doesn't get up high enough to go over the scoreboard. So that part of the field is frozen. The rest of the field might be fine. So you know all those things. So, I think, on bad weather, I was better at it in preparing the players, to keep them focused on the game."

Grant recalled how George Allen, the coach of the Washington Redskins, brought his players to Minnesota three days before a playoff game so that they would have time to get used to the cold. "He had a whole locker room all full of all kinds of things to wear," Grant said. "You know, shoes and gloves and mittens and turtlenecks. They spent the whole three days figuring out what they were going to wear instead of getting ready for the game. We won the game.

I took all that away. I said to my players, 'Here, this is what we are going to do. I'll tell you what to wear. That's over with.'" Grant said he liked to look over at the other bench, where players were turned to face the heaters "with their backs to the field. We had to stand up to stomp our feet to stay warm," Grant said, "but we were watching the game."

Grant was flexible about the personalities of players he would employ. One of them, who also came down from Canada, was Joe Kapp, a quarterback whose competitive instincts were greater than his skills. Although not known as a passer, Kapp earned a share of an NFL record on Sept. 28, 1969, when he threw seven touchdown passes in a 52-14 victory over the Baltimore Colts.

But Grant's teams weren't known primarily for talent on offense. They were led by the defense and the defense was led by a front four of linemen called "The Purple People Eaters." They included Marshall, Carl Eller, Alan Page, and Gary Larsen.

Page was the most valuable player in the league for the 1971 season, the first defensive lineman so honored. He and Tarkenton are the only Vikings who have been inducted into the Pro Football Hall of Fame. Page was an amazingly quick and cerebral lineman. He was described thus by author Denis J. Harrington in the book *The Pro Football Hall of Fame, Players, Coaches, Team Owners and League Officials, 1963-1991.* "Perhaps the appropriate theme for the NFL career of Alan Page would be the popular pop standard 'I Did It My Way,'" Harrington wrote. "Page played on the Notre Dame 1966 national championship team. He was the number one pick of the 1967 draft. From 1969 through 1975, he was All-Pro six times and received nine invitations to the Pro Bowl." In his book, Rashad wrote about Page's personality. "Alan Page was the most composed of them all," Rashad said. "You just never saw a trace of pressure on his calm face. He was the most professional ass-kicker in the business. One year, Bud let him miss the entire training camp because Alan was enrolled in law school." Page became a marathon runner. After football, he pursued a career in law and is now an associate judge of the Minnesota State Supreme Court.

Super Bowl Frustration

Part of the legacy of Grant and his teams of that era is, unfortunately, that of Super Bowl defeats. The team reached the championship game four times and lost all of them.

The first was Super Bowl IV, a 23-7 loss to the Kansas City Chiefs on January 11, 1970, at Tulane Stadium in New Orleans. It was the last Super Bowl played under circumstances in which the AFL was a separate league; the two leagues officially merged the next year.

Prior to the contest, both starting quarterbacks received some unwelcome press attention. The week before the game, NBC television implicated Chiefs quarterback Len Dawson in a gambling investigation. Despite the tension and suspicion of the week, he played well.

The Vikings' quarterback, Joe Kapp, bristled at suggestions made by the national press that he lacked a classic throwing style. "Classics are for Greeks," he said. "Who's a classic quarterback? I think I can play some ball." When Sunday came and the game was played, however, Dawson outplayed him and Grant had to take Kapp out of the game.

Before the game, a hot-air balloon with the legend "Vikings" emblazoned across it crashed into the stands, an omen of things to come. Minnesota's Charlie West couldn't handle a wind-blown kickoff and the Chiefs recovered the fumble. The Chiefs used a trap scheme to neutralize Page and they held a 16-0 lead at halftime.

Chiefs coach Hank Stram, wearing a microphone as he was being filmed during the game, was heard saying of the Vikings "They can't figure it out, they don't know what they're doing. It's like a Chinese fire drill out there." The Chiefs cruised in the second half to a comfortable victory.

The second championship defeat was Super Bowl VIII, a 24-7 loss to the Miami Dolphins on January 13, 1974, at Rice Stadium in Houston. Tarkenton had returned, reacquired in a trade with the Giants. The pre-game controversey centered around the Vikings practice facilities at Delmar Field. The dressing rooms had no lockers, only nails on the wall. Birds had built a nest in the shower room, where many of the nozzles didn't work. "This is shabby treatment. This is the Super Bowl. Not some pickup game," Grant told reporters in a press conference early that week. "The NFL sets up the practice facilities and they had a year to do it. Go look for yourself. We don't have any lockers. Our seven coaches get to share one table for spreading out our clothes. The facilities definitely give the Dolphins the advantage." The Dolphins were at the Houston Oilers' facility. The NFL commissioner, Pete Rozelle, fined Grant for his remarks.

By this time the NFL was a powerful institution and the Super Bowl dominated the yearly sports calendar. Some people, including some players, found the hyperbole a bit much. Before the game, lineman Gary Larsen told reporters:

"I hope you don't think I'm a wise guy when I add one thing: We've sweated a long time for this, and a whole bunch of people will be watching on TV. But there are eight hundred million Chinamen who don't give a good goddamn about what happens in Houston this Sunday afternoon."

Those who cared will remember that Miami scored on its first possession of the game, a 68-yard drive, then drove 66 yards on its second possession and led by 17-0 at halftime. The Dolphin quarterback, Bob Griese, had to throw only seven passes, as the Vikings proved unable to stop Miami's formidable rushing attack, spearheaded by fullback Larry Csonka.

The Vikings' third championship defeated occurred in Super Bowl IX, a 16-6 loss to Pittsburgh on January 12, 1975, at Tulane Stadium in New Orleans. The Vikings were favored to win this one, although Page was quoted as having said: "This team is not as good as our other two Super Bowl teams. It is my opinion, just a feeling I have."

At halftime, Pittsburgh led by the score of 2-0. The Steelers scored when Tarkenton turned to hand off the ball and dropped it, resulting in a safety. The Vikings didn't cross their own 35-yard line on their first four possessions as Tarkenton was playing with an injured shoulder and the fierce Steel Curtain defense of Pittsburgh was in fine form. After Bill Brown of Minnesota fumbled the opening kickoff of the second half, the Steelers recovered and scored the first touchdown of the game four plays later. The Vikings were never able to mount a serious challenge.

The club's fourth unsuccessful trip was to Super Bowl XI, a 32-14 loss to the Oakland Raiders on Jan. 9, 1977, at the Rose Bowl in Pasadena. Tarkenton had said "There's an obsession with this team to win this game," but the Vikings came out fumbling. The Raiders jumped to a 19-0 lead and their coach, John Madden, said his team had played tougher games in the conference playoffs. Afterward, Tarkenton said "What we're trying to do is run through all the AFL clubs to see if there's one we can beat."

Reflecting on the Super Bowl losses years afterward, Grant said "I don't think my life would have been any different today if we would have won four Super Bowls. I don't think there is one thing I would have changed in my life," he said. "This is the entertainment business. This is not life and death. You enjoy it, and then it's over. There's nothing older than yesterday's sports page. And then there's a new hero tomorrow. The one thing you have to learn to survive in this business is to lose. It's easy to win. You've got to survive the losses. They are what take the toll on coaches. Yes, we would have liked to have won. We tried our best. We did our best. We got beat by better teams.

"The only thing I feel bad about in losing the Super Bowl is that if we had won a couple of them, I'm sure we'd have three or four more players in the Hall of Fame. Somebody like Paul Krause, with 81 interceptions. No one will ever come close to that record and his name never even comes up. Ron Yary, offensive tackle, played for many years. Jim Marshall. Mick Tinglehoff. Durable players who never missed a game, let alone a season. They played every week and when things got tough and tight, they won close ball games."

Tarkenton and Foreman

Tarkenton had returned to the Vikings in time for the 1972 season, ready to disprove Van Brocklin's earlier knock that he was a "7-7 quarterback." The Vikings, before his return, had won 23 of their previous 28 regular-season game. His first year back the team went 7-7, but the club soon improved. Paul Flatley, a teammate, recalled that Tarkenton was "a take-charge guy who took advantage of everything anybody gave him on the field."

"There were a few people on the team who felt that sometimes he was more concerned with himself than he was about anything else," Flatley is quoted as saying, in Tarkenton's book. "I never paid that much attention. You hear that about almost any successful person. He was probably the first of the businessmen football players. I mean, guys who were serious about using their football careers as a springboard into the business life. Away from there, he was more aloof from the guys than most ballplayers are, even the stars. He gave you the impression he knew exactly where he was going." Of his business interests, Tarkenton said "I'm a capitalist without apology."

Page, at the time, wasn't overly impressed with the quarterback. "I don't think I would give him great grades as a motivator," Page said at the time, according to Tarkenton's book. "I mean, when you compare him with a guy like Joe Kapp. Kapp got involved in every way. He revved up the team."

Tarkenton nonetheless had an outstanding pro career. In 18 seasons with the Vikings and the Giants, Tarkenton became the NFL's all-time leader in attempts (6,467), completions (3,686), yards passing (47,003) and touchdowns (342).

The other stellar player on the offense in the era of the 1970s was Chuck Foreman, a running back who could carry the ball on handoffs and catch it in pass patterns out of the backfield. From 1973 through 1979, Foreman set team records for yards rushing (5,879) and yards combined rushing and receiving (8,936). He led the team in rushing for six consecutive seasons. His best game rushing was on Oct. 24, 1976, when he carried for 200 yards against the Philadelphia Eagles.

Foreman was a first-round draft choice from the University of Miami, which had originally recruited him as a defensive tackle because he stood 6-foot-2 and weighed 195 pounds. In an interview in *The First Fifteen Years,* Foreman tried to describe his running style. "I am sometimes surprised when I look at film of myself," he said. "I just do what's natural out there and live by instinct.... It's like when you're riding your bicycle and all of a sudden, a mad dog starts chasing you. There's a little bit of fear in your heart. You've got to get away.... I look at running as an art."

Some Lean Years

After the fourth trip to the Super Bowl, the decline of the team toward mediocrity was gradual but evident. In the seven seasons from 1977 through 1983, Grant's Vikings finished with records of 9-5, 8-7-1, 7-9, 9-7, 7-9, 5-4 (in a strike-interrupted season) and 8-8. In this span, the team reached the post-season playoffs in four years, but won only two of six playoff games.

Grant retired following the 1983 season, but after the new head coach, Les Steckel, went only 3-13 in 1984, Grant was persuaded to return for a single season, 1985, when his team went 7-9 and finished third in the Central Division of the National Football Conference.

During these unsettled 1980s, many changes were taking place that would alter the infrastructure of the team, its personnel, and its personality. According to the Harris book, *The League,* Winter was dissatisfied with a home stadium that had been adequate for the 1960s but didn't measure up to the improving standards of the 1970s.

The capacity of Metropolitan Stadium, below 50,000, was small. The Vikings didn't have many luxury boxes, which were becoming an important profit center in newer stadiums; these expensive suites drew high priced lease fees from the wealthiest fans. The Vikings could look east to suburban Detroit and see a domed stadium, the Pontiac Silverdome, where fans and players enjoyed climate-controlled comfort no matter how hot or cold the weather was outside.

"Max Winter had been complaining about the stadium for more than a decade," Harris wrote. "His options were either to get a new stadium built or move to another city, and Max had a lot of roots in Minnesota. When nothing had happened by 1973, Winter made his first noises about moving the Vikings, and scheduled an exhibition game in Phoenix, Arizona. In February, 1976, a proposal for a $47 million stadium in downtown Minneapolis was formally submitted to the legislature, but was almost immediately hamstrug by the pro-Bloomington forces."

At that point, according to Harris's history, Winter sent the team's general manager, Mike Lynn, to New York to discuss the possiblity of moving east to play in Yankee Stadium. Lynn next visited Memphis to discuss possibilities there. The Vikings signed nothing more than a one-year lease on the stadium they had.

"In May, 1977, the Minnesota House of Representatives moved 70-60 to start the process again and established the Metropolitan Sports Facilities Commission," Harris wrote. "The commission was empowered to select a site for a new stadium and then issue bonds for construction.

By July, the commission had narrowed the field down to three locations: Minneapolis, Bloomington and suburban Egan.... Max Winter was ready to play his hometown off against whoever was available."

The stadium, called the Metrodome, was built in downtown Minneapolis and became the home of both the Vikings and the baseball Twins. The Vikings moved there in 1982. Seating capacity for football is 63,000. The building features 115 private suites, owned and operated by the Vikings, who control them for all events. The league played Super Bowl XXVI there in 1992, the same year the Metrodome hosted the final four teams in the championship culmination of the basketball tournament of the National Collegiate Athletic Association.

On the field—an artificial field, now—the Vikings were respectable but no longer the dominant and feared team of the Grant era. Jerry Burns, long a Grant assistant, took over as head coach in 1986 and his teams compiled regular-season records of 9-7, 8-7, 11-5, 10-6, 6-10, and 8-8. In 1987, another strike-marred season, the team won its first two playoff games before losing 17-10 to the Washington Redskins in the conference championship.

The Herschel Walker Trade

Late in the decade, the Vikings were involved in one of the biggest and most one-sided trades in the history of professional sports. It involved 18 players, the most famous of them Herschel Walker, a running back and the central figure of the deal, who moved from Dallas to Minnesota on Oct. 13, 1989. Walker had been a star in college at the University of Georgia and had been a key signing of the United States Football League, which briefly challenged the NFL in the early 1980s by playing football in the spring months.

In the deal, the Vikings also got from the Cowboys a third-round draft choice for 1990, a tenth-round draft choice in 1990, and a third-round draft choice in 1991. In exchange, the Vikings sent to Dallas a huge number of players: linebacker Jesse Solomon and David Howard, cornerback Issiac Holt, defensive lineman Alex Stewart, first-, second-, and sixth-round draft choices in 1990, first- and second-round choices in 1991, and first-, second-, and third-round choices in 1992. The Vikings also sent running back Darrin Nelson to Dallas, which traded Nelson to San Diego for the Chargers' fifth-round draft choice in 1990, which Dallas then sent to Minnesota.

Walker played with the Vikings until the end of the 1991 season. He led the team in rushing all three seasons, with totals of 669, 770, and 825 yards in the three seasons. Respectable numbers, but not the sort of statistics expected from a player upon whom the Vikings were hanging championship hopes. After that, Walker was released and signed by the Philadelphia Eagles. The Cowboys, in part with the players they acquired from Minnesota, rebuilt quickly and won the 1993 Super Bowl.

The trade was made by Lynn, the long-time general manager who was also part of a group that purchased the team from Winter in 1987. But the ownership situation remained unsettled, with many disputes among investors, until Roger L. Headrick became president and chief executive officer in 1991, leading a united group that took control of the franchise.

On another front, the Vikings made a change on the coaching staff that will be seen as significant in the league's history. In January of 1992, Headrick hired Dennis Green as head coach. It was Green's first head-coaching position in the NFL. Perhaps more importantly, Green is African-American and was only the second person of color to be appointed to a head coaching position in league history. (The first, two years before, was Art Shell of the Los Angeles Raiders.) In his first season, 1992, Green's team, lightly regarded prior to the season, posted a record of 11-5 and won a division title.

Born on February 17, 1949, Green grew up in Harrisburg, Pennsylvania. He began his coach-

AP/Wide World Photos

Before the start of the 1993 season Minnesota signed colorful ex-Bears quarterback Jim McMahon—a players' favorite—to provide the Vikings with on-field leadership and experience.

ing career in 1972 as a graduate assistant at Iowa, where he had played as a running back. In 1981 he was named the head coach at Northwestern. He moved on to Stanford, then joined the staff of the San Francisco 49ers. After several years on the West Coast, Green returned to the Midwest.

In an interview with writer Frank Deford in *Newsweek,* Green said "I guess they hired me because they were desperate. But why not? Northwestern hired me because they were desperate and so did Stanford." In previous seasons, the Vikings' white front office had been criticized by some of the black players for allegedly insensitive racial attitudes.

Joe Browner, a defensive back, led the criticism during a contract dispute, saying that Lynn showed more willingness to negotiate with white players. The Vikings at that time were the only team in pro football without a single black assistant. Under Green, the 1993 Vikings press guides showed 14 assistant coaches; four of them were black, including Tony Dungy, the defensive coordinator.

Green doesn't enjoy discussing football through a filter of race, although he knows such questions are inevitable. "Yes, yes, I know I'm a trailblazer," he told Deford. "I know all that. But I also know I've never had to apply for a job yet."

As the Vikings begin their second season under Green's guidance, it is possible to see similarities between the Vikings of the 1990s and those of the 1960s. One is at quarterback, where, like Joe Kapp, the Vikings are led by a hard-living, slightly eccentric veteran who had moved around his profession before getting what could be a final chance in Minnesota. Jim McMahon, the controversial quarterback best known for his antics on the Chicago Bear squads of the mid-1980s, has signed with the Vikings and assumed the role of their top signal-caller.

Another similarity is the dominance of the defense. Although not yet as popular as the Purple People Eaters, it is expected to be the strength of the team.

Whether Green, McMahon, and the club's strong defense can lead the team to a return to its prominence of yesteryear is unclear. Longtime Viking fans, however, yearning for a return to winning football exemplified by those Bud Grant-led squads of the 1960s and 1970s, will certainly lend their support.

Sources

Books

Green, Jerry, *Super Bowl Chronicles: A Sportswriter Reflects on the First 25 Years of America's Game,* Masters Press, 1991.

Harrington, Denis J., *The Pro Football Hall of Fame,* McFarland & Company, 1991.

Harris, David, *The League: The Rise and Decline of the NFL,* Bantam Books, 1986.

Neft, David S., Richard M. Cohen, and Jordan A. Deutsch, *The Sports Encyclopedia: PRO FOOTBALL, The Modern Era,* Gosset and Dunlap, 1978.

Rashad, Ahmad, with Peter Bodo, *RASHAD: Vikes, Mikes and Something on the Backside,* Viking, 1988.

Tarkenton, Fran, and Jim Klobucher, *Tarkenton,* Harper & Row, 1976.

Whittington, Richard, *Sunday Mayhem, A Celebration of Pro Football in America,* Taylor Publishing, 1987.

Periodicals

Newsweek, November 23, 1992.

Other

Joe Lapointe, interviews with Jim Klobuchar, Bud Grant, and Fran Tarkenton, October, 1993.

—Joe Lapointe

Tampa Bay Buccaneers

The quest for a quarterback is intertwined throughout the history of the Tampa Bay Buccaneers. Only once in the first two decades of the Florida team's existence has it had a quarterback who seemed able to lead them to the promised land—and it couldn't hang on to him. The list of Tampa Bay hopefuls is an impressive one: Steve Spurrier, Gary Huff, Doug Williams, Jack Thompson, Steve DeBerg, Vinny Testaverde, and Craig Erickson. There have been lots of memorable names, but the only one who won a Super Bowl—Williams—did it for somebody else, the Washington Redskins.

Williams and the Buccaneers' management became embroiled in a bitter contract dispute in 1983. The reasons Tampa Bay wouldn't give in to the quarterback's demands seemed sound at the time, but the Bucs have been paying the consequences ever since. When Williams left, they scrambled to find a replacement; when they found one, they overpaid for him, rather than biding their time and drafting another young prospect to groom. Furthermore, when the replacement didn't work out, the team compounded the mistake by making it all over again.

The Bucs also made mistakes with their top picks, for example drafting Bo Jackson and then not signing him. And regarding quarterback Vinny Testaverde, a Heisman Trophy winner who did not perform well for the Bucs, time will tell whether Tampa once again panicked and cast him away too soon.

Team Origins

Tampa Bay, though, is a dream franchise, and its fortunes seem destined to change. The team has everything going for it: weather, location, fans, and television market with little competition. The franchise dream began in 1968 when the Tampa Bay area first started to push for a professional football franchise. The dream became a reality on April 24, 1974, when the National Football League gave the region the league's 27th team. Attendance had averaged 41,000 for 13 exhibition games, and this display of interest impressed NFL brass. It also expanded the geographic boundaries of the league and increased the size of the television audience, no small consideration.

Tampa Stadium was to be expanded to 72,000 seats as part of the plan, but ownership of the new franchise was nearly as swashbuckling as its name: Buccaneers. Philadelphian Tom McCloskey, a construction man, was originally named the franchise owner, but he declined ownership on October 30th of that year. A quick search turned up Hugh F. Culverhouse, a Jacksonville attorney and real estate investor who turned down ownership of the Seattle franchise for geographic reasons. A 30-year lease was signed committing the Bucs to Tampa Stadium.

Culverhouse settled a year later on his choice to guide the new entry, John McKay, who had coached Southern California to four national championships and was searching for new worlds to conquer. The Bucs stocked their team with 39 players—whom many considered rejects—from the other teams in the veteran allocation draft. This was a gesture merely to give them the bodies to put a team on the field. The real plums were in the draft. The first player McKay chose in 1976 was defensive end Lee Roy Selmon of Oklahoma, whose No. 63 jersey is the only number Tampa Bay has seen fit to retire in its brief history. Selmon's brother Dewey was drafted in the second round.

Dismal Beginnings

To call the first season a disaster is almost like terming Hurricane Andrew a windstorm. Tampa Bay won zero of the season's 14 games, the closest being a 13-10 loss to fellow expansionist Seattle, followed by a 23-20 loss to in-state rival Miami. Shut out five times that season, the Bucs played as a member of the AFC West before settling permanently with the NFC Central.

Only twice did Tampa Bay give up less than 20 points, and its last three losses were by scores of 49-16, 42-0, and 31-14. Spurrier—a journeyman pro quarterback acquired from San Francisco for two players and a second-round draft choice because he won the Heisman Trophy playing for Florida—was so impressive he was quickly waived after the season.

That earned the Bucs the No. 1 overall selection in the draft for the second straight year, and McKay reached into his memory for that one, taking Southern Cal running back Ricky Bell. To back Bell up, he acquired his predecessor, Anthony Davis. He also picked up another veteran backup quarterback whom he hoped would be ready to move up, Mike Boryla, but he suffered a knee injury and never played a game.

Rudderless for their second season, Tampa Bay lost its first 12 games—six by shutout—and looked like a cinch to make it 0-28 for two years. But while everybody was noting the horrible offense, few realized the defense had improved markedly. Only four times did it give up 20 or more points with a second draft and a year of experience behind it.

Successful Defense

Tampa Bay was getting noticed around the league for its punishing defense (teams that played the Bucs noticed it Monday morning). The franchise recorded its milestone first victory on December 11th, with a 33-14 win over the Saints in New Orleans. It was the defense showing the way, returning three interceptions for touchdowns to tie an NFL mark. More than 8,000 fans welcomed the team on its return home that evening. They were rewarded the very next Sunday with Tampa Bay's first home victory, a 17-7 upset of the St. Louis Cardinals.

Suddenly, midway through the 1978 season, everybody was waking up to the strength of the Bucs' defense. The Buccaneers had the top pick

TEAM INFORMATION AT A GLANCE

Founding date: 1974

Home stadium: Tampa Stadium
1 Buccanner Pl.
Tampa, FL 33607
Phone: (813) 870-2700
Seating capacity: 74,296

Team colors: Florida orange, white, and red
Team nickname: Bucs
Logo: The face of a swashbuckling pirate wearing a feathered hat and holding a dagger in his mouth

Franchise record	Won	Lost	Tie
(1976-1992)	74	173	1

in the draft for the third straight year, but McKay traded down to Houston, drafting 17th. He believed the 17th player would automatically help his struggling team (and he was right because that turned out to be quarterback Williams) and that Oilers' Jimmie Giles would upgrade the tight end position dramatically for the Bucs as well. He also got Houston's second pick that year, plus two more choices in 1979.

Selmon by now was an All-Pro defensive end while top linebackers Dewey Selmon, David Lewis, and Richard Wood made up a hard-hitting defense that helped Tampa Bay reach 4-4 by midseason. The lack of depth and inexperience, combined with the fact that strong-armed Williams was learning on the job, contributed to seven losses in the last eight games. Still, 5-12 was a big step up for a team that obviously was going to be heard from in the near future.

McKay again traded his top choice, to Chicago for defensive end Wally Chambers, and made guard Greg Roberts the franchise's top choice in Round 2. Additional experience enabled Tampa Bay to win its first five games. The NFC Central Division race seemed to be over early as the other alleged contenders stumbled around. Bell, working behind a much improved offensive line, became a dominant back with 1,263 yards. Meanwhile, the defense allowed fewer yards rushing and passing than anybody else's, a fact dramatically pointed out at season's end.

Despite the good start, a three-game stretch in which the Bucs could net only 10 points meant Tampa Bay had to win its last game of the season to qualify for its first playoffs. The defense throttled Kansas City, and Neil O'Donoghue's fourth quarter field goal provided a 3-0 victory. And the Bucs didn't stopped here. Tampa Bay's first venture into the playoffs was a success, with Bell running for 142 yards and scoring twice, and Williams hitting Giles with a nine-yard touchdown pass in the fourth quarter to provide a 24-17 victory over Philadelphia.

That put Tampa Bay in the NFC championship game against Los Angeles, which only had a 9-7 record but, like the Bucs, had an outstanding defense. The Rams played ball control to eke out three Frank Corral field goals, while the Bucs could get nothing off the Rams' defense, netting just 177 yards as Williams misfired on his first eight passes. Lee Roy Selmon was named NFC Defensive Player of the Year.

Fleeting Success

Did the success in the third year spoil the team? Maybe so, as Tampa Bay dropped back in 1980 to mental mistakes and mediocrity at 5-10-1, tied with Green Bay for last in the NFC Central. The draft yielded offensive lineman Ray Snell and wide receiver Kevin House, but Chambers retired and injuries curtailed the seasons of nose tackle Randy Crowder and Bell. Nobody was taking Tampa Bay lightly any more, especially divisional foes who were 6-1-1 against them. The Bucs lost six of their last seven overall.

The lack of a dominant team in the division gave Tampa Bay time to regroup and rebound in 1981, allowing the Bucs to win the division with a 9-7 record. It also was the year in which Culverhouse fronted a drive that resulted in Tampa Stadium landing the 1984 Super Bowl.

McKay felt the quality of his linebackers' play declined sharply in 1980, so he drafted No. 1 Hugh Green to prod them. Back James Wilder also came on board to back up Bell. And Williams continued to develop. He came into the league known as a kid who could throw a ball through a brick wall—and sometimes was accused of treating his receivers like brick walls.

Williams still threw a 60-yard line drive, but now was getting a touch and a feel for running an offense. He moved up to become the sixth-rated passer in the NFC, threw 19 TD passes, and his interception rate dropped to three percent. Green sparkled as a rookie, and House blossomed with 1,176 yards and a conference-best average of 21 yards per catch. Tampa Bay stumbled around like the rest of the division and was 5-6 through 11 games, two games out of first.

But three straight wins put the team in a first-place tie, which Tampa Bay settled with a 20-17 victory at Detroit. House caught an 84-yard TD pass, and David Logan turned a Selmon sack into a touchdown to provide the victory margin.

The Playoffs

The playoffs were a different story. Dallas picked off four of Williams' passes, stuffed the Tampa Bay running game, and carried off a 38-0 victory to show the Bucs they still had a lot of growing up to do. Guard Sean Farrell and defensive end Booker Reese were McKay's first two choices in the 1982 draft. Bell, Dewey Selmon, and Lewis were traded to San Diego.

That was the season the players went on strike after two games, which put a sense of urgency on the season when it resumed November 21st. The regular season was extended through January's first weekend, and a Super Bowl tournament was set up involving the top eight finishers in each conference.

Tampa Bay had lost both pre-strike games and split its first four after play resumed. But McKay rallied his team for three wins down the stretch. The last came when Bill Capece kicked a game-tying 40-yard field goal with 26 seconds left in regulation, and added a 33-yard field goal 3 minutes and 14 seconds into overtime to produce a 26-23 victory over Chicago. The Bucs had won by scoring 17 points in 22 minutes.

The offense became as predictable as hot weather and rain in the tropics—Williams handed off to Wilder or Williams threw to Wilder. The defense returned to its body-thumping best of earlier seasons, enabling the team to secure all five of its victories in the final minute of play. A player might know Wilder was coming, but that didn't mean he could stop him. The opposing offense wasn't going to move the ball on the suffocating Buccaneer defense.

Finishing seventh in the tournament slotting meant Tampa Bay caught Dallas in its playoff opener again, and the Cowboys licked the Bucs one more time, although 30-17 was not indicative

Quarterback Debacle

It isn't hard to pinpoint when things started coming apart for the Tampa Bay Buccaneers. It was the summer of 1983 when negotiations between Tampa Bay and quarterback Doug Williams came undone. With Williams, the Buccaneers were a team on the way up. Without him, they went straight to the bottom and have been starting over ever since. Coach John McKay made Williams his first-round draft choice in 1978, the franchise's third year. The Bucs had gone 0-14 and 2-12 before Williams arrived. McKay made the first black quarterback to be drafted in the first round his starter from his very first game, and Tampa Bay improved to 5-11. His second year they were 10-6, division champions, and won the first play-off game they didn't have to watch on TV.

A year of regression to 5-10-1 followed, but 1981 was another NFC Central championship year at 9-7. Tampa Bay made the play-offs with a 5-4 record during the 1982 strike season when Williams' contract was in its last year. Negotiations broke down, Williams took bigger money from the USFL, and when that league folded after two seasons, he signed with the Washington Redskins. Washington won the 1988 Super Bowl, 42-10, over Denver, with Williams as quarterback. He was MVP for throwing four touchdown passes in the second quarter when the Redskins blew the Broncos away.

Injuries followed and Williams was forced to retire after 1989. "He was becoming—not there yet, but on the way—one of the better quarterbacks in the game," McKay told *Sports Illustrated* the season after Williams left, the one where it all came unglued for Tampa Bay. "The biggest thing he had to control was his emotions.... That thing about being the first great black quarterback might have been the problem, but I thought he was controlling that. I had to tell him, 'No matter what happens, Doug, you're the quarterback. Nobody's going to come out there and take your place.'"

Looking back, especially considering the kind of money being thrown around for quarterbacks today, the amount Williams and Bucs' owner Hugh Culverhouse differed by was small change. Williams wanted $875,000 annually (he said that in public, but when it was all over he said he'd have taken $600,000 a year), while Culverhouse offered $400,000 a year on a three-year contract. The owner made a final offer, tacking on an additional $500,000 year, then a fifth season at $600,000. Culverhouse and Williams started exchanging public insults, hardening both positions. McKay didn't want to get involved because it wasn't his place. Williams felt racism was involved, saying a white quarterback would have gotten what he asked. He ended up signing a two-year contract with the Oklahoma Outlaws of the USFL in early August.

McKay felt Williams and Culverhouse would come to terms, so he didn't draft a quarterback in the spring. But when training camp neared and it became obvious that there was no resolution to the problem, McKay told General Manager Phil Krueger to go fishing. What they caught was Cincinnati's No. 2, Jack Thompson. The price was a first-round draft choice and Thompson's $200,000 salary. It didn't take a genius to figure out that Thompson's salary added to what they were offering Williams might have brought the incumbent quarterback back. Tampa Bay, though, proceeded with the deal, and Williams signed with Oklahoma. The Bucs played ten games before they finally won one without Williams as their quarterback; entering 1993, they still had not had a winning season.

Would their record have improved with Williams? No one knows for sure. One thing for certain was that Tampa Bay would have a first-round draft choice in 1984, and a second-round pick in 1985, which they gave to Denver to get Steve DeBerg. These two factors might have ensured they would have picked lower than first overall in 1986—when Tampa Bay drafted Bo Jackson and never signed him. Somebody else would have drafted Vinny Testaverde the next year, 1987. And Tampa Bay would have had a first-round choice in 1992—the one they gave Indianapolis for quarterback Chris Chandler. Maybe Doug Williams would have quarterbacked Tampa Bay to the 1988 Super Bowl title--or, maybe not. So far, McKay's been right. Nobody has come out there to take Williams' place. They made a decision. And they've been paying for it ever since.

of the game's closeness. Dallas outgained Tampa Bay, 456-218, and this year picked off three of Williams' passes, one of which was run into the end zone in the fourth quarter to turn a 17-16 Cowboy deficit into a 23-17 lead. A late TD pass by Danny White, who outpassed Williams 312-113, sewed it up.

Williams Moves On

The honeymoon lasted seven years. It ended for Tampa Bay in 1983. A starter since his rookie season five years previous, Williams was not only growing up professionally, he was feeling underpaid and underappreciated by the Bucs. So he signed with the fledgling USFL when he normally would have been in training camp, leaving Tampa Bay scrambling to find somebody other than journeyman Jerry Golsteyn to run the show. It never dawned on McKay that his quarterback and owner wouldn't find a meeting of the minds, so he neglected to take a quarterback in the spring draft. It was a problem that would continue to haunt the Bucs for years.

Shopping around, McKay found Cincinnati willing to part with Thompson, Ken Anderson's backup, but the price was steep. Tampa Bay had to part with a No. 1 draft choice in 1984. With no No. 1, Tampa Bay's top draftee was linebacker Keith Browner. Thompson's numbers weren't bad—2,906 yards and 18 touchdowns—but he wasn't consistent, and Tampa Bay couldn't score when it needed to. Great defense was no longer good enough. The fans weren't interested in reasons or excuses; they had had enough. There had to be someone on whom to pin the blame.

McKay didn't have a top-flight quarterback, and his offensive line had been thinned by injuries plus the trade of veteran Charley Hannah. So McKay turned to doing in the professional ranks that had worked so well at the collegiate level: student body left, student body right, and student body up the middle. It became a question of who was going to break down first, enemy defenses or James Wilder. Enemy defenses won.

The bull-like running back ran 42 times against Pittsburgh on October 30th, gained 219 yards against Minnesota a week later, then went out for the season with broken ribs the next week. An undefeated preseason had given the fans hope that the loss of Williams would not be critical. But the Bucs struggled. They lost by a touchdown here and a field goal there; they lost nine straight games. Neither Thompson or Golsteyn could move the team, and after winning its first game of the year, Tampa Bay dropped the next two by shutout. And when Wilder went out, it was all over. The Bucs finished 2-14, and the fans found their scapegoat. It was McKay.

The always aloof McKay may have been tiring of being on the pro scene firing line anyway. While running a critic-free show at USC and during the Bucs' formative years, McKay never had to get used to having his decisions questioned. Now, everybody was an expert. Times were changing on the player scene, too. No longer would the athletes take their money and be quiet. Not only did they talk, they often voiced how they thought things ought to be. McKay certainly wasn't used to players telling him how the team should be run.

Possessor of a biting wit, his humor now turned sour. Lines that used to draw laughs now drew sneers. Soon McKay was hurling humor harpoons at his own players. The atmosphere grew decidedly sour. Knowing a quarterback was essential to his team's chances in 1984, McKay took out a second mortgage on the future, but not going for No. 1—the boss had learned that lesson. He had to find another good backup, but one not so expensive.

A New Quarterback

The presence of John Elway made Denver's backup expendable, so Steve DeBerg was purchased at the cost of a current No. 4 draft choice plus 1985's No. 2. DeBerg ranked eighth in the NFC in passing (3,554 yards), House caught 1,005 yards worth of passes, and Wilder ran for 1,544, but now Tampa Bay began having trouble on the other side of the line of scrimmage. An October automobile crash took Green out of the lineup, leaving too much of the burden on Selmon and Logan.

The squad had scratched and clawed its way to a 3-3 record when it lost four straight, the last a 27-24 defeat at Minnesota on November 4th. The next day McKay announced he would not return as coach in 1985, retreating to the club presidency. The Bucs won their next game but dropped three more before sending McKay to the safety of the front office with two straight wins and a 6-10 season that was good for third place in the shabby NFC Central. Selmon made Pro Bowl starter for the sixth straight year.

The Bucs decided to go with a proven pro for their second coach and chose former Atlanta boss Leeman Bennett. Defensive end Ron Holmes (1st) and kicker Donald Igwebuike (10th) were the notable draftees in 1985. Nine straight losses took care of the Bucs' chances to be a winner. They shut out St. Louis, 10-0, to break that streak, but after getting hammered, 62-28, by the Jets the following game, Bennett got the idea it might be time to change quarterbacks.

Exit DeBerg and enter Steve Young, a young man who didn't have Williams' arm but who did know something about throwing on the run and reading defenses. Bennett may have been reluctant to go to Young earlier because he was culled from the USFL. The newcomer guided his team to a 19-16 overtime win over Detroit, but Tampa Bay lost its last four to finish 2-14. Wilder gained 1,300 yards and led the team in receptions again, but House fell off to 803. More trouble loomed.

There was only one choice for the first overall pick in the 1986 draft—super-back Bo Jackson. So Tampa Bay drafted him, then didn't do what it took to sign him. Tired of the hardball tactics of the Bucs, Jackson decided to play a little hardball himself—of the baseball variety, with the Kansas City Royals. Kansas City soft-talked and sweet-talked and finally, paying enough money and guaranteeing him a major league roster spot, got Jackson to sign a baseball contract.

Tampa Bay had a second first-round choice in the draft, from Miami for Green, and took cornerback Rod Jones to beef up its secondary. The season started with two straight losses and quickly got to 1-7. Both ends went down with injuries, hurting an already meek defense, and Bennett cut mainstay tight end Giles plus wide receiver House in mid-year. Young showed progress but had no help, and a second straight 2-14 season earned Bennett the door and Tampa Bay another shot at picking first in the draft. Young was another quarterback who suffered for a rocket arm by comparison with Williams. They also thought he flushed from the pocket too easily.

Enter Third Coach

Having gone to the college ranks for their first coach and the pros for their second, Tampa Bay opted for a hybrid for its third coach, Ray Perkins. Perkins coached the New York Giants in 1979 (6-10), 1980 (4-12), 1981 (9-7), and a 4-5 mark in 1982's strike season before leaving to succeed legendary Bear Bryant at Alabama, where he'd gotten the Crimson Tide rolling again. Perkins wanted the moon to get back into the pros, so the Bucs gave him that plus Mars and Venus, too. Perkins got total control of Tampa Bay's fortunes on the last day of 1986, but it didn't take a rocket scientist to figure who his 1987 draft choice was going to be—1986 Heisman Trophy winning quarterback Testaverde.

Shortly after the draft, the NFL went through six ballots before naming Tampa Stadium the site of the 1991 Super Bowl, the second Super Bowl game to be held there. The presence of Testaverde made Young superfluous. San Francisco believed Young was a quarterback in the Joe Montana mold and got him by giving Tampa Bay draft choices who turned out to be linebacker Winston Moss and wide receiver Bruce Hill. Guard Sean Farrell was traded to New England for a couple of draft picks, and Perkins chose wide receiver Mark Carrier in the third round. Defensive back Ricky

Reynolds was taken second, while tight end Ron Hall was a fourth-round selection.

A 4-3 start that included a 1-2 record with strike replacement players had Tampa Bay fans with short memories thinking playoffs. But the St. Louis Cardinals, trailing 28-3 after three periods, scored 28 points for the biggest fourth quarter comeback in NFL history to take a 31-28 win. "If I believed in a turning point," Perkins admitted after the season, "I'd say that was probably it."

Tampa Bay didn't win a game the rest of the year, the last four with Testaverde getting valuable experience—at running for his life, if nothing else. Testaverde made his debut as a starter on December 6th and passed for 369 yards with two touchdowns. Carrier's 212 receiving yards in the game were a club record.

There were holes to fill on the offensive line, and Perkins plugged one with first-round draftee Paul Gruber, a tackle. DeBerg, too high-priced to sit on the bench, was shipped to Kansas City for a low draft choice. That meant Testaverde was being thrown in the bay to sink or swim. He tread water. Veteran Joe Ferguson was obtained from Indianapolis at a low cost (low 1989 draft choice) for backup duty and perhaps to teach Testaverde how to harness his bullet ball.

AP/Wide World Photos

Vinnie Testaverde (14)

Testaverde Becomes Starter

Perkins formally installed Testaverde as his starter, and his second-year status showed an incredible 35 interceptions, an efficiency rating of 48.8 (inefficiency rating in this case), and a ranking of 14th among NFC quarterbacks. The promise of the man was shown in a game against Indianapolis when Testaverde threw for 469 yards, a 35-31 loss. However, the state of the NFC Central Division was so dismal at that time that there were two teams worse than Tampa Bay—Detroit and Green Bay—so a 5-11 record put the Bucs third.

Second-round draft choice Lars Tate supplanted the worn-down Wilder as the backfield workhorse, while Hill (1,040) and Carrier (970) returned the emphasis on the passing attack to the wideouts, rather than backs and tight ends. The season produced one other notable: Tampa Bay's 10-5 win over eventual AFC East winner Buffalo was the first game in NFL history decided by such a score.

Linebacker Broderick Thomas was the top draft choice for 1989, a season in which Tampa Bay stayed still yet dropped to the bottom of the standings. A second 5-11 record wasn't good enough to remain ahead of the Lions and Packers—or the sagging Bears. Tampa Bay opened the season by sandwiching wins against Green Bay, New Orleans, and Chicago around two losses. In came winless Detroit and out went Tampa Bay's hopes of mounting an assault on its recent losing tradition. The Lions won, 17-16, behind a rookie quarterback, Rodney Peete, who reminded some Bucs fans of Young.

Carrier set club records with 86 catches for 1,422 yards that season, but no ground game and a toothless defense hurt the Bucs. Testaverde climbed to 11th in the rankings, cut his interceptions to 22, and threw for 20 touchdowns, but continued to play inconsistently. Perkins went for yet another linebacker with the first choice in the 1990 draft, but Keith McCants, whom he'd had at Alabama, was flopped first at linebacker and then at defensive end before being slashed from the roster during 1993's training camp.

Running back Reggie Cobb was drafted No. 2 to shore up the lagging ground attack, and Gary Anderson, who could be utilized as a double threat, running as well as catching the ball coming out of the backfield, was obtained from San Diego for a third-round choice in 1990 and a second-round pick in 1991. Anderson was available because he'd sat out the previous season in a salary dispute with the Chargers.

The Bucs started out 3-1 and 4-2, giving rise to unrealistic expectations. Then a last-minute loss to Dallas started a six-game losing streak. You could hear the whispers of blame during the tailspin and see fingers pointing through the flames as the season crashed. Having total roster control made Perkins subject to criticism when things didn't work out, and he was another coach who didn't take kindly to having his judgment questioned by those whom he considered to be less knowledgeable. His testiness increased with the losses, which finally ended with a 23-17 win over Atlanta on December 2nd. But the next day Perkins was fired, and his chief assistant, Richard Williamson, was named to replace him.

Tampa Bay toppled Minnesota in Williamson's first game. But the club lost its last two, and a debate began over whether to give the former assistant his own shot at the job or go outside for another name boss. In the meantime, the New York Giants edged Buffalo, 20-19, in the Tampa Bay-hosted Super Bowl XXV. Shortly thereafter Tampa Bay settled on naming Phil Krueger general manager and giving Williamson a chance to create his own coaching identity.

Tackle Charles McRae was the Krueger team's pick in the first round of the draft. The second choice belonged to San Diego as a result of the Anderson deal, but Tampa Bay made a good choice in the third round when they took wide receiver Lawrence Dawsey.

Continued Quarterback Disappointment

The other whisper to come out of the previous season concerned Testaverde and his potential to become a franchise quarterback. His continual throwing into coverage, resulting in too many drive-stopping interceptions, plus a lack of a knack of knowing when to eat the ball or when to throw it away were leading to disenchantment with the quarterback from press and public.

The 1991 season began with five losses, and Testaverde hit the sidelines twice during the season, only to reclaim his job when Chris Chandler wasn't any better. Chandler himself was an indication of the team's dissatisfaction with Testaverde, because Tampa Bay had traded Indianapolis its 1992 first-round draft choice to get the backup. His confidence shaken, Testaverde dipped to 17th in the rankings. His TD passes plummeted to eight, but his interceptions remained high at 15. His passing yardage dropped from 2,800 yards to 2,000.

The team scored only 199 points, but there were bright spots as Cobb ran for 752 yards and rookie receiver Dawsey led the team with 818 yards. Thomas began to star at linebacker for a defense that performed well except in interceptions and stopping opponents from getting across the goal line. The 3-13 record and the desultory way it came about got Williamson fired. Sam Wyche, who lost his cool and his job at Cincinnati, was brought in as coach and director of football operations to do the things Perkins was unable to do.

With the Bengals, Wyche had grown paranoid over a woman sportswriter coming into his locker room and, before he left, was reacting badly to anyone who wanted to talk to his teams. Wyche found himself without a first-round pick because of the Chandler deal, so his top choice was second-rounder Courtney Hawkins, a wide receiver who only caught 20 passes but averaged 16.8 yards doing it. Just in case, he also picked one of Testaverde's successors with the Miami Hurricanes' Craig Erickson in the fourth round. (Erickson had a knee injury coming out of school and could not agree on a contract with Philadelphia, which had made him its fifth choice in 1991. Erickson spent the year as an assistant coach at Georgia and became a free agent again on 1992 draft day.)

Wyche was widely credited with the making of Joe Montana during his days as a Walsh assistant with San Francisco, then developing Boomer Esiason at Cincinnati. Perhaps Testaverde didn't have the makings of either of those illustrious quarterbacks, but Wyche viewed one of his first tasks as that of restoring Testaverde's shattered image.

If the problems Testaverde was having came from being hounded on the field and in the press, Wyche could do something about that. He took the young man under his wing, re-drilled him, and turned him loose on the field. Tampa Bay won three of its first four games before Testaverde passes again began winding up with the wrong jerseys. The Bucs lost six straight, won one, then lost five in a row before finishing with a victory that made Wyche 5-11, tied with Chicago and Detroit for worst record in the NFC Central.

Testaverde Let Go

Testaverde finished ranked 10th in the NFC among quarterbacks, although his completion percentage was up to 57.5 and his yardage to 2,554. But he only countered his 16 interceptions with 14 TD tosses. So when the decision had to be made whether to re-sign Testaverde or let him go, Wyche opted to let Cleveland sign the quarterback to a big contract to back up Bernie Kosar. DeBerg, returning to the Bucs as a Plan B free agent signee from Kansas City, started two games for Testaverde in 1992 and provided Wyche with experienced help (at 39 he is the oldest player in the league), while Erickson was being groomed to take over. Erickson's size and arm may not compare to Testaverde, but he may have the intellect to run Wyche's no-huddle offense and recognize defensive coverages.

Dawsey and Courtney provided bodies to throw to, while Cobb ran for 1,058 yards and scored nine times in 1992. Defense was another subject, however, so Wyche moved to beef up that area with the drafting of defensive end Eric Curry first, and linebacker Demetrius DuBose in the second round. The play of both Thomas and McCants declined along with the defense, which finished 21st in the conference. The defense did develop some good players in 1992. Reynolds became one of the league's best at his position, while rookie defensive linemen Santana Dotson, a fifth-rounder, and Mark Wheeler, the third-round choice, showed exceptional promise.

The franchise has in Wyche a coach who has been to the Super Bowl and knows what it takes to get there. Tampa Bay fans have to hope Erickson can develop into the quarterback the franchise has been looking for ever since Williams left town.

Sources

Books

Neft, David S., Richard M. Cohen, and Rick Korch, *Sports Encyclopedia: Pro Football,* 11th edition, St. Martin's, 1993.

Odioso, Rick, and Tampa Bay Public Relations Staff, *Tampa Bay Buccaneers Media Guide,* Tampa, FL, 1993.

Riffenburgh, Beau, *The Official NFL Encyclopedia,* NAL, 1986.

Periodicals

Sport, October 1983.

Sports Illustrated, October 24, 1983.

—Richard Shook

National Football Conference

Eastern Division

Dallas Cowboys

Known as "America's Team," the Dallas Cowboys are arguably the most talked-about franchise in the history of the National Football League (NFL). Winners of three Super Bowls, the Cowboys have built a solid record of achievement since forming in 1960. Off years have been rare indeed for a squad that one sportswriter called "the best characterization of the pro football team imaginable."

That same writer, Leigh Montville, is quoted in *Tex! The Man Who Built the Dallas Cowboys* as saying that the team "should be put in a time capsule. If the dominant sport of our generation has been pro football—and it has been—the Cowboys are the logical choice. No team better describes pro football and stay-at-home Sundays of the past decade.... They are a team of efficiency and controversy and rhinestone glitter."

In *The Great Teams: Why They Win all the Time,* Robert A. Liston wrote, "There are few things as predictable as the appearance of the Dallas Cowboys in the playoffs of the National Football League.... Even in losing they have provided some of the monumental moments in the history of the sport. The Cowboys are truly dynastic." Remarkably, that dynasty has been engineered by less than a half-dozen people. For nearly 30 years the team was led by general manager Tex Schramm and coach Tom Landry, who sent the Cowboys to five Super Bowls and 11 divisional first-place finishes.

More recently, owner Jerry Jones and coach Jimmy Johnson have stemmed the tides of decline and restored the Cowboys to Super Bowl glory. As Dave Caldwell remarked in the *Philadelphia Inquirer,* after the Cowboy victory in Super Bowl XXVII in 1993 "the message was Texas-size, there for 27 NFL teams to read and tremble over.... *The Cowboys are back. Get used to it....* If they keep this up, Lord knows what the next few years will be like for the rest of the league."

The "America's Team" nickname grew out

of a perception that the Cowboys had a national following. Television's Nielsen ratings bear this out: year after year, the team draws larger viewing audiences than its rivals—even in losing seasons. Bob St. John wrote in *Tex!* that at CBS "the admitted policy ... has been, when in doubt televise the Cowboys." This is not to suggest that the team basks in a limelight of total national approval, however. The Cowboys' glittering image—shiny silver uniforms, palatial offices and stadium, and scantily-clad cheerleaders—has drawn equal amounts of admiration and loathing. The hot spotlight of fame has magnified each Cowboy controversy, intensified each Cowboy defeat, and—most important—has made Dallas "the team to beat" in every other city housing an NFL team.

Before achieving championship form, the Cowboys suffered years of dramatic struggle and setback in the early years of the franchise. Texans remember vividly that theirs was an NFL team better known for losing big games than for winning. What brought the Cowboys to greatness in the 1970s was a stable organization—an owner who gave his staff votes of confidence and blank checks, a general manager who knew how to promote the team, and a coach who was both a football genius and a Christian gentleman.

Many NFL teams are remembered for the outstanding contributions of individual players or for particularly aggressive units. Dallas has had its share of superstars, but the names most closely associated with the team for 30 years were the men running the show: Tex Schramm and Tom Landry. Both were enshrined in the Football Hall of Fame on first ballots in the early 1990s.

The Men Who Built the Cowboys

Texas E. Schramm was born and raised in San Gabriel, California. His parents were Texans who relocated to the West Coast but still retained pride in and dedication to their native state. A hyperactive child who struggled with learning disabilities throughout his youth, Schramm blossomed only in high school. There, at Alhambra High, he became sports editor of the school paper and a varsity athlete as well.

Tex Schramm

In order to qualify for admission to the University of Texas—his father's alma mater—he had to study briefly at Pasadena Junior College. Finally he was accepted at the University of Texas, where he joined the football team as a walk-on and played until injuries put an end to his career.

Schramm wanted to be a sportswriter. He majored in journalism at college and wrote for the *Daily Texan,* the university's newspaper. After receiving his degree he took a job as afternoon sports editor of the *Austin American-Statesman.* In the meantime, his father found out that the fledgling Los Angeles Rams were looking for a publicity director. In the mid-1940s, Schramm went to work for the Rams. By dint of hard work and enthusiasm, Schramm found favor with Rams' owner Dan Reeves.

Team Information at a Glance

Founding date: January 28, 1960

Home stadium: Texas Stadium
2401 E. Airport Freeway
Irving, TX 75062
Phone: (214) 566-9900
Seating capacity: 65,024

Team colors: Blue, silver, and white
Team nickname: Cowboys, 1960—
(Also unofficially known as "America's Team," 1979—)
Logo: Royal blue five-point star outlined in white

Franchise record	Won	Lost	Pct.
(1960-1993)	284	191	.594

Super Bowl wins (3): 1972 (Super Bowl VI), 1978 (Super Bowl XII), 1993 (Super Bowl XXVII)
Super Bowl losses (3): 1971 (Super Bowl V), 1976 (Super Bowl X), 1979 (Super Bowl XIII)
National Football Conference Championships (6): 1970, 1971, 1975, 1977, 1978, 1992
National Football Conference East division first-place finishes (12): 1966, 1967, 1970, 1971, 1973, 1976, 1977, 1978, 1979, 1981, 1985, 1992
Wild-card playoff appearances (6): 1972, 1975, 1980, 1982, 1983, 1991

Over the years the enterprising Schramm showed talent in scouting, recruitment of players, contract negotiation, and publicity. By the time he left the Rams in 1956, he was a highly regarded general manager. Insiders in the football business were surprised when he took a job as assistant sports director at CBS.

All of Schramm's work prior to the move to Dallas helped prepare him to field and sell a professional football team in Texas. From his days with the Rams he learned the practical business of building and running a football program. From his days with CBS he learned extra techniques for publicity, media management, and computerization. He was, in short, an extremely knowledgeable, canny executive who would wield enormous power in the NFL, both on behalf of the Cowboys and the league.

Unlike Schramm, who labored for football behind a desk, Landry served his apprenticeship on the field. Born in tiny Mission, Texas in 1924, he grew up dedicated to perfecting his athletic abilities. In his senior year of high school, his football team went 12-0 and won a state championship. From Mission, Landry moved to the University of Texas, where he played quarterback, punted, and played fullback.

His college career was interrupted by World War II. Trained as a bomber co-pilot on a B-17, he flew 30 combat missions over Europe before returning to finish his education. As a postwar collegian, he distinguished himself in University of Texas performances at the Sugar Bowl one year and the Orange Bowl the next.

In 1949 Landry signed to play professional football with the New York Yankees in the All-American Football Conference. The conference folded the following year, and he moved to the better-known Giants. He played defensive halfback and also served as a punter, but his real talents lay in his ability to grasp the nuances of the game and devise new tricks to help the team. In 1954 he was named player-coach for the Giants' defense. At 29 he was the youngest assistant coach in the league—younger, in fact, than some of the players he coached.

By 1958 Landry was perhaps the best-known assistant coach in football. His experimental 4-3 defense, with major emphasis on the middle linebacker, gave the game a new dimension. The Giants became a championship contender, and coach Jim Lee Howell touted his young protege as "the best coach in football."

That year the Giants advanced to the national championship, losing to the Baltimore Colts in sudden death overtime, 23-17. The game ranks among the most memorable ever played in pro football, and it only enhanced the reputation of Landry, the Giants' defensive coach, and Vince Lombardi, the offensive coach.

Even then Landry did not feel his future lay in professional football. Salaries were not high in those days, and during the off-season he supplemented his income by selling insurance back home in Dallas. Still, he was consumed by the game and spent hour after hour absorbed in films and diagrams of defensive alignments. The luck of good timing and his own hard work would provide Landry with a dream job—one that he would hold for almost 30 years.

The Cowboys Come to Dallas

Texas millionaire Clint Murchison had tried for years to bring an NFL franchise to Dallas, Texas. Murchison had offered to buy the failing Dallas Texans in 1952, but the team left town for Baltimore. In 1959 NFL officials became aware that Lamar Hunt, an owner in the rival American Football League (AFL), planned to field a team in Dallas by 1960. The officials quietly let Murchison know that he could purchase an expansion NFL team to compete with Hunt's AFL squad. Even before they were sure they had a team, Murchison and partner Bedford Wynne began to lay the groundwork. The first man recruited was Tex Schramm.

"I kept hearing rumors about Dallas being awarded an expansion team, and that was what I really wanted," Schramm remembered in his biography, *Tex!* "I mean, I wanted to start something from scratch and build it into a success." Schramm went to work for Murchison in October of 1959 at an annual salary of $36,500. Schramm thus became general manager of the Cowboys even before they became a team.

The inclusion of an NFL expansion franchise in Dallas would be decided by vote at the annual league meeting in January of 1960. This date was well after the pro football draft for that year. Schramm took immediate steps to assure that the new team in Dallas would not be totally bereft of talent. He signed popular Southern Methodist University quarterback Don Meredith to a "personal services contract" that would help the team obtain NFL rights to Meredith. Then, in an even more audacious move, Schramm had counterfeit copies of the standard NFL contract printed so he could sign free agents in December of 1959. "I had to do something to get us started, because we would miss the draft regardless of what happened," Schramm explained in his biography.

Schramm received help in his free agent search from Gil Brandt, a scout he had known in Los Angeles. Although he had not played much football, Brandt was able to spot football talent in other people. He had also forged bonds with agents and college coaches all over the country, and thus Brandt was able to sign 28 free agents to the counterfeit contracts.

For his head coach Schramm looked no further than Tom Landry, a native Texan, fundamentalist Christian, and defensive wizard for the Giants. After the Giants lost another title game to the Colts in 1959, Landry announced that he would be head coach of the new NFL franchise in Dallas. In a book called *The Man Inside ... Landry,* the taciturn coach recalled that the Dallas job "just seemed ideal. It was where we [Landry, his wife and children] were living, we liked the city and the area, and the idea of such a big challenge intrigued me." At 35, Landry became the youngest head coach in the league.

The Hands-Off Approach to Management

The Dallas Cowboys formally came into existence on January 28, 1960. The owners were Clint Murchison and Bedford Wynne. Tex Schramm was the general manager, Tom Landry the head coach, and Gil Brandt the director of scouting. The ownership of the Cowboys was atypical from the start. Murchison declared that he would not interfere, or even attempt to influence, Schramm in the day-to-day business of the club. In turn, Schramm adopted the same hands-off policy with Landry. St. John described the setup in *Tex!:*

"Schramm would be the overseer of the organization itself and any and all things pertaining to the Cowboys that did not involve coaching or actual competition on the field. Landry would control these things and make the final decision on trades, draft choices, and the hiring and firing of assistant coaches. Suggestions might be made, but no pressure would be applied. And to either's knowledge they've never had a serious clash." The relationship endured in harmony for more than two decades.

A challenge was what Schramm and Landry wanted, and a challenge is what they got. First they faced a personnel problem—the new team consisted of free agents with dubious talent, a handful of rookies, including Meredith, with desire but no experience, and 36 veterans deemed expendable by the existing NFL franchises. "I knew I didn't have a lot of talent to work with," Landry stated in his autobiography, *Tom Landry.*

To make matters worse, the Cowboys faced competition for the spectator dollar from both Hunt's Texans and from the ever-popular college teams in the area. Games were played in the cavernous Cotton Bowl in front of less than 10,000 fans. The "front office" was a handful of cubicles on the second floor of an auto club, and the practice facilities teemed with rats.

"Perhaps the most encouraging thing about that first season was how few hometown fans came out to see us lose," Landry recalled in his autobiography. "I remember trotting out onto the field at the Cotton Bowl before one game and wondering if we'd shown up on the wrong date. So few fans came to another home game, that when rain began to fall, the entire crowd moved back under the shelter by the concession stands while we continued to play in what looked from the field to be a completely deserted stadium." The Cowboys finished their debut season without a win, going 0-11-1. The season's only highlight was a 31-31 tie with Landry's former team, the Giants. In 18 years no team had posted a worse showing.

A Challenging Start

No one expected early miracles, however. Landry figured he would need five years to build a team that could handle his complicated offensive plays and unorthodox defensive strategy. He knew that the Cowboys would need several draft years to strengthen the talent. Improvement came slowly in 1961 with the acquisition of tackle Bob Lilly, running back Don Perkins, and linebacker Chuck Howley—all of whom would go on to have multiple Pro Bowl seasons for Dallas. Meredith too showed promise, even though his easy-going personality rankled the businesslike Landry. The Cowboys finished 4-9-1 in 1961 and 5-8-1 in 1962 as Landry shuttled between Meredith and veteran Eddie LeBaron at quarterback.

The 1963 season began with high hopes. The Cowboys had added middle linebacker Lee Roy Jordan and defensive back Cornell Green, and Meredith continued to play strong despite multiple injuries. Still the Cowboys were able to post only a 4-10 season. Worse, in the aftermath of the John F. Kennedy assassination in November, fans in rival cities booed the team lustily, as if the players themselves were responsible for the sad event in Dallas. The only highlight of the year was a victory of sorts: after losing an estimated $3 million, Lamar Hunt announced that he would move his team to Kansas City. Dallas would be the home of one professional franchise—the Cowboys.

Interest in professional football was growing enormously in the 1960s thanks to television, and the Dallas market was no exception. Despite their lackluster play, the Cowboys were drawing audiences who wanted to see victories. When the team finished 4-10 in 1963, some people began to call for a new coach. The stone-faced Landry had not endeared himself to fans. Nor could they understand his baffling "quarterback shuffle" between Meredith and LeBaron.

Bob Lilly

Schramm detected greatness in Landry, and a few words to Murchison convinced the owner too. With a year to go on his original contract, Landry was re-signed in 1964 to a ten-year extension. The new 11-year deal was thought to be unprecedented in the sport.

"I had concluded in my mind that Tom was a damned smart coach and had all the ingredients to make a winner of the Cowboys," Schramm said in *The Man Inside ... Landry*. "I talked to Clint about this and we felt we should make a commitment that this was the direction we were going and let everybody, the players or fans or whomever, know how we felt."

For his part, Landry accepted the new contract as proof of divine intervention. "I had been praying and asking God for some sort of direction and guidance about my future," he said. "And now it seemed I had my answer. I took that remarkable ten-year contract as clear indication of God's will for my life. And I never again doubted that coaching was to be my life's calling."

Landry for the Long Haul

Thus Landry achieved a phenomenal amount of control over the destiny of the Cowboys. He had enough time built into his contract to teach his esoteric plays and to recruit the best young talent. No one above him second-guessed his decisions, and his players knew they would have to work with him for many years to come. As if on cue, the Dallas fans began to support their team and to see its potential. Meredith started throughout 1964 despite sustaining even more injuries, and rookie wide receiver Bob Hayes added some dash to the offense.

Free to implement his strategies, Landry developed the Flex defense and began using it as early as 1963. The Flex is not simple to explain or to execute. St. John wrote, "Basically, Landry had refined the original 4-3 defense he installed with the Giants to combat the 'run to daylight' offensive theory of his friend and rival, Vince Lombardi, at Green Bay. Lombardi's reasoning was to have a blocker hit a man and let the defender react to the block, moving one way or another against the pressure. A running back then would go to the hole created as the defender reacted to the pressure of the block. The specific hole varied, depending on the easiest direction the blocker would take the defender. Certainly, this made it easier to block because the offensive player would just take a defender the direction he was trying to go. The back would adjust to the available hole."

St. John continued, "Landry sought a system in which the defender *would not* react to pressure. Thus, in theory, Cowboy defenders will not react to false keys or pressure, and no holes will be created. Each has a gap responsibility and will simply go to that gap, no matter what appears to be happening. A defender for Dallas, such as a defensive lineman, will first hold his gap, wait, and then react. The natural instinct of an athlete is to react immediately to what he sees and so it takes two or three years to teach a player to wait and then react." Once the Cowboy defenders learned the Flex, they also earned the title "Doomsday Defense." Rival teams spent a great deal of time and energy devising strategies to counter the Landry system.

Landry's "Exotic" Offense

Landry's offense was, if possible, even more complicated. His years as a defensive coach for the Giants had prepared him to anticipate what other teams might run against him—now he devised ways to move the ball that would penetrate such a defense. His playbook was thick with trick plays he liked to call "exotics" as well as the fine-tuned basics. Flanker Pete Gent, who would one day skewer the Dallas organization in the novel *North Dallas Forty,* once quipped to a rookie Cowboy, "Don't bother reading the playbook, kid. Everybody gets killed in the end."

For years Don Meredith got battered behind a weak offensive line. By 1966, however, the Cowboys were beginning to reap the fruits of Landry's harsh tutelage. In the same year that saw the merger of the NFL and the AFL—a deal engineered by Tex Schramm and Lamar Hunt—the Cowboys went 10-3-1 and captured their first Eastern Conference title. Canny draft moves by Gil Brandt had stocked the team with talent. Some of the players, like Hayes, Gent, and Cornell Green, had been college basketball stars or track men.

The dominant characteristic of the 1966 Cowboys, though, was youth—at 29 Meredith was one of the oldest starters. Many others were in their mid- to early-twenties. The team not only looked like a strong contender for immediate games, but it also held the promise of providing a dynasty of winning football for eager Texas fans. Unfortunately for the Cowboys, that promise proved more elusive than any of them might have expected.

Spirits were high as Dallas traveled north to meet the Green Bay Packers for the 1966 NFL title. The game pitted Landry against his former Giants associate Vince Lombardi and also demonstrated two vastly different football philosophies; where Landry favored finesse, Lombardi preferred brute strength. The game was closely contested throughout. The Packers jumped to a 14-0 lead in the first quarter, but the Cowboys tied the score. Late in the game the score stood 34-20, Packers.

The Cowboys drove for a touchdown, then recovered the ball on a squibbed punt. With the clock running down, Meredith managed to move the ball to a first-and-goal at the two yard line. On the first down the Cowboys ran it to the one yard line, but they could not cross the goal line. Three botched plays later, Green Bay had won the championship, 34-27. The loss stung, but Cowboys fans found much to praise, as the young team was finally winning. Meredith was named NFL Player of the Year, and all the cogs seemed to be in place for a series of championship years.

One source of anxiety in 1967 turned out to be Don Meredith. "Dandy Don," the affable antithesis of Landry, had always played with injuries, but in one series of mishaps that year he suffered two cracked ribs, a twisted knee, a broken nose, and pneumonia that robbed him of 20 pounds. Landry eased the pressure on Meredith by playing backup quarterback Craig Morton, and the Cowboys finished 9-5 during the regular season. A spectacular 52-14 drubbing of the Cleveland Browns assured the Cowboys the Eastern division crown again, and that set the stage for another showdown with Green Bay.

December 31, 1967 proved to be one of the coldest days in Wisconsin's recorded history. Despite temperature readings of 13 degrees below zero, the NFL championship game went on as scheduled. During the contest the thermometer dipped to 20 below. Somehow the Cowboys managed to remain competitive even as they developed frostbite. With less than five minutes remaining in the game, Dallas held a 17-14 lead on the frozen field. Then Packers quarterback Bart Starr launched a drive that sent his team to the one yard line with a first-and-goal. Two plays later Starr sneaked the ball across the goal line as the clock ran out. Green Bay had won in dramatic fashion, cheating the Cowboys out of a second Super Bowl trip. Rumors began to fly, saying that the Cowboys were good, but they could not win "the big one." Landry feared that the back-to-back losses to Green Bay would erode his team's confidence, and he was right.

Team Loses Meredith

The 1968 Cowboys finished their regular season 12-2, but lost the Eastern Division championship to the Cleveland Browns. Meredith played so badly in the second half of the Browns game that Landry pulled him and substituted Morton. The upset shook the entire team, and even Landry admitted, "This is my most disappointing day as a coach." Meredith skipped the flight home to Dallas and went to New York City instead. Nevertheless, Landry bounced back quickly and the Cowboys did too. In the next draft, the team acquired Calvin Hill in the first round. Hill was a relative unknown, having played football at Yale University. His solid performance over the years at Dallas would lead other franchises to utilize more liberal criteria when judging potential professional talent.

Dallas would begin its 1969 campaign without the services of Don Meredith, who retired early to the surprise of fans. Although frequently injured, he was not yet 35 years old. Much speculation surrounded Meredith's decision, and some felt that his relationship with Landry—or lack thereof—contributed to his departure. Others noted that Meredith was rarely popular with Dallas crowds, who had booed him even in the winning 1968 season. Certainly Meredith could not have liked the way he was pulled in favor of Morton, especially in the 1968 Cleveland game. Whatever the reason, Meredith left the Cowboys and joined ABC as a television personality. He thus had ample opportunity to air his views of Landry from the broadcast booth, and he did just that from time to time.

Meredith's departure left the Cowboys with Morton as a starter and only one backup quarterback—Roger Staubach. Staubach, a Heisman Trophy winner, had been drafted some years before by Dallas, but as a Naval Academy graduate, he was required to serve four years of active military duty before playing pro football. Throughout his years in the Navy, Staubach retained his ties to the Cowboys, and in 1969 he came to the team as a rookie.

The year belonged to Morton, however, and to Hill, a sensation at halfback. Once again the Cowboys captured their division title with an 11-2-1 season, and once again the team journeyed to Cleveland to try to win the Eastern title. Showing more panache than they had the previous season, the Browns easily beat Dallas 38-14. The Cowboys seemed permanently saddled with the "can't win the big one" reputation.

To make matters worse, the team began 1970

with a shaky start. Staubach and Morton both vied for the starting quarterback position, and—remarkably, given his rookie-of-the-year season in 1969—Calvin Hill competed at halfback with another rookie, Duane Thomas. At mid-season Dallas stood at 5-3, facing a must-win situation in a Monday night game against the St. Louis Cardinals. The televised game was played at the packed Cotton Bowl, and the Cowboys lost 38-0. To add to the humiliation, the crowd began chanting for Meredith, who was supplying commentary in the television booth with Howard Cosell. Landry was almost driven to tears by the loss and its implications for the season. At the next practice, he told the players: "just go out today and play touch football."

Finally, a Trip to the Super Bowl

Somehow that simple game of touch football inspired the struggling team. The Cowboys won five straight to finish the season 10-4. They subsequently beat the Detroit Lions 5-0 in the first round of the playoffs and downed San Francisco 17-10 for the NFC crown. The Cowboys had finally made it to the Super Bowl, where they would meet the Baltimore Colts.

Super Bowl V initially looked promising for the Cowboys. Dallas led 6-0 early after a big Morton-to-Hayes play set up a second field goal. The Colts tied the score in the second quarter, but Dallas jumped ahead again after Jethro Pugh recovered a fumble. Late in the first half, Dallas was on the verge of another touchdown when Duane Thomas fumbled the ball inside the ten yard line. A snatching melee ensued, and the referee ruled that the Colts had recovered the fumble. Despite the second half loss of Colts' quarterback Johnny Unitas, Baltimore came from behind to beat the Cowboys 16-13. The controversial Thomas fumble turned out to be the play that turned the tide for the Cowboys. At game's end, Cowboy Bob Lilly threw his helmet half the length of the football field in frustration.

"For the Dallas Cowboys, it hadn't been enough just to make the Super Bowl," Landry said in his autobiography. "We'd lost again. Yet I saw reason for hope. The way the team pulled together at the end of the '70 season had been the most rewarding experience I'd ever had as a coach. When someone made a mistake, everyone else on the team worked even harder. Because no one else believed we had a chance—not the writers, not our fans—our players realized they had to believe in themselves. We had won seven straight big games just to make it to the Super Bowl. So despite the loss to Baltimore, I thought maybe, just maybe, we'd broken through the mental barrier that had kept us from becoming champions. If so, I believed 1971 would be our year."

The Cowboys opened their 1971 season in a brand-new facility. Texas Stadium, in Irving, provided a gleaming, luxurious palace for the determined Dallas team. Controversy surrounded the 1971 Cowboys, and Landry did his best to keep control in an era when athletes began to demand more attention, more money, and more input on the field. First Landry faced a quarterback quandary. Morton had played injured in 1970 but seemed better in 1971. On the other hand, Staubach had matured and was ready to start. After several weeks of hopping from one to the other, Landry chose Staubach. Staubach was determined to prove worthy of his permanent promotion, and he led the Cowboys to an 11-3 record. Dallas beat the Vikings in the first playoff round 20-9 and won the NFC again on a 14-3 victory over the 49ers to waltz into Super Bowl VI.

Problems With Thomas

One of their biggest controversies followed them to the Super Bowl. Duane Thomas was a brilliant player, but was also moody and disgruntled. Without his performance while Calvin Hill was injured, the Cowboys might never have made the Super Bowl. Still, Thomas was one superstar who would not talk to the press or conform to Landry's rules. His behavior was tolerated through 1971, and he responded by dominating Super

Bowl VI and helping Dallas to win 24-3 over the Miami Dolphins.

The victory of Super Bowl VI showed the Cowboys at peak strength. Staubach had veterans such as Hayes, Mike Ditka, and Lance Alworth on his offense as well as Hill, Thomas, and Walt Garrison. The "Doomsday Defense" was in top form with Lee Roy Jordan, Bob Lilly, Chuck Howley, and Mel Renfro all playing. Dallas rushed for a then-Super Bowl record 252 yards. As Cowboys fans celebrated the long-awaited victory, Murchison commented that the Super Bowl win was "just the successful conclusion of our twelve-year plan."

Roger Staubach

The tense situation with Duane Thomas did not improve as the 1972 season dawned. Landry had regretted his holding Thomas to a double standard and did not intend to do it anymore. Thomas, still fuming over a salary he felt was inadequate, was traded. Hill stepped in and became the first Cowboys' rusher in history to gain more than 1,000 yards in a season. Other injuries slowed the defense, and Staubach missed some games with a separated shoulder. Nevertheless, Dallas advanced to the playoffs as a wild-card team.

Victory begets victory, as Landry knew. In the first-round playoff game, the Cowboys—with Staubach at quarterback—trailed the 49ers by 12 points with less than two minutes to play. So sure were the 49ers of the win that they taunted the Cowboys at the line of scrimmage. The jibes only served to ignite Staubach, who threw for two touchdowns to give the Cowboys a 30-28 edge. Fans began to talk about Staubach as a never-say-die player, a "comeback kid" who could pull miracles for the team. An NFC playoff loss to the Redskins was shrugged off as incidental to an otherwise highly satisfying year.

"We went into the '73 season feeling optimistic, despite a sizable turnover in the team with Chuck Howley, George Andrie, Lance Alworth, and Mike Ditka all retiring," Landry said in his autobiography. "We'd drafted Robert Newhouse and Jean Fugett in '72 and our rookie crop of '73 included Billy Joe Dupree, Harvey Martin, Golden Richards, and a free agent by the name of Drew Pearson." Staubach took the Cowboys to another 10-4 season and led the league in passing. Dallas won the first round playoff against Los Angeles 27-16 but lost to the Minnesota Vikings 27-10 in the NFC Finals. It was the third straight year the Cowboys had missed the Super Bowl by one game, but the eighth straight year that the team had been in postseason play.

The following year, 1974, saw the departure of Calvin Hill and the arrival of a top draft choice—Ed "Too Tall" Jones, a 6'9" 260-pound defensive end from Tennessee State. Jones would become a pivotal player in the "Doomsday II" defense that would help muscle the Cowboys to future Super Bowls. In the meantime, an injury to Staubach forced the use of rookie quarterback

Clint Longley. Longley engineered some come-from-behind victories of his own, but he is best known in Dallas today for his 1975 locker room fistfight with Staubach. After only one season with the Cowboys, Longley disappeared from the NFL. Dallas finished the 1974 season with an 8-6 record, failing to qualify for the playoffs for the first time since 1966.

Enter "The Dirty Dozen"

Observers wondered if the team was on its way to mediocrity when Bob Lilly, Cornell Green, and Walt Garrison retired in 1975. Landry drew more dire predictions when he traded Hayes. Fortunately, Dallas had drawn a trump card, a cadre of 1975 draft choices so talented that they became known as "the dirty dozen." Having several of the players would have been a delight, but having all of them put Dallas right back into contention. The "dirty dozen" were Randy White, Burton Lawless, Thomas "Hollywood" Henderson, Bob Bruenig, Rolly Woolsey, Pat Donovan, Kyle Davis, Randy Hughes, Mike Hegman, Herb Scott, Mitch Hoopes, and Scott Laidlaw. Nine of the men became Cowboys starters.

News of the "dirty dozen" marked the zenith of the Cowboys' scouting procedures. The Cowboys had been using computerized rankings for athletes since 1965 and had devised a standardized checklist that scouts could complete. Brandt, the scouting director, also held the opinions that top athletes in any sport could be taught football, and that no college was too small to yield a potential NFL player. Brandt once signed an Austrian soccer star, Toni Fritsch, to the Cowboys. In 1978 Liston wrote, "The Dallas scouting system is now used routinely throughout the National Football League. But Dallas, by working at it harder, still manages to find more than their share of talent. In their long dynasty, the Cowboys have never faded for long. They feed in a couple of players a year, replacing the old with the new. Other teams can blame this continuity of talent on the club's peerless organization."

In 1975 the Cowboys became a Cinderella team with their stellar draft choices, their timely signing of veteran running back Preston Pearson, and their novel use of the Spread, or Shotgun formation in passing situations. Staubach was particularly suited to the Shotgun, and he used it to advantage during the season. A Cowboy team that had been written off as past its prime went 10-4 during the season and earned a wild-card berth in the playoffs. The first round game was played in icy conditions against the Vikings of Minnesota, and it gave football a new phrase for the game's most dramatic play.

The Cowboys trailed the Vikings 14-10 with only 1:50 to play and the ball on their own 15 yard line. After five plays and two completions by Drew Pearson, the Cowboys faced a fourth and 16 from their own 25 yard line. Staubach tried desperation passes to two players named Pearson—Drew and Preston. With no time-outs remaining, Staubach heaved a last-chance, desperation pass of 50 yards to Drew Pearson. The receiver caught it, and the Cowboys won 17-14. The last drive was 85 passing yards in 1:27. After the game, Staubach, a Roman Catholic, called the pass a "Hail Mary." The name has stuck to all such passes, complete and incomplete, in the years since. The Staubach-Pearson combination teamed up for numerous last-second pass completions; Staubach's never-say-die attitude was bolstered by Pearson's ability to catch passes—seemingly beyond the sidelines—while staying in bounds.

Two Different Approaches to Super Bowl X

The underdog 1975 Cowboys traveled to Los Angeles for the NFC showdown and won handily, 37-7. The stage was set for Super Bowl X, one of the most exciting Super Bowls to date. The game pitted Dallas against the Pittsburgh Steelers. Two more different teams would be hard to find. Dallas was known for poise and finesse, for tricky plays and the Flex defense. Pittsburgh relied on muscle and force to get the job done. As

Phil Musick put it in *The Super Bowl,* "If the Steelers were a stiff finger in your eye, the Cowboys were an unfelt hand lifting your wallet. To Pittsburgh, football was muscle and meanness; to Dallas, it was guile and trickery. The Cowboys wouldn't have wanted to live in Pittsburgh's neighborhood, and the Steelers knew it." The hostility between clubs was barely concealed prior to the game, and it was openly expressed once the contest began.

The Cowboys led 7-0 after the first quarter, 10-7 at halftime, and 10-9 in the fourth quarter. But Dallas just simply couldn't stop the attack by Terry Bradshaw, Lynn Swann, and Franco Harris. The Steelers pulled ahead 12-10, then they kicked a field goal, and then put the game away 21-10 on a pass to Swann. The Cowboys rallied to finish the game at 21-17. Super Bowl X crowned the achievements of the blue-collar Steelers over the high-tech Cowboys.

Injuries to Staubach, Preston Pearson, and Robert Newhouse notwithstanding, the Cowboys turned in a strong 1976 showing with an 11-3 season record and the NFC East championship. A surprising first round playoff loss to the Rams, 14-12, ended the year. Landry realized that his team had suffered from the loss of Calvin Hill and Duane Thomas. The coach made it a priority to find a dominant runner. With a high draft choice in 1977, the Cowboys picked Heisman Trophy winner Tony Dorsett, perhaps the essential man for future postseason glory.

Dorsett lived up to his advance billing, and the Cowboys went 8-0 to begin the 1977 season. The team finished 12-2, one of its strongest showings, and easily beat the Chicago Bears and the Minnesota Vikings to advance to Super Bowl XII. This time the Cowboys met the Denver Broncos in the Super Bowl, and the Bronco quarterback was none other than Craig Morton. Any advantage Morton might have had from his years on the Dallas team was quickly scuttled, as the "Doomsday II" defense, led by Randy White and Harvey Martin, shut Denver down. The Cowboys won handily, 27-10, for their second Super Bowl win in four appearances. Landry said in his autobiography: "Super Bowl six was special because people had said we couldn't win the big one. But I felt pretty darned good about Super Bowl twelve, too."

Tex Schramm, who had been a high-profile NFL executive longer than Landry had been a coach, spent countless hours devising ways to increase the Cowboys' media exposure. One of his successes was entirely his brainchild. The other came quite by chance. Together they assured that Dallas would rank right at the top in sales of NFL merchandise, in televised games, and in overall recognition.

The Schramm brainchild was the Dallas Cowboy Cheerleaders. From his days in television, Schramm knew that the cameramen would try to find a pretty woman in the crowd and then flash her face on the screen between plays or just before a commercial break. To Schramm's way of thinking, Dallas's profile could only be helped if the pretty woman in the quick camera shot was associated with the Cowboys. He therefore recruited a large team of beautiful young girls who, clad in skimpy halter tops, short shorts, and go-go boots, became the famous cheerleaders.

By 1980 the Dallas Cowboy Cheerleaders were—for better or worse—national celebrities in their own right. They made tours to foreign military bases, did charity work, and performed intricate dance routines at each Cowboys game. At the height of their popularity, a made-for-television movie based on their exploits drew Nielsen ratings almost as high as those for the mini-series *Roots.* Landry, a committed Christian, did not approve of the sexy cheerleaders. He did not object strongly, however, as any interference in Schramm's sector of the business might lead to a loss of his own autonomy.

Cowboys Become "America's Team"

The other stroke of lasting publicity came from a highlight film of the Cowboys' 1978 season. The film editor could not seem to come up with a title that suitably captured the Cowboys. Then he noticed that the team had been televised nationally 12 times in 16 games. He also noted that every city the Cowboys visited seemed to have clusters of Dallas fans. He decided to call the film "America's Team." Newspapers picked up the concept, and within months the Cowboys were known as America's Team.

The nickname has remained, and—like the cheerleaders—it is a mixed blessing. As recognition for a winning ball club and its millions of fans, the name is an endearment. For fans of other teams, and especially for the personnel on those other teams, the name is a mockery, a suggestion that somehow the Cowboys are superior. "America's Team. The moment I heard it I thought, *Oh no! Everybody's really gonna be gunnin' for us now,"* Landry recalled in his autobiography. "I don't know anyone on the Cowboys who liked that label to start with.... Other teams used it as a motivational tool against us. However, what seemed so presumptuous at first eventually became part of the proud Cowboys' tradition."

As the Cowboys became America's Team, Landry became God's Coach, a nod to his numerous activities on behalf of his Christian faith. The emotional baggage—America's Team, God's Coach, the "proud Cowboys' tradition"—eventually would become a curse rather than a joy as Landry tried to maintain his national image.

Little chinks began to show in the Landry armor by the late 1970s. Although he enjoyed a good relationship with Staubach in general, the

AP/Wide World Photos

Dallas end Ed "Too Tall" Jones closes in on Steelers' quarterback Terry Bradshaw (12)

two feuded over who would call the plays during games. Sometimes Staubach changed Landry's plays in the huddle or during an audible. Other players rebelled too against Landry's stern discipline, demanding higher wages and less intimidation during meetings. Needless to say, the tension was lower when the team won, but it is fair to say that some of the Cowboys players did not react well to Landry's stern, businesslike attitude.

Landry addressed this issue in his autobiography. "The explanation for my cool sideline image isn't that I don't have any emotions, but that I deliberately control them," he explained. "By the time I left the football field as a player and began coaching on the sidelines, I realized that the expression of emotion interfered with my ability to think clearly and make the complex judgments and snap decisions needed to coach defense in the NFL. My intense, competitive nature had always come out in the aggressive way I'd played football. But standing on the sidelines, I had to do something with all that pent-up intensity. I rechanneled it into a total concentration of focus."

Bob Lilly, perhaps speaking for a number of his fellow Cowboys, told St. John: "Tom Landry is a fine man, a very high caliber person and he did an awful lot for me. But I don't think anyone really knows him personally, except his family. We respect him an awful lot but don't really know him. Tom never interfered with the way we lived our lives and I assume he doesn't want anyone to interfere with the way he lives his." Lilly concluded: "I guess a man today in business can't get too involved in the personal lives of his employees. Things are so darned complex."

Super Bowl X Reunion

Life in the NFL did become more complex for Landry as other teams began incorporating his ideas and opposing players came gunning for America's Team. The change began to be noticeable in the Cowboys' 1978 season. After a slow 6-4 start, the team won six in a row to finish 12-4 and garner another NFC East title. In the playoffs, Staubach and company downed Atlanta 27-20 and Los Angeles 28-0 to qualify for Super Bowl XIII. The game would be a rematch of Super Bowl X with the infamous Steelers, and tempers ran short on both sides.

Dallas's chances for victory were not helped by the caustic comments of Thomas "Hollywood" Henderson, who told reporters that Steelers quarterback Bradshaw "is so dumb he couldn't spell cat if you spotted him the 'c' and the 'a.'" That chance comment—as well as veiled threats toward the frail but effective Swann—galvanized the Steelers and brought them another Super Bowl win.

Terry Bradshaw was at his peak in Super Bowl XIII. Relying on a passing game to neutralize Landry's Flex defense, Bradshaw completed 17 of 30 passes for 318 yards and four touchdowns. Lynn Swann torched Dallas for seven receptions worth 124 yards and scored the winning touchdown. Still, the game was close throughout, and Dallas fans raged after a controversial pass interference call on Cowboy defender Ben Barnes. The 33-yard penalty gave the Steelers a first down at the Dallas 23 and a chance to take a commanding lead in the fourth quarter. Pittsburgh led 35-17 with six and a half minutes remaining to play, and the clock ran out on Staubach's hardy comeback attempt. The controversial referee decision and a dropped Staubach-to-Jackie Smith end zone pass were considered the decisive moments in the 35-31 Cowboy loss.

As the Cowboys' second decade wound down with another 11-5 season in 1979—and a first-round playoff loss to the Los Angeles Rams—Landry and his methods seemed vindicated. From 1970 through 1979, Dallas had played in five Super Bowls, won two World Championships, and missed the playoffs only once. The Cowboys' won-loss record from 1970-79 was the very best in professional football. Small wonder that the America's Team label stuck as football fans flocked to the winners in blue, silver, and white.

The Cowboys began the 1980s with a new quarterback. Staubach announced his retirement in March of 1980 and, again, some felt he stepped down prematurely. Charlie Waters said, "You know, I don't think I realized at the time how special a team we were. Roger was special. We always believed we could win—unless Roger was hurt." In Staubach's place, Landry started Danny White. White proved himself equal to the task, compiling a 1980 won-loss record of 12-4 as the Cowboys scored a league-leading 454 points. Right on cue Dallas won a wild-card playoff game against the Rams, 34-13 and pulled off a stunning come-from-behind victory against the Atlanta Falcons, 30-27. The drive to yet another Super Bowl was cut short when the Philadelphia Eagles won the NFC championship game 20-7.

"Oh, what stars the 1980 team had," writes Skip Bayless in *God's Coach: The Hymns, Hype, and Hypocrisy of Tom Landry's Cowboys.* "White was surrounded by an embarrassment of prime-timers in their prime. By veterans who had learned and made peace with Landry's systems. By receivers Butch Johnson, Drew Pearson, Tony Hill, Billy Joe DuPree, Doug Cosbie, Preston Pearson, and Ron Springs. By tailback Tony Dorsett and fullback Robert Newhouse. By Pro Bowlers Pat Donovan and Herb Scott in the offensive line. The defensive line—a Doomsday II of Ed Jones, Randy White, John Dutton, and Harvey Martin—remained one of football's most feared. Cowboy mystique was at its Transylvanian peak."

The 1980s' Slide

From that peak, a slow descent began. Bayless quotes a 1982 *Sports Illustrated* article entitled "Dallas Can Have 'em," in which a reporter wrote: "The Cowboys may be hot stuff in Big D, but in the rest of the country America's Team seems to have attracted a multitude of haters turned off by its attitude, image, and success."

The first noticeable erosion in Dallas's seeming invincibility came through its draft choices of the late 1970s and early 1980s. Few of the first- and second-round picks between 1980 and 1986 went on to have productive years with the team. Drafted players kept by the Cowboys tended to suffer career-ending injuries. Some promising rookies were traded to other teams, where they performed well. Dallas passed on chances to draft Joe Montana in 1979 and Dan Marino in 1983.

Nevertheless, the Cowboys continued to win on the backs of veteran stars. In 1981 the Cowboys advanced to the NFC championship game, but lost in stunning fashion to the Joe Montana-led 49ers. Montana connected with Dwight Clark on a touchdown pass following and 89-yard drive. The 49ers won 28-27, and Clark's reception became known simply as "The Catch"—much to the chagrin of Cowboy fans used to seeing last-minute heroics from their own team. In 1982 the team advanced to the NFC championship game for the third year in a row, only to be defeated by the Washington Redskins, 31-17. The following year the Cowboys finished the regular season 12-4 and loss a wild-card playoff game to the Rams, 24-17. Even in these winning years, a few columnists dared to question Landry's competency. God's Coach had not changed his strategies significantly since the early 1970s. He still insisted upon calling each play during games. Worse, in an age of substance abuse and other social excesses, he showed little concern about his players' off-field activities.

Team Ownership Changes Hands

These concerns were considered minor quibbles in Dallas, where an economic boom seemed to coincide with the Cowboys' winning ways. In 1984 the franchise ownership changed hands for the first time. The new owners were headed by Texas businessman Bum Bright, who—taking a lead from Clint Murchison—adopted the same "hands-off" policy and expressed nothing but confidence in Landry and Schramm. Murchison had awarded Landry a bonus and a contract extension in 1983, and Bright stuck by the deal. Bright also helped to foot the bill for a fabulous new Cowboys Center outside of Dallas that would house the front-office staff, provide training fields and state-of-the-art fitness facilities, cheerleader practice studios, and even a souvenir stand.

Just before the team sale, player Butch Johnson told Skip Bayless that he and some other Cowboys felt that they had become "media darlings." Johnson added, "We were on national TV almost every week. But Tex marketed the package, not individuals. This was never Roger Staubach and the Cowboys. It was America's Team. But *we* weren't America's Team; Tom [Landry] and Tex [Schramm] and Gil [Brandt] were. People on the outside had no idea what was really happening on the inside."

Nor did most people question the illusion as long as the victories continued. In 1985 the Cowboys were expected to finish third or fourth in their division behind strong Washington and New York teams. Instead they topped the NFC East after the regular season and looked strong for the playoffs behind a renegade group of defenders known as "Thurman's Thieves," after defensive back Dennis Thurman. The upstart Cowboys, relative newcomers in the NFL, appeared in their 36th playoff game—an NFL record. Unfortunately for them, the Los Angeles Rams were able to contain Tony Dorsett in a 20-0 drubbing, and the Cowboys were eliminated in the divisional final.

The 1985 divisional loss capped a stressful year for Landry. Danny White was injured, and backup quarterback Steve Pelluer was nearly a rookie. Worse, the rank-and-file players—led by Thurman's Thieves—began to show signs of rebellion against the aging Landry. After the Rams loss, a disgruntled Tex Schramm told reporters: "We won't be playing with the same deck next year."

Beginning of the End for Landry

What Schramm did then was unprecedented in the long history of the Cowboys: he suggested—strongly—that Landry hire a new offensive coordinator, Paul Hackett, from the San Francisco 49ers. Landry seemed to accept the interference with good grace, and hired Hackett. Unfortunately for all involved, Hackett's coaching philosophies were quite different than Landry's. The two men tried to integrate a new offensive approach with Landry's old one. At first it worked, and the Cowboys went 6-2 behind Danny White. Then White suffered a season-ending injury, and Pelluer could not handle the vast amount of information he was supposed to learn. Dallas lost seven of the last eight games of 1986 and did not advance to the playoffs. The Cowboys' 7-9 record represented the team's first losing season in 20 years.

Landry took the 1986 setback in stride. Sensing that more troubles lay ahead, he asked for—and received—a new, three-year contract from Schramm. The coach felt he could rebuild the team around the still-effective Tony Dorsett and a newly signed halfback, Herschel Walker. Walker signed a five-year, $5 million contract in 1986 that made him the highest paid Cowboy ever.

Not surprisingly, the deal infuriated Dorsett, who had complained about his own contract for years. During the 1987 season, Dorsett remained with the Cowboys, but he was critical and dissatisfied. His 12,036 career yards rushing for the team placed him in certain position for the Pro Football Hall of Fame, but he still demanded to be traded.

In the meantime, many of the problems from 1986 resurfaced. Danny White began the season but was injured again. Landry decided to scrap the new offensive ideas Hackett had contributed and resort to his former methods. The result was near-chaos. Although Walker rushed for more than 100 yards in several games, the Cowboys managed only a 7-8 regular season record. Owner Bum Bright and some of his partners began complaining about Landry.

After one particularly dispiriting loss, even Schramm said: "It's very seldom I put myself in a position of giving the players a reason for losing, but I'm not sure it's all on the players. When things aren't working and you continue to see the same things, it shakes your confidence.... There's an old saying, 'If the teacher doesn't teach, the students don't learn.'" The quote is reprinted in

Cowboys Super Bowl Appearances

Super Bowl V (January 17, 1971) Baltimore 16, Dallas 13

Two Mike Clark field goals and a 7-yard pass from Craig Morton to Duane Thomas brought Dallas 13 points by the half. The Cowboys led 13-6 going into the fourth quarter, but Baltimore added a touchdown and a last-minute field goal by rookie kicker Jim O'Brien to win dramatically, 16-13. Chuck Howley, a Dallas linebacker, was named Most Valuable Player.

Super Bowl VI (January 16, 1972) Dallas 24, Miami 3

The Cowboys rushed for a record 252 yards, and their defense did not permit a single Dolphins touchdown. Dallas led at halftime 10-3 after Chuck Howley recovered a Larry Csonka fumble to set up a field goal by Mike Clark. The touchdown came on a 7-yard pass from Roger Staubach to Lance Alworth. Running back Duane Thomas spearheaded a 71-yard drive for a touchdown after the half, taking the ball in from the 3 for a 17-3 lead. Early in the fourth quarter, Howley intercepted the ball at the 50, setting up a final touchdown pass from Staubach to Mike Ditka. Clark kicked the extra points. Roger Staubach was named Most Valuable Player.

Super Bowl X (January 18, 1976) Pittsburgh 21, Dallas 17

Offensive drives by Terry Bradshaw, including a 64-yard touchdown pass to Lynn Swann in the fourth quarter, helped to ease the Steelers past the Cowboys in a close game. The Cowboys scored touchdowns on a 29-yard pass from Roger Staubach to Drew Pearson in the first quarter and on a 34-yard pass from Staubach to Percy Howard in the fourth. Dallas's only other scoring opportunity came on a 36-yard field goal by Toni Fritsch, a former Austrian soccer star.

Super Bowl XII (January 15, 1978) Dallas 27, Denver 10

Dallas converted two first-half interceptions into 10 points. First came a 3-yard run by Tony Dorsett for a touchdown. Then Efren Herrera added a 35-yard field goal. In the second quarter, Herrera completed a 43-yard field goal to make the score 13-3 at the half. In the third quarter, Butch Johnson pulled down a 45-yard pass for a touchdown that put the Cowboys ahead 20-3. A Broncos touchdown in the third quarter cut the lead to 20-10, but Dallas clinched the victory on a play-action pass from running back Robert Newhouse to wide receiver Golden Richards. Herrera kicked the extra points. Randy White and Harvey Martin of the Dallas defense were named co-Most Valuable Players.

Super Bowl XIII (January 21, 1979) Pittsburgh 35, Dallas 31

With Terry Bradshaw at the top of his form throwing for four touchdowns, the Steelers became the first team to win three Super Bowls. The contest was close until the fourth quarter, when the Steelers scored two touchdowns in 19 seconds. Pittsburgh led 35-17 with 6:51 to play, but Roger Staubach found Billy Joe DuPree for an 8-yard touchdown pass with 2:23 remaining. The Cowboys then recovered an onside kick, and Staubach drove for another score, passing 4 yards to Butch Johnson with 22 seconds left. Another onside kick attempt was recovered by Steeler Rocky Bleier, effectively ending the game.

Super Bowl XXVII (January 31, 1993) Dallas 52, Buffalo 17

The Bills burst to a 7-0 lead early in the first quarter, but Dallas responded with two touchdowns. The first—Troy Aikman to Jay Novacek—capped a 47-yard drive off an intercepted pass. Another, only seconds later, came on a 2-yard fumble return by defensive tackle Jimmie Jones. Dallas added two more touchdowns in the second quarter, including a one-play, 18-yard pass from Aikman to wide receiver Michael Irvin. The score at halftime stood 28-10, Dallas. Buffalo came back in the third quarter to score a touchdown, answered by a Dallas field goal. The Bills lost control of the game entirely in the fourth, as Aikman passed for a 45-yard TD and handed the ball to Emmitt Smith for a 10-yard touchdown run. The last Dallas score came on another Buffalo fumble—Ken Norton, Jr. recovered and ran the ball 9 yards for a touchdown. Lin Elliott kicked a field goal and the extra points. Troy Aikman was named Most Valuable Player.

Landry's autobiography.

At the beginning of the 1980s, no one would have thought to ask Landry to retire. By 1987, more and more people were suggesting he do just that. Skip Bayless felt that Landry began to fail when he stopped being a coach and started being a celebrity. "Landry had become a prisoner of his myth," Bayless writes. "He ... had been overwhelmed by the team's runaway fame. Beneath Landry's 'best dressed' awards was just a small-town guy with a mild speech impediment who sometimes couldn't remember the names of his players. The real Landry was called 'nerdy' by some around him. The real one, according to many assistants and players, at times was overwhelmed by major game plan or personnel decisions and sometimes made irrational moves seldom criticized by the media.... Yes, beneath the stoneface facade, the coat and tie, Landry sometimes came unraveled, at the expense of his quarterback. Yet the real Landry was too insecure to ever accept any blame."

Many Dallas supporters believed that Bayless's portrait of Landry was unduly critical and failed to take into account the coach's many phenomenal years. Nevertheless, by the end of a 3-13 season in 1988, the future looked bleak for the man in the hat and tie. Landry was aware that he had fallen out of favor. Minority owner Ed Smith in particular criticized the state of team affairs, even trying at one point to purchase the Cowboys.

Through all the turmoil, Landry maintained his confidence and predicted that he could turn the team around by 1989. He even stated that he would "stay on" into the 1990s, in order to assure the Cowboys' strong return in the NFC East. But Landry did not foresee the arrival of Jerry Jones.

Jones grew up in Arkansas and had made a very large fortune in oil and gas exploration, energy production, banking, real estate, crude oil shipping and refining, and poultry processing. He was also a football fanatic, having been a co-captain of a 1964 University of Arkansas team that won the Cotton Bowl. In the fall of 1988, Jones found out that Bright wished to sell the Dallas Cowboys. The Arkansas businessman jumped at the opportunity to own a team he had cheered for his entire adult life. Negotiations dragged on into early 1989, but Jones finally obtained the team, and Texas Stadium, on February 25, 1989. The deal was formalized that April.

The Arrival of Jones and Johnson

Jerry Jones never made a secret of the fact that he wanted to name his friend Jimmy Johnson head coach of the Cowboys. Johnson had been Jones's teammate and roommate at the University of Arkansas (although Johnson later claimed that they had never been close friends). While Jones went into business, Johnson stayed with football, coaching on the college level at Wichita State, Iowa State, the University of Oklahoma, Oklahoma State, and the University of Miami. In 1987 Johnson's Miami team won the collegiate national championship, and the coach himself was showered with honors.

When Jones and Johnson arrived in Dallas in 1989, Landry and Schramm saw the writing on the wall. Landry was fired immediately—a gesture that seemed callous to most Cowboys fans. Schramm's tenure under the new ownership was brief, ending when Jones named himself president and general manager of the team.

The new owner did not endear himself to the Dallas faithful when, just after firing Landry, he announced: "This is like Christmas to me. The Cowboys are America. They are more than a football team.... My entire office and my entire business will be at this [Cowboys] complex. I intend to have an understanding of the complete situation, an understanding of the player situation, of the jocks and socks."

To make matters worse, Jones added: "What Jimmy [Johnson] will bring us is worth more than if we had five first-round draft choices and five Heisman Trophy winners. History will show that one of the finest things that ever happened to the Dallas Cowboys is Jimmy Johnson."

Many Dallas fans sneered. Jones had dispatched God's Coach and replaced him with a

PROFILES

A Tale of Two Coaches

The Dallas Cowboys have had only two coaches in the history of the franchise: Tom Landry and Jimmy Johnson. The two men are polar opposites in many respects. Throughout his 29 years as a pro football coach, Landry made a point of spending time with his wife and children. Johnson divorced his spouse, calling her a "distraction" from football. Landry lent countless hours to Christian causes, from the Fellowship of Christian Athletes to the Billy Graham Crusade. Johnson works 16 to 18 hours a day and makes no apologies for his schedule. Landry was detached, cool, forbidding on the sidelines. Johnson is active, visibly tense, and emotional.

Landry on the demands of coaching: "You can read any number of books on stress relief. But for me, two major factors explain my long survival. The first is my faith.... Knowing your job isn't the most important thing in your life relieves a lot of the pressure. And because I felt I was doing God's will for my life I knew I didn't have to do it all in my own strength; God promises the necessary strength to those who follow him."

—Tom Landry in *Tom Landry: An Autobiography*.

Johnson on the demands of coaching: "I used to think it would be great to be a CEO of some major company, work 40 hours a week and make all this money and be the best at my business. Then I started meeting some of those CEOs and they were working Saturdays and Sundays, they were working 12 hours a day. I saw the people that are truly at the top and want to stay at the top, they don't put a token effort into it. So as long as I want to stay at the top, I'm going to work this schedule. Now, when I get to the point where I've had enough of it at the top, that's when I'll pull back and go back to the beach and have a cold one."

—Jimmy Johnson in the *Philadelphia Inquirer*

Jimmy Johnson photo (above, right): *AP/Wide World Photos*

man who had never held a clipboard in the NFL. Jones ignored the hallowed Dallas tradition of hands-off ownership and openly planned to run the show. As if to mock the new owner and his upstart coach, the city of Dallas held a Tom Landry Day, during which over 100,000 people lined the streets to cheer their longtime hero. The prognosis did not look great for the new Dallas Cowboys regime.

Their first year at the helm was the Cowboys' worst in decades. The team finished the 1989 regular season with a 1-15 record. Jones, who often stood on the sidelines along with his team during games, was soundly booed at every opportunity.

Johnson Upsets the Status Quo

Johnson was not about to win any popularity contests, either. The new coach told Bayless he was astonished at the poor team he had inherited. "I really had no idea how far the talent had slipped," he said. "I mean, they were the Dallas Cowboys, and it looked like they were competitive in most of their losses." Johnson made changes at an astonishing rate. One of the first of 46 trades was that of star Herschel Walker, who went to the Vikings. Danny White was waived and Steve Pelluer was traded. Johnson announced that he intended to build a new team around first-round draft pick Troy Aikman. Young talent arrived in the persons of running back Emmitt Smith, tight end Jay Novacek, and linebacker Ken Norton, Jr.

By 1991 the Cowboys were back in contention with an 11-5 regular season record and a 17-13 victory over the Chicago Bears in the wild-card playoff game. Dallas ended the 1991 season with a 38-6 loss to the Detroit Lions, but the Jones-Johnson strategy was vindicated: in just two seasons, the high-stakes owner and his workaholic coach had turned the Cowboys around.

Jones made other changes in the Cowboys' organization as well. Gil Brandt was summarily fired, and budget controls were implemented for scouting and administration. The Cowboys began holding training camp in Texas rather than California, and the palatial Cowboys Center underwent architectural adjustments. By 1992, just about the only recognizable remnant of Landry's Cowboys was the color of the uniforms.

AP/Wide World Photos

Troy Aikman

The 1992 Dallas Cowboys posted a 13-3 record. The team ranked in the top five in total offense (4th), rushing offense (5th), passing offense (5th), total defense (1st), rushing defense (1st), and passing defense (5th). *Philadelphia Inquirer* correspondent Bill Lyon wrote: "What everyone so gravely misjudged was the will of these two [Jones and Johnson], their willingness to commit, their cold purposefulness, their unbending desire. There is no sacrifice they aren't prepared to make and no one they aren't willing to sacrifice. They have made ... 56 draft picks. They play the Plan B market like takeover raiders on the scent of a vulnerable company. These boys are corporate killers. They could swim with the big sharks on Wall Street."

A Winning Trip to the Super Bowl

Dallas finished first in the NFC East behind a maturing Troy Aikman. The Cowboys passed for 200 yards in a 34-10 playoff rout of the Philadelphia Eagles and then captured the Super Bowl bid by defeating the San Francisco 49ers 30-20. Overnight, Johnson's carefully-arranged hairdo became as well known as Landry's hat.

The Cowboys landed in Super Bowl XXVII against the favored Buffalo Bills. For the Bills it was a third Super Bowl appearance in as many years, and the previous two losses made the Buffalo players hungrier than ever for a victory. The game, held at the Rose Bowl in Pasadena, California, featured a war-torn but solid veteran team versus a youthful, exuberant squad just ripening for NFL competition. And the game turned out to be one of the most lopsided Super Bowls ever. The Cowboys trounced the Bills 52-17, forcing a Super Bowl-record nine turnovers.

The Cowboys' fantastic victory led *Sports Illustrated* contributor Paul Zimmerman to comment: "Get used to the Dallas Cowboys, folks, because they're going to be with us for a long time. Here comes that dread word—*dynasty*. Oh, my, yes. Everything points to it.... Troy Aikman and Emmitt Smith and Michael Irvin and Ken Norton Jr. and Charles Haley—all those implements of destruction that embarrassed and humiliated a proud, battle-tested team are just starting to feel their oats. Coach Jimmy Johnson and his hair spray; Jerry Jones, the owner who hungers for the limelight. You say you're tired of them already? Gee, that's tough, because the whole gang's going to be with us for a while."

Sources

Books

Bayless, Skip, *God's Coach: The Hymns, Hype, and Hypocrisy of Tom Landry's Cowboys,* Simon & Schuster, 1990.

Landry, Tom and Gregg Lewis, *Tom Landry: An Autobiography,* HarperCollins, 1990.

Liston, Robert A., *The Great Teams: Why They Win All The Time,* Doubleday, 1979.

St. John, Bob, *Tex! The Man Who Built the Dallas Cowboys,* Prentice-Hall, 1988.

St. John, Bob, *The Man Inside ... Landry,* Word Books, 1979.

Wiebusch, John, editor, *The Super Bowl,* Simon & Schuster, 1990.

Periodicals

"Dallas Cowboys 1986 Season Preview," *Dallas Cowboys Weekly,* 1986.

New York Times, January 17, 1993.

Philadelphia Inquirer, January 18, 1993; January 28, 1993; January 31, 1993; February 1, 1993; February 2, 1993.

Sports Illustrated, February 8, 1993.

—*Mark Kram*

New York Giants

After more than six decades the New York Giants prevail as one of the most successful and storied franchises in the history of the National Football League (NFL). Many of the pro game's greatest performers have worn the Giant colors at one time or another through the years.

Beginning with the likes of the fabled Jim Thorpe, Red Badgro, and Cal Hubbard, and proceeding to such luminaries as Ken Strong, Tuffy Leemans, Mel Hein, and Benny Friedman a decade later, the Giants resolutely evolved into a perennial contender for league honors.

Later, when Charlie Conerly and Y. A. Tittle were calling the signals and throwing to Frank Gifford, Kyle Rote, and Del Shofner the Giants' stalwart defense featured Andy Robustelli, Jim Katcavage, Rosey Grier, Dick Modzelewski, Sam Huff, Emlen Tunnell, and Jimmy Patton. They kept the opposition at bay as the Giants ruled the Eastern Conference with an iron hand and made five appearances in the NFL championship game within a six-season span.

More recently the Giants returned to prominence with a new generation of title-hungry talent. Lawrence Taylor, Harry Carson, Jim Burt, Leonard Marshall, Phil Simms, Joe Morris, and Mark Bavaro were the headline makers who led this resurgence that resulted in a Super Bowl championship following the 1986 campaign. The squad turned the trick again in the 1990-91 season with a rich mix of much decorated veterans and aspiring newcomers. And so the beat goes on.

But victories are not the sole criteria by which attainment should be measured. The Giants also pioneered several advances in football philosophy and strategy that fundamentally changed the way the game is played today, for the Giants boast a long roster of innovative coaches who roamed the sidelines for New York over the years. Under long-time (1931-1953) field boss Steve Owen they introduced two-platoon substitution and the umbrella defense that served as the forerunner of the various zone defense systems employed today.

From the mid- to late-1950s the club enjoyed the services of two staff assistants who would go on to make NFL history on their own behalf. Vince Lombardi functioned as offensive coordinator and Tom Landry headed the defensive coaches. Under Lombardi's direction New York boasted a strong, balanced attack that effectively meshed a power-oriented running game with an incisive, quick-strike aerial scheme. On the other side of the ball, Landry's charges installed the 4-3 alignment that yet persists as the basic method of defense favored by the majority of teams in the NFL.

After this came Allie Sherman with his variation on the themes already established. He took the Giants to three consecutive conference titles from 1961 through 1963, but failed to nail down a league title, losing to the Green Bay Packers—twice—and the Chicago Bears in the championship game. From this point the team's fortunes slipped until Bill Parcells took over as head coach in 1983 and brought the franchise two Super Bowl crowns.

Currently, the Giants are seeking to regain their once feared status under newly acquired mentor Dan Reeves, who comes to them after an 11-year tenure with the American Football Conference Denver Broncos. While with the Broncos he amassed an impressive 117-79-1 record and led them to three Super Bowl appearances.

Tim Mara

1925: Taking A Chance

It was quite a gamble even for a bookmaker of Timothy J. Mara's stature. But the dapper man of means and many connections anted up the $2,500 required to purchase an NFL franchise without hesitation. In doing so he commented, "I'm gonna try and put pro football over in New York."

The venture was originally rejected by Billy Gibson, a sporting entrepreneur, who suggested to NFL Commissioner Joe Carr that Tim Mara might be of a mind to buy into the league.

He was right. The big Irishman well understood that the odds were against him making a success of a pro team in New York City, especially at the height of the Great Depression. But he was a man who liked a challenge and this one would surely test his mettle.

Marshaling his own resources and utilizing loans, Mara raised the $25,000 necessary to cover salaries, the cost of equipment and transportation, leasing a stadium, and sundry other business expenses.

His first personnel move was to put Dr. Harry March, a retired army physician, in charge of the club's day-by-day affairs. He then hired Bob Folwell, a former college coach whose most recent position had been at the U.S. Naval Academy, to conduct the on-field operations.

As an experienced promoter, Mara knew he needed players who commanded at least

Team Information at a Glance

Founding date: 1925

Home stadium: Giants Stadium
East Rutherford, NJ 07073
Phone: (201) 935-8111
Capacity: 77,311

Team colors: Blue, red, and white
Team nickname: Giants
Logo: Word "Giants" in white and underlined.

Franchise record	Won	Lost	Tie
(1925-92)	496	408	32

Super Bowl victories (2): 1986, 1991.

minimal public recognition and could comprise a team that would give the customers full value for the price of their ticket. With this in mind he acquired an aging and out-of-condition Jim Thorpe from the Rock Island (Illinois) Independents as a drawing card although the once-fabled Indian athlete could no longer produce the gridiron heroics of bygone days. But the remainder of the roster was peopled with the likes of Century Milstead, an All-America tackle at Yale; Henry "Hinkey" Haines, a standout tailback from Penn State; fullback Jack McBride of Syracuse; and center-guard Joe "Doc" Alexander, who had been a solid performer for several seasons with the Rochester Jeffersons.

In early October of 1925 the Giants played one non-league game as a warmup against an aggregation called Ducky Pond's All-Stars in New Britain, Connecticut, and easily prevailed, 26-0. A week later the first of two road contests got the New York regular season schedule underway. The Providence Steam Roller club was the initial opponent and won convincingly, 14-0. Moving on to Philadelphia, the Giants dropped a 5-3 decision to a veteran Frankford Yellow Jackets team, a safety accounting for the narrow margin of victory.

The following afternoon the Yellow Jackets again provided the opposition, only this time at New York's Polo Grounds. Some 25,000 spectators, only half of whom had bought a ticket, were on hand in the famed horseshoe-shaped stadium for the Giants debut. It couldn't have been more disappointing. The home club went down to defeat, 14-0, sagging to an 0-3 record. Due to a knee injury Thorpe played less than a half and was released shortly thereafter. He returned to Rock Island and finished the campaign with the Independents.

Despite this disheartening commencement the Giants rallied to win their next seven contests. The streak included four successive shutouts, over the Cleveland Bulldogs, 19-0; the Buffalo Bisons, 7-0; the Columbus Tigers, 19-0; and the Rochester Jeffersons, 13-0. Armed with a respectable 7-3-0 season mark, the club began to attract the attention of the New York press. But this all-conquering streak did little to draw more fans into the cavernous reaches of the Polo Grounds. And so it was that Mara found himself $40,000 in debt.

Friends, relatives, and colleagues ardently urged the big bookmaker to bail out and cut his losses. Even New York Governor Al Smith urged him to wash his hands of the venture. "Pro football will never amount to anything," Smith said. "Why don't you give it up?" Mara looked around at his two sons, Wellington and Jack, and replied, "The boys would run me right out of the house if I did."

He was going to hold on a bit longer for another reason. The Chicago Bears, with their much celebrated all-purpose back Harold "Red" Grange, were due at the Polo Grounds for a game on December 6. Easterners had never seen the fabulous "Galloping Ghost" work his ball-carrying magic and Mara hoped they would turn out in droves for the opportunity.

Working the promotional mills for all they were worth, Mara sold more than 70,000 tickets for the game and issued in excess of 100 press credentials. Come game time the Polo Grounds groaned with a capacity crowd while thousands of other onlookers availed themselves of whatever lofty spot they could find.

Damon Runyon, present for the festivities along with other noted sports writers such as Grantland Rice, Paul Gallico, and Westbrook Pegler, wrote of the scene: "Seventy thousand men, women and children were in the stands, blocking the aisles and runways. Twenty thousand more were perched on Coogan's Bluff and the roofs of apartment houses overlooking the baseball home of McGraw's club, content with an occasional glimpse of the whirling mass of players on the field below and wondering which was Red Grange."

The course of the contest itself was almost anticlimactic as the Bears forged an early 12-0 lead. Both touchdowns were the result of faked handoffs to Grange sweeping wide of one end, drawing the Giants defense with him like bees to honey. Diminutive Chicago tailback Joey Sternaman, hiding the ball on his hip, simply headed in the opposite direction and scored unmolested.

A tenacious second-quarter drive capped by fullback Phil White's three-yard touchdown plunge put the Giants back into the game, 12-7. This remained the score until late in the final period, when Grange intercepted a pass and raced 35 yards to the New York end zone. The Bears thus triumphed, 19-7. But the balm of losing for Mara was the big payoff he reaped as his share of the gate receipts. The contest enabled him not only to erase his $40,000 debt, but also to post an $18,000 profit at the end of the year.

Looking back on that moment of salvation for the Giants, Wellington Mara said, "I remember my father was losing a lot of money on the team in their first year. But everything changed when Red Grange came out to the Polo Grounds at the end of the season. My father had wanted him in a Giants uniform, but he came as a Chicago Bear instead. Nevertheless, the Galloping Ghost, the most famous football player of his day, drew the fans into the Polo Grounds, more than 70,000 of them, and the franchise was saved."

A week later the Giants and Bears went at it again in Chicago at Cubs Park (Wrigley Field), a game tacked onto the NFL slate as part of a hastily arranged Bears/Grange barnstorming tour. New York got sweet revenge, besting the Bears 9-0 for a respectable 8-4-0 record and a fourth-place finish in a league comprised of 20 clubs.

With the onset of 1926, Mara and the Giants found Grange back in New York, though not in a helpful capacity this time. Grange had quit the Bears in a salary dispute and left for New York with his agent, C.C. "Cash and Carry" Pyle. Grange joined a rival American Football League (AFL) with his own club, the New York Yankees, holding forth in the Bronx, just a pitchout from the Polo Grounds. To make matters worse, two more AFL franchises were set up in Brooklyn and nearby Newark, New Jersey. As if the increased competition wasn't enough, Giants lineman Century Milstead and coach Bob Folwell deserted to the enemy ranks.

Not one to cry over spilt milk, Mara gave Doc Alexander the coaching reins and set about recruiting new talent. One of his finds was a burly tackle named Steve Owen, who had previously plied his talents for the Kansas City Cowboys and Cleveland Bulldogs. He was destined to become an important part of the organization for the next 27 years. Other notable acquisitions included halfbacks Jack Hagerty and Walt Koppisch, both college stars.

The Giants labored their collective way to an 8-4-1 season and seventh place in a 22-team NFL. With scheduled hostilities now history Mara invited the neighboring Yankees to come over to his yard and settle their differences with an "intra city championship game." Pyle thought better of it so the challenge was issued to the AFL titlist Philadelphia Quakers, the team to which Milstead and Folwell had defected. The Quakers agreed and the date of the contest was set for December 12 at the Polo Grounds.

On game day snow covered the field and both teams played conservatively. At intermission the Giants went to their locker room with a tenuous 3-0 advantage. But with the start of the third period the New York offense opened up and the contest quickly degenerated into a rout. At the end of the proceedings the final score was Giants 31, Quakers O. The AFL had been appropriately quieted. Unfortunately, only 5,000 hardy fans viewed the lopsided triumph.

In the aftermath of the bloodletting, New York tackle Babe Parnell said, "Everybody on the Giants wanted to win this one. The Quakers thought we were pushovers, but we kicked the bleep out of them." With the close of the 1926 slate Mara again found himself $40,000 in the red. The AFL fared even worse, however, and went out of business. But the Yankees survived and were absorbed into the NFL, where they were consigned to play all but four of their next season's games on the road.

During the 1927 campaign the Giants finally hit their stride, at least on the field. That year they went 11-1-1 to win their first league title. The club finished the season with a 13-7 win over the Bears in the concluding contest for both clubs. It was a particularly brutal showdown. "That was the roughest, toughest game I ever played," Owen said. "I played 60 minutes at tackle opposite Jim McMillan, who later became a world wrestling champion. When the gun went off, both of us just sat on the ground in the middle of the field. We didn't say a word. We couldn't. It was fully five minutes before we got up to go to the dressing room."

Although there were no notable changes in the team's personnel, the 1928 Giants played poorly from start to finish and tumbled all the way from the league pinnacle to sixth place with a 4-7-2 record. Mara went another $40,000 in the hole and so decided to shake things up. Before he was done the club had been purged of no less than 18 players. Now the principal objective was to find a new coach and put some punch in the offense.

To do this Mara had no choice but to purchase the nearly defunct Detroit Wolverines franchise, acquiring part-owner and coach LeRoy Andrews and passing sensation Benny Friedman, who would lead the Giants back to the fore of the NFL. Grange said of Friedman: "He was the best quarterback I ever played against. There was no one his equal in throwing a football in those days." It cost Mara $10,000 to sign Friedman for the 1929 campaign. But he more than earned his keep, passing for 19 touchdowns on the year while directing New York to a 13-1-1 mark. Following a season-opening tie the Giants set about bludgeoning their next eight opponents, scoring a total of 204 points while giving up just 29. But the rejuvenated Green Bay Packers were also making a mockery of the other teams in the league.

The two unbeaten clubs slugged it out at the Polo Grounds in late November. Green Bay went up 7-0 after recovering a fumble deep in New York territory and held that edge through the initial half. In the third quarter Friedman hit fullback Tony Plansky with a touchdown pitch but missed the PAT and the Giants' deficit was narrowed to 7-6. But the Packers managed a pair of late scores to pull out the win 20-6. As a result they stood alone atop the NFL with a 12-0-1 record.

The 1930s: Getting That Championship Feeling

If ever there was a match that seemed destined to be made it was a mating of New York University All-America back Ken Strong with the Giants. Everybody in the know simply considered it to be a done deal. But complications arose in salary negotiations and Strong signed instead with the Staten Island Stapletons.

This was a particularly damaging blow to the Giants as the Bears acquired sensational rookie fullback Bronko Nagurski and the champion Packers added bomb-throwing back Arnie Herber to their roster. Strong later claimed that the Giants made him one offer during negotiations, then lowered the price when it came time to put his name on the dotted line. Though still young at the time Wellington Mara remembered quite vividly the conversation his father had with Strong when he ultimately joined the Giants in 1933.

"My father said, 'Well, Ken, you are three years too late. I never understood why you went over there (Staten Island) for less money than we offered you.' Ken said, 'What do you mean?' My father replied, 'Why we offered you $10,000 a year.' Strong shook his head. 'No, you didn't. You offered me $5,000.' Apparently our employee was going to pocket the $5,000 difference, or else he thought he was going to save the club some money and make points for himself. I don't know which; all I know is that's how we lost Ken Strong."

The Giants began the 1930 campaign with two victories before losing 14-7 to Green Bay. After that they put together a string of eight wins that included a 12-0 shutout of the Bears despite the presence of Grange and Nagurski, two drubbings of the Ernie Nevers-powered Chicago Cardinals, a 53-0 humiliation of the Frankford Yellow Jackets, and a pleasing 9-7 squeaker over the Stapletons, who featured Strong in their backfield.

Late in the year the Bears visited the Polo Grounds seeking vengeance. Heavy rains held the crowd to just 4,000 faithful and reduced the field to a quagmire. Friedman was unable to pass effectively while the Chicago running attack all but ground to a halt. Late in the going Nagurski tallied twice, once on a 6-yard blast and then on a sloshing 20-yard canter during which he shook off would-be New York tacklers like so many bothersome flies. The Bears triumphed, 12-0.

Ken Strong

Next on the schedule were the defending champion Packers, and 45,000 fans turned out to see them taken on the Giants at the Polo Grounds. A Friedman pass in the second quarter put New York out front, 7-0. This score stood until the third period, when the Giants' Hap Moran faked a punt and then legged the ball 84 yards to the Green Bay one-yard line. Friedman went in from there to give New York a 13-0 advantage.

The Packers struck back in the last quarter with a sustained drive to close the gap, 13-6. With the clock running down they reached the Giant one-yard line and pushed in for an apparent score. However, both teams were ruled offside on the play and the down had to be repeated. This time the New York defense held and the home team escaped with the victory. Now the Giants boasted an 11-2 record and looked to be headed for another NFL title.

However, it wasn't to be as they promptly fell before the Stapletons, as Strong ironically tallied the deciding touchdown. The Giants then suffered an upset loss to the Brooklyn Dodgers, a new franchise in the league. The Packers suffered only one more defeat that season and so retained their championship laurels with a 10-3-1 mark. New York played the bridesmaid at 13-4-0. The team's stumbling finish resulted in Andrews' ouster as head coach. From hero to goat in a matter of two weeks, such are the vagaries of sport.

The 1931 Giants were singularly undistinguished, posting a 7-6-1 record for fifth place in the 10-team NFL. But off the field the club made two well-advised moves, promoting Steve Owen to the head coaching position and signing Washington State standout Mel Hein to a contract. He would become a mainstay at center and a charter member of the Pro Football Hall of Fame.

As a rookie Hein played for $150 a game. Years later, he said, "I think at the time that was probably the highest pay of any lineman in the league. It was pretty good money even though it doesn't sound that way today. Back then you could buy a loaf of bread for a nickel and get a whole meal for only 35 cents at the Automat. And there was no income tax."

Friedman left the Giants for good prior to the 1932 season when his request for a piece of the team was rejected. He moved to the Brooklyn Dodgers, who in turn released former Giant tailback Jack McBride. The Giants promptly claimed McBride to replace Friedman.

After dropping five of their first six games, the lone victory coming at the expense of the Friedman-led Dodgers, it was painfully obvious the Giants weren't going anywhere. They did rally during the remainder of the schedule, however, with three wins against a single loss to close at 4-6-2.

A number of changes took place in the NFL during the early days of 1933. With a view to enhancing offensive play, league officials further reduced the circumference of the ball, making it more adaptable for throwing. In a related action they ruled that a forward pass could be initiated from anywhere, not just five yards deep, behind the line of scrimmage. Another aid to scoring was the shifting of the goal posts from the back of the end zone to the goal line. Also, hash marks were to be drawn on the field 10 yards in from the sideline for ball spotting purposes, thereby keeping the course of the game more oriented toward the center of the field.

To best take advantage of these alterations in the status quo, Mara signed University of Michigan All-America tailback Harry Newman, a passer in the Friedman mold. He joined Strong, freshly salvaged from the bankrupt Stapletons, in the New York backfield, giving the Giants a touchdown threat equal to that of the Bears.

With the onset of the season the league was divided into Eastern and Western Divisions. The Eastern Division included the Giants, Dodgers, and Boston Redskins along with two new franchises, the Philadelphia Eagles and Pittsburgh Pirates. Mara felt confident his team would give a good account of itself, armed as it was with the passing of Newman, Strong's running and kicking, and sound defensive play. Mara harbored hopes the squad might become the division representative in the league's inaugural championship game.

After the first four contests of the year, however, Mara's lofty expectations took a nose dive as his club could do no better than a 2-2 start, with the toughest part of the schedule remaining. The Eagles were the opposition for the home opener at the Polo Grounds and Mara pleaded with his players to put forth their best effort. He needn't have worried. They demolished the Philadelphia entry, 56-0.

Some 30,000 spectators were in attendance the following week to see the Giants take on the visiting Dodgers. Besides Friedman the Brooklyn backfield contained another New York alumnus, ex-Army star Chris "Red" Cagle. On the third play from scrimmage Newman looked to pass but saw no open receivers so he tucked the ball under his arm and ran 25 yards for a touchdown.

Then, just before the end of the half he hit end Glenn Campbell with an 18-yard scoring pitch. It was New York, 14-0, at the intermission. On the opening play from scrimmage of the third quarter halfback Elvin "Kink" Richards weaved his way through the entire Brooklyn team en route to a 70-yard touchdown jaunt. The Giants went up 21-0 and from that juncture they limited the Dodgers to a single TD to gain the much-needed victory.

New York would lose only one more game during the remainder of their schedule, a 14-10 decision to the Bears. The club finished with an 11-3-0 record, good enough to capture the Eastern Division title. Chicago went 10-2-1 and won the Western Division crown. So a rubber match between the two teams for the NFL Championship was set for the Windy City on December 17.

A chilling mist greeted the 26,000 spectators who paid their way into Wrigley Field for the contest. They came to cheer for the hometown club and the Bears didn't make them wait long. Early in the first quarter placement specialist "Automatic Jack" Manders booted a pair of field goals to put Chicago ahead 6-0. In the second period the Giants finally got on the scoreboard with a 29-yard pass from Newman to end Red Badgro. Strong kicked the PAT and it was New York 7-6 at the half.

Manders gave Chicago the lead again with another field goal at the top of the third quarter. But the Giants promptly drove 62 yards on Newman's aerials to reclaim the edge, 14-9. The Bears marched right back down the field and tallied via an 8-yard Nagurski pitch to end Bill Karr. Chicago, 16-14. The New York contingent, though, would not be denied. With a bit of free-lance razzle dazzle they surged in front once more, 21-16. Afterward, Strong related how the touchdown was accomplished.

"Newman handed off to me on a reverse to the left, but the line was jammed up," he said. "Then I saw Newman standing back on the (Chicago) 15-yard line, so I threw the ball to him. He took off to the right, but got bottled up. By then I had crossed into the end zone and was wildly waving my hands. Newman threw the ball to me. I caught it and fell into the first-base dugout."

With time quickly dwindling away, Chicago took to the air and reached the New York 33-yard line. From that point Nagurski faked a run and tossed a pass over the middle to end Bill Hewitt. When trapped along the sideline Hewitt flipped a lateral to the streaking Kerr and he went in to score. The Bears had the advantage once again, 23-21.

On the last play of the game Newman hit Badgro far downfield for the Giants. Badgro sprinted for the Chicago end zone with only Grange in his path. Grange made the stop, hitting Badgro up high so he couldn't toss the ball to a trailing teammate. For the Giants it was a matter of close, but no cigar. Following the exciting contest, Mara said, "Red Grange saved the day for Chicago. His quick thinking prevented a score at the end."

In 1934 the Giants and the Bears again dominated their respective divisions, thus setting the stage for a league championship rematch at the Polo Grounds. On game day, December 9, the temperature was a bone-rattling nine degrees above zero and a sheet of ice coated the playing field. Due to the treacherous footing the contest became little more than a test of balance and brute force. The Bears enjoyed a perceptible size advantage and used it to wedge their way to an early touchdown with the trip-hammer running of Nagurski. A Manders' field goal capped another drive and it was Chicago 10-3 at the intermission.

But unknown to the Bears a Giants' equipment manager had been sent to nearby Manhattan College to procure enough basketball sneakers to shod the team. During halftime most of the New York players exchanged their cleats for the rubber soled footwear. Back on the field they found themselves better able to cut and change directions than their stumbling, surprised opponents.

Steve Owen

Due to markedly improved traction the Giants were able to exploit their edge in team speed, tallying 27 points in the fourth quarter to overwhelm the slipping and sliding Chicagoans, 30-13, and win their first NFL title game. With evident glee Wellington Mara recalled the famed sneakers championship.

"In the second half we began moving the ball," he said. "And one of the Bears' players went over to Halas and told him we were wearing sneakers. 'Step on their toes,' Halas shouted to his team. After we had won Halas vowed, 'I'll never get caught like that again.' But the damage had already been done."

The Giants continued to dominate with a 9-3-0 mark in 1935. Over in the West the Detroit Lions finished atop the standings with a 7-3-2 record. Versatile tailback Dutch Clark directed the Lions' offense. Playing alongside him were Glen Presnell, an elusive ball carrier who also possessed the sure hands of a fine receiver, and Ace Gutowsky, a premier short-yardage pounder.

Steady rains had reduced the University of Detroit field, the site of the league title showdown, to a literal morass. Then, shortly before the opening kickoff, the precipitation became snow, which only served to render the already hazardous conditions that much more so. Undaunted by the deplorable state of the playing surface, the Lions took charge early on with a pair of touchdowns and never looked back. Detroit methodically increased their advantage and the Giants were unable to mount a rally. At the closing gun it was Detroit in a runaway, 26-7.

In 1936 New York could do no better than third place in the division; the club finished second the following year. During this interim away from the championship scene the Giants acquired premier running back Alphonse "Tuffy" Leemans and changed their uniform color scheme to blue jerseys and silver pants.

With an 8-2-1 record in 1938, the Giants moved back to the head of the Eastern Division pack. Their only losses came at the hands of the Philadelphia Eagles, 14-10, and the Pittsburgh Pirates, 13-10. Easily the high point of the regular schedule was a 36-0 drubbing administered to the Washington Redskins that clinched division honors. Green Bay, meanwhile, attained the West crown with an 8-3-0 slate. The Packers attack featured the sterling aerial combination of Cecil Isbell to glue-fingered end Don Hutson and the power running of Clarke Hinkle.

When New York and Green Bay got together at the Polo Grounds that year to determine the matter of league supremacy, what resulted was one of the most physically-demanding games ever played in the history of the NFL. The Giants scored first with a field goal after blocking a punt. A few minutes later they blocked another punt and this time converted the turnover into a touchdown, Leemans finally reaching the Packers's end zone from a few yards out. New York thus built a 9-0 advantage.

Early in the second period an intercepted pass put Green Bay back in contention. Arnie Herber whistled a 40-yard TD pitch to Carl Mulleneaux and the Packers trailed by a scant two points, 9-7. But the Giants mustered a sustained drive that ended with a 20-yard touchdown toss from tailback Ed Danowski to running mate Hap Barnard, pushing their lead back up to nine points, 16-7.

As the waning minutes of the half ticked away Isbell connected on a short throw to end Wayland Becker who scampered 66 yards before being hauled down at the Giants' 17-yard line. From there Hinkle battered the New York defense on five straight carries, the last of these efforts netting six points. Once again the Packers closed the gap to two points, 16-14, at the intermission.

Mute testimony to the savagery of the contest was a list of those missing in action at the midway point of the hostilities. Hutson went out due to a knee injury while New York lost Hein with a concussion and guard Johnny Dell Isola to a severely contused spine that required hospitalization.

At the onset of the third quarter Green Bay drove the length of the field to the Giants' five-yard line. But the New York defense stiffened and the Packers had to settle for a field goal by 240-lb. guard Tiny Engebretsen. Green Bay now owned the lead, 17-16. Not to be denied, the Giants promptly generated a drive that consumed 62 yards and culminated with a touchdown pass from Danowski to halfback Hank Soar. New York was on top once again, 23-17.

Utilizing all their offensive weapons, the Packers repeatedly threatened the Giants' end zone during the fourth period but were unable to score. In each instance alert defensive play frustrated the Green Bay probes, and so New York became the first franchise to win two NFL title games. A record crowd for the postseason classic of 40,120 fans went home hoarse but happy. The following day sports writers expended their best superlatives in eulogizing the ruggedly contended matchup.

International News Service reporter Arthur "Bugs" Baer wrote in part, "They went at each other like dogs meeting in a sausage machine... It was mostly a barroom fight outdoors. Close to 50,0000 innocent bystanders looked upon the resumption of gang warfare in America. It was terrific." Added the *New York Times*' Arthur Daley: "What a frenzied battle this was! The tackling was fierce and the blocking positively vicious.... Tempers were so frayed and tattered that stray punches were tossed around all afternoon. This was the gridiron sport at its primitive best."

In 1939 the Giants again found themselves contending with the Redskins for Eastern Division laurels and the right to play in the league title game. Both New York and Washington owned identical 8-1-1 records on the eve of their deciding matchup at the Polo Grounds. Despite a persistent rain, more than 62,000 spectators showed up for the much anticipated contest.

The defenses of both teams dominated the sloppy affair, with the Giants converting a trio of field goals for a 9-0 advantage after three quarters. But in the final period the Redskins managed to score via a touchdown pass from tailback Frank Filchock to end Bob Masterson. Now New York led by only a 9-7 margin.

With less than a minute left in the game Washington prepared for a field goal from the Giants' 10-yard line. Kicker Bo Russell launched the ball and it appeared to sail cleanly between the uprights. However, referee Bill Halloran didn't see it that way and indicated the attempt had been unsuccessful. An uproar resulted but Halloran could not be swayed, so New York topped the East standings once more.

For days thereafter the controversy raged on. Photographs of the disputed field goal were inconclusive so the matter was forever consigned to the realm of conjecture. Owen said, "I thought the call was right, but I didn't have the best angle to judge." Redskins' coach Ray Flaherty, once an end with the Giants, said, "If that guy (Halloran) has got a conscience, he'll never have another good night's sleep as long as he lives."

The Packers survived a tough division fight with the Bears and as West champions hosted the NFL title tilt. In actuality, the game was to be conducted at the State Fair Park in Milwaukee, which could accommodate more spectators than the Green Bay stadium.

A cold, windy December day greeted the members of the two clubs as they trotted onto the frozen field prior to the opening kickoff. Midway through the first quarter a Herber pass to end Milt Gantenbein went for a touchdown and the Packers kept a 7-0 edge to the halftime break. The Pack then added 10 points in each of the remaining two quarters for a 27-0 win and league honors.

The 1940s: World War II and Beyond

Changes in personnel contributed substantially to a disappointing 6-4-1 campaign for the Giants in 1940. But the following season they bounced all the way back to first place in the Eastern Division with an 8-3 mark. This was due in large part to Leemans' recovery from a debilitating back injury and the decisions of Danowski and Hein to forego retirement. On December 7, the last Sunday of the regular schedule, New York lost 21-7 to the Dodgers at the Polo Grounds. But no one really had their mind on football. For it was that very day the Japanese attacked Pearl Harbor and plunged the United States into war.

Both Chicago and Green Bay boasted 10-1-0 records in the Western Division. The Bears won the playoff that was played to determine who would face the Giants. The NFL Championship game took place at Wrigley Field before only 13,341 paying customers, the smallest crowd ever to view a league title contest.

The Giants took a 6-3 lead by virtue of a TD pass from Leemans to halfback George Franck. New York held the lead into halftime. Chicago dominated the latter stages of the game, however. The Bears tallied four touchdowns and coasted to a 37-9 victory, giving Halas his revenge for the earlier sneakers embarrassment. They became the first team to win back-to-back championship games.

Beginning in 1942 there was a mass exodus of personnel from the NFL into the various branches of the military. Overall, 638 players served their country through 1945, and 21 of this number were killed while serving their country. No less than 52 Giants were in uniform and two of them died in action—tackle Al Blozis and end Jack Lummus.

With the loss of many key performers the 1942 New York aggregation struggled through a 5-5-1 campaign and finished third in the Eastern Division. Some time later Leemans said, "I took one look at the squad, and I felt like crying. It hurt to see the Giants I loved having as miserable a group as we had there."

Early in 1943 the Pittsburgh and Philadelphia franchises melded together and formed one team. For the second year attendance around the league was down considerably and most clubs were making do with aging and second-class talent. But the NFL kept going and with it the Giants, moving back into title contention yet one more time.

A memorable blot on that season, however, was a 56-7 beating administered by the Bears. In that contest Chicago quarterback Sid Luckman threw for seven touchdowns and 453 yards, both new single-game marks. More than 56,000 spectators in the Polo Grounds watched the carnage in disbelief.

Thereafter, New York enjoyed a string of four wins, two of these coming at the expense of the despised Redskins on consecutive Sundays. Both teams completed the regular schedule with 6-3-1 records and met again to decide divisional honors. From the opening kickoff at the Polo Grounds the visiting Washingtonians had things pretty much their own way. During the course of the afternoon quarterback "Slinging Sammy" Baugh threw for three touchdowns and further added insult to injury by intercepting a pair of New York aerials. The final score was 28-0, Redskins.

By September 1944 the manpower shortage problem in the NFL had reached critical proportions. So it was that Owen phoned Union College in Schenectady, New York, where Hein, retired since 1942, was teaching and coaching football. He talked the 35-year-old former All-Pro into playing for the Giants on weekends. Their agreement went like this. After Friday classes Hein boarded a train for Manhattan and rejoined the club. On Saturdays he practiced with the team, then played center and linebacker Sunday afternoons. Following the game he returned to Schenectady.

"It wasn't easy," he recalled. "Before our first game I hadn't done any contact work at all. We were in Boston on the hottest day ever up there and I went the full 60 minutes. What a toll it took. I could hardly get on the train for Schenectady that night. I didn't get rid of all that soreness for about three weeks. But I still had to go 60 minutes every Sunday."

In addition to Hein, Owen coaxed 38-year-old Strong and former Green Bay passing great Arnie Herber, then 34, into uniform once more. Leemans decided to stay retired. While the Giants were admittedly a bit creaky, so were the other clubs in the league. Nonetheless, it was still surprising that this odd amalgam of over-the-hill talent, coupled with a handful of promising newcomers, could produce a sparkling 8-1-1 record, good enough to top the Eastern Division standings. The Giants met the Western champion Packers at the Polo Grounds to decide the matter of league supremacy.

Neither team could move the ball with any consistency in the opening period. But the Packers tallied twice in the second quarter. The first touchdown came on a one-yard plunge by fullback Ted Fritsch and the other resulted from a 27-yard bit of catch-and-run that again featured Fritsch. Green Bay led 14-0 at the intermission.

The third period was scoreless. New York finally got on the board when halfback Ward Cuff bulled into the Packers' end zone from a yard out. But the Giants were unable to push another score across and Green Bay again became league champion, 14-7. The loss went down particularly hard for Mara as his club had gone to the title game seven times since its inception and emerged as the winner on only two occasions.

Following a disappointing 3-6-1 mark in 1945, the Giants climbed to the pinnacle of the Eastern Division once more in 1946. They did it with a marked change in personnel. Gone for good were Hein and Herber while in came a flow of new talent. Frank Filchock was acquired from Washington to get the Giants' passing attack back in gear and rookie tackles Dewitt "Tex" Coulter and Jim White significantly bolstered the New York interior line.

With Filchock throwing for a club-record 1,252 yards and leading all rushers with 371 yards the Giants compiled a record of 7-3-1 and earned their eighth trip to the NFL title game. The Bears provided the opposition, fresh from an 8-2-1 season in which Luckman tossed for 1,826 yards and 17 touchdowns. The day before the big matchup Mara and Owen learned that Filchock and fullback Merle Hapes were under investigation concerning bribe offers to throw the championship game. Bert Bell, then in his initial year as NFL commissioner, ruled that Filchock could play against Chicago after hearing testimony to the effect he had not actually been approached by gambler Alvin Paris. Hapes was suspended indefinitely because he didn't report the illicit overture to either his team or the league front office.

On Sunday, December 15, 58,346 fans paid a total of more than $282,000 to enter the Polo Grounds, a record gate for a title contest at that time. Early in the first quarter Luckman hit end Ken Kavanuagh with a 21-yard strike for a score. Dante Magnani then picked off a Giants' aerial and returned it 19 yards for a touchdown, putting the Bears up 14-0. But Filchock, choking on blood from a broken nose, connected with end Frank Liebel for a 38-yard TD toss to close the gap to 14-7.

The second period was scoreless. After the intermission Filchock came out throwing with deadly accuracy. One of his offerings, to running mate Steve Filipowicz, brought the Giants even with the Bears, 14-14. But in the final 15 minutes Luckman faked beautifully to fleet-footed halfback George McAfee and then, as the New York defenders shifted to intercept the breakaway star, he bootlegged the ball around the opposite end for the deciding six points of the game. A field goal followed and Chicago again held sway over the NFL, 24-14.

After the disheartening loss Filchock was also suspended for having lied about his involvement with Paris. The year 1946 was otherwise notable in that the All-America Football Conference (AAFC) started play. And with the birth of the new league came the Cleveland Browns. In the 1950s the Browns as well as their founder and coach Paul Brown were destined to become arch-rivals of the Giants.

Hard times befell the New York franchise from 1947 to 1949 as the club struggled to records of 2-8-2, 4-8, and 6-6. But it was merely a transition phase during which the club concentrated on rebuilding. Perhaps the cornerstone of this renovation project was Charlie Conerly, an All-American quarterback from the University of Mississippi. His draft rights were acquired from the Redskins in 1948. He took over the quarterbacking chores as a rookie and didn't relinquish them for more than a decade. That same year Emlen Tunnell came calling on Mara unannounced and asked for a tryout. He got it and became the first black player to wear a Giants uniform.

Prior to the 1949 campaign Owen adopted the T-Formation to better utilize Conerly's passing skills. The lean freshman quarterback lived up to expectations, throwing for 2,138 yards and 17 touchdowns. Receiver Bill Swiacki, another rookie, set single-season club records for catches (47) and yardage (652), while sophomore halfback Gene "Choo-Choo" Roberts led the NFL in scoring, tallying 102 points on 17 TDs. Other "finds" who portended better things for the future were defensive tackle Al DeRogatis, offensive guard Bill Austin, and placekicker Ben Agajanian, who had defected from the AAFC.

In the wake of the 1949 slate the AAFC died and bequeathed three of its teams—the Cleveland Browns, San Francisco 49ers, and Baltimore Colts—to the NFL.

The 1950s: Cleveland and the New NFL

With the advent of the 1950 schedule the NFL underwent realignment. The Eastern and Western Divisions became known as the American and National Conferences. New York was assigned to the American Conference along with Philadelphia, Pittsburgh, Cleveland and Chicago (Cardinals). Comprising the National Conference were the Los Angeles Rams, Chicago Bears, New York Yanks, Detroit Lions, Green Bay Packers, and Baltimore Colts.

The Giants fell heir to such standout AAFC veterans as tackle Arnie Weinmeister and defensive backs Tom Landry and Otto Schnellbacher. Weinmeister, Landry, and Schnellbacher would each play an integral part in leading the franchise back to glory. Via the college draft the club obtained much needed offensive talent in quarterback Travis Tidwell, fullback Eddie Price, and end Bob McChesney.

From the outset of the season the Browns proved to be more than a match for the best teams in the NFL. But the Giants, utilizing Owen's revolutionary "umbrella defense," served to sufficiently blunt Cleveland's offensive spread formation and thereby defeated the Browns twice during the regular schedule. At campaign's end both teams boasted 10-2-0 records which made necessary a playoff to determine who would represent the conference in the league championship game.

The contest took place at Cleveland's Municipal Stadium in 17-degree weather. An icy wind swept in from adjacent Lake Erie that made passing a very hazardous proposition indeed. Caution and defense dominated the confrontation, with the Browns going ahead on a field goal in the first quarter. This three-point margin stood up until the Giants kicked a field goal of their own in the final period. With less than a minute on the clock Cleveland notched another field goal and then trapped Conerly as he attempted to pass from his own end zone for a safety. The Browns thus won the American title, 8-3.

Cleveland repeated as conference champs from 1951 to 1955, while New York sought vainly to keep pace. All the while the club was enhancing its offensive arsenal with such draft acquisitions as running backs Kyle Rote (1951) and Frank Gifford (1952) and linemen Roosevelt Brown, Jack Stroud, and Ray Wietecha (1952).

After New York went 3-9-0 in 1953 the Maras figured the time for change had come. Owen was fired as head coach and replaced with Jim Lee Howell, a former player who had been tutoring the ends. Then Weinmeister jumped to the Canadian League and Conerly quit, soured on the game after six seasons of being battered. Howell went after him in the hope he would change his mind.

"I tracked him down," Howell said. "He was putting out fertilizer on his farm. When I asked him about coming back, he replied he didn't want to be hurt anymore. I told him I'd get a line that would protect him, so he said okay, he'd come back."

Allie Sherman

With Conerly in the fold again Howell set about rebuilding the club with a rich mix of new talent and established veterans. He also put Landry in charge of the defense and hired Vince Lombardi, then an assistant coach at Army, to direct the offense. Both these moves paved the way for the Giants steady climb back to prominence. At the close of the 1955 campaign the Giants left the Polo Grounds for their new home in Yankee Stadium.

The fruits of the rejuvenation process were first realized in 1956. New York moved to the top of the now Eastern Conference standings with an 8-3-1 record and so advanced to the NFL Championship game. With the Yankee Stadium turf frozen and slippery the Giants reverted to a tactic employed successfully in 1934, sneakers. Putting on rubber sole gym shoes once more, they ran all over the Bears, 47-7, to become league titlists for the fourth time.

In 1957 New York dropped to second place in the conference but regained the top spot the following year with a 9-3-0 record. Cleveland equalled this mark and the two teams met in a playoff game at Yankee Stadium. The Giants prevailed in a defensive struggle, 10-0, holding the great Jimmy Brown in check all afternoon. From there the Giants moved on to battle the Baltimore Colts, Western Conference winners, for league supremacy.

The venue for what eyewitnesses would term "the greatest football game ever played" was Yankee Stadium. Some 15,000 Baltimore fans swelled the crowd to over than 64,000 spectators and millions more watched via the magic medium of television. It proved to be the event that put pro football on the map as an entity of national interest.

New York got on the board with a field goal in the first period to lead 3-0, but the Johnny Unitas-led Colts tallied a pair of touchdowns in the second quarter and went up 14-3 at the intermission. The Giants made a valiant goal-line stand early in the third period, then put together an 86-yard play comprised of a completed pass and a recovered fumble that took them to the Baltimore one-yard line. From there fullback Mel Triplett scored. The Colts still led, however, 14-10.

At the top of the fourth period a 15-yard Conerly-to-Gifford pass capped a New York drive for yet another touchdown. New York forged ahead, 17-14. Now time became a very vital factor. The Giants were marching again with little more than two minutes left to play.

At that juncture Colts' end Gino Marchetti broke a leg and in the resulting confusion the referee neglected to spot the ball. When he finally did so some observers claimed that the spot was nearly a foot shy of the actual point of forward progress. In any event New York was forced to punt.

With one eye on the clock, Unitas drove his team 62 yards in seven plays to the Giants' 13-yard line. On came kicker Steve Myhra who booted a field goal that deadlocked the score at 17-17. For the first time in league history the championship would be settled in a sudden-death overtime quarter. New York won the toss and received the kickoff but failed to move the ball and so punted. Starting from the Baltimore 20-yard line Unitas directed the Colts to the Giants' two-yard line, where fullback Alan "The Horse" Ameche burst over for the winning touchdown. The Colts were victorious, 23-17.

Y.A. Tittle

In a subdued New York locker room tackle Dick Modzelewski said, "You can't come any closer to winning the championship than we did. We outfought Baltimore, but they outplayed us."

On February 13, 1959, Tim Mara died, leaving the management of the club to his two sons. Then Lombardi left to take over the reins of the lowly Green Bay Packers and Allie Sherman became the offensive coordinator. On a roll now, the Giants swept to a 10-2-0 record and a rematch with the Colts in Baltimore's Memorial Stadium.

A 59-yard aerial from Unitas to back Lenny Moore got the Colts out to a 7-0 lead in the initial quarter. But for the next two periods the New York defense was able to effectively hold the powerful Baltimore attack in check. And so going into the last 15 minutes of play the Giants enjoyed a 9-7 edge.

Then the dormant Colts came alive, with Unitas running for one TD and throwing for another. Shortly thereafter cornerback Johnny Sample snared a pair of Conerly pitches and returned them for scores. Baltimore's fourth quarter explosion enabled them to triumph, 31-16, for a second successive NFL crown. Tom Landry then departed New York to become head coach of the expansion Dallas Cowboys.

The 1960s

Injuries bit deep into the New York lineup. One of a particularly serious nature occurred in a battle against the Philadelphia Eagles, when Frank Gifford was knocked unconscious in a game by linebacker Chuck Bednarik. One of the most famous plays in NFL history, "Bednarik hit [Gifford] like a lifetime supply of bad news," according to *Sports Illustrated.* Sam Huff called it "the greatest tackle I've ever seen."

In any event, the blow, delivered cleanly in 1960, knocked Gifford out of football until 1962. Age played its part as well, especially at quarterback, where 37-year-old Conerly required relief

Frank Gifford

on numerous occasions from backup George Shaw. These factors resulted in a 6-4-2 mark and third place in the 1960 conference standings.

When the last gun had sounded Howell quit the bench for a place in the front office. The Maras sought mightily to entice Lombardi to leave Green Bay and assume control of the Giants. But he declined the offer and Sherman took over as the team's field boss. Even as this was taking place the rival American Football League (AFL) was already a year old and would soon be contending with the NFL for playing talent.

In one of the better trades the Giants have made they procured 34-year-old quarterback Yelberton Abraham Tittle from San Francisco to run Sherman's pass-oriented offense. Also acquired was another jewel in the rough, gazelle-like end Del Shofner from the Los Angeles Rams. He was especially needed as Gifford, still not fully recovered from the notorious hit laid on him the previous season, had decided to retire and pursue a career in broadcasting. On defense secondary standout Erich Barnes was added to an already formidable array of talent that included Andy Robustelli, Jim Katcavage, and Sam Huff.

After the first two contests of the 1961 campaign Y.A. Tittle took over at quarterback from Conerly and the Giants began putting points on the scoreboard in bunches. Following an opening loss they strung together five wins, dropped a one-point decision to Landry's Cowboys, and then ran off four more victories. They finished at 10-3-1 under the new 14-game regular schedule format to claim Eastern Conference laurels.

On December 31, Tittle and company traveled to the frigid climes of northern Wisconsin to contend with Lombardi's Packers for the NFL title. Early in the first period the Giants missed on two fine scoring opportunities and thereafter were methodically ground under by the Green Bay juggernaut, 37-0. For New York it was just another case of so close but yet so far.

Prior to the 1962 campaign retirement claimed Conerly, Rote, and kicker Pat Summerall. But Gifford returned to the weekend wars in the capacity of a flanker, or what has come to be known as a wide receiver. Surprisingly enough, those in the know picked Cleveland, armed with the great Jim Brown at running back, to win conference honors. But the Giants didn't quite see it that way.

At first it appeared as though the prognosticators might be right. The Browns stopped New York 17-7 in the season opener for both clubs at Cleveland's Municipal Stadium. But from that juncture on the Browns plummeted and the Giants soared, winning 12 or their next 13 games to close with a 12-2-0 mark and repeat as conference champions.

During this victory run Tittle enjoyed the finest afternoon of his lengthy career when he completed 27 of 39 pass attempts for seven touchdowns, tying an NFL record, and 505 yards as New York bombed the Redskins, 49-34. With fans screaming for an eighth TD toss the "Bald

Eagle" declined and kept the ball on the ground. In the wake of his electrifying performance, he said, "It would have been in bad taste to go for eight touchdown passes. If you're leading by so much, it just doesn't sit right with me to fill the air with footballs. It would be showing off." During the regular schedule Tittle threw 33 scoring aerials to eclipse a league mark of 32 held jointly by Unitas and Sonny Jurgensen, then with the Eagles.

Confident and primed for action the Giants hosted Green Bay, the 13-1-0 Western Conference winners, for the NFL title contest in Yankee Stadium. On the day of the hostilities, December 30, the temperature was a chilling 19 degrees and raw, gusting winds of up to 40 miles per hour raked the field. These were not conditions that favored the forward pass.

From start to finish it was a brutal, ground-oriented battle that gave the 64,892 partisan fans in the stands little to cheer about during the long, bitter afternoon. A field goal provided the Packers with a 3-0 lead in the first period. Then, in the second quarter, they recovered a fumble at the New York 28-yard line. It took them just two plays to score, fullback Jim Taylor tallying the touchdown from seven yards out. Green Bay led 10-0 at the half.

The Giants' only TD resulted from a third-period blocked punt that they grounded in the enemy end zone. But the Packers countered with a field goal and another in the final quarter to successfully defend their league crown, 16-7. Once again New York was left with that empty feeling. "I never saw a team that tried so hard and lost," said Rote, now an assistant coach.

Contending with age and the odds, the Giants once more scaled the conference heights in 1963 with an 11-3-0 record and a bushel basket full of passing achievements. As a team they amassed 3,558 yards via the air while Tittle surpassed his own single-season mark with 36 touchdown tosses. But New York's overhead attack would be sorely tested by the Western Conference champion Bears, who boasted the best zone defense in the league.

The matchup took place in Chicago's Wrigley Field on a nine-degree day. A 14-yard pitch from Tittle to Gifford put the Giants on top 7-0 early in the first quarter. But a few minutes later Chicago linebacker Larry Morris ran back an interception to the New York five-yard line. From there the Bears tied the score at 7-7. In the second period a field goal enabled the Giants to take a 10-7 lead to their locker room at the half. But the downside of this situation was an injury to Tittle's left knee, the one that bore the brunt of his weight when he threw the ball.

With their quarterback severely hobbled the New York offense became a sitting duck for the fierce Chicago defense. During the last 30 minutes of play no less than five of Tittle's aerial efforts were intercepted. One of them was returned 62 yards and set up a Bears' touchdown. At the final gun it was Chicago, 14-10, giving Halas his last league crown.

That year the floundering crosstown AFL franchise was sold to new monied interests and renamed the New York Jets.

Sam Huff

In 1964 the Giants began a slide that reduced them to also-ran status for the remainder of the decade. Quickly and incisively one illustrious name after another disappeared from the New York roster. Huff, Gifford, Robustelli and Tittle all retired during this time. Tittle's retirement announcement in January 1965 coincided with the Jets' announcement of their quarterback of the future—Joe Namath.

The warring NFL and AFL reached an accommodation in 1966 that allowed for a postseason World Championship Game (Super Bowl) between the representatives of the two leagues commencing in 1967 and concluding in 1969. With the start of the 1970 regular schedule the leagues would merge into one expanded NFL with the Super Bowl to be conducted annually between the American Football Conference (AFC) and the National Football Conference (NFC) winners.

As the result of a trade with the Minnesota Vikings, passing sensation Fran Tarkenton, dubbed "The Scrambler" for his freelance style of dashing about behind the scrimmage line, joined the Giants for the 1967 campaign. Under his generalship the club played .500 ball that year and again in 1968 with identical 7-7-0 records.

On January 26, 1969, the New York papers reported that Wellington Mara was considering the construction of a stadium in the Hackensack (N. J.) Meadowlands area. During the preseason the Giants lost a 34-14 decision to the rival Jets and drew poorly at the gate. As a result Sherman lost his head coaching position to former star fullback Alex Webster. But despite this change and the presence of Tarkenton at quarterback the team's record dropped to 6-8-0.

The 1970s: Old Problems and a New Home

After losing three games at the top of the 1970 season the Giants did a complete turnaround, winning their next six starts. The club went into the last week of the regular schedule tied with Dallas. But they fell before the Rams, 31-3, while the Cowboys were crushing Houston, 52-10, and so finished as runner-up in the NFC Eastern Division with a 9-5-0 mark.

Prior to the onset of the 1971 campaign Tarkenton quit the team over a salary dispute. He returned four days later and agreed to a new contract. On August 26, Wellington Mara and New Jersey Governor William T. Cahill jointly announced that the Giants had signed a 30-year lease to play all their home games in a new stadium that was to be completed by 1975 on a 750-acre parcel of land near the town of East Rutherford, New Jersey.

Little went right for the club during the season and even Tarkenton was benched for the last game of the slate. The once proud franchise suffered a drop to last place in the division with a 4-10-0 record. For the first time in the history of the Pro Bowl no New York players were invited to participate.

Tarkenton asked to be traded and was, back to the Vikings for Norm Snead and other considerations. Surprisingly enough, the Giants rebounded to an 8-6-0 record in 1972 and actually challenged for a wild card spot in the playoffs. The team placed third in the NFC Eastern Division standings. Just before the season ended ground was officially broken for the new stadium in New Jersey's Meadowlands.

With Yankee Stadium set for major renovations in the fall of 1973 the Giants were forced to find a ballpark in which to play five of their seven home games. After much consternation and political maneuvering, even at the congressional level relative to TV blackouts for home contests, the team arranged to use the Yale University Bowl in New Haven, Connecticut. Finally, U.S. President Richard M. Nixon signed legislation that eliminated restrictions on telecasts of home games that had been sold out at least 72 hours in advance of the opening kickoff.

The Giants commenced the 1973 season with a pair of contests at Yankee Stadium, whipping Houston 34-14 and deadlocking with Philadelphia 23-23, then bid farewell to the famous ballpark. During the remainder of the schedule they managed to win only once, a 24-13 decision over the St. Louis Cardinals at Yale Bowl. Before the last game Webster resigned. His team posted a 2-11-1 record.

On the bright side, New Jersey Governor-elect Brendan T. Byrne announced that he had come to terms with the Maras and the building of the new stadium complex went forward as planned.

Bill Arnsparger, who had been defensive coordinator for the two-time Super Bowl champion Miami Dolphins, became the Giants' new head coach on January 16, 1974. He made a concerted effort to bolster an aging offensive line with top draft choices and trades. But his efforts had little immediate effect as the club went 2-12-0 that year, still plagued by a lack of scoring punch.

The one saving grace of the dismal campaign had been the acquisition of quarterback Craig Morton, formerly of the Cowboys. He called the signals for only half of the schedule but nearly doubled the point production of the first seven games. When he joined the team Snead went to San Francisco in a trade.

As the 1975 season drew near it became clear that the new stadium would not be ready in time to accommodate the Giants. The City of New York, under new mayor Abraham Beame, granted the club permission to play its home games at Shea Stadium on Long Island and so ended the two-year sojourn to Yale Bowl. Again the offensive effort was lacking, with Morton dropping to eighth among NFL passers, and the defense surrendered 306 points, third worst mark in the NFC. The record stood at 5-9-0.

On October 10, 1976, Giants Stadium was dedicated in the New Jersey Meadowlands with considerable fanfare. Then the capacity crowd of 76,042 sat back and watched the Cowboys maul the displaced New Yorkers, 24-14. Midway through the schedule Arnsparger got the ax and assistant John McVay became head coach. In all, another dreary season closed with the Giants finishing at 3-11-0.

Morton was traded to Denver early in 1977 and so missed suffering through another 5-9-0 campaign. After a 5-3 start in 1978 the club won only once more and stumbled to a 6-10 record in the NFL's first season to feature a 16-game schedule. McVay received his walking papers at the conclusion of the season.

In February 1979 the Giants took a big step toward the restoration of past glory with the hiring of George Young as general manager (director of football operations). He would prove to be the architect of the club's not too distant successes. Ray Perkins left his offensive coordinator duties with the high-scoring San Diego Chargers to become the club's next head coach.

That year the team finished 6-10-0 once again but a pair of rookies, quarterback Phil Simms and receiver Earnest Gray, along with veteran linebackers Harry Carson and Brad Van Pelt and punter Dave Jennings, provided a gleam of hope that the future would indeed be brighter.

The 1980s: On to the Super Bowl

As expected Simms showed signs of brilliance during the 1980 schedule, his best performance coming against Dallas in the Meadowlands when he threw for 351 yards and three touchdowns in a 38-35 winning cause. But a shoulder injury consigned him to the bench during the final three games of the season and the Giants logged a disappointing 4-12-0 mark.

Prior to the 1981 campaign a number of Giants' veterans complained loud and clear about the $750,000 salary club officials were supposedly willing to pay rookie linebacker Lawrence Taylor, their first round draft choice. By the time Taylor did sign on the tumult and the shouting had died. Other acquisitions of note were draftee Billy Ard, a guard, and veteran defensive tackle Jim Burt.

With Taylor and Carson leading a rejuvenated defense and the offense starting to put larger numbers on the scoreboard the Giants rebounded to a 9-7 mark and earned a wild card spot in the playoffs. But their first postseason appearance in more than 15 years wasn't assured until they scratched out a 13-10 overtime victory against Dallas in the last regular season contest for both clubs. Then they had to wait for the New York Jets to beat Green Bay before the celebrating could begin. At long last they were again in the title hunt, only without the services of Simms, who had suffered a shoulder separation earlier in the year.

The defending NFC titlist Eagles provided the first postseason hurdle for the Giants at Veterans Stadium. With a newfound aggressiveness the New Yorkers jumped all over their hosts, scoring three times in the opening period on a pair of passes by backup quarterback Scott Brunner and an end zone fumble recovery. At the half they enjoyed a comfortable 27-7 advantage. From that point they hung on for a 27-21 victory with a ball-control offense and a smothering defense.

AP/Wide World Photos

Phil Simms

A week later they went out to San Francisco to meet the 49ers in Candlestick Park. It was a hotly contested matchup all the way. The 49ers scored first, but the Giants quickly retaliated with a 72-yard Brunner-to-Gray bomb to knot the count at 7-7 in the initial period.

Shortly after the onset of the second quarter a field goal put the 49ers up 10-7. Moments later a Brunner pass was intercepted and promptly converted into a TD when San Francisco quarterback Joe Montana lofted a 39-yard strike to receiver Dwight Clark for a 17-7 lead. On the 49ers' next possession running back Ricky Patton rambled 25 yards to make it 24-7. New York kicker Joe Danelo converted a 48-yard field goal attempt just before the half ended to close the gap to 24-10, San Francisco.

In the third period Brunner threw a 59-yard strike to receiver Johnny Perkins, further reducing the Giants' deficit to 24-17. Then came the turning point in the contest. With the ball at the opposition's four-yard line a third-down Brunner pass was knocked away in the end zone. So on came Danelo for the game-tying field goal. But the 21-yard attempt deflected wide off the right upright.

If that wasn't enough of a heartbreaker New York defensive end Gary Jeter lost his temper shortly thereafter and took a swing at his tormentor. The resulting penalty kept a 49ers' drive alive and they scored again, making it 31-17. Both sides tallied once more and San Francisco prevailed, 38-24.

During the 1982 preseason Simms tore ligaments in his knee and was lost for another campaign. Brunner took over again and veteran Jeff Rutledge was obtained from the Rams as a backup. The Giants lost their first three games of the schedule, which had been severely truncated by a players' strike, and they never got back into the playoff picture, finishing at 4-5-0. Immediately thereafter, Perkins left to replace Bear Bryant at the University of Alabama. Just as immediately, defensive coordinator Bill Parcells was named head coach.

Just before the 1983 season got underway Parcells announced that Brunner would be the Giants' number one quarterback, with Simms and Rutledge the backups. Reacting bitterly, Simms asked to be traded. Midway into the campaign he replaced Brunner only to be lost for the rest of the schedule due to another debilitating injury. The team stumbled to a 3-12-1 mark.

The Giants hit it big in the 1984 draft with linebackers Carl Banks and Gary Reasons, quarterback Jeff Hostetler, and wide receiver Lionel Manuel. Each of them would play an important role in the club's rise to prominence in the years immediately ahead.

Simms reclaimed his quarterbacking chores and directed the Giants to a pair of victories at the top of the regular schedule. But by the midway point they were only playing .500 ball. Diminutive running back Joe Morris was inserted into the lineup and promptly responded with a three touchdown performance. At about the same time the offensive line got its pass protection act together. The result was a 9-7-0 record and a wild card spot.

When the Giants met the Rams at Anaheim Stadium in the first round of the playoffs they were intent upon avenging an earlier loss. They notched a field goal on their first possession of the game and then converted a Los Angeles fumble into a TD for a 10-3 halftime lead. The Giants managed to hold on for a 16-13 win.

The following week Candlestick Park was the battle ground and the 49ers were the enemy. A pair of Montana aerials put San Francisco out front 14-0 in the first period. But New York converted two second-quarter interceptions into a field goal and a TD, making it 14-10. Then Montana threw another scoring strike to give the 49ers a 21-10 lead, which they maintained through the second half for the victory.

Perhaps the 1985 season can best be depicted as a roller coaster ride. The Giants opened with a victory, dropped their next start, added two more wins then lost a pair and so it went. In the end the club patched together a 10-6 record to share NFC Eastern Division laurels with Dallas and Washington. When all the figuring was done New York had earned a wild card spot once more.

In the first round of the playoffs the Giants hosted the 49ers and sent them packing, 17-3. Simms passed for two TDs and the defense sacked Montana four times. Revenge was sweet. The following week the Bears provided the opposition in Soldier Field. Little went right for New York as Simms was sacked six times and Morris could only manage 32 yards rushing. Chicago prevailed easily, 21-0.

AP/Wide World Photos

Lawrence Taylor (56)

After dropping their 1986 season opener to Dallas, 31-28, the Giants hardly seemed like a team of destiny. But thereafter New York won all but one of their remaining games to top the NFC Eastern Division standings at 14-2-0. They then crushed San Francisco, 49-3, in the divisional playoff round at Giants Stadium and sent Mon-

Continued on page 372

PROFILE

Lawrence Taylor

Even before Lawrence Taylor had so much as slipped on a New York Giants' jersey displaying the now-familiar number 56 he was the subject of considerable publicity and no little controversy. Just prior to the NFL college draft on April 28, 1981, word got around that Taylor, an All-America linebacker from the University of North Carolina and the Giants' first-round pick, was seeking a $750,000 per-year contract. Outraged that an untried rookie would receive that much money, a number of the veteran players vowed not to report for the preseason training camp if this unsettling rumor did indeed become fact. When eight-year linebacker Brad Van Pelt was asked about a possible revolt against the team's front office, he replied, "I haven't been a party to any type of discussion on the matter, but I know about it."

Taylor also heard of the reaction to his agent's bargaining efforts and such talk upset him. "Yeah, I was told some of the Giants would walk out if I got a lot of money," he said. "I didn't want people to get mad at me. So I sent the Giants a telegram saying that under the circumstances I would rather not be drafted by them." His missive elicited an immediate response from New York. "That night I got calls from some of the players, on both the offense and defense, and some of the coaches," he recalled. "They said there was nothing to the story, and there would be no walkout. They said they wanted me. That made me feel better."

During his freshman campaign as a pro, Taylor was in on 133 tackles, 94 of them solo efforts, and logged 9.5 sacks. This creditable debut earned Taylor All-Pro honors. He put on a particularly awesome show of defensive versatility in a 1982 nationally televised Thanksgiving Day game against the Detroit Lions. After sitting out much of the first half with a minor knee ailment, he entered the fray and immediately made his presence felt. He quickly forced a hurried throw that was intercepted and set up a New York field goal. When the Lions again got possession of the ball he caused a fumble that led to another Giants' field goal. On the next Detroit set of downs his tremendous one-handed sack of quarterback Gary Danielson stopped a potential scoring drive in its tracks. Finally, in the last quarter, he nabbed a Lions' aerial at the New York four-yard line and returned it 96 yards for a touchdown. The Giants won, 13-6.

With each passing year Taylor added more to his image as an almost legendary figure. Opposing teams devised all manner of schemes to impede his effectiveness, but to no avail. Joe Woolley, the Philadelphia Eagles director of player personnel, perhaps best put in words the feeling of futility that was sweeping those clubs faced with playing the Giants. "Teams are putting tight ends on him," Woolley said, "backs on him, tackles on him, and he's still going right through them. He hampers your offense totally. He's the most dominating player in football, offense or defense."

Following the 1985 schedule any number of observers, both on and off the field, detected a change in Taylor's performance. By any measure he had a good year with 83 solo tackles, 21 assists and 13.5 sacks, attainments which again merited him postseason laurels. But still, those in the know perceived that something was missing. Call it verve or that certain electrifying element which so marked his play in earlier seasons. On March 20, 1986, Taylor's critics were vindicated in their judgment. At that time he stated, "In the past year, due to substance abuse, I have left the road that I had hoped to follow both as a player and a public figure. Recently, I have sought professional assistance to help me with these problems. I have just completed the first phase in what I know will be a difficult and ongoing battle to overcome these problems." There was a dour shaking of heads all around and muted predictions that Taylor's days as a singular force in pro football were at an end. But Giants' head coach Bill Parcells did not hold to such a pessimistic view. "Let me tell you something about Lawrence Taylor," he said. "You're going to be surprised. He's going to play better than ever this year." Parcells proved to be prophetic. Taylor bulwarked the best defense in the NFL during the 1986 weekend wars and discharged his duties in Player of the Year fashion with 79 solo tackles and a league-high 21.5 sacks. Not incidentally, the Giants went to Super Bowl XXI and won.

Lawrence Taylor

PROFILE

In summarizing Taylor's value to the team, New York general manager George Young said, "Lawrence has been so much of a bigger factor in games than stats indicate. It's amazing how just his presence on the field influences a quarterback." In support of these sentiments signal caller Jay Schroeder said, "You always have to be aware of where Taylor is in the scheme of things. And you know that sooner or later he's going to be on your case. He hits like nobody else. Afterward you need to take an inventory of your parts."

Even during the Giants' decline in 1987 and their subsequent return to the top three seasons later with another Super Bowl victory it was the defense that remained the one constant element in the ever changing team mix. And Taylor continued to prevail as the unit's heart and soul. Nonetheless, passing time was taking its toll on the man wearing number 56. He could no longer shake off the nettling nicks and bruises inherent to his position as in bygone days. Increasingly, he played with less than his usual prowess and on occasion missed a start. Not a few of his critics, both within and without the club, pointed to his disdain for an off-field training regimen as being part of the problem.

Once the season was over Taylor headed for the nearest golf course dismissing such bothersome offseason regimens as running and weightlifting programs. And he was a big enough star that the coaching staff didn't press him on the matter. More than once he reported late to training camp with the cavalier excuse that "the foursome in front of me was playing slow." Under new head coach Ray Handley in 1991 discussion surfaced that had Taylor becoming more of a situational performer than a starter. He rebelled and threatened to retire. The matter didn't come up again. But a year later Handley told Taylor, "Even though you may have earned the right (to star status), you're going to have to give that up, because we can't treat anybody differently."

Taylor was back to playing like his old self in 1992 when he tore the Achilles' tendon in his right leg and was lost for the season and maybe for good. Would he make a comeback at age 34, or leave pro football with his niche in the Hall of Fame assured? Former Giants' defensive end Leonard Marshall said, "I would seriously consider retirement if I were Taylor. He's done everything he can possibly do as a player. But if it (the game) is still in his blood, if he still tastes it, if he's still yearning for the glory, then I'd tell Lawrence to go for it. But not just for the money."

The people who knew Taylor weren't surprised that he opted to come back from surgery. It was largely a matter of self-esteem. He didn't want to leave the game on his shield. Only he would have to make certain adjustments to get the job done. This point was driven home early in 1993 when Dan Reeves took over the Giants' coaching reins. "I don't know of anybody who's rehabbed an Achilles tendon on the golf course," Reeves said. "I've heard what his feelings have been in the past about training camp. But this is the future. He certainly needs to be here and to be physically ready to go."

Cutting short a golfing excursion, Taylor flew back to New Jersey with the promise he would be in top shape for the onset of training camp. "I didn't want to get off on a bad foot with him (Reeves)," he said. "He's the coach and I'm just an employee. But we're both working for the same thing." True to his word, Taylor began working out regularly in the gym and playing racquetball three times a week. "Yeah, it's kind of different for me," he said of his regimen. "But it's something you have to do at my age. It's strange because I feel better. I'm doing a lot of stomach work, agility work and stuff like that. I feel good, and I may even go to camp on time and do the running test because I feel I'm in shape."

As for the status of his injury, he said, "All that's behind me. I don't give it a second thought. I do things I know maybe I shouldn't. And I did things when I was in a cast that maybe you shouldn't do. Only I think if you baby any type of injury, it's going to heal like a baby. It's over with, and if I get hurt, I'm going to get hurt full speed." Not since his early years in the NFL has Taylor been so determined to do well. That burning desire bodes well for the Giants in 1993 and beyond.

tana to the hospital with a concussion. In a post-mortem critique Parcells said, "Not a perfect game, but it was pretty close to it."

Now the only obstacle that stood between New York and the conference title was the Washington Redskins. During the regular season the Giants had beaten Washington twice. They did it a third time before 76,600 fans on their home field, scoring early to win 17-0 and gain the NFC crown.

Super Bowl XXI took place January 25, 1987 at the Rose Bowl in Pasadena, California, before 101,643 spectators. On their first possession of the game the AFC champion Denver Broncos notched a 48-yard field goal to go ahead 3-0. But the Giants went up 7-3 when Simms capped a 78-yard drive with a six-yard touchdown pitch. Shortly thereafter Denver quarterback John Elway passed his team to the New York 24-yard line. A pair of penalties moved the ball to the six and from there the Broncos reclaimed the lead, 10-7. Just before the half Elway was tackled in his end zone for a safety. Denver, 10-9.

In the third period the Giants took charge early as Simms threw a 13-yard TD strike. A field goal followed, then Morris tallied from a yard out to put New York on top, 26-10. A deflected pass was caught by wide receiver Phil McConkey for another Giants' touchdown early in the fourth quarter. Denver retaliated with a field goal but running back Ottis Anderson's two-yard scoring plunge further fattened the New York advantage. Shortly before the conflict ended Elway connected on a 48-yard TD toss. But it was too little, and too late. The Giants were again masters of all they surveyed, 39-20.

Simms earned Super Bowl MVP honors for his 22 of 25 passing performance, which netted 268 yards and three touchdowns. Lawrence Taylor was named NFL Player of the Year in recognition of his season-long mauling of the opposition from his linebacker position. Parcells got the nod as the league's best coach.

Yet another players' strike cut the 1987 schedule to 15 games and allowed replacement teams to fill in three other weekends. The Giants' sub squad was 0-3 and the regulars weren't much better at 6-6. Injuries reduced the running attack to nil and internal strife did the rest. The result was a last place finish in the NFC Eastern Division.

Bill Parcells

Simms continued to play well in 1988 and Morris got back on track, rushing for more than 1,000 yards. But defensively there were problems. Taylor was out four games for substance abuse and fellow linebacker Harry Carson missed as many starts due to injuries. Still, the Giants tied Philadelphia for division honors with a 10-6-0 record. However, two losses to the Eagles dealt them out of the wild-card shuffle.

In 1989 the Giants won the NFC East title with a 12-4-0 mark. But their four losses came at the hands of playoff-bound teams, which didn't bode well for the postseason. The Rams were the opposition in the divisional round at Giants Stadium. A pair of field goals gave New York an early 6-0 lead but quarterback Jim Everett's TD toss in the second period put Los Angeles out front, 7-6. In the third quarter the Giants went up

13-7 on a short scoring run. But the Rams rallied with two field goals before the gun to knot the count at 13-13. Another Everett pass settled the issue in overtime: Los Angeles, 19-13.

The 1990s: To the Top One More Time

Like a sprinter coming off the blocks the Giants got out to a fast start in 1990 with 10 straight wins before stumbling. The squad put on a strong finishing dash for a 13-3-0 record to again head the NFC East. Of their three losses only one was by a margin greater than four points, that being a 31-13 hiding at the hands of the ever nettlesome Eagles. But they also dropped a 17-13 decision to the Buffalo Bills at Giants Stadium. It was this defeat that remained very much on their minds as the year progressed.

Going into the playoffs the Giants were at full strength save for Simms, who was sidelined with a foot injury. Hostetler took over at quarterback in week 14 and acquitted himself well. Against the Bears in the divisional round he completed 10 of 17 passes for 112 yards and two touchdowns as the Giants romped 31-3 before 77,025 home field fans.

Then it was on to San Francisco for yet another confrontation with the 49ers in the NFC Championship game. Both teams could muster only field goals in the first 30 minutes of the contest and so were deadlocked 6-6 at the half. During the third period Montana and wide receiver John Taylor combined for a 61-yard scoring play that put the 49ers up 13-6. But kicker Matt Bahr converted three consecutive field goal attempts to give the Giants a 15-13 victory.

In Super Bowl XXV at Tampa (Fla.) Stadium the Giants and the Buffalo Bills, AFC titlists, matched field goals in the opening quarter for a 3-3 standoff. The Bills went ahead 10-3 in the second period on a one-yard plunge by running back Don Smith. A few minutes later Hostetler was tackled in his end zone to make it 12-3, Buffalo. But he quickly vindicated himself with a 14-yard TD pass and New York trailed 12-10 at the half.

On their initial possession of the third quarter the Giants drove 75 yards to go ahead 17-12. Then, at the top of the last period, running back Thurman Thomas scored on a 31-yard jaunt and the Bills went up again, 19-17. But a field goal put New York right back in the lead, 20-19. As the waning seconds of the game expired a Buffalo field goal attempt from 47 yards out went inches wide and the Giants were Super Bowl champs once more. Ottis Anderson, who led the New York ground attack with 102 yards rushing, was named MVP. Hostetler hit on 20 of 32 attempts for 222 yards and a touchdown. Parcells resigned as head coach on May 15, 1991, for health reasons and was replaced by Ray Handley, the Giants' offensive coordinator.

From Super Bowl winner to a .500 ball club is the way it went for the Giants in 1991. Immediately following the preseason schedule Handley announced that Hostetler would be the starting quarterback and Simms the backup. So began the second guessing and it continued throughout the season. Everyone got into the act regarding the quarterback controversy—the media, the players and the fans. Despite the many disruptions the Giants were competitive in every game but could do no better than an 8-8-0 record. Nothing told the story of their demise quite so starkly as the statistic that showed that the opposition outscored them in the fourth quarter during the course of the season by a total of 129 points to 53.

Lack of a consistent pass rush plagued the Giants throughout the 1992 campaign, particularly after Taylor was lost with a torn Achilles tendon in week nine. At that juncture they were a respectable 5-4, but the club posted a 1-6 record for the remainder of the slate and finished an embarrassing 6-10-0. Injuries and indecision which caused Hostetler and Simms to play musical quarterbacks was another disconcerting factor. Moreover, as the year wore on it seemed increasingly apparent that Handley didn't really have charge of the program. So it came as no surprise when he lost his job at season's end.

Early in 1993 the Giants hired Dan Reeves to be their 15th head coach. He came to New York after a dozen years in Denver, where he compiled an impressive 117-79-1 record. Under his tutelage the Broncos played in three Super Bowls and won as many AFC titles. Recently, he said, "I wouldn't have taken this job if I hadn't thought that this is a winning organization." So once again the Giants look to take the high road back to glory.

Sources

Books

Aaseng, Nathan. *Football's Cunning Coaches.* Lerner Publications Company, 1981.

Beall, Alan. *Braves on the Warpath.* Kinloch-Books, 1988.

Cohen, Richard, & Neft, David S. *The Sports Encyclopedia-Pro Football.* St. Martin's Press, 1990.

Fifty Years of NFL Excitement. NFL Properties, Inc., 1986.

Fitzgerald, Ed. *My Own Story-Johnny Unitas.* Grosset & Dunlop, Inc., 1968.

Giants Information Guide. New York Football Giants, Inc., 1993.

Gola, Hank. *Hard Nose.* Harcourt Brace Jovanovich, 1987.

Harrington, Denis J. *The Pro Football Hall of Fame.* McFarland & Company, Inc., 1991.

Izenberg, Jerry. *No Medals for Trying.* Macmillan Publishing Company, 1990.

Leckie, Robert. *The Story of Football.* Random House, Inc., 1974.

Maule, Tex. *The Gladiators - The Men of Professional Football.*

Rutledge Books, 1973.

Miller, J. David. *The Super Book of Football.* Time Inc. Magazine Company, 1990.

Nelson, Kevin. *Football's Greatest Insults.* Perigee Books, 1991.

NFL Special Report. Super Bowl XXV, XXI. NFL Properties, 1987, 1991.

Schaap, Dick. *Simms to McConkey - The Story of the 1986 Giants.* Crown Publishers, Inc., 1987.

Smith, Ron. *The Sporting News Chronicle of 20th Century Sport.* Mallard Press, 1992.

The Official 1992 National Football League Record & Fact Book. NFL Properties, Inc., 1992.

The Sporting News Pro Football Guide. The Sporting News Publishing Company, 1991, 1990.

Whittingham, Richard. *The Giants: From the Polo Grounds to Super Bowl XXI.* Harper & Row, 1987.

Periodicals

Football Digest, January/April/July/August, 1993; February/March, 1989; September/October/November, 1988; April/May/June, 1987; September/October, 1986.

Pro Football Illustrated Annual, 1988, 1987.

Pro Football Weekly, August 1, 1993.

Redskins News, September 26-October 3, September 6-12, 1988.

Redskins Report, November 17, 1985; September 24, 1984; October 15, 1984; November 19, 1984.

The Sporting News, March 25, 1991; May 27, 1991; July 15, 1991; September 2, 1991; September 16, 1991; September 23, 1991; September 30, 1991; October 7, 1991; October 14, 1991; May 25, 1992; June 8, 1992; June 22, 1992; July 6, 1992; July 13, 1992; July 27, 1992; August 3, 1992; August 10, 1992; August 31, 1992; September 14, 1992; September 21, 1992; October 12, 1992; November 2, 1992; November 9, 1992; November 16, 1992; November 23, 1992; November 30, 1992; December 28, 1992; January 11, 1993; March 22, 1993; April 5, 1993; April 12, 1993; April 26, 1993; May 3, 1993; May 17, 1993; May 24, 1993; May 31, 1993; June 1, 1993; June 7, 1993; June 28, 1993; July 5, 1993; July 12, 1993.

Sports Illustrated, September 6, 1993.

—Denis J. Harrington

PHILADELPHIA EAGLES

From the deepest days of the Great Depression to the present, the Philadelphia Eagles have been one of the most colorful franchises in the National Football League. Founded in 1933 by the legendary Bert Bell, the Eagles have been a continuous presence in the City of Brotherly Love for six decades. Fans have flocked to a succession of stadiums to see the team meet such perennial rivals as the New York Giants, Washington Redskins, Dallas Cowboys, and Chicago Bears.

Loyalty to the underdog franchise remains high despite years of dismal or disappointing performance. In his book *Pigskin Power,* Ken Rappoport notes that the team has won only three NFL championships and appeared in one Super Bowl, with a handful of outstanding seasons offset by years of struggle. Nevertheless, the author concludes, "fewer teams have given more tradition and panache to NFL history than this proud bunch of birds."

Mere records alone do not do justice to the Eagles' history. The Philadelphia story includes names that are enshrined in the top echelon of professional football: Sonny Jurgensen, Norman Van Brocklin, Bert Bell, Steve Van Buren, and the heart-stopping defensive end Reggie White. Recent years have seen an Eagles defense so effective that it has been lifted almost man-for-man straight into the Pro Bowl, and quarterback Randall Cunningham, who has delighted the crowd with his dramatic rushing and scrambling techniques.

Despite its fallow years and its dubious tradition of early-round playoff losses, the Eagles team is the single most profitable franchise financially in the entire NFL. Season tickets to spacious Veterans Stadium sell out every year, and home game television blackouts are rare indeed.

A packed Veterans Stadium can be a mixed blessing for the Eagles, however. Philadelphia fans are notorious for their propensity to boo the home team and jeer the quarterback when he fails to produce touchdowns. The tradition of vocal dissent goes back decades. Upon his induction to the Pro Football Hall of Fame, quarterback Jurgensen told the *Philadelphia Daily News* that his most pleasant memory of his seven years with the Eagles (1957-63) was "getting traded." Jurgensen added: "Philly is a tough town. My rookie year I won three of my four starts and they still threw beer cans at me when I came through the tunnel."

The Eagles are certainly a paradox. Teams that were thought to be mediocre at best have won championships, while others loaded with fresh, young talent have been disappointments. The current owner, Norman Braman—a Philadelphia native who bought the team for "sentimental" reasons—is a notorious cost-cutter who lost a star player in 1992 in a salary dispute.

Perhaps the largest hurdle the Eagles must overcome is the team's position in the National Football Conference East, a division perennially regarded as one of the toughest in all of professional football. In addition to meeting traditional Super Bowl champions like the Redskins and the Cowboys, the embattled Birds often draw other NFC rivals such as the Chicago Bears and the San Francisco 49ers. Year after year the Eagles face daunting schedules in which, at least since 1980, they have held their own in admirable style.

Modest Beginnings

Professional football's earliest roots lie in Pennsylvania and Ohio. The first man ever to accept payment for appearance in a football game was John Brallier, who offered his services to a team in his hometown of Latrobe, Pennsylvania. The concept was warmly embraced elsewhere, and by the turn of the century numerous cities in the east were recruiting college stars for professional work. Philadelphia hosted two professional teams at the time—the Athletics and the Nationals. As early as 1902, Connie Mack of baseball fame organized the Athletics with a partner named Rube Waddell. The Athletics had the distinction of playing in the first professional night game, a 39-0 victory at Elmira, New York. Not to be outdone, the Nationals became the first team to bring professional football indoors, losing 6-0 at Madison Square Garden to rivals from Syracuse, New York.

Recruiting fan support for professional football was an uphill battle from the start. College football remained the favorite among football devotees. Most of the first professional football players earned little more than pocket change to supplement their daytime jobs in factories and industry. The best way to float a team, promoters found, was to build its identity around a city or a neighborhood, thereby fostering local loyalty. One such neighborhood-based professional football team was the Frankford Yellow Jackets.

The team was founded in 1924 in a working-class section of Philadelphia called Frankford. Players were recruited from the graduating classes of local colleges such as the University of Pennsylvania, Temple University, and Princeton University. Funding came from a group of Frankford businessmen who each kicked in fifty dollars to cover expenses. Home games were played in a 9000-seat stadium in the neighborhood.

Throughout their seven-year tenure, the Yellow Jackets endured a dizzying schedule. Laws on the Philadelphia books prohibited professional sporting events on Sundays, so the team often played at home on Saturday, then took a night train to a Sunday game elsewhere. In one weekend the players might range as far afield as Chicago, Detroit, or New York City.

An 18-member roster left no room for injuries, let alone special team play. The average player earned less than $40 per game and had to provide his own equipment. Bill Hoffman, the last surviving member of the 1926 Yellow Jackets, told the *Philadelphia Daily News:* "We didn't get rich in our day, but we had a lot of fun. We had to love what we were doing or else we wouldn't have lasted. Of course, we won, and winning is fun anytime."

The Yellow Jackets drew capacity crowds in 1926 when they won the National Football League championship by compiling the best won-loss

Team Information at a Glance

Founding date: 1933

Home stadium: Veterans Stadium
Broad St. and Pattison Ave.
Philadelphia, PA 19148-5201
Phone: (215) 463-2500
Seating capacity: 65,356

Team colors: Kelly green, silver, and white
Team nickname: Eagles, 1933--
Logo: Silver eagle wing trimmed with white

Franchise record:	Won	Lost	Tie
(1933-1990)	196	185	13

NFL Championships (2): 1948, 1949

record of the year. The team's coach, Guy Chamberlin, also played end and did his share of the scoring in the two years he spent in Philadelphia.

Forty years later, in 1965, Chamberlin was elected to the Pro Football Hall of Fame, ensuring the Yellow Jackets a noted place in the early history of pro football. The team continued to play into the 1930s, and then the depressed economy took its toll. Frankford's ball park fell into disrepair and its backers could not afford to rebuild it. The Yellow Jackets declared bankruptcy in 1931.

At this juncture a wealthy man named Bert Bell entered the picture. Bell loved football and dreamed of owning a professional team. Since he had grown up in the posh suburbs of Philadelphia known as the Main Line and had attended the University of Pennsylvania, he decided to buy a new franchise for his home city. In 1933 Bell and partner Ludlow Wray formed a syndicate to purchase the rights to the Yellow Jackets. They managed to amass $2500, settled the debts of the Yellow Jackets, and bought the team.

They called their new club the Philadelphia Eagles, in honor of the symbol Franklin Roosevelt had chosen to represent his New Deal and National Recovery legislation. Bell and Wray chose blue and yellow for team colors because those were Philadelphia's city colors. They also recruited a few seasoned veterans from the Yellow Jackets to help guide the fledgling Eagles.

If the Eagles had really been birds, they would have left the nest with a resounding crash onto the pavement. In the 1933 season opener, they lost 56-0 to the New York Giants, followed by a 25-0 trouncing from a Portsmouth team in their home debut. With Wray as coach, the Eagles finished their first year with a 3-5-1 record. The only small consolations were a 3-3 tie with the mighty Chicago Bears and a repeal of the Blue Laws that had previously forbidden Sunday play in the city.

Within three years the Eagles had lost $80,000. One by one, Bell's investors dropped out, finally leaving him in sole control of the franchise. Undaunted, he proceeded to serve as coach, general manager, scout, public relations director, and even ticket hawker in order to produce support for the team.

Philadelphia Inquirer correspondent William Ecenbarger describes the early years: "Bell did everything he could to keep the Eagles aloft. Because the rent was cheap, the team played in the 102,000-seat Municipal Stadium before at least 100,000 empty seats. One rainy Sunday, only 50 people showed up for a game against the inept Brooklyn Dodgers; Bell invited them all up to the covered press box, where he provided free coffee and hot dogs. The original team colors were blue and yellow, but there were so many derisive comments about the symbolism of the latter color that Bell switched to kelly green and white. Players traveled to games in wheezing, unreliable buses, and sometimes Bell would order the driver to stop at an open field for an impromptu practice. To build fan interest, Bell hired Alabama Pitts, who had recently been the mainstay on the Sing Sing prison team. But the Eagles continued to lay eggs."

From 1933 until 1942, Bell did not have a single winning season. Rappoport claims that those years did have some highlights, however. He cites a "smattering of good players in the Eagles' lineup," including local heroes Dave Smukler and Thomas Hanson from Temple. "This explosive pair gave the Eagles some of the best running in the league, Smukler at fullback and Hanson at halfback," the author notes. End Joe Carter, another stand-out, led the NFL in 1934 with 16 receptions for 238 yards.

On more than one occasion, the Eagles actually dressed their water boy so the bench would not look too anemic. As the sole financial backer of the team, Bell watched in disgust as wealthier franchises lured star college players with lucrative offers. Bell found it unfair—a classic case of the rich getting richer—when the best players were automatically signed by the dominant clubs. At last he hit upon a plan that he felt would help to equalize the talent on all the NFL teams.

At an owners' meeting in 1935, Bell proposed a draft of eligible college players in which the NFL team with the worst record would get first choice from the talent pool. The other owners agreed, and in 1936 the pro football draft was begun. It continues to this day and is one of many lasting changes Bell wrought on professional football.

Bert Bell

The Eagles finished 1935 with a 2-9 record, giving Bell the first pick in the very first football draft. He chose Jay Berwanger, the Heisman Trophy-winning halfback from the University of Chicago. Berwanger was dissatisfied with the deal. He wanted a higher salary than the lowly Eagles could afford, so Bell traded his rights to the Chicago Bears. Even that powerful team could not meet Berwanger's asking price, so the first-ever first-round draft pick never actually played professional football.

Other draft picks for the Eagles fared somewhat better. Quarterback Davey O'Brien from Texas Christian University became a crowd-pleaser in the late 1930s and helped Bell to keep the franchise narrowly profitable. O'Brien joined the team in 1938. The following year he set an NFL record for passing yardage in one season, with 1,324 yards. His abilities notwithstanding, the Eagles won only two games in 1938 and 1939. O'Brien retired in 1940.

That same year saw a complicated series of transactions involving the Eagles and their counterpart in Pittsburgh, the Pirates. Like the Eagles, the Pirates had struggled since their formation in 1933. Their owner, Art Rooney, sold the club to Alexis Thompson, a 26-year-old steel heir from Boston. At first Thompson announced plans to ship the Pittsburgh franchise to Boston. Rooney bought a share of Bell's Philadelphia Eagles with the intention of staging home games in both Philadelphia and Pittsburgh.

The good intentions never materialized—Thompson kept his team in Pittsburgh, and Rooney became successful promoting boxing in Pittsburgh as well. Bell made everyone a proposition. He simply suggested a swap: he and Rooney would move the Philadelphia franchise to Pittsburgh, and Thompson could move the Pittsburgh franchise to Philadelphia. The idea appealed to Thompson because Philadelphia was closer to his home base in New York City.

Mystery shrouds the fine details of the scheme. Rappoport reports that Bell and Rooney sold their holdings in Philadelphia to Thompson. Ecenbarger suggests that the transaction was more like an actual swap, with the Pittsburgh players moving east and the Philadelphia players moving west. In fact, neither scenario is exactly complete. By the time the dust cleared in 1940, the Philadelphia Eagles did have some new players from Pittsburgh, and vice versa, but the only dramatic change in Philadelphia was the leadership.

Neale Takes the Helm

Thompson had no desire to coach his own football team as Bell had. Instead, he hired Earle "Greasy" Neale, former backfield coach at Yale University, to guide the Eagles. Neale caught Thompson's attention because Thompson was a Yale graduate. As an inside choice, however, it was inspired. Neale went on to transform the Eagles from the league's worst losers to the national champions in the space of a decade. Rappoport maintains that the stubbornly independent Neale "was acknowledged to have one of the finest football minds of his era, or any era for that matter."

Neale decided to concentrate on the T formation on offense with his Philadelphia Eagles. It was less than an overnight success. Relentless drilling notwithstanding, the Eagles managed only a 2-8-1 record in 1941 and a 1-9 record in 1942. Fans came to the games anyway, in part because they enjoyed the spectacle of Neale pacing the sidelines like a caged wildcat.

World War II created a severe manpower shortage in the entire NFL by 1943. President Roosevelt declared that no professional sportsman found eligible for service should be exempted, and rosters were soon depleted. Some teams responded by calling back long-retired veterans. The Eagles met the challenge by merging with the Pittsburgh Steelers. The one-year experimental team, quickly dubbed the "Steagles" in the press, was jointly presided over by Thompson, Rooney, and Bell. The players practiced in Philadelphia at the University of Pennsylvania and took the field in the Eagles' green-and-white uniforms. Half the home schedule was played in Philadelphia and half in Pittsburgh.

Jack Hinkle, an offensive star for the Steagles—and later for the Eagles as well—received a discharge from the Air Force for stomach ulcers. He was a typical player of the time. He worked 40 hours a week in a defense plant in north Philadelphia, then spent three hours each evening practicing for the Sunday game. For an entire season's participation he earned $1,350. "Most of us played because we loved the game," he told the *Philadelphia Inquirer.*

The unorthodox union kept both teams alive. For the players it was a happy merger, but the coaches were another matter. The crusty Neale bridled at the idea of sharing his coaching duties with Pittsburgh's Walt Kiesling, and both coaches conspired to win the most talented rookie players for their own respective teams. By mid-season the two men were barely speaking, and the Steagles disbanded after one year. The team's 5-4-1 finish at season's end was the best record the Eagles had compiled in their first decade of existence.

The shortage of quality players worsened in 1944. Of 300 men selected in the draft that year, only a dozen ended up on the field. Fortunately for the Eagles, one of those 12 was their first round draft choice, a halfback out of Louisiana State University named Steve Van Buren.

Van Buren Takes the Spotlight

"Steve Van Buren was the marquee name of that era, a 6-foot, 210-pound halfback with 9.8 speed," writes Ray Didinger in the *Philadelphia Daily News*. "He led the league in rushing four of five seasons (1945-49). He was the first NFL player to surpass the 1,000-yard season-rushing mark twice..... Greasy Neale called Van Buren the greatest runner he'd ever seen. Better than Jim Thorpe, better than Red Grange.... Van Buren took the Philadelphia franchise off skid row and made it a two-time world champion. He made the Pro Football Hall of Fame.... And, for all this, Big Steve earned $15,000 in his best year, 1950."

Van Buren, a fan favorite, was simply one cog in a mighty machine that Neale assembled piece by piece in the mid-1940s. A former end himself, Neale carefully chose pass catchers who could also block, such as Pete Pihos, Jack Ferrante, Neil Armstrong, and Dick Hubert. Van Buren was joined at halfback by Bosh Pritchard, another powerful runner. As early as 1944 it was evident that a new era had begun in Philadelphia. The Eagles finished in second place with a 7-1-2 record as Neale began to see the fruits of his devotion to the T formation.

No one dominated the NFL more thoroughly than Steve Van Buren from 1945 until 1949. He notched 77 touchdowns in eight years and even scored several times on kickoff returns. Despite his talent and tenacity, Van Buren never courted fame, either in Philadelphia or elsewhere. He turned down product endorsements, baffled that anyone would want to use his name. He shunned the media. He preferred to live quietly, as he does today, in a middle-class Philadelphia neighborhood. Van Buren told the *Philadelphia Daily News* that on one occasion, during a contract negotiation, then-owner James Clark offered him three shares of the Eagles as part of his deal. He turned Clark down, convinced that the shares would not appreciate. "What would they be worth today?" Van Buren asked in 1983. "A quarter of a million dollars? Regrets? Nah. Some guys were meant to be rich and some guys were meant to be happy. I'm happy."

Eagles fans were happy too as the team began to flex its muscles in 1947. By that time the roster was full-strength again after the war years. Neale pushed his players with all the vitriol a football coach can muster, and the team grew disciplined and close-knit. Veteran quarterback Tommy Thompson, who was blind in one eye, became legendary for his nonchalant optimism. More than once, when the team trailed late in a game, the quarterback would yell at Neale: "Don't worry, old man, we'll run them right out of the ballpark." By 1947 the Eagles finished at the top of the Eastern Division with a 21-0 victory over Pittsburgh in a playoff. A championship was denied them when the Chicago Cardinals beat them 28-21 in Chicago's Comiskey Park.

The following two years belonged to the Eagles. They compiled a 20-3-1 record over the 1948 and 1949 seasons and outscored their opponents 761-290. No other NFL team has ever won back-to-back championships by shutout, as the Eagles did in 1948 and 1949. Didinger observes that most of the players were as modest as Van Buren. "They didn't mind riding a trolley to practice or working another job in the offseason," the reporter notes. "They were happy just to be home [from the war] and playing football again. The money wasn't that great, but so what? The players were more concerned with winning games and having fun. The old Eagles led the league in both departments."

What stands out most about the two national championship games is not a particular player's performance, but the weather. The 1948 contest was played in Philadelphia in the midst of a blinding snowstorm. Conditions were so bad that some of the players assumed the game would be called off. Jack Ferrante, an end for the team that year, told Rappoport: "I looked out the window of my house and said, 'We're not going to play today.' The snow was a couple of feet deep. I got to the park some way—I don't remember how—and we had a short meeting with Greasy Neale in the locker room. Everybody from out of town had their bags packed and didn't want to stay over another week. I know Greasy didn't. He thought we'd lose our competitive edge if we had to wait more time to play the game. I remember he said, 'You fellows practiced all week, and now if we stay over another week, you have a chance of losing." The team voted to play, and although it snowed a few inches during the game, the Eagles managed to defeat the Chicago Cardinals 7-0 on a Van Buren touchdown.

Steve Van Buren

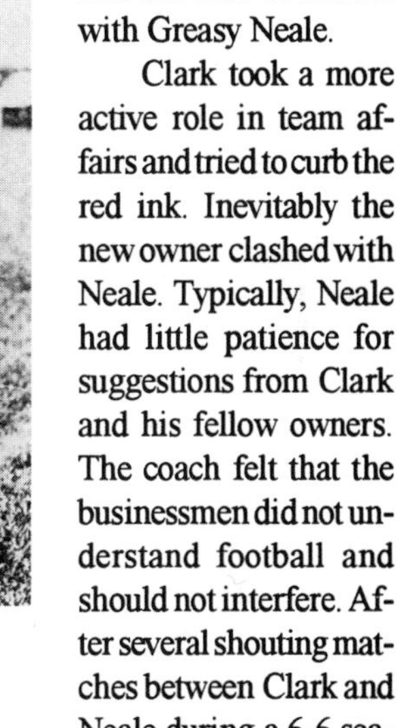

Snow was not a factor the following year, but rain was. A rare 24-hour rainstorm struck Los Angeles the day before the Eagles were set to meet the Rams. Ankle-deep in mud, the team rushed for 274 yards and two touchdowns, winning 14-0. Van Buren contributed 196 of those yards himself for a NFL championship game record that stands to this day. All told, five contributors to the back-to-back Eagles championships eventually were inducted into the Pro Football Hall of Fame: Van Buren, Neale, end Pete Pihos (who had 63 career touchdowns), center Alex Wojciechowicz, and linebacker Chuck Bednarik, who would endure on the roster into a second championship era.

In 1949 Thompson sold the Eagles franchise to a syndicate headed by local businessman James Clark. Clark named Vince McNally general manager. At first all was well. The Eagles rode a 12-1 season record to their second championship, and Van Buren was in his prime. The following year the elements of success began to unravel. Thompson—who actually lost money on the Eagles even while they were winning—was a hands-off owner and the best of friends with Greasy Neale.

Clark took a more active role in team affairs and tried to curb the red ink. Inevitably the new owner clashed with Neale. Typically, Neale had little patience for suggestions from Clark and his fellow owners. The coach felt that the businessmen did not understand football and should not interfere. After several shouting matches between Clark and Neale during a 6-6 season in 1950, Neale was fired. Early in 1951 Van Buren retired after sustaining multiple playing injuries. An era had ended.

"The dismissal of Neale signaled a general decline for the Eagles in the 1950s," writes Rappoport. Clark's first choice for coach, Alvin "Bo" McMillan, became ill with cancer before the start of the 1951 season and was only able to coach two games. He was replaced by Wayne Millner, who only lasted one season. The following year, coach Jim Trimble took the helm and helped guide the Eagles to second-place finishes in 1953 and 1954. Clark's frugality with the Eagles did not damage the team beyond repair—end-placekicker Bobby Walston was signed in 1951, became rookie-of-the-year, and went on to become a league-leading scorer by 1954. Pete Pihos remained with the team despite some dissatisfaction with his salary, and he led the league in touchdowns with ten in 1953. The receiving combination of Pihos and Walston kept the Eagles competitive, as did a strong defense.

Coaching remained a sore point for the team as the 1950s progressed. After a 4-7-1 season in 1955, Trimble was replaced in 1956 by Hugh Devore. His showing was equally dismal, 3-8-1 during a year in which Pihos retired. The series of losing seasons continued in 1957, as the Eagles only managed a 4-8 record. The only solace the team could find was in a series of promising draft choices.

The genesis of a new champion began modestly with the acquisition of defenseman Tom Brookshier from the University of Colorado and the signing of halfback Tommy McDonald of the University of Oklahoma and quarterback Sonny Jurgensen of Duke. McDonald, who at 5'10" had to overcome the idea that he was too small to play professionally, began to make a mark as a receiver in 1957.

Still, the 1957 and 1958 seasons provided Eagles fans with little to cheer and plenty to jeer. Future Hall-of-Famer Jurgensen was soundly booed most of the time when he played—a memory that would come back to haunt Eagles fans years later when he was traded to the Washington Redskins. After finishing 4-8 in 1957, the Eagles once again changed coaches.

This time the new skipper was Buck Shaw, a strategist who managed to remain optimistic in the face of seemingly insurmountable odds. Shaw detected the seeds of greatness in Jurgensen but felt the young quarterback did not have sufficient experience to lead the team through a whole season. In a trade with the Los Angeles Rams, Shaw acquired a 32-year-old, seasoned quarterback named Norman Van Brocklin. Nicknamed "The Dutchman," Van Brocklin joined the Eagles, predicted a championship, and began to bully his teammates into line.

The Dutchman Takes the Team by Storm

"Norm Van Brocklin was perhaps the most complex and fascinating personality to flash across the pro football horizon in ... decades," writes Didinger in the *Philadelphia Daily News.* "He was a man of consummate talent and temper, a man who could ooze charm one moment, spew volcanic ash the next. He was a man who clung to old, hard-line principles, a man who dug his heels into the 1940s and refused to budge."

For Van Brocklin, winning a championship with the Eagles by 1960 became an obsession. His determination and enthusiasm soon infected his teammates. Didinger concludes of Van Brocklin: "His was a triumph of attitude over ability, of fire over logic. He won as many games with the gravel in his belly as he did with his strong right arm. He was cranky and vulgar, perhaps the worst loser the league ever saw, but, in his own earthy way, he embodied the spirit of pro football."

Teammates and sportswriters alike compared the Dutchman to General George Patton. Former New York Giants defensive back Dick Lynch told the *Philadelphia Daily News:* "Dutch ... went at every game as if he were leading his men across the Rhine, and God help anybody who let him down. Patton slapped his troops. Dutch kicked his in the rear end. I remember covering his receivers and hearing them almost whimper after they dropped a pass. They'd be on the ground, holding their heads, saying, 'Now I've gotta go back to the huddle and Dutch is gonna kill me.'"

On the flip side, the Dutchman instituted a series of informal Monday morning get-togethers at a Philadelphia tavern. Every player who attended had a chance to air his concerns, voice his complaints, or accent the team's assets. These team meetings helped build camaraderie on the squad. Gradually a team that seemed mediocre at best on paper became a championship contender.

Van Brocklin favored the pass, and with the Eagles he found two able receivers—McDonald and Pete Retzlaff. Both McDonald and Retzlaff became threats for the long "bomb" as well as the short-to-medium routes.

While the Van Brocklin-to-McDonald combination became a favorite for Philadelphia's spectators, Retzlaff topped the league in catches in 1959 and 1960. "I didn't have great natural ability," Retzlaff told the *Philadelphia Daily News.* "I worked to become a good receiver.... I was very fortunate. I came to [Philadelphia] ... literally looking for a job. I never dreamed all this would happen."

By 1959 the Eagles had improved to 7-5 and a tie for a second place finish with Cleveland. As the 1960 season dawned, optimism ran high—at least among the Eagles players—for a championship year. After an opening day loss to the Browns, 41-24, the Eagles went on to win nine games in a row.

Retzlaff recalled the feat in the *Philadelphia Daily News:* "We were putting things together, but no one believed in us. We had won two in a row but people said, 'They can't win three.' When we won three in a row they said, 'They can't win four.' It went on like that. We won nine in a row, clinched the division, and people were still saying we weren't that good. The only ones who believed were the guys on the team. Yeah, we got a few breaks, but we had a lot to do with making those breaks." Retzlaff concluded: "Cinderella team? I don't buy it. We had a lot of guys who had kicked around (the NFL) but they had ability. All they needed was a chance."

The idea of a Cinderella team originated with the style in which the 1960 Eagles won. Many times they trailed in the fourth quarter, only to mount a near-miraculous comeback. No one epitomizes the determination of the 1960 Eagles better than Hall-of-Famer Chuck Bednarik, the only Eagle who remained from the 1949 championship year. A battered veteran, Bednarik was called to work on both offense and defense midway through the 1960 season. He played center on offense and linebacker on defense and is widely known as the "last of the 60-minute men." In the 1960 NFL championship game he played 58 minutes.

Chuck Bednarik

"The name, Chuck Bednarik, means football in this city," writes Didinger in the *Philadelphia Daily News.* "He is the greatest player in Penn history. He is the only man to serve on both Eagle championship teams, the Greasy Neale dynasty of the '40s and Shaw's miracle workers of '60. He was the center on the NFL's First 50-Year Team... He is one of only three players—Jim Thorpe and Don Hudson are the others—elected to both the college and pro football halls of fame." As late as 1992, Bednarik still held the Eagles record for most Pro Bowls attended, with eight appearances.

In 1960 the Eagles won six of ten victories by eight points or less, including a thrilling 31-29 revenge game against the Browns. The national championship game found them facing the Green Bay Packers at home in Philadelphia's Franklin Field stadium.

That game more or less followed the pattern the Eagles had established over the season: they were outgained (401 yards to 296), trailed in the fourth quarter (13-10), and won on a 5-yard touchdown run by a rookie fullback, Ted Dean. With a final score of 17-13, the Eagles became champions. The average salary for an Eagle player that year was $14,000.

The 1960 championship team was certainly a one-year wonder, a group of football-smart veterans and talented younger stars who made magic happen through one season. The most remarkable aspect of that Eagle team is the contribution many of its members made to football *after* 1960.

Of 22 starters, 12 wound up in an NFL front office. Four of its players became Eagles head coaches—Jerry Williams, Nick Skorich, Eddie Khayat, and Marion Campbell. Van Brocklin coached two expansion teams, the Minnesota Vikings and the Atlanta Falcons. Retzlaff became Eagles general manager from 1969-72. Both Van Brocklin and Bednarik have been inducted into the Pro Football Hall of Fame.

Ironically, Eagles founder Bert Bell did not live to see the 1960 championship. After a long career as Commissioner of Football, he died of a heart attack in 1959—during a football game.

At the end of the 1960 season both Van Brocklin and coach Shaw retired. Jurgensen took over as starting quarterback and Nick Skorich won head coaching duties in a controversial decision—Van Brocklin claimed he had been promised the job.

Despite the front office turmoil, Jurgensen blossomed as a quarterback in 1961. He led the league in every passing category, compiling 235 completions and 3,723 total yards. The Eagles finished in second place with a strong 10-4 record, but then the situation began to deteriorate.

Rappoport writes: "The Eagles quickly went from a winner to a loser and stayed that way for the better part of two decades. From 1962 through 1977, the Eagles were only able to manage one winning season (9-5 in 1966) and five times lost ten games in a season and once as many as twelve."

Grim Days Ahead

That dismal long-term performance seems to have begun with the purchase of the team in 1963 by Jerry Wolman, a developer. Wolman hired Joe Kuharich as head coach. Determined to revamp the struggling team, Kuharich traded McDonald to Dallas—a devastatingly unpopular move—and dealt Jurgensen and safety Jim Carr to Washington. "The reports were that Kuharich had made all these trades to break up cliques on the Eagles that had formed on the 1960 championship team," maintains Rappoport. "Kuharich protested loudly, of course, and defended his position with the remark: 'We weigh all the factors and do what we think is best for the team.' But many of Kuharich's trades were largely unpopular, especially the one that sent Jurgensen, the best pure passer in the league, to Washington."

Kuharich was probably the most hated coach in the history of the Eagles. Disgruntled fans wore "Joe Must Go" buttons and formed a "Get Rid of Kuharich Club." Once someone even hired an airplane to fly over Franklin Field with the banner "Goodbye, Joe Baby" flapping behind it in the wind. Indeed, some of the coach's decisions were baffling to everyone concerned. In 1966, the only winning season during the period, he platooned three quarterbacks and literally did not tell who would be starting until the National Anthem was playing on game day.

Norman Snead was the main starting quarterback after Jurgensen's departure. Reminiscing on Kuharich, Snead told the *Philadelphia Daily News:* "We (the quarterbacks) didn't know what Joe was thinking half the time. We'd be looking at each other in the locker room before the game, saying, 'Did he tell you anything? No, he didn't tell me anything either.' I remember a game we played against Dallas at Franklin Field. Joe came up to me before the warmup and said, 'Are you ready?' I said, 'You bet.' He said, 'Good. You're going in today.' I was all charged up. Then during the warmup, Joe came over to King [Hill]. He said, 'Be ready. If we get the ball inside our own 40, you're starting.' King said to me, 'Didn't he say you were starting?' At that point, we were both confused. Then, as we were going back in, Joe said to [Jack] Concannon, 'Look, if we get the ball inside their 20, you're starting.' We all looked at each other.... There just didn't seem to be a whole lot of logic to what was going on."

The same could be said of the team's progress in general. After a winning year in 1966, the Eagles went 6-7-1 in 1967, 2-12 in 1968, 4-9-1 in 1969, and 3-10-1 in 1970. Snead was the starting quarterback most of those years, and he defended the team in the *Philadelphia Daily News*. "It's a shame we never put it together in Philadelphia," he said. "It seemed like we were right on the verge a few times, then one or two key guys would go down with injuries." Another victim of the perennial booing crowds, Snead concluded: "Philadelphia is a passionate sports city. As an athlete, you have to be prepared to deal with both sides of that passion. It can be real good or real bad. Let's face it, nobody likes to be booed, but it's not personal, really. It's part of the business."

The team's misfortunes notwithstanding, the Eagles were sold in 1969 for a then-record price of $16.1 million. Trucking magnate Leonard Tose, the new owner, named Pete Retzlaff the new general manager and Jerry Williams the coach. The losing continued, and Williams lasted just one full season and three games into 1971.

Tose fired Williams, setting off a storm of protest from the players. After recording a 6-7-1 season under new head coach Ed Khayat in 1971, the Birds fell to a dismal 2-11-1 in 1972. Retzlaff resigned in frustration, and Tose released the entire Eagles coaching staff. The Eagles had never seemed so hapless.

The 1973 season began with another new coach, Mike McCormack, and a new quarterback—at least for the Eagles—Roman Gabriel. Gabriel had enjoyed a productive career with the Los Angeles Rams but had suffered a collapsed lung and an injury to his passing arm in 1972. Signing him was a gamble, but he rose to the occasion. With the help of league-leading receiver Harold Carmichael, Gabriel managed to pull the Eagles back up to 5-8-1. At season's end Gabriel was named NFL Comeback Player of the Year. The following year Gabriel led the Eagles to a 7-7 record, the best mark posted by the club in nearly a decade.

Rappoport writes: "McCormack left in 1975 after three years, but his contribution to the Eagles' success in the late Seventies was inestimable. While his Eagles teams never won more games than they lost, he laid the foundation for a series of winners to come." Draft picks such as Jerry Sisemore from the University of Texas, Charlie Young from the University of Southern California, and Randy Logan from the University of Michigan formed part of a nucleus of talent that also included linebacker Bill Bergey and wide receiver Harold Carmichael. Bergey, for instance, became a mainstay of the Eagles defense and attended four Pro Bowls. Carmichael too was a Pro Bowl invitee four times.

Vermeil Takes Over

In 1976 the Dick Vermeil era began in Philadelphia. Tose hired the 39-year-old Vermeil from the University of California, Los Angeles. The best showing Vermeil could muster in his first professional season was a 5-9 record. In what was a rather unpopular move at the time, Vermeil traded for quarterback Ron Jaworski of the Los Angeles Rams in 1977.

"Jaws" became yet another target of raucous booing, now echoing through the bowl-shaped Veterans Stadium, but Vermeil adamantly refused to change starters. "I'm not going to let the fans dictate what quarterback I use," he said, as quoted by Rappoport. "They can boo for six months and I'm not going to take [Jaworski] out of a game. That's the way a guy matures—going nine innings."

Jaworski went nine innings, and more. He

matured from an erratic, gambling quarterback into a powerful, disciplined player who could read a defense efficiently and who showed strength on both the pass and the run. With more help from the mighty Bergey, Jaworski's Eagles posted a 9-7 record in 1978 and made the playoffs for the first time since 1960.

Their 14-13 wild card playoff loss to the Atlanta Falcons was a heartbreaker, with two Falcons touchdowns in the fourth quarter and a missed Eagles field goal in the final two minutes of play. Rappoport notes that even though they lost early in the playoff rounds, "the 1978 season did prove that Vermeil's Eagles were competitive and launched them toward higher levels in successive years."

Improvements continued in 1979, as running back Wilbert Montgomery became a potent force on the offense, along with Carmichael. Montgomery broke a club record with 1,512 rushing yards, and Carmichael scored 11 touchdowns on 52 catches and extended his league record of receptions to 106 consecutive games.

AP/Wide World Photos

Harold Carmichael

The Eagles went 11-5 in the regular season—including a dramatic 31-21 victory over the Cowboys in a nationally-televised game—and once again advanced into the playoffs as a wild card team. This time the Eagles won their wild card game, defeating the Bears 27-17, but were upset in the divisional playoff round against Tampa Bay. Vermeil's tenacity paid off as he was named NFL Coach of the Year.

The 1980 season brought another high water mark for the Eagles. They won 11 of their first 12 games and easily clinched the NFC East Championship with a 12-4 season record. Jaworski had his best year to date with 3,529 passing yards and 27 touchdowns, Montgomery and Carmichael turned in fine performances, and five other Pro Bowl choices—tackle Stan Walters, Sisemore, Logan, wide receiver Wally Henry, and Charlie Johnson brought depth to the squad.

Walters told Rappoport that the 1980 Eagles worked together so well because each player had faith in Dick Vermeil. "The thing that got the veterans in Dick's corner right away is that he didn't come in here with the idea of cleaning house," Walters said. "He said, 'You're my players, and there's enough talent here to win with.'" Vermeil's confidence in his personnel was a strong motivator. The Eagles trounced the Minnesota Vikings 31-16 in the divisional playoff round and secured the NFC crown with a 20-7 victory over the Cowboys in Philadelphia—possibly the sweetest moment for Eagles fans in twenty years.

Super Bowl XV featured the highly-favored Eagles against the Oakland Raiders. The Eagles had beaten the Raiders 10-7 in Oakland earlier in the year and seemed poised to dish out yet another round of punishment. Instead, the Raiders upset Philadelphia 27-10, denying the Eagles a victory in their first-ever Super Bowl appearance.

The loss did not deprive the Eagles of all the laurels, however. Jaworski was named NFL Player of the Year by the Maxwell Club and NFC Player of the Year by United Press International. "Jaworski was a solid professional and, above all, a survivor," concludes Didinger in the *Philadelphia Daily News.* "He took some terrible poundings, but he kept coming back."

For ten years, from 1977 to 1986, Ron Jaworski held the starting quarterback position for the Eagles. He remained among the best in the league throughout most of that period, but the Eagles were unable to repeat their success of 1980.

Philadelphia returned to the playoffs in 1981 as a wild card team but were upset at home by the Giants, 27-21. The following season was shortened by a player strike, and the Eagles missed the playoffs for the first time since 1977. At the end of the 1982 season, Dick Vermeil retired and was replaced by Marion Campbell.

Campbell strengthened a trend that has charted a course for the Philadelphia Eagles of the present. Armed with his experience as a defensive coordinator before he became head coach, he accented the defense and began to build a defensive unit that would eventually dominate the league.

The process took time, however, and for the remainder of Jaworski's tenure the Eagles were best known for their offensive stars, such as wide receiver Mike Quick, who joined the team in 1982, kicker Paul McFadden, who scored 116 points for the Eagles in 1984 and won NFC rookie of the year, and the consistent Wilbert Montgomery, who established a new Eagles career rushing record with 6,538 yards.

Norman Braman Buys the Eagles

Leonard Tose had owned the Eagles for almost two decades and had indicated that he wanted his daughter to succeed him as primary owner at some point. Tose experienced financial setbacks, however, and by 1984 he was trying to sell the team. The franchise almost passed to a group of Phoenix businessmen, but Philadelphia mayor Wilson Goode stymied the sale by reducing the Eagles' stadium rent and agreeing to construct luxury boxes in Veterans Stadium.

Just as matters looked bleak for the Eagles, a savior appeared. Norman Braman acquired the franchise for an estimated $65 million. The new owner was a Philadelphia native and the owner of two dozen major luxury automobile franchises in Florida and Colorado. Braman had earned not one but two fortunes: the first, in the early 1960s, came from self-service department and drugstores.

A millionaire by his mid-30s, he "retired" to spend more time with his family. After seven years he returned to the business world with a Cadillac dealership and amassed one of the nation's largest personal fortunes. For many years the Braman family had lived in Florida, but Braman wanted to own the team he had grown up watching.

As a teen Braman had watched the championship Eagles teams hold their summer practices and preseason games at West Chester State. On one occasion he even served as water boy during a scrimmage. This was the thrill of a lifetime for the youngster—he could not afford to pay to see the team he worshipped. "They're still my heroes," Braman told the *Philadelphia Inquirer,* "and I don't have too many heroes in life. Those are the pictures I had up on my wall when I was a kid—Bosh Pritchard, Steve Van Buren, Alex Wojciechowicz.... If you ask me what my greatest pleasure has been in owning the Eagles, it's been getting to know the older players that I worshiped as a boy."

It sometimes seems that Braman has drawn little enjoyment from his team otherwise. At the news conference announcing his purchase of the team, he boasted, "I don't know what the words losing money mean" and called the Eagles "a solid business deal that's deeply immersed in sentimentality."

Philadelphia Inquirer reporter Glen Macnow describes the Florida businessman as nervous and irritable during games, joyous when the team wins and morose after each loss. "He is a man who loves the sheer violence of football, who raises his flute-sized cigar to toast a ferocious Reggie White sack," Macnow writes. Over the years, however, another picture of Norman Braman has emerged—one that accents his "solid business deal" approach to Eagles ownership. "When Norman came in, the feeling was that business came first and winning came second," Jaworski told the *Philadelphia Inquirer*. "The impression was that he was going to make his money and then worry about taking care of us."

Jaworski was one of the casualties of the Braman regime. He was put on waivers early in 1987 when the club refused to guarantee his contract. On the other hand, Braman realized that he would have to court big-salary players in order to compete in the NFC East.

Deals with stars like Mike Quick and the newly-arrived Reggie White were competitive with the pay scales of other clubs, and Randall Cunningham, who joined the Eagles in 1987, has been among the top paid quarterbacks in the NFL since 1988. Overall, the Eagles' pay scale ranks near the NFL's middle.

In the waning days of the Tose ownership, the Eagles had once again slumped, finishing 7-9 in 1985 and 5-10-1 in 1986. Braman vowed he would make the team a Super Bowl contender again, and he hired yet another new coach, Buddy Ryan. A colorful character whose reputation for tough talk, action, and blue-collar ethics preceded him, Ryan had gained notoriety as the defensive coordinator for the Super Bowl champion Chicago Bears.

AP/Wide World Photos

Buddy Ryan (standing)

He and Braman bought a hard-line attitude to the Eagles, releasing older players and recruiting young, boisterous talent, especially for the defense. Almost from the outset, Ryan and Braman were at odds personally. Ryan was an outspoken, blunt man who supported his players when they asked for more money and who scorned the "replacement team" he was given to coach during the 1987 players' strike. Braman may have winced at Ryan's methods, but the owner was satisfied that his surly coach had begun to work miracles with the team.

Ryan's fortunes in Philadelphia were helped by a veritable landslide of fresh young talent. White became the anchor of a defense that, by 1992, sent four players to the first-team Pro Bowl. Tight end Keith Jackson, named rookie of the year in 1988, added double punch to Mike Quick's threat on the pass.

Undoubtedly the most exciting component of the Ryan Eagles was number 12, Randall Cunningham. No quarterback before Cunningham had played the game quite like he did. In 1988 he became the first NFL quarterback in history to lead his team in rushing yards, an indication of promising things to come. Highlight films abounded with footage of Cunningham streaking from the pocket, leaping, dodging, and sliding for a first down or a touchdown. By 1992 Cunningham had become the greatest rushing quarterback in the history of the NFL.

With Cunningham at the helm, the Eagles took a 10-6 record to the NFC East Eastern division title in 1988. At season's end the team traveled to Chicago to meet the Bears in a divisional playoff game. Not since the 1948 national champions slogged through a blizzard had weather been so much a factor in a playoff game. After a first half played in bright sunlight, a thick fog rolled in from Lake Michigan, obscuring the field from cameras and commentators alike. The "Fog

AP/Wide World Photos

The ever-elusive Randall Cunningham (12) has given new meaning to quarterback mobility

Bowl," as it was later called, ended with a 20-12 victory for the Bears. The loss was bittersweet, because Cunningham later earned Pro Bowl Most Valuable Player, the Maxwell Club's Bert Bell Award, and was named Top Player of the Year by the NFL.

Ryan's defense blossomed in 1989, and the Eagles improved to an 11-5 regular season record. This was only good for a second place finish in the NFC East, however, and the Eagles drew a wild card game against the Rams at home in Veterans Stadium. They lost that contest 21-7, leading critics to question Cunningham's ability to handle the pressures of post-season play. The questions followed Cunningham into the 1990 season, when the Eagles once again earned a wild card berth and then lost to the Washington Redskins, 20-6.

The Eagles' early departure from post-season play in 1990 was more than Norman Braman could bear. As *Philadelphia Inquirer* correspondent Mark Bowden puts it, the owner "determined to make a change not just of head coaches but in the very character of his football team." Bowden adds: "Much of the owner's distress, front-office sources say, stemmed from the off-field conduct Ryan tolerated in some of his favorite players. And Braman was convinced that lax discipline had left him with a team that was often out of control—even in games. Especially in games."

Charges of gambling and womanizing in hotel rooms by some of the players were never substantiated, but Braman felt that Ryan was actively undermining morale on the team. Bowden writes: "Braman saw a very young team that had achieved tremendous success two seasons earlier, when it won the NFC East title, but then had failed to progress for two straight seasons. Instead of progress, the owner saw deterioration."

Braman was also embarrassed by Ryan's rudeness to reporters and front office personnel. The owner told the *Philadelphia Inquirer:* "Sitting in my seat, you get to that point of really saying to yourself, 'Is winning worth it? Is winning worth it?' Or winning at what price? At the price of ridiculing your opponents? At the price of ridiculing decent people? At the price of not acknowledging the support of other individuals who help you win: I won, but it's always somebody else's fault when I don't win? And I reached the point where I said to myself, 'Well, if we go into the playoffs and win a couple of games, maybe I can live with it for another few years.'"

When Ryan's contract expired in the second week of 1991, Braman did not renew it. Amidst a strong showing of support from the Eagles players, Ryan left town and was succeeded by his offensive coordinator, Rich Kotite. The major difference between Ryan and Kotite was not football philosophy, but personality. The reserved Kotite promised a "more disciplined" team and made steps to curb the perception that the Eagles players were unruly off the field.

Kotite's mettle as a head coach was tested early. In the very first game of the 1991 season, Cunningham was dealt a severe injury to his knee. The injury sidelined the starting quarterback for the rest of the season, and Kotite was forced to use five quarterbacks in eight games—including former Bears star Jim McMahon—in order to keep the team alive. A phenomenal showing from the Eagles defense was the highlight of the year. The Eagles ranked number one in the NFL in terms of fewest yards overall, fewest yards versus the run, and fewest yards versus the pass.

This same Eagles defense led the NFL in quarterback sacks and fumble recoveries. Not surprisingly, the Eagles sent five defenders to the 1992 Pro Bowl—Jerome Brown, Reggie White, Seth Joyner, and Clyde Simmons on the first team, and Eric Allen on the second.

In 1992, Eagles fans had reason to remember Jaworski's ominous predictions about Braman's business techniques. Star tight end Keith Jackson held out for a salary increase and eventually became a free agent as a result of an antitrust lawsuit filed against the NFL. The loss of Jackson served as a warning that Braman would not necessarily bow to his best performers' demands in order to keep them in town.

More importantly, records released to the courts as part of the antitrust suit indicated that the Eagles ranked first in the NFL in profits, if the owner's salary was included. Documents from the 1990 season revealed that Braman paid himself $7.5 million that year, more than double the amount of the next closest owner. This news was particularly distressing to Eagles season ticket holders, who had seen price increases every year since Braman bought the team.

In 1993 the Eagles also lost star defensive end Reggie White to the Packers because of an acrimonious salary dispute that featured a significant amount of verbal sniping between White and Braman.

These quibbles about profits and owner salaries are muted by the knowledge that Braman has every intention of keeping the Eagles in Philadelphia and owning the team for years and years to come. Braman's daughter works in the Eagles front office, and the owner has indicated that he wants her to have the team some day.

Having observed the 60th anniversary of the franchise in 1993, Eagles fans can follow the team with a measure of security. If life in the NFC East is a constant struggle for playoff contention, at least Philadelphia will always be part of that struggle—a squad in kelly green, holding its own in tough company.

Sources

Books

Rappoport, Ken, *Pigskin Power,* Tempo Books, 1981.

Periodicals

Philadelphia Daily News, March 1, 1983; May 3, 1983; September 5, 1985; September 10, 1987; November 4, 1988; September 7, 1989; September 27, 1990; August 29, 1991.

Philadelphia Inquirer, September 9, 1990; January 13, 1991; July 8, 1992; August 19, 1992; September 9, 1992.

Philadelphia Inquirer Magazine, December 4, 1988; September 2, 1990.

—*Anne Janette Johnson*

Phoenix Cardinals

The Cardinals can lay claim to being the oldest surviving charter member (along with the Chicago Bears) of the National Football League. Joining the league in 1920 as the Chicago Cardinals, only they and the Chicago Bears (then the Decatur Staleys) are still left from that 13-team circuit.

In fact, the Cardinals trace their roots back even farther than the Bears, establishing themselves as Chicago's first professional team in 1898. The team disbanded twice because of lack of professional competition, in 1910 and World War I. Since 1918, however, the Cardinals have operated continuously until the present day.

The team's founder, Chris O'Brien remained as Cardinal owner for more than 30 years, selling the NFL franchise in 1929 to a Chicago doctor named David Jones. The transaction price was \$25,000. O'Brien paid just \$100 nine years earlier to enter the Cardinals in the NFL.

Doctor Jones lasted just three years as Cardinal owner, finding a buyer in the oddest of places. With Paddy Driscoll being sold to the Chicago Bears in 1926 and Ernie Nevers retiring after the 1931 season, the Cardinals were without a star and floundering in the standings. Jones found his buyer while having dinner aboard the yacht of Chicago tycoon Charles Bidwill in 1932. Jones made an off-handed remark that he would gladly get rid of the Cardinals for a price. Bidwill offered \$50,000 and Jones agreed. The odd part is that Bidwill was a vice president of the Bears at the time. Bidwill divested his holdings in the Bears and assumed ownership of the Cardinals for the 1932 season.

The Bidwill family has owned the Cardinal franchise ever since, seeing the team through a move to St. Louis in 1960 and to Phoenix in 1988. Charles Bidwill himself, however, never got to see his team win an NFL championship. Just eight months after he died in 1947, the Cardinals (whose only previous title was tainted by controversy after the 1925 season) won the NFL championship with a 28-14 victory over the Philadelphia Eagles.

According to the Associated Press, Bidwill's widow, Violet Bidwill broke into tears after the championship game. "It's just too bad that Charles couldn't have seen this," she sobbed. Violet Bidwill remarried in 1949 to St. Louis businessman Walter Wolfner and the couple ran the team operations in tandem.

When Violet Bidwill Wolfner died, January 29, 1962, she left the Cardinals to her two sons, Charles Jr. and Bill. Walter Wolfner contested the will and it was only during those proceedings that Charles and Bill learned that they were adopted. The will was ruled valid by a probate court in Chicago. In 1972, Bill Bidwill, who had worked with the Cardinals as a water boy, program ad salesman and scout, bought out his brother's shares in the team to become the principle owner.

Longevity notwithstanding, the Cardinals have tasted success very few times in their history. They were named NFL champions just once (1925), but only after the league president stripped the title from Pottsville. What the Cardinals have amassed through the years is a string of football superstars. From Paddy Driscoll in the 1920s right on through Ernie Nevers in the 1930s, Charley Trippi in the 1940s, Ollie Matson in the 1950s, Charley Johnson in the 1960s and Terry Metcalf in the 1970s, the Cardinals have had their share of gate attractions.

As Normal As Can Be

The Cardinals' roots can be traced back to the 19th century when football was a sport for amateurs and strategies were in their infancy. The birth of the team now known as the Cardinals was in 1898 when a neighborhood group of predominantly Irish descent that lived on Chicago's south side began playing games as the Morgan Athletic Club. One year later, the team was purchased by a Chicago painting and decorating contractor named Chris O'Brien. When the team was moved to a field at the corner of Normal Boulevard and Racine Avenue, it adopted the nickname "Normals."

It wasn't until the owner found an equipment bargain that the team acquired its current nickname. O'Brien purchased second-hand uniforms from the University of Chicago in 1901—they were old and appeared to be faded maroon in color. O'Brien countered, "That's not maroon, it's cardinal red." The nickname "Cardinals" has been with the team ever since, through three different cities.

The Racine Cardinals—drawing their first name from the cross-street of their home field—lasted until 1906 when the team was disbanded. With football in Chicago being a predominantly amateur sport, the professional Racine Cardinals found it difficult to find competition.

Seven years later, O'Brien reorganized the Racine Cardinals. This time, the franchise found enough opponents to play from 1913 through 1917. The Chicago Football League provided the competition and in 1917, the Cardinals were league champions with just two losses. Before that season, Marston Smith was hired to coach the team and new uniforms—still keeping the cardinal red—were purchased.

The toll that World War I took was evident by 1918. Losing players and fans to the service, coupled with a flu epidemic that swept through the nation, forced the Racine Cardinals to suspend operations. After Armistice Day, however, O'Brien brought the Racine Cardinals back into existence after a one year absence. Ever since, the Cardinals have fielded a professional football team. Of the 13 teams in the American Professional Football League in 1920, only the Cardinals and the Decatur Staleys (later the Chicago Bears) would still be in operation 50 years later.

The First Cardinal Star

In 1920, for the sum of $100, O'Brien bought the Racine Cardinals, a franchise in the newly-formed American Professional Football League.

TEAM INFORMATION AT A GLANCE

Founded in 1898 as the Chicago Cardinals;
relocated and became the St. Louis Cardinals, 1960;
relocated and became Phoenix Cardinals, 1988

Home stadium: Sun Devil Stadium
P.O. Box 888
Phoenix, AZ 85001
Phone: (602) 379-0101
Seating capacity: 74,707

Team colors: Red and white
Team logo: A stylized cardinal's head in profile
Team nickname: Cardinals; Cards

Franchise record:	Won	Lost	Tie
(1898—)	366	481	38

To obtain former Northwestern University standout and football barnstormer John "Paddy" Driscoll, O'Brien had to pay $3,000 for one season. The deal proved to be financial genius.

Many athletes through the years have been touted as "franchise" players. But how many can say that they actually saved their team from disbanding with one game's brilliant performance? Were it not for Paddy Driscoll, a quarterback, halfback and dropkicker, the Racine Cardinals would have died as a franchise on the field, November 7, 1920.

With two Chicago franchises in the APFL (the Racine Cardinals and the Chicago Tigers), both teams' ownership felt that competition for Windy City fans would be ruinous for both franchises. Thus, O'Brien arranged a game with the Tigers in which each team's owner staked his franchise upon the outcome.

Prior to the arrangement, the Cardinals and Tigers played to a 0-0 draw on October 11, 1920. The Chicago Daily Tribune reported: "Twenty-six college alumni, representing two professional football teams, scuffled to a draw, 0 to 0, before 10,000 gridiron fans yesterday at Cub Park. But the opinions of the critical rooters gave a shade decision to the Racine Cardinals, piloted by Paddy Driscoll, over their opponents, George Falcons' Chicago Tigers."

That set the stage for a winner-take-all showdown, November 7, in which Driscoll scored the game's only touchdown on a 40-yard run. The Cardinals won, 6-3. The Tigers, so named for the stripes on their uniforms, disbanded immediately. Chicago was now the domain of the Cardinals.

And the Cardinals were Paddy Driscoll's team. In addition to being a superb runner and defender, the future Hall of Famer was noted for being a wizard at kicking a football. Said George Sullivan in his book *Pro Football's All-Time Greats:* "Charley Brickly, Frank Nesser, Jim Thorpe and Paddy Driscoll were artists when it came to drop-kicking, but Driscoll is rated by many as the greatest of them all. His skilled right foot rendered him the greatest name in Chicago football until a fellow named Red Grange exploded upon the scene in 1925."

It was the Cardinals, in fact, who were the first to greet Grange upon his entry into the NFL on November 26, 1925. With a remarkable crowd of 36,000 watching at Wrigley Field, the Bears (with their new sensation) and the Cardinals played to a 0-0 tie. Most of the credit for stopping Grange was showered upon Driscoll, who punted away from the rookie with accuracy. Of Driscoll's 23 punts, only three were returned by Grange.

According to Sullivan, as thousands booed from the stands, Driscoll spoke with his wife. "It's a shame to hear the fans boo Grange," said Driscoll. "It wasn't his fault." "Don't feel sorry for him," she said. "They're booing you."

Driscoll was a native of Evanston, Illinois, who went on to captain a Northwestern football team that lost just one game in 1916. As a member of the Great Lakes Naval Station team, Driscoll was a member of the Rose Bowl championship team of 1919. Driscoll kicked a 30-yard field goal and passed to George Halas for a touchdown in a 17-9 win over the Mare Island Marines. A versatile athlete, Driscoll played 13 games for the Chicago Cubs in 1917.

After a 0-0 finish between the Cardinals and Chicago Staleys on December 18, 1921, the Chicago Herald Examiner reported: "During a good share of the time the Cardinals kept the ball in the Staley territory due largely to Paddy Driscoll's superb play."

When the Cardinals beat the Bears, 9-0, December 10, 1922, the Chicago Herald Examiner reported: "Paddy Driscoll, star of the Cards, kicked three goals from the field. Whenever the Bears got their powerful attack started it seemed as if somebody would fumble and then Paddy Driscoll would punt the ball out of danger. Paddy was very much in evidence, making a field goal in each of the first three quarters."

Driscoll drop-kicked four field goals in a 19-9 win over the Columbus Tigers, October 11, 1925. One travelled what was then an NFL record of 50 yards.

By 1926, the Cardinals were in jeopardy of losing their first star. A rival league to the NFL, the American League, started a franchise in Chicago called the Bulls. The upstart team forced the Cardinals out of their Comiskey Park home (they'd moved there in 1922) by leasing the stadium. Forced to move back to smaller Normal Field, the Cardinals couldn't match the salary offered to Driscoll by the Bulls.

Opportunistic George Halas, however, stepped in and paid the Cardinals $3,500 for Driscoll and then signed the gridiron star. Halas' Bears had just lost Red Grange to the new league and thus remained a box office draw with Driscoll moving into their north-side park.

The Cardinals didn't recover for years. In Driscoll's last four years with the south-siders (1922-25), the Cardinals went 32-13-2, winning the NFL championship in 1925. It wouldn't be until 1947 that the Cardinals again won more than six games in any one season.

Tainted Title

Success came early to the Chicago Cardinals (the team's name was changed to Chicago when a Racine, Wisconsin, franchise entered the NFL in 1922). It has not, however, come often.

In their sixth season in the NFL, the Cardinals were crowned the 1925 league champions. That, unfortunately, is an accomplishment that the franchise has been able to match only once. The irony of the Cardinals' 1925 title is that they were the second team to be named NFL champions that season. The Pottsville (Pennsylvania) Maroons were a veteran independent team that was new to the NFL that year. Their 9-2 record, however, put them in a position to win the title if they could beat the Cardinals, who were 9-1-1, in Comiskey Park, December 6. The Maroons outshined the home team, winning, 21-7. Their top player, Walter French of West Point, was the star of the game.

With a fresh championship in tow, the Maroons agreed to play a Notre Dame all-star team that included the Four Horsemen in a post-season exhibition game in Philadelphia. The game was played one week after the Maroons won the title in Chicago. After the exhibition game, however, the Frankford (a Philadelphia suburb) Yellowjackets protested to NFL president Joe Carr that the Maroons had infringed upon their territorial rights.

In one of the oddest decisions in sports history, Carr upheld the Yellowjackets' claim and stripped the Maroons of their title, banning Pottsville from the NFL (they were allowed back in the fold in 1926). Carr then ordered the Cardinals to play two more games—a penalty that would not help the Yellowjackets, but was aimed at handing the Cardinals the NFL title. This was at a time when there was no standard number of games that a team was required to play in the 20-team NFL. For example, the Chicago Bears played 20 games in 1925. Canton played eight games, Pottsville played 12 and Columbus played nine.

The Philadelphia Inquirer reported on December 13, 1925: "Some important results of Pottsville's pro grid champions of 1925 meeting with the Four Horsemen yesterday afternoon at Shibe Park are that they have forfeited their franchise in the National League of Professional Football Players, have been outlawed from the league and been deprived of their title, according to disclosures made public yesterday by the president of the league ... Dr. Streigel, the well-known Pottsville physician and owner of the Maroons ... claims that he had a verbal permission from the secretary of the league to play the game ... Pottsville had won the league title by defeating the Chicago Cardinals for titular honors in the post season tilt waged out in the Windy City recently."

The Cardinals quickly scheduled games against the Milwaukee Badgers and the Hammond (Indiana) Pros. The Badgers had already broken up for the post-season and bowed without a fight, 59-0, on December 10. Hammond, which had been the only team other than the Maroons to beat the Cardinals, fell 13-0 two days later. With an 11-2-1 record, the Cardinals now officially held a better record than the 10-2 Maroons and Carr declared Chicago's south-side team to be NFL champions.

The post-script to the 1925 title is as odd as the season itself. It was later determined that Milwaukee used four high school players in their final game against the Cardinals. Carr canceled the Badgers' NFL franchise and suspended the team's manager, Arthur Folz, for life. Folz is the only man in NFL history to receive a lifetime banishment.

Rivalry

From the inception of the American Professional Football Association in 1920 through the Cardinals' move to St. Louis after the 1959 season, the football battle in Chicago between the Cardinals and Bears formed one of sports' all-time great rivalries.

Ironically, the Bears could have been stopped from ever playing a home game in Chicago by the Cardinals themselves. After the Cardinals played a winner-take-all game for the league rights to Chicago on November 7, 1920, the triumphant Cardinals held the power to veto any new franchise being established in the nation's Second City. When the Decatur Staleys petitioned NFL president Joe Carr to move to Chicago in the 1921 season, Carr deferred to Cardinal owner Chris O'Brien, who had the right to block such a move.

Remarkably, O'Brien approved the deal, opening the door for Coach George Halas and his Staleys to invade Chicago's north side. The Staleys were required by their Decatur sponsor to keep their nickname for one year after the move. In 1922, the franchise became the Chicago Bears.

The rivalry immediately took hold. Although the Cardinals finished with just a 2-3-2 record in 1921, they closed their season with a 0-0 tie at the home of the Staleys. The northsiders had a chance to win the game when they recovered a second-half fumble on the Cardinals' 20-yard line. The

Staleys, however, surrendered the ball on downs.

The Chicago Herald Examiner reported: "Chicago's pro football title remains undecided as a result of yesterday's 0 to 0 game between the national champion Staleys and the Cardinals at the Cub Park. Several thousand shivering rooters braved the cold to see one of the hardest fought battles of the season."

The Staleys wound up as the league champions in 1921 with just their tie with the Cardinals and a loss to the Buffalo All-Americans staining the Staleys' record.

Cardinal back Ernie Nevers saved his finest single-game performance for the Bears on Thanksgiving Day, 1929. Rushing for six touchdowns and kicking four extra points, Nevers scored all 40 of the Cardinals' points in their 40-6 win over the Bears. Perhaps the most meaningful game in the Cardinals/Bears rivalry was played at Wrigley Field on December 14, 1947. With the NFL's Western Division title going to the winner, the Cardinals outfought the Bears, 30-21.

Cardinal team owner Charles Bidwill had died eight months before the title-clinching game. The Associated Press reported after the game: "The inspired Chicago Cardinals scored on an 80-yard touchdown play the first time they got the ball today to touch off a drive that carried them to a 30-21 triumph over the Chicago Bears and to their first Western Division pennant in the history of the National Football League."

Two weeks after beating the Bears in 1947, the Cardinals earned their second NFL title with a 28-21 win over the Philadelphia Eagles.

The Cardinals included two wins over the Bears (by scores of 28-14 and 24-14) among their three in 1951. Had the Bears beaten the last-place Cards just once, they would have tied the Los Angeles Rams for first place in the NFL's National Conference race. The 1951 entry for the Cardinals in *The Official Encyclopedia of Pro Football* reads, "The season's only solace was two victories over the Bears, the last of which spoiled that team's chances for a conference title."

In 1956, the Cardinals posted their best record since winning the NFL's Western Division eight seasons earlier. The Cards' 7-5 mark under Coach Ray Richards was, however, good only for second place in the Eastern Conference behind the New York Giants.

Of course, any Cardinal fan would point to their team's 10-3 loss to the crosstown Bears on December 9 as a major part of the south-siders' failure to win the title. Hall of Fame running back Ollie Matson rambled for touchdowns of 65 and 83 yards. Both, however, were called back on penalties and the Cardinals never did find the Bears' end zone.

The rivalry was finally laid to rest after the 1959 season. The Cardinals announced their move to St. Louis. The Bears have been Chicago's team ever since.

Ernie Nevers

His time with the Chicago Cardinals was brief—from 1929 through 1931—but the franchise may never see another like Ernie Nevers. Pop Warner, who coached both Nevers and Jim Thorpe was asked which of the two was the better player. "Nevers," answered Warner. "He could do everything Thorpe could do and he tried harder. No man ever gave more of himself than Ernie Nevers."

Warner coached the Wisconsin-raised Nevers at Stanford University. A winner of 11 letters, Nevers missed most of his senior season after breaking both of his ankles—one in pre-season and the other in Stanford's next-to-last game.

Warner, however, pieced together two crude braces that allowed Nevers to play for Stanford in the Rose Bowl that year against Notre Dame and its Four Horsemen. Playing the entire 60 minutes, Nevers rushed for 114 yards on his heavily-encased legs as Stanford outgained the Irish, 391 yards to 192, despite being outscored, 27-10. Nevers' individual performance earned him national recognition.

Walter Eckersall, one of the Rose Bowl officials, wrote two days later in the *San Francisco*

Chronicle, "Nevers is about the best fullback who ever graced a gridiron ... a terrific line smasher ... an accurate forward passer and an excellent blocker."

Upon graduation in 1926, Nevers barnstormed with a team from Duluth, Minnesota, that was renamed Ernie Nevers and the Iron Men of the North. With the team playing 29 games that season from September through February, Nevers was the iron man of the Iron Men, being on the field for 1,713 minutes out of a possible 1,740.

From 1926 through 1928, Nevers pitched for the St. Louis Browns of the American League, surrendering two of Babe Ruth's 60 home runs in 1927. In 1929, the Cardinals were sold to a Chicago doctor named David Jones. One of the new owner's first acts was to bring Nevers out of a football retirement to be the team's player/coach. Still just 26, Nevers showed that he was still in top form, scoring an NFL-record 40 points in the Cardinals' 40-6 Thanksgiving Day win over the Chicago Bears.

The Cardinals of Nevers' day were not, unfortunately, a strong football team. In 1929, they finished 6-6-1. They followed that with a 5-6-2 season in 1930 and a 5-4 record in 1931. Nevers, however, was the undisputed team star and workhorse. With 19 games on the schedule (including exhibitions), Nevers played every minute of every Cardinal game in 1931.

He came close to leaving a game against the Brooklyn Dodgers, November 1, when he was knocked unconscious after being tackled. Carried off the field, Nevers regained consciousness as he neared the sidelines. The player/coach turned and bolted back onto the field. Nevers then called his own number again and again, carrying the ball for 16 consecutive plays until the Cardinals scored a touchdown. The Cardinals' 14-7 victory that day was the beginning of a four-game winning streak.

On November 15, 1931, Nevers led the Cardinals to a 21-13 upset of the defending champion Green Bay Packers. The Associated Press reported: "It was the first time in ten years a Chicago Cardinal eleven has been able to defeat a Green Bay team, and also the first defeat for the Packers in ten starts this year. The Cardinal-Packer rivalry started in 1921, and sixteen games have now been played. Nevers gave one of his greatest exhibitions in lifting the Cards to victory over the great team from the north. In the first period he tossed a 15-yard pass to Bill Glasgow for a touchdown and place kicked for the extra point. With Nevers slashing through the Packer line the Cards (then) took the ball to the Packer 5-yard mark from where Beldin plunged over and the former Stanford ace again place kicked for the point."

Before the 1932 season began, Nevers retired from football. Being the focal point of 60 minutes of football every week had taken its toll on his body. Although he returned to coach the team in 1939, the Cardinals managed just a 1-10 record for their former star.

"Ernie Nevers was great in spite of the fact that he was always playing with lousy teams," said Jimmy Conzelman, coach of the Chicago Cardinals in the 1940's and an NFL player during Nevers' day. "He was able to lift them beyond their capacities."

A Marquee Performance

The stage was set on Thanksgiving Day, 1929. Crosstown NFL rivals the Chicago Bears and the Cardinals were scheduled to play at Comiskey Park. Both teams were slightly below the .500 mark (the Bears were 4-6-1, the Cardinals 4-5-1), but any notion of a wasted season would be dispelled with a win in the season's lone meeting between the NFL's two Windy City franchises. Toss a little snow on the ground and the sound of 8,000 fans to create the proper atmosphere and get ready to turn on the footlights.

With Red Grange carrying the ball for the Bears and a 40-something Jim Thorpe called out of retirement for a one-game appearance, there were a pair of widely-known names to adorn the marquee. It was, however, Cardinal fullback Ernie Nevers—a star in his own right—who became the leading performer. He scored all of the Cardinals' points in a 40-6 victory. His six rushing touchdowns set a long-standing NFL record as did the 40 points that he amassed with the help of four extra point kicks.

In a 1972 nation-wide poll of 1,437 sports editors and writers for the book *Professional Football's Greatest Games,* the Cardinals/Bears Thanksgiving Day game of 1929 was ranked as No. 8 all-time.

How impressive was Nevers' feat in the context of football in 1929? The Cardinals had scored a total of 67 points in their first 10 games of the season for an average of 6.7 per game. Their opponents had totalled just 53 points in 10 games.

The Cardinals' previous best in terms of points scored in 1929 was a 19-0 win over the Dayton Triangles one week before the Thanksgiving Day game. Nevers scored all 19 points. The Associated Press: "Ernie Nevers threw passes, ran and smashed the line to score three touchdowns and give the Chicago Cardinals a 19-0 victory."

The Stanford graduate scored on carries of 20, 4, 6, 1, 1 and 10 yards. Nevers missed wide on his first extra point try, but then missed only one more because of a bad snap.

Said Benny Friedman, quarterback of the New York Giants in 1929, "I never saw anyone who epitomized the idea of a will to win more so than Ernie. He was a tremendous football player, tremendous leader both on offense and defense. And you always knew you were in a battle when you played against one of his teams."

Nevers followed the blocking of Duke Slater off tackle and into the end zone for two of his first three touchdowns. Those scores along with Nevers' four-yard dive up the middle gave the Cardinals a 20-0 halftime advantage. Cobb Rooney set up the first score of the third quarter when he carried the ball 40 yards. Nevers then ran it in from the 1-yard line.

Only a 60-yard touchdown pass from Bear Walt Holmer to Garland Grange (younger brother of Red) interrupted Nevers' historic performance. Nevers scored a pair of fourth-quarter touchdowns—of one and 10 yards—to cap his day. One of those in attendance that Thanksgiving Day was Notre Dame head coach Knute Rockne, who brought his Irish team in from South Bend. After Nevers scored his sixth touchdown, the legendary Rockne said to his players, "That, gentlemen, is how to play football."

Pooling Resources

For one season, the struggling Chicago Cardinals and the equally destitute Pittsburgh Steelers combined forces. With World War II depleting the supply of both football talent and fans, the two teams joined together to form one franchise in 1944.

The results were dismal. After posting a 0-10 record in 1943, the Cardinals didn't fare any better in 1944. The Card-Pitt team, as it became known, went 0-10 in 1945, finishing last in the NFL's Western Division. It allowed 328 points, including no fewer than 21 in any one game. The Card-Pitt offense managed to score just 108 points, being held to single-digits in seven of its 10 games.

The combined squad used a co-coach system. Cardinal leader Phil Handler and Steeler boss Walt Kiesling equally shared the coaching responsibilities. The home games were shared as well with three games being played in Pittsburgh and two in Chicago. Inexplicably, Card-Pitt scheduled its season finale against the Chicago Bears in Pittsburgh. Two weeks earlier, Card-Pitt played Cleveland in Chicago. The teams went their separate ways in 1945. The Steelers went 2-8, finishing last in the Eastern Division. The Cardinals were at the bottom of the Western Division with a 1-9 record.

Renaissance Man and the 1947 Title

The only coach to guide the Cardinals to an undisputed NFL title in their many decades in the league was Jimmy Conzelman. Ironically, he was born and raised in St. Louis (the Cardinals' home from 1960 through 1987), but coached the Cardinals to the 1947 league title when their home was Chicago. In his lifetime, Conzelman was a professional football player and coach, an amateur boxing champion, a major league baseball official and executive, an artist, a newspaper owner, a magazine writer and an advertising executive. He is also a member of the Football Hall of Fame.

Despite his many achievements in life, Conzelman will always be remembered in Cardinals' lore as a championship-caliber coach. His association with the Chicago Cardinals, however, started as an unsuccessful venture.

He was hired in 1940 by Cardinal owner Charles Bidwill with a recommendation from Bears' owner and a former teammate of Conzelman's, George Halas. In the three seasons prior to Conzelman's hire, the Cardinals won just eight games. In Conzelman's first three seasons, the Cards won only eight games. "One of the first things I did when I took over the Cardinals was write a fight song called, 'It's in the Cards to Win'," said Conzelman. "Oh how wrong I was for the first three years!"

With a thin Cardinal talent base growing rapidly thinner as men went off to World War II, the losing became enough to drive Conzelman back to St. Louis. After the 1942 NFL season, Conzelman left the Cardinals to join the front office of major league baseball's St. Louis Browns. As an assistant to the team's president, Don Barnes, Conzelman was with the Brown when they won the American League pennant in 1944.

After the war was over, Bidwill convinced Conzelman to rejoin the Cardinals as head coach. In his second stay with the team, Conzelman presided over a steadily improving franchise. In 1945, one year before he took over, the Cardinals had the NFL's worst record at 1-9. In Conzelman's first year back, the Cards improved to 6-5. In 1947, the team went 9-3 and won the NFL championship. In 1948, Conzelman's team posted the NFL's best record (11-1) before falling to the Philadelphia Eagles in the championship game.

Conzelman was key in scouting and signing one of the best backfields in Cardinals' history. It became known as the "Million Dollar Backfield" and the "Dream Backfield". Charles Trippi was brought in from the University of Georgia. Elmer Angsman was signed from Notre Dame. They joined Marshall Goldberg, Paul Christman and Pat Harder. "I had heard that Elmer had lost two teeth in the Navy game in his senior year and yet showed up for practice on Monday," said Conzelman. "I figured I wanted him if he was that tough."

Conzelman's on-field managerial moves were instrumental in winning the championship in 1947. When the Cardinals needed to beat the Chicago Bears in the season finale to advance to the championship game, Conzelman hatched a play that gave the Cards a 7-0 lead on their first play.

Unique in its day, Conzelman's play called for two Cardinal receivers to both run pass patterns through one Bear defensive back's zone. When Mal Kutner went by, Bears' DB Mike Holovak went with him. That left Boris Dimancheff open when he entered Holovak's zone.

"The Bears were stronger than we were," said Conzelman. "We thought we'd have to score first to have a chance ... So we designed a pass play, taking into account the defense our scouts said the Bears would use deep in our territory." The play covered 80 yards and the Cardinals never trailed after going up 7-0 on the game's first play from scrimmage.

In the 1947 championship game against the Philadelphia Eagles, Conzelman again helped his Cardinals gain momentum from the start. After learning before the game that the Eagles were wearing longer spikes than normal, Conzelman waited until an opportune moment in the game to protest to the referees. They assessed the Eagles a five-yard penalty on two consecutive plays before the Philadelphia players changed their shoes in the middle of the game.

The Associated Press reported: "While the Chicago Cardinals hilariously celebrated their first National Football League title triumph since 1925, the crestfallen Philadelphia Eagles bitterly bemoaned their 28-21 `tennis shoe' defeat on cement-like Comiskey Park gridiron today ... (Eagles coach Greasy) Neale had a bone to pick with officials who called the Eagles after the first five minutes for `illegal equipment'—sharply honed cleats on regular football shoes. The Cardinals trotted onto the field in `sneakers' while the Eagles tried to play with regular football shoes, but switched to gym shoes when the officials objected to their irregular shoe cleats ... `It won't show in the final score, but at the start of the game we were penalized five yards for illegal equipment when we could have made a first down, and that cost us plenty,' added the Eagle skipper."

In 1948, Conzelman led the Cardinals to their finest single-season record (11-1) and an appearance in the championship game—one that the Eagles won, 7-0. "The Eagles game was my farewell," said Conzelman. "I was still looking for more security than I felt I could find in football. Remember, we had no pension plans then. That winter I went back to St. Louis to work for an advertising agency." The impression Conzelman left on Cardinal history, however, has remained to this day. His 1947 NFL champions were the last Cardinal team to win a post-season game.

The Trade

On February 28, 1959, NFL commissioner Bert Bell received this telegram from Los Angeles Rams general manager (and future NFL commissioner) Pete Rozelle: "Los Angeles Rams trade to Chicago Cardinals tackle Ken Panfil, tackle Frank Fuller, tackle Art Hauser, tackle Glenn Holtman, end John Tracey, fullback Larry Hickman, halfback Don Brown, the Rams' second draft choice in the 1959 selection meeting, plus a player to be delivered during the 1959 training camp season, in exchange for fullback Ollie Matson."

It was a trade that was bold and unique. It was a trade that would be talked about for decades. The Cardinals gave up one player and received nine in return. True, Matson was the Cardinals' leading ground-gainer every season from 1954 through 1958, setting what was then a franchise record with his 924 yards in 1956. Matson rushed for 21 touchdowns in those five seasons combined and added six more scores on kick returns. And he was a member of the 1952 United States Olympic track team.

The Associated Press reported: "The Rams gave up four first-string veterans—defensive tack-

Cardinals' Team Tragedies

Although the 1947 and 1948 seasons were filled with on-field glory for the Chicago Cardinals, the team suffered through a series of off-field tragedies. On April 19, 1947, team owner Charles Bidwill died of pneumonia. Bidwill had been the sole owner of the Cardinals since purchasing the franchise from David Jones in 1932. His death occurred only months before the Cardinals were to win the NFL championship.

On October 24, 1947, Cardinal halfback and punter Jeff Burkett was killed in a plane crash. The Associated Press reported: "Jefferson Davis Burkett, 26, Chicago Cardinals punting star, was aboard a United Airlines DC-6 plane which crashed today at Bryce Canyon, Utah, the airlines said. Burkett underwent an appendectomy last Saturday and was unable to return to Chicago with his professional football team Monday after its game last Sunday with the Los Angeles Rams. Burkett, former three-sport athlete at Louisiana State University, prior to missing Sunday's game against Los Angeles, led the National Football League in punting with an average of 47.4 yards on 11 kicks. It was his first professional season."

Following the opening game of the 1948 season, lineman Stan Mauldin collapsed and died of a heart attack in the middle of the Cardinals' dressing room. Mauldin was 27 at the time and father of a 5-year-old son. The Texas graduate had complained during the game to Line Coach Phil Handler that he felt dizzy and had a headache. Handler caught Mauldin in his arms when the tackle collapsed in the locker room. Mauldin died in the room, lying atop the rubbing table.

les Frank Fuller and Art Hauser, offensive tackle Ken Panfil and defensive end Glenn Holtzman. They also yielded three top draft choices—halfback Don Brown of Houston (their No. 2 choice); fullback Larry Hickman, Baylor (No. 3); and end John Tracey, Texas A&M (No. 4) ... 'Our entire coaching staff feels that these additional top-flight players will, without a doubt, make the Cardinals a strong contender this year,' said Walter Wolfner, managing director."

Wolfner was wrong. In fact, the Cardinals and the Rams finished in last place in their respective divisions in 1959, posting identical 2-10 records. Matson played four seasons with the Rams, only one of which he lead the team in rushing.

Meet Me In St. Louis

The formation of a rival league—the American Football League—played a role in the Cardinals moving from their Chicago home of some 60 years. By 1960, the NFL was considering expansion and all studies pointed to St. Louis as a prime location. At the same time, the newly-formed AFL was looking for cities to host franchises and St. Louis, with its growing population and lack of NFL competition, was an obvious candidate.

With the Cardinals posting a 39-89-4 record from 1949 through 1959, they had lost the battle of Chicago to the more-successful Bears. The team studied moving the franchise to St. Louis, but initially found too many drawbacks. The moving costs alone would total more than $500,000. The only football facility was 34,000-seat Busch Stadium and would have to be shared with the baseball Cardinals. There was no place to hold regular practices.

On March, 13, 1960, however, the NFL voted to compensate the Cardinals for their move south, ending the franchise's relationship with Chicago. The Associated Press reported: "The transfer, which was emphatically denied just yesterday by Managing Director Walter Wolfner of the Cardinals, is subject to two conditions: The Cardinals must work out a satisfactory stadium lease at Busch Stadium, and television arrangements. Commissioner Pete Rozelle said the league does not anticipate that either will be a problem. The league agreed to pay the Cardinals $500,000 to move to St. Louis to relieve the club of the expense of the shift. Part of this is for the club's lease with Soldier Field. Rozelle admitted that the rival Chicago Bears agreed to assume a large portion of the $500,000, realizing the now-open television territory will produce added revenue.... "[St. Louis brewer Joseph] Griesedieck said he and his associates had guaranteed the Cardinals 25,000 season ticket sales, adding a survey currently under way indicated St. Louis would support professional football. He pointed out the Missouri city was the largest town in the country that did not have a pro club." Wolfner was himself a St. Louis native who had married team owner Violet Bidwill in 1947.

At that time, the Chicago Cardinals were the only team left from the 1920 NFL season that still remained in the league in its original city. The Bears were the only other remaining team that had joined the league in 1920, but were then the Decatur Staley. The Bears moved to Chicago in 1921.

On October 2, 1960, the Cardinals played their first home game in St. Louis, losing to the New York Giants by the score of 35-14 in front of 26,089 fans. Griesedieck's projection for season-ticket sales was high. The Cardinals averaged 23,336 fans per game in their first season in St. Louis.

Broadway Joe

With their first-round draft pick in 1964, the St. Louis Cardinals became involved in one of the most storied bidding wars in football history. Having selected Joe Namath, the Alabama quarterback and 1964 Heisman Trophy winner, the Cardinals became the NFL's representative in a battle in the war against the American Football League. The five-year old AFL desperately sought name players to legitimize itself in the eyes of the public.

On January 2, 1965, one day after leading the Alabama Crimson Tide to a national championship with an Orange Bowl win over Texas, Namath announced that he had signed a contract with the AFL's New York Jets. The Cardinals had lost their chance at a first-rate quarterback. The AFL had won a major publicity battle.

The Associated Press reported: "Brawny Joe Namath, son of a struggling Beaver Falls [PA] steelworker, signed the contract today that made him the richest rookie in the history of pro football—and probably any other sport. The Horatio Alger story of the former shoeshine boy who led Alabama to the national college championship was climaxed at a luxury hotel at Miami Beach. Here, he concluded a deal with the New York Jets, of the American Football League, that reportedly will bring him $400,000 for three years' work ... Namath disclosed that the Jets and the St. Louis Cardinals, who drafted him in the American Football League, made 'about the same' offers. It had been reported that St. Louis dropped out when the bidding reached $400,000. 'I took both teams into consideration,' said the 6-foot-2 194-pound quarterback who is one of the most promising passers to enter the pro ranks. 'I wanted more than money. I was interested in the coach and the organization. New York City is a fine place. The sports fans are great and Weeb Ewbank is an outstanding coach.'"

On January 12, 1969, Joe Namath quarterbacked the Jets to a 16-7 upset of the Baltimore Colts in Super Bowl III. One year later, the NFL and AFL officially merged.

Winning And Losing In The Draft

One of the wisest decision that the Cardinals ever made in a draft was to select quarterback Charley Johnson out of New Mexico State in the 10th round in 1960 as a "future". It was one of the last decisions made when the Cardinal franchise was still in Chicago.

It was the St. Louis Cardinals that reaped the benefits of that draft pick. Johnson joined the team in 1961, riding the bench behind Sam Etcheverry and Ralph Guglielmi. In the middle of the Cardinals' 31-14 loss to the New York Giants on October 7, 1962, however, Coach Wally Lemm inserted Johnson at quarterback. The 23-year-old completed the first seven passes that he threw and became the Cardinals starting quarterback for the next five seasons. "I wish I was Charley Johnson's age," said Hall of Fame quarterback Y.A. Tittle in 1963. "And I wish I had his future."

Johnson soon became a prolific passer despite his penchant for throwing interceptions. In 1963, his 3,280 yards through the air were second in the NFL only to Johnny Unitas. One year later, he led the league with 3,045 yards. The Cardinals went 18-8-2 in 1963 and 1964 combined after suffering through 10 losing marks in their previous 13 seasons.

"Charley throws a soft ball, and he knows when to zing it and when not to zing it," said Cardinal receiver Sonny Randle in the 1966 Murray Olderman book, *The Pro Quarterback*. "His first season as a regular he was three years ahead of any quarterback that's ever come along."

The Cardinals, however, lost Johnson to a different sort of draft in August of 1967. The New Mexico native and his Cardinal teammate Larry Stallings were both inducted into the army. Johnson's once promising career had been reduced to spot playing time while he was on weekend passes that year. He was a footnote in the game stories. Jim Hart took over as the full-time signal-caller. Johnson was out of football after 1969.

Getting A Kick Out Of The Game

One of the bright spots for the Cardinals during the 1960s and 1970s was the place-kicking of Jim Bakken. The Wisconsin graduate was an old-fashioned straight-on kicker in the days of transition to soccer-style kicking. On September 24, 1967, Bakken broke an NFL record by kick-

Larry Wilson (8)

ing seven field goals in a 28-14 win at Pittsburgh. Bakken was good on kicks of 18, 24, 24, 32 and 23 yards going into the wind. He also made two kicks—of 33 and 29 yards—with the wind at his back. With misses from 50 and 45 yards, Bakken also set an NFL record with his nine field goal attempts.

Bakken's regular holder, Larry Wilson, left midway through the game because of a cut hand. Bobby Conrad held for Bakken's final three field goals. "I don't think you can make any distinction between the holder, the kicker and the center," said Bakken to the Associated Press. "If any one of them doesn't do his job, the kick won't be any good. I knew about the record and it almost cost me," Bakken added. "When I kicked the seventh one, I wanted to see if it was any good almost before I kicked it. So I looked up and almost dubbed it. It just made it."

Bakken, who led St. Louis in scoring for 16 consecutive seasons, retired after the 1978 season, owning virtually all of the Cardinal records for place kicking.

A Return To Post-Season Play

The Cardinals last played for an NFL title following the 1948 season. They then waited 26 years—and had moved from Chicago to St. Louis—before they'd play in another post-season game. The Cards' 10-4 record in 1974 under second-year coach Don Coryell marked an improvement of six victories from the previous season. St. Louis' 26-14 win over the New York Giants at Busch Stadium, December 15, clinched the NFC's Eastern Division title.

Coryell was a former San Diego State head

coach and became the 26th coach in Cardinals' history when he was hired on January 18, 1973. Two personnel moves in his first season helped make Coryell a success with the Cardinals. First, he ended a prolonged quarterback controversy, naming Jim Hart as his starter. And it was in 1973 that the Cardinals drafted running back Terry Metcalf of Long Beach State.

St. Louis was an immediate success in 1974. Hart led the conference in completions and touchdown passes (20) while only being intercepted eight times. Metcalf became the game's greatest all-around offensive threat. The second-year player led the NFC with a 4.7 yards per carry average in gaining 718 yards on the ground. He caught a team-high 50 passes and was the league's top kick returner, averaging 31 yards per kickoff return and 13 yards per punt return. Dan Dierdorf and Conrad Dobler were standouts on the offensive line. The Cardinal defense cut the number of points it allowed from 365 in 1973 to 218 in 1974. It all added up to an NFL-best start of seven straight wins.

The Cardinals lost their first game of 1974 in Dallas on November 3. The Associated Press reported: "The cliff-hanging odds finally turned on the St. Louis Cardinals Sunday. St. Louis, owning the National Football League's only unblemished record, tumbled, 17-14, to the Dallas Cowboys on Efren Herrerra's 20-yard field goal with four seconds left. The Cardinals had won seven consecutive games—five of them in the final minute—prompting Coach Don Coryell to say, 'Well, if we're not for real we're damn lucky and I'd rather be lucky than real.'"

The upstart Cardinals came back to earth after that game, losing four of their final seven regular-season games. Their win over the Giants in the season finale, however, did give the Cardinals the division title and a ticket to the playoffs.

On December 21, 1974, the Cardinals' dream season came to an end on the field in Minnesota. A 30-14 Viking victory eliminated the Cardinals in an NFC playoff game. The Associated Press reported: "Fran Tarkenton fired two touchdown passes to John Gilliam and cornerback Nate Wright scored with a fumble recovery, leading the Minnesota Vikings ... Minnesota scored 10 points in a 64-second span early in the third quarter to take command of the game, which was tied 7-7 at the half."

The Cardinals bettered their 1974 season with an 11-3 record and another NFC Eastern Division title in 1975. This time St. Louis saved its hot streak for the end of the season, closing with nine wins in its last 10 games. Metcalf set an NFL record for total yardage, gaining 2,462 yards. The Cardinals clinched the division title in their second-last game of the regular season with a 34-20 win over the Chicago Bears.

The playoffs, however, were again unkind to the Cardinals as they were eliminated in the first round for the second consecutive year. This time it was by a 35-23 margin at the hands of the host Los Angeles Rams.

The Associated Press reported: "Reserve quarterback Ron Jaworski learned just two minutes before kickoff that he'd be starting for the Los Angeles Rams and then, with the help of a near-perfect defense, led his club to a 35-23 victory."

The playoffs appeared to be on the horizon once again when the Cardinals went 8-3 in their first 11 games of 1976. Two straight losses, however, to Washington (16-10) and Dallas (19-14) contributed to the Cardinals finishing in a second-place tie with the Redskins. St. Louis' 10-4 record wasn't good enough for a Wild Card berth.

The Cardinals slid backwards in 1977, being shutout for the first time since 1974, in their season opener, 7-0, at Denver. The Cardinals had their six-game winning streak snapped at home against Miami with a 55-14 embarrassment. The Cardinals never regained form. St. Louis lost its last four games of the season.

Coryell resigned as head coach. He had guided the Cardinals to three consecutive 10-win seasons for the first time in franchise history. The team had waited since 1948 for even one campaign with a double-digit victory total.

Cardinals Nest in The Arizona Desert

After 28 years in St. Louis, the Cardinals ended their relationship with the Gateway to the West in the spring of 1988. The once-Chicago Cardinals, once-St. Louis Cardinals were to be the Phoenix Cardinals. Cardinal owner Bill Bidwill found Arizona to be the promised land.

After years of fighting a losing battle with the Bears in Chicago and more years of lackluster attendance figures in St. Louis, the Cardinals found a strong backing in Phoenix in 1988. In their first season in Phoenix, the Cardinals set a franchise record by drawing an average of 59,117 fans per home game. To top that, the Cardinals were charging NFL-record ticket prices for games at the Arizona State University's 72-000-seat Sun Devil Stadium.

Early in the 1988 season, the Cardinals gave the fans of Phoenix hope for the chance to buy post-season tickets. With their 7-4 start, the Cardinals were in contention for a playoff spot. But when quarterback Neil Lomax's arthritic hip acted up, causing him to miss time, the Cards began to fall. Closing the season with five consecutive losses left the Cardinals with a 7-9 record.

Unfortunately for the franchise's sake, those seven wins were a figure that the Cardinals couldn't match in their next four seasons. Slumping to a 5-11 record in 1989 cost the Cardinals dearly at the box office. There was an amazing 26.9 percent drop in attendance at Sun Devil Stadium.

That was only the start. The Cardinals finished in last place in the NFC Eastern Division in their second, third and fourth seasons in Phoenix, posting records of 5-11, 4-12 and 4-12.

Sources

Books

Cohen, Richard M., Jordan A. Deutsch and David S. Neft. *The Scrapbook History of Pro Football.* Indianapolis: The Bobbs-Merrill Company, Inc., 1979.

Curran, Bob. *Pro Football's Rag Days.* Englewood Cliffs, New Jersey: Prentice-Hall, Inc., 1969.

Herskowitz, Mickey. *The Golden Age of Pro Football.* New York: Macmillan Publishing Co. Inc., 1974.

Neft, David S., Richard M. Cohen and Rick Korch. *The Sports Encyclopedia Pro Football - 11th edition.* New York: St. Martin's Press, 1993.

The Official NFL Encyclopedia of Pro Football. New York: NAL Books, 1982.

Olderman, Murray. *The Pro Quarterback.* Englewood Cliffs, New Jersey: Prentice-Hall, Inc., 1966.

Olderman, Murray. *The Running Backs.* Englewood Cliffs, New Jersey: Prentice-Hall, Inc., 1969.

Sullivan, George. *Pro Football's All-Time Greats.* New York: G.P. Putnam's Sons, 1968.

Treat, Roger. *The Encyclopedia of Football - 16th revised edition.* Garden City, New York: Dolphin Books, 1979.

Periodicals

Sports Illustrated, September 13, 1993.

Associated Press reports, 1940—.

—*Bruce MacLeod*

Washington Redskins

Washington, D.C., is well known as the seat of the United States federal government and its attendant monuments, museums, and tourist attractions. The city is also renowned as the home of the Washington Redskins, a pioneer franchise in the National Football Conference East and a favorite team throughout the Mid-Atlantic region. A football powerhouse in the 1940s and again since the 1980s, the Redskins team has been a vital presence in the nation's capital since 1937.

Not only have the men in burgundy and gold won three Super Bowls and numerous playoff appearances, they have also given the professional game such football staples as a fight song, a band, and a halftime show. In his book *The Washington Redskins: An Illustrated History*, Richard Whittingham characterized the team's history in Washington, D.C., as "more than 50 years of sustained entertainment."

The most entertaining part of that history has come since 1980. The Redskins have made four Super Bowl appearances since 1983. Challenging tough rivals in the National Football Conference East, the team has forged a dynasty behind head coach Joe Gibbs, quarterbacks Joe Theismann, Doug Williams, and Mark Rypien, an offensive line known as the "Hogs," and stellar receiver Art Monk. Recent achievements have added luster to a team whose championship tradition began during the Great Depression, reached a peak in the years of the World War II, and began a resurgence in the 1970s.

"The Redskins are a good team, a very good team—a damn good team," wrote Rick Telander in *Sports Illustrated*. "They are a team of remarkable strength and determination. Boring, perhaps, but disciplined and smart." Redskins center Jeff Bostic might have summed it up perfectly in 1992 when he stated in *Sports Illustrated*: "If the rest of Washington ran as efficiently as this football team, there wouldn't be any deficit."

Born of Laundry

The Redskins were the pet project of one George Preston Marshall of Washington, D.C. In the depths of the Great Depression Marshall had amassed a comfortable fortune through a string of 57 laundry outlets in Washington and its environs. Marshall had inherited one run-down laundry shop from his father in 1918 and had proceeded, through hard work and a flair for promotion, to dominate the local market with his "Wet Wash King" business. A thwarted actor himself, Marshall loved both sports and show business. With the Redskins he would combine the two in dramatic fashion.

In 1932 Marshall and three partners purchased a football franchise within the fledgling National Football League. The team's first name—the Braves—was an obvious attempt to gain fan support in the new location, Boston. Marshall, who appointed himself chief executive officer of the new team, arranged to have his Braves play their home games at Boston's Braves Field, home of the successful baseball team. With no professional football competition in the city at that time, the dapper laundryman felt assured his team would draw well at the box office.

In his book *The Team Nobody Wanted*, author George Solomon called Marshall a promoter who "used every gimmick and trick in the book to sell tickets," adding: "Marshall regarded professional football as entertainment to be sold to the public in much the same manner as a barker sells at a carnival." Such flamboyant entrepreneurship was hardly welcomed in staid Boston, a city that had already rejected one professional football team after only two dismal seasons.

"The National Football League in 1932 was a world away from the NFL of today," Whittingham wrote. "There were only eight teams, no divisions or conferences, no playoffs or formal championship game. Of the eight teams, only five franchises besides Mr. Marshall's would survive into the modern NFL: the Chicago Bears, the Green Bay Packers, the New York Giants, the Chicago (later St. Louis and still later Phoenix) Cardinals, and the Portsmouth (Ohio) Spartans, who would eventually relocate in Detroit and change their name to the Lions." In those days, team officials would arrange the game schedules themselves, with no regard to uniformity. In 1932, for instance, the Bears played 14 games, Marshall's Braves just 10.

George Preston Marshall

Building a Team

Marshall's first coach was Ludlow Wray, a gridiron star of the 1920s who had subsequently coached at the University of Pennsylvania. Wray set about the task of assembling a team in advance of the 1932 season. The coach signed 40 players and invited some three dozen more to try

Team Information at a Glance

Founding date: July 9, 1932

Home stadium: R.F.K. Stadium
Washington, D.C. 20003
Phone: (202) 546-2222
Surface: Natural turf
Seating capacity: 55,585

Team colors: Burgundy and gold
Team nickname: Braves, 1932; Redskins, 1933—
Logo: Indian brave in profile

Franchise record	Won	Lost	Pct.
(1932-1992)	392	316	.553

Super Bowl wins (3): 1983 (Super Bowl XVII), 1988 (Super Bowl XXII), 1992 (Super Bowl XXVI)
Super Bowl losses (2): 1973 (Super Bowl VII), 1984 (Super Bowl XVIII)
National Football Conference Championships (5): 1973, 1983, 1984, 1988, 1992
National Football Conference East division titles (5): 1972, 1982, 1983, 1987, 1991
NFL Championships prior to Super Bowl (2): 1937, 1942
NFL Championship appearances prior to Super Bowl (6): 1936, 1937, 1940, 1942, 1943, 1945

out at their own expense. One of the signees, tackle Glen "Turk" Edwards, drove a rented bus from his home in Washington State across the country, picking up recruits at various locations. The six-foot-two-inch, 230-pound Edwards was one member of the new franchise who would go on to greatness as a Brave and a Redskin.

Another promising rookie in 1932 was halfback Cliff "Gip" Battles, who was heavily recruited after Marshall happened to see him play at obscure West Virginia Wesleyan University. Other important acquisitions included two backs from the University of Southern California, Erny Pinckert and Jim Musick, ends Paul Collins and George Kenneally, and a quarterback with the colorful name of Honolulu Hughes.

The Braves opened the 1932 season before some 6,000 fans in Boston on October 2. They lost to the Brooklyn Dodgers 14-0. The following week they earned their first-ever home victory with a 14-6 win over the New York Giants. At season's end the team had compiled a respectable 4-4-2 record, and Battles had led the league in rushing with 576 yards on 148 carries.

As Whittingham observed, however, the future did not look bright: "Although the Braves played some good football and showcased some exciting players, Bostonians for the most part interested themselves in other Sunday activities, and the team ended the season with a loss of about $46,000. It was enough to induce Marshall's three partners to look for a safer investment, but the laundryman was hooked on pro football, and announced he was in it to stay."

Redskins Are Born

At season's end Marshall lost Coach Wray. The first of a string of coaches to chafe under Marshall's constant interference both during and between games, Wray took a job with the Philadelphia Eagles. Marshall replaced him with William "Lone Star" Dietz, a full-blooded Indian.

Dietz was a welcome addition, to Marshall's mind, because the meddling owner had just changed the franchise name to "Redskins" and had moved the home games to Boston's Fenway Park. The days of Native American anger over pejorative Indian names in football were well in the future—in 1933 Marshall had his players pose in "war paint" with feathered headdresses and encouraged Dietz to appear in full Indian garb.

The ploy did not lead to better play on the field. The Redskins compiled a 5-5-2 record and failed once again to lure customers. Legend has it that money was so scarce by midseason that Marshall personally sought to retrieve any football that wound up in the stands during the game.

Lackluster play and attendance continued through the next two seasons. At the close of the 1934 campaign Marshall fired Dietz and hired Ed Casey, the football coach at neighboring Harvard University. It was Casey's turn to suffer through a year with Marshall next to him on the bench during Redskins games, and the team finished 1935 with a 2-8-1 record. Then Casey was fired in favor of Ray Flaherty.

Flaherty took the job on one condition: he wanted no interference from the ownership, namely Marshall. Himself a former All-Pro end, Flaherty proceeded to make the best of football's first college draft, signing tailback Riley Smith in the first round and receiver Wayne Millner from Notre Dame in the eighth round. Millner would still be around—and in the prime of his career—when passing became an essential Redskins staple by decade's end.

The 1936 NFL season provided plenty of excitement for the few Redskins fans in Boston. The Skins battled to a first-place tie with two games to go against the rival Pittsburgh Pirates and the Giants. In the final home game at Fenway Park, Boston trounced the Pirates 30-0 to keep Redskins' championship hopes alive.

Only 4,800 customers turned out to watch the crucial contest. Marshall was furious, even though he himself had raised ticket prices just prior to the game. Then and there he decided he had seen enough of Boston. When the Redskins beat the Giants to secure the NFL East title the following week, Marshall announced that the NFL championship game would be played not in Boston, but in New York, at the Polo Grounds. There, on December 13, 1936, the Redskins lost their first championship bid to the Green Bay Packers, 21-7.

Team Moved to D.C.

Just a week after the game, Marshall announced that the Redskins were moving to Washington, D.C. Home games would be played at Griffith Stadium, the facility that housed the Washington Senators. If fans in Boston had been hostile or indifferent to the team, fans in the nation's capital welcomed the franchise with open arms. Whittingham wrote: "The love affair that developed that 1937 season between the city and the Redskins never wilted, despite frustrating times and an unholy 25-year drought between two championship eras."

Marshall took steps to assure his franchise the same degree of popularity he had seen in other NFL cities. Within years he had arranged for radio broadcast of Redskins games on stations throughout the mid-Atlantic region and the deep South. He recruited a 150-piece band, outfitted it in feathered headdresses and mock leather, and produced the first-ever halftime shows. He also provided the team with its own fight song, not the first for a professional franchise, but certainly the best-known in football history. Marshall's wife, Corinne, supplied the lyrics for the song, "Hail to the Redskins." Composer/band leader Barnee Breeskin wrote the music.

In a reflection of more sexist times, Marshall said he devised the musical entertainment and the halftime shows in order to attract female fans. Whittingham quotes the Redskins owner: "For the women, football alone is not enough. I always try to present halftime entertainment to give them something to look forward to—a little music, dancing, color, something they can understand and enjoy."

It was presumably for the benefit of the male fans that Marshall signed a tall, lean Texas tailback named Sam Baugh. Some observers felt that Baugh, at six-foot-two and 180 pounds, might be too brittle for professional football. Instead, "Slingin' Sammy" spent 16 seasons in Washington and helped to revolutionize football from a game run primarily on the ground to a balanced contest of ground and air attack.

Baugh was a lethal passer who also set some NFL punting records in his day. On defense, in those days before specialized play, he intercepted passes with the best in the league. According to Whittingham, "Baugh's on-field brilliance helped the Redskins establish the support they had found sorely lacking in Boston. The fact that fans in the nation's capital are among the most ardently loyal in the league can be traced directly to the arrival of Slingin' Sam, cowboy hat and all, back in Washington's first season in the NFL."

Skins Capture NFL Championships

During Baugh's debut year with the Skins in 1937, he led the NFL in passing, while Battles took the rushing record. The team played to abundant home crowds and compiled a won-loss total of 8-3-0. The divisional championship was decided on the last week of the regular season when the Redskins journeyed north to meet the New York Giants. In a spectacle that warmed Marshall's heart (he now called himself "The Big Chief"), 10,000 Washington fans boarded 15 special trains for the trip north on game day. When the trains arrived at New York's Penn Station, Marshall grandly announced, "The Indians have come to reclaim Manhattan Island." Then Marshall led his band and the throng of fans on a parade up Seventh Avenue. That afternoon the Redskins annihilated the Giants, 49-14.

Thus the Redskins returned to the NFL championship game for their second consecutive year. This time they met the Chicago Bears, the quintessential running team of the era with future Hall-of-Famer Bronko Nagurski leading the offensive attack. The game was played under frigid conditions at Wrigley Field in Chicago.

With temperatures in the teens and a gusty wind, the players took the field for an exciting championship contest. The score stood at 14-7, Chicago leading, at halftime. It was tied at 21 after Baugh lobbed a long pass to Millner, who ran for a 78-yard touchdown play. Another Baugh pass, to Ed Justice, gave the Redskins a 28-21 lead, and they carried it to game's end for the championship.

Sammy Baugh

Marshall's Redskins were just beginning a string of notable seasons in which they would make six championship game appearances (1936, 1937, 1940, 1942, 1943, and 1945) and win two of them. Washington supporters argue that the Skins were robbed of yet another championship bid in 1939. That year, the Redskins and Giants advanced to a last-day showdown with identical 8-1-1 records. Once again trainloads of die-hard Redskins fans flocked to the Polo Grounds, singing "Hail to the Redskins."

The game was tightly contested, and the Giants carried a slender 9-7 lead into the final minute of play. Washington obtained possession of the ball and drove to the New York ten-yard line. From there, kicker Bo Russell attempted the winning field goal. The kick looked good, and the Redskins fans went wild. A moment later, however, the stunned audience watched as referee Bill Halloran declared the kick a miss. Flaherty protested the call to no avail.

The Giants went on to the championship game. Whittingham noted that subsequent measurements based on where the ball landed, as well as slow-motion viewing of the game film, vindicated the Redskins. "It was impossible to have been called anything but a field goal by anyone but the most calloused official," concluded the author.

Frustration in 1940

The 1940 Redskins advanced to the championship game again. Baugh and Frank Filchock combined to pass for more than 1,800 yards, and Dick Todd led the team in rushing. The perennial Edwards continued to be the defensive anchor. The Skins compiled a 9-2 record for an easy first place finish and prepared to meet the Chicago Bears for the NFL championship.

Oddsmakers predicted a tough battle between the two hardy teams. The Redskins had beaten the Bears 7-3 during the regular season, and Marshall had added insult to injury by telling a reporter after the game that the team from Chicago consisted of "front-runners," "quitters," and "cry-babies." Needless to say, his comments made it into the Chicago newspapers. On the day of the championship game, Bears coach George Halas taped copies of the newspaper clipping all over the Bears locker room. He exhorted his players to prove Marshall wrong, and they did just that—in humiliating fashion.

"Washington fans prefer not to dwell on the cataclysm," recalled Whittingham. Cataclysm it was, indeed: the Bears stomped the Redskins 73-0. It was one of the largest margins of victory ever amassed in a post-season game, and it was played out in front of a home team crowd at Griffith Stadium. When asked if the score might have been different if his receiver had caught what appeared to be a touchdown pass in the first quarter, Baugh responded: "Hell, yes, the score would have been 73-6."

A mediocre 6-5-1 season in 1941 was punctuated by a strange event. The Redskins had a home game on December 7, 1941—their last of the season. A crowd of more than 27,000 came to Griffith Stadium despite the team's being out of playoff contention. During the game, the public address system crackled on to page some prominent government officials, including the Secretary of War and the Secretary of the Navy, who were told to contact the White House. The persistent paging by public address threw a damper on the afternoon. The crowd left in uneasy silence, only to discover later that the Japanese had bombed Pearl Harbor that day.

Wartime Football

World War II robbed professional football of a number of players, coaches, and other personnel. Still the games went on, however—they were considered morale-boosters in an uncertain time. At the outset of the 1942 season, Redskins coach Flaherty announced that he would be leaving at year's end for the U.S. Navy. The Redskins were not favored to win their division, even though they had lost relatively few players to the service at that time.

Washington had not won a title for five years, and only Sammy Baugh and Ed Justice remained as starters from that championship season. The bulk of the team had arrived in the meantime: a huge tackle with the misnomer "Wee Willie" Wilkin and center/linebacker Ki Aldrich, fullback Andy Farkas, ends Bob Masterson and Ed Cifers, and quarterback Ray Hare (Baugh still played tailback). This Redskins lineup turned in a 10-1 season, the best won-loss ration in the team's history. The NFL championship showdown returned to the nation's capital, and the opponents were the Chicago Bears.

Marshall and his Redskins relished this opportunity to revenge themselves for the 73-0 humiliation in 1940. Just prior to the game, the Big Chief sauntered into his team's locker room, wrote "73-0" on the blackboard in big, bold letters, and stalked out again without a word. A crowd of 36,006 gathered in the bitter cold in Washington to watch the game. Not only did the Redskins win 14-6, but the fans were treated to the halftime spectacle of the 150-member Native American band, in long white beards, playing Christmas carols as a salute to the brave Americans fighting the war.

Whittingham quotes sportswriter Bob Considine, who was appalled at the show: "First the loudspeaker boomed that the National Football League was extending the wish of a Merry Christmas to our soldiers and sailors, which will come as a great comfort to the boys in foxholes and probably bring Hitler to his knees. Then to cap it all, George's ... Indian band [played] 'Jingle Bells.' At a late hour last night a war council of the Sioux, Iroquois, Blackfeet, and Choctaw nations was considering secession." However garish the halftime show, the Washington faithful were pleased to bring another NFL championship to the banks of the Potomac.

Between 1942 and 1945, a total of 44 Redskins players left the team to serve in World War II. The most notable loss was Flaherty. In 1943 he was replaced by Arthur J. Bergman, a former coach of Washington, D.C.'s Catholic University. The somewhat talent-depleted Redskins turned in another good season in 1943, finishing the year in a 6-3-1 tie with the Giants.

The identical records brought on a divisional playoff game, scheduled for the Polo Grounds on December 9. Only two weeks earlier the Skins had been trounced by the Giants 31-7, so they were considered the underdog in the playoff. The underdog ranking irritated Baugh, who in 1943 led the NFL in passing, punting, and interceptions. Behind his fired-up play, including 16 of 21 passes for 199 yards, the Redskins defeated the Giants 28-0 and clinched the division.

This set up yet another showdown with the Bears. Whittingham wrote: "The NFL championship game was set for Sunday, December 16, at Wrigley Field in Chicago. Both teams figured they had something going against them before they even took the field. Because the Bears had begun their season two weeks before the Redskins and because the title game had to be pushed back a week to accommodate the NFL East playoff game, Chicago had not played a football game in a month. On the other hand, the Redskins were coming off three crucial, pressure-filled games in a row. The gamblers wondered which would dull the edge, or perhaps if both might exact a toll. When the day had ended, it was safe to say that three intense games in succession had been more damaging than four weeks of rest and relaxation."

In the opening play Baugh was kicked in the head. He suffered a concussion, missed the first half, and staggered through the second half at only a fraction of his usual ability. Baugh completed eight of 12 passes for 123 yards and two touchdowns, but his Chicago counterpart, Sid Luckman, passed for 286 yards and five touchdowns—then a championship record. At game's end the Bears stood victorious, 41-21. In four title appearances against one another, the Redskins and Bears had split evenly, two each.

Team Adopts T-formation

Another new coach arrived in 1944. Marshall hired Dudley DeGroot from Rochester University to replace Bergman. Marshall also recruited Clark Shaughnessy, an offensive specialist from Stanford University, and gave him the mandate of initiating the T-formation. Most other NFL teams had adopted the T-formation by that time. Only the obvious talent of Baugh from the tailback position had kept the popular option out of the Redskins' arsenal. Now Baugh, a seven-year veteran, and Frank Filchock, also a seasoned player, were faced with the task of adjusting to the T. Filchock proved more readily adaptable, leading the NFL in passing in 1944. Despite his success, the Redskins finished at 6-3-1 that season, behind both the Giants and the Philadelphia Eagles.

By 1945 Baugh had mastered the T-formation and found it much to his liking. "I could play it in top hat and tails," he bragged before making a then-record 70.3 per cent of his passes during the season. With a fine 8-2 record, the 1945 Redskins easily won the NFL East divisional title for a fifth time. This time they drew not the Bears but the Cleveland Rams in the championship showdown. Home field advantage went to the Rams, who invited the Skins to Municipal Stadium, a solid block of ice on Lake Erie.

Temperatures hovered around zero when the game began. Although the Washington players had brought their sneakers for better traction on the icy field, the Rams players had only cleats. In a spirit of fairness, DeGroot declared that his players would wear their cleats as well. The decision probably cost Washington the game. The Rams won, 15-14 on two freak plays. The first occurred when Baugh tried to pass from the Redskins' three-yard-line. Just as he released the ball, a gust of wind caught it, and it hit the goal post. At that time the goal posts were located on the goal lines. The referee ruled a safety for the Rams and awarded Cleveland two points. Later in the game, a Rams kick for an extra point after a touchdown struck the crossbar on the goal post and literally wobbled across for the extra point. The strange kick provided the crucial difference in a very close game.

In *Pro Football's Great Moments*, Jack Clary wrote: "In the end it was the weather that doomed the Skins. The cold, for which the Redskins' players had been prepared with their sneakers, might have been an advantage if they had gone ahead and worn the rubber-soled footwear. The wind, which blew Baugh's pass into the goal posts and [a Redskins] field-goal attempt wide, punished the Skins more than the Rams. Yet weather, as essentially beyond man's control, somehow escaped the blame. It was the rule on safeties that inflamed the Washington management. It took the Skins' fiery owner, George Preston Marshall, precisely 27 days, until the next rules committee meeting, to have that rule amended." Marshall was also instrumental in moving the goal posts to the position they occupy today in the end zones.

25-year Coma

"After royally entertaining their fans with five divisional titles and two world championships during Washington's nine seasons in the nation's capital, the Redskins lapsed into a coma that lasted more than a quarter of a century," wrote Whittingham. "Certainly they played football on Sunday afternoons, and sometimes they won, although that was the exception rather than the rule. They showcased some certified stars, as well as a variety of memorable characters, but after the 1945 season, Washington would not advance to the playoffs again until 1971."

Through that long, dreary hiatus from post-season play, Washington only topped the .500 mark four times. Ten head coaches came and went as the ownership struggled to return the team to its pre-war form. George Solomon gave two reasons for the long fade. First, Solomon noted, the Redskins salaries were notoriously low, save for the few stars like Baugh who won Marshall's favor. Good players would pray for release or trade, knowing they could earn more elsewhere. They might also jump to other leagues, that were not bound by NFL recruitment restrictions.

The other reason made itself felt in the 1950s and early 1960s. Marshall, to put it plainly, would not hire blacks. His Redskins team was popular via radio and television throughout the South, and most observers think he avoided integration to keep that audience. While other franchises integrated, Washington remained all-white. As late as 1962 it took persuasion from the Kennedy Administration and threats by the U.S. Department of the Interior to sway the stubborn owner from his unstated hiring policies. Overlooking talented black players—and underpaying the members of the team—contributed greatly to Washington's decline.

Whatever the reasons, a Redskins team that had once visited the playoffs regularly fell into decline. Baugh held on as quarterback through the rest of the 1940s, leading the NFL in passing in 1948, but the Skins never finished better than second place. At decade's end in 1949, the best the team could do was 4-7-1 under head coach John Whelchel.

The mediocrity continued into the 1950s, although receiver Hugh "Bones" Taylor earned national recognition by catching 12 touchdown passes in the 1952 season. Ironically, Taylor's best year found him catching passes from young quarterback Eddie LeBaron. At long last, after 16 seasons, Sammy Baugh retired at the end of 1952. Baugh was nothing less than a superhero in Washington, D.C., but he chose to return to his ranch in Texas for his retirement. He was 38. Baugh was elected to the Pro Football Hall of Fame as a charter member in 1963.

Head coaches came and went through the Redskins' dormant period. Whelchel lasted one season, 1949. He was succeeded by Herman Ball, who in two years posted a 4-16 record. In 1951, Dick Todd took over and the Redskins finished in third place with a 5-4 record. Todd could not abide Marshall's interference, so he quit prior to the 1952 season. Marshall then hired Earl "Curly" Lambeau, who lasted through the 1953 season with a 10-13 record. Lambeau was yet another veteran coach who quarreled with Marshall and quit in a fit of pique. His replacement was Joe Kuharich. Kuharich managed to hold on for four years, until 1958.

The 1950s were not devoid of all excitement, however. On October 1, 1955 the Redskins scored 21 points in 137 seconds in the third quarter to wrest a come-from-behind victory from the Eagles. The scoring blitz included three fumble recoveries—one for a touchdown—and some clutch play by quarterback LeBaron. That same year saw the Redskins post a respectable 8-4 record for second place, with halfback/kicker Vic Janowicz scoring 88 points on seven touchdowns, six field goals, and 28 extra points.

The task of filling Sammy Baugh's shoes fell to Eddie LeBaron through much of the 1950s. Nicknamed the "Little General" for his diminutive height, LeBaron quarterbacked the Skins from 1952-53 and again from 1955-59. The mid-career hiatus saw LeBaron jump to the Canadian Football League due to conflicts with Redskins coach Curly Lambeau.

When Lambeau resigned, LeBaron returned. He was the starter when the Skins finished 8-4 in 1955, and he had a personal best season in 1957 when he completed 99 passes for 1,508 yards during a 5-7-1 campaign. LeBaron retired from the Redskins in 1960. He was enticed back into the game by Dallas Cowboys coach Tom Landry, and played another four years in Texas.

Needless to say, the years of lackluster play eroded fan support in Washington, D.C. Marshall was constantly on the prowl for promotions that would stimulate demand for tickets. One perennial stunt was the arrival of Santa Claus at Griffith Stadium. Each year Marshall would try to think of a new way for the jolly elf to make his appearance. Once, a gusty wind completely foiled everyone as a parachuting Santa was blown past the stadium and onto the roof of a nearby apartment building.

New Stadium for Skins

Marshall's franchise got a boost late in 1959 when Congress approved the construction of a new football stadium for the District of Columbia. The facility, first called D.C. Stadium and later renamed R.F.K. Stadium in honor of slain politician Robert F. Kennedy, was completed in time for the 1961 season. The Redskins signed a 30-year lease.

The brand new stadium was just what the team needed to keep afloat. In 1960 the Redskins completed their worst-ever year, earning a dismal 1-9-2 record under head coach Mike Nixon. Nor did a new park improve the sagging Skins' fortunes. In front of 37,767 fans on D.C. Stadium's Opening Day, the home team blew a 21-0 lead for a 24-21 loss to the hated Giants.

At season's end Washington's record stood at 1-12-1, with the sole victory at the expense of the struggling expansion franchise in Dallas. Whittingham noted: "As it turned out, those two forgettable years are the only two in Redskins history in which the team failed to win more than one game."

By 1962 pressure was being brought to bear on Marshall from all sides. Every other team in the NFL had been integrated in the 1950s. Marshall had held out, feeling that he would lose his television audience in the South if he hired black players. Finally, in 1962, he relented. He had first pick in the college draft that year, and he selected Heisman Trophy-winner Ernie Davis of Syracuse.

Immediately he traded Davis for running back/flanker Bobby Mitchell of the Cleveland Browns. Mitchell would prove to be one of the most exciting flankers in the history of the NFL and would go on to a Hall of Fame career with the Redskins. "I wasn't too worried about being the first black man on the team," he later told George Solomon. "My feeling dealt with going from a winner in Cleveland to a loser in Washington." Mitchell added: "I enjoyed the experience of playing football in Washington. I always made good money and saved for the future. I also became part of the black community in town. The worst thing a football player can do is restrict his life solely to football. If you do that, when you're finished, you have nothing. I have something today."

The Redskins had something too: a quick, sure-handed receiver who could fake his way past the quickest defenders. Whittingham called him "a pure hellion on the football field." In his first season at Washington, Mitchell became the first Redskin to break the 1,000-yard mark as a receiver. He spent six more seasons in a burgundy-and-gold uniform, gaining 8,162 net yards on offense and kick returns. Mitchell was voted into the Pro Football Hall of Fame in 1983.

Mitchell could not stem the tide of losing seasons, however. In 1963 the Redskins managed only three victories. The worst had passed, however, and a new set of players were about to take up the Washington cause.

The personnel change began at the very top of the ranks. By 1963 George Preston Marshall was too ill to run the team anymore. He turned his administrative duties over to his board of directors: Leo De Orsey, Edward Bennett Williams, and Milton King. Soon the trading began. Washington fans were astonished when their quarterback, Norm Snead, was sent to the Eagles for their backup quarterback, Sonny Jurgensen.

Jurgensen was just making a name for himself as a passer, but at five-foot-eleven and 200 pounds he hardly typified the lean-and-hungry professional athlete. Another important acquisition for the 1964 season was future Hall of Fame linebacker Sam Huff. From the draft the Redskins selected halfback Charley Taylor from Arizona State, probably their most important selection in years.

In Jurgensen's first year with Washington, he completed 207 passes for 2,934 yards and 24 touchdowns, and the Redskins bettered their record to 6-8. It was the most wins the team had earned since 1956. Unfortunately, Jurgensen was not able to build upon this foundation. The following year the Redskins lost their first five games in a row before finishing with an identical 6-8 tally. The continuous sub-.500 play brought the firing of head coach Bill McPeak, who was succeeded by Otto Graham.

Graham was a former star quarterback who emphasized the passing game. He found much to his liking on the Redskins offense. One of his first steps was to move Charley Taylor to wide receiver. It was a controversial decision at the time. Taylor had tallied 755 yards rushing in 1964 and led the Skins in rushing in 1965.

As potent as he appeared at halfback, however, he was even better at wide receiver. In his first six games at the position in 1966, he caught 54 passes. Taylor spent the next 11 years with Washington and was one of the few links between its worst years and its best. He made eight Pro Bowl appearances and was named to the Hall of Fame in 1984.

One of the highlights of the 1966 season was a game best known as the "TD Jamboree." The Redskins and the Giants met in Washington for what is still the highest-scoring NFL contest of all time. When the dust settled Jurgensen, Taylor, and company had won 72-41. The Skins scored two touchdowns in the first quarter, three in the second, two in the third, and three in the fourth—plus a field goal with seven seconds on the clock. The slugfest was the most notable Redskins victory in a 7-7 season.

Graham had molded the Redskins into a powerful passing team, but the running game and the defense lagged, and the Redskins continued to struggle. Jurgensen set Redskin and NFL passing records for most attempts, completions, and yards in 1967. Even more remarkably, Taylor, Jerry Smith, and Mitchell ranked first, second, and fourth in the NFL on offense—the highest finish ever by receivers on the same team. Still the Skins could only manage a 5-6-3 record in 1967, just slightly better than the basement-dwelling first-year New Orleans Saints. Washington fell even further in 1968, when injuries sidelined Jurgensen and the team limped to a 5-9 finish.

Team president Edward Bennett Williams had seen enough. He fired Graham and somehow persuaded football legend Vince Lombardi to take the challenge of coaching the Redskins. Lombardi's Green Bay Packers were one of the certified dynasties of the 1960s. Fans in Washington expected nothing less than a miracle from the crusty coach.

Lombardi's Brief Reign

Lombardi had only held the head coaching job for a few months when longtime Redskin owner George Preston Marshall died in August of 1969. Marshall's absence from the front office since 1963 did little to diminish feelings about him in the city. Black players for the Redskins refused to attend his memorial service until they were ordered to do so by management. In his eulogy for the *Baltimore News-American*, reprinted in Whittingham's book, John F. Steadman wrote of the controversial owner: "He was ... a strong-willed, unbending, non-compromising man with the strength of his convictions in all matters, be it in the area of politics, sports, religion or racial relations.... Suffice to say that George Preston Marshall was not a hypocrite. Whether you liked him or found him repulsive, you knew the stand he had taken because he let the world know it."

Marshall's passing truly marked the end of an era in Washington, D.C. Gone were the days

Sonny Jurgensen

when fans surged through the streets singing "Hail to the Redskins" behind a band bedecked in feathers. Gone too were the long years of frustration, poor finishes, and thwarted potential. The Redskins were about to move into the 1970s as serious competitors in the National Football Conference East.

Whittingham wrote that the gap-toothed Lombardi "successfully developed a balanced offensive attack and ... inspired a defense to be intimidating" as the Redskins compiled a 1969 record of 7-5-2. Sellout crowds had been packing D.C. Stadium since 1966, but now the fans really had something to cheer about. Even better, Lombardi vowed that his 1970 Redskins would be tougher still. Then tragedy struck. Just prior to summer training camp in 1970, Lombardi discovered he had cancer. He promised to return to Washington in time for the regular season, but he died before the season began. As Whittingham put it, "A football nation mourned the passing of one of the game's greatest figures."

As if reeling from the loss of Lombardi, the Skins sank back to 6-8 in 1970 under new head coach Bill Austin. The only highlight of that season was the performance of All-Pro Larry Brown who, in his sophomore season with Washington, became the first Redskin to break the 1,000 yard rushing barrier. Brown ended the year as the NFL's top rusher.

Allen Improves Club's Fortunes

Dawn had definitely come for the Redskins, and now a new, bright morning arrived. On January 6, 1971, president Williams announced that the Redskins had hired yet another new coach, George Allen. Allen had spent the previous five years with the Los Angeles Rams, who had won two divisional titles under his guidance. Volatile and controversial, Allen felt that success could be won by trading for proven performers who might be nearing the ends of their careers. He came to Washington and gave the city a new football slogan: "The future is now." No more waiting for young players to develop. No more trusting fate to draft picks who might take years to mature. Allen planned to win right away.

Allen recruited veteran players and paid them high salaries. He demanded—and got—a new practice facility for the team. Part-owner Edward Bennett Williams quipped at the time: "I gave George an unlimited expense account and he exceeded it in the first month with us."

Allen's moves brought results, however. His Redskins, dubbed the "Over the Hill Gang," racked up five straight victories to start the 1971 season, including one against the arch-rival Cowboys. Ironically, this new season of promise found a new starter at quarterback. Jurgensen had been injured during the preseason, so the quarterbacking duties fell upon 31-year-old Billy Kilmer, an Allen recruit from the New Orleans Saints.

Despite injuries to such key players as Charley Taylor, Larry Brown, and Jerry Smith, the Redskins earned a wild card playoff bid with a 9-4-1 record. It was their first visit to post-season play since 1945 and the most victories the team had won since 1942.

The wild card playoff featured the Redskins against the San Francisco 49ers in Candlestick Park on December 26, 1971. A Kilmer-to-Smith touchdown pass provided the first scoring in the game, and at halftime Washington led 10-3. The momentum turned in the second half. San Francisco scored two touchdowns in the third quarter and went on to win the game 24-20. The Redskins returned home to watch their hated rivals, the Dallas Cowboys, win the Super Bowl.

Redskin/Cowboy Rivalry

Virtually from the moment the franchise from Dallas joined the league, the Cowboys/Redskins competition became less a matter of games won than of wars fought. The feud began slowly in the 1960s, with two losing franchises trying to eke at least a few victories at the other's expense each year. Both clubs had ascended by the early 1970s, and the rivalry took on personal tones as head coaches Tom Landry and George Allen sniped at each other in the press. In *The Semi-Official Dallas Cowboys Haters' Handbook*, Mark Nelson and Miller Bonner suggested that coach Allen "turned hating the Dallas Cowboys into a religious experience. He made it personal. The Cowboys, with their computerized organization, didn't know how to react. They accused him of spying, lying, and cheating." From these roots grew a level of inter-divisional competition that remains one of the toughest rivalries in professional football.

One of Landry's observations about Allen was that the Washington coach tended to stock his team with older players by trading away draft choices—it was a questionable way to run a franchise. Allen replied, as quoted in Whittingham's book: "An aging team is the least of my worries. If you do things right at the start of any football operation, you don't have to build and rebuild. We have a solid club in Washington. They win because they want to win." In 1972 Allen further predicted the demise of the Super Bowl Champion Cowboys: "This is the year Dallas falls from grace, and we're going to do the pushing."

The Over-the-Hill Gang strode into the 1972 season with confidence, winning four of their first five games. The sixth game pitted them against Dallas, and first place in the division hung on the outcome. The Cowboys jumped to an early 13-0 lead, but Kilmer and his receivers—and a powerful Redskins defense—turned the tide and brought the Skins a 24-20 win. Washington went on to win its next six straight, and the team finished the season 11-3 with the NFC East title firmly in hand.

"The entire team contributed to the 1972 regular-season glory," noted Whittingham. "The defense gave up the fewest points in the NFC, 218.... Larry Brown led the NFL by gaining 1,216 yards rushing, which was also a new club record. Billy Kilmer, who had regained the starting job at quarterback after Sonny Jurgensen suffered a season-ending injury in the seventh game that year, was the fourth-ranked passer in the league. Charley Taylor gained 673 yards on 49 receptions, and Roy Jefferson picked up 550 on 35 catches. And six Redskins earned invitations to the Pro Bowl: Larry Brown, Billy Kilmer, Charley Taylor, Len Hauss, Chris Hanburger, and Speedy Duncan."

In the 1972 playoffs the Redskins handily defeated the Green Bay Packers, 16-3 and then met their nemeses, the Cowboys, for the NFC Championship. The game was played on New Year's Eve in Washington, and the Skins rolled over Dallas, 26-3. For the first time since the big game's inception, the Redskins were going to the Super Bowl.

As luck would have it, the Washington Redskins drew as Super Bowl opponents the undefeated Miami Dolphins. Miami had won all of its regular season games and two playoff matches to advance to the championship with a 16-0 record. Allen was undaunted by the feat, but in a pregame interview he humbly said: "Miami is the best team I've seen in my career. We'll be lucky to stay on the same field with them." The Redskins

AP/Wide World Photos

George Allen

stayed on the field in Super Bowl VII, but they could not de-rail Don Shula's Dolphin juggernaut. The Dolphins held a 14-0 lead by the half. The only Redskins score came on a strange play in the fourth quarter, when Miami kicker Garo Yepremian had his field goal attempt blocked, then recovered the ball briefly, before bobbling it into the hands of Washington cornerback Mike Bass, who ran it 49 yards for a touchdown. The lucky Skins touchdown notwithstanding, Miami won 14-7, for a perfect season.

Washington fans had become accustomed to a winning team, and Allen did not disappoint them. While he was unable to return the Redskins to the Super Bowl again during his tenure as head coach, he did guide the team to the playoffs five times in seven years. Whittingham observed that after Super Bowl VII, "Allen's teams ... were always in the war but for some reason could not win a postseason battle. It was, however, a most entertaining segment in Washington Redskins lore."

In 1973 Allen platooned his two aging quarterbacks, Jurgensen and Kilmer, and the Skins finished the season with a 10-4 record. To their dismay, the Cowboys had finished with an identical record—and an identical 6-2 tally for the division—to tie for the NFC East title. The title was awarded to Dallas on a points differential. The Redskins had beaten the Cowboys by seven points in one seasonal encounter, but the Cowboys had won by 20 in the other. Washington had to settle for a wild card game, which they lost to the Minnesota Vikings, 27-20.

A new owner appeared on the scene in 1974. Canadian businessman Jack Kent Cooke had been a minority shareholder in the Redskins since 1960. He purchased a majority of the stock in the franchise and took over as general manager soon thereafter. Cooke was no stranger to the professional sports business. He had owned the Toronto Maple Leafs in the National Hockey League and would reap international renown for his Los Angeles Lakers in the 1970s and 1980s. Cooke was not an interfering and anxious owner in the George Preston Marshall mode, but he did make his presence felt from the stands at games, as well as on the practice fields.

Allen's "the future is now" policy became strained in 1974 and 1975 as his Over-the-Hill Gang began to retire and the Redskins faced few prime draft choices. Still, in 1974 the Skins earned a wild card playoff bid, which they lost to the Los Angeles Rams 19-10. The 1974 playoff game marked the last appearance of Sonny Jurgensen in a Redskins uniform.

At 40, Jurgensen had long served as backup to quarterback Kilmer. Sonny could still work the old magic, though. In his last season he completed 107 of 167 passes and guided the Skins to important victories over the Dolphins and the Giants. He did not want to retire but was asked to do so by coach Allen. On May 1, 1975, he stepped aside. He was inducted into the Pro Football Hall of Fame in 1983.

The Redskins failed to make the playoffs in 1975, posting an 8-6 record—their poorest since Allen's arrival in 1971. The season's highlight was significant, however. Thirty-four year-old Charley Taylor caught his 634th career pass to become the all-time reception leader in the NFL. The record-breaking catch came in the final game of the season against the Philadelphia Eagles. Taylor's achievements, good enough for a Hall of Fame induction in 1984, have since been eclipsed by another Redskin receiver, Art Monk, who broke a passing record with more than 800 catches by 1992.

Allen promised Washington's fans that the aging Redskins would be back in 1976, and he exhorted his team of veterans to play at their best. The season came down to the final game, of course a showdown with the Cowboys in Dallas. Dallas had already clinched the NFC East title, but Washington had to beat them to gain a wild card berth. The Skins had never won in Landry's Texas Stadium, but this time they proved equal to the task. A 27-14 win gave them the wild card bid, and they traveled to Minnesota to meet the Vikings. In a contest some called an "Old-Timers' Game," the veteran Vikings thrashed the Redskins 35-20. Once again Washington had failed to advance in the playoffs.

Whittingham called the loss to Minnesota "an enduring blow to George Allen, despite the fact that he was named NFC Coach of the Year [for the third time]. It was no longer merely being whispered around town that Allen could not win the big ones; it was now quite vocal. Winning seasons, yes, but he could not lead his team to victories in the playoffs, many were saying." Relations between Allen and the front office—now bossed by Edward Bennett Williams and Jack Kent Cooke—took a turn for the worse. Nor did they improve as the 1977 Redskins went 9-5 behind Kilmer and a new young quarterback named Joe Theismann. At the close of the 1977 season, Allen was fired after making it known that he was a candidate for a head coaching job with the Rams.

The George Allen years might have ended on a sour note, but few fans in Washington had anything critical to say about him. In his seven years as coach he had posted a record of 67-30-1, the winningest in Skins history at the time. He had also led his Over-the-Hill Gang to five playoff appearances and one Super Bowl. Whittingham concluded: "In the Redskins' saga, the Allen era—controversial, exciting, frustrating, and above all, memorable—had come to an end."

In Allen's place the Redskin owner hired Jack Pardee, a former Over the Hill Gang member who had served several years as head coach of the Chicago Bears. Pardee's first decision was to bench Kilmer in favor of the younger Theismann at quarterback.

From 1974 until 1978 Theismann chafed on the sidelines while Kilmer and Jurgensen held onto the spotlight under Allen. When he finally got a chance to start as Pardee's choice, Theismann spearheaded the Skins to victory in their first six games of 1978.

Then the team took a nosedive, losing eight of the remaining ten contests. The year was not a complete loss, however. Theismann had proven himself capable of working as a starter. Within a few short years he would demonstrate his capacity to win a Super Bowl.

Riggins Rushes In

Theismann's attack was strengthened by the advent of a tempestuous and flamboyant running back named John Riggins. Riggins was another Redskin who had been relegated to minor duties under Allen but liberated by Pardee. Over the ensuing seasons he would become one of the most productive, and certainly the best-known, Redskins.

An improved defense and the explosive Riggins helped the Redskins to improve in 1979. A tight NFC rivalry extended into the last game of the season against—as always—the Cowboys. The Redskins found themselves in a three-way tie with the Cowboys and the Eagles for the NFC East crown. They had to win against Dallas in order to be in the playoffs at all. At a hostile Texas Stadium, Theismann engineered a 17-0 lead through the second quarter, but the Cowboys behind Roger Staubach roared back with two touchdowns to end the half at 17-14. In the second half the Redskins at one point held a 31-21 lead, but Dallas hung tough and pulled off a stunning 35-34 upset in the last two minutes of play. Meanwhile, the Chicago Bears scored a massive victory to edge Washington out of a wild card spot. It was certainly one of the most devastating losses in Redskins history. Pardee groused: "One little point takes us from division champs to the outhouse."

Better Times Lay Ahead

The 1980 season marked the arrival of Art Monk and the departure of Jack Pardee. It had been some time since the Redskins had the luxury of a first-round draft choice, but they did that year. They used it to secure Monk, a tall, steel-nerved wide receiver from Syracuse. Monk became a starter in his rookie year, but his presence in the Redskins offense was offset by the loss of Riggins, who sat the year out in a contract dispute. Despite the efforts of a fine defensive secondary, anchored by Lemar Parrish, Joe Laven-

AP/Wide World Photos

Joe Theismann

der, and Mark Murphy, the Skins finished a dismal 6-10 without a glimmer of playoff hope. Pardee was fired before the 1980 post-season had ended. His replacement was a deeply religious workaholic with a long assistant coaching history, Joe Gibbs.

Gibbs came to Washington from the San Diego Chargers, where he had been offensive coordinator. What he proposed to do in Washington was initiate his imaginative offensive schemes while maintaining the already solid defense. It took some time for the Redskins to adapt to his complex offensive strategy. The team began the 1981 season with five straight losses, all of them shellackings. Owner Cooke expressed his confidence in Gibbs, however, and sure enough the Redskins rebounded. After finishing 8-8 in 1981, they surged to a Super Bowl year in 1982.

The 1982 season was shortened by a players strike that lasted a full seven weeks in the middle of the season. When it ended and the dust cleared, Washington climbed to the top of the NFC East with an 8-1 record. Because the season had been so short, the football commissioner decreed longer playoffs. Thus the Redskins had to defeat the Detroit Lions, the Minnesota Vikings, and the hated Cowboys to advance to the Super Bowl. It was a daunting task, but Theismann and company did it: a win over Detroit, 31-7, a win over Minnesota, 21-7, and a thrashing of Dallas, 31-17. Each game was played for the home crowds at R.F.K. Stadium, providing a post-season orgy of joy for fans in the District of Columbia.

Hogs In Heaven

Super Bowl XVII was billed as "The Hogs versus the Killer Bees." The "Hogs" were Gibbs's offensive linemen, a group of massive men who had provided almost superhuman protection for Theismann during the season. The "Killer Bees" were the renowned defensive unit for the Miami Dolphins, Washington's Super Bowl opponents.

It had been ten years since the "perfect" Dolphins had spoiled Washington's first Super Bowl outing. This time John Riggins and the Hogs triumphed. Riggins made 38 carries and compiled 166 rushing yards as the Redskins easily defeated Miami, 27-17.

At game's end, Riggins—himself a designated Hog—was named Super Bowl Most Valuable Player. He had successfully rushed for more than 100 yards in each four of the playoff games. The Redskins had finally won a Super Bowl; it was the franchise's first national title since Sammy Baugh had won one for Washington in 1942.

In 1983 Washington cast away any doubts that their Super Bowl season had been helped by the strike. The Redskins roared to a 14-2 regular season record, the most wins in the team's long history. The 541 points the Skins scored on the way to this record was the most any NFL team had ever amassed in a single year. Whittingham related: "Mark Moseley led the league in scoring with 161 points, the most ever by a kicker in a single season.... John Riggins set the club record for rushing yardage with 1,347 as well as number of carries, 375. Joe Theismann again topped 3,000 yards passing.... Charlie Brown became only the third Redskin receiver to surpass 1,000 yards gained on receptions, with 1,225.... And, needless to say, the Hogs clearly controlled the trenches, or 'trough,' as it was now being called around Washington."

Back to the Super Bowl the Redskins went, after trouncing the Rams 51-7 and then hanging on for a thrilling 24-21 victory over the 49ers. Super Bowl XVIII was held in Tampa, Florida on January 22, 1984. There the Redskins met the Los Angeles Raiders for a game that was predicted to hinge on offensive prowess. In the final analysis, Los Angeles effectively stifled the Redskins' scoring threats, while quarterback Jim Plunkett found his receivers. The Raiders cruised to a 38-9 blowout and denied Washington back-to-back Super Bowl crowns. After the game, a disconsolate Gibbs told reporters: "We were emotionally spent. We just weren't up for it today."

Jack Kent Cooke optimistically predicted a third straight Super Bowl appearance in 1984, but it was not to be—the Skins won the NFC East division but were defeated by the Bears in the playoffs. Then Cooke talked of three Super Bowls in four years in 1985, but that too proved a pipe dream.

AP/Wide World Photos

Joe Gibbs

By mid-season in 1985 the Skins were a dismal 5-5 as they prepared to meet the Giants. In the second quarter of that game, Theismann was sacked by the Giants' All-Pro linebacker Lawrence Taylor. The sack was performed with such ferocity that Theismann sustained a compound fracture of his leg that effectively ended his career. He attempted a comeback after the injury healed but was never able to play again.

The 1985 season was also Riggins's last due to recurring back problems. Despite the promising performance of quarterback Jay Schroeder, the Redskins took second place in the NFC East and did not earn a wild card bid.

Championship-winning Black Quarterback

Prior to the 1986 season, Gibbs acquired the rights to quarterback Doug Williams from Tampa Bay. Williams was something of a pioneer—the first black quarterback to be selected in the first round of the NFL draft. Tampa Bay had selected him in 1978, and he had played five years there before leaving for the United States Football League. Gibbs hired Williams merely as a backup—there was some question of injuries to the former Buccaneer, and no other team had bid for his services. It was to prove a singularly fortunate move for the Redskins as Williams went on to make Super Bowl history.

A 12-4 record behind Schroeder in 1986 was good enough to secure the Redskins a playoff opportunity. In the NFC playoffs the Redskins defeated the Rams 19-7 and then stunned the defending-Super Bowl champion Bears 27-13. This set the stage for an NFC title game against the surging Giants at Rutherford, New Jersey. The bad blood between the Giants and the Redskins was almost as potent as that between Washington and Dallas, especially since the Giants had ended Theismann's career. It was therefore particularly galling that the Giants shut Washington out by a score of 17-0 to advance to the Super Bowl. The Redskins took small consolation in the fact that seven of their members were voted onto the Pro Bowl roster that year: Schroeder, Monk, receiver Gary Clark, lethal defensive end Dexter Manley, "Hogs" Joe Jacoby and Russ Grimm, and cornerback Darrell Green.

Talk of a players' strike was again in the air as the 1987 football season opened. The games began on schedule, however, and disaster seemed imminent for the Redskins right away. In an Opening Day romp over the Eagles, Washington lost Schroeder to a shoulder injury. Williams was called off the bench, and he executed the victory.

After a loss to the Atlanta Falcons the following week, the Redskins players walked out on strike, as did many of their NFL mates. This time the NFL ownership fielded "replacement" teams, staffed by athletes who had been unable to obtain roster positions under ordinary circumstances. Despite bitter disputes with the regular players, the replacement Redskins won all three of their games during the strike. The walkout ended in its fourth week, and Gibbs's players returned to the field.

Williams and Schroeder alternated as quarterbacks for the remainder of the season, with Gibbs leaning more and more toward his recruit from Tampa Bay. With the Hogs in fine form again and Manley a stalwart on defense, the Skins easily won the NFC divisional title with an 11-4 record. For the second year in a row Washington drew the Bears in a playoff game, and in a tight contest beat Chicago 21-17.

Then the Redskins hosted the NFC championship game in Washington, defeating the Minnesota Vikings 17-10 in an outing that rested upon the Skins' defense. The Redskins had advanced to the Super Bowl again. The last time they had won it had been in a strike year—now, in the wake of another strike, they would try again.

Super Bowl XXII took place in San Diego, California, on January 31, 1988. The Redskins were set to meet the Denver Broncos, who were led by power quarterback John Elway. Although Williams had seemed to struggle in the NFC championship game, he still got called to start for

AP/Wide World Photos

Doug Williams (with ball)

Washington. The Broncos were favored to win, and they seemed to get an extra edge late in the first quarter when Williams dropped back to pass, slipped, and strained his knee. After one quarter of play, Denver led 10-0. The second quarter of Super Bowl XXII proved the single most exciting 15 minutes of play in Redskins' history.

Williams limped onto the field at the beginning of the quarter. With a first-and-ten at his own 20, he lofted a pass to wide receiver Ricky Sanders, who streaked downfield for an 80-yard touchdown. The Skins defense allowed Denver three downs and a punt, then Williams cut loose again, earning a second TD on a 27-yard pass to Gary Clark. Two minutes later, Washington had the ball again. Williams handed it off to running back Timmy Smith, who raced 58 yards for another seven points.

Remarkably, after a brief Denver possession, Williams came in again and hefted yet another pass to Sanders for a 50-yard touchdown. The Skins defense held after the kickoff, and Washington roared back again, behind the running of Smith, two passes to Sanders, and one to Clint Didier, for another Redskins touchdown. At the end of the second quarter, Washington led 35-10. As Whittingham put it, "The Broncos ... had just suffered the ignominy of having allowed the most points ever scored in a single quarter, not just in Super Bowl annals, but in the entire history of NFL playoffs."

Super Bowl XXII was essentially over after that. Williams was named Super Bowl MVP in the 42-10 drubbing of Denver, and Sanders and Smith reaped their own laurels for their gritty offensive performances. Asked how he felt after his record-breaking day, Williams quietly replied: "When you win, everything feels fine. This is the best moment I've ever had as a player." It was indeed Williams's last great moment in the sun. Although he played parts of the 1988 and 1989 seasons, he was always plagued with injuries. He retired in 1989.

Rypien Assumes Helm

On the bench during Super Bowl XXII was a young quarterback from Washington State, Mark Rypien. Rypien (pronounced RIP-pen) spent most of the 1986 and 1987 seasons on injured reserve, but in 1988 he began to see some playing time. He was eased in as a starter after Schroeder was traded in 1988 and Williams continued to suffer injuries. It was the reserved Rypien who would lead the Skins to another Super Bowl.

The quarterback shuffle took some time to resolve itself. In 1988 Washington only managed a 7-9 record, the team's worst since Gibbs's arrival. The following season showed improvement, although the Redskins' 10-6 record did not qualify them for the playoffs. By the mid-point in 1990, Rypien had finally shrugged off the last of his injuries and was ready to contend. The Redskins again compiled a 10-6 record, earning a wild-card bid. In the wild card game, the Skins beat the Eagles 20-6, but the following week Washington bowed to the streaking 49ers, 28-10.

Rypien said he felt great at the outset of the 1991 season, and he proceeded to prove it. With the Hogs still providing him plenty of protection and the likes of Sanders, Gary Clark, and Monk on his line, he quickly established himself as a quarterback of note. The 1991 Redskins compiled a 14-2 regular season record, giving Gibbs well over 100 wins in his coaching career. Having snared the NFC East title, Washington went on to defeat the Falcons 24-7, and the Lions 41-10 to advance to Super Bowl XXVI.

Rypien and his Hogs seemed at a decided disadvantage in the Super Bowl. Their opponents—the Buffalo Bills—were returning for a second consecutive Super Bowl appearance under veteran quarterback Jim Kelly. The soft-spoken Rypien may have lacked the looks and snappy personality of a media darling, but with the Super Bowl on the line he performed in the grand tradition of Kilmer, Theismann, and Williams. Rypien completed 18 passes in 33 attempts for 292 yards and two touchdowns as the Redskins crushed Buffalo 37-24. At game's end Rypien was named Super Bowl Most Valuable Player.

The victory in Super Bowl XXVI brought many milestones to the Redskins. Gibbs's three Super Bowl wins surpassed Vince Lombardi, Don Shula, and Tom Landry in the record books and tied him with 49ers coach Bill Walsh.

Observers were quick to note, however, that no other coach in the history of the NFL had ever won three Super Bowls with three different starting quarterbacks. In addition, Gibbs' dozen seasons with the Redskins brought the team eight playoff appearances, five division titles, four NFC championships, and four Super Bowl appearances.

The 1992 season was a rocky one for Redskin fans. The defending champs, hampered by key injuries and Rypien's training camp holdout, never really got untracked. Nonetheless, Gibbs was able to guide the Redskins into the playoffs once more on the strength of a 9-7 regular season

AP/Wide World Photos

Mark Rypien (11)

record. Washington won their first-round playoff game, defeating Minnesota 24-7, but succumbed to the 49ers in the conference playoff game, 20-13. Joe Gibbs retired as head coach of the Redskins in 1993 and was replaced by his longtime defensive coordinator, Richie Petitbon.

In a time when the Washington, D.C., area has struggled with inner city crime and middle-class flight to suburbia, nothing has united the spirits of the citizenry like the Redskins. Not everyone will be happy when Cooke takes his team to a new football stadium in Alexandria, Virginia, scheduled to open by the end of the 1990s. Continued protests by Native Americans over the use of the title "Redskins" may even force management to find a new name for the franchise some day.

Whatever the future holds for the team in burgundy and gold, however, one fact is established: the Redskins have won big behind efficient coaching, a disciplined organization, and attention to fundamentals. Their future as a premier box-office draw in the mid-Atlantic states is assured.

Sources

Books

Clary, Jack, *Pro Football's Greatest Moments*, Sammis Publishing, 1985.

Nelson, Mark and Miller Bonner, *The Semi-Official Dallas Cowboys Haters' Handbook*, Macmillan, 1984.

Rambeck, Richard, *The Washington Redskins*, Creative Education, Inc., 1991.

Solomon, George, *The Team Nobody Wanted: The Washington Redskins*, Regnery, 1973.

The Super Bowl, Simon & Schuster, 1990.

Whittingham, Richard, *Sunday Mayhem: A Celebration of Pro Football in America*, Taylor Publishing, 1987.

Whittingham, Richard, *The Washington Redskins: An Illustrated History*, Simon & Schuster, 1990.

Periodicals

Sports Illustrated, January 27, 1992; February 3, 1992.

—Mark Kram

National Football Conference

Western Division

Atlanta Falcons

Not since the days of the Civil War and Generals William Sherman and Robert E. Lee had Atlanta been such a sought-after prize. Both the National Football League and American Football Leage jockeyed for position to place a franchise in the Empire City. At the time, the NFL fold numbered 14 while the AFL had eight franchises.

Both leagues were correct in their prediction that Atlanta would support professional football at its highest level. Only the NFL, however, would reap such rewards. A poll of Atlanta citizens showed that the locals overwhelmingly favored a franchise in football's senior circuit. Although the AFL had already granted a franchise to a local businessman, the NFL's franchise was given a home in Atlanta's only viable professional stadium—the newly-constructed Atlanta Fulton County Stadium.

The NFL collected immediate dividends. The Falcon franchise surpassed the league record for season ticket sales within days. In a matter of weeks, the team had to stop season ticket sales for fear of overselling the available seating. Since the franchise's first game in 1966, the Falcons have averaged more than 46,000 fans per home game.

Who knows what sort of attendance figures the Falcons could reach if their on-field product was top-flight? The team has reached the NFL post-season only four times in its 27-year history—once being after the strike-shortened 1982 season. Only twice has Atlanta been able to fly a division-championship flag over its home turf.

The Falcons have had their share of football talent. Their first-ever draft pick, University of Texas linebacker Tommy Nobis, turned into a five-time Pro Bowl selection. Defensive end Claude Humphrey earned five consecutive trips to the Pro Bowl in the early 1970's and added a sixth in 1977. Center Jeff Van Note made six Pro Bowl appearances from 1974 to 1982. His linemate, guard Bill Fralic, was named to the NFL's

Team of the 80's Second Team. Quarterback Steve Bartkowski collected a dozen 300-yard passing games. Chris Miller had eight such games in his first five full seasons. Gerald Riggs rushed for 6,631 yards in seven seasons as a Falcon and William Andrews carried for 5,986 yards in his eight seasons. Andre Rison became the only receiver in NFL history to catch 300 passes in his first four years. In 1977, the Falcons' defense set a modern NFL record by allowing just 129 points in a 14-game season.

All the while, the Falcons have struggled to find success in the standings. When they have, the Falcons have been unable to prolong their winning ways. Only six times in their first 27 seasons have the Falcons posted a winning record. On each of those six occasions, the team's encore was a below-.500 campaign.

The franchise has had a handful of headline-grabbing coaches. The Falcons' second head coach, Hall of Famer Norm Van Brocklin, brought the franchise its first measure of success with a pair of seven-win seasons (1971 and 1972) followed by a 9-5 campaign in 1973 that saw the team finish second in the NFC West. A 2-6 start in 1974 was all the front office needed to hand the volatile "Dutchman" his pink slip.

Leeman Bennett guided the Falcons' star-filled teams of the late 1970's and early 1980's to a wild-card playoff berth (1979) and the franchise's only title—the NFC West crown in 1980. Bennett was replaced, however, after the strike-torn 1982 campaign.

The 1990's saw the introduction of a dressed-in-black, Elvis Presley fan of a head coach, Jerry Glanville. Glanville had been a Falcons' defensive coach from 1977 through 1982, taking part in the 1977 NFL record performance for fewest points allowed in a season. The former Houston head coach guided the Falcons to their second wild-card finish in 1991. That team, however, was bounced from the playoffs after a first-round loss to the eventual Super Bowl champions, the Washington Redskins.

After attendance began to dip to franchise-low figures in the late 1980's, the Falcons found the cure. Making the 71,000-seat Georgia Dome their home in 1992, the Falcons set a franchise record for single-season attendance with an average home crowd of 63,566.

Alphabet Soup

Ironically, it was major league baseball that opened the door for professional football in Atlanta. When the National League's Milwaukee Braves announced in 1964 that they planned to move to Georgia, the only hurdle was a major league stadium. On April 15, 1964, Atlanta mayor Ivan Allen, Jr. presided over groundbreaking ceremonies at Atlanta Fulton County Stadium—an $18 million project that was proceeding "with money we didn't have, for teams that didn't exist," according to Allen.

With the football-fanatical South waiting for its first franchise (the AFL's Houston Oilers and the NFL's Dallas Cowboys were the closest franchises in 1964, with the Miami Dolphins joining the AFL in 1966), the construction of a stadium in Atlanta opened the door for football at its highest level. The NFL and its junior competitor, the AFL, immediately began researching the Atlanta area. The NFL did so despite an earlier timetable outlined by Commissioner Pete Rozelle, calling for expansion no sooner than 1967.

The AFL acted first, awarding an expansion franchise to J. Leonard Reinsch of the Cox Broadcasting Corporation on June 8, 1965. The NFL reacted, however, by sending public opinion pollster Louis Harris to Atlanta. The resulting Harris Poll showed that city's population preferred—by a large margin—to see an NFL expansion franchise rather than an AFL team in Atlanta. That gave the Atlanta Fulton County Stadium Authority enough ammunition to openly choose between the two professional leagues. The winner was the NFL.

On June 30, 1965, 41-year-old Rankin M. Smith, executive vice president of the Life Insurance Company of Georgia, was awarded an NFL franchise for Atlanta at the cost of $8.5 million.

Team Information at a Glance

Founding date: June 30, 1965
Home stadium: The Georgia Dome
1 Georgia Dome Drive
Atlanta, GA 30313
Phone: (404) 223-9200
Seating capacity: 70,500

Team colors: Black, red, silver, and white
Team nickname: Atlanta Falcons
Logo: Silhouette of a falcon in flight

Franchise record:	Won	Lost	Tie
(1966-1992)	150	245	5

Division titles (1): 1980

The ownership of the franchise was named "Five Smiths, Inc." in honor of Smith's five children. "Doesn't every adult male in America want to own his own football team?" asked Smith at the time. By August 29, the franchise had selected its nickname from entries in a radio station contest. Julia Elliott, a school teacher from Griffin, Georgia, was chosen from the many who suggested "Falcons." "The Falcon is proud and dignified, with great courage and fight," said Griffin. "It never drops its prey. It is deadly and has a great sporting tradition." The team logo—a long-winged falcon with outstretched talons—was designed by Wayland Moore Studios of Atlanta and remains unchanged to this day.

All that was left for the Falcons to do was sell tickets for their upcoming 1966 inaugural season.

Cashing In

It took all of 54 days for the Falcons to become a success. Monetarily, at least. The previous NFL record for season-ticket sales was held by the Minnesota Vikings with 26,000. The Falcons opened their ticket windows on November 1, 1965. Before November was over, the Falcons had surpassed the Vikings' record sales. By December 24, the front office stopped season-ticket sales which had reached an amazing 45,000. General seating tickets were selling for $6 per game with club level seats priced at $10.

In their first season, the Falcons averaged 52,017 fans per game at Atlanta Fulton County Stadium. It didn't take long, however, for ticket sales to become a reflection of on-field performance.

Expansion team failure led to a slight decline in attendance, eventually bottoming out at 37,874 per game in 1974. The team's successes—two playoff berths in three years—in the late 1970's boosted attendance to a new team record of 54,366 per game in 1979, followed by 60,957 per game in 1980.

When the team slumped in the 1980's, going eight years without reaching post-season play or a .500 record, attendance figures again dropped.

By 1987, the Falcons drew an anemic 23,727 fans per game at home—still a club record for futility.

A wild-card playoff berth in 1991 lifted attendance back up to 50,366 per game. After reaching the 50,000 mark in attendance nine times in the franchise's first 16 seasons, 1991 marked the first time in 10 years that the Falcons had drawn that well.

A new stadium, the Georgia Dome, opened in 1992, giving the Falcons what they had lacked since expansion—a drawing card that didn't depend on the team's success in the standings. An average of 63,566 fans came out to see the Falcons in 1992, despite the team's third-place finish in the NFC West with a 6-10 record. The attraction was the Georgia Dome itself, a 71,594-seat stadium, second only to Detroit's Silverdome in domed-stadium seating capacity.

Camp Run Amuck

The Falcons' first summer training camp home was a YMCA camp in Black Mountain, North Carolina. The assorted cast that would soon be sorted out to form the first-ever edition of the Atlanta Falcons included: 25 draft choices; 42 supplemental picks from the existing 14 NFL franchises; 63 free agents (bringing the total number of players in camp to 130); and a 39-year-old head coach, Norb Hecker, who had been the defensive backfield coach for Vince Lombardi's Green Bay Packers.

Alex Hawkins was drafted off the Baltimore Colts roster and became the Falcons' leading receiver in 1966 with 44 catches for 661 yards. This is how the veteran viewed the Falcons' remote training facility, which was visited by its neighbor, the Reverend Billy Graham: "Pro teams always try to locate their training camps in out-of-the-way, secluded areas, but the Falcons had outdone themselves.... The authorities had come in, cut down 300 trees, planted grass, lined the field with lime, and erected two goal posts. The rookies had been practicing for almost a week, and by now the grass was almost gone. The field itself was full of rocks and as hard as Peachtree Street. The large mountain pines on three sides of the field blocked off any possible breeze." Hawkins said that "in just a matter of days this place would be forever remembered and referred to as Camp Run Amuck."

The abilities of Hecker as a coach were suspect in the eyes of his Falcon players. The process of hiring the first coach in the team's history included talks with Paul Brown and Vince Lombardi. Both, however, wanted partial ownership of the team—something that was out of the question. In fact, when Lombardi was asked about one of his assistant coaches, Norb Hecker, he gave an unfavorable recommendation.

"Vince told (owner Rankin Smith) that Norb was not yet ready for head coaching responsibility," said Hawkins. "For Rankin Smith, that was enough; he figured that Lombardi had said that because he did not want to lose Hecker. It was a classic case of a vain and inexperienced man trying to outsmart a simple, honest one."

Hecker's record with the Falcons wound up being 4-26-1 in slightly more than two seasons. He had an expansion team's talent base with which to work. From the supplemental draft came the Falcons' inaugural-season leading rusher (Junior Coffey from Green Bay), leading receiver (Hawkins), and a defensive captain (linebacker Bill Jobko from Minnesota).

The team's initial draft produced a starting linebacker in Tommy Nobis (the Outland Trophy winner from the University of Texas), a starting cornerback in Ken Reaves of Norfolk State, and the starting quarterback, Randy Johnson of Texas A&I.

What Hecker accomplished with that expansion talent wasn't enough for him to retain his position as head coach for even three seasons. Said Hawkins, "(It was) the strangest and most ill-advised front office in the history of the NFL. Not a single one of these men was qualified for the position he held. The Falcons were well on the way to their gloomy destiny from the start. It was the blind leading the blind, as together they stumbled down a dark, dead-end street."

Abandoned By The Mascot

There has never been an expansion team that stepped right into championship cleats in its first season. The Falcons were no exception. "Our opening game was against the Rams in Atlanta," said wide receiver Alex Hawkins. "The mayor of Atlanta, the governor of Georgia, and the commissioner of the NFL were there along with 54,418 fans, to welcome the debut of the Atlanta Falcons football team. Before we took the field a live falcon was to be released in the stadium. Our mascot was to circle the field three times and land back on its trainer's perch. I watched that bird as it circled the field once, then flew out of the stadium, never to return. Our mascot had abandoned us before the first snap. It was a preview of things to come."

That first game was played on September 11, 1966. The Falcons were introduced to the NFL by the Rams with a 19-14 loss. Atlanta was also introduced to NFL-style mind games. An Associated Press report of the game stated: "Coach Norb Hecker charged today a disappointed player cut last week disclosed Atlanta's offensive plans to Los Angeles before the Falcons' National Football League debut.

"Hecker did not name the player, but Los Angeles coach George Allen admitted that former Falcon kicker Bob Jencks had talked with the Rams. 'Jencks came over to try to get a job with us,' Allen said. 'He was disappointed about being cut and he talked to Bill George a while.' George is a Los Angeles linebacker, but Allen denied knowing all about the Falcons' offense. 'If we knew what they were going to do, we wouldn't have gone down to the last minute of the game in a position to lose,' Allen said."

That was the first of nine straight losses by the expansion Falcons. A twelve-point loss was the closest they would come to victory during that losing streak. The Falcons hit bottom on October 23, when the host Green Bay Packers, the defending NFL champions, beat Atlanta 56-3.

The expansion Falcons featured: a place kicker, Wade Traynham, who injured himself on an opening kickoff by missing a ball that was sitting on a tee; a defensive back, Billy Lothridge, who had just one kidney and jeopardized his life by playing; and a rookie bonus baby, Charles Casey, who took a $100,000 signing bonus and then refused to even practice, telling Hawkins that he hated football.

The Falcons' first win came on November 20, 1966, by a 27-16 margin over the New York Giants at Yankee Stadium. This assortment of professional football players, however, managed just four wins in the franchise's first 32 games. Hecker's career as Falcon head coach lasted 31 games.

The Dutchman

On October 1, 1968, two days after losing their third straight game to open the season, the Falcons announced the firing of Norb Hecker as head coach and the hiring of Norm Van Brocklin.

The Associated Press reported: "Norm Van Brocklin, one of pro football's most colorful characters, today was given the job of building the hapless Atlanta Falcons into a National Football League contender. 'Van Brocklin has been controversial,' said Atlanta owner Rankin Smith. 'But he has one of the finest minds in pro football.' Van Brocklin, 42, has been given a long-term contract and promised a free hand in trading and drafting players, Smith said. Terms of the contract were not disclosed. The former NFL quarterback and coach of the Minnesota Vikings for six years was still at his home in Medicine Lake, Minn., when the Falcons announced the coaching change."

Ironically, a 1966 loss to the Falcons—which featured a woeful performance by then-Viking and future-Falcon quarterback Bob Berry—played a role in Van Brocklin's firing at Minnesota. The "Dutchman" had been angered by Viking quarterback Fran Tarkenton and benched the future Hall of Famer. Van Brocklin started Berry, a second-teamer, against the expansion Falcons on December 4—a day that saw temperatures across

Minnesota drop below zero and six inches of snow fall on the Vikings' field. The Falcons intercepted five of Berry's passes and went on to win for the second time in franchise history, 20-13. Van Brocklin was fired as Viking head coach after the 1966 season.

What the fiery coach brought to the Falcons was a measure of success that moved Atlanta from expansion status to that of a legitimate NFL threat. In his first full season (1969), Van Brocklin guided the Falcons to a 6-8 record. After the team took a step backwards in 1970 with a 4-8-2 mark, the Falcons won at least seven games in each of the next three seasons— something that the franchise has not been able to duplicate, despite an expanded 16-game schedule.

Atlanta's 7-6-1 record in 1971 was good for third place in the NFC West, while in 1972 (7-7) and 1973 (9-5) the Falcons finished second in their division.

The Falcons' first big step forward came in the final game of Van Brocklin's first full season. Atlanta had won two straight games going into its finale against the powerful Minnesota Vikings at Atlanta Fulton County Stadium. Minnesota would go on to be the last champion of the NFL before the league's merger with the AFL would take effect in 1970. The Vikings opened 1969 with a loss to the New York Giants, but went on to win their next 12 games before traveling to Atlanta for what seemed like a breather before the playoffs. The Falcons, however, upset the Vikings 10-3. The loss left Minnesota one win short of tying the NFL record for consecutive victories, set by the Chicago Bears in 1934.

The Associated Press reported: "A 24-yard touchdown run with a recovered fumble by defensive end Claude Humphrey gave the Atlanta Falcons a 10-to-3 upset victory over Minnesota today, ending the Vikings' hope of tying a National Football League record for consecutive wins ... Minnesota had taken a 3-0 lead on a 19-yard field goal by Fred Cox in the first period and the two teams exchanged fumbles and pass interceptions the rest of the half in an icy rain, occasionally mixed with snow and sleet. But with 25 seconds left in the half, defensive end John Zook forced Viking quarterback Gary Cuozzo to fumble at the Minnesota 24 and Humphrey, last season's defensive rookie of the year, picked up the loose ball and scampered into the end zone to give Atlanta a 7-3 halftime lead."

The Falcons flourished under the Van Brocklin because of their defensive prowess, particularly their pass defense. In their three most successful seasons under the "Dutchman" (1971-73), no NFC team allowed fewer passing yards or had a lower opposition completion percentage. In 1971, the Falcons allowed an NFL-low 1,895 yards passing on just a 47.8 completion percentage. In 1972, those figures were a solid 1,911 yards on an NFC-best 45.5 percentage. In the Falcons' 1973 campaign, they allowed NFC lows in passing yardage (1,619) and completion percentage (46.6). Meanwhile, the overall defense improved from 277 points allowed in 1971, to 274 points in 1972, to 224 points in 1973.

Falcon defensive standouts under Van Brocklin include: end Claude Humphrey, a Pro Bowl selection from 1970-74 and in 1976; end John Zook, a Pro Bowl selection in 1973; linebacker Don Hansen, who was named the Falcon Player of the Year in 1971; linebacker Tommy Nobis, who earned his fifth Pro Bowl selection in 1972; and defensive back Ken Reaves, who led the team in interceptions in 1967, 1970, and 1971.

The offense, however, was sluggish under Van Brocklin. In his first full season, the "Dutchman" replaced young Randy Johnson—the Falcons' first quarterback—with 27-year-old Bob Berry, who played under Van Brocklin in Minnesota. Berry remained the Falcons' number-one quarterback from 1969 through 1972, peaking with a 2,158-yard season in his final year in Atlanta. Only once did a Falcon receiver gain more than 700 yards in Van Brocklin's regime—Jack Snow's 859 yards in 1970.

The Falcons reached their pinnacle under Van Brocklin in 1973, winning seven consecutive games to give them an 8-3 record with three games to play. Dick Shiner, the starting quarterback during Atlanta's 1-3 start, was put on waivers and replaced by Bob Lee. The 27-year-old guided the Falcons to a 28-20 win on the New York Jets' home field on November 25, for the Falcons' seventh consecutive victory.

Back-to-back losses at home to Buffalo and St. Louis in weeks 12 and 13, however, dropped Atlanta from post-season contention. Their 9-5 record fell one game shy of the Washington Redskins in the race for a wild-card playoff spot. Falcon running back Dave Hampton finished the 1973 season with 997 yards rushing while place kicker Nick Mike-Mayer made all 34 of his extra point attempts and booted a league-best 26 field goals.

When the Falcons faltered early in 1974, losing their first three games, rumors abounded that Van Brocklin would not last long in Atlanta. Five full seasons of the "Dutchman's" stern rule had the players bristling. When the Falcons put together another three-game losing streak in mid-season, Van Brocklin felt the pressure. At one November press conference, he challenged a reporter to a fist fight.

On November 6, 1973, defensive coordinator Marion Campbell was named as Van Brocklin's replacement.

A Thousand Reasons

Falcon running back Dave Hampton was the team's top offensive threat from 1972 through 1975. The Falcons traded lineman Malcolm Snider to the Green Bay Packers after the 1971 season to obtain the second-year player. Hampton's battle with a number, however, proved to be just as challenging for the University of Wyoming product as getting around a defensive end or powering over a linebacker.

In his first season in Atlanta, a 25-year-old Hampton did what no Falcon had ever done—rushed for 1,000 yards. Earlier in the 1972 campaign, Hampton set a club record with a 161-yard game against Los Angeles in the Falcons' first win over the Rams in 11 meetings. Hampton reached the magic mark of 1,000 yards with a one-yard run around end on the second play of the fourth quarter in the season finale at Kansas City. The game was stopped. Hampton was presented the ball.

Coach Van Brocklin, however, called Hampton's number again on the Falcons' final drive of the season. This time, the Chiefs threw the Falcon runner for a six-yard loss when he fumbled a pitchout. Hampton then gained one yard on his final carry. The Falcons had lost, 17-14, and Hampton had lost his 1,000-yard distinction, finishing the season with 995 after a 65-yard game against Kansas City. He did, however, get to keep the ball.

The next season, Hampton added to his hard-luck label when it came to the 1,000-yard barrier. Carrying the ball 263 times during the Falcons' stellar 9-5 season, Hampton came up short of the individual accomplishment during the last game against the New Orleans Saints. The Falcon back finished the 1973 season with 997 yards.

When the Falcons slipped in 1974, so did Hampton. He carried the ball just 127 times for 464 yards and only two touchdowns.

At the age of 28, however, Hampton finally joined the 1,000-yard club. With 61 yards rushing in the 1975 finale versus Green Bay, Hampton pushed his season total to 1,002 yards, becoming the Falcons' first 1,000-yard rusher ... again.

Money Matters

After five years of constant ticket prices and healthy attendance figures, the Falcons decided to raise ticket prices for the 1971 season. What had been \$6 seats would now cost \$7.50. The first ticket rate hike in team history was a victim of bad timing, coming during a national wage-and-price freeze. By trying to charge more per ticket, the Falcons ended up in federal court.

The Associated Press reported on September 28, 1971: "The Justice Department filed suit yesterday against the Atlanta Falcons for allegedly violating President Nixon's wage-price freeze by raising the price of football tickets. According to a suit filed in U.S. District Court in Atlanta, regular-game admission prices were raised by $1.50 after the freeze took effect August 15. The action against the National Football League club is the third to be taken by the Justice Department to enforce the 90-day wage-price freeze.... The two previous legal actions were taken against a Louisiana school district that granted a raise to its teachers and against a Texas landlord who increased the rent on two apartments. Secretary of the Treasury John B. Connally, chairman of the Cost of Living Council, said in a statement, 'I am indeed disappointed that such a flagrant violation of the wage-price freeze should occur in the world of professional sports, which has benefitted from widespread public support. I am hopeful that the owners of the Falcons will not prolong this case and will quickly make restitution to their many loyal supporters.' The suit filed by the government maintains the team should make refund to approximately 58,000 ticket-holders."

The Falcon ticket hike was eventually allowed.

Twice The Price

Marion Campbell has the odd distinction of serving as the Falcons' head coach on two separate occasions. The odd thing about Campbell's two tenures in Atlanta is that they came more than a decade apart.

Campbell replaced Norm Van Brocklin midway through the 1974 season and continued as the Falcons' chief until five games into the 1976 season. When Dan Henning was fired after the 1986 season, the Falcons again turned to Campbell, who remained as head coach during his second term until he resigned 12 games into the 1989 campaign.

Both of Campbell's terms had one thing in common—a total lack of success in the standings. In his first term, the Falcons compiled records of 1-5 (partial season) 4-10 and 1-4 (partial season). In Campbell's second term, the Falcons went 3-12, 5-11, and 3-9 (partial season).

Campbell's lifetime record coaching the Falcons was 17-51 for a winning percentage of .250. In every season that Campbell was in Atlanta, except for one, the Falcons finished fourth in their division. The exception was 1975 when the Falcons' 4-10 record put them ahead of the 2-12 New Orleans Saints in the NFC West race.

Despite tremendous success as a defensive coordinator, Campbell, as a head coach, produced teams that were woefully inadequate at stopping—or even slowing—the opposition. In 1987, opponents marched through Atlanta for an NFL-high 436 points. In 1989, only the Phoenix Cardinals allowed more points than the Falcons' 437.

Campbell's teams were also box-office failures. Before his first term, the Falcons had four straight seasons of averaging more than 49,000 fans per home game. In 1974 (when Campbell took over in mid-season), Falcon attendance dropped to a new low of 37,858 per game. That was followed by a mark of 40,723 in 1975 and 37,874 in 1976, the year Campbell was released. With Campbell on the sidelines, December 1, 1974, there were an NFL-record 40,202 no-shows at Atlanta Fulton County Stadium as the Falcons lost, 30-7, to the Los Angeles Rams.

In Campbell's second term, Falcon attendance took another turn for the worse. In 1987, the Falcons set a franchise record that still stands by averaging just 23,727 fans per home game. That was followed by a mark of 33,477 in 1988 and 40,069 in 1989, when Campbell was fired.

In all, the six full or partial seasons that Campbell was head coach of the Falcons saw six of the eight lowest attendance figures in team history, including the two worst marks.

The Bart Man

George Kunz turned out to be an important name in the Atlanta Falcons' history. The offensive tackle from Notre Dame was a member of the Falcons from 1969 through 1974, but on the day before the January 28, 1975 NFL draft, Atlanta traded him to the Baltimore Colts. The Falcons sent Kunz and a draft choice to the Colts in exchange for Baltimore's sixth-round selection and the rights to the number-one selection in the draft.

That sixth-rounder wound up being linebacker Fulton Kuykendall of UCLA, who wore the Falcons' colors from 1975 through 1984. More importantly, Atlanta selected 6'4" quarterback Steve Bartkowski of California with the number-one pick. In Bartkowski's 11 years with the Falcons, he led the team to three playoff berths, bringing Atlanta to within one win of the NFC championship game in 1978.

By the time Bartkowski retired, he could lay claim to a dozen 300-yard passing games as well as the top 10 passing games in Atlanta history. Three times in his career, Bartkowski passed for 3,000 yards in a season. He was released by the Falcons five weeks into the 1985 season with 23,468 career passing yards.

Bartkowski's best seasons came back-to-back in 1980 and 1981, when he threw for a combined 61 touchdowns. In 1980, Bartkowski's 31 TD passes led the NFL. He followed that with a 30-touchdown performance in 1981, second only to Hall of Famer Dan Fouts' 33 touchdown passes that season.

Bartkowski spread the aerial attack around all quadrants of the field, including his wideouts, tight end, halfback, and fullback as frequent targets. In 1980, Bartkowski was blessed with Alfred Jenkins (57 receptions, 1,026 yards, 6 touchdowns), Wallace Francis (54 receptions, 862 yards, 7 TD), and Alfred Jackson (23 receptions, 412 yards, 7 TD), as wideouts. The Falcon tight end was Junior Miller (48 receptions, 584 yards, 9 TD), a 6'4", 235-pound target. Both Atlanta running backs, Williams Andrews (51 receptions, 456 yards, 1 TD) and Lynn Cain (24 receptions, 223 yards, 1 TD), were strong receivers when it came to picking up short yardage.

That core of six pass-catchers remained intact for the Falcons in 1981, and again posted formidable numbers: Jenkins (70 receptions, 1,358 yards, 13 TD); Francis (30 receptions, 441 yards, 4 TD); Jackson (37 receptions, 604 yards, 6 TD); Miller (32 receptions, 398 yards, 3 TD); Andrews (81 receptions, 735 yards, 2 TD); and Cain (55 receptions, 421 yards, 2 TD). Together they helped the Falcons' passing attack account for 3,986 yards.

Not coincidentally, the Falcons' ground game was potent in both 1980 and 1981. Complementing Bartkowski's arm were Andrews and Cain who combined for 2,222 yards rushing in 1980 and 1,843 yards in 1981.

Bartkowski directed the Falcon attack to its two most successful seasons in franchise history. In 1980, Atlanta scored 405 points, followed by a team-record 426 points in 1981. While the offense soared both years, a defensive drop-off in 1981 accounted for the Falcons tumbling from the 1980 NFC West title to a 7-9 record and second place in 1981. The Atlanta defense allowed just 272 points in the Falcons' first title season. That figure ballooned to 355 points a year later and denied the Falcons a trip to the playoffs.

Bartkowski had perhaps his finest game during a franchise-record nine-game winning streak in 1980. On October 26, at Atlanta Fulton County Stadium, Bartkowski rallied the Falcons to a 13-10 comeback victory. An improbable 54-yard touchdown pass from Bartkowski to Alfred Jackson on a third-and-38 play, came with just 1:15 left to play in the game, which turned out to be the second of nine straight Falcon wins.

One week earlier, Bartkowski had thrown for four touchdowns in a 41-14 win over the New Orleans Saints to start the streak.

On November 9 in St. Louis, with the streak in jeopardy, Bartkowski threw for a team-record 378 yards to help the Falcons pull out a 33-27 overtime victory—their fourth straight win. Bartkowski would break his own single-game yardage record a year later when he totaled 416 yards through the air against the Pittsburgh Steelers on November 15, 1981. That remains as the lone 400-yard passing day in Falcons' history. Unfortunately for the Falcons, Pittsburgh quarterback Terry Bradshaw threw for five touchdowns in a 34-20 Steeler victory.

Bartkowski's 28th, 29th, and 30th touchdown passes of the 1980 season came during a 35-10 win over Bill Walsh's San Francisco 49ers on December 14. That, coupled with William Andrews' sixth 100-yard rushing game of the season, helped the Falcons win for the ninth straight time. The win over San Francisco clinched the NFC West title—the only time that the Falcons finished first in a non-strike season.

Bartkowski made his only Pro Bowl appearances after the 1980 and 1981 seasons. The second game included a franchise-record seven Falcons: Bartkowski; offensive tackle Mike Kenn; center Jeff Van Note; guard R.C. Thielemann; Jenkins at wide receiver; Andrews at running back; and Miller at tight end.

In the Pro Bowl that followed the 1981 campaign, Bartkowski passed for a game-record 173 yards and threw a 55-yard touchdown pass to Jenkins.

A Capital "D"

A franchise that has seen numerous offensive heroes competing for headlines, the Falcons can also boast of one of the most impressive one-year defensive performances in NFL history. By allowing just 129 points during their 1977 campaign, the 7-7 Falcons set an NFL record for fewest points allowed during a 14-game schedule and earned the nickname "Grits Blitz."

The 1977 Falcons were opportunistic on defense. Their 26 interceptions and 22 fumble recoveries both led the NFC. They were strong, allowing just five rushing touchdowns all season and only 3.7 yards per carry. And the Falcons were sophisticated, confusing opposition passing attacks and allowing an NFL-best 1,384 yards through the air.

Consistency was a part of the Falcons' defensive success in 1977. Only twice did they allow more than 16 points in a game. Both were losses—21-20 to the New Orleans Saints and 23-7 to the Los Angeles Rams. In 14 games, the Falcons allowed a scant 14 touchdowns, holding the opposition to single-digit scoring seven times.

Defensive end Claude Humphrey was in the midst of his sixth Pro Bowl season at the age of 33. Defensive back Rolland Lawrence, also a Pro Bowl selection, led the Falcons in interceptions (with seven) for the third of five consecutive seasons.

Darrell Simmons of *Pro Football Weekly* reported after the Falcons' season finale: "There's never been a grin wider in celebration of a .500 season than Claude Humphrey was wearing last Sunday afternoon. But there was a lot more to the Atlanta Falcons' 35-7 victory over New Orleans than just breaking even for Atlanta. The defensive record that was at stake may have meant almost as much as the game and a 7-7 year. 'We are the best defensive team in the whole world, in the whole wide world,' said Humphrey, the defensive end who will be one of three Falcons in the Pro Bowl this season. At the beginning of the year, it looked as if Humphrey wouldn't even be a Falcon anymore. He had asked to be traded, but new Coach Leeman Bennett sold him on sticking around. And Humphrey became a key in a record season for the Atlanta defense. The record is one that will never be broken."

Simmons wasn't looking into a crystal ball. He was referring to the fact that the NFL had already planned to increase the number of games that each of its teams play—from 14 to 16—beginning in 1978. The Falcons' mark of 129 points allowed in 14 games broke the modern record set by the Minnesota Vikings of 133 in 1969. The Falcons became the kings of defense in a 14-game schedule in the last season of the 14-game schedule.

Playoff Payoff

It took 12 seasons of frustration and four head coaches before the Atlanta Falcons finally found the road to the NFL's post-season in 1978. The Falcons' 9-7 record earned them second place in the NFC West and a spot in the playoffs as a wild-card team.

The Falcons' 1978 success was buoyed by a

series of close victories and come-from-behind miracles. Seven of Atlanta's nine victories were by six points or less. The Falcons even fought through the loss of defensive standout Claude Humphrey, who retired after the fourth game of the season, and a 1-3 start.

On October 30, quarterback Steve Bartkowski went down with an injury in the second quarter of the Falcons' first nationally-televised game in four years. But back-up quarterback June Jones led Atlanta to a 15-7 upset over the NFC West's defending champions, the Los Angeles Rams. Place kicker Tim Mazzetti accounted for all of the Falcon's scoring in that game with five field goals. That win, in front of 57,250 fans in Atlanta, lifted the Falcons record to 5-4.

One of the most notable Falcon comebacks ever led to a 20-17 win in New Orleans on November 12. The Falcons actually trailed 17-6 with just 2:23 to play before beginning their rally on their own 20-yard line. An 80-yard touchdown drive cut the deficit to 17-13, but only 59 seconds remained on the clock. After the defense held, Bartkowski let loose a bomb on the Falcons' "Big Ben Right" play.

The 57-yard pass went into a cluster of players, deflected off Falcon Wallace Francis, and landed in the hands of Alfred Jackson for the winning touchdown with just 10 seconds left in the game. Two weeks later, Bartkowski threw a touchdown pass with just five seconds left, to beat the Saints, 20-17.

On December 9, Mazzetti had the chance to kick a game-winning 37-yard field goal against the Washington Redskins with no time remaining. Mazzetti's kick was wide. A Washington penalty, however, gave the 22-year-old a second chance. Mazzetti connected from 32 yards out for the Falcons' ninth win of the season.

Six days later, the Falcons clinched their first-ever playoff berth on an off-day. The Redskins lost to the Chicago Bears on December 15, closing Washington's season with an 8-8 mark. Already having won their ninth game, the Falcons were assured of a wild-card berth even before losing their season finale at St. Louis.

Atlanta hosted the 1978 NFC wild-card game between the Falcons and the Philadelphia Eagles on Christmas Eve. The Eagles were ahead, 13-0, through the first three quarters. A failed point-after by Philadelphia kicker Mike Michel would prove costly to the Eagles as Bartkowski engineered another Atlanta comeback in the game's final eight minutes. First came a 19-yard touchdown pass to tight end Jim Mitchell. Mazzetti's kick brought the Falcons to within 13-7. Then a 37-yard touchdown pass in the rain from Bartkowski to wide receiver Wallace Francis made the score even. Mazzetti's extra point gave the Falcons a one-point lead.

It wasn't until Michel missed a 34-yard field goal attempt in the final seconds that the Falcons had wrapped up the playoff win. Ironically, the Falcons fell victim to a Dallas Cowboy comeback in their NFC semifinal game, December 30, at Dallas. The Falcons led 20-13 at the half, but Dallas back-up quarterback Danny White led the Cowboys to a pair of second-half touchdowns after replacing Roger Staubach, who was injured in the first half.

The Falcons' win over Philadelphia would be one of only two Atlanta playoff wins in the franchise's first 27 seasons.

Teaching Success

Ironically, the debut of the most successful coach in Atlanta's short history, Leeman Bennett, drew little attention the day after he coached the Falcons to a 17-6 win over the Los Angeles Rams. After all, on the other sidelines stood "Broadway" Joe Namath wearing the colors of the Rams for the first time since being traded by the New York Jets.

The Associated Press reported on September 19: "Haskel Stanback and Scott Hunter scored touchdowns on 1-yard runs as the Atlanta Falcons took advantage of a punting breakdown and upset Los Angeles, 17 to 6, yesterday in Joe Namath's debut with the Rams."

That, however, was the first victory in a career that would see Bennett, a former Rams' assistant coach, lead the Falcons to their first three playoff appearances. His 46-41 record with the Falcons is more impressive when you consider that he inherited a franchise that had gone 50-100-4 in its brief history.

The Falcons gave an early indication of their future success under Bennett when they posted a 7-7 record in his first year (1977) after having tallied just 11 wins in their three previous seasons combined. That Falcon team also set the NFL record for fewest points allowed over a 14-game schedule (129).

In his second season, Bennett led the Falcons to the playoffs with a 9-7 mark. According to *The Pro Football Sports Encyclopedia*: "Bennett took his overachieving Falcons into the playoffs for the first time in their history. The defense used a lot of blitzing and came up with big plays that kept the Falcons in several close games."

After seeing the Falcons slip back to a 6-10 record in 1979, Bennett's team posted the NFL's best record (along with Philadelphia and Dallas) in 1980 with a 12-4 mark. Bennett had brought a division title to Atlanta in his fourth season at the helm.

A defensive collapse led to a 7-9 record and a second-place finish in 1981. But the Falcons rebounded in 1982 to earn a playoff berth—their third in Bennett's sixth season. A players' strike tarnished the achievement, but the Falcons were officially the NFC West champions with their 5-4 record. Atlanta traveled to Minnesota's Metrodome on January 9, 1983, for a first-round playoff game, losing, 30-24. The Falcons led from the first quarter until midway through the fourth, but Viking Ted Brown carried the ball in for a five-yard touchdown to cap a 14-point Minnesota fourth-quarter rally.

The playoff defeat became Bennett's final game as Falcon's head coach. Five days after the game, he was released after six seasons. Dan Henning, an assistant coach with the Super Bowl champion Washington Redskins, was named as Bennett's replacement on February 1, 1983.

When the Atlanta Falcons drafted a cornerback out of Florida State in 1989 named Deion Sanders, they got more than just a football player. The Falcons drafted a one-man show whose athleticism put him in the same company as Bo Jackson and Jim Thorpe. The self-proclaimed "Prime Time" decided to pursue careers in both professional football and baseball, thus grabbing headlines across the nation.

Prime Time

Already a member of the New York Yankees farm system, Sanders pointed to a full-time baseball career when contract negotiations with the Falcons slowed in 1989. A late-season call-up to New York only helped "Prime Time"'s cause. After holding out for much of September of the 1989 season, however, Sanders and the Falcons came to terms on a contract that would allow him to play both sports, with football taking precedence.

Sanders' legend blossomed as a two-sport player. Signing late with the Falcons left him only enough time to attend a Friday practice and a Saturday walk-through before his first NFL game. Nevertheless, Sanders didn't play like someone who hadn't put on football pads in seven months.

In the first quarter of the season-opener at Atlanta Fulton County Stadium against the Los Angeles Rams, Sanders returned a punt 68 yards for a touchdown. Having hit a home run earlier that week for the Yankees, Sanders thus became the only athlete to hit a home run in the majors and score a touchdown in the NFL in the same week.

On October 13, 1991, at San Francisco, Sanders returned a kickoff 100 yards for a touchdown, setting a club record and helping the Falcons hand the 49ers their only home loss of the season. Hammer, a rap star, was on the sidelines that day—the first of many 1991 Falcon games that he attended. Hammer, in fact, became the Falcons' official good luck charm in a season that brought Atlanta a wild-card playoff berth. The

Falcons adopted "Too Legit to Quit"—the title of Hammer's hit song—as their team motto, and Sanders, Andre Rison, and coach Jerry Glanville all appeared in Hammer's "Too Legit To Quit" video.

Later in 1991, the media attention that surrounded Sanders and the Falcons drew other celebrities out to Atlanta Fulton County Stadium. In the Falcons' final home game of the season on December 15, Hammer, heavyweight boxing champion Evander Holyfield, Wayne Newton, and country music group Diamond Rio were all in attendance, along with a sellout crowd.

Sanders proved, however, to be the ultimate showman. When Falcon defensive back Tim McKyer intercepted a Seattle Seahawk pass, he immediately turned and lateraled the ball to Sanders, who raced to pay dirt for a 55-yard touchdown. That play made highlight shows across the country as the Falcons won, 26-13.

By the time the 1992 football season began, Sanders had become a success in baseball. After two less-than-impressive seasons with the Yankees (.234 batting average in 1989, .158 in 1990), Sanders' rights were traded to the Atlanta Braves. "Prime Time" showed no signs of baseball excellence in 1991, batting just .191 for the National League-champion Braves.

In 1992, however, Sanders emerged as a full-fledged baseball star. He finished 1992 with an impressive batting average of .304 and a league-leading 14 triples. Sanders was a key part of a four-man outfield rotation employed by the Braves (which also included Otis Nixon, David Justice, and Ron Gant), and reworked his contract with the Falcons, making baseball his first priority.

Sanders, however, couldn't resist attempting to do what no athlete before him had done. While helping the Braves successfully defend their National League title during the week, Sanders exchanged his baseball hat for a football helmet on Sundays.

On Sunday, October 11, "Prime Time" took part in his second professional sporting event in a week. The night before, a Saturday, Sanders played for the Braves in a National League playoff game in Pittsburgh. He immediately jumped on a plane after the game, flying to Atlanta for a Sunday afternoon game against the Miami Dolphins. Sanders helped the Falcons contain Dolphin quarterback Dan Marino, denying Miami even one touchdown pass. Sanders jumped on a plane after the football game, arriving back in Pittsburgh in time for Sunday night's baseball game.

A two-sport celebrity. A popular commercial spokesman. Owner of one of the nation's flashiest fashion senses. All that aside, Sanders was a prime time football player. He led the Falcons in punt returns in each of his first three seasons, scoring two touchdowns and averaging more than eight yards per return each year.

Sanders also led the Falcons in kickoff returns in each of his first four seasons, scoring three touchdowns, including a league-leading two in 1992. From his cornerback position, Sanders tallied 17 interceptions over his first four seasons, leading the Falcons each year and scoring three touchdowns.

Elvis Has Left The Stadium

The 1990's began for the Falcons as the decade of Jerry Glanville. Hired on January 14, 1990, Glanville brought with him four years of head-coaching experience with the Houston Oilers. The Ohio native also represented a link to the Falcons' past glory, having been the Falcons' defensive coordinator from 1979 through 1982. In 1977, Glanville was the team's defensive backfield coach when they set their NFL record for fewest points allowed in a 14-game schedule.

Early in his career, as head coach of the Oilers, Glanville became a media darling. Before a pre-season game that Houston played in Memphis, Tennessee, Glanville toured the Elvis Presley estate, Graceland. Glanville decided to leave tickets for Presley at the will-call window at that night's game. The gesture has become a Glanville trademark ever since.

Glanville's eccentricities include: wearing black from head to toe; keeping a collection of

Elvis memorabilia; and having a life-size stand-up cutout of James Dean in his office. Glanville has also appeared in three music videos: Hammer's "Too Legit To Quit"; and Confederate Railroad's "She Took It Like A Man" and "Queen of Memphis." He also had a bit part in the movie "Hoffa" and is a member of the Atlanta Country Music Hall of Fame.

Glanville has backed his brashness with on-field success. In his first six years of being a head coach, Glanville's teams reached the playoffs four times. In 1991, he took the Falcons to the post-season for just the fourth time in franchise history and led the team to its second playoff victory.

The Falcons' 1991 campaign ranks as the franchise's second-most successful ever. A 10-6 record earned the Falcons second place in the NFC West, marking only the second time that Atlanta had a double-digit victory total. Finishing one game behind the New Orleans Saints, the Falcons knocked division rival San Francisco (which also finished with a 10-6 record) out of playoff contention, beating the 49ers twice during the regular season.

Glanville had installed a run-and-shoot offense in Atlanta labeled the "Red Gun." Throwing for at least 30 touchdowns in both 1991 and 1992 is a feat that no other NFL team could match. One key to the Falcons' 1991 success was the health of quarterback Chris Miller. Knocked out of the 1990 campaign with a broken collarbone and the 1992 season with an injured knee, Miller, the 13th pick overall in the 1987 draft, threw all but 87 of the Falcons' passes in 1991.

Miller's favorite targets that year were wide receivers Andre Rison (81 receptions, 976 yards, 12 touchdowns) and Michael Haynes (50 rec., 1,122 yds., 11 TD). The Falcons' passing game became all-important because of the weakness of the running attack. No Falcon rusher totaled as much as 450 yards in 1991.

One of the Falcons' biggest wins of the 1991 season came in front of an ESPN audience. In beating New Orleans, 23-20 on November 24, the Falcons were forced to score 10 points in the last two minutes of regulation to force overtime. Miller then completed a 54-yard bomb to Haynes that set up a 50-yard field goal by Norm Johnson for the overtime victory.

One week earlier, Atlanta set a franchise record with a 33-point outburst in one quarter of their 43-7 win over visiting Tampa Bay. In that game, Rison tied a team record with three touchdown receptions.

The playoffs brought about a third game with division foe New Orleans. The Saints won the first meeting, 27-6, back on September 29, but the Falcons countered with their 23-20 overtime win in November.

It turned out that the Falcons would need another comeback to earn their second playoff victory in franchise history. Playing in New Orleans, on December 28, the Falcons trailed 20-17 midway through the fourth quarter.

A 36-yard field goal by Johnson, however, tied the score at 20-20. Miller then connected with Haynes (a New Orleans native) on a 61-yard touchdown pass for the game-winning points. When cornerback Tim McKyer intercepted a Bobby Hebert pass in the game's waning moments, Atlanta had secured a trip to the NFC semifinals.

Washington, however, stymied the Falcon attack in the second-round playoff game, holding Atlanta to just 12 first downs in a 24-7 Redskin victory. Washington went on to defeat Detroit in the NFC Championship Game and Buffalo in the Super Bowl.

Sources

Books

Atlanta Falcons, 1993 Fact Book.

Cohen, Richard M., Jordan A. Deutsch and David S. Neft. *The Scrapbook History of Pro Football.* Indianapolis: The Bobbs-Merrill Company, Inc., 1979.

Hawkins, Alex. *My Story (And I'm Sticking To It).* Chapel Hill, North Carolina: Algonquin Books of Chapel Hill, 1989.

Neft, David S., Richard M. Cohen, and Rick Korch. *The Sports Encyclopedia: Pro Football 11th edition*. New York: St. Martin's Press, 1993.

The Official NFL Encyclopedia of Pro Football. New York: NAL Books, 1982.

—Bruce MacLeod

Los Angeles Rams

Those helmets. Those great helmets. Even though the Los Angeles Rams' National Football League championships have been few (two) and far between, they still have those helmets. Moreover, the club has been in postseason play more than any other team, a mark of the Rams consistency over the years, although they have been forced to deal with a "choke" label acquired over the years for losing so many playoff games.

"Rams" seems an ideal name for a football team. Players, after all, do plenty of ramming. And to have rams horns painted on the helmets seems the perfect touch. All the players look like charging rams when they barrel toward the goal line, or toward an opponent they plan to tackle or block.

It wouldn't be surprising to learn that someone's clearest and dearest memories of the early days of television sports might involve watching the Rams play. Those unique helmets were so easy to notice, although they were black and white on 10-inch TV screens, not blue and yellow on a poster-sized projection set like today. As it so happens, those early days of TV coincide with the Rams' biggest glory years, the late 1940s and early 1950s. That's when the team lived up to the glitz and glamour befitting the first NFL franchise on the West Coast, the land of palm trees and movie stars.

Magical names jump out from that era, such as Tom Fears, Elroy "Crazylegs" Hirsch, Bob Waterfield, Norm Van Brocklin, Les Richter, Tank Younger, Deacon Dan Towler, Don Paul, Andy Robustelli. There would, of course, be other great players who would become associated with the Rams, but there was something extra special about that early group.

From 1946, their first year in Los Angeles, through 1955, the Rams would finish first in their division or conference four times and second twice. In the year before their move from Cleveland, 1945, they won the championship. In 1951 the Rams won it again. It's been a dry spell since, at least as far as overall championships go.

But no one could say the squad didn't come close. In fact, no league team has had more playoff appearances than the Rams. Overall, they have made 22 trips into postseason play in their 55-year history.

From the Hirsch-Waterfield era, Rams' fans would have to wait until Coach George Allen came on the scene in the late 1960s before any real glory was to return. Excitement drifted away a little again before Chuck Knox became coach and started a new winning era, from 1973 through 1977. In 1992 he was brought back to try and restore the winning ways, which began to slip away from the sometimes-successful John Robinson.

Their first 55 years, though—including eight in Cleveland—show more victories than defeats, a 53-percent winning percentage on a record of 402-346-20. That may seem just a bit above mediocrity, but there have been plenty of great players and great moments in the team's history.

Fifteen Rams have earned enshrinement into the NFL Hall of Fame in Canton, Ohio, including owner Dan Reeves (1967) and Coach Sid Gillman (1983). Others accorded the honor, who spent at least some time with the Rams, are: Waterfield (1965), Hirsch (1968), Fears (1970), Robustelli and Van Brocklin (1971), Ollie Matson (1972), Dick "Night Train" Lane and Bill George (1974), David "Deacon" Jones (1980), Merlin Olsen (1982), Joe Namath and executive Pete Rozelle (1985), and executive Tex Schramm (1991). The Rams have retired two numbers, Waterfield's 7 and Olsen's 74.

"Waterfield could do it all," said *Petersen's 1971 Pro Football Annual*. "He punted beautifully, placekicked with the best, played well as a defensive back, and also was the best prober of defenses and strongest leader the Rams ever had." He once slugged a running back in the jaw in the huddle, the magazine said, because the player vetoed a Waterfield play once too often.

Perhaps the most significant achievement by the Rams in all their years was simply that Reeves challenged the NFL hierarchy in the first place by bringing a team from the Midwest to the West Coast when no major league sports franchise ever had tried it. It opened the floodgates for other sports leagues moves and expansion that to this day have proved healthy for franchisees' bank accounts and a boon to sports fans everywhere.

As *Petersen's 1971 Annual* noted, "It was, of course, the original gamble by Reeves...that inspired the remaking of the map in professional sports—not only in football, but in everything else, as well." Wellington Mara, president of the New York Giants, said in that article: "Dan broke the barrier. I very well remember sitting in at the league meetings with my father and brother when Dan had to overcome the severest of opposition from all sides, particularly the Giants, in order to get permission to make the move."

The Move Westward

Of course, when Reeves decided to move the Rams from Cleveland, the team's Ohio fans also were less than thrilled. After all, their Rams had just won the NFL championship for the first time since local businessman Homer Marshman was granted the franchise on February 12, 1937. There had been a team in Cleveland belonging to the rival American Football Association, founded in 1921. That club was known as the Indians and would not enjoy the same esteem as the Rams.

When Marshman was awarded his NFL franchise, he and General Manager Buzz Wetzel endeavored to settle on a nickname. "There is one college team that has a name I really like," Wetzel said. "The Fordham Rams." Marshman, according to *Great Teams' Great Years: Los Angeles Rams*, agreed immediately, saying, "That's wonderful. That's what we'll call them. The Rams."

Besides, Wetzel knew it would fit easily in newspaper headlines, an important consideration when the nation was still climbing out of the Great Depression and sports teams wanted any publicity they could get.

Team Information at a Glance

Founding date: 1937 (Cleveland) ;1946 (Los Angeles)

Home stadium: Anaheim Stadium
2327 West Lincoln Ave.
Anaheim, CA 92801
Phone: (714) 535-7267
Seating capacity: 69,008

Team colors: Royal blue, gold, and white
Team nickname: Rams
Logo: Rams horns

Franchise record:	Won	Lost	Tie
(1937-92)	403	344	19

Super Bowl appearances (1): 1979

Unfortunately, Coach Hugo Bezdek's team finished with a 1-10 record. Assistant coach Art Lewis took over from Bezdek three games (all losses) into the 1938 season. He was able to coax three victories out of the final seven games. Then all-time great Detroit Lions quarterback Earl "Dutch" Clark became head coach in 1939 and kept Lewis on as his assistant. With the help of rookie tailback Parker Hall of Purdue, Clark guided the Rams to a 5-5-1 record. Hall got the Joe Carr Trophy as the NFL's Most Valuable Player.

The 1940 Rams slipped a bit, to 4-6-1, but fullback Johnny Drake became their first all-league player. Then, in 1941, Reeves and Fred Levy, Jr., bought the club from Marshman and his syndicate in June for $125,000, installing Billy Evans, a former sports columnist and American League umpire, as general manager.

The 1941 opener was in the Rubber Bowl in Akron, Ohio, against Pittsburgh. Rams halfback Dante Magnini caught the opening kickoff and returned it all the way for a touchdown. Levy pounded Reeves on the back and exclaimed, "Is it this easy?"

It wasn't. The Rams won that game, and the next, then lost their last nine to finish in the cellar. Evans resigned before the 1942 season and Charles Walsh replaced Lewis as assistant coach. World War II had begun and both owners entered the Army, Reeves as a lieutenant and Levy as a major. The team finished with a 5-6 record, good for third place in the five-team Western Division.

1943 saw Clark resign, Walsh become coach, and the Rams receive permission from the league to suspend operations because of wartime difficulties in fielding a competitive team. Reeves, meanwhile, bought out Levy. Walsh had to be content with a 0-0 coaching record for, in 1944, he became general manager and appointed Buff Donelli as coach. The Rams managed a 4-6 record, not good enough for Donelli to keep his job. Walsh named his brother Adam as Donelli's successor in 1945 and Donelli entered military service.

The previous year the Rams had drafted Waterfield as a future pick out of UCLA. He joined the squad in 1945 as a T-formation quarterback and led the Rams to a 9-1 season and their first divisional title. On an icy field in Cleveland they nipped the Washington Redskins 15-14 for the "world championship." Washington quarterback Sammy Baugh was the victim of a strange play in that contest. The Rams got a safety when Baugh, throwing from his own end zone, hit the goal post upright and a Ram pounced on it for a safety and two points. Waterfield became the first player to receive a unanimous vote as the league's MVP, Walsh was named Coach of the Year—and the business lost $50,000.

Climbing on board that year, the first of a 29-year tenure, was business manager Bill John. He was the person responsible for softening the frigid field at Municipal Stadium for the title game. He did it by buying enough straw to fill six boxcars and part of a seventh. It worked out well, although he still had most of the straw when it was determined the team would be moving to Los Angeles. He tried to sell a bale or two at a time to stables and farmers. "I thought I'd never see California," he said. "But eventually a circus came to town and bought me out."

Tom Fears

Reeves didn't just snap his fingers, though, and move the team. There were obstacles to surmount, namely other team owners who weren't enamored with the prospects of having a team move so far away from everyone else. At one point in the league meeting Reeves stalked angrily out of the room, followed by some other owners.

"I remember how strongly he felt about the West Coast," recalled Art Rooney, the late president of the Pittsburgh Steelers. "Some of the owners, including myself, reacted to a West Coast franchise as if Indians were still lurking on the other side of the Mississippi. Dan clinched the deal when he offered to pay, out of his own pocket if necessary, $5,000 over the existing guarantee when NFL teams played against his team on the Coast."

Convincing the officials at the 101,296-seat Memorial Coliseum in Los Angeles to let his club play there was the next step. Originally built for the 1932 Olympic Games, the Coliseum had long been considered a sanctuary for amateur sports. The University of Southern California and UCLA, along with the other members of the Pacific Coast Conference, were not enthusiastic about sharing their turf (and ticket-buying public) with a professional team.

Reeves enlisted the help of influential Redskins owner George Preston Marshall and they persuaded Coliseum authorities to allow the Rams to play there by agreeing to have funds from an exhibition game against Washington benefit Los Angeles Times Charities Inc. Still, USC and UCLA only had to pay the Coliseum operators 10 percent of their gate. The Rams had to pay 15 percent.

"The first season of 1946 was a nightmare in Los Angeles," wrote an analyst in *Petersen's 1971 Annual*. "USC and UCLA, the two colleges which considered the Coliseum their exclusive playground, fought the invasion of the pros. The fans were cool to the NFL, figuring it was still a back-alley sideshow. Reeves didn't waver. He was ready to go all the way with the family fortune—$11 million realized from the sale of his father's grocery chain to Safeway."

After early reversals, the Los Angeles Rams hit with a roar, became world champions in 1951 and the electricity of the Bob Waterfield-Norm Van Brocklin-Elroy Hirsch-Tom Fears-Tank Younger-Dan Towler scoring machines of the early 1950s captivated the town. Suddenly, professional football's first 100,000-plus crowds were jamming the Coliseum. Now the whole world was watching.

Besides prominent college teams, the Rams found themselves in competition in Los Angeles with the Dons, a team in the new All-American Football Conference. To bolster their image, the Rams acquired such players as Tom Harmon, the superstar Heisman Trophy winner from Michigan who, as a pilot in the war, was shot down by a Japanese fighter plane over China. (He would write a book about it, *Pilots Also Pray*. He married actress Elyse Knox and became a Los Angeles sportscaster after his football career ended.)

The Rams also signed former UCLA All-American Kenny Washington and Woody Strode, the first African-American players in the NFL since 1933. Washington was a UCLA teammate of Jackie Robinson, who broke baseball's color barrier in 1947, a year after Washington did it in the NFL. There were stories that Washington could consistently throw a ball 60 yards.

One of the wedges Reeves used to gain use of the Coliseum was to sign Washington, who already was 28. The NFL had an unwritten "no blacks" rule and anti-Rams factions could point to that as a reason the Coliseum shouldn't allow them to use the facility. Bob Snyder, the backfield coach who signed Washington, said "all hell broke loose" among the owners, but Reeves had them over a barrel.

"When all those NFL people began thinking about all those seats and the money they could make filling 'em, they decided my kind wasn't so bad after all," Washington said. Strode, who later became an actor, was a UCLA teammate of his and became his roommate. Washington rushed for 859 yards in his two years, averaging 6.14 a carry. "While I was with the Rams we had three Heisman Trophy winners," Snyder recalled, "Les Horvath, Tom Harmon, and Glenn Davis. He was better than all three. There's no comparison."

Emil Sitko, an All-American running back from Notre Dame, was their Number 1 draft choice, but he signed with the AAFC. But the Rams did secure Fred Gehrke as a halfback, Jim Hardy as a backup quarterback, and Fred Naumetz as a center and linebacker.

Over in Cleveland, the Browns took up the gauntlet thrown down by the Rams' departure and established themselves as the standout team of the rival AAFC. The Browns won the title in 1946, beating the New York Yanks 14-9 in the championship game. The Rams, meanwhile, found themselves in second place in their division of the NFL with a mediocre 6-4-1 record. Waterfield wasn't mediocre, though, completing 127 of 251 passes for 1,747 yards and 18 touchdowns. End Jim Benton caught 63 passes for 981 yards.

Before that season started, the Rams lost to the College All-Stars 16-0 in Chicago, with Elroy Hirsch one of the college heroes. In an article entitled "A Game I'll Never Forget" in the July-August 1972 issue of the *Football Digest*, Hirsch said: "Like a lot of other guys, I had spent the last few years wearing a different kind of uniform.... After a couple years away from the game (in military service), away from the top competition, you have to wonder if you can still do it, if you've still got that something, whatever it was, that made you. I was scared. I've never been more scared."

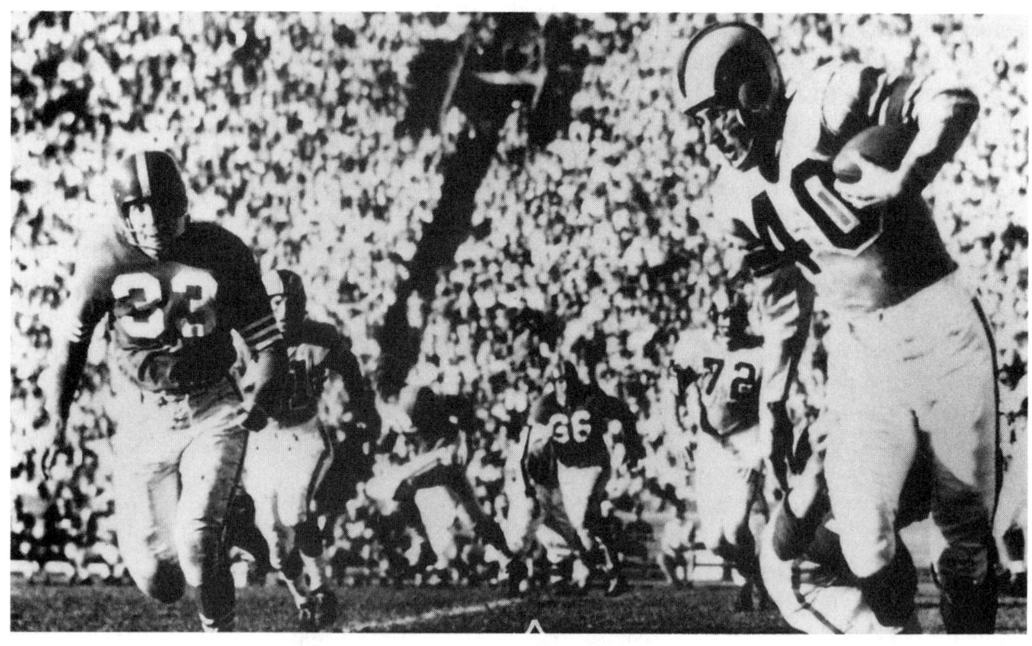

Elroy "Crazylegs" Hirsch (40)

Hirsch had one long touchdown run and caught a TD pass from Otto Graham for another score. Hirsch would later ignore the Rams, who drafted him, and sign on with the AAFC's Chicago Rockets and play with them for three years. He didn't join the Rams until 1949.

"I had to prove to myself that I could make it with the best and prove to the Rams that they shouldn't have let me get away," he said. When he finally hooked up with LA, he was converted from halfback to wide receiver. "I wasn't really crazy about it at first. ... But finally I started to get the hang of shaking loose real fast."

According to a story in *GameDay*, Hirsch honed his running skills by racing through the woods "aiming straight for the trees," Hirsch said, "then cut as close to a tree as possible. It's amazing what fear can make you do. I never hit a single tree, and I picked up some pretty good moves."

The 6-4-1 record in 1946 prompted Chile Walsh to fire his brother, Adam. Then he himself was given the sack by Reeves, who assumed the GM duties in 1947. Snyder was named head coach and Joe Stydahar came on as a new assistant. The team was talent-laden, but injury riddled. It wound up 6-6. Reeves sold part interests to former partner Levy, to Edwin and Harold Pauley, and to Hal Seley. The new investors agreed to shoulder a proportionate share of the losses and in the process got one of the best bargains in sports history. For $1, Pauley bought 30 percent of the stock.

All-American halfback Herman Wedemeyer of St. Mary's was drafted by the Rams, but chose to play for the Dons. The preseason game against Washington drew a pro football record of 80,889. In the regular season, Waterfield led the offense, Harmon was a star defensive back and the defensive line standout was 250-pound tackle Dick Huffman.

Snyder "is remembered as the coach whose personal instruction turned Waterfield into one of the game's great quarterbacks," wrote Steve Bisheff in *Great Teams' Great Years: Los Angeles Rams*. In an early preseason game that was going badly in 1948, however, Snyder told his minions at halftime, "There had better be a change this second half or some of the guys in this room will not be here tomorrow." The next day, Snyder was fired.

"It was to become a pattern for the professional football team in Los Angeles," Bisheff said. "Except for the all-winning years of 1949-55, this was an organization beset by controversy and change. The tone was established, in fact, before the club even moved west."

Clark Shaughnessy was named head coach September 3. Some consider him the originator of the flanker position. In the second game of the season, the Rams trailed Philadelphia 28-0 with 16 minutes left. But Waterfield threw four TD passes and kicked four extra points for a 28-28 tie.

The team lost four of its next five before winning four of the last five to end up 6-5-1. Hardy, subbing for an injured Waterfield, set a club passing record of 406 yards in a 27-24 loss to the Chicago Cardinals. Benton had retired, but rookie Fears picked up his mantle and led the league with 51 catches for 698 yards. Linebacker Paul of UCLA was another prominent rookie.

The Rams lost $250,000 and only kept afloat by virtue of the new partners, who absorbed the losses. The team averaged 34,000 spectators—about 7,000 fewer than the Dons. Syndicated columnist Jim Murray wrote that the league warned Reeves that "everybody went to the beach on Sunday in California," which, of course, wasn't really the case.

1949 was a superb, yet bittersweet, year for the Rams. They won their first six games, but went 2-2-2 the rest of the way, yet edged the 9-3 Chicago Bears for first in the West. Rookie Van Brocklin had joined the team and shared quarterback duties with Waterfield.

"I used Waterfield to test the defenses and set things up for the big play," Shaughnessy said. "Then I'd put the kid (Van Brocklin) in and with that great arm he'd throw the bomb and get all the applause. But Bob was a real pro. He didn't care for the situation, but he helped make it work. He was a real pro. He didn't depend on cheers for his satisfaction."

Another rookie that season was the University of Wisconsin's Hirsch, fresh from the AAFC. Also prominent were running backs Verda "Vitamin T" Smith of Abilene Christian and Tank Younger, from the then little-known Grambling College. Washington State defensive back Jerry Williams also was one of Shaughnessy's top players.

The NFL championship, however, wasn't to be theirs. Heavy rains held down the crowd to 27,980 and hurt the Rams' attack in a 14-0 title game loss to persistent nemesis Philadelphia. Fears repeated as the top pass catcher in the league, with 77 receptions for 1,013 yards and nine touchdowns. A controversy started brewing, however, because of the shared quarterbacking between superstar Waterfield and budding superstar Van Brocklin.

The NFL Expands

As the 1950s began, the NFL absorbed three AAFC teams. The Dons weren't one of them, but the Cleveland Browns, who had filled the gap caused by the Rams' departure from Ohio, were added, along with the Baltimore Colts and San Francisco 49ers.

Meanwhile, the Rams front office remained an unpredictable one. Although he was considered very innovative, Shaughnessy was fired because of "internal friction" within the organization. Stydahar, 39, took his place and appointed Hampton Pool, Mel Hein, and Howard "Red" Hickey as assistants.

Glitz and glamour still were at the forefront of the owners minds when acquiring players. The Rams secured the services of Army superstar back Glenn Davis, the famed "Mr. Outside" Heisman Trophy winner who had teamed at the Academy with "Mr. Inside," Doc Blanchard. End Bob Boyd, a local player from Loyola of Los Angeles joined the club as well. In addition, the Rams added defensive back Woodley Lewis, halfback Towler, and middle guard Stan West to the roster. In 1950 the Rams became the first NFL team to have all its games, home and away, televised. It reversed policy the next year and only televised away games so as not to hurt ticket sales.

With so many weapons, Los Angeles piled up points at a stunning rate, including 70 against Baltimore and 65 against Detroit. Fears caught an NFL single-game record of 18 passes. The Rams rung up six consecutive victories en route to a 9-3 record to tie the Bears for first in the National Conference, setting 22 league records in the process, scoring 466 points and 64 TDs. The club also racked up 3,709 yards passing and 1,711 rushing.

Los Angeles beat the Bears 24-14 in a playoff game. Then the Browns, who had something to prove to the folks in Cleveland, won a classic championship game 30-28 on Christmas Eve on a Lou Groza field goal in the closing seconds and four touchdown passes by Otto Graham. The game featured an 82-yard scoring pass from Waterfield to Davis on the first play from scrimmage. Dick Hoerner scored on two short runs and defensive end Larry Brink ran six yards for a touchdown on a recovered fumble to account for the Los Angeles scoring.

Cleveland coach Paul Brown called it "the greatest game I had ever seen" because of the aerial exhibition by both teams. The Browns had Max Speedie, Dante Lavelli, and Dub Jones as star receivers, while the Rams countered with Fears, Hirsch, and Davis. Waterfield completed 18 of 22 for 312 yards and a TD. Graham hit on 22 of 33 passes, with 11 of the strikes going to Lavelli, who scored two touchdowns. "Both teams had shown all of football that there was a new way to play the game," according to *The First 50 Years: The Story of the NFL.*

It was another great year for Fears, who led the NFL with 84 catches for 1,116 yards and seven TDs. What did players like Fears make in those days? "Our salaries were fair because a lot of teams weren't making any money," he said in *Great Teams' Great Games.* "Do you know that an established star back then was lucky to be drawing five figures. I don't think there was anyone in the league making $20,000, unless it was Otto Graham or someone like that."

Van Brocklin led the passers in that near-miss title year, getting 127 completions in 223 attempts for a team-record 2,061 yards and 18 touchdowns. The team's success earned Stydahar a three-year contract and he would begin the tenure with the Rams' first—and only—NFL championship in Los Angeles.

He kept the players happy and Pool devised ways to utilize their offensive strengths. As a result the Rams continued with their winning ways in 1951. Draftees included defensive end Andy Robustelli, defensive back Norb Hecker, linebacker Dick Daugherty, and tackle Charley Toogood. In an exhibition game, Towler and Younger joined Hoerner in what was known as the "Bull Elephant" backfield. Towler weighed 225 pounds and the others were 220 each.

When Towler joined the Rams he heeded the advice of his Grambling coach, soon-to-become-legendary Eddie Robinson, who told him to run 30-35 yards with the ball in practice plays, instead of 10 like everyone else. "The longer you have the ball under your arm, the longer the man is watching you," Robinson said, as noted in *The Golden Age of Pro Football: A Remembrance of Pro Football in the '50s.*

Hirsch and Fears remained the main targets of Waterfield and Van Brocklin, who set an NFL record by passing for 554 yards in a 54-14 victory over the New York Yanks in September. Hirsch caught four of his scoring passes as he again led the NFL, totaling 66 receptions for 1,495 yards. Waterfield took over the passing leadership from Van Brocklin, going 88-for-176 for 1,566 yards and 13 touchdowns. The team amassed more yards, 5,506, than any in NFL history. They wound up with a division-best 8-4 record, edging the Lions and San Francisco 49ers by a half game for the division crown.

A rift developed in the final game of the season, however, at home against Green Bay. Stydahar benched Van Brocklin, who refused a play from his coach from the sidelines. Waterfield went in the rest of the way, passing for five touchdowns and 256 yards to nip Van Brocklin for NFL season passing honors. Later, the coach and Van Brocklin got in a shouting match, so Waterfield quarterbacked the first 50 minutes of the playoff game against Cleveland.

With the game tied 17-17, Van Brocklin was sent in, threw a 73-yard scoring pass to the double-teamed Fears, and the Rams won 24-17 for their first championship since moving west. Hoerner and Towler scored on one-yard plunges and Waterfield kicked a 17-yard field goal in the game to account for the rest of the Rams' scoring. The game was the first to be televised coast-to-coast. The Dupont Network paid $75,000 for the broadcast rights.

The 300-pound Stydahar didn't have much time to savor the title. The following season the team lost three straight preseason games and lost the regular season opener by a big score, prompting his resignation and earning a promotion for the innovative Pool. Stydahar had grown weary of a serious rift with Pool and brought his concerns to Reeves, only to lose out in the squabble.

Los Angeles lost two of the next three games after its season opener, but won the last eight to tie for the conference championship, only to lose 31-21 to Detroit in a playoff. Van Brocklin succeeded Waterfield as the top quarterback in the league and Towler became the first Ram to finish first in rushing, with 894 yards.

Waterfield announced his retirement after the season and Rozelle, sports information director at the University of San Francisco, was hired to the team's public relations staff. He would eventually become the commissioner of the league. Also in 1952, the Rams drafted Vanderbilt quarterback Bill Wade and guard Duane Putnam from College of the Pacific. Other new additions included local star Skeet Quinlan of San Diego State and free agent defensive back Dick "Night Train" Lane.

The Rams shook the football world with a blockbuster trade, too, sending 11 players to the Dallas Texans, including Hoerner, for the rights to linebacker Richter, who then, along with Wade, entered military service for two years.

In 1953 Pauley died and the Rams' No. 1 draft choice, All-American linebacker Donn Moomaw of UCLA, chose to go into the ministry instead. Among the newcomers was rookie quarterback Rudy Bukich from Southern Cal, linebacker Harland Svare from Washington State, and a massive defensive tackle from Detroit who didn't go to college, Gene "Big Daddy" Lipscomb. The Rams finished the season with an 8-3-1 record, beating world champion Detroit twice, but finished third in the West. The losses were by a total of eight points.

Van Brocklin won the passing title for the third time in five years when he set an NFL record in 1954 with 139 completions in 260 passes for 2,637 yards. But the team's record skidded to 6-5-1. Hirsch retired. All Pool's assistants resigned and soon he did, too.

In *Great Teams' Great Years: Los Angeles Rams* Pool talked about the team's reputation that earned it the nickname, "Hollywood Rams": "I'll tell you this much: They were far from playboys. We got that reputation because so much of the scoring was done the easy way—with bombs, reverses, fake runs and passes, etc. We had a flashy style, sure. But then, the main thrust of our offense was passing, so we had to do things in a way which would best utilize the talents of the players we had."

In January 1955, the Rams hired Gillman, head coach at the University of Cincinnati, to replace Pool. Hirsch was talked out of retirement for a year. A fine defensive season and clutch field goal kicking by Richter gave the Rams an 8-3-1 record and the conference championship. Rookie Ron Waller led the team in rushing with 716 yards. Other top newcomers were linebacker Larry Morris and defensive back Don Burroughs.

A record crowd of 85,693 attended the championship game against perennial rival Cleveland. The Browns intercepted seven Rams passes, six thrown by Van Brocklin, en route to a 38-14 victory. It was the final game for Browns' superstar QB Graham. As if the loss wasn't enough, problems developed that year among the team owners and Reeves' old friend Levy switched his support. Reeves was relieved as the franchise's director. Towler retired as well after a fine career in which he amassed a club-record 3,493 yards and a 5.2 average per carry.

Lean Years

In the mid-1950s the Rams were poised on the cusp of an inauspicious period in the franchise's history. The Rams of 1956 were about to begin a skid, interrupted briefly by an 8-4 mark in 1958, that would hit bottom in 1962 with a 1-12-1 record and last until George Allen's arrival in 1966.

1956 featured a new quarterback controversy when Wade received more playing time at the expense of Van Brocklin. Fears, Quinlan, and Toogood retired and Lipscomb was sent to Baltimore for the $100 waiver price. He would become a star with the Colts. The Rams lost five in a row early and ended up in the cellar at 4-8. A defensive tackle, Bud McFadin, had his career interrupted by a near-fatal gunshot wound in Texas.

Club owners named Rozelle general manager in 1957 succeeding Schramm, who went to CBS-TV after 11 years with the Rams. When Rozelle was inducted into the Hall of Fame, he recalled his beginnings with the Rams, when his ambition was to become a sports editor. Publicity director Maxwell Stiles hired him in 1946 for $50 a game (and four free tickets) to edit the programs.

The 1957 Rams team lost some close games en route to a 6-6 record, but with such new players as halfback Jon Arnett and defensive back Del Shofner, things looked promising. The 49ers-Rams game in November at the Coliseum drew an NFL-record 102,368 spectators. LA won 37-24. For the season, including exhibitions, the Rams played before more than one million fans. Attendance for its home games reached 711,924. It was easy to see that Reeves was right to believe football would go over big in Los Angeles.

Hirsch, perhaps the most popular Ram, retired for the second time. He tried it once before and after his "final game" he was mobbed as he left the field. By the time he got to the locker room all he had left on was his athletic supporter.

The Rams would rebound in 1958 to 8-4 behind the passing of Wade, the running of Arnett, and the receiving of Shofner, who was switched to offense. Among the victories was a 41-35 decision over Chicago before 100,470 at home that featured an all-purpose yardage day of 298 for Arnett. For the year Wade hit on 181 of 341 passes for 2,875 yards, only 63 yards short of Baugh's NFL record. Shofner caught 51 and averaged 21 yards a catch. Van Brocklin, who briefly retired after the 1957 season, was traded to the Eagles.

Injuries contributed to a 2-10 season in 1959, the Rams' worst since their 1937 Cleveland debut. Ollie Matson, acquired for nine players from the Cardinals, was the workhorse at fullback, gaining 837 yards. New draft picks who were to

Matson Magic

When the Rams acquired halfback Ollie Matson from the Chicago Cardinals in exchange for nine players in 1959, they probably still were getting the best of the deal. He only played four years for the Rams, but he was a sensational player and drawing card. In 1972 he was inducted into the Pro Football Hall of Fame in Canton, Ohio.

Matson arrived in the NFL from the University of San Francisco, where he had been an All-American. He was fresh from the 1952 Olympics, where he finished third in the 400 meters and also had run on the relay team. At 6' 2", 208 pounds, he was unlike almost any back the league had ever seen because he could run the 100-yard dash in 9.6 seconds, a sensational time for the era and for a person of his size.

After leaving the game, Matson turned to a career as a high school football coach.

become standouts were defensive back Ed Meador and running back Joe Marconi. On the last day of the season, Gillman and his staff resigned and he went on to success at San Diego of the AFL.

During his term, the Rams "kept discarding heroes as fast as they were grown—Red Phillips, Del Shofner, Jon Arnett," wrote Mickey Herskowitz in *The Golden Age of Pro Football*. Three quarterbacks were traded away who went on to win titles elsewhere: Van Brocklin, Wade, and Frank Ryan.

The Rams lost their general manager as Rozelle, a compromise candidate on the 23rd ballot, succeeded the late Bert Bell as NFL commissioner on January 26, 1960. Hirsch became Los Angeles' GM and Bob Waterfield came to the rescue (folks thought) as the new coach, "but the most popular of all Ram players was to become the least popular of all Ram coaches," reported *Fawcett's 1963 Pro Football* magazine. Fears, Pool, and Paul were among his assistants.

The following year was one of bad trades, bad recruiting and bad judgment, according to *Fawcett's*. The team finished 4-7-1. The Rams lost more than a lot of games. They also lost their top draft choice, Heisman Trophy-winning halfback Billy Cannon of Louisiana State, to the upstart American Football League. The case went to court and Cannon was ruled the property of the AFL's Houston Oilers.

A trade sent Wade to the Bears for quarterback Zeke Bratkowski. Shofner was also traded away. Two players were sent to the New York Giants for defensive back Lindon Crow and a first draft choice, which turned out to be North Carolina State's prized quarterback Roman Gabriel. The team still struggled, finishing 4-10.

"In 1961, the Rams could not brag of great coaching, of a superior front office, or even high morale," wrote Arnold Hano in an article headlined "The Rams—Football's Most Fouled Up Team," in the 1962 *Pro Football Stars* magazine. "Coaches squabble. The front office feuds. The players backbite." Halfback star Arnett said at least 10 Rams weren't NFL caliber, according to Hano, and Hirsch was the "real power behind the Rams." Everyone had an opinion as to the nature of the team's difficulties. "It's not our morale that is ruining our play," one player said. "We're ruining our morale. Once we start winning we'll smile."

Reeves Ousted

In January 1962, businessmen Levy and Hal Seley and oil tycoon Ed Pauley deposed Reeves as president of the Rams by pooling their shares. Pauley, who owned just under 31 percent, became the new president. Bob Hope owned 11.2 percent, with Levy voting Hope's stock. Hirsch was accepted by both disparate groups.

The result of the split, Hano wrote, was "a dispirited ball club playing below its potential to ever-dwindling crowds. Los Angeles fans are historically the most knowing, most critical and most fanatical of all football spectators. Through league history they have also been the most numerous."

Four of the first five losses early in 1962 were narrow, but losses just the same, and the team plunged to 1-12-1. Waterfield resigned after the eighth game and Svare became interim coach. "I'm not concerned with troubles this club has had in the past or mistakes it has made," Svare said when he got the job. "I'm not concerned that I have only a one-year contract. In this league, you try to win every ball game, right here and now, anyway. I have the job for a year and if I do it well, in my own way, the future will take care of itself."

Fullback Dick Bass became the first Ram to rush for 1,000 yards, gaining 1,033. In the backfield with him were Arnett, Matson and Bratkowski. Despite the poor showing of the Rams, Arnett was still considered one of the more exciting players in the league.

Two days after Christmas, Reeves reacquired control of the Rams, buying full interests of co-owners Pauley, Levy, Seley, and Bob Hope in a sealed-bid process. Reeves now owned 51 percent and had 11 minority partners. Before the bids were submitted, Reeves, in a ploy, told the press he thought the value of the club was between $4 million and $4.5 million. His partners bid $6.1 million and he bid $7.1 million.

The low bidder had the option of raising its bid by 20 percent within 30 minutes, but that would have meant they'd have to pay $8.6 million for a franchise they figured (by Reeves reckoning) was worth only $4.5 million, tops. They came in the room without an intention of raising the bid, grinning over the belief that Reeves had just agreed to pay $1.6 million more than the Rams were really worth. It was what Reeves hoped would happen.

The Rams tried to rebuild through the draft that season, getting such players as defensive tackle Merlin Olsen from Utah State and Notre Dame tackle Joe Carollo. Olsen, a 6-foot-5, 270-pounder, would become a superstar and mainstay for 15 years. Said Cleveland All-Pro guard Gene Hickerson, in 1970, "The only man in pro football who really scares me is Merlin Olsen."

Svare, 32, had replaced Paul as defensive line coach before being promoted to head coach, whilst Waterfield went back to his movie star wife Jane Russell. For a time, Glenn Davis competed with Waterfield for Hollywood headlines, keeping the Rams' flashy image intact by courting another beautiful movie star, Elizabeth Taylor.

Fawcett's said that from a record average of 83,000 fans a game a couple years earlier, the Rams had fallen to about 42,000 a game in 1962, "most of whom sat on their hands and yawned through dreary defeats.... Football's finest franchise, playing in its most spacious stadium, has hit rock bottom."

On Reeves' battle to control the team, the publication said, "Maybe he just liked to have his pals around. In the ensuing years, his pals almost got a noose around his neck. They took equal control and turned policy meetings into grand debates. The Ram ship floundered, rudderless. They came finally to fight it out in the back rooms, newspapers and courts until this past winter when they were persuaded to settle the issue in sealed bids. Everyone, including the players and press who were sympathetic to the Reeves cause, assumed the wealthy Pauley would win."

In 1963, Reeves sold 49 percent interest in the club to Gene Autry, Bob Reynolds, Leonard Firestone, Paul A. O'Bryan, Robert Lehman, J.D. Stetson Coleman, and Joseph A. Thomas. Svare was retained before the season started and Richter retired. The Rams lost their first five games before Gabriel was installed at quarterback. He went the rest of the season without relief, guiding the team to a 5-4 record, for a 5-9 overall slate.

Fourteen rookies made the 1964 team, which finished 5-7-2, mostly behind the quarterbacking of a first-round draft pick, Bill Munson. Then the 1965 team won just one of the first 10 before winning three of the last four as Gabriel resumed the starting job for an injured Munson. But the late push wasn't enough to save Svare's job.

Commented *Fawcett's*, "Coaching the Rams has been tantamount to being one of Tommy Manville's wives," referring to the man who at one time held the record for most marriages. "The pay is good, but not the security, and it ruins your reputation."

George Allen Takes the Helm

After a court fight, George Allen was released from his assistant coach position with the Bears and hired in 1966 to coach the Rams. The NFL and AFL merged in the spring. Bob Kelley, the Rams' play-by-play radio broadcaster since 1937, died in September.

Allen would build his winning foundation by acquiring as many veterans as possible, emphasizing sturdy defense and an offense that, according to one critic, "was careful to the point of being stodgy." One of Allen's first decisions was to make Gabriel the No. 1 quarterback. Allen's maneuvers paid off, as the Rams became competitive again. The Rams had a chance to finish second in the Western Conference until the final game, a 27-23 loss to champion Green Bay. They wound up 8-6.

The club's first round draft pick that year was Tom Mack of Michigan. Some years later Allen was to say of Mack, "It's not often that the fan notices a guard in a football game. But people notice Tom. There's no better blocker on sweeps." Mack became a perennial Pro Bowl player and All-Pro or all-conference selection and never missed a game due to injury.

In 1967, for the first time in their history, the Rams went unbeaten (6-0) in the preseason. The would go on to post an 11-1-2 record, winning eight in a row to end the regular season and capture the Coastal Division championship, their first title of any kind since 1955. The club was swatted 28-7 in the conference title game by Green Bay. As a consolation, the Rams crushed Cleveland 30-6 in the short-lived Playoff Bowl, which matched conference runners-up. Gabriel had a club re-cord 25 TD passes for the season; he totalled 2,779 yards as he completed 196 of 371 attempts. There wasn't a better quarterback in football than Gabriel in his first four years under Allen.

David "Deacon" Jones (75)

He posted a gaudy 42-15-3 record and took the Rams to two division titles and two second-place finishes. "We had been losers for so long we almost forgot what it was like [to win]," he said in an article in the 1970-71 *Hall of Fame Yearbook.* "We were accepting defeat too easily then, but now when we lose, we suffer."

Gabriel's receivers, meanwhile, sometimes suffered in practice. "If I find a receiver is not running his route, I'll hit him in the back of the head with the ball," Gabriel said.

Attendance in 1968 passed the million mark for the second consecutive year as the Rams posted a 10-3-1 record, good for second in their division. The club's defense set a 14-game NFL record for fewest yards allowed, 3,118. Deacon Jones was one of the reasons.

"You can't pick an all-time All-Pro team today without picking Deacon Jones," Allen said. Jones used to lead his team at South Carolina State in prayers, hence the nickname "Deacon." When he began his pro career in 1961, "There were 10 pages of Joneses in the phone book when I came to town," he said, "and 15 or 20 of them had my name, David Jones. So I changed it to Deacon. I thought a name like that would be remembered."

In a stunning turn of events, Allen was fired the day after Christmas, only to be rehired two weeks later. In 1969 Hirsch ended a 20-year relationship with the Rams by leaving to become athletic director at his alma mater, Wisconsin. He was replaced by public relations director Jack Teele. The Rams kept winning, grabbing their division title with an 11-3 mark, although the last three games of the season were all losses. They lost to Minnesota in the West championship game, 23-20. Gabriel completed 217 of 399 passes for 2,549 yards and 24 TDs for the season and was named the league's MVP. Bass retired with a Rams' career best rushing total of 5,417 yards. In the Playoff Bowl against the Dallas Cowboys, Los Angeles won 31-0.

The Allen revival boosted what would have been a horrible decade record to a fair 60-67-6 mark. One reason for the upsurge might be found in the caliber of players he had, in character, as well as raw ability. Tackle Bob Brown was such a player. The 6-4, 275-pounder from Nebraska made the Pro Bowl in his only two years with the Rams, 1969 and 1970, after spending five years with Philadelphia. He finished out his career as a star with the Oakland Raiders through 1973. "I have an urgent need to be successful," he said during his last year with Los Angeles. "The only things I fear are obscurity and being ordinary. I want to be singled out. ... All I do the year around is train and practice. I have no off-season job or interest except football. This is just like playing the concert piano. There's no off-season for a great pianist. He keeps at it and so do I."

The 1970s began the Rams' 25th year in Los Angeles. Among their draftees in 1970 was No. 1 overall pick Jack Reynolds, a linebacker from Tennessee. Center Rich Saul from Michigan State also was chosen. The Rams would win nine, lose four and tie one, finishing second in the West to in-state rival San Francisco. At the end of the season it was announced Allen's contract would not be renewed. His record was 49-17-4 and his five-year tenure tied him with Gillman for longevity in the franchise's revolving-door operation.

In April 1971, Reeves died of cancer in New York. He had Hodgkin's Disease and two other types of cancer, but had maintained active control of the Rams until his death. "But even the life-loving, fighting, tough little delight of an Irish pixie that was Dan Reeves, as stubborn as he was sentimental and as soft as he was hard, couldn't beat this one," wrote John Hall in *Petersen's 1971 Pro Football Annual.*

Reeves' longtime friend and business associate, William A. Barnes, became president and general manager and Tommy Prothro moved over from UCLA to become coach. One of Barnes' first moves was to made a youth-for-veterans trade with Allen, who had taken the coaching job at Washington. Barnes sent linebackers Jack Pardee, Myron Pottios, and Maxie Baughan, plus defensive tackle Diron Talbert, to the Redskins for linebacker Marlin McKeever and numerous draft choices. The Rams used the picks to draft linebacker Isiah Robertson from Southern University, defensive end Jack Youngblood from Florida, and defensive back Dave Elmendorf from Texas A&M. All of these players would be staples of the Ram defense over the coming years. The Rams played the league's toughest schedule and ended up 8-5-1, second again to the 49ers in the West.

In a history-making move in 1972, Chicago-based industrialist Robert Irsay bought the Rams from the Reeves estate, then traded the franchise to Baltimore Colts owner Carroll Rosenbloom, who was the NFL's most successful owner over the previous two decades. He brought Don Klosterman, once a backup quarterback with the Rams, with him to Los Angeles to serve as the club's general manager.

The Chuck Knox Era

After a 6-7-1 season all the coaches were fired. Entering through the revolving door as new coach was a relative unknown, former Detroit assistant Chuck Knox, with a three-year contract. He had been on the staff of fired Joe Schmidt of the Lions and registered at the hotel in Los Angeles as "Chuck Mills" to fend off reporters' queries. In the job interview, Klosterman asked Knox if he thought he could win right away. Knox replied, "I don't think we can win this year, I know we can win." A week later he was called for a second interview.

"I had coached 19 years, 10 as a pro assistant, four as a college assistant, five in high school," remarked Knox in his 1988 book, *Hard Knox, The Life of an NFL Coach.* "I had just recently been slapped in the face and cast out into football oblivion by an NFL general manager, Russ Thomas, who thought he would never hear from me again. I had never played pro ball. I had not played big-time college ball. I had no big-league connections . . . and suddenly here I was, the head coach of the fastest team in the fastest lane in America."

It didn't take long for criticism to fly after the Rams had a 0-3-1 exhibition start. He told his team: "Don't you dare put the full accountability for your performance on me. Don't dare say, 'Well, there's been a change of coaches so we're missing some intensity.' Be a man about your job and yourself. While our job is to prepare you, your job is to execute. So don't blame us when things go bad. There will be no Alibi Ikes here."

"An early tipoff that there was something special about Chuck Knox was seen through the eyes of the Rams players," wrote Doug Krikorian, in *Petersen's 1974 Pro Football Annual.* "Athletes are notorious for laying blame on their coach when things are going poorly. But no one was blaming Knox."

Merlin Olsen (74)

All he did was take the team to its best record ever, 12-2, and earn NFL Coach of the Year honors. Roman Gabriel was traded to Philadelphia and former San Diego Charger John Hadl was given the nod at quarterback. He became the National Conference Player of the Year. Lawrence McCutcheon gained 1,097 yards rushing. The Rams won the West division, but lost in the opening playoff round, 27-16, to Dallas.

"Chuck Knox found himself in an uneasy situation," Krikorian said. "He had promised Rosenbloom he would turn the Rams into winners—immediately. He was taking over a troubled team (with a tradition of dissension) from a coach, Tommy Prothro, who many felt wasn't responsible for the Rams' inadequacies during their 6-7-1 season in 1972. Knox was so unknown in a town that puts a high priority on name personalities that he was unable to line up his own TV show." Said Rosenbloom, "I feel Chuck Knox is the best choice I've made yet in picking a football coach. When God made the mold for football coaches, he must have been thinking of Chuck Knox. Chuck has all the qualities—patience, intellect, discipline, enthusiasm, and charisma."

There are many who might dispute the "charisma" tag. Knox became noted for speaking in cliches and rarely giving a reporter an exciting quote. Said Krikorian, "He's agreeable but guarded, friendly but cautious, responding to most questions with discretion, his answers freighted with platitudes." Knox then revamped the team with 12 new starters and 16 new players. "The Rams under Tommy Prothro were not a buoyant team," Krikorian reported. "They went their own way and lacked esprit de corps . . . But the Rams united under Chuck Knox. He made sure of it; demanded it."

He put in 14- to 16-hour days, listened to his players and didn't criticize them in public. He was good at delegating authority, demanded strict grooming and curfew rules, and instituted weight limits. "Chuck's secret isn't a secret," Klosterman said. "He's a highly-organized individual who believes in hard work, a lot of hard work, and it's paid off."

Hadl was not the only player to emerge as a star during Knox's first season at the reins. Wide receiver Harold Jackson came from Philadelphia in a trade for Gabriel and would end up catching 13 touchdown passes in an All-Pro first season with Los Angeles. "He's the greatest deep threat in the league," Hadl said. "I try to wait for his last move and after that I have to hope I can throw it far enough." McCutcheon starred as a rookie, with help from Jim Bertelsen in the backfield. They had holes opened by players like 34-year-old Charlie Cowan, Ken Iman, and Joe Scibelli. They became known as "The Piano Movers." Fred Dryer, Merlin Olsen, Larry Brooks, and Jack Youngblood anchored the defense.

Receiver Jack Snow found himself on the end of fewer passes because of Jackson. However, he said, "If it had been my first or second year in the league I might have said something. But a real pro loves to win, above all. ... Any desire I may have had to catch more passes was less important to me than the fun of having a 12-2 season."

Rosenbloom installed his son, Steve, as assistant to the president in 1974. After a 3-2 start, management traded Hadl to Green Bay for five draft choices, with backup James Harris becoming the starter and leading the Rams to a 10-4 record and its second consecutive West crown. Harris became the first African-American to quarterback a team to a title. The Rams also posted their first playoff victory since 1951, upending Washington 19-10. But, in the NFC title game, the often-bridesmaid Rams lost 14-10 to the Minnesota Vikings. McCutcheon was the running star again, piling up 1,109 yards rushing for the season, plus 408 receiving.

Defense ruled in 1975 as the team allowed the second fewest points in NFL history over a 14-game season (135), en route to its third straight NFC West title in a 12-2 campaign. Olsen, Youngblood, Brooks and Dryer were the keys as they formed an awesome front four. One coach would say of them, "The way these four guys play together is unique. They're like four cylinders in a sports car."

Youngblood spoke of the Rams' famous defensive line of the 1960s: Jones, Roosevelt Grier, Lamar Lundy, and Olsen. "Merlin was the key then, just as he is today, but the Deacon was the greatest lineman of all time. I'm thankful I got to play with him on the same club one year."

Bob Oates, writing in the January 1975 issue of *Football Digest*, spoke of Dryer, who would one day become a TV star in a detective series: "The handsome Dryer, 6-6, 240, is constructed like a broad-shouldered ballet dancer. He has the same grace and moves. A witty free-thinker, Dryer is the best impersonator the club has had since Dick Bass." Oates called Olsen "the most remarkable Ram" because he was "a forceful speaker, an engaging companion and a perennial All-Pro."

The Rams clinched the NFC West title for the third straight year by winning a Thanksgiving Day game in Detroit before 80,000 at the Silverdome and a national TV audience. Harris threw for three TDs, two to Jackson and one to ex-Lion Ron Jessie. "It's just great to come back here and clinch our division. That's the biggest thing. It doesn't make any difference who we're playing against," Knox said in the *Associated Press* wire story.

Durable Records

Three of the most legendary Rams still own three of the most durable NFL records: Wide receiver Tom Fears holds the mark for most receptions in a game, 18, in the Rams' game against the Green Bay Packers, December 3, 1950. Quarterback Norm Van Brocklin owns the record for most yards passing in a game, 554, set September 28, 1951, against the New York Yanks. Defensive back Dick "Night Train" Lane's all-time record is for most interceptions in a season, 14, in 1952. All three Rams are in the Pro Football Hall of Fame.

Ron Jaworski took over for an injured Harris late in the season. The Rams beat St. Louis 35-23 in the divisional playoff, then bowed to the Cowboys in the conference championship matchup, 37-7. Over three years the Rams' 34-8 record was the best in the NFL.

"They're a super team," said Minnesota coach Bud Grant. "They are better now than the team they had in 1969, which won 11 games in succession. That team concentrated on mistake-free football. This team goes after you. They're the most dominant team that anyone has seen in quite a while." Still, a championship eluded them.

In 1976, for the fourth straight year, the Rams won their division, with a 10-3-1 record. Dallas was a 14-12 playoff victim on the road, then the Rams once again suffered a setback in the NFC title game, 24-13 at Minnesota. Quarterback injuries marred the season and rookie Pat Haden became the fourth different playoff QB in four years under Knox. The Rams' 351 points were the most in the conference.

"One of the things I like best about Knox is that he's open to ideas," Haden said. "In the end, everything goes back to the head coach. He makes us what we are. Chuck is the same, win or lose. He never broods over mistakes but always looks ahead. ... Knox and his staff have a way of keeping everything positive."

A typical Rams quarterback controversy ensued in 1977, with former Southern Cal star Haden, a Rhodes Scholar who had been with the now-defunct World Football League, ultimately getting the job. Former New York Jets star Joe Namath wound up his great career with the Rams in 1977, but bad knees forced him to turn the job over to Haden.

In training camp in 1976 Haden weighed just 173 pounds. "The food at Oxford was worse for me than I thought," he said of his Rhodes Scholar days in his book, *Pat Haden, My Rookie Season with the Los Angeles Rams.* Haden's book discussed the myriad personalities that compose a professional football team, quoting Merlin Olsen, who said "a good defensive lineman has to be part charging buffalo and part ballet dancer," and that, "The Rams look for more than raw football ability. These guys are intelligent, well-spoken, and they have a lot of things going for them off the field." Mack, for instance, was cited for his nuclear engineering graduate degree from Michigan. Indeed, it takes all kinds. Olsen said kicker Tom Dempsey "drinks beer like a prospector just come in from three weeks on the desert" and punter Rusty Jackson "has aspirations of becoming a male nurse."

When Olsen retired after the 1976 season, he had appeared in an NFL record 14 Pro Bowl games and a record 208 games as a Ram, including 198 consecutive appearances. He would go on to prominence as a color TV commentator for football broadcasts and an acting career on the "Little House on the Prairie" television series.

The Rams of 1977 found themselves in a Coliseum with a new configuration that reduced seating capacity from 91,000 to 71,000. The club rolled to its fifth successive division crown and a 10-4 record, with McCutcheon setting a club career rushing record of 5,523 yards. Once again, though, the Rams lost in the playoffs, 14-7 to Minnesota at home. Knox resigned to take the head coaching job with the Buffalo Bills. He had wanted to bail out sooner but said Rosenbloom made it impossible with compensation requirements he waved at tampering teams.

"I've just about had it with Carroll Rosenbloom's overbearing direction," Knox would write. "I've taken so much in four years, I'm having trouble swallowing. ... Everything had to be show business, from the long passes at the end of the first half to the Friday night appearances in Bel Air. I'm not showbiz. I'm not anything, really, but a western Pennsylvania football coach. The LA experience made me realize this."

Carroll Rosenbloom decided perhaps it was time to bring Allen back. He did, Feb. 1, 1978, but fired him after the second exhibition game, giving the job to assistant Ray (Raymondo Giovanni Baptiste) Malavasi. He guided the team to a 12-4 record and a sixth consecutive division title, tying an NFL mark. Finally, the Rams won a playoff game, beating the Vikings 34-10. But next came a 28-0 shutout by Dallas in the NFC championship game.

"I don't know if anyone other than Ray could have come in under such trying circumstances, two weeks before the season began, and pulled the pieces together the way he did," said Youngblood in his 1988 book *Blood.* Of Rosenbloom, Youngblood said: "Each man on the Rams—player and coach alike—knew beyond a doubt that Carroll Rosenbloom was the one to call the final shots. Of all the other owners, maybe only the Raiders' Al Davis commanded similar respect from his employees."

Also in 1978, the Rams announced plans to move to Anaheim in Orange County to the south. 1979 took a shocking turn early when, on April 2, the 72-year-old Rosenbloom drowned while swimming of the Florida coast, leaving, said Youngblood, "a pall over the team and a vacuum at the power center." Rosenbloom's widow, Georgia Frontiere, became majority owner and Steve Rosenbloom was named executive vice president in charge of day-to-day operations. Klosterman soon replaced him and he left the organization.

Super Bowl Bound

After a 4-2 start, injuries took their toll and the Rams lost four games in five weeks. Defense remained tough and, in a 24-0 victory over Seattle, the Rams completely dominated the Seahawks, holding the Seattle offense to an NFL record minus seven yards in offense. Haden set a club mark with 13 consecutive completions in that game, but was lost for the season with a broken finger. Vince Ferragamo took over and quarterbacked the Rams to four victories in a row and a seventh-straight NFC West crown with a 9-7 record. In the divisional playoff, Ferragamo threw three TD passes, the last with 2:06 left, as Los Angeles defeated the Cowboys 21-19.

This time, there wasn't an NFC title-game collapse. The Rams shut out Tampa Bay 9-0, earning their first trip to the Super Bowl—Super Bowl XIV. The Rams weren't successful there, though, losing to AFC champ Pittsburgh 31-19 as the Steelers came from behind in the fourth quarter. It was a valiant effort, however, as the underdog Rams nearly denied the Steelers' their fourth Super Bowl championship in the decade. Youngblood played with a broken leg, as he would do later in the Pro Bowl game.

Los Angeles could look back on its most successful 10-year stretch. The 1970s produced a fantastic regular season record of 98-42-4. The 1980s didn't begin with an eighth straight division title. The Rams had to settle for second place with an 11-5 record, selling out the last six home games in the 69,045-seat Anaheim Stadium. Safety Nolan Cromwell, a former Kansas quarterback, was named the conference's Defensive Player of the Year by UPI. Ferragamo set records for completions (240), passing yards (3,199) and touchdown passes (30). Los Angeles, which set 15 team records for the year and led the league in rushing for the first time since 1957, played Dallas in a playoff game for wild card teams and was trounced 34-13 in December.

1981 showed an uncharacteristic 6-10 record, as the Rams missed the playoffs for the first time since 1972. Ferragamo departed for the Canadian Football League as a result of an acrimonious contract dispute with the club, and the Ram defense proved unable to match its performance of past years. Bright spots included LeRoy Irvin's league mark of 207 punt return yards in a 37-35 triumph over Atlanta and Wendell Tyler's season, in which he rushed for 1,074 yards and tied Hirsch's team record of 17 touchdowns in a season. By the end of the season, the starting quarterback was Dan Pastorini, a free agent acquisition. He replaced injured Haden and backup Jeff Rutledge.

The NFL players' strike wiped out seven games of the 1982 regular season, one in which the Rams finished last in the conference with a 2-7 record. Haden had retired in the spring. During his watch as a starter, the Rams were 35-18-1. Quarterback Bert Jones, acquired on draft day in a trade with Baltimore, missed the last five games of the season with a neck injury. Ferragamo re-

HISTORY | **Blockbuster Trades**

When it comes to blockbuster trades, no team in NFL history has been more prolific than the Los Angeles Rams. Four of the league's top six trades of all time in terms of volume have involved the Rams: With 10 players switching teams twice, 12 once and 15 once. The Rams even posed a picture once with two of their big trade acquisitions surrounded by 20 helmets, signifying how many Rams players had departed.

The first of the big deals involved 12 players and was consummated on June 13, 1952. Eleven players left the Rams in the deal. The Rams got draft rights to linebacker Les Richter of California from the Dallas Texans in exchange for running backs Dick Hoerner, Billy Baggett, Dave Anderson, and Dick McKissack; defensive backs Tom Keane and George Sims; centers Joe Reid and Aubrey Phillips; linebacker Vic Vasicek; tackle Jack Halliday; and end Richard Wilkins.

The team's next huge move came March 23, 1959, when ten players switched teams, and once again the Rams received only one player in the deal. The Rams got halfback Ollie Matson from the Chicago Cardinals for tackles Frank Fuller and Ken Panfil, defensive end Glenn Holtzman, defensive tackle Art Hauser, end John Tracey, running backs Larry Hickman and Don Brown, the Rams' second-round 1960 draft choice, and a player to be delivered during the 1959 training camp.

Blockbuster deal number three for the Rams was made on January 28, 1971, and involved 15 players. Los Angeles received linebacker Marlin McKeever; first- and third-round choices in the 1971 draft; and third-, fourth-, fifth-, sixth-, and seventh-round picks in the 1972 draft from the Washington Redskins in exchange for linebackers Maxie Baughan, Jack Pardee and Myron Pottios; running back Jeff Jordan; guard John Wilbur; defensive tackle Diron Talbert; and a fifth-round 1971 draft pick.

On October 31, 1987, the Rams were involved in a 10-player deal. Running back Eric Dickerson was the only one to leave the Rams. He went to the Indianapolis Colts, who in turn dealt the rights to linebacker Cornelius Bennett to Buffalo and running back Owen Gill, the Colts' first- and second-round choices in 1988, and their second-round selection in 1989 to the Rams. The Bills, to complete the three-way trade sent Bills running back Greg Bell and Buffalo's first-round choice in 1988, as well as their first- and second-round picks in 1989, to the Rams.

gained his starting job and in a game against Chicago threw for 509 yards, second best in league history. Malavasi got the ax at the end of the season.

Frontiere wasted no time shaking things up in 1983, hiring Robinson away from Southern Cal to become coach, revamping the front office and engineering a dozen trades. Eric Dickerson was drafted on the first round and the running back would become one of the NFL's all-time greats. Robinson installed a new single-back offense and a new 3-4 defense, and Frontiere signed all the players to contracts.

"John was a breath of fresh air," Youngblood wrote of Robinson. "He invigorated the team almost immediately." The Rams went 9-7, making the playoffs as a wild card team. They defeated the Cowboys at Dallas 24-17, but were crushed by the Redskins in Washington in the next round, 51-7. Dickerson set a rookie rushing record of 1,808 yards and Robinson was named Coach of the Year. "I just don't see many teams win that don't dominate physically," Robinson said. "One of the things you get from being physical is that you run the football. I can't imagine coaching a team that didn't run the football well."

A 10-6 record in 1984 put the Rams in the playoffs again and they hosted their first postseason game in Anaheim, only to lose the wild card game 16-13 to the New York Giants. Dickerson had 2,105 yards for the year to break O.J. Simpson's NFL record of 2,003.

Youngblood set a team mark by playing in his 201st consecutive game. The new quarterback was Jeff Kemp, replacing the injured Ferragamo three games into the season and leading the team to nine victories. Dickerson was the NFC Player of the Year. "It's a thrill to watch him," Youngblood said of Dickerson. "He's the greatest thing I've ever seen."

1985 saw the Rams fall one game short of a conference title again as they were blanked by Chicago 24-0, after having won the division championship by blanking Dallas 20-0 behind Dickerson's playoff record 248 yards rushing. Canadian League transplant Dieter Brock completed just 16 of 53 passes in the two playoff games. The regular season team record was 11-5.

The Oakland Raiders, meanwhile, had been the Los Angeles Raiders since 1982 and shared the Coliseum with the Rams."I don't feel we really compete," Robinson said in a 1986 article in *The Sporting News Pro Football Yearbook*. "I don't see them as anything. They are no threat to me whatsoever." Others, however, felt the Raiders had eaten away at the Rams' fan base. "The Rams still have plenty of fans in town—their often superior television ratings prove that—but their marketing focus is on the conservative, upper-scale residents of Orange County."

Raiders owner Al Davis felt, the article said, that Frontiere conspired to keep his team out of Los Angeles and sued, but the case was thrown out of court. However, it still cost the Rams' owner $1 million to settle.

Jim Everett Joins the Rams

The Rams again made the playoffs in 1986, compiling a 10-6 record. They had acquired rookie quarterback Jim Everett from Houston in a trade and he became a starter the last five games. Dickerson had 1,821 yards rushing for the season and, in just his fourth year, brought his total to a Rams' best 6,968 for a career.

In 1987, however, the Rams dropped to a 6-9 record. A players' strike shorted the season by a game. Trades gave the Rams six draft picks, three number one's and three number two's, over the next two years from the Colts, who got Dickerson. He won the league rushing title with 1,374 yards.

Making it back to the playoffs as a wild card team in 1988 with an 10-6 record, the Rams lost in the first round, 28-17 to Minnesota. Robinson, though, became the franchise's winningest coach during the course of the season. Everett led a wide-open offense, setting four team passing records, and Henry Ellard set a club record for most catches in a season with 86. On defense, 56 quarterback sacks were a club record and led the league.

The Rams didn't win the Western Division in 1989, but once again the Rams were a wild card team. This time, though, they won a couple games before getting roughed up 30-3 by San Francisco, the dynasty team of the 1980s behind the quarterbacking of Joe Montana.

Everett became the first Ram to pass for more than 4,000 yards (4,310) and Ellard (1,382) joined Flipper Anderson (1,146) as the first two Rams receivers to total more than 1,000 yards in the same season. Anderson also set a league mark with a 336-yard game on 15 catches against New Orleans. The Rams finished out the decade with a 10-year record of 86-66.

The early 1990s would bring little good news, except perhaps the return of Knox, who replaced Robinson before the 1992 season. In 1990 Ellard was one of the few bright spots in a 5-11 season, setting career team marks for receptions (412) and yards receiving (7,037). Tackle Jackie Slater became the team iron man, playing in his 209th game. Ellard and Anderson both passed the 1,000-yard receiving mark again. Only two other teams ever had two receivers hit that total in the same year twice.

1991 was one of the most dismal in the franchise's history, a 3-13 record that including 10 losses in a row. Robinson resigned before the last regular season game and in 1993 returned to the college ranks as coach of USC. Slater, meanwhile, became the first Ram to play 16 seasons. For the first time since the game's inception in 1950, the Rams didn't have a player named to the Pro Bowl team.

Knox began what was hoped would be a new revival, boosting the victory total in 1992 up to six in a 6-10 season. Included was a 31-27 victory at Tampa Bay in which the Rams overcame a 24-point deficit. They also dealt a 27-23 setback to eventual Super Bowl champion Dallas, the Cowboys' only loss at home during the campaign.

The 1993 season began a new era in the NFL with a free agency system for players with five years experience. Everett and defensive tackle Sean Gilbert were named transition players, giving the Rams the right of refusal once their contracts expire. Los Angeles picked Notre Dame running back Jerome Bettis as their top draft choice (No. 10 overall).

SOURCES

BOOKS

Bisheff, Steve. *Great Teams' Great Years: Los Angeles Rams.* MacMillan Publishing, 1973.

First 50 Years, The Story of the NFL. Simon & Schuster, 1969.

Haden, Pat, with Robert Blair Kaiser. *Pat Haden, My Rookie Season with the Los Angeles Rams.* William Morrow & Co., 1977.

Harmon, Tom. *Pilots Also Pray.* Thomas Y. Crowell Co., 1944.

Herskowitz, Mickey. *The Golden Age of Pro Football: A Remembrance of Pro Football in the '50s.* NFL Properties, 1974.

Knox, Chuck, and Bill Plaschke. *Hard Knox, The Life of an NFL Coach.* Harcourt-Brace-Jovanovich, 1988.

Los Angeles Rams Media Guide. Los Angeles Rams, 1993.

Neft, David S., and Richard M. Cohen. *The Football Encyclopedia.* St. Martin's Press, 1991.

Official National Football League 1993 Record & Fact Book. National Football League, 1993.

Youngblood, Jack, with Joel Engel. *Blood.* Contemporary Books, 1988.

PERIODICALS

Associated Press, November 28, 1975.

Detroit Free Press, September 9, 1993.

Fawcett's 1963 Pro Football, 1963.

Football Digest, January 1972; July-August 1972; February 1974; January 1975.

GameDay, December 15, 1975; December 10, 1984; December 16, 1984.

Hall of Fame Yearbook, 1970-71, 1970.

Insider!, 1988; Spring 1991; Winter 1991; Winter 1993.

NFL Report, Fall 1988; Spring 1989; Spring 1990; Summer 1990; Fall 1990; Spring 1991; Winter 1992; Spring 1992; Fall 1992.

Petersen's Pro Football Annual, 1958; 1971; 1974; 1981.

PRO!, August 1981; September 1984; March-April 1985.

Pro Football Stars, 1962; 1964.

Pro Quarterback, January 1978.

Pro Football Almanac, 1971.

Pro Football Handbook, 1961.

Rams Report, Winter 1982.

Sporting News Pro Football Yearbook, 1986.

Street & Smith's 1960 Football Yearbook, 1966.

—Larry Paladino

New Orleans Saints

"They ain't 'Aints' no more." The New Orleans Saints, whose fans gained notoriety by going to games with paper bags over their heads during the sad-sack days of 1980 and 1981, have returned to respectability, just as they were in their beginning, November 1, 1966, All Saints Day. The National Football League, long impressed by support fans gave exhibition games in Tulane Stadium, announced it was granting New Orleans a professional football franchise.

What could you name a team in a city where Dixieland and jazz are king and one of the classic songs is "When the Saints Go Marching In"? "Saints" seemed appropriate. But after New Orleans shook the tag "expansion team" quicker than any new franchise had, the club regressed, and it took the patience of a Saint to be a fan as the team constantly flip-flopped philosophies and changed directions. But after finally growing up—and it took a full 21 years—the Saints seem finally to be back on the track for success.

New Orleans got off to a good start as a franchise. Millionaire sportsman John W. Mecom, Jr., was designated majority stockholder and president of the franchise, and on December 22, 1966, he appointed Vic Schwenk director of player personnel. Among Mecom's limited partners was famed trumpeter Al Hirt. The first coach was Tom Fears, all-time great end with the Los Angeles Rams and assistant to Green Bay's Vince Lombardi. The first player to sign with the Saints was former Mississippi and L.A. Ram kicker Paige Cothren, who didn't make the roster.

Fears leaned heavily on veterans in the expansion draft. The first quarterbacks were Billy Kilmer and Gary Cuozzo. Jim Taylor was taken to provide a pounding, and inside runner and defensive end Doug Atkins was selected despite being 37 years old. Other key, aged original Saints included defensive tackles Lou Cordileone (30) and Earl Leggett (33), center Joe Wendryhoski (28), linebackers Jackie Burkett (30), Steve Stonebreaker (29), and Fred Whittingham (28), and defensive back Dave Whitsell (31).

Pro football may have been late in coming to the South, but the South was no stranger to football. High school football was great, and college football was king. The pro game? Until television, nobody much cared, because pro teams were all on the coasts or up North. But nationally televised pro games changed things—as did the formation of the American Football League in 1959.

New teams meant new markets, so when the Saints were formed, New Orleans fans were ready. They bought 20,000 season tickets the first day they went on sale and had guaranteed attendance of 33,400 before the first game was played. Pro football had come to New Orleans—and it would be a long time between the Saints and the "Aints."

New Orleans traded one of its two first-round selections to Baltimore for Cuozzo and made fullback Les Kelley the first player taken with the second. The list from the Saints' first draft includes defensive end Dave Rowe and, way down at No. 17, a slow but sure-handed wide receiver by the name of Danny Abramowicz.

New Team Falters at First

The Saints surprised everybody by going 5-1 in the exhibition season, but when the season started, the victories stopped. Rookie John Gilliam returned the kickoff of the opening game 94 yards for a touchdown, but the Los Angeles Rams recovered for a 27-13 victory in front of 80,879 fans at Tulane Stadium.

The first seven games were losses before flanker Walt Roberts scored all three of his season's touchdowns to lead New Orleans to a 31-24 victory over Philadelphia. New Orleans won two other games to finish 3-11, and Whitsell's ten interceptions tied for the league lead. He was named UPI's Comeback Player of the Year, invited to participate in the Pro Bowl, and selected second team All-NFL.

Having traded away their first-round choice for 1968, New Orleans dumped Cuozzo on Minnesota and chose defensive end Kevin Hardy. The NFL old-boy club liked to squeeze the new kids whenever they could, and got New Orleans to give Los Angeles its second-round draft pick when the Saints joined the Rams' scouting combine.

Schwenk, promoted to general manager, teamed with Fears on a daring maneuver July 17th by signing San Francisco wide receiver Dave Parks, who played out his option after getting in a contract squabble with the 49ers and decided to test the NFL's contract system. On July 26th the NFL, reluctant to get into a legal battle that could well cost it control of its player pool, condoned the signing by not contesting it. However, Commissioner Pete Rozelle awarded first-round choice Hardy to the 49ers along with the Saints' top 1969 choice.

Grateful to be in the league, New Orleans meekly complied. What came to be called the "Rozelle Rule" was struck down by a federal judge in the winter of 1975-76 and modified in 1977 through negotiations between owners and players. Taylor went through a painful second training camp before deciding on September 10th to retire despite leading Saints' rushers that first season with 390 yards. The ex-Packer was also their No. 2 receiver with 38 catches.

Taylor (No. 31) and Atkins (No. 81) are the only Saints to have the uniform numbers retired. Both are members of the Pro Football Hall of Fame. Parks was nowhere near New Orleans' leading receiver in 1968 as the team improved to 4-9-1 and climbed out of the Century Division basement over the dismal Pittsburgh Steelers, 2-11-1. Rowe was picked for the Pro Bowl. Abramowicz caught 54 passes for 890 yards and seven touchdowns, more than twice as many catches and triple the yardage of Parks.

Fifth-round choice Don McCall led the team with 156 carries and 637 yards. Kilmer was the No. 1 quarterback and the 10th rated passer in the NFL. New Orleans got a second No. 1 pick for Cuozzo in 1969 and used it on guard John Shinners. Fears obtained Andy Livingston from Chicago and promoted Tony Baker from the taxi

TEAM INFORMATION AT A GLANCE

Founding date: 1966

Home stadium: Louisiana Superdome
6928 Saints Dr.
Metairie, LA 70003
Phone: (504) 733-0255
Seating capacity: 69,065

Team colors: Old Gold, black, and white
Team nickname: Saints
Logo: Fleur-de-lis

Franchise record:	Won	Lost	Tie
(1967-92)	152	229	5

squad, and they combined for 1,400 yards. Kilmer threw for six touchdowns in a 51-42 outslugging of St. Louis, and his brainy leadership helped New Orleans—shifted to the Capital Division of the NFL's Eastern Conference—again beat out an established team. A 5-9 mark bettered Philadelphia's 4-9-1.

A field goal kicker had been found, Tom Dempsey, born with no right hand and wearing a square-toed kicking shoe over a toeless right foot. Dempsey kicked four goals November 16th, the last with 11 seconds, to pin a 25-24 loss on the New York Giants and start a three-game Saints' winning streak. Kilmer improved to eighth among QBs, and his touchdowns exceeded his interceptions for the first time (20-17). Abramowicz was 15 yards over 1,000 with 73 receptions.

Abramowicz was All-NFL as the league's leading receiver, while Atkins finished a 17-year career with a second-team spot. Livingston, Baker, Dempsey, and guard Jake Kupp were picked for the Pro Bowl along with the entire Saints' coaching staff.

NFL Transition

The NFL was realigned in 1970 to complete its merger with the old AFL, New Orleans moving to the NFC West to be with Los Angeles, San Francisco, and geographic rival Atlanta. New Orleans was no longer regarded as an expansion team by that time, so a 1-5-1 start cost Fears his job. J. D. Roberts, formerly a coach in the minor league Atlantic Coast Football League, was hired to replace him. The Saints responded with a 19-17 victory over Detroit—on an NFL record 63-yard field goal by Dempsey on the last play of the game—but didn't win again and finished last, 2-11-1.

Kilmer's interceptions outnumbered his TD passes, 17-6, and Edd Hargett began seeing more playing time. Abramowicz was down to 55 catches for 906 yards, but he caught half the club's ten TD passes. The ground game was nonexistent, and the defense very weak. Looking for a young quarterback around which to build the team, New Orleans traded Kilmer to Washington for line-

AP/Wide World Photos

Tom Dempsey (19) kicks his legendary, record-setting 63-yard field goal with two seconds left in the Saints' victory over the Detroit Lions, 19–17. Bill Cody (66) blocks Lion Alex Karras (71). Holding the ball for Dempsey is Joe Scarpati.

backer Tom Roussel plus two mid-range draft choices, and made Mississippi pass-run star Archie Manning its top pick in 1971.

Right in the middle of training camp came the exciting news that construction was finally beginning on the controversy-dogged Superdome, though it would be four more seasons before the Saints would play a game in their new dome. With a new coach and new quarterback on the scene, and a new stadium in the future, New Orleans opened the year with a bang.

Manning symbolized the transition of the Saints from rag-tags to a young team on the march when he completed 16 of 29 passes for 218 yards and a touchdown against the Rams. He capped his excellent debut with a one-yard touchdown sneak on the final play to give his team a 24-20 victory. The rookie also ran for two touchdowns on October 17th in a 24-20 win over eventual Super Bowl champion Dallas.

Foot and leg problems plagued Manning much of the season, though, and Hargett wound up with half the playing time for the Saints. The two ranked 11th and 10th, respectively, in the conference.

The addition of veteran tackle Glen Ray Hines improved the line, as did center John Didion and a fourth-round draftee, tackle Don Morrison. Abramowicz's production declined even further, to 37 catches for 657 yards, but both figures still led a balanced offense. Parks continued his steady play with 35 receptions for 568 yards, but a bad defense and the lack of a consistent running game contributed to a 4-8-2 record, easily last in the NFC West.

Former astronaut Richard F. Gordon was named executive vice-president at the start of 1972 in a continuation of the face parade through the front office. Though the defense was badly in need of help, New Orleans added a guard, Royce

Smith, to its improved line at the top of the 1972 draft. It added safety Tommy Myers in the third round and a good middle linebacker, Joe Federspiel, in the fourth.

Other Expansion Teams Faring Better

Compounding New Orleans' problems was that Cincinnati, Atlanta, and Miami, the other expansion teams of the era, were all much better off than the Saints. Each was directed by a strong, visionary individual, and the Saints suffered greatly by comparison. The Bengals were the creation of legendary Paul Brown, the Falcons were temporarily performing for taskmaster Norm Van Brocklin, while Don Shula had just shifted from Baltimore to replace George Wilson with the Dolphins.

Roberts got a full season out of Manning. Second-year receiver Bob Newland led the club with 47 catches and 579 yards, while Abramowicz closed out his career with the Saints by taking 38 passes 668 yards. Parks caught 32 for 542 yards. But the quarterback was the team's second-leading rusher at 351 yards, and when a QB is only 30 yards shy of being the leading grounder gainer, there are problems. The team dropped back to 2-11-1 as morale slipped badly, a problem reflected in the NFC's highest amount of penalty yards and badly timed turnovers.

The defensive problems were addressed with the shipping of the team's No. 1 draft pick to Baltimore for defensive end Billy Newsome. Roberts was fired during the next training camp, replaced August 26th by the easy going but knowledgeable and highly respected John North. Ex-Marine North learned his football under Blanton Collier at Kentucky. Atlanta welcomed North to the league with a 62-7 whomping in the first game.

It couldn't get worse than that, North figured, so he patiently went to work and the Saints showed improvement in the second outing. They lost at Dallas, 40-3.

Things Start Looking Up

The margin of defeat declined to 14-10 at Baltimore, and New Orleans returned home the fourth week to find Chicago that hadn't been paying attention. New Orleans won, 21-16, to start a stretch of four wins in five games. The defense was improving. It had three 40-point games, but in eight contests New Orleans held opponents to 17 points or less. Newsome, Federspiel, plus defensive backs Ernie Jackson (seventh-round rookie) and Bivian Lee (third round, 1971) showed promise. All-time leading receiver Abramowicz was traded to San Francisco in midyear.

The defense's progress was shown November 4th when New Orleans recorded the seven-year-old franchise's first shutout, 13-0, over Buffalo. It limited O.J. Simpson, on his way to the league's first 2,000-yard rushing season, to only 79 yards on 20 carries. Manning cut his interceptions to 12, still two more than his TD tosses, and added 293 yards rushing. Manning threw just 267 passes.

New Orleans traded draft positions with Detroit and got linebacker Rick Middleton. No. 8 choice, Alvin Maxson, turned into the team's leading rusher with 714 yards and its leading pass-catcher with 42. But as the season went on it was obvious that the 163 points the punchless Saints scored the year before were no fluke. People began to think Manning should be traded to get more players.

North apparently shared some of the dissatisfaction with Manning, who finished with only six TD passes and 16 interceptions, because he benched the quarterback to start first Bobby Scott (14th-round draftee the same year as Manning) and then rookie Larry Cipa. The defense cut its points allowed from 312 to 263, but a 166-point season by the offense doomed New Orleans to another 5-9 season.

The quest for more offense led to the drafting of swift wide receiver Larry Burton, and the Saints got a second first-round selection by trading Newsome to the Jets, taking guard Kurt Schumacher.

They added center Lee Gross, back Andrew Jones, and defensive end Elois Grooms—all in the first three rounds. Manning cut down his roaming, but the offense was geared to throwing to the backs. Maxson was the leading receiver and No. 2 runner, while ninth-round draft choice Mike Strachan was the top runner and No. 2 receiver—neither reaching the end zone.

The three leading deep threats—Burton, Andy Hamilton, and tight end Henry Childs—caught a combined 38 passes. Manning threw only seven touchdown passes with 20 intercepted, as the offense produced just 10 points in the first three games, 165 all season. What made the year memorable was that the 72,000-seat Superdome finally opened—so what if the Saints got shut out by Cincinnati, 21-0? On October 27th, North was fired with the team sinking at 1-4, replaced on an interim basis by Director of Pro Personnel Ernie Hefferle.

Losing Streak Continues

That emotional lift got New Orleans a 23-7 victory over Atlanta, but then the thrill was gone; the Saints closed 0-for-7. Points allowed went back up to 360. Hank Stram's "offense of the '70s" deteriorated with the Kansas City Chiefs, but New Orleans brought him back from a season in the television booth to turn the Saints into the kind of team the Chiefs were. He did just that, New Orleans closely resembling the 5-9 Chiefs who got Stram fired after the 1974 season.

Stram traded Middleton to San Diego for quarterback Bobby Douglass and a third-round draft choice. Running backs Chuck Muncie and Tony Galbreath were Stram's first draft picks. New Orleans got out of the basement—but only because the NFL put expansion Seattle in the NFC West. However, the Saints also tied the suddenly sad-sack Falcons, despite a 4-10 record in Stram's first year.

Manning missed that entire season with tendinitis in his throwing arm (bad news or good news depending on whether one was a Manning booster) that required surgery, leaving the quarterbacking to be divvied up between the two Bobbys—Scott and Douglass. Scott threw just six interceptions while Douglass had eight, and they split eight touchdown passes as Stram instituted a "Thunder and Lightning" offense based on the power of Muncie (659 yards) and the speed of Galbreath (570). Again, a back was the leading receiver as Galbreath caught 54 passes in an effort to exploit his open field abilities.

After helping the offense increase its 1976 point production to 253, Stram turned his attention in the 1977 draft to a defense that had trouble halting a parked bus. He went for defensive end Joe Campbell, defensive tackle Mike Fultz, and linebacker Robert Watts in the first three rounds, trading the fourth pick to Los Angeles for linebacker Ken Bordelon.

Manning returned but again spent much of his effort running to stay alive. He threw eight TD passes and cut his interceptions to nine, which helped him go up to fifth in the QB rankings. Muncie set a club record with 811 yards rushing (Galbreath had 644), and again the No. 2 runner was the favored passing target. Tight end Childs was second, and his nine touchdowns were a club record.

Field goals figured prominently in the Saints' season again. Rich Szaro hit the right upright with a last-second kick, and it went through for a 27-26 victory over the Rams after punter/holder Tom Blanchard threw a touchdown pass to tackle-eligible Grooms on a fake field goal attempt. Two weeks later Szaro hit the upright and saw the ball bounce back in a 10-7 overtime loss to the 49ers.

New Orleans allowed an NFC high 336 points and finished at the bottom of the NFC West again, Seattle having been switched over to the AFC West. The embarrassment of that season came December 11th, when New Orleans became the first team to lose to Tampa Bay. The Buccaneers returned three interceptions for touchdowns in a 33-14 victory. So much for long-term planning, too. The 4-10 and 3-11 records cost Stram his job.

A New Coach

The new franchise game plan involved hiring former San Francisco head coach Dick Nolan, in the forefront of the complex defenses that were becoming popular. Nolan came aboard February 6, 1978, with Eddie Jones named executive vice-president and Harry Hulmes vice-president of player personnel. These moves recognized the increasing sophistication of the football operation.

The draft brought wide receiver Wes Chandler plus help for both sides of the line. Nolan moved to plug holes through trades that netted All-Pro guard Conrad Dobler and receiver Ike Harris from St. Louis. His first game was a 31-24 victory over Minnesota, and New Orleans was 5-4, including a 10-3 upset of the previously unbeaten Rams on October 22, before the balloon deflated. Dobler and Emanuel Zanders both went out with injuries in September.

The line did offer enough protection for Manning to become the conference's No. 2 passer. His TD passes finally exceeded his interceptions, 17-16, and he completed 62 percent of his throws for 3,416 yards. He was named Player of the Year in the NFC. Galbreath was the favorite target again, this time catching a club record of 74 passes. Childs was again second with 53, but his 869 yards led the team. Galbreath also got the call more than Muncie and led rushers with 635 yards.

A 17-10 revenge victory at Tampa Bay gave the Saints their best record, even if it was 7-9, and a step up to third place. The success of punter Ray Guy with the Raiders—he was their No. 1 draft choice in 1973—made all NFL teams re-examine the importance of special teams. Guy led the AFC in punting three of the next four years but, even when he didn't, was a critical part of the team's success—his distance and hang time contributed to good field position.

New Orleans figured it had the ultimate when it opened its 1979 draft by taking Russell Erxleben, who could both punt and placekick. He was a disaster, having problems adjusting to kicking without a tee. Garo Yepremian had to be signed to placekick and Rick Partridge to punt. The team drafted linebacker Reggie Mathis in the second round of another undistinguished draft. It sent its third-round choice to Miami as compensation for the signing of defensive end Don Reese.

An overtime loss to Atlanta started the season, and New Orleans found itself 0-3 before victories over San Francisco and the New York Giants started a stretch of seven wins in ten games. Suddenly the Saints were tied for first place with the Rams. In fact, they had even been alone in first place October 28 after a 14-10 win at Washington.

The return of Zanders and Dobler helped protect Manning, and the quarterback was hitting Chandler, Childs, and Harris downfield with regularity. Muncie was on his way to becoming the first 1,000-yard New Orleans rusher (1,198), and Galbreath was both running (708 yards) and catching (58-for-484). Chandler gained 1,069 yards with 65 receptions.

But there was a hitch. The offense couldn't control the ball 60 minutes a game. Things looked good for the playoffs when New Orleans jumped out to a 28-7 lead over Oakland in the second quarter and were up, 35-14, six minutes into the third quarter. Safety Tom Myers, who would join Manning, Muncie, Chandler, and Childs in the Pro Bowl, was a key player on a defense that sparkled in that earlier win at Washington. The defense stopped the Redskins seven times inside the two and 18 times on a down with goal to go to preserve the win.

Back to the Losing Side

But in this Monday night game on December 3rd, it was unequal to the task. The Raiders rattled off 28 unanswered points to take a 42-35 victory, and the Saints dropped out of playoff contention the next week with a 35-0 loss to San Diego. The team responded with a 29-14 victory over the division champion Rams, though, to become the first Saints' team to post an 8-8 record.

Then came another change. Steve Rosenbloom was hired as executive vice-president and general manager four days after the final regular season game, replacing Jones and Hulmes. Rosenbloom had left the Rams after the death of his father in a dispute over his role on the team with his stepmother, Georgia Frontiere. Dick Steinberg, another ex-Ram, was named director of player personal in June.

Manning ranked fourth among NFC quarterbacks, completing 60 percent of his passes and with 15 TD passes and 20 interceptions. Muncie capped his excellent year with an MVP Pro Bowl game, a 37-27 win by his conference. He ran for touchdowns of 1 and 11 yards and threw a 25-yard TD pass to Tony Hill on an option play.

The distance from the penthouse to the outhouse isn't very far, however, and from the franchise peak the Saints plummeted back to the bottom the very next season. The problems started with the draft; the club was unable to address its defensive needs. There was a trade for a tackle, Steve Riley, that sent choices three and five to Minnesota. The No. 1 was an excellent tackle, Stan Brock, and the No. 2 was a solid cornerback, Dave Waymer. Ominously, three unnecessary running backs were drafted including the hulking 300-pound George Woodard.

The season started with a 26-23 loss to San Francisco (rebuilt from 2-14 by Bill Walsh)—and that was as close to a win as the team got until a 23-20 loss to Minnesota on November 30th. Abominable defense and probable realization things weren't going to get any better quickly sent an attitude of bickering and defeat through the squad. Nolan shipped the disagreeable Muncie to San Diego after the fourth game but didn't have anybody to replace him.

On November 24th the team sleepwalked through a 27-7 loss to the Rams, not much different than any of the earlier losses except that this one was a Monday night game. Nolan was fired immediately after the game, and Dick Stanfel, a former All-Pro lineman, was chosen to clean up.

The 23-20 loss followed, and the next week New Orleans blew a 35-7 halftime lead to San Francisco, losing 38-35 in overtime. They escaped the indignity of an all-losing season with a 21-20 victory over the New York Jets in a Shea Stadium snowstorm but swallowed a come-from-ahead 38-27 loss to New England to close out the 1-15 year. The defense surrendered a nightmarish 487 points.

Manning was almost heroic in the terrible season, though. He ranked sixth in the NFC, but his 309 completions and 3,716 yards were conference bests. His touchdown passes exceeded his interceptions, 23-20, and he completed 61 percent of his throws. Chandler gained 975 yards with a team-high 65 receptions, while Galbreath caught 57 for 470. But no runner carried the ball 100 times. And Erxleben averaged a disappointing 39.3 yards for 89 punts and was unable to outkick veteran Bennie Ricardo, who managed converting just 10 of 17 field goals.

Fans Embarrassed by Their Team

Fans of the Saints felt such humiliation and degradation during their season of disappointment that they initiated one of those classic moments of expression. Although many stayed away in protest, thousands began showing up to watch the sad-sack Saints wearing paper bags over their heads. With holes cut out for viewing and clever faces drawn on the bags, these individuals who wanted to express their embarrassment over the team began to be called "The Aints."

The name—derived from "Saints" stripped of its first letter—conveyed such sentiments as, "Aint nobody gonna see me at one of these games" and New Orleans "aint no good." Club and league officials were infuriated, but the rest of the nation saw the humor.

Fallout from the dismal season included yet another front office shift, the resignations of Rosenbloom and Steinberg. Two days later, O. A. "Bum" Phillips was hired as coach. Phillips was the colorful good 'ol boy Texan who had kept getting the Houston Oilers into the playoffs but couldn't get them into the big game. His famous statement was, "Last year we walked up to the door. This year we knocked on it. Next year we're going to crash the danged thing down."

He never did, and that frustration caused the Oilers to dump the possession-minded, defensive oriented coach. The Saints moved quickly to snap him up. Phillips immediately went to work fashioning a similar style team in New Orleans. The top choice in the draft was his, so he took George Rogers, the 1980 Heisman Trophy winner and a big power back who could be more effective after his 25th carry than he was with his first. Galbreath was traded to Minnesota.

The Saints also had chosen a hoped-for successor to Manning, quarterback Dave Wilson of Illinois, in a supplemental draft, costing them their second first-round pick in 1981. Safety Russell Gary was the first of two second-round picks with linebacker Rickey Jackson coming from a San Diego pick acquired in the Muncie trade. New Orleans had two third-round picks and took defensive end Frank Warren plus tight end Hoby Brenner. The club found a gem in the 12th round, nose tackle Jim Wilks.

Attitude readjustment was the next project, and Phillips got help there from his background and also from the fact the club won its second game of the season, beating the Rams, 23-17. Injuries reduced the effectiveness of Harris and Manning, but Wilson got valuable experience running the club. A 4-12 finish might not have been acceptable the year before, but it was certainly good enough following a one-win year. Rogers led the NFC with 378 carries and set a rookie yardage record with 1,674. Erxleben improved to 40.5 yards per punt, but Ricardo barely made half his field goal tries (13 of 25).

The general manager's duties were added to Phillips' coaching title on February 17th, and Eddie Jones, executive vice-president in the Nolan regime, returned as Saints' president. Lack of a dominant receiver prompted Phillips to use the choice he got from San Diego for Muncie to take Lindsay Scott. Center Brad Edelman was the second-round pick, while cornerback Rodney Lewis and wide receivers Eugene Goodlow and Kenny

AP/Wide World Photos

Morten Andersen (7)

Duckett plus safety John Krimm were third-round picks as Phillips traded players to stockpile draft choices.

But the Saints' best draft that year, maybe their best ever, came in the fourth round: kicker Morten Andersen, who has enjoyed an ongoing career that arguably has made him the best in NFL history. When Houston cut Ken Stabler, Phillips' quarterback with the Oilers, New Orleans snapped him up. One game into the season Phillips responded to Houston's frantic call for a replacement and sent Manning in exchange for tackle Leon Gray.

It was revealed during the offseason that Rogers had spent some $10,000 on cocaine, but after assurances that the habit was broken, the workhorse runner was welcomed back. Progress continued during the 1982 season, interrupted by a player strike after the second game. New Orleans was 1-1 when players walked out, won its first two when play was resumed on November

21st, and looked on the verge of its first playoff berth with the wily Stabler running the offense and a considerably improved defense.

Hopes Are Dashed Again

Four straight losses took care of notions of grandeur, but Phillips rallied the team for a season-ending victory to get back to 4-5. It was good enough to edge the 49ers for second place in the NFC West, but not good enough to put the Saints among the top eight qualifiers for the strike-revamped playoffs.

Phillips also had a plan, and when it required a change in philosophy, Bum did not hesitate to do so. Stockpiling draft choices was no longer necessary since the talent level had risen considerably. Now, he targeted specific needs and would send draft choices to fill them. A hole was plugged by swapping the No. 1 draft choice to the Packers for defensive end Bruce Clark, who wanted out of Green Bay. Guard Steve Korte and tight end John Tice were second- and third-round picks with an additional third-round choice obtained from St. Louis in the person of back Cliff Austin.

St. Louis fell, 28-17, to New Orleans in the season-starter as Rogers ran for a club record 206 yards. The team bumped off Miami, 17-7, then took a last-second 19-17 victory at Atlanta to improve to 4-2 and raise playoff hopes. But either age alone or the hard living that Stabler had done through most of his 37 years finally started to catch up with him. All he could muster was short passes, which allowed defenses to begin keying more and more on the runners.

The Saints were shut out twice in the last six games (a 21-20 loss to Dallas on September 25th came because of a safety in the final two minutes) and held a 24-23 lead over Los Angeles late in the fourth quarter, with 70,148 fans screaming their support. But the Rams eked out a field goal in the final two seconds to leave the Saints 8-8 and out of the playoffs yet one more year.

Jackson, safety Gary, and cornerback Johnnie Poe were emerging young players on a defense that was getting better. Stabler threw twice as many interceptions (18) as touchdown passes and wound up 13th among QBs. Andersen, though, took care of the placekicking problem by hitting 75 percent of his 24 tries. Erxleben kept his punting average up to 41.0.

Realizing Stabler was showing his age, Phillips gambled by sending his No. 1 1984 draft choice to the New York Jets for Richard Todd, a respectable veteran quarterback coming off a sub-par year. The move didn't pan out, and Phillips shot himself in the foot on October 9th by swapping the Saints' top 1985 choice to Houston for his workhorse with the Oilers, Earl Campbell. Center Joel Hilgenbert was a good fourth-round pick, while the Saints' choice in the ninth round was a Pro Bowl pick as a rookie, punter Brian Hansen.

Todd won the quarterbacking job, but 'Snake' Stabler didn't like playing backup so he slithered off into retirement after eight games. The presence of Campbell gave New Orleans two wheelhorses on a one-horse wagon. Rogers had the lead role, but his yardage dropped to less than 1,000. Add to that Campbell's 468, and the two totaled close to what Rogers made by himself as a 1981 rookie.

Clark had a Pro Bowl season and formed the backbone of a good defense with fellow Pro Bowler Jackson, who had surged to prominence the season before by leading NFL linebackers in sacks with 12. Atlanta beat New Orleans, 36-28, in the opening game, but the Saints struggled back to 3-2 before a three-game losing streak put them in a big hole. The Saints won two straight but dropped four of their last five to wind up 7-9, meaning they had still never broken .500. At season's end, owner John Mecom, Jr., announced he would take $75 million for the franchise.

Todd was 15th among NFC QBs, but he only threw one touchdown pass and had 19 interceptions. And two of the top three pass-catchers were backs. Having already mortgaged the future, Phillips tried to pay it off by trading Rogers to Washington, plus 5th-, 10th-, and 11th-round choices, for the Redskins' No. 1 choice. He drafted linebacker Alvin Toles.

When the USFL went under after its 1984 campaign, the NFL held a special draft, and the Saints got linebacker Vaughan Johnson, back Mel Gray, and linebacker Steve Bearden. They also signed Bobby Hebert, who had quarterbacked the Michigan Panthers to the first USFL title in 1983.

Todd demonstrated that his best years were over, so Phillips tried both Wilson and Hebert during the season. Campbell's skills were fading, the defense was giving up three touchdowns a game, and there was no standout wideout. Dave Wilson threw 11 touchdown passes (and 15 interceptions), but the best part of the New Orleans offense was Andersen, who tried 35 field goals and made an incredible 31 of them.

Franchise Sold

Complicating matters was the sale of the franchise. Negotiations with A. N. Pritzker didn't pan out, but by March 12th, Mecom had reached agreement with Tom Benson, Jr., an automobile dealer who later got into banking. On May 31st, Benson took ownership of the Saints from Mecom for $70.204 million and assumed the position of managing general partner.

New Orleans was losing two-thirds of its games when it upset Minnesota, 30-23, on November 24th. Phillips resigned the next day and let his son Wade, the defensive coordinator, run the team for the last four games. Eddie Jones, director of football operations Pat Peppler, and offensive coordinator King Hill also resigned as Benson formulated his own management plans.

Wade Phillips coached New Orleans to a second straight upset, but the Saints closed out with three more defeats to finish 5-11. He went on to coach at Denver. Jim Finks, who masterminded success at Minnesota and Chicago and had hopes of succeeding Rozelle as commissioner, was hired to bring his blueprint for success to New Orleans. The Saints had such plans in the past, of course, but kept changing them every few years.

Finks had joined the Vikings when they were four years old, and by the time he left, they had lost two Super Bowls and were about to lose two more. He quit to rebuild the Bears in 1974. Three years later they were in the playoffs, and by the time he resigned in 1983, the building was almost complete on the team that would win the Super Bowl in 1985. He was allowed to become part-owner of the Saints when he joined the organization January 14th and two weeks later had settled on the most successful USFL coach, Jim Mora, as his coach.

Director of scouting Joe Woolley was allowed to work through the draft before being let go. Bill Kuharich, son of late former pro and college head coach Joe Kuharich, had worked with Mora in Philadelphia and was made director of player personnel. Tackle Jim Dombrowski, injured early in his rookie season but a regular since then, was the first choice in a very productive draft. Back Dalton Hilliard was second, while back Rueben Mayes, linebacker Pat Swilling, and back Barry Word were all taken in the third round. There was also a free agent find, linebacker Sam Mills. Swilling has been in four recent Pro Bowls; Mayes and Hilliard have been in one each. Johnson, the linebacker the club got in the USFL draft, has also been in the last four Pro Bowls.

Campbell retired in training camp as it became clear Mayes was going to carry the load in 1986. New Orleans got out of the gate slowly, winning just once in five tries, but the Saints responded to the whip Mora was using. He fined players. He benched them. He cut non-producers. He worked them hard. And gradually they got better.

The Picture Improves

Indianapolis fell, 17-14, in the sixth game, as did Tampa Bay in the next game. After a loss, three straight wins put the Saints over .500. They lost three out of four and took a 33-17 defeat in the season's last game to wind up 7-9. The offense scored less points than the year before, 288-

AP/Wide World Photos

Pat Swilling (56) sacks Steelers quarterback Bubby Brister, one of three he made in the first quarter

294, but the excellent linebacking helped the defense trim its total by more than 100, to 287 from 401. The average of 3.2 yards permitted per rush was lowest in the NFC, and its special teams coverage the best.

Mayes finished with 1,353 yards rushing, fourth best in the NFL, and was the NFC's Rookie of the Year. Gray averaged 27.9 yards returning kickoffs. Dave Wilson only stood 11th among NFC quarterbacks, though, and his TD/interception ratio was 10/17. Hebert was sparingly used. Defensive end Shawn Knight was a wasted top 1987 draft choice, lasting just one season. No. 2 choice Lonzell Hill, a wide receiver, contributed for a couple of seasons, but the best players for the Saints were their Nos. 7 and 8 picks, safety Gene Atkins and cornerback Toi Cook.

Regardless of the outcome of the draft, the Saints were about to grow up. It seemed about time—they were 21 years old. The Saints marched in the season with a 28-21 win over the Cleveland Browns, getting a team-record two safeties in the game and a 147-yard rushing effort from Mayes.

Following a second-game loss, NFL players went on strike. New Orleans' replacement team put the regulars in good position by winning two of its three games. Quarterback of the irregulars was John Fourcade, a New Orleans native. San Francisco beat New Orleans, 24-22, in the first game following the return of the regulars. It was the last game the Saints were to lose in a 12-3 seasons that was the best the club ever had.

Guiding the team during that stretch was Hebert, who only placed 14th on the table of NFC quarterbacks but whose balancing of running and passing, both the long game and the short game, was superb. Hebert had just nine interceptions and threw 15 TD passes, although he passed for just 2,119 yards.

Mayes nearly got to 1,000 yards (missing by 83), while Gray continued as the most feared returner in the league, averaging 21.2 yards on kickoffs and 14.7 on punts. The defense maintained its level from the previous season, allowing just 283 points, on the excellent play of linebackers Johnson, Jackson, Swilling, and Mills. It was tested the fewest number of times on the ground of any defense in the league, intercepted the most passes, and was sixth in fumble recoveries. It was among the stingiest in first downs allowed.

A Playoff Spot

The only thing the nine-game winning streak got the Saints was a spot in the playoffs, though, since the 49ers finished a game ahead of them. At least the Saints got to host their first playoff game, since they were the wild card team with the best record. Minnesota spotted New Orleans a 7-0 lead on Hebert's ten-yard scoring pass to Eric Martin, then scored 24 unanswered points and took a 31-10 halftime lead on the way to a 44-10 victory. Mayes suffered a knee injury in the game, requiring surgery, and Hebert, intercepted twice, could only manage 84 yards passing. New Orleans had just 149 yards net offense.

A reward for the good season was that six Saints—Andersen, Brenner, Edelman (now playing guard), Mayes, Mills, and Waymer—were selected to play in the Pro Bowl game. Finks was named Executive of the Year and Mora Coach of the Year. Coming off the glow of the best season in the Saints' history, one would figure 1988 to be a struggle. And it was. The draft yielded another heavy duty runner (literally—his weight was a squatty 250 pounds packed on a 5-11 frame), Craig 'Ironhead' Heyward at the top of the list, with wide receiver Brett Perriman second as the only other major contributor.

Hebert progressed to sixth on the NFC passing chart, his touchdown count again exceeding interceptions, 20-15. But with Mayes slow to recover from knee surgery, his passing yardage went up to 3,156. Hilliard ran for 823 yards, Mayes 628, and Heyward 355 as he battled weight problems as much as opposing tacklers. Martin again led receivers with 1,083 yards, while he and Hill each scored seven times.

New Orleans opened against San Francisco, not a good thing in those years, and lost a hard-fought 34-33 decision, rebounding with seven straight wins. Nicks here and there began to hurt the thin Saints, who split their next four. On November 27th the team lost a particularly frustrating game, 13-12, to the New York Giants because Andersen showed his mortality, missing a 29-yard field goal. It lost two more before closing the season with a 10-9 victory over Atlanta. The record of 10-6 was the second best in New Orleans' history. But it also left the Saints in third place in the NFC West, out of the playoffs again. Andersen, Mills, and Martin were Pro Bowl players.

The Saints were easier to pass on in 1988. The excellent linebacking corps was getting stretched to the limit because of a weak defensive line, having to pay more attention to the ground game and putting more emphasis on pass rushing.

How far the Saints had come was shown in the Plan B limited free agency the owners put in place for the 1989 season, their ploy to forestall complete free agency. New Orleans lost eight players and signed only three. Finks targeted the defense for draft help by taking defensive end Wayne Martin first and cornerback Robert Massey second. Other helpful picks from that draft included tackle Kevin Haverdink (5th) and wide receiver Floyd Turner (6th), both on some All-Rookie teams.

Finks was the lone candidate to succeed retiring Rozelle at a summer NFL meeting, falling short of election and leading to the selection of Paul Tagliabue in the middle of the season. Jackson got hurt in an automobile accident before the season, and Swilling held out in a contract dispute to get the Mora's fourth season off to a poor start.

The first opening day shutout in the club's history preceded four straight losses before New Orleans righted itself with five wins in the next six games. Then, on December 3rd, Detroit beat New Orleans, 21-14. That left the Saints at 6-7, and Mora benched Hebert for the next game in favor of Fourcade, who had been sharpening his skills in the summer Arena Football League.

Fourcade became the franchise's darling by leading New Orleans to three season-closing wins, throwing seven touchdown passes and running for one. It was the third winning season in a row for a franchise that had not had any until Finks and Mora arrived. But it still wasn't good enough to put the Saints in the playoffs for the second time.

Despite the benching and criticism that he wasn't generating enough offense, Hebert threw 15 TD passes (and 15 interceptions). He also completed 62.9 percent of his 353 passes for 2,686 yards. Hilliard had a Pro Bowl year (Johnson and Swilling were also honored) with 1,262 yards rushing and 18 touchdowns (13 rushing, 5 passing), while Martin led the team with 1,090 yards and 68 catches.

The Saints lost ten players in the Plan B signings, picking up just two. The defense drew first priority in the first four rounds of the 1990 draft: defensive end Renaldo Turnbull, cornerback Vince Buck, and linebackers Joel Smeenge and DeMond Winston. The club also acquired nose tackle Robert Goff in a trade with Tampa Bay.

Hebert, smarting over the benching and feeling financially underappreciated, declined to report to training camp and began a bitter protracted negotiation on a long-term contract. Finally, Hebert requested a trade to another team, preferably the Raiders, and the Saints granted him permission to negotiate one on his own. Mora, a proponent of team play over the star system, shrugged his shoulders and went on. He opened the season with the man from nowhere, Fourcade, as his quarterback, but San Francisco won the opener, 13-12; New Orleans was drubbed in the second game and won its first game by beating a poor Phoenix team, 28-7.

With Fourcade showing little, and a feeling the season was too promising to throw away, Finks paid Dallas a stiff price to get Steve Walsh, a softer-throwing graduate from the Miami quarterback factory who was backing up Troy Aikman. It took 1991's first- and third-round choices plus a No. 2 in 1992 to make the deal.

Hilliard suffered a season-ending knee injury October 21st, the game Walsh made his debut as a starter, and New Orleans struggled. Walsh, though inconsistent, produced a winning record while at the helm, and two straight wins at the close of the season brought the Saints to .500. But 8-8 this year was good enough to make the playoffs, thanks to the expanded playoff system that was a function of the league expanding television coverage in an effort to offset the declining worth of its network TV contracts.

Wild-Card Game

The Saints went to Chicago to play the Bears in a wild card game, with the result only marginally better than their first post-season experience. New Orleans managed just 193 yards net offense in a 16-6 defeat. Hilliard returned to the lineup, but the ground game produced just 65 yards. The inexperienced Walsh completed just 6 of 16 passes and was intercepted once before Fourcade replaced him with similar results.

Special teams excelled for New Orleans, which had conference lows in field goals against (just 60 percent) and the lowest numbers on kickoff returns. It also was among the leaders in overall defense. The strength of the New Orleans linebacking crew was acknowledged in the naming of Johnson and Swilling to the Pro Bowl team again. Andersen also made the NFC team again.

Turnbull led conference rookies with 11 sacks. Walsh ranked 13th among conference quarterbacks but kept his interceptions to a minimum (13) and threw 12 touchdown passes. His completion rate was low (53.3), even though Mora kept him to possession passes to reduce risk. Martin nearly made 1,000 yards (912) and caught a team-best 63 passes.

Despite being cleaned out, the 1991 draft was not a washout. The highest choice was second-rounder Wesley Carroll, a wide receiver. Other choices who lasted included cornerback Reginald Jones (5th), back Fred McAfee (6th), and tight end Frank Wainwright (8th). Guard Derek Kennard was picked up in a trade with Phoenix. Hebert and the team settled their differences in the off-season in a minimally acrimonious fashion. Walsh was returned to understudy.

The 1991 season began with seven straight victories, and visions of Super Bowl danced in their heads. Then reality aimed a kick to the ribs. Chicago stopped the streak, 20-17, but New Orleans regrouped to win two more before Hebert suffered a shoulder injury that sidelined him for the remainder of the season in a 24-21 loss at San Diego. Walsh returned as the starter with an opportunity to guide the Saints to their first division crown.

Atlanta stalled the first bid to clinch with a 50-yard overtime field goal for a 23-20 victory. New Orleans also dropped the next two before snapping the four-game skid with a 27-0 blanking of the Raiders to sew up its first division title. The Saints also ran up 27 points in beating the Cardinals to finish 11-5.

Because the defensive line now got off a good pass rush to complement the best linebackers in the conference, the Saints allowed fewer points than anyone in the NFL (211). They were second in yardage given up, while Swilling led both leagues in sacks (17) and was named Defensive Player of the Year.

Atlanta and New Orleans had each won on the other's turf during the regular season, but the host Saints were still favored in the post-season meeting of the NFC West's top two teams. Hebert returned to quarterback and guided New Orleans to a 13-10 halftime lead. Atlanta wide receiver Michael Haynes put his team ahead with a 20-yard pass from Chris Miller in the third quarter. Hilliard got the Saints back on top, 20-17, at the start of the fourth quarter with a one-yard run, but Norm Johnson tied it with a 36-yard field goal; the Falcons kept New Orleans winless in post-season play when Haynes caught a 61-yard touchdown pass. The game was close statistically, but New Orleans made one more turnover.

Statistically, there wasn't much to choose between Hebert and Walsh, either. The veteran was 10th in the QB standings, while the younger man was ninth. Walsh threw eleven TD passes to Hebert's nine and had six picked off while the older player threw eight to the wrong guys. Walsh had 1,638 yards, Hebert 1,676. Hebert completed 60.1 percent of 248 passes, Walsh 55.2 percent of 255.

Turner blossomed into a top receiver, leading the team with 927 yards on 64 receptions. Martin had the most catches, 66, for 803 yards. Johnson, Mills, and Swilling were all named to start for the NFC in the Pro Bowl game, with special teams expert Bennie Thompson also making the team.

A running back, Vaughn Dunbar, was drafted first in 1992 to beef up a weak ground game. It looked like another slip-back when New Orleans broke even in its first four games, but a 9-1 surge saw them stay near San Francisco at the top. Unfortunately, two of those first three losses were to the 49ers, who finished two games ahead of the Saints. A defeat to Buffalo left New Orleans 12-4, the four defeats by a cumulative total of 11 points.

The defense was even better than the previous season, limiting teams to 202 points, easily the lowest in both conferences, and was at the bottom of the NFL in net yards allowed (2,470). In nearly every important statistical category the Saints were near the lead. The team had returned to their success of 1977, when it led the league in most sacks (57) and fewest sacks allowed (15).

PROFILE	Jim Finks

The legacy of Jim Finks is that he built winners. Finks turned losers into winners at all three stops of his professional football sojourning: Minnesota, Chicago, and New Orleans. Diagnosed with lung cancer in April of 1993, Finks continued to keep in touch with the workings of the Saints as he battled the illness. When he came into the organization in 1986, Saints fans were so far beyond cynicism it took a winning season just to get back there.

"There was a certain cynicism," Finks told *Business Week* in 1991, "because they had heard so many times that 'This is the year.' Then it was the same old Saints, so no one believed us." Finks has made it look so easy that it's hard to believe just anyone can't walk into an NFL front office and turn a moribund franchise into a vibrant entity with just a few drafts and deals. But if it were so easy, then anyone could do it.

There are two common threads through Finks' turnarounds. First, he finds the best coach he can and then sticks with him. Then, he hires good scouts and player personnel people. He joined the Minnesota Vikings in 1964 when the Norm Van Brocklin-coached franchise was four years old. In 1967 Van Brocklin took his worn-out welcome to Atlanta, and Finks selected a relative unknown named Bud Grant to coach the team.

When Finks left in 1974 to rebuild the Chicago Bears, Grant was no longer a nobody. He inherited Abe Gibron as a coach in Chicago but the next year selected Jack Pardee, who left after 1977 to be replaced by Neill Armstrong, who was replaced in turn by Mike Ditka. It was under Finks' guidance that the majority of the players on Chicago's 1985 Super Bowl champions were drafted, although he left the club in 1983.

New Orleans made Finks an offer he couldn't refuse in 1986: some equity in the club, the presidency, and general managership. Searching around for a coach, he settled on a new face (instead of the NFL merry-go-round of faces), Jim Mora, late of the Philadelphia entry in the USFL. Mora had been that league's most successful coach in its short existence.

The former Pittsburgh Steelers' quarterback took some shots for running a tight ship and a tight pocketbook, but that's the way he is. Quarterback Bobby Hebert wanted $2 million a year in 1990, at least double what Finks thought he was worth. Hebert sat out a season, then came back to play for $1 million. He was waived after the 1992 season. The Saints had made the play-offs four times with Hebert on the roster, and he had quarterbacked three of the games. New Orleans' play-off record is 0-4.

But while he's tough with players, he's soft with fans. Finks gave New Orleans its first marketing department, inaugurated a news letter for fans, started up a fan club with 15,000 dues-paying members, has the team host an indoor tailgate party before every home game, and stages an annual festival to give fans a chance to meet the stars. Games at the 69,065-seat Superdome are regularly sold out now. Before Finks arrived, fans came to games with paper bags over their heads and called themselves "The Aints." Not a bad legacy for any person to have.

Aspiring to Greatness

Only an inability to get important points kept New Orleans from being a great team. The Saints scored 330 but had trouble moving the ball against better defenses. It showed in the playoffs when Philadelphia, another team with an excellent defense, limited New Orleans to just one field goal in the second half. New Orleans had a 20-7 margin after that field goal, but the Eagles matched it, then scored 26 unanswered points in the fourth quarter for a 36-20 victory. Hebert was intercepted three times, although he threw for 291 yards, and that just happened to be the difference. The Eagles had 349 yards offense, the Saints 360.

Hebert finished as the sixth-rated quarterback in the conference, throwing for 3,287 yards, completing 59 percent of his passes, throwing 19 touchdowns, and having 16 passes intercepted. Martin caught 68 passes for 1,041 yards, while Dunbar only marginally improved the running attack with 565 yards on 154 carries. Hilliard got to 445, while Heyward ran for 416.

Feeling Hebert was unable to get them over the hump, New Orleans did not offer the quarterback a contract for the 1993 season. It signed veteran free agent Wade Wilson and let him battle with Walsh, who did not see any action in 1992, for the starter's job. More shakeups followed. Linebacker Pat Swilling, who signed an offer sheet with Detroit the previous year to force New Orleans to match it, was traded to the Lions on draft day for first- and fourth-round draft choices. Turnbull inherited his spot.

After the draft, the Saints signed tackle Tootie Robbins, a free agent from Green Bay, and announced they would not offer a contract to their own tackle, 13-year veteran Brock, who left the Saints as the leader in games played with 186. New Orleans "traded" running backs with Chicago, too, signing Bears free agent Brad Muster and declining to offer a contract to Heyward, which allowed Chicago to sign him.

In the draft, the Saints used the Lions' choice to take tackle William Roaf, then sent San Francisco two draft choices to switch first-round selections and get tight end Irv Smith. Linebacker Reggie Freeman is the second-round choice. Shortly after the draft, the club announced that Finks has lung cancer, a development that will put a cloud on the team's future.

Sources

Books

Kasmiersky, Rusty, and Media Relations Staff, *New Orleans Saints Media Guide,* New Orleans, LA, 1993.

Neft, David S., Richard M. Cohen, and Rick Korch, *Sports Encyclopedia: Pro Football,* 11th edition, St. Martin's, 1993.

Porter, David L., editor, *Biographical Dictionary of American Sports: Football,* Greenwood Press, 1987.

Riffenburgh, Beau, *The Official NFL Encyclopedia,* NAL, 1986.

Periodicals

Business Week, December 16, 1991.

—Richard Shook

SAN FRANCISCO 49ERS

In the early 1970s, the National Football League added the San Francisco 49ers' volume to its book series, *Great Teams' Great Years*. Who could have known the Niners' greatest years were a decade away? No one could say the highlights detailed in the book weren't significant. There were great 49ers games and great 49ers players from the time of the team's birth in the old All-American Football Conference in 1946 through the 1950s, 1960s, and 1970s in the NFL. But today—and maybe for decades to come—when people speak of San Francisco's professional football history, they are bound to zero in on the 1980s.

There isn't much dispute that the Niners were the "Team of the Decade," winning four Super Bowl championships and 104 regular season games. In fact, a book on the 49ers entitled, *The San Francisco 49ers: Team of the Decade*, by Michael W. Tuckman and Jeff Schultz, was published in 1989. Bill Walsh is regarded as the coaching genius who engineered that incredible team. Joe Montana is considered the quarterback genius who was the catalyst. And Jerry Rice is the pass receiver who made both the quarterback and the coach look so smart.

There were, to be sure, many other heroes in the Niners' greatest decade, including wide receiver Dwight Clark, safety Ronnie Lott, running back Roger Craig, nose tackle Michael Carter, guard Randy Cross, and defensive end Fred Dean.

The club's owner since 1977, Eddie De Bartolo, was one of the most obvious beneficiaries of that magic decade. "There is no doubt that the team has dominated my life during this period," he told Tuckman and Schultz. "Owning an NFL franchise is similar to being a parent. One day your child will come through the door with a straight-A report card and three community service awards. The next week you'll receive a call advising you that he or she just wrecked your new automobile after attending a wild party. The wins are exhilarating, but the losses can be incredibly depressing to an owner who has made a strong commitment to winning."

Exhilaration came in fits and starts in the early years. Depression crept in often. But the success of the 1980s—and similar achievements early in the 1990s—helped San Francisco fans forget the failings of earlier Niners' teams.

But no one could argue the 49ers didn't have great achievers before the 1980s. Seven players who wore the scarlet and gold for at least part of their careers are enshrined in the Professional Football Hall of Fame in Canton, Ohio: Fullback Joe Perry and defensive tackle Leo Nomellini (inducted in 1969); halfback Hugh McElhenny (1970); quarterback Y.A. Tittle (1971); running back O.J. Simpson (1985); fullback John Henry Johnson (1987); and tackle Bob St. Clair (1990). Coach Walsh earned the honor in 1993.

The 49ers have also retired the numbers of seven players: Perry (34), McElhenny (39), Nomellini (73), quarterback John Brodie (12), defensive back Jimmy Johnson (37), defensive tackle Charlie Krueger (70), and wide receiver Dwight Clark (87). There also have been countless All-Pro, All-Conference, and Pro Bowl performers over the last nearly five decades of the franchise.

Lawrence "Buck" Shaw had a fine record (72-40-4) as the 49ers' first head coach. And there were others before Walsh who had made their marks with decent records, including Frankie Albert, Howard "Red" Hickey, and Dick Nolan.

In the beginning

In light of the rate at which records were being set in the 1980s and 1990s—with star players filling Pro Bowl rosters and fans delighting at championships—the previous "glory years" of the 49ers seem to have gotten shunted aside. But there were other significant successes, all the way back to 1946 when the team debuted in the All-American Football Conference.

Anthony J. Morabito, a partner in a San Francisco lumber firm, had tried but failed to get an NFL franchise, so he formed the 49ers in 1946 as a charter member of the AAFC. One of Morabito's partners in Lumber Terminals of San Francisco—either Allen E. Sorrell or E.J. Turre—is believed to have nicknamed the team. John Blackinger was named general manager.

The original 49ers emblem showed a booted prospector in a lumberjack's shirt and checkered pants, his hat blown off and his hair askew. His feet were spread apart and two revolvers were in his hands. In those days, instead of "49ers," the name was spelled out, "Forty-Niners."

Morabito raided NFL teams for players, as did other AAFC teams. He signed notable Bay Area college players, such as quarterback Frankie Albert and fullback Norm Standlee of Stanford (and an ex-Chicago Bear). Santa Clara's Lawrence T. "Buck" Shaw was named coach, and the team rented Kezar Stadium for its games.

In 1946, the Forty-Niners finished second to the Browns (12-2) in the AAFC with a 9-5 record. Highlights of the season included a 34-20 victory over Cleveland in one of two games against the eventual champs. (The other was a 14-7 loss.) Former Santa Clara end Alyn Beals of the Niners, who often ran deep patterns, led the conference in receiving with 40 catches for 586 yards. The top lineman was former Eagle Bruno Banducci.

Morabito would be accused of putting the area's Catholic colleges out of the football business. His alma mater, Santa Clara, as well as the University of San Francisco and St. Mary's all played their games on Sundays at Kezar Stadium, because they could not compete on Saturdays with Stanford and the University of California. The Niners' Sunday games in Kezar pushed out the Catholic schools and resulted in a great deal of negative publicity for the team.

The 1947 San Francisco team again finished second behind Cleveland, with an 8-4-2 record. The 5-10, 160-pound Albert kept fans interested with his fine ball handling and unpredictable play calling. He completed 128 of 242 passes for 1,692 yards and 18 touchdowns. "Little Frankie dealt out fakes in the backfield ... by sending defenders

Team Information at a Glance

Founding date: 1946 (AAFC)

Home stadium: Candlestick Park
4949 Centennial Blvd.
Santa Clara, CA 95054
Phone: (408) 562-4949
Seating capacity: 66,390

Team colors: Forty niners gold and scarlet
Team nickname: 49ers
Logo: Capital letters "S" and "F"

Franchise record	Won	Lost	Tie
(1946-92)	360	281	15

Super Bowl victories (4): 1981, 1984, 1988, 1989

in hot pursuit of runners who didn't even have the ball," said David Neft and Richard Cohen in *The Football Encyclopedia*. "Close to the end zone, he often would fake to all three backs, hide the ball behind his hip, and roll unmolested around end for a touchdown. Although his long passes wobbled like a crippled pigeon, Albert never hesitated to throw the ball to ends Alyn Beals and Nick Susoeff on quick, short patterns or on deep bombs. With Albert deftly shuffling pass plays, handoffs to his running backs, and bootleg keepers, enemy defenders never knew what was coming next."

Albert was named co-MVP of the league in 1948, sharing the honors with Cleveland quarterback Otto Graham. The Forty-Niners had a 12-2 record—the kind of mark that wasn't to return for decades—yet were runners-up again to the undefeated, untied Browns.

Joe "The Jet" Perry got his career off the ground with the Niners, beginning with a 58-yard run on his first play. Perry, an African-American, would face insults and violence because of his race, but he would lead San Francisco to the greatest team rushing yardage in pro football history. The team gained 3,663 yards on the ground, averaging 6.1 per carry and 262 per game, with 35 rushing touchdowns for the year and 495 points in all. Perry averaged 7.3 yards, with a 562 total; but Johnny Strzykalski led that year with 915 yards, averaging 6.5. Banducci, Visco Grgich, Riley Matheson and John Woudenberg were the ones opening up the holes on the offensive line.

Perry had scored 22 touchdowns in his first season at Compton Junior College in California. San Francisco tackle John Woudenberg saw him play for the Naval Training Station team at Alameda and told Shaw and Tony Morabito about him. "Just point him in the right direction and watch him go," Woudenberg said. Perry accepted an offer from the Forty-Niners, turning down 14 good college offers.

He was first called "The Jet" after becoming one of the AAFC's stars. Albert is credited with giving him the nickname when he said, "I'm telling you, when that guy comes by to take a handoff his slipstream darn near knocks you over. He's strictly jet-propelled." In a 16-year pro career, Perry was to rush for 9,723 yards, second only to Cleveland's Jim Brown at the time of Perry's retirement.

Nineteen forty-nine was the last year for the AAFC, and it provided one last opportunity for San Francisco to finish second behind Cleveland. They did it with a 9-3 record, to the Browns' 9-1-2. A 56-28 victory at home over Cleveland at mid-season put the Forty-Niners in first place in what had become a one-division league that year. They wouldn't lose the lead until they dropped two consecutive games late in the campaign after being crippled by injuries to halfbacks Strzykalski and Ed Carr.

The Niners and the Browns played in Cleveland for the championship before 22,550 spectators. San Francisco lost 21-17 to Paul Brown's team. Albert wound up with 27 TD passes for the year. "I'd never even met Paul Brown," Shaw said. "Now I scheme to beat him, dream of beating him, and wind up screaming because I haven't beaten him."

Joining the NFL

On December 9, 1949, the AAFC went out of existence, and the Niners joined the Browns and Colts in moving to the National Football League. But the 1950 season would be uncharacteristically difficult for the team. The Niners won only three games, losing nine. A rival coach said they were "not big enough or tough enough." Shaw, though, uncovered two fine rookies: offensive-defensive tackle Leo Nomellini and end-placekicker Gordy Soltau. The league change didn't matter to the Browns; they won the championship again, beating the Rams in their first NFL title opportunity.

Nomellini was from Chicago—by way of Lucca, Italy. After Pearl Harbor Day he enlisted in the U.S. Marines and, in 1942, started to play football on a Leatherneck team at Cherry Point, North Carolina. The University of Minnesota offered him a scholarship after his term in the service, and he became a freshman starter. He would go on to be an All-NFL offensive performer in 1951 and 1952, then All-NFL defensive player in 1953, 1954, 1957, and 1959. He missed just two Pro Bowl games in 12 years.

In 1955, Nomellini, nicknamed "The Lion," averaged nearly 60 minutes per game. Soltau was first drafted by Green Bay then traded to Cleveland, where Lou Groza was firmly entrenched as the placekicker and where Dante Lavelli and Mac Speedie were standout ends. He was told by Coach Paul Brown he could make the team but wouldn't play much, so he welcomed the chance to be traded to San Francisco. "It's something I've never been sorry for," Soltau said.

A great rookie crop in 1951 helped the Niners to a 7-4-1 record, finishing just a half game out of first in the National Conference. Defense led the way, with the help of shoulder tackler Hardy Brown. Quarterback Y.A. Tittle and end Billy Wilson joined the 49ers that year. Tittle had come from the Colts, who sold their franchise back to the league after the 1950 season. Although two-platoon football was now common, many players still had to play both offense and defense because the roster limit was only 33 players.

In 1952 the 49ers won their first five games before hitting a slump on their way to a 7-5 record. A fake punt by Albert went awry when San Francisco was leading Chicago 17-10; this created strained relations between the quarterback and Shaw and led to a 20-17 loss, which precipitated the skid. Meanwhile, halfback Hugh McElhenny, a rookie from the University of Washington, became the league's Player of the Year as he averaged nearly seven yards per carry.

Albert and Strzykalski retired after the 1952 season. Morabito suffered a heart attack during the year, Lou Spadia became general manager, and Standlee was stricken with polio and never would play football again.

Nineteen fifty-three featured the 49ers' best NFL showing so far, a 9-3 record. Normally that would be good for first place, but Detroit was 10-2 that year. The three losses were by a total of nine points, and two came while Tittle was sidelined because of a severe facial injury. Perry became one of the few players in the league to hit the 1,000-yard rushing mark in a season. For his 1,018-yard total, Perry was awarded a bonus of $5,090 by Morabito—$5 for each yard.

Perry was the lone African-American on the team for quite a while, until Bob Mike was signed from UCLA in 1948. The next, Charley Powell, arrived in 1952, right out of San Diego High School. "I think the nucleus of our team in the forties was southern boys, and we got along fabulously," Perry said. "We were like one big, happy family. If one guy [on another team] got angry, it didn't do any good. He couldn't fight, because he'd have to fight all of us. And hell, I was part of the family. This team has always been like that.... Although I guess the big business factor has entered into football and most of the young players don't think like the older players. They didn't go through the same things we did. Consequently, I don't think they're as close-knit as the clubs were back in those day."

For the second consecutive year, Soltau led the NFL in scoring (94 points on seven touchdowns from his end position, 34 extra points, and six field goals). The 6'9", 260-pound tackle Bob St. Clair was in his rookie year. In practice St. Clair was matched against Nomellini—both future Hall of Famers. Their confrontations were described as being "like a couple of bull elephants trying to get out of a phone booth," according to Mickey Herskowitz in *The Golden Age of Pro Football*.

Undefeated after five games in 1954, the 49ers then lost three in a row to fall back in the standings. The slide began when McElhenny suffered a shoulder separation, with Tittle and Perry also incurring injuries. Perry still became the first player in the league to pass the 1,000-yard rushing mark in consecutive seasons. Joining him in the backfield was John Henry Johnson, an acquisition from the Canadian Football League. The two backs finished 1-2 in rushing in the NFL. Together with McElhenny, they were known as the "Million Dollar Backfield." Shaw was fired at the end of the season, although he had a .638 winning percentage on a record of 72-40-4.

"Those who were close to the San Francisco 49ers—including the bankers who held the team's notes—insist that Hugh McElhenny saved the franchise" during those years, Herskowitz wrote. "He was never able to convert his immense talents into a title for San Francisco, not in nine seasons of trying, but he became the dominant running back of the fifties. And the 49ers were fun to watch. It was an eternal contest to see if McElhenny and Y.A. Tittle could score touchdowns as fast as the 49ers defense gave them away."

With Norman "Red" Strader at the helm, the 1955 team struggled through a 4-8 record. Strader was quickly fired and soon suffered a fatal heart attack. Former superstar quarterback Frank Albert, only 36, was given the coach's job in 1956, and the 49ers finished 5-6-1—after starting out 1-6. Halfback Joe Arenas made his debut and became a standout kick returner. Early in the season, Albert benched Tittle in favor of rookie Earl Morrall of Michigan State, but Tittle soon got his job back, rallying the Niners to four victories and a tie in the last five games.

San Francisco drew 522,339 spectators, an NFL record at the time. "He looked about 10 years younger," Brodie said of Albert in his book, *Open Field*. "They called him 'The Boy Wonder.' He hadn't changed much. He coached the same way he had played and this gave the whole team a kind of free-wheeling vitality both on and off the field."

Nineteen fifty-seven would turn into one of the 49ers' most memorable seasons. A three-game winning streak at the end of the year gave them an 8-4 record and a first-place tie with Detroit. The teams had a Western Conference playoff game to see who would earn the right to meet perennial East champ Cleveland in the title game.

It looked like the 49ers were a shoo-in when Tittle passed them to a 27-7 halftime lead. But substitute quarterback Tobin Rote rallied the Lions to an incredible 31-27 victory, considered one of Detroit's all-time greatest games. It would be San Francisco's last postseason competition until

1970. "If you'd walked into our dressing room after that game, you would have seen 35 grown men crying," Perry said.

Still, Tittle, McElhenny, Perry, Wilson, and new receiver R.C. Owens would perform well all year, along with defenders Nomellini and Marv Matusak. Tittle and the 6'5" Owens perfected the "Alley-Oop" pass, a long, high bomb into a crowd, with Owens just out-jumping the defenders for the ball.

The season had begun with a 20-10 loss to Chicago, and it seemed something different was needed to spice up the offense. In practice, disgusted with the pass rush, Tittle flung the ball high and deep down the field, with former Idaho basketball player Owens leaping to snare it. According to Herskowitz, Hickey exclaimed, "Hey, there's our Alley-Oop play." The duo worked on it all week, and the play succeeded twice in a 23-20 triumph over the Rams.

"Tittle was no loser," said Herskowitz. "But his legend was reduced by the fact that he never quarterbacked a team that ran the course. He is remembered best, ironically, for a gimmick: The Alley-Oop play. Yet he was a tough, persistent operator whose thoughts were often original, and as a passer he was nearly an artist."

Brodie was a rookie in 1957, and Morrall was another promising star already with the club. At a team meeting one day, Brodie wrote in his book, he told Morrall, "With this many quarterbacks it looks like one of us ain't gonna do much playing." His rival leaned over and said, "Hey, John. If you think either one of us is going to play any football here, you'd better take another think, because the best quarterback in the league [Tittle] is right here in this room."

The 49ers, Brodie said, were "held together by a special spirit and sense of loyalty," because they were one of only two West Coast teams. "The 49ers had entered big league football late in 1946, like a brash upstart from some uncharted part of the country. From the beginning it had been a loose, wide-open team. Win or lose, they played colorful football."

Such promise would erode into a 6-6 season the next year, Albert's last as coach. Tony Morabito, only 47, had collapsed during a game and died of a heart attack during the 1957 season, and 1958 was his brother Vic's first year as club president. The star players were getting old, and younger talent had to be woven in. Brodie played a lot in place of Tittle in 1958. Abe Woodson was a welcome addition as a defensive back and kick returner.

In 1959, Hickey replaced Albert, who had resigned as coach. Brodie gained more valuable experience as the leader-to-be at quarterback, and converted defensive back J.D. Smith became the team's second 1,000-yard rusher. Charlie Krueger was a rookie defensive tackle. The team finished with a 7-5 record and a tie for third in the NFC West. The 49ers ended the 1950s with a record of 63-54-3, and a two-decade mark of 101-68-5.

The 1960s

Innovation by Hickey highlighted the beginning of the 1960s. His newly-installed "shotgun" attack helped save the 1960 season from disaster, with Brodie beating out Tittle as starter. The formation led to victories in four of the last five games for a 7-5 record. In the shotgun, the quarterback stands three to five yards behind the center and takes a long snap. It allows for more time, because defenders have farther to go to reach him.

In addition to the more potent offense—which now featured future coach Monte Clark at tackle—defense was a season-long strength. Veteran linebacker Matt Hazeltine, Nomellini, Woodson, and his secondary mates Jerry Mertens, Eddie Dove, and Dave Baker were important contributors.

Nineteen sixty-one was another winning season, 7-6-1, but it nevertheless featured the kind of mediocrity that would dog the Niners throughout the 1960s. Hickey's shotgun was the talk of the football world, especially after a 49-0 drubbing of the Lions three weeks into the season. Rookie Bill Kilmer from UCLA was employed at quarterback often, because his running ability better complemented the passing advantages of the new formation. But Brodie and Bobby Waters sometimes were used alternately with Kilmer, with Brodie being used in the more conventional T-formation.

The 49ers took a 4-1 record into Chicago, where the Bears had devised a strategy to control the shotgun, thanks to scouting work by Clark Shaughnessy. It worked, to the tune of a 31-0 Bears victory. Thus exposed, the shotgun wasn't very effective again, although partly because Hickey was reluctant to use it much after getting burned so badly.

At 6-8 in 1962, the 49ers finished under .500 for the first time in four years. They won five of seven road games, but just one at Kezar Stadium. St. Clair, Hickey's best offensive lineman, suffered an Achilles tendon injury. Seven players underwent knee operations during the season. Kilmer broke a leg in a car accident and missed the last three games. Age had cut down Nomellini's quickness. And flanker Bernie Casey, who went on to a movie acting career, led the receivers with 819 yards on 53 catches.

Eventual champion Chicago lost only one game all season in 1963, 20-14 to San Francisco. But that was one of the only bright spots for the Niners that year. They finished with a 2-12 record, by far their worst ever. Woodson returned three kickoffs for touchdowns, forcing some teams to resort to squib kicks so he wouldn't get the ball. One of the returns was for 105 yards, led by unbelievable blocking by St. Clair. According to one report, he blocked six opponents on the play, two of whom had to be helped off the field.

St. Clair built a successful chain of liquor stores in San Francisco. And he later became the mayor of Daly City, California, for a term. He was nicknamed "Geek" because of some of his habits, which included eating raw meat, raw fish, and raw eggs. While having dinner with a sports writer, St. Clair ate his steak raw. "Good liquor and a big sweat relax me," he said. "I'm a guy under a good deal of tension."

Brodie broke an arm in 1963, and veteran Lamar McHan took over. Other injuries spelled disaster, including those to Krueger and Mertens. At mid-season Hickey was fired and replaced by ex-Lions superstar defensive back-kick returner and eventual Hall-of-Famer Jack Christiansen. Nomellini retired with an NFL record 184 consecutive games played.

In May 1964, Vic Morabito died of a heart attack at the age of 44. Injuries to key personnel kept the offense from blossoming, but the defense was among the league's best. Taking some of the sting out of the 4-10 season were good rookie performances by end Dave Parks, quarterback George Mira, and linebacker Dave Wilcox, as well as Casey and receiver Monte Stickles.

The 1965 49ers led the league in scoring and total offense, finishing 7-6-1. Brodie was the

Milestone Makers

• Six players for San Francisco have rushed for 1,000 yards in a season, topped by Roger Craig, who hit that mark three times, and Joe Perry on two occasions. Craig's 1,502 yards in 1988 leads the way. The others were J.D. Smith, Delvin Williams, Wendell Tyler, and Ricky Watters.

• Four 49ers quarterbacks have passed for 3,000 yards in a season. Joe Montana did it seven times, including the all-time best of 3,944 in 1990. Others to reach the level were John Brodie, Steve DeBerg and Steve Young. Brodie hit it twice.

• On the receiving end, seven players have accumulated 1,000 yards in a season, led emphatically by Jerry Rice with seven such years. John Taylor did it twice, while R.C. Owens, Dave Parks, Gene Washington, Dwight Clark, and Roger Craig did it once each. The best total was 1,570 by Rice in 1986.

league's most productive quarterback, completing 262 of 381 passes for 3,112 yards and a whopping 30 touchdowns. Parks led the league in receptions with 80 for 1,344 yards. Rookie Ken Willard and veteran John David Crow, acquired in a trade from St. Louis in the off-season, paced a solid ground attack. In the season opener, the Niners beat Chicago 52-24. It was the most points ever given up by the Bears.

San Francisco ended the 1966 season with a 6-6-2 record. Parks and guard John Thomas were All-Pro. The American Football League had tried to lure Brodie to the Houston Oilers, giving him contract leverage which he used to bargain for a $900,000 multi-year contract with the 49ers. That deal eventually helped push the AFL and NFL into a merger: Teams started going broke trying to outbid rivals from the other league.

After an auspicious 5-1 start, San Francisco wound up 7-7 in 1967 as injuries and a six-game losing streak took the team out of contention. The 49ers were the only team to beat Los Angeles in the regular season. Mira came off the bench to lead them to victory twice at the end of the season, after which Christiansen was canned.

Dick Nolan was named the new head coach for 1968 and experienced some success right away, as the improved 7-6-1 record indicated. Spadia took the title of president and Jack White became general manager. But the 49ers happened to be in the NFL's strongest division, the Coastal Division of the Western Conference, and three losses and a tie were against division rivals Baltimore and Los Angeles. Receiver Clifton McNeil and guard Howard Mudd were chosen to the All-NFL team.

Unfortunately, the decade closed on a sour note, a 4-8-2 campaign that was injury-plagued. It was six weeks into the 1969 season before the 49ers won a game. Cornerback Jimmy Johnson emerged as an All-Pro. Hazeltine had retired. Among the promising rookies were wide receiver Gene Washington and tight end Ted Kwalick. Mudd and Crow were named to the All-NFL team of the decade. But the 1960s closed for the Niners with a none-too-impressive 57-74-7 total record.

Reorganization

In 1970, to San Francisco's benefit, the league was reorganized by a merger with the AFL. After years of near misses and disappointing finishes, the 49ers finally put just about everything together, winning the new West Division with a 10-3-1 record. The Niners met the Vikings in the playoffs and won 17-14 on two fourth-quarter Brodie TD passes to win a spot in the NFC championship game. They met Dallas at Kezar Stadium, but the Cowboys won a 17-10 decision.

Still, it was easily the team's best year ever. "San Francisco fans were accustomed to finishing as also-rans and they took the loss to Dallas ... philosophically," said Petersen Publishing's 1971 annual, *Pro Football*. "Even the press seemed not to want to pick the game apart." Brodie was named NFC Player of the Year, defensive back Bruce Taylor Rookie of the Year, and Nolan Coach of the Year. Washington caught 53 passes for 1,100 yards. Brodie threw for nearly 3,000 yards and 24 touchdowns.

Brodie was a San Francisco native who went to Stanford without a football scholarship. He broke all the passing records there—formerly held by Albert—and was an All-American, as well as MVP in the 1957 College All-Star Game. The 49ers made him their No. 1 draft choice. "I didn't know if I'd make it," he said. "In those days clubs only carried two quarterbacks."

The team kept Brodie and Tittle and traded Morrall in 1956. "John has a great deal of ability and confidence in himself," Nolan said in 1970. "The players believe in him and what he does. He's not a holler guy—he does things positively." Washington, who was one of his teammates at Stanford, agreed, "Although he is a star, he's the kind of guy who helps everybody on the club." The 1971 *Pro Football Almanac* said: "For years Brodie had to live with the reputation of being a quarterback who couldn't win the big game. But last year he led his team to its first title in 49er history, and the boos at Kezar Stadium became cheers, the beer cans were raised in tribute instead of anger."

CLIFFHANGERS | **Top Games**

San Francisco was involved in three of the all-time top-10 games, as determined by the National Football League (numbers 2, 3, and 9):

No. 2 San Francisco 20, Cincinnati 16 in Super Bowl XXIII, January 22, 1989, at Joe Robbie Stadium in Miami, Florida. Joe Montana completed eight of nine passes in an 11-play, 92-yard drive in the final two minutes and 46 seconds, climaxed by a 10-yard touchdown pass with 34 seconds left to John Taylor, giving the 49ers their third Super Bowl title.

No. 3 San Francisco 28, Dallas 27 in the 1981 National Football Conference championship game, January 10, 1982, at Candlestick Park, San Francisco. Wide receiver Dwight Clark of the 49ers made a leaping catch of a decisive 6-yard touchdown pass from Joe Montana to close an 89-yard drive with 51 seconds left.

No. 9 San Francisco 38, New Orleans 35, December 7, 1980, at Candlestick Park, San Francisco. After trailing 35-7 at halftime, the 49ers became the first NFL team ever to overcome a 28-point deficit and win. San Francisco running back Lenvil Elliott had a 7-yard TD run, and Ray Wersching kicked the extra point for a 35-35 tie with 1:50 left in regulation. At 7:40 of overtime Wersching kicked a 36-yard field goal.

Nineteen seventy-one brought more successes and a 9-5 record. In addition to capturing the division title, the Niners beat Washington 24-20 at their new home, Candlestick Park, in an NFC playoff game. San Francisco clinched its division when it beat Detroit 31-27, ironically the identical score the Lions handed the 49ers in 1957 to knock them out of the championship.

The 1970 nemesis, Dallas, was host of the conference championship matchup, which they won, 14-3. Wilcox, Johnson, and center Forrest Blue were accorded All-Pro honors. A good rushing year from Willard (856 yards) helped take some of the pressure off Brodie, who threw for 2,600 yards and 18 touchdowns.

"Candlestick Park is an excellent example of the Morabitos versus the outside world," according to *Great Teams' Great Years*. "Candlestick was built by the city to house the baseball Giants when they came west. It was renovated a decade later, at enormous additional cost, to accommodate the 49ers as well. The process of renovation not only increased the seating capacity but, with its completed double-decking, provided an effective baffle against the winds that had frozen fans for 10 years and reduced the quality of competition at times to the level of a bad joke....

"Why wasn't Candlestick built for football as well as baseball to begin with? Why didn't the 49ers, destined to play there anyway, move in with the Giants in 1960? The city fathers were all for it, not only for the increased revenues from extra customers and extra dates, but because big crowds at Kezar Stadium were a constant headache. The lack of parking there caused game traffic to block private driveways." But the Morabitos, who wanted an extra deck put on Seals Stadium (which never happened), balked at going to Candlestick, and it would be 11 years before they made the move.

There was only a slight dropoff in 1972, to 8-5-1, and a two-point playoff loss to the Cowboys, 30-28. Dallas had trailed 28-13 before quarterback Roger Staubach led a great comeback. Former Heisman Trophy winner Steve Spurrier was an able nine-game replacement for the injured Brodie and helped the 49ers win the division for the third straight year. To finish first, San Francisco had to beat the Vikings in the final regular-season game.

The Niners won 20-17 with the aid of two more Brodie fourth-quarter TD passes.

That year, center Forrest Blue, defensive back Jimmy Johnson, tight end Ted Kwalick, wide receiver Gene Washington, and linebacker Dave Wilcox were All-Pro selections.

Nineteen seventy-three would see a slide to a 5-9 record, partially due to more key injuries and an unsettling quarterback situation. Washington and Johnson suffered with bad knees and had down seasons. Brodie, who retired along with Krueger after the season, was on the bench behind Spurrier and Joe Reed after a slow start.

He did start the November 5 game in Detroit, a 30-20 loss in which he threw six interceptions. It was his first start in four games—and one of the worst days of his career. "I'll have to look at the films to see what happened," Brodie said in an Associated Press story. "I just had an off day, that's all." Nolan, knowing the 38-year-old Brodie would retire, made him the starter in the final game in 1973 but had to pull him in the first half against Pittsburgh due to a sore arm.

After a preseason injury to Spurrier in 1974, Nolan tried five different quarterbacks. The team won the first two games, lost seven in a row, then closed with a rush to finish 6-8. One of the losses was in Detroit, 17-3, in a game that featured the starting debut of left-handed quarterback Dennis Morrison. He wouldn't get too many more opportunities, after completing 17 of 40 passes, with three interceptions.

On the other side of the line, though, Danny Abramowicz caught a five-yard pass that tied him with Lance Alworth for the all-time record of receptions for 96 consecutive games. He would go on to break that mark in a great career. Running back Wilbur Jackson was one publication's Rookie of the Year. Blue and punter Tom Wittum were All-NFC picks. Wilcox ended an 11-year career by retiring at the end of the season.

A 24-23 victory over Los Angeles ended a string of 10 straight losses to the Rams, but that wasn't enough to help salvage the 1975 season, which the 49ers finished with a 5-9 record. Ends Tommy Hart and Cedric Hardman led a capable defense, but it was clear the early promise of the Nolan regime was fizzling fast. The 49ers lost their last four games—and Nolan lost his job.

Enter Monte Clark, the burly former 49er tackle, as new coach in 1976. He had come from the Miami Dolphins where he was an assistant. Meanwhile, Jim Plunkett came to the Niners in a trade from New England in hopes of solving the quarterback dilemma. The 49ers won six of their first seven games before a 23-20 overtime loss to St. Louis sent them into second place in the division behind the Rams. But they ended with the first winning season since 1972.

A quarterback-sacking defense was a key element in this modest success, along with productive running from Jackson and Delvin Williams. But Clark had a falling out with team owners and was gone after the season, later to land with Detroit as the Lions' head coach. Johnson retired after a great 16-year career.

New Ownership

With the unlikely help of Al Davis—owner of the Oakland Raiders, San Francisco's rival across the bay—Niners management found a buyer for the team: Eddie DeBartolo Sr., who quickly designated his son Eddie Jr. as sole owner. The purchase price was reported to be $17 million, with Davis earning a substantial finder's fee. Ten percent of the stock was to remain with the previous owners.

The deal was completed on March 31, and DeBartolo Jr. quickly installed Joe Thomas (formerly of Minnesota, Miami, and Baltimore) as general manager. Thomas would be presiding over a strife-torn 1977 campaign and beyond. It was the first ownership change in the 32-year-old franchise, one of the most stable in the NFL, and at 31 DeBartolo became the league's youngest owner. Thomas named Ken Meyer as coach.

In 1977 the Niners revived the 5-9 record they'd had twice in the previous four years. After a 5-6 start, they lost their final three games, one of them a 28-27 decision to Minnesota after having led the Vikings 27-7 in the fourth quarter. The late slide cost Meyer his job. Williams and Jackson combined for 1,711 yards rushing, and Plunkett passed for 1,693 yards.

Through the coaches' revolving door came Pete McCulley for 1978. Thomas shuffled the team with a series of personnel maneuvers. He gave up draft choices to Buffalo for running superstar O. J. Simpson, hoping to salvage a final season or two out of his aching knees. He got wide receiver Freddie Solomon from Miami and traded Williams to the Dolphins. Hart was traded to Chicago. Washington was cut. Plunkett was released (only to become a Super Bowl winner with Oakland) and Steve DeBerg became the starting quarterback.

The Niners lost their first four games in 1978, beat Cincinnati 28-12, then won just one more the rest of the way to finish with the worst record in team history, 2-14. Simpson gained only 593 yards in nine games before suffering a shoulder injury in former assistant Fred O'Connor's first game as McCulley's replacement. Injuries to DeBerg and his backup, Scott Bull, forced O'Connor to use Solomon and defensive back Bruce Threadgill at quarterback against Detroit.

AP/Wide World Photos

Bill Walsh

O'Connor was released at the end of his 1-6 trial—and DeBartolo had enough of Thomas, giving him the axe, as well. Walsh, in his book, said Thomas made bad trades and draft picks and once cut the team's best defensive back after he had a bad game. "If Joe suffered, the players would suffer," Walsh said. "Of course, people simply do not respond to that kind of tension and vindictiveness."

After all the turmoil and the years of mediocrity, who could have predicted that the next coaching choice would provide the magic elixir to take San Francisco to new heights of competitive prominence? Enter Walsh. Enter Montana. Enter the San Francisco 49ers into NFL history. And out with that dreadful 1970s total record of 60-86-2. The team of the decade was about to arrive.

Bill Walsh Takes Command

The modern era in the history of the 49ers began in 1979 with the arrival of Bill Walsh, who was the coach at Stanford University in California, after stints as an NFL assistant with the Oakland Raiders (1966), Cincinnati Bengals (1968-75), and San Diego Chargers (1976).

He had become known for molding outstanding quarterbacks, including Ken Anderson at Cincinnati and eventual Hall of Famer Dan Fouts at San Diego. Another hallmark would be his method of personally scripting the offensive game plan. In San Francisco, "we had taken it beyond that pattern of failure and finger pointing, so that the responsibility for the success of an offense started with the coach," Walsh said in his 1990 book, *Building a Champion*, co-authored with Glenn Dickey.

Dickey said, in contrast to other winners where players peak together and the team goes into decline, "Walsh kept changing, rebuilding as he was winning, with six division championships and seven playoff appearances in his last eight years. Each Super Bowl team was quite different; only five 49ers played in all three Super Bowls and only three of them—quarterback Joe Montana, center Randy Cross and defensive back Ronnie Lott—played key roles in all three games.... Walsh did it his way. Whether it was his offensive system or his method of evaluating players, he was a step ahead of his competitors."

At San Francisco Walsh inherited a team that won two games and lost 14 in 1978. His first team duplicated that record, but he tripled the victory total in 1980 and more than sextupled it in 1981, going 13-3 en route to San Francisco's first NFL championship in Super Bowl XVI. Before Walsh turned things over to assistant George Seifert in 1989, the Niners were to win two more Super Bowls (1984 and 1988). Seifert kept it rolling with another Super Bowl title in 1989.

The decade closed with an amazing regular season record of 104-47—plus a postseason mark of 13-4. "Bill Walsh inherited a team that was the NFL's worst," Tuckman and Schultz wrote. "To make the job even more difficult, the 49ers also finished dead last in total offense in 1978 and next-to-last in defense. The situation seemed hopeless for the veteran coach."

Before the 1981 season Walsh said: "When I was hired, one of the most difficult hurdles was the team's low motivation. I feel the current mood has overcome that. We've become competitive psychologically and emotionally." When the 49ers hired Walsh as head coach, they gave him the general manager's job as well. The previous coach was Fred O'Connor, the Niners' second coach to be relieved of his duties in a 2-14 season (1978). Walsh spent his first disastrous season, 1979, "rummaging through the rubble he inherited and through the waiver list for serviceable football players," according to David S. Neft and Richard M. Cohen in their *Football Encyclopedia.*

The Niners lost their first seven games on the way to the 2-12 record. New faces manned the defense, and their mistakes often helped inflate opponents' scores. Walsh emphasized the pass on offense and had a good, young quarterback in Steve DeBerg, who would still be starting and winning games elsewhere into the 1990s. DeBerg set NFL records for passing attempts (578) and completions (347) in a season, throwing for 3,652 yards and 17 touchdowns.

His backup, a rookie from Notre Dame named Joe Montana, completed 13 of 23 for 96 yards and one touchdown. There were other highlights in the dismal season. Ray Wersching set a club record with an 83.3 percent field goal success average, tops in the NFL. After the season, O.J. Simpson—whose fame was made at Buffalo—ended his two years with San Francisco and his 11-year NFL career by retiring as the second-leading rusher of all time, with 11,236 yards.

Keeping 'Em Loose

Coach Bill Walsh's visit to Detroit for Super Bowl XVI with his San Francisco 49ers began on a light note—not to mention finish on a bright one with a victory over the Cincinnati Bengals at the Pontiac Silverdome. Walsh dressed up as a bellhop and fooled most of his players when they arrived at the team hotel.

"I was the first one to get off the bus, and I see this guy coming up to me," former wide receiver Mike Shumann recalled. "I started thinking, 'Great, here's somebody who's already trying to make some money off of us.' So when he reached for my bag, I literally armed him away from me. I didn't know it was Bill until later on when I was riding down the elevator with John Ayers and he said, 'What do you think of Bill dressing up as a bellhop?'"

A Decade of Brilliance

The rebuilding program made headway in 1980. The Niners opened the season with a three-game winning streak. Their other three wins were also in succession, from week 12 through 14. On

AP/Wide World Photos

Dwight Clark

December 7, San Francisco made NFL history by overcoming a 35-7 halftime deficit against the New Orleans Saints to win in overtime, 38-35. The 28-point comeback set a league record. Second-year man Dwight Clark's sure hands and quick moves earned him a starting spot, and he caught 82 passes to break the team mark for wide receivers.

In addition, Montana set the club passing percentage record at .645 by completing 176 of 273 passes for 1,795 yards and 15 TDs. He shared quarterbacking chores fairly evenly with DeBerg, but his superior mobility and intelligent play hinted at the glory to come. Top 49er rookies in 1980 included end Jim Stuckey, punter Jim Miller, and fullback Earl Cooper, who led the National Conference with a team record 83 receptions, the most ever by an NFL first-year man.

Montana "is no Cinderella," said an analyst in the NFL's *ProLog* magazine. "No one ever touched him with a magic wand. Since he was a little kid, Montana has had to work. He's had to fight for every starting position he's had. He's had to lead comebacks for most of the important victories in his career. In truth, the guy with the storybook name is a hard-working Joe who only seems to have a fairy godmother looking over him."

Nineteen eighty-one was a year of firsts—and bests—for the 49ers. Not only were they 13-3 for the regular season, they slid through the postseason with three triumphs, climaxing with a 26-21 decision over the Cincinnati Bengals in Super Bowl XVI at the Silverdome in Pontiac, Michigan. To get there San Francisco first beat the New York Giants 38-24 in the NFL playoffs at home in Candlestick Park. Next came the conference championship game, also at home, with the Niners nipping the Dallas Cowboys 28-27 in a game that featured six lead changes. Not only was the championship their first, they had reached the playoffs for the first time since 1972.

The one-point conference title victory over Dallas featured the Montana the football world would learn to expect. With just under five minutes left, he began a do-or-die drive from his own 10-yard line. He moved the 49ers downfield with pinpoint passes and tough running gains, driving the team to the Dallas six. On third down, Montana rolled right, eluded huge Larry Bethea and threw a scoring pass to Clark. Wersching got the winning point-after kick, and the pattern was set for future dramatic last-ditch drives.

Walsh was named everybody's coach of the year. Montana led the NFC in passing (311-of-488 for 3,585 yards and 19 TDs) and was chosen Super Bowl Most Valuable Player. Dean, who left San Diego in a salary dispute, got numerous postseason honors for his tenacious pass-rushing performance.

San Francisco became the first team since the Chicago Bears (1945-47) to go from the league's worst record to the best in three years. And it happened with three rookies in the defensive backfield: Lott, Eric Wright, and Carlton Williamson. Other standouts were Cross, wide receiver Freddie Solomon, defensive back Dwight Hicks, and veteran linebacker Jack "Hacksaw" Reynolds.

The Detroit-area Super Bowl was the first outside the Sun Belt. It was snowy, icy, and near zero in temperature outside—but about 72 degrees inside. Both opponents had been regular losers in the past, but many considered Coach Forrest Gregg's Bengals the favorite. San Francisco led 20-0 at halftime then fought off a resurgent Cincinnati, which scored 14 points in the final quarter. "People didn't believe and, in a way, it was disheartening to us," Montana said about the Bengals being favored. "Even the coaches around the league, most of them picked Cincinnati to win the game. But we believed." After being named the game's MVP, Montana was asked what he could do for an encore. "Maybe they'll name a state after me," he joked. (Actually, a small town in Montana—prompted by a radio disc jockey's gimmick in the 1990s—did change its name to "Joe".)

AP/Wide World Photos

Joe Montana

Nobody would expect the newly-crowned 49ers to fall flat on their faces in 1982, but they did. The season was abbreviated to nine games by a players' strike, and the Niners wound up 3-9, failing to win any of their five home games, although Clark led the NFL with 60 catches, and Montana set an NFL record with five consecutive 300-yard-plus passing games.

But 1983 would bring good times back to San Francisco. The team won the West Division with a 10-6 record, clinching first place on the final Monday night of the season with a 42-17 thrashing of Dallas. Next came the Detroit Lions in the NFC playoffs at home. It wasn't so easy, but San Francisco pulled it out, 24-23. But in the conference championship matchup at Washington, the Niners lost 24-21 to the Redskins. Solomon averaged a team-record 21.4 yards per catch for the year. Dean led the NFC with 17.5 sacks and defensive end Dwaine Board had 13. And rookie Roger Craig had 752 yards rushing and 427 receiving.

In the old days, what the Niners accomplished in 1983 would have been monumental; in the 1980s it was considered bad news. But 1984 would be different, with a return to the Super Bowl and the club's all-time best record, 15-1, in the regular season. And they scored victories in all three postseason encounters: 21-10 over the New York Giants at Candlestick in the NFC playoffs; a 23-0 whitewashing of Chicago in another home game in the conference championship clash; then a 38-16 trouncing of Miami in Super Bowl XIX at Walsh's old stomping grounds, Stanford University in Palo Alto, California.

No NFL team had ever won 15 games, nor had anyone been able to win eight road games in a regular season as the 49ers had done. And they broke 14 club records while becoming the only team to win all the games within its conference and division. The Niners scored their most points ever, 475, and the defense was the league's stin-

AP/Wide World Photos

Jerry Rice

giest, allowing just 227 points. Ten players earned Pro Bowl berths, including the entire secondary of Lott, Wright, Williamson, and Hicks.

In the Super Bowl, Montana completed 24 of 35 passes for 331 yards and three touchdowns. Two were to Craig, who also ran for a score, as did Montana. It was the most-watched event ever on television, with an estimated 116 million viewers. The economic impact to the Bay Area was pegged at $113.5 million. "From start to finish the 49ers simply were the most dominant team in the NFC," said a reporter in *PRO!* magazine. The article went on to quote defensive back Dwight Hicks: "You look around the locker room and you see the commitment from our owner and head coach in getting talented players."

Craig and Rice were potent weapons for the 1985 team that qualified for a wild-card playoff berth with a 10-6 mark before losing an away game against the Giants 17-3 in the opening round. Craig became the fist player in the league to pass 1,000 yards running (1,050) and receiving (92 catches for 1,106 yards). Rice was the NFC's Rookie of the Year, piling up 927 receiving yards. Four new defensive starters emerged: Carter, linebackers Todd Shell and Michael Walter, and end John Hardy.

In 1986 the 49ers captured their fourth NFC West title since 1981. Rice developed into an All-Pro, leading the NFL with 1,570 yards receiving and 15 touchdowns. The Niners set club records with 39 interceptions, five of them for TDs. Lott had 10 interceptions, equalling Dave Baker's 1960 mark; after one interception for a touchdown against Green Bay it was discovered he had a hairline leg fracture. Injuries hit some veterans. Montana missed weeks two through nine due to back surgery, and his backup, Jeff Kemp, was out four weeks with a hip injury. That gave Mike Moroski some playing time.

Nobody had a better record in 1987 than the 49ers' 13-2, but it didn't translate to a championship—or even a single playoff victory. And the season had looked so promising. They whipped their last three opponents by a composite score of 124-7, including the Rams' most one-sided loss ever, 48-0. But in their NFC playoff matchup at home against Minnesota, the Niners lost 36-24.

San Francisco amassed 5,987 yards—the most in the league—and was best on defensive yardage, allowing only 4,095. Rice set a league standard with 22 receiving touchdowns, including a mark for getting at least one in 13 consecutive games, becoming the league's MVP. Montana won the first NFL passing title of his nine-year career and set a club mark with 31 scoring passes.

The next two years would bring two more Super Bowls and two more Super Bowl championships. Surprisingly, it didn't look like the 1988 season would be truly outstanding, in view of a modest (by San Francisco's latest standards) 10-6 record. The team's game against the Patriots had to be moved from Candlestick Park to Stanford's stadium because of damage from the October 17 earthquake. In the NFC playoff game at home, the 49ers clobbered the Vikings, 34-9, with Rice catching three TD passes. They then faced the Bears in Chicago in the NFC title game, which the Niners won, 28-3.

Super Bowl XXIII at Miami loomed, a rematch with San Francisco's first Super Bowl opponent, Cincinnati. The 49ers won again, 20-16, with Rice earning game MVP distinction with a sensational 11 catches for a Super Bowl record 215 yards and a touchdown. The Bengals led 16-13 with 3:20 remaining when Montana started one of his patented clutch drives from his own eight-yard line. Passes to tight end John Frank and Rice helped get the team into Bengal territory. With 1:15 on the clock and a second-and-20 situation, Montana threw over the middle to Rice, who got to the Cincinnati 18. An eight-yarder to Craig followed. Then Montana hit John Taylor in the end zone for the winning score, completing an 11-play, 92-yard march and giving the Bengals just 34 seconds left.

"All of a sudden, things were just happening," guard Guy McIntyre recalled of that comeback drive. "Nobody panicked. Everything was so calm. It was almost like not being there. It was like looking down on everything that was happening. Before you knew it, we had scored."

The league's newsletter, *NFL Report*, quoted the *New York Times*: "For nearly a quarter of a century the Super Bowl had been searching for this scenario: Pro football's best quarterback taking pro football's best team the length of the field for the winning touchdown in the final minute. And now, at last, Joe Montana has played the part." The *Houston Post* agreed: "Team of the Eighties. Wide receiver of the Ages. Check, double check. It was all there, every last cliche. And when it was over, this was one Super Bowl that lived up to its name." Concluded the *Indianapolis Star*, "This was the state-of-the-art game, the one future Super Bowl contestants will take as a model."

Walsh left the 49ers for a short career as a television color analyst before winding up back at Stanford in 1992. His regular-season record at San Francisco was 92-59-1—not to mention the postseason successes. Subtract that 2-14 campaign in 1979, and his teams went 90-45-1 in nine years. In addition to a still-talented team, Walsh left a quarterback controversy brewing, having given left-hander Steve Young an opportunity to play a great deal in place of Montana.

Still, Montana remained a Walsh fan. What set the coach apart, he said, was "his knowledge of the game.... He's always analyzing and coming up with new things. And he listens. If someone else comes up with a good idea, he's not afraid to put it to good use." Said Walsh of his star quarterback: "He most likely is the best in football right now at reading defenses and calling audibles. In terms of the mental aspects of the game, the only other quarterbacks I've coached who come close would be Fouts and Anderson."

The 49ers won five of their first seven games in 1988, but by week 12 their 5-2 record had fallen to 6-5, and they were two games out of first with only five left. They rose to the challenge with a four-game winning streak, earning a third successive NFC West crown. Along the way, Craig broke the team's single-season rushing record, finishing with 1,502 yards, and kicker Mike Cofer established a Niners' single-season standard for field goals attempted (38) and made (27). Lott, Carter, and linebacker Charles Haley were among the defensive stars.

Defensive coordinator George Seifert, who had been an assistant under Walsh at Stanford, was named head coach just four days after the Miami Super Bowl. Walsh said that at Stanford, Seifert "was an excellent technician and taskmaster. He had a gifted mind and was extremely well-organized.... One of the basic tenets in establishing the [49ers] organization was to make it so solid that it could survive anyone's departure, including mine. I take real pride in the team continuing to thrive, winning the Super Bowl the following year with George Seifert as coach. In all honesty, the team was revitalized; it was to become one of the best teams in National Football League history."

Seifert's 1989 team didn't skip a beat. In fact, it stepped up the tempo, raising its regular season mark to 14-2 and sweeping its three postseason contests, beginning with an NFC playoffs home-game victory against Minnesota, 41-13. In the conference title clash at Candlestick, the intrastate rival Los Angeles Rams went home 30-3 losers.

The 49ers traveled to New Orleans for Super Bowl XXIV and annihilated the Denver Broncos 55-10. The Niners set or tied 40 Super Bowl records. Montana was the game's MVP for an unprecedented third time as he completed 22 of 29 passes for 297 yards and a Super Bowl record five touchdowns. Rice caught seven passes for 148 yards, including TD grabs of 38 and 28 yards. Taylor had a 35-yard scoring grab and Rathman ran for two scores.

Seifert became only the second rookie coach to lead a team to a Super Bowl championship. After the game, he said of Walsh, "It has really been the strength of Bill's personality, his demands and his intelligence, and the structure that he has established and people he has hired that have enabled us to do all this. Granted, you like to feel a part of it. But you have to be realistic about it, too."

Among the early victories that season was a 38-28 triumph in Philadelphia, in which Montana threw four fourth-quarter touchdown passes. For the game he threw for 428 yards and five TDs. Elbow and knee ailments sidelined Montana five weeks into the season, but Young played superbly. A six-game victory string helped the Niners dominate the division, and when the Rams came into town two games behind in the standings they had their work cut out for them. The Rams jumped to a 17-0 first-quarter lead and led 27-10 in the fourth quarter before San Francisco rallied for a 30-27 triumph.

Cofer's 136 points led the NFL, and he set a team record with 29 field goals. Lott set a career team interception record (48) and one for interception return yardage (617), while linebacker Michael Walter's 103 tackles gave him the NFL lead for the third straight season. Rice again led the league in receiving with 1,483 yards. He caught 17 scoring passes to boost his six-year total to 66. Fellow wide receiver John Taylor snared 60 passes for 1,077 yards and 10 TDs. Craig had a 1,054-yard rushing year, and fullback Tom Rathman led conference running backs with 73 pass catches.

And, as if to emphasize who should start, Montana had the best season of his 11-year career and was the consensus Player of the Year with an NFL record 112.4 rating. Montana, Rice, and Lott were first-teamers on the All-1980s team selected by a Hall of Fame panel. Craig was chosen to the second team, with Taylor selected as a punt returner.

Continued Success

The first three years of the 1990s produced a 34-10 record, including 14-2 marks in 1990 and 1992. Both those years, the 49ers won their first playoff game, only to lose in the NFC title matchup.

AP/Wide World Photos

Ronnie Lott

A "three-peat" wasn't to be in 1990, despite an impressive won-lost record and a club-record 10-game winning streak to begin the season. Age and injuries ruined the season for Craig. The Montana-to-Rice combo, though, continued to carry the team.

Montana took over the career team passing lead from John Brodie, reaching 34,998 yards, and was the league's Player of the Year again. He completed 68 percent of his passes, 26 for touchdowns, and totaled 3,944 passing yards. Craig became the team record-holder in receptions, with 508, to edge ahead of Clark. Defensively, linebacker Bill Romanowski had 79 tackles, and cornerback Darryl Pollard had 74. Haley led the NFC with 16 sacks. San Francisco ousted Washington in the playoffs, 28-10 at home, then was nipped by the Giants 15-13 in the NFC championship game at Candlestick.

In 1991, the 49ers went 5-0 in the pre-season, including a victory over Washington in London, England, in the NFL's third "American Bowl" exhibition game in Europe. But when the games counted, they lost six of their first 10 (by a total of 26 points). They won their last six and missed the playoffs for the first time since 1982. The record did earn the team an NFL-best ninth straight double-digit victory season.

Rice extended some of his records, and Steve Young supplanted the injured Montana as passing hero. In fact, he helped guide the 49ers to the highest-rated offense in the conference, with statistics that included the most first downs (336). Despite missing six games with a knee injury, Young topped the NFL with 2,517 yards passing, 17 TDs, and a 101.8 rating.

When the 49ers first brought Young to San Francisco in May of 1987 in a trade from the Tampa Bay Buccaneers, he hadn't brought any cleats for a workout. Niners equipment manager Bronco Hinek gave him a pair of Montana's cleats, not expecting Montana to be around. But about a half-hour later, Montana showed up and was introduced to the guy who eventually would literally fill his shoes. Young stood with his heels to the wall so Montana couldn't see his number 16

AP/Wide World Photos

Steve Young (8)

on them. "Frankly, I didn't know how he'd react," Young told authors Tuckman and Schultz. "Maybe he would think I was walking right in and trying to take over. I mean, this guy is a legend. We all went into a room and talked and watched some football film, until Joe had to go. As he left, he smiled at me and said, 'Steve, a pleasure meeting you. And, oh, by the way, nice shoes you're wearing.'"

The 1992 season brought another fine 14-2 record and an opening-round playoff opening triumph, 20-13, at home against the Redskins. But Dallas handed the Niners a 30-20 setback to earn the NFC championship in San Francisco. It still had to be regarded as a great year, especially considering that there were five new assistant coaches and a schedule that included the last

Super Bowl team, three division champs, and five division winners.

Rice became the all-time touchdown reception leader at 103, passing Steve Largent's 100. Young hauled in 34 awards for his many accomplishments, including league MVP, after passing for 3,465 yards and 25 TDs, with a 107 rating—the first time any quarterback put together back-to-back 100-plus ratings.

Montana, sidelined nearly two years with elbow problems, played well in the season finale and earned a comeback try in 1993 with the Kansas City Chiefs. Ricky Waters gained 1,013 yards to establish a club mark for rookies. And Cofer became the first 49er to register four 100-point seasons. Among the team records set were single-game total offense (598 yards) and points (56).

During the 1993 exhibition season, 49er rookie quarterback Elvis Grbac from Michigan passed San Francisco to a victory by utilizing Rice as a prime target. Rice, he said, "is the best receiver of all time. If you don't use him, you're a fool. I just try to get the ball in his hands as much as possible." Thus Grbac, working with the Niners in the early 1990s, came to the same conclusion as had two quarterbacks before him: Hit Rice and you'll look like a genius.

SOURCES

BOOKS

Brodie, John, and James D. Houston, *Open Field*, Houghton-Mifflin, 1974.

First 50 Years: The Story of the NFL, Simon & Schuster, 1969.

Great Teams' Great Years: San Francisco 49ers, Macmillan, 1974.

Herskowitz, Mickey, *The Golden Age of Pro Football: A Remembrance of Pro Football in the '50s*, NFL Properties, 1974.

Neft, David S., and Richard M. Cohen, *The Football Encyclopedia*, St. Martin's Press, 1991.

Official National Football League 1993 Record & Fact Book, NFL Properties, 1993.

San Francisco 49ers Media Guide, San Francisco 49ers Football Club, 1993.

Tuckman, Michael W., and Jeff Schultz, *The San Francisco 49ers: Team of the Decade*, Prima Publishing, 1989.

Walsh, Bill, with Glenn Dickey, *Building a Champion*, St. Martin's Press, 1990.

PERIODICALS

Associated Press, November 23, 1970; November 5, 1973; October 15, 1974.

Football Digest, November 1971; January 1972; December 1990.

GameDay, December 15, 1979; September 2, 1984; November 22, 1984; October 22, 1989.

Insider!, 1988; Summer 1989; Fall 1989; Winter 1992.

NFL Report, Fall 1988; Spring 1989; Summer 1990; Fall 1990; Fall 1991; Spring 1992; Fall 1992.

Petersen's Pro Football, 1971; 1974; 1977; 1981.

PRO!, March-April 1985; August 1981.

Pro Football Almanac, 1971.

Pro Football Stars, 1964.

ProLog, 1982.

—Larry Paladino

Index

A

Abramowicz, Danny 472, 473, 475, 498
Abrams, Nate 289
Adams, Bud 49, 50, 51, 52, 53, 148, 175
Adderley, Herb 297
Agajanian, Ben 210, 363
Aikman, Troy 94, 348, 349
Albert, Frankie 194, 490, 491, 492, 493, 494
Alderman, Grady 169
Aldridge, Lionel 214, 297
Alexander, Charles 27
Alexander, Doc 353, 354
Allen, Chuck 211, 213, 226
Allen, George 215, 254, 255, 310, 422, 423, 424, 425, 439, 450, 458, 460, 461
Allen, Ivan Jr. 436
Allen, Marcus 201, 202, 205, 206, 227
Alworth, Lance 212, 213, 214, 337, 338, 498
Alzado, Lyle 163, 167, 168, 169, 200, 201
Ameche, Alan 102, 103, 104, 105, 106, 107, 365
Andersen, Morten 479, 481, 483
Anderson, Bobby 166
Anderson, Dick 120, 124, 125
Anderson, Edwin J. 274
Anderson, Flipper 468
Anderson, Gary 79, 218, 325
Anderson, George 204
Anderson, Hunk 247, 248, 249
Anderson, Ken 23, 25, 26, 28, 29, 31, 322, 499
Anderson, Neal 263, 264, 265
Anderson, Ottis 374, 375
Anderson, Ralph 210
Andrews, William 436, 443, 444
Andrie, George 338
Ane, Charley 275, 276
Angsman, Elmer 403
Arbanas, Fred 176
Ard, Billy 369
Arenas, Joe 493
Armstrong, Neil 382
Armstrong, Neill 258, 259, 260
Armstrong, Otis 167
Arnett, Jon 458, 459
Arnold, Jim 282, 283
Arnsparger, Bill 368
Artoe, Lee 247
Atkins, Doug 253, 254, 255, 261, 269, 471, 472
Atkins, Gene 482
Atkinson, Butch 153
Atwater, Steve 173
Auer, Joe 119
August, Steve 223
Austin, Bill 67, 363, 422
Austin, Cliff 480
Autry, Gene 460
Avelini, Bob 258

B

Bach, Joe 60, 65
Bacon, Coy 25, 214
Badgro, Red 351
Bahr, Matt 77, 375
Bailey, Edwin 225
Bailey, Mark 182
Baker, Archie 84

Baker, Dave 494
Baker, Tony 472, 473
Bakken, Jim 406
Ball, Herman 419
Banaszak, Pete 153, 191
Banducci, Bruno 491
Banks, Carl 370
Banks, Chip 45, 46
Barbaro, Gary 183
Barber, Stew 84
Barkett, Jackie 105
Barnard, Hap 359
Barnes, Ben 342
Barnes, Don 403
Barnes, Erich 366
Barnes, Roosevelt 281
Barnes, William A. 462
Barney, Lem 278, 279
Bartkowski, Steve 436, 443, 444, 445
Bartle, H. Roe 177
Barwegan, Dick 100, 101, 250, 251
Bass, Dick 459
Bass, Glenn 85, 86, 191
Bass, Mike 424
Battles, Cliff 7, 413
Baugh, Sammy 8, 9, 51, 148, 157, 194, 245, 247, 248, 361, 415, 416, 417, 418, 419, 452
Baughan, Maxie 462
Bavaro, Mark 351
Baxter, Brad 158
Beals, Alyn 491
Beame, Abraham 369
Bean, M. Lamont 222
Bearden, Steve 480
Beathard, Bobby 218, 220
Beathard, Pete 182
Becker, Wayland 360
Bednarik, Chuck 2, 12, 365, 383, 385, 386
Beeson, Terry 223
Behring, Ken 230
Belichick, Bill 47
Bell, Bert 7, 9, 62, 101, 148, 175, 306, 377, 379, 380, 381, 386, 404, 459
Bell, Bobby 178, 181
Bell, Ricky 318, 320
Bell, Todd 261
Bemiller, Al 84
Bengston, Phil 137
Bengtson, Phil 299
Benirschke, Rolf 127, 216, 217
Bennett, Cornelius 92, 115
Bennett, Leeman 323, 436, 444, 445, 446
Benson, Tom 481
Benton, Jim 453, 455
Bergey, Bill 22, 24, 387
Bergman, Arthur J. 417, 418
Bernstine, Rod 164, 174, 218
Bero, Tubby 289
Berry, Bob 439, 440
Berry, Mort 37
Berry, Ray 98, 102, 103, 104, 105, 106, 107, 108, 110, 112
Berry, Raymond 139, 140, 142, 144
Berry, Royce 22
Bertelsen, Jim 464
Berwanger, Jay 7, 380
Bethea, Larry 501
Bettis, Jerome 469
Bettis, Tom 182
Bezdek, Hugo 450
Biasucci, Dean 116
Bickett, Duane 116
Bidwell, Charles 175
Bidwill, Bill 396, 409
Bidwill, Charles 395, 400, 403, 404
Bidwill, Charles Jr. 396
Bidwill, Violet 396
Biggs, Verlon 150
Biles, Ed 55
Biletnikoff, Fred 153, 187, 191, 192, 193, 197
Billups, Lewis 30
Bingaman, Les 274, 275, 276
Birdwell, Dan 192
Bishop, Sonny 51
Blackinger, John 490
Blackledge, Todd 183
Blackmon, Robert 231

Blackwood, Lyle 222
Blades, Brian 230
Blair, George 211
Blanchard, Doc 455
Blanchard, Tom 476
Blanda, George 50, 51, 52, 57, 101, 153, 187, 191, 193, 194, 196, 210, 211, 251, 260, 269
Bledsoe, Drew 146, 232
Blier, Rocky 72, 75, 76, 77, 78
Blount, Mel 59, 68, 69, 78
Blozis, Al 361
Blue, Forrest 497, 498
Board, Dwaine 502
Bodenger, Maury 272, 273
Boozer, Emerson 151, 154
Bordelon, Ken 476
Bortz, Mark 263, 264
Boryla, Mike 318
Bostic, Jeff 411
Bosworth, Brian 230, 231
Bowlen, Pat 174
Box, Cloyce 274, 276
Boyd, Bob 107, 108, 109, 455
Braase, Ordell 109
Braatz, Tom 303
Bradshaw, Terry 59, 68, 69, 70, 71, 72, 73, 74, 75, 76, 77, 78, 193, 215, 340, 341, 342
Brallier, John 4, 378
Braman, Norman 378, 389, 390, 391, 392
Branch, Cliff 193
Brandt, Gil 332, 333, 335, 348
Brandy, Bill 116
Bratkowski, Zeke 459
Bray, Ray 250
Brazile, Robert 55
Breech, Jim 27, 29, 30
Breeden, Louis 26
Breen, John 49, 50, 53
Brenner, Hoby 483
Brettschneider, Carl 277
Brickly, Charley 397
Bright, Bum 343, 344
Brink, Larry 456
Briscoe, Marlin 88
Brister, Bubby 78, 79
Brister, Buddy 80
Brock, Dieter 468
Brock, Pete 138
Brock, Stan 478, 487
Brodhead, Bob 53
Brodie, John 490, 494, 495, 496, 497, 498, 505
Brodie, Steve 40
Brooker, Tommy 51, 177, 178
Brooks, James 27, 28, 29, 30, 217
Brooks, Larry 464
Brown, Bill 312
Brown, Bob 461
Brown, Charlie 426
Brown, Dave 222, 227, 230, 231
Brown, Don 404
Brown, Ed 67, 251, 252
Brown, Eddie 29, 30
Brown, Hardy 492
Brown, Jerome 392
Brown, Jim 1, 12, 13, 34, 40, 41, 42, 261, 276, 364, 366
Brown, Larry 72, 422, 423
Brown, Lomas 281, 283
Brown, Paul 10, 13, 17, 21, 22, 25, 33, 34, 36, 37, 39, 40, 41, 296, 363
Brown, Ray 105
Brown, Roger 277
Brown, Roosevelt 363
Brown, Tim 205, 207
Brown, Willie 187, 191
Browner, Joe 315
Browner, Keith 322
Browner, Ross 26, 28
Bruenig, Bob 339
Brunbaugh, Carl 242
Brunner, Scott 370
Bryant, Cullen 77
Buchanan, Buck 178
Buchanon, Willie 215
Buck, Vince 484
Budde, Ed 178
Bukich, Rudy 255, 457
Bulaich, Norm 112

Bull, Scott 499
Bulloch, Hank 92
Bullough, Hank 83, 138
Buoniconti, Nick 121, 124, 125, 126
Burk, Adrian 100
Burkett, Jackie 471
Burkett, Jeff(erson Davis) 404
Burley, Gary 26
Burns, Jerry 314
Burns, Mike 113
Burroughs, Derrick 30, 92
Burroughs, Don 457
Burruss, Lloyd 184
Burt, Jim 351, 369
Burton, Larry 475, 476
Burton, Ron 135
Bush, Blair 26, 226
Bussey, Dexter 279, 281
Bussey, Young 247
Butkus, Dick 2, 3, 255, 256, 257, 259, 268
Butler, Jack 65, 66, 67
Butler, Jerry 89, 91
Butler, Keith 224
Butler, Kevin 262, 263, 264, 265
Butts, Marion 218
Byner, Earnest 45, 46
Byrd, Butch 213

C

Caddel, Ernie 272, 273, 274
Cagle, Red 357
Cain, Lynn 443
Calhoun, George 288, 289
Campanella, Joseph 108
Campbell, Earl 53, 54, 55, 76, 480, 481
Campbell, Glenn 358
Campbell, Hugh 55
Campbell, Joe 476
Campbell, Marion 386, 389, 442
Canadeo, Tony 10
Cannon, Billy 49, 50, 51, 148, 192, 459
Capece, Bill 320
Cappelletti, Gino 134, 135, 136, 144
Cardwell, Lloyd 274
Carlson, Cody 57
Carlson, Roy 244
Carmichael, Harold 387, 388
Carollo, Joe 460
Carpenter, Lew 276
Carpenter, Rob 55
Carpenter, Ron 22
Carr, Ed 492
Carr, Fred 297
Carr, Jim 386
Carr, Joe 240, 242, 246, 291, 352, 399, 451
Carr, Roger 113
Carrier, Mark 264, 323, 324
Carroll, Wesley 485
Carson, Bud 47
Carson, Carlos 183, 184
Carson, Harry 351, 369, 374
Carter, Dale 185
Carter, Michael 489, 503, 504
Carter, Rubin 168
Carter, Virgil 23
Casanova, Tommy 24
Casares, Rick 245, 252, 253, 258
Casey, Bernie 495
Casey, Charles 439
Casey, Ed 414
Casper, Dave 54, 197, 199, 203
Cassady, Howard "Hopalong" 276
Caster, Rich 154
Cefalo, Jimmy 126
Chamberlin, Guy 378
Chambers, Rusty 126
Chambers, Wally 257, 258, 319
Chandler, Bob 88
Chandler, Bobby 201
Chandler, Chris 325
Chandler, Don 108, 297
Chandler, Wes 216, 217, 477, 478
Cherry, Deron 183, 184
Chester, Raymond 199, 201, 203
Childs, Henry 476, 477
Christensen, George 272, 273, 274

Christensen, Todd 203, 205
Christiansen, Jack 271, 276, 495, 496
Christie, Dick 148
Christie, Steve 94
Christman, Paul 249, 403
Christy, Earl 152
Cifers, Ed 417
Cipa, Larry 475
Clancy, Jack 120
Clark, Boobie 24
Clark, Bruce 480
Clark, Dutch 271, 272, 273, 274, 359
Clark, Dwight 343, 489, 490, 500, 501
Clark, Earl 451
Clark, Gary 428, 429
Clark, Harry 248
Clark, James 382, 383, 384
Clark, Monte 280, 281, 494, 498
Clark, Potsy 271, 272, 273
Clarke, Earl 7
Clayborn, Raymond 138, 144
Clayton, Mark 129, 130
Clement, Johnny 64
Coan, Bert 180
Cobb, Marvin 24
Cobb, Reggie 325, 326
Cockroft, Don 45
Cody, Bill 474
Cofer, Michael 283
Cofer, Mike 30, 505
Coffeen, Jim 289
Cogdill, Gail 277
Collier, Blanton 34, 42, 43, 101
Collier, Joe 86, 173, 179
Collins, Gary 42, 43
Collins, Paul 413
Collins, Tony 134, 140, 144
Collinsworth, Cris 26, 29
Concannon, Jack 261
Conerly, Charlie 38, 351, 363, 364, 365, 366
Conkright, Red 189
Conlan, Shane 92
Connor, George 250, 251, 252, 258, 268
Connors, Dan 192, 195, 196
Conrad, Bobby 407
Conzelman, Jimmy 238, 402, 403, 404
Cook, Greg 22
Cook, Toi 482
Cooke, Jack Kent 424, 425, 426, 427
Cooper, Earl 27, 501
Cordileone, Lou 471
Corral, Frank 320
Coryell, Don 209, 215, 217, 218, 407, 408
Cosbie, Doug 343
Cosell, Howard 337
Coslet, Bruce 147, 158
Costa, Dave 166, 167
Cothren, Paige 471
Coulter, Tex 362
Covert, Jim 262, 263
Cowan, Charlie 464
Cowher, Bill 80
Cox, Fred 440
Craig, Dobie 51
Craig, James 139
Craig, Neal 24
Craig, Roger 205, 489, 502, 503, 504, 505
Creekmur, Lou 275, 276
Cribbs, Joe 27, 83, 91
Croft, Don 88
Cromwell, Nolan 466
Cronan, Peter 223
Cross, Randy 489, 499, 501
Crow, John David 495
Crowder, Randy 320
Crowe, Clem 100
Crusan, Doug 120
Cryder, Bob 227
Csonka, Larry 1, 15, 119, 120, 121, 122, 123, 125, 126, 154, 181, 311
Culverhouse, Hugh F. 318
Cunningham, Bennie 77
Cunningham, Randall 377, 390, 391, 392

Cunningham, Sam 134, 137
Cuozzo, Gary 108, 440, 471, 472
Curry, Bill 112
Curry, Eric 326
Curtis, Issac 24, 29
Curtis, Mike 108, 112, 113, 222
Custer, Rudy 261

D

Dalby, Dave 201
Danelo, Joe 370
Daniels, Clemon 190, 192
Danielson, Gary 47, 280
Danowski, Ed 359, 361
Darden, Thom 44
Darragh, Dan 86
Daugherty, Dick 456
Davenport, Ron 129
David, Jim 276
Davidson, Ben 192, 193, 196
Davidson, Cotton 101, 102
Davis, Al 187, 188, 190, 191, 192, 193, 196, 198, 200, 201, 202, 205, 206, 207, 221
Davis, Anthony 318
Davis, Clarence 194, 197, 198
Davis, Ernie 41, 420
Davis, Fred 249
Davis, Glenn 453, 455, 456, 460
Davis, Kyle 339
Davis, Lamar 98, 99
Davis, Mike 54
Davis, Milt 103, 105
Davis, Sam 78
Davis, Wendell 264
Davis, Willie 297
Dawsey, Lawrence 325, 326
Dawson, Len 40, 176, 179, 180, 181, 182, 213, 311
De Orsey, Leo 420
Dean, Fred 215, 216, 489, 502
Dean, Ted 386
DeBartolo, Eddie, Jr. 489, 498, 499
DeBartolo, Eddie, Sr 498
DeBerg, Steve 170, 184, 185, 227, 317, 322, 323, 324, 326, 499, 500, 501
Degan, Dick 213
DeGroot, Dudley 418
Delaney, Joe 183
Dell, Johnny 360
DeLong, Steve 213
Delpino, Robert 174
Demory, Bill 154
Dempsey, Tom 14, 465, 473, 474
Dent, Richard 261, 262, 263, 264
DeRogatis, Al 363
Deschaine, Dick 297
Devine, Dan 302
Devore, Hugh 384
Dewveall, Willard 13, 50
Dial, Buddy 66
Dibert, Grant 4
Dickerson, Eric 16, 115, 116, 117, 205, 466, 467, 468
Dickey, Curtis 114
Dickey, Lynn 53, 302
Didier, Clint 429
Didion, John 474
Dierdorf, Dan 408
Dierking, Scott 155
Dietz, William 414
Dillon, Bobby 297
Dimancheff, Babe 249
Dimancheff, Boris 403
DiMelio, Luby 60
Ditka, Mike 253, 254, 255, 260, 261, 262, 263, 264, 265, 269, 337, 338
Dixon, Hewritt 192
Dobler, Conrad 408, 477
Doll, Don 274
Dombrowski, Jim 481
Domres, Marty 112
Donaldson, Ray 115, 116, 232
Donelli, Buff 62
Donovan, Art 98, 101, 102, 103, 104, 105, 106, 110
Donovan, Pat 339, 343
Dooley, Jim 257

Dorais, Gus 64, 274
Dorow, Al 148
Dorsett, Tony 173, 223, 340, 343, 344
Dotson, Santana 326
Douds, Jap 60
Douglass, Bobby 476
Dove, Eddie 494
Dowhower, Rod 115
Dowler, Boyd 297
Drake, Johnny 451
Dreith, Ben 138
Dressen, Charley 238
Driscoll, John 252, 255
Driscoll, Paddy 5, 242, 267, 395, 396, 397, 398
Driskill, Walt 100
Dryer, Fred 464
Dubenion, Elbert 85
DuBose, Demetrius 326
Duckett, Kenny 479
Dudley, Bill 63, 64, 274
Duerson, Dave 262, 263
Duhe, A.J. 157
Dunbar, Vaughn 485, 486
Duncan, Curtis 56
Duncan, Leslie 213
Duncan, Speedy 423
Dungy, Tony 315
Duper, Mark 128, 129, 130
Dupre, L.G. 102, 105
Dupree, Billy Joe 338, 343
Dutton, John 113, 343
Dwyer, Dutch 289
Dwyer, Reggie 289
Dyer, Ken 23

E

Easley, Kenny 225, 226, 227, 229
Eason, Tony 140, 144, 145
Eaton, Vic 65
Ebding, Harry 273
Eddy, Jim 58
Edelman, Brad 479, 483
Edmunds, Ferrell 232
Edwards, Dan 101
Edwards, Glen 69, 74, 413
Ellard, Henry 468
Eller, Carl 224, 310
Elliott, Lenvil 24
Ellis, Allan 258
Elmendorf, Dave 462
Elway, John 46, 114, 163-64, 170-74, 227, 374, 428
Embry, Jake 100
Emerson, Ox 272, 273
Emtman, Steve 117
Engebretsen, Tiny 360
English, Doug 281
Enke, Fred 101, 274
Erdelatz, Eddie 188, 189
Erhardt, Ron 138, 139
Erickson, Craig 317, 326
Erxleben, Russell 477
Esiason, Boomer 28, 29, 30, 31, 158
Essink, Ron 224
Etcheverry, Sam 406
Evans, Billy 451
Evans, Norm 222
Evans, Vince 259, 260
Everett, Jim 374, 468, 469
Ewbank, Weeb 14, 65, 97, 98, 101, 102, 104, 106, 107, 111, 114, 147, 149-54, 157

F

Fairbanks, Chuck 137, 138, 146
Faison, Earl 211, 212, 214, 216
Famiglietti, Gary 247
Fantetti, Ken 281
Farkas, Andy 417
Farr, Mel 278
Farrell, Sean 320, 323
Faulkner, Jack 164, 165
Favre, Brett 303
Fears, Tom 449, 450, 452, 453, 456, 458, 471
Feathers, Beattie 245

Federspiel, Joe 475
Feldman, Marty 189
Fencik, Gary 259, 260
Fenner, Derrick 231
Fergerson, Duke 223
Ferguson, Joe 27, 72, 83, 88, 89, 90, 91, 324
Fernandez, Manny 124, 125
Ferragamo, Vince 467
Ferrante, Jack 382, 383
Ferry, Martins 34
Fest, Howard 22
Fields, Joe 156
Filchock, Frank 9, 164, 360, 362, 416, 418
Filipowicz, Steve 362
Finks, Jim 65, 261, 481, 483, 486, 487
Firestone, Leonard 460
Flaherty, Ray 35, 360, 414, 417
Flanagan, Ed 279
Flatley, Paul 312
Fleming, Marv 181
Fletcher, Simon 173
Flores, Tom 86, 188, 191, 193, 197, 198, 200, 203, 204, 205, 221, 231, 232
Flowers, Charlie 50, 210
Floyd, Don 51
Flutie, Doug 144, 145
Follis, Charles 4
Folwell, Bob 352, 354
Folz, Arthur 399
Fontes, Wayne 272, 282, 284
Ford, Len 39
Ford, William Clay 278
Foreman, Chuck 313
Fortmann, Dan 246, 247, 248, 255, 267
Fortunato, Joe 254, 255
Forzano, Rick 279
Foss, Joe 120, 148, 191, 306
Foster, Barry 79, 80
Foster, Gene 213
Fourcade, John 482, 484
Fouts, Dan 27, 127, 130, 209, 214, 215, 216, 217, 218, 499
Fralic, Bill 435
Francis, Russ 138
Francis, Wallace 443
Franck, George 361
Frank, John 30, 503
Franklin, Byron 91, 223
Franklin, Tony 134, 142
Fraser, Jim 178
Frazier, Willie 214
Freeman, Reggie 487
French, Walter 398
Frerotte, Mitch 232
Friedman, Benny 351, 355
Friesz, John 218
Frietas, Jesse 215
Fritsch, Ted 362
Fritsch, Tony 77, 339
Frontiere, Georgia 466, 478
Fryar, Irving 140
Fugett, Jean 338
Fulcher, David 29, 30
Fuller, Frank 404
Fuller, Steve 182, 183
Fultz, Mike 476
Fuqua, Frenchy 69, 71, 193

G

Gabriel, Roman 279, 387, 460, 461, 463
Gagliano, Bob 220
Gaines, Clark 155
Galbreath, Tony 476, 477, 478
Galimore, Willie 253
Gallarneau, Hugh 249
Gallery, Tom 8
Gallico, Paul 354
Gansz, Frank 183, 184
Gantenbein, Milt 294, 360
Garrett, Carl 137, 257
Garrett, Mike 179, 180, 181, 214, 215
Garrison, Gary 213
Garrison, Walt 338, 339

Garron, Larry 136
Gary, Russell 479, 480
Gastineau, Mark 147, 156, 157, 158
Gatski, Frank 33, 38, 41
Gault, Willie 263
Gavin, Fritz 289
Gay, William 281
Gayle, Shaun 264
Gedman, Gene 275
Gehrke, Fred 10, 453
Gelbaugh, Stan 232
Gent, Pete 335
Gentry, Dennis 264
George, Bill 251, 252, 253, 258, 268, 450
George, Jeff 116, 117
Gerela, Roy 69, 70, 71, 72, 73, 74, 76
Gibbs, Joe 411, 425, 427, 428, 430
Gibron, Abe 257, 258
Gibson, Billy 352
Gifford, Frank 2, 3, 351, 363, 364, 365, 366, 367
Gilbert, Gale 229
Gilbert, Sean 469
Gilchrist, Carlton 84, 85
Gilchrist, Cookie 165
Giles, Jimmie 53, 319, 323
Gill, Owen 229
Gilliam, Joe 71, 72
Gilliam, John 472
Gilliam, Jon 179
Gillman, Sid 53, 68, 85, 209, 210, 212, 213, 214, 219, 450, 457, 458, 462
Gilmer, Harry 278
Gipp, George 289
Givins, Ernest 56, 57
Gladishar, Randy 163
Glanville, Jerry 55, 56, 436, 446, 447, 448
Glasgow, Bill 401
Glenn, Howard 148
Goff, Robert 484
Gogolak, Pete 84
Goldberg, Marshall 403
Goldman, Julian 152
Golic, Bob 45
Golsteyn, Jerry 322
Gonsoulin, Goose 164, 165
Goodlow, Eugene 479
Gordon, Dick 256, 257
Gossett, Jeff 206
Grabowski, Jim 120
Gradishar, Randy 168, 169, 170
Graham, Otto 11, 33, 34, 36, 37, 38, 39, 98, 99, 275, 420, 421, 453, 456
Grange, Garland 402
Grange, Red 5, 6, 240, 241, 242, 243, 244, 245, 254, 258, 266, 354, 356, 358, 398, 401
Grant, Bud 279, 305, 308, 309, 310, 311, 313, 316
Grantham, Larry 148
Gray, Carlton 232
Gray, Earnest 369, 370
Gray, Leon 53, 143, 479
Gray, Mel 480, 481, 483
Grayson, David 47, 192
Grbac, Elvis 506
Green, Bobby Joe 257
Green, Cornell 333, 335, 339
Green, Darrell 428
Green, Dennis 305, 314, 315, 316
Green, Ernie 42
Green, Gary 183
Green, Harold 30
Green, Hugh 130, 320, 323
Green, Jacob 224, 226, 227, 229
Green, Johnny 84
Greene, Joe 59, 68, 69, 71, 72, 78, 169
Greenwood, L.C. 68, 69, 71, 76, 78
Gregg, Forrest 26, 28, 44, 297, 302
Grgich, Visco 491
Grier, Roosevelt 351, 464
Griese, Bob 119, 120, 121, 122, 123, 125, 126, 128, 181, 311
Griesedieck, Joseph 405
Griffin, Archie 27
Grimm, Russ 428
Grogan, Steve 133, 138, 142, 144, 145, 156

Groman, Bill 50, 210
Grooms, Elois 475, 476
Gross, Lee 475
Gross, Pete 231
Grossman, Burt 218
Grossman, Randy 73
Grossman, Rex 99
Groza, Lou 33, 34, 39, 41, 456
Gruber, Paul 324
Guglielmi, Ralph 406
Gutowsky, Ace 243, 273, 274
Guy, Ray 194, 205

H

Habib, Brian 174
Hackett, Paul 344
Haden, Pat 465, 466
Hadl, John 53, 209, 212, 213, 214, 218, 302, 463
Hagerty, Jack 355
Haines, Henry 353
Halas, George 1, 4, 7, 130, 213, 237, 238, 239, 240, 242, 244, 246, 247, 249, 250, 251, 252, 254, 255, 256, 260, 261, 266, 291, 294, 306, 361, 398, 399, 403, 416
Haley, Charles 349, 504
Hall, Parker 451
Hall, Ron 324
Halloran, Bill 360, 416
Halloway, Brian 142
Ham, Jack 59, 69, 71, 72, 76, 78
Hamilton, Andy 476
Hamilton, Raymond 138
Hampton, Dan 259, 261, 262
Hampton, Dave 441
Hampton, Lorenzo 129
Hanburger, Chris 423
Handler, Phil 402, 404
Handley, Ray 375
Hannah, Charley 322
Hannah, John 134, 137, 140, 143
Hanner, Dave 297
Hanratty, Terry 69, 71, 74
Hansen, Don 440
Hanson, Thomas 380
Hapes, Merle 9
Harbaugh, Jim 264, 265
Harder, Pat 403
Hardison, Dee 89
Hardman, Cedric 498
Hardy, Bruce 217
Hardy, Jim 453, 455
Hardy, John 503
Hardy, Kevin 472
Hare, Ray 417
Harmon, Ronnie 218, 220
Harmon, Tom 453, 454
Harper, Bruce 155
Harper, Jack 121
Harris, Cliff 74
Harris, Dick 211
Harris, Duriel 126
Harris, Franco 14, 59, 68, 69, 70, 71, 72, 73, 75, 77, 78, 169, 193, 340
Harris, James 464
Harris, Jim 150
Harris, Louis 436
Harris, M.L. 27
Harry, Dr. March 352
Hart, Jim 406, 408
Hart, Leon 274, 275
Hart, Tommy 498
Hauser, Art 404
Hauss, Len 423
Haverdink, Kevin 483
Hawkins, Alex 438
Hawkins, Courtney 325, 326
Hawkins, Wayne 189, 192
Hay, Ralph 237
Hayes, Bob 334, 335, 337, 339
Hayes, Lester 54
Hayes, Wendell 181
Haymond, Alvin 108
Haynes, Abner 165, 166, 178
Haynes, Michael 448, 485
Haynes, Mike 138, 143, 205
Hays, Ralph 291
Hazeltine, Matt 494
Headrick, Roger L. 314

Healey, Ed 254
Hebert, Bobby 448, 480, 481, 482, 483, 484, 485, 486, 487
Heck, Andy 231
Hecker, Norb 438, 439, 456
Heffelfinger, William 4
Hefferle, Ernie 476
Hegman, Mike 339
Hein, Mel 351, 357, 361, 362, 455
Heinz, Bob 121, 124, 125
Henderson, Thomas 339, 342
Henderson, Wymon 173
Hendricks, Ted 54, 98, 111, 112, 116, 187, 195, 205
Hennigan, Charlie 50, 51, 52
Henning, Dan 218
Henry, Bill 8
Henry, John Johnson 1
Henry, Wally 388
Herber, Arnie 6, 356, 359, 362
Herman, Dave 150
Herrerra, Efren 408
Herring, George 164
Herrmann, Mark 114, 218
Herron, Mack 137
Herzeg, Ladd 55
Hess, Leon 149
Hewitt, Bill 244, 245, 249, 257, 268, 358
Heyward, Craig 483, 487
Hickerson, Bob 43
Hickerson, Gene 460
Hickey, Red 455, 490, 494, 495
Hickman, Larry 404, 405
Hicks, Dwight 501, 502
Highsmith, Alonzo 56
Hilgenberg, Jay 262, 263, 264
Hilgenbert, Joel 480
Hill, Bruce 323, 324
Hill, Calvin 336, 337, 338, 340
Hill, Drew 56
Hill, Harlon 251, 252
Hill, J.D. 89
Hill, Jerry 153
Hill, King 481
Hill, Tony 343, 478
Hillenbrand, Billy 98, 99
Hilliard, Dalton 481, 484, 485, 486
Hilton, Barron 209, 210, 213
Himmelman, Lyman P. 222
Hines, Andre 224
Hines, Glen Ray 474
Hinkle, Clarke 1, 6, 294, 360
Hinkle, Jack 381
Hinton, Chris 98, 114, 115, 116
Hinton, Eddie 23
Hipple, Eric 281
Hirsch, Elroy "Crazylegs" 449, 450, 453, 454, 456, 459
Hirt, Al 471
Hoaglin, Fred 222
Hoern, Bob 275
Hoerner, Dick 456, 457
Hoffman, Bill 378
Hofman, Ken 230
Hoge, Merrill 79
Holland, Vern 23
Holman, Rodney 29
Holmer, Walt 402
Holmes, Ernie 69
Holmes, Robert 180, 181
Holmes, Ron 323
Holmgren, Mike 303
Holovak, Mike 136, 137, 403
Holt, Issiac 314
Holtz, Lou 154, 155
Holtzman, Glenn 404
Holub, E.J. 176
Hoopes, Mitch 339
Hope, Bob 459
Horan, Mike 173
Hornung, Paul 3, 13, 40, 277, 287, 297
Horvath, Les 453
Hostetler, Jeff 206, 371, 375
House, Kevin 320
Houston, Jim 43
Howard, David 314
Howard, Thomas 183
Howell, Jim Lee 332, 364
Howfield, Bobby 154
Howley, Chuck 333, 338

Howsam, Bob 164, 175
Huarte, John 150
Hubbard, Cal 292, 351
Hubbard, Marv 194, 195, 201
Hubert, Dick 382
Hudson, Don 385
Hudspeth, Tommy 279
Huff, Gary 317
Huff, Sam 2, 351, 366, 367, 420
Huffman, Dick 454
Hughes, Chuck 279
Hughes, Ed 52, 53
Hughes, Randy 339
Hulmes, Harry 108, 477
Humphrey, Bobby 173
Humphrey, Claude 435, 440, 444
Humphries, Stan 209, 220
Hunley, Rickey 170
Hunt, Lamar 12, 148, 164, 175, 176, 177, 178, 188, 332, 334, 335
Hunter, Patrick 229, 230
Hunter, Tony 91
Hush, Frank 114
Huston, Don 7
Hutson, Don 294, 359

I

Igwebuike, Donald 323
Iman, Ken 464
Infante, Lindy 302
Irons, Gerald 193
Irsay, Jim 115
Irsay, Robert 98, 112, 115, 462
Irvin, LeRoy 466
Irvin, Michael 349
Isbell, Cecil 98, 99, 100, 106, 294, 359
Iselin, Philip H. 149, 151
Ivy, Pop 51

J

Jackson, Alfred 443, 445
Jackson, Bo 205, 206, 317, 323, 446
Jackson, Bob 51
Jackson, Bobby 212, 217
Jackson, Ernie 475
Jackson, Harold 139, 463
Jackson, Keith 390, 392
Jackson, Mark 164, 171
Jackson, Michael 224
Jackson, Rich 166, 167
Jackson, Ricky 479, 480, 483
Jackson, Rusty 465
Jackson, Tom 168
Jackson, Wilbur 498
Jacoby, Joe 428
Jaeger, Jeff 206
Jagade, Chick 251
Jakowenko, George 195
James, Craig 134, 140
James, Lionel 217
James, Robert 88
Jamison, Al 50, 51
Jankovich, Sam 145
Jaworski, Ron 387, 388, 389, 408
Jefferson, John 215, 216
Jefferson, Roy 23, 423
Jeffires, Haywood 56, 57
Jencks, Bob 439
Jenkins, Alfred 443, 444
Jenkins, Melvin 230
Jennings, Dave 369
Jennings, Stanford 30
Jessie, Ron 464
Jeter, Bob 297
Jeter, Gary 370
Jobko, Bill 438
Joe, Billy 165
Johnson, Andy 138
Johnson, Billy 26, 53
Johnson, Bob 22
Johnson, Butch 343
Johnson, Charley 163, 167, 388, 396, 406
Johnson, Essex 22, 24
Johnson, Gary 215, 217
Johnson, Harvey 86, 88
Johnson, Jimmy 329, 346, 347, 348,

349, 490, 496, 497, 498
Johnson, John Henry 66, 67, 490, 493
Johnson, Johnny 158
Johnson, Norm 227, 232, 448, 483, 484, 485
Johnson, Pete 26, 217
Johnson, Randy 438, 440
Johnson, Stone 178
Johnson, Vance 164, 170, 171
Johnson, Vaughan 480
Johnsos, Luke 244, 247, 248, 249
Joiner, Charlie 215, 216, 217
Jones, Andrew 475
Jones, Bert 113, 114, 466
Jones, Dave R. 39
Jones, David 395, 401
Jones, Deacon 214, 215, 450, 461
Jones, Dub 38
Jones, Ed 338, 341, 343
Jones, Eddie 477, 479, 481
Jones, Homer 43
Jones, James 281
Jones, Jerry 329, 346, 348, 349
Jones, June 445
Jones, Ralph 242, 244
Jones, Reginald 485
Jones, Rod 323
Jones, Rulon 163, 170
Jones, Stan 251, 252
Jordan, Henry 296, 297
Jordan, Lee Roy 333, 338
Joyce, Don 105
Joyner, Seth 392
Jurgensen, Sonny 366, 377, 378, 384, 386, 420, 421, 423, 424

K

Kaiser, Edgar F. 169
Kane, Tommy 230
Kapp, Joe 137, 181, 305, 310, 311, 312, 315
Karlis, Rich 46, 170, 171, 173
Karr, Bill 244, 245, 358
Karras, Alex 13, 197, 276, 277, 278, 279, 474
Kasay, John 232
Katcavage, Jim 351, 366
Kavanaugh, Ken 247, 249, 362
Keane, Jim 249, 250
Keane, Tom 101
Keating, Tom 192
Kelcher, Louie 215, 217
Kellett, Don 101, 108
Kelley, Bob 460
Kelly, Jim 30, 47, 83, 90, 92, 93, 174, 430
Kelly, Leroy 43
Kemp, Jack 83, 85, 86, 88, 209, 210, 211, 212, 213
Kemp, Jeff 232, 467, 503
Kenn, Mike 444
Kennard, Derek 485
Kenneally, George 413
Kennedy, Cortez 231
Kenney, Bill 183, 184
Kerkorian, Gary 101
Khayat, Eddie 386
Kiam, Victor 134, 143, 144, 145
Kiesling, Walt 60, 64, 65, 66, 381, 402
Kiick, Jim 15, 120, 121, 123, 125
Kilmer, Billy 422, 423, 424, 425, 430, 471, 472, 473, 494, 495
Kilroy, Bucko 11
King, Milton 420
Kinlaw, Reggie 203
Klecko, Joe 147, 156, 157, 158
Klein, Eugene 213, 214, 215, 217
Klingler, David 31
Klosterman, Don 109, 176, 462, 466
Klosterman, Ron 52
Knight, Shawn 482
Knox, Chuck 83, 89, 90, 91, 221, 224, 226, 227, 229, 230, 232, 450, 462, 463, 465, 468
Kocourek, Dave 210, 211, 212, 213
Kolb, John 78
Kolen, Mike 124

Komlo, Jeff 281
Kopcha, Joe 245
Koppisch, Walt 355
Korte, Steve 480
Kosar, Bernie 29, 45, 46, 47, 173
Kotite, Rich 392
Kramer, Jerry 297
Kramer, Ron 297
Krieg, Dave 185, 221, 226, 227, 229-32
Krimm, John 479
Krouse, Ray 105
Kruczek, Mike 75
Krueger, Charlie 490, 494, 495, 498
Krueger, Phil 325
Krumrie, Tim 29, 30
Krupa, Joe 67
Kuharich, Bill 481
Kuharich, Joe 386, 419
Kunz, George 113, 442
Kupp, Jake 473
Kush, Frank 114, 115
Kutner, Mal 403
Kuykendall, Fulton 443
Kwalick, Ted 496, 497

L

Ladd, Ernie 211, 213, 214, 216
Laidlaw, Scott 339
Laird, Bruce 112
Lambeau, Earl "Curly" 10, 288, 289, 290, 292, 293, 419
Lambeau, Marcel 291
Lambert, Jack 2, 59, 69, 72, 74, 78
Lammons, Pete 153, 154
Lamonica, Daryle 52, 85, 86, 152, 153, 191, 192, 193, 194, 214
Landry, Greg 114, 279
Landry, Tom 15, 64, 169, 178, 329, 330, 331, 332, 333, 334, 335, 336, 337, 338, 340, 341, 342, 343, 344, 346, 347, 352, 363, 365, 422, 430
Lane, Dick "Night Train" 277, 278, 450, 457
Lane, MacArthur 182
Langer, Jim 119, 125, 126
Lanier, Willie 22, 179, 181, 182
Laraba, Bob 211
Largent, Steve 221, 223, 225, 227, 228, 229, 230, 231, 294
Larsen, Gary 310, 311
Lary, Yale 271, 276, 277
Lavelli, Dante 33, 34, 36, 38, 39, 41
Lavende, Joe 425
Lawless, Burton 339
Lawrence, Henry 205
Lawrence, Rolland 444
Layden, Earl 35
Layden, Elmer 247
Layne, Bobby 11, 41, 66, 67, 250, 251, 271, 274, 275, 276
Leahy, Frank 209
Leahy, Pat 157
LeBaron, Eddie 333, 334, 419
LeBeau, Dick 279
LeClair, Jim 24
Lee, Bivian 475
Lee, Bob 440
Lee, Dave 109, 112
Lee, Jacky 50, 165, 180
Lee, Mack Hill 178
Leemans, Tuffy 351
Leggett, Earl 471
Lehman, Robert 460
Lemm, Wally 50, 52, 406
Levy, Fred 451
Levy, Marv 83, 91, 92, 93, 94, 182, 183
Lewis, Art 451
Lewis, David 319, 320
Lewis, Frank 69, 91
Lewis, Rodney 479
Lewis, Woodley 455
Liebel, Frank 362
Lillis, Donald 149, 151
Lilly, Bob 333, 334, 337, 338, 339, 342
Lincoln, Keith 136, 212, 213
Linhart, Toni 113
Lippett, Ronnie 140, 145
Lipps, Louis 78

Lipscomb, Gene 67, 103, 104, 105, 106, 457, 458
Liske, Pete 166
Little, Floyd 163, 166
Little, Larry 119, 121, 125, 126
Little, Lloyd 167
Livingston, Andy 472, 473
Livingston, Mike 180, 182
LoCasale, Al 21, 192
Lofton, James 294
Logan, Jerry 108, 112
Logan, Randy 387, 388
Lomax, Neil 409
Lombardi, Vince 12, 287, 288, 293, 296, 297, 298, 299, 332, 335, 352, 364, 365, 421, 422, 430, 438
Long, Chuck 204, 281
Long, Howie 204
Long, Ken 155
Longley, Clint 338
Lothridge, Billy 439
Lott, Ronnie 158, 206, 489, 499, 501, 502, 504, 505
Lowe, Paul 210, 211, 212, 213
Lowery, Nick 178
Lucci, Mike 279
Luck, Oliver 55
Luckman, Sid 105, 246, 247, 248, 249, 251, 267, 361, 417
Lujack, Johnny 249, 250, 251, 253
Lummus, Jack 361
Lumpkin, Roy 272, 273
Lundy, Lamar 464
Lycas, Richie 84
Lyles, Lenny 105, 108
Lyman, Roy 244, 254
Lynch, Jim 179, 181, 182
Lynch, Tom 223
Lynn, Mike 313, 314
Lyons, Marty 156

M

Maas, Bill 183, 184
Mack, Connie 378
Mack, Kevin 45, 56
Mack, Tom 460
Mackey, Dee 149
Mackey, John 98, 107, 108, 109, 111, 214
Mackovic, John 183
MacPherson, Dick 145
Madden, John 169, 192, 193, 194, 195, 196, 197, 198, 200, 206, 312
Maggs, Don 174
Magnani, Dante 362
Maguire, Paul 211
Majkowski, Don 303
Malavasi, Ray 465, 466
Malone, Mark 78
Mandel, Fred 274
Manders, Jack 244, 245, 246, 358
Maniaci, Joe 247
Manley, Dexter 428
Manning, Archie 55, 474, 475, 476, 477, 478
Manuel, Lionel 371
Mara, Tim 12, 352, 362, 365
Mara, Wellington 354, 356, 359, 368
Marchetti, Gino 98, 101, 102, 103, 104, 105, 106, 107, 108, 110, 112, 364
Marchibroda, Ted 65, 113, 114, 117
Marconi, Joe 254, 458
Marino, Dan 16, 119, 128, 129, 130, 131, 343, 447
Marinovich, Todd 206
Marshal, Leonard 352
Marshall, George Preston 6, 7, 8, 14, 100, 412, 414, 415, 416, 417, 418, 419, 420, 421, 452
Marshall, Jim 308, 309, 310, 312
Marshall, Leonard 351
Marshall, Wilbur 263
Marshman, Homer 451
Martin, Eric 483, 485, 486
Martin, Harvey 338, 340, 343
Martin, Kelvin 232
Martin, Rod 203, 205
Martin, Townsend B. 149
Martin, Wayne 483

Massey, Robert 483
Masterson, Bernie 245
Masterson, Bob 360, 417
Matheson, Riley 491
Mathews, Bo 215
Mathis, Bill 148, 154
Mathis, Reggie 477
Matson, Ollie 65, 400, 404, 450, 458, 459
Matsos, Archie 84
Matte, Tom 106, 107, 108, 109, 112
Mattes, Ron 229
Matthews, Clay 47
Matusak, Marv 66, 494
Matuszak, John 53, 198, 200
Maxson, Alvin 475, 476
Mayes, Rueben 481, 483
Maynard, Don 148, 151, 152, 153, 154
Mays, Jerry 176
Mazur, John 137
Mazzetti, Tim 445
McAfee, Fred 485
McAfee, George 247, 249, 250, 256, 267
McBride, Jack 353, 357
McBride, Mickey 33, 34, 39
McCafferty, Don 98, 109, 112, 279
McCall, Don 472
McCants, Keith 325, 326
McCaskey, Edward 261
McCaskey, Michael 264, 265
McChesney, Bob 363
McClinton, Curtis 176, 177, 178
McCloskey, Tom 318
McCloughan, Dave 232
McCloughan, Kent 192
McConkey, Phil 374
McCormack, Mike 114, 226, 231, 387
McCormick, John 166
McCulley, Pete 498
McCulloch, Earl 279
McCullum, Sam 222, 226
McCutcheon, Lawrence 77, 463, 465
McDaniel, Ed 150
McDaniel, Terry 207
McDermott, Gary 86
McDonald, Ricardo 31
McDonald, Tommy 384, 385, 386
McDowell, Bubba 57
McElhenny, Hugh 308, 490, 492, 493
McElroy, Vann 205
McFadden, Paul 389
McFadin, Bud 458
McGah, Ed 189, 202
McGee, Max 294, 297
McGee, Tim 29, 30
McGraw, Thurman 274, 275
McGwire, Dan 232
McHan, Lamar 495
McIntyre, Guy 504
McKalip, Bill 272, 273
McKay, John 318, 319, 320, 322, 323
McKeever, Marlin 462
McKenzie, Reggie 226
McKnight, Ted 182
McKyer, Tim 130, 447, 448
McMahon, Jim 142, 218, 261, 262, 264, 305, 315, 316, 392
McMakin, John 69
McMichael, Steve 263
McMillan, Bo 274, 383
McMillan, Jim 355
McMillan, Randy 115
McMurtry, Chuck 84
McNally, Johnny 6, 60, 292, 294
McNally, Vince 383
McNeil, Clifton 496
McNeil, Freeman 28, 147, 156, 157, 184
McPeak, Bill 420
McRae, Charles 325
McVay, John 369
McVea, Warren 181
Meadows, Ed 276
Mecklenburg, Karl 170, 173
Mecom, John, Jr. 480
Mecom, John W. 471

Mehl, Lance 157
Mellus, John 100
Mercer, Mike 178, 179
Meredith, Don 332, 333, 334, 335, 336, 337
Merriweather, Mike 78
Mertens, Jerry 494, 495
Mertes, Buzz 99
Metcalf, Terry 396, 408
Metzelaars, Pete 223
Meyer, Ken 498
Meyer, Ron 115, 117, 139
Michaels, Walt 147, 155, 157
Michalske, Mike 292
Michel, Mike 445
Michelosen, John 65
Middleton, Rick 475, 476
Mike, Bob 493
Millen, Matt 205
Miller, Anthony 220
Miller, Bill 191
Miller, Chris 436, 444, 448, 485
Miller, Fred 109, 112
Miller, Jim 501
Miller, Junior 443
Miller, Red 163, 165, 167, 168, 169
Miller, Terry 89
Millner, Wayne 383, 414
Mills, Sam 481, 483, 485
Milstead, Century 353, 354
Mims, Chris 220
Mingo, Gene 163, 164
Minnifield, Frank 45
Mira, George 495, 496
Mirer, Rick 232
Mitchell, Bobby 41, 420, 421
Mitchell, Jim 445
Mitchell, Lydell 113, 116, 215, 216
Mix, Ron 187, 210, 211, 212
Modell, Art 34, 41, 45, 47
Modzelewski, Dick 42, 44, 351, 365
Molesworth, Keith 101, 244
Monk, Art 16, 411, 424, 425, 428
Montana, Joe 17, 27, 29, 30, 129, 173, 343, 370, 371, 375, 489, 499, 500, 501, 502, 504, 505, 506
Montgomery, Wilbert 388, 389
Montoya, May 29, 30
Moon, Warren 55, 56, 57, 58
Moore, Lenny 98, 103, 104, 105, 106, 107, 108, 110, 113
Moore, Nat 194
Moore, Wilbur 247
Mora, Jim 481, 483, 484
Morabito, Anthony J. 490, 492, 493
Morabito, Vic 495
Moreau, Doug 121
Morgado, Arnold 182
Morgan, Stanley 134, 138, 139, 144
Moroski, Mike 503
Morrall, Earl 66, 109, 112, 123, 125, 126, 153, 278, 493, 494, 496
Morris, Joe 351, 371, 374
Morris, Johnny 253, 255
Morris, Larry 367, 457
Morris, Mercury 24, 121, 123, 125, 154
Morrison, Don 474
Morton, Craig 75, 163, 167, 168, 169, 336, 337, 340, 369
Mosebar, Don 207
Moses, Haven 169
Moss, Winston 323
Motley, Marion 1, 33, 36, 38, 39
Mudd, Howard 496
Muhlmann, Horst 22
Mulleneaux, Carl 359
Mumpford, Lloyd 121
Muncie, Chuck 216, 217, 476, 477, 479
Munoz, Anthony 29, 31
Munson, Bill 279, 460
Murchison, Clint 332, 333, 334, 343
Murphy, Don 292
Murphy, Kevin 232
Murphy, Mark 425
Murray, Francis 144
Musick, Jim 413
Musso, George 244, 245, 261, 269
Muster, Brad 264, 487

Mutryn, Chet 100
Mutscheller, Jim 103, 105
Myers, Chip 24
Myers, Tommy 474, 477
Myhra, Steve 106, 365

N

Nagurski, Bronko 1, 6, 242, 243, 244, 245, 246, 248, 254, 258, 266, 272, 356, 358, 415
Namath, Joe 14, 86, 109, 125, 147, 150, 151, 152, 153, 154, 155, 170, 191, 367, 405, 406, 445, 450, 465
Nance, Jim 134, 136
Nash, Joe 227
Nathan, Tony 126, 127
Nattiel, Ricky 164, 171, 173
Naumetz, Fred 453
Naumoff, Paul 279
Neale, Greasy 37, 38, 64, 381, 382, 383, 385, 404
Neely, Ralph 52
Nelsen, Bill 67
Nelson, Andy 105
Nelson, Steve 144
Nesbitt, Dick 243
Nesser, Frank 397
Nevers, Ernie 1, 242, 395, 396, 400, 401, 402
Newhouse, Robert 338, 340, 343
Newman, Harry 357
Newsome, Billy 475
Newsome, Ozzie 44, 45, 46
Niehaus, Steve 222
Nielsen, Gifford 53, 55, 216
Ninowski, Jim 277
Nitschke, Ray 2, 287, 297
Nixon, Mike 67, 420
Nobis, Tommy 52, 438, 440
Nock, George 154
Nolan, Dick 476, 477, 478, 490, 496, 498
Noll, Chuck 15, 66, 68, 69, 71, 75, 77, 78, 79, 80
Nomellini, Leo 490, 492, 493, 494, 495
Nordstrom, John 226
Nordstrom, Lloyd W. 222
Norman, Joe 224
North, John 475
Norton, Don 212
Norton, Jim 52
Norton, Ken Jr. 348, 349
Norton, Rick 120
Norwood, Scott 17, 30, 94
Nowatzke, Tom 112
Nutter, Buzz 105

O

O'Brien, Chris 395, 396, 397, 399
O'Brien, Davey 380, 381
O'Brien, Jim 14, 112
O'Brien, Ken 141, 147, 157, 158
O'Bryan, Paul A. 460
O'Connell, Tom 40, 41
O'Connor, Fred 499, 500
Odoms, Riley 167
O'Donnell, Neil 80
O'Donoghue, Neil 319
Offerdahl, John 130
Okoye, Christian 184, 185
Olsen, Merlin 164, 450, 460, 463, 464, 465
Olson, Lisa 145
O'Neal, Leslie 218, 220
Orr, Jimmy 66, 108
Orthwein, James B. 134, 146
Osborne, Jim 258
Osborne, Robert 189
Osmanski, Bill 246
Otto, Jim 180, 187, 188, 189, 191
Owen, Steve 244, 273, 351, 354, 357, 359, 361, 362, 363
Owen, Tom 138, 199
Owens, R.C. 494
Owens, Steve 279

P

Page, Alan 310, 311
Pagel, Mike 47, 114, 115
Paige, Stephone 183
Panfil, Ken 404
Parcells, Bill 146, 370, 374, 375
Pardee, Jack 56, 258, 425, 462
Parilli, Vito 40, 134, 135, 137, 153, 189
Park, Ernest 213
Parker, Buddy 65, 66, 67, 68, 271, 274, 276
Parker, Jim 98, 103, 104, 105, 106, 107, 108, 112
Parks, Billy 214
Parks, Dave 472, 475, 495
Parnell, Babe 355
Parrish, Lemar 23, 425
Parros, Rick 170
Parsons, Bob 260
Partridge, Rick 477
Pastorini, Dan 53, 54, 76, 126, 138, 199, 200, 216, 466
Pastrana, Al 166, 167
Patera, Jack 222, 224, 226
Patton, Jimmy 351
Paul, Don 449
Pauley, Ed 459
Payton, Walter 1, 16, 173, 258, 259, 260, 261, 262, 263, 270
Pearson, Drew 338, 339, 343
Pearson, Preston 339, 340, 343
Peete, Rodney 283
Pegler, Westbrook 354
Pellington, Bill 105
Pelluer, Steve 344, 348
Pennacchia, Tony 143
Peppler, Pat 481
Percival, Mac 256
Perkins, Don 333
Perkins, Johnny 370
Perkins, Ray 323, 324, 325, 369
Perriman, Brett 483
Perry, Joe 11, 106, 490, 491, 492, 493
Perry, William 141
Peterson, Bill 53
Petibon, Richie 254, 255, 265, 430
Phillips, Bum 53, 54, 55, 173, 478, 479, 480, 481
Phillips, Jess 22
Phillips, Wade 164, 173, 174
Phipps, Allan R. 169
Phipps, Gerald H. 169
Phipps, Mike 43, 44
Pickel, Bill 205
Pickens, Carl 31
Pietrosante, Nick 276
Pihos, Pete 382, 383, 384
Pinckert, Erny 413
Pinkett, Allen 56
Pitts, Elijah 179
Plum, Milt 41, 278
Plummer, Gary 218
Plunkett, Jim 137, 146, 188, 199, 200, 201, 204, 205, 216, 498
Podolak, Ed 181
Poe, Johnnie 480
Pool, Hampton 247, 455, 457
Post, Dickie 214
Pottios, Myron 462
Powell, Art 86, 148, 191, 192
Powell, Charley 493
Powell, Marvin 155, 156
Powers, Sam 289, 290
Presnell, Glenn 272, 273, 359
Price, Eddie 363
Pritchard, Bosh 382
Pritzker, A.N. 481
Prothro, Tommy 215, 462, 463
Pruitt, Gary 44
Pucker, Reggie 137
Pugh, Jethro 337
Putnam, Duane 457
Pyle, C.C. 5, 241, 354
Pyle, Mike 254

Q

Quick, Mike 389, 390
Quinlan, Skeet 458

R

Rabb, Warren 84
Ralston, John 163, 167
Ramsey, Buster 84
Ramsey, Derrick 140
Ramsey, Steve 167
Randle, Sonny 406
Rashad, Ahmad 89, 309, 310
Rathman, Tom 505
Ratterman, George 40, 41, 100
Rauch, John 86, 88, 153, 191, 192
Ray, Darroll 156
Reasons, Gary 370
Reaves, John 25
Reaves, Ken 438, 440
Rechichar, Bert 101, 102, 103
Redman, Rick 213
Reece, Geoff 223
Reed, Andre 30, 84, 92, 93
Reed, Joe 498
Reed, Tony 182
Reese, Don 477
Reeves, Dan (Team Owner) 330, 450, 451, 452, 453, 454, 457, 459, 460, 462
Reeves, Dan (Coach) 33, 163, 164, 169, 171, 173, 174, 352, 375
Reich, Frank 93
Reid, Mike 22
Reimers, Bruce 30
Reinsch, J. Leonard 436
Renfro, Mike 53, 216
Renfro, Ray 39
Retzlaff, Pete 385, 387
Reynolds, Bob 460
Reynolds, Jack 462, 501
Reynolds, M.C. 84
Reynolds, Ricky 323, 326
Ric, Homer 26
Rice, Grantland 354
Rice, Jerry 26, 30, 294, 489, 503, 504, 505, 506
Richard, Stanley 220
Richards, Elvin 358
Richards, George A. 271, 272
Richards, Golden 338
Richards, Ray 400
Richardson, Gloster 180
Richardson, Willie 108, 109, 122
Richter, Les 449
Riggins, John 1, 2, 154, 425, 426, 428
Riggs, Gerald 436
Riley, Ken 22, 25
Riley, Steve 478
Ringo, Jim 89, 297
Rison, Andre 116, 436, 446, 448
Rizzo, Joe 168
Roaf, William 487
Robbie, Joseph 120, 121, 130
Robbins, Tootie 487
Roberts, Choo-Choo 363
Roberts, Greg 319
Roberts, J.D. 473
Roberts, Ray 232
Robertson, Isiah 462
Robinson, Dave 297
Robinson, Eddie 456
Robinson, John 203, 450, 466, 467, 468
Robinson, Johnny 50, 177, 181
Robinson, Matt 169
Robinson, Mike 155
Robinson, Paul 22
Robustelli, Andy 351, 366, 367, 449, 450, 456
Rockne, Knute 288
Rodenberg, Bob 98
Rodgers, Johnny 215
Rogers, Darryl 281, 282
Rogers, George 479
Romanik, Steve 251
Romanowski, Bill 505
Ronzani, Gene 294

Rooney, Art 9, 16, 59, 60, 61, 62, 64, 65, 67, 68, 72, 78, 381
Rooney, Cobb 402
Rooney, Dan 78
Rosenbloom, Carroll 101, 107, 112, 462, 464, 465
Rosenbloom, Steve 466, 477
Rosenow, Gus 289
Ross, Bobby 220
Ross, Kevin 183
Rote, Kyle 351, 363, 366
Rote, Tobin 41, 212, 213, 276
Roussel, Tom 473
Rowe, Dave 472
Rozelle, Pete 12, 14, 17, 27, 109, 191, 215, 277, 311, 404, 405, 436, 450, 457, 458, 472, 481, 483
Rozier, Mike 56
Rucker, Reggie 44
Rudnay, Jack 183
Rush, Clive 137
Russell, Andy 69, 71
Russell, Bo 360, 416
Rust, Rod 144, 145
Rutigliano, Sam 44, 45
Rutledge, Jeff 370, 466
Rutowski, Ed 86
Ryan, Buddy 58, 390, 391, 392
Ryan, Frank 42, 459
Ryan, Pat 157, 158, 184
Rymkus, Lou 50, 52
Rypien, Mark 411, 429, 430

S

Saban, Lou 83, 84, 86, 88, 89, 135, 166, 167
Salaam, Abdul 156
Salata, Paul 100
Sample, Johnny 365
Sanders, Barry 281, 282, 283, 284
Sanders, Charlie 279
Sanders, Deion 446, 447
Sanders, John 215
Sanders, Ricky 429
Sandusky, John 112
Sandusky, Mike 66
Sanford, Lucius 89
Sarkowsky, Herman 222, 226
Sauber, Charlie 289
Sauer, George 150, 151, 153, 154
Saul, Rich 462
Saunders, Al 218
Savoldi, Joe 242
Sayers, Gale 178, 255, 256, 257, 258, 262, 268
Scarpati, Joe 474
Schafrath, Dick 43
Schmidt, Joe 1, 271, 275, 276, 277, 278, 279, 462
Schnelker, Bob 214
Schnellbacher, Otto 363
Schnellenberger, Howard 112, 113
Schonert, Turk 28
Schottenheimer, Marty 45, 47, 175, 184
Schramm, Tex 17, 329, 330, 332, 333, 334, 335, 340, 343, 344, 450, 458
Schroeder, Jay 30, 206, 428
Schuh, Harry 192, 193
Schulman, Sam 213
Schumacher, Kurt 475
Schwedes, Gerhardt 135
Schwenk, Bud 98, 99
Schwenk, Vic 471, 472
Scibelli, Joe 464
Scott, Bo 43
Scott, Bobby 475
Scott, Herb 339, 343
Scott, Jake 124
Scott, Lindsay 479
Seau, Junior 220
Seifert, George 303, 500, 504
Seley, Hal 459
Sellers, Goldie 166
Selmon, Dewey 318, 319, 320
Selmon, Lee Roy 318, 320
Septien, Raphael 76
Sewell, Harley 275
Shanahan, Mike 205

Shanklin, Ron 69
Sharpe, Sterling 303
Shaughnessy, Clark 8, 495
Shaw, Billy 84, 86
Shaw, Buck 384, 386
Shaw, Dennis 88
Shaw, George 102, 104, 365
Shaw, Lawrence 490, 492, 493
Shea, Bill 148
Shell, Art 17, 187, 196, 197, 205, 206, 207, 314
Shell, Donnie 69, 78
Shell, Todd 503
Shepherd, Bill 273
Sherer, Dave 105
Sherk, Jerry 44
Sherman, Allie 364, 365
Shiner, Dick 440
Shinners, John 472
Shinnick, Don 105, 109
Shipp, Ken 154
Shofner, Del 351, 366, 458, 459
Shofner, Jim 47
Shonta, Chuck 135
Shula, David 30, 31
Shula, Don 15, 68, 76, 97, 98, 101, 107, 108, 109, 112, 119, 120, 122, 123, 124, 125, 126, 129, 130, 131, 153, 157, 423, 430
Shuler, Mickey 157
Silverwood, Tom 290
Simmons, Clyde 392
Simms, Phil 351, 369, 370, 371, 374, 375
Simpson, Keith 224
Simpson, O.J. 15, 72, 83, 86, 87, 88, 89, 91, 475, 490, 500
Sims, Billy 280, 283
Sims, David 224
Singletary, Mike 16, 261, 262, 263, 264, 265
Sinkwich, Frank 274
Sipe, Brian 44, 45
Sisemore, Jerry 387, 388
Sistrunk, Otis 193, 197
Skinner, Ned 222
Skorich, Nick 43, 44, 386
Skoronski, Bob 297
Slater, Jackie 468
Slusher, Howard 143
Smeenge, Joel 484
Smerlas, Fred 90
Smith, Billy Ray 218
Smith, Bruce 92, 93
Smith, Bubba 112
Smith, Charlie 152
Smith, Dave 53
Smith, Don 375
Smith, Ed 346
Smith, Emmitt 348, 349
Smith, Irv 487
Smith, J.D. 494
Smith, Jackie 342
Smith, Jerry 167, 421, 422
Smith, Jim 274
Smith, John 134
Smith, Marston 396
Smith, Neil 184, 185
Smith, Nolan 179
Smith, Paul 163, 167
Smith, Rankin 436, 438
Smith, Riley 7, 414
Smith, Ron 77, 216
Smith, Royce 474
Smith, Sammie 130
Smith, Sherman 222, 226
Smith, Verda 455
Smolinski, Mark 149
Smukler, Dave 380
Snead, Norm 368, 386, 420
Snell, Matt 150, 151, 154
Snider, Malcolm 441
Snow, Jack 440, 464
Snyder, Bob 453
Snyder, Harry 243
Soar, Hank 360
Solomon, Freddie 501
Solomon, George 418
Solomon, Jesse 314
Solt, Ron 116
Soltau, Gordy 492
Songin, Butch 135

Sorrell, Allen E. 490
Spadia, Lou 492, 496
Spanos, Alex G. 217
Spavital, Jim 100
Speedie, Mac 34, 36, 38, 165, 166
Spencer, Ollie 275
Spielman, Chris 184, 283
Spikes, Jack 176
Spinney, Art 105, 106
Springs, Ron 343
Spurrier, Steve 317, 497
St. Clair, Bob 490, 493, 495
Stabler, Kenny 54, 55, 70, 138, 156, 193, 194, 195, 197, 199, 200, 479, 480
Stallworth, John 69, 72, 73, 75, 76, 77
Standlee, Norm 490, 492
Stanfel, Dick 275, 478
Stanfill, Bill 121, 124, 125
Stark, Rohn 114, 115, 117
Starr, Bart 287, 297, 299, 302, 336
Staubach, Roger 76, 123, 336, 337, 338, 339, 340, 341, 342, 425, 445
Stautner, Ernie 65, 67
Steadman, Jack 176
Steckel, Les 313
Steinberg, Dick 158, 478
Steinfort, Fred 169
Stenerud, Jan 178, 179, 180, 181
Stephens, John 134, 144
Stephenson, Kay 91
Sternaman, Dutch 239, 242, 244
Sternaman, Joey 354
Stevens, Howard 113
Stewart, Alex 314
Stickle, Monte 495
Still, Art 182
Stingley, Darryl 137, 138, 198
Stofa, John 21
Stonebreak, Steve 471
Storck, Carl 246, 247
Stoudt, Cliff 78
Stouffer, Kelly 230, 231, 232
Stoyanovich, Pete 130
Strachan, Mike 476
Strader, Red 493
Stradford, Troy 129
Stram, Hank 176, 177, 179, 180, 181, 182, 311, 476
Stratton, Mike 85, 213
Strickland, Larry 251, 252
Strock, Don 47, 125, 126, 127, 128
Strong, Ken 351, 356, 362
Stroud, Jack 363
Stroud, Morris 181
Strzykalski, Johnny 491, 492
Stuckey, Jim 501
Studley, Chuck 55
Studstill, Pat 278
Stydahar, Joe 245, 246, 247, 249, 256, 268, 454, 457
Sulliva, Don 112
Sullivan, Bill 134, 136, 138, 140, 143, 144
Sullivan, Chuck 143
Sullivan, Pat 142, 143, 144, 145
Suman, Don 50
Summerall, Pat 366
Susoeff, Nick 491
Sutherland, Jock 64, 66
Svare, Harland 214, 215, 457, 460
Swann, Lynn 59, 69, 72, 73, 74, 75, 76, 77, 78, 340, 342
Sweeney, Walt 212, 215
Swenson, Bob 169, 170
Swiacki, Bill 363
Swift, Doug 124
Swilling, Pat 481, 482, 483, 484, 485, 487
Symank, Johnny 104
Syzmanski, Dick 102
Szaro, Rich 476
Szymanski, Dick 107, 114

T

Tagliabue, Paul 17, 483
Talbert, Diron 462
Taliaferro, George 101
Taliaferro, Mike 150

Talley, Darryl 93
Tarkenton, Fran 130, 305, 308, 309, 312, 313, 368, 439
Taseff, Carl 105
Tatum, Jack 71, 138, 193, 198, 200
Taylor, Altie 279
Taylor, Charley 420, 421, 422, 423, 424
Taylor, Hugh 419
Taylor, Jim 1, 12, 287, 297, 298, 367, 471, 472
Taylor, John 29, 375, 503, 505
Taylor, Keith 116
Taylor, Lawrence 2, 3, 351, 369, 371, 372, 373, 374, 375
Taylor, Lionel 163, 164, 165
Taylor, Otis 178, 179, 180, 181
Taylor, Roosevelt 254, 256
Taylor, Terry 227, 230
Teele, Jack 461
Tensi, Steve 166, 167
Testaverde, Vinny 47, 317, 324, 325, 326
Theismann, Joe 411, 425, 426, 427, 430
Thielemann, R.C. 444
Thomas, Bob 214
Thomas, Broderick 325, 326
Thomas, Danny 120
Thomas, Derrick 184
Thomas, Duane 214, 336, 337, 338, 340
Thomas, Emmitt 182
Thomas, Eric 29
Thomas, Joe 112, 113, 121, 199, 498
Thomas, Joseph A. 460
Thomas, Pat 58
Thomas, Skip 196
Thomas, Thurman 84, 92, 93, 94, 375
Thompson, Alexis 62
Thompson, Bill 166, 168, 169
Thompson, Jack 317
Thompson, John 222
Thompson, Tommy 381, 382, 383
Thornton, James 158, 264
Thornton, Sidney 77
Thorpe, Jim 1, 4, 238, 240, 292, 351, 353, 385, 397, 400, 401, 446
Threadgill, Bruce 499
Thurman, Dennis 344
Thurston, Fuzzy 105, 297
Tice, John 480
Tidwell, Travis 363
Tinglehoff, Mick 312
Tippett, Andre 140, 141
Tittle, Y.A. 99, 100, 351, 365, 366, 367, 490, 492, 493
Todd, Dick 416, 419
Todd, Richard 154, 155, 156, 157, 480
Tofflemire, Joe 231
Tolar, Charlie 50, 51
Tomczak, Mike 264
Toogood, Charley 456, 458
Toon, Al 147, 157, 158
Torczon, Lavern 84
Tose, Leonard 387, 389, 390
Towler, Dan 449, 453, 455, 457
Townsend, Greg 205, 206
Tracey, John 404, 405
Tracy, Tom 66
Trafton, George 241, 242, 254
Traynham, Wade 439
Treadwell, David 57
Trimble, Jim 383, 384
Triplett, Mel 364
Trippi, Charley 396, 403
Tripucka, Frank 163, 164, 165
Trudeau, Jack 115, 116, 117
Trumpy, Bob 22
Tuiasosopo, Manu 224
Tunnell, Emlen 169, 351, 363
Turnbull, Renaldo 484, 487
Turner, Bake 149
Turner, Cecil 256, 257
Turner, Clyde 148, 247, 248, 250, 251, 256, 267
Turner, Daryl 227
Turner, Floyd 483
Turner, Jim 150, 151, 152, 153, 168
Turre, E.J. 490

Twilley, Howard 120, 121, 122
Tyler, Wendell 466
Tyrer, Jim 176

Unitas, Johnny 2, 11, 23, 65, 97, 98, 102, 103, 104, 105, 106, 107, 108, 109, 111, 112, 114, 123, 130, 153, 214, 337, 364, 365, 366
Upchurch, Rick 168
Upshaw, Gene 144, 187, 191, 192, 193, 196, 197, 199, 201

V

Vainisi, Jack 296
Vainisi, Jerry 261
Valley, Wayne 189
Van Brocklin, Norm 305, 308, 309, 312,377, 384, 385, 386, 436, 439, 440, 441, 442, 449, 450, 453, 455, 456, 457, 458, 459, 475
Van Buren, Steve 1, 9, 10, 37, 377, 382, 383
van Eeghen, Mark 199, 201
Van Note, Jeff 435, 444
Van Pelt, Brad 369
Vanhorse, Sean 220
Vataha, Randy 137
Veeck, Bill 239
Venturi, Rick 117
Verdin, Clarence 116
Vermeil, Dick 200, 387, 388, 389
Villapiano, Phil 193
Vogel, Bob 107, 108, 109, 112
Volk, Rick 108, 109, 112

Waddell, Rube 378
Wade, Bill 254, 457, 458, 459
Wagner, Mike 69, 71, 76, 78
Wainwright, Frank 485
Walker, Doak 271, 274, 275, 276
Walker, Herschel 314, 344, 348
Walker, Wayne 279
Walker, Wesley 28, 155, 157, 158
Wallace, Steve 30
Waller, Charlie 214
Waller, Ron 215, 457
Walsh, Adam 454
Walsh, Bill 215, 303, 430, 443, 489, 490, 499, 500, 501, 504
Walsh, Charles 451
Walsh, Chile 454
Walsh, Steve 484, 485, 487
Walter, Joe 29
Walter, Michael 503, 505
Walters, Stan 388
Walton, Joe 147, 157, 158
Wannstedt, Dave 265
Warfield, Paul 15, 42, 43, 119, 122, 123, 125, 126
Warlick, Ernie 213
Warner, Curt 226, 227, 229, 230, 231
Warner, Glenn 4
Warner, Pop 400
Warren, Chris 232
Warren, Frank 479
Warren, Jimmy 71, 213
Washington, Brian 158
Washington, Gene 496, 497
Washington, Joe 114
Washington, Russ 217
Waterfield, Bob 9, 449, 450, 452, 453, 455, 456, 457, 459
Waters, Bobby 494
Waters, Ricky 506
Watner, Abraham 100
Watson, Steve 163, 169, 170
Watts, Robert 476
Waymer, Dave 478, 483
Weathers, Robert 140
Webster, Alex 368
Webster, George 52, 53, 55
Webster, Mike 69
Wedemey, Herman 454

Weinmeister, Arnie 363
Wells, Warren 192
Wendryhoski, Joe 471
Werblin, Sonny 149, 150, 151
Wersching, Ray 27
West, Charlie 311
Westmoreland, Dick 213
Wheeler, Mark 326
Whelan, Tom 100
Whelchel, John 419
White, Byron 8, 60, 61, 274
White, Danny 322, 344, 348, 445
White, Dwight 69, 71, 76
White, Jack 496
White, Jim 362
White, Lorenzo 56, 57
White, Phil 354
White, Randy 339, 340, 343
White, Reggie 302, 303, 377, 390, 392
White, Sherman 24
White, Stan 113
Whitley, Wilson 26
Whitsell, Dave 472
Whittingham, Fred 472
Wietecha, Ray 363
Wiggin, Paul 182
Wightkin, Bill 251
Wilcox, Dave 495, 497, 498
Wilder, James 320, 322
Wilkerso, Doug 217
Wilkin, Wee Willie 417
Wilks, Jim 479
Willard, Ken 495, 497
Williams, Darryl 31
Williams, Dave 215
Williams, Delvin 498
Williams, Doug 317, 319, 320, 322, 411, 428, 429, 430
Williams, Edward Bennett 420, 421, 422, 425
Williams, Eric 170
Williams, Fred 102
Williams, Harvey 185
Williams, Jerry 386, 387, 455
Williams, John L. 229, 230, 232
Williams, Lee 218
Williams, Win 99
Williamson, Carlton 501, 502
Williamson, Fred 192, 193
Williamson, Richard 325
Willis, Bill 33, 39
Willis, Peter Tom 265
Wilson, Billy 492
Wilson, Dave 479, 482
Wilson, George 119, 120, 122, 271, 276, 278
Wilson, George, Jr. 120
Wilson, Larry 407
Wilson, Marc 145, 204, 205
Wilson, Nemiah 166
Wilson, Otis 262
Wilson, Ralph C. 84, 86, 88
Wilson, Stanley 29
Wilson, Tim 55
Wilson, Wade 487
Winder, Sammy 163, 170, 173
Winner, Charley 154
Winslow, Kellen 27, 216, 217
Winston, DeMond 484
Winter, Max 306, 313, 314
Wismer, Harry 148, 306
Wisniewski, Steve 206
Wittum, Tom 498
Wojciechowicz, Alex 271, 274, 383
Wolf, Ron 303
Wolfner, Mrs. Walter 175
Wolfner, Walter 405
Wolman, Jerry 386
Wood, Dick 149, 150
Wood, Richard 319
Wood, Willie 179, 297
Woodall, Al 154
Woodard, George 478
Woodard, Milt 191
Wooden, Terry 231
Woodley, David 126, 128
Woods, Don 215
Woods, Ickey 29, 30
Woods, Tony 230
Woodson, Abe 494
Woodson, Ron 78

Woolsey, Rolly 339
Word, Barry 185, 481
Worley, Tim 78
Woudenberg, John 491
Wray, Ludlow 379, 412, 414
Wright, Elmo 181
Wright, Eric 501, 502
Wright, Howard S. 222
Wright, Louis 163, 168, 170
Wyche, Sam 28, 30, 325, 326
Wyman, David 230
Wynne, Bedford 332, 333

Yarno, John 223
Yary, Ron 312
Yepremian, Garo 14, 123, 181, 278, 424, 477
Youell, Frank 188
Young, Buddy 98, 101
Young, Charles 226, 387
Young, Fredd 227, 231
Young, George 369
Young, Steve 323, 504, 506
Young, Wilbur 215
Youngblood, Jack 462, 464, 465, 467
Younger, Tank 449, 453, 455

Z

Zanders, Emanuel 477
Zendejas, Tony 56
Zimmerman, Roh 247
Zoll, Carl 289
Zoll, Martin 289
Zook, John 440
Zorn, Jim 221, 222, 224, 225, 226, 229, 231
Zupke, Bob 238